FRONTIERS IN COMPUTER COMMUNICATIONS TECHNOLOGY

Proceedings of the ACM SIGCOMM '87 Workshop
Stowe, Vermont
August 11-13, 1987

COMPUTER COMMUNICATION REVIEW
Volume 17, Number 5, Special Issue

edited by:

J. J. Garcia-Luna-Aceves
Information Sciences and Technology Center
SRI International
Menlo Park, California
USA

Sponsored by ACM SIGCOMM with support given
by the Information Sciences and Technology
Center of SRI International and Cybertree, Inc.

The Association for Computing Machinery
11 West 42nd Street
New York, New York 10036

©1988 by the Association for Computing Machinery, Inc. Copying without fee is permitted provided that the copies are not made or distributed for direct commercial advantage, and credit to the source is given. Abstracting with credit is permitted. For other copying of articles that carry a code at the bottom of the first page, copying is permitted provided that the per-copy fee indicated in the code is paid through the Copyright Clearance Center, 27 Congress Street, Salem, MA 01970. For permission to republish write to: Director of Publications, Association for Computing Machinery. To copy otherwise, or republish, requires a fee and/or specific permission.

ISBN 0-89791-245-4

Additional copies may be ordered prepaid from:

ACM Order Department *Price*
P.O. Box 64145 Members $23.00
Baltimore, MD 21264 All others $30.00

ACM Order Number: 533870

PREFACE

Since its inception in 1969, the objectives of SIGCOMM have been to advance the state of the art in computer communications by promoting the interchange of new technical ideas and approaches to the solution of problems in data communications. This workshop was the result of an initiative made to ACM by Walter Kosinsky, General Chair of the Workshop, and myself. The intent of this event was to bring together some of the best researchers in computer communications within a stimulating atmosphere for the discussion of novel ideas, representative of the frontiers in computer-communications technology.

The original planning of the Workshop was aimed at informal technical presentations. However, as the planning of the event progressed, it became apparent that publication of the results presented at the Workshop was a must for the benefit of the SIGCOMM community at large. Following Michael Ferguson's encouragement, I decided to put together a technical program consisting mostly of full papers. This special issue of the CCR is the end result of the undertaking.

The workshop started with the keynote address by Dr. Vinton Cerf, and was followed by technical sessions arranged mainly one track at a time. The workshop consisted of 13 technical sessions and brought together 48 international speakers and was attended by 100 people.

In the past, much of the discussion on new directions in computer communications had taken place within companies or in the relatively quiet confines of such research communities as the Internet task forces. The results of that work took years to percolate to the user community at large. Today, however, we are witnessing a great acceleration in the way in which new computer communication technology is developed and, subsequently, adopted by users. The workshop reflected this trend throughout its various sessions, which dealt with research issues, implementation problems, and experience.

A great deal of work is involved in planning an international meeting of the caliber of the SIGCOMM symposia and workshops. The quality of the papers in this volume is an indication of the efforts by members of the technical program committee. Of these, special mention should be made of Jun Murai, Steve Wolff, Al Thaler, Dan Lynch, and Lou Schreier, for their efforts in putting together many of the technical sessions of the Workshop.

As program chairman of the workshop, I would finally like to acknowledge the invaluable support received from Michael Frankel, Earl Craighill, and JoAnn Hodges of the Information Sciences and Technology Center of SRI International.

J.J. Garcia-Luna-Aceves
Information Sciences and Technology Center
SRI International

SYMPOSIUM COMMITTEE

General Chair
Walter Kosinsky
Central China University of
Science and Technology
Dept. of Computer Science
H.U.S.T. Wuham, Hubei
China

Program Chair
J. J. Garcia-Luna-Aceves
SRI International
333 Ravenswood Avenue
Menlo Park, CA 94025
USA

Conference Registrar
John Trono
Computer Science Department
Saint Michael's College
P.O. Box 243
Winooski, VT 05404

PROGRAM COMMITTEE

L. Chapin, *Data General, USA*
S. Lam, *University of Texas at Austin, USA*
D. Lynch, *Advanced Computer Environments, USA*
J. Mathis, *Apple, USA*
Jun Murai, *University of Tokyo, Japan*
L. Schreier, *SRI International, USA*
A. Thaler, *National Science Foundation, USA*
Y. Wang, *Tongzi University, China*
S. Wolff, *National Science Foundation, USA*

KEYNOTE SESSION

Keynote Address: Rarefied Protocols - A Look at the Upper Layer
Vinton Cerf, Corporation for National Research Initiatives, USA

TABLE OF CONTENTS

PART 1. TCP/IP ISSUES 1

Chair: D. Lynch, Advanced Computer Environments, USA

Improving Round-Trip Time Estimates in Reliable Transport Protocols 2
P. Karn, Bellcore, and C. Partridge, BBN Laboratories, Inc., USA

Internet Protocol Implementation Experiences in PC-NFS 8
G. Arnold, Sun Microsystems Inc., USA

The Kiewit Network: A Large AppleTalk Internetwork 15
R. Brown, Darmouth College, USA

Supercomputers on the Internet: A Case Study 27
C. Kline, University of Illinois, USA

PART 2. PERFORMANCE ANALYSIS 34

Chair: J. Garcia-Luna-Aceves, SRI International, USA

Performance Modeling of the Orwell Basic Access Mechanism 35
M. Zafirovic and I. Niemegeers, Univ. of Twente, The Netherlands

Efficient Point-to-Point and Point-to-Multipoint Selective-Repeat 49
ARQ Schemes with Multiple Retransmissions: A Throughput Analysis
S. Mohan, J. Qian, N. Rao, Clarkson University, USA

Performance of Priorities on an 802.5 Token Ring 58
J. Peden and A. Weaver, University of Virginia, USA

PART 3. COMPUTER NETWORKS IN JAPAN 67

Chair: Jun Murai, University of Tokyo, Japan

Researches in Network Development on JUNET 68
J. Murai, University of Tokyo, and A. Kato, Tokyo Institute of Technology, Japan

Computer Networking for Large Computers in Universities 78
J. Matsukata, University of Tokyo, Japan

The SIGMA Network 88
K. Saito, SIGMA Project, Japan

PART 4. EXPRES: NEAR- AND LONG-TERM IMPLICATIONS OF THE 98
NSF SPONSORED PROJECT ON EXPERIMENTAL RESEARCH IN
ELECTRONIC PROPOSAL SUBMISSION.

Chair: Al Thaler, National Science Foundation, USA

    An Overview of the Andrew Message System 99

    J. Rosenberg, C. Everhart, N. Borenstein, Carnegie Mellon University, USA

PART 5. PROTOCOL VERIFICATION AND CONVERSION 109

Chair: S. Lam, University of Texas at Austin, USA

    A Verified Connection Management Protocol for the Transport Layer 110
    S. Murphy and U. Shankar, University of Maryland, USA

    Protocol Verification Using Reachability Analysis: The State Space 126
    Explosion Problem and Relief Strategies
    F. Lin, P. Chu, M. Liu, Ohio State University, USA

    New Communication Protocols from Old 136
    Z. Bavel, J. Grzymala-Buse, and Y. Hsia, University of Kansas, USA

    An Exercise in Deriving Protocol Conversion 151
    K. Calveret and S. Lam, University of Texas at Austin, USA

PART 6. ROUTING IN LARGE NETWORKS 161

Chair: L. Chapin, Data General, USA

    Modeling, Analysis, and Optimal Routing of Flow-Controlled 162
    Communication Networks
    S. Lam and C. Hsieh, University of Texas at Austin, USA

    Adaptive Routing in Burroughs Network Architecture 173
    J. Rosenberg, S. Gruchevsky and D. Piscitello, UNYSIS Corporation, USA

    An Architecture for Network-Layer Routing in OSI 185
    P. Tsuchiya, MITRE Corporation, USA

    The NSFNET Backbone Network 191
    D. Mills, University of Delaware, and H. Braun, University of Michigan, USA

PART 7. PROTOCOL DEVELOPMENT AND PERFORMANCE 197
Chair: W. Kosinsky, Norwich University, USA

Algorithms for The Reduction of Timed Finite State Graphs 198
G. Masapati and G. White, University of Ottawa, Canada

Extensions to Hoare's Communicating Sequential Processes to Allow 217
Protocol Performance Specification
J. Zic, University of Sydney, Australia

The IC* System for Protocol Development 228
D. Cohen and T. Guinther, Bell Communications Research, USA

PART 8. RESOURCE SHARING IN DISTRIBUTED SYSTEMS 234
Chair: L. Schreier, SRI International, USA

A Yellow-Pages Service for a Local Area Network 235
L. Peterson, University of Arizona, USA

Resource Management in the Cronus Distributed Operating System 243
R. Schantz, K. Schroeder, and P. Neves, BBN Laboratories Inc., USA

Strategies for Decentralized Resource Management 245
Michael Stumm, University of Toronto, Canada

Resource Management in a Distributed Internetwork Environment 254
G. Skinner, J. Wrabetz, and L. Schreier, SRI International, USA

PART 9. COMPUTER-SUPPORTED COLLABORATIVE WORK 259
Chair: J. Garcia-Luna-Aceves, SRI International, USA

A Network Environment for Computer Supported Collaborative Work 260
J. Whitescarver, P. Mukherji, and M. Turoff, New Jersey Institute of Technology, USA

Integrating X.400 Message Handling into the IBM VM/SP Environment 273
K. Fischer and W. Racke, IBM European Networking Center, West Germany

Laboratory for Emulation and Study of Integrated and 283
Coordinated Media Communication
L. Ludwig and D. Dunn, Bell Communications research

Telescience and Advanced Technologies 292
B. Leiner, Research Institute for Advanced Computer Science, USA

PART 10. DISTRIBUTED SYSTEMS ... 293
Chair: L. Schreier, SRI International, USA

Models of a Very large Distributed Database ... 294
M. Blakey, Monash University, Australia

A Threaded/Flow Approach to Service Primitives Architectures ... 306
L. Ludwig, Bell Communications Research, USA

Distributed Shared Memory in a Loosely Coupled Distributed System ... 317
B. Fleisch, UCLA, USA

Resource Management Schemes in Distributed Environment ... 328
O. Nakamura and N. Saito, Keio University, Japan

PART 11. COMMUNICATION PROTOCOLS ... 335
Chair: J. Mathis, Apple, USA

Receiver-Initiated Busy-Tone Multiple Access in Packet Radio Networks ... 336
C. Wu and V.O.K. Li, University of Southern California, USA

A Reliable and Efficient Multicast Protocol for Broadband Broadcast Networks ... 343
A. Erramilli and R. Singh, Bell Communications Research, USA

NETBLT: A High Throughput Transport Protocol ... 353
D. Clark, M. Lambert, L. Zhang, Massachusetts Institute of Technology, USA

Measurement Management Service ... 360
P. Amer and L. Cassel, University of Delaware, USA

PART 12. NETWORK INTERCONNECTION AND SWITCHING ... 368
Chair: Y. Wang, Tongzi University, China

LAN-HUB: An Ethernet Compatible Low Cost/High Performance Communication ... 369
I. Chlamtac, University of Massachusetts, USA, and A. Herman, Codex Corporation, USA

Transparent Interconnection of Incompatible Local Area Networks Using Bridges ... 381
G. Varghese and R. Perlman, Digital Equipment Corporation, USA

Fragmentation Considered Harmful ... 390
C. Kent and J. Mogul, Digital Equipment Corporation, USA

A Case for Packet Switching in High-Speed Wide-Area Networks ... 402
Z. Haas and D. Cheriton, Stanford University, USA

PART 1. TCP/IP ISSUES

D. Lynch

Advanced Computer Environments, USA

Improving Round-Trip Time Estimates in Reliable Transport Protocols

Phil Karn
Bell Communications Research, Incorporated

Craig Partridge
Harvard University/BBN Laboratories Incorporated

1. Abstract

As a reliable, end-to-end transport protocol, the ARPA Transmission Control Protocol (TCP) uses positive acknowledgements and retransmission to guarantee delivery. TCP implementations are expected to measure and adapt to changing network propagation delays so that its retransmission behavior balances user throughput and network efficiency. However, TCP suffers from a problem we call *retransmission ambiguity*: when an acknowledgment arrives for a segment that has been retransmitted, there is no indication which transmission is being acknowledged. Many existing TCP implementations do not handle this problem correctly.

This paper reviews the various approaches to retransmission and presents a novel and effective approach to the retransmission ambiguity problem.

2. Introduction

Dynamically estimating the round-trip time, the interval between the sending of a packet and the receipt of its acknowledgement, is a key function in many reliable transport protocols [5,15,22]. Such estimates are used to ensure that data is reliably delivered. If a packet remains unacknowledged for too long, it is assumed to have been lost and is retransmitted. Estimated round-trip times are used to determine when these retransmissions will occur.

Three developments in IP networking [19,20,21] have led to increased interest in the problems of estimating round-trip times.

First, there has been an explosive growth in the size and complexity of IP *internetworks*, built by interconnecting existing subnetworks. The best known example is the ARPA Internet. (The ARPANET is just one component subnetwork in the ARPA Internet.) The ARPA Internet has highly variable round-trip times. Because its paths are very complex, it also tends to lose more packets.

Second, there has been a large increase in traffic on some of the major IP networks. Higher traffic loads have led to serious network congestion on some parts of the ARPA Internet [16,18]. Like network size, congestion is known to cause highly variable round-trip times and higher packet loss rates.

Finally, recent research has shown that the standard approaches to estimating round-trip times for the Transmission Control Protocol (TCP) are inaccurate if packets are lost or round-trip times are highly variable [9,24]. This discovery is distressing because it suggests that the mechanism reliable protocols depend upon to handle loss and variable round-trip times, namely the estimation of round-trip times, may not work well.

Concern about the accuracy of estimated round-trip times has led to some interesting research into reliability mechanisms which are less dependent on round-trip estimates [2,24]. The authors, however, take a different approach that tries to improve the data used to compute round-trip time estimates. In this paper we present an analysis of this work.

3. The TCP Algorithm

TCP implementations attempt to predict future round-trip times by sampling the behavior of packets sent over a connection and averaging those samples into a "smoothed" round-trip time estimate, *SRTT*.

When a packet is sent over a TCP connection, the sender times how long it takes for it to be acknowledged, producing a sequence, S, of round-trip time samples: $s_1, s_2, s_3 \ldots$.

Permission to copy without fee all or part of this material is granted provided that the copies are not made or distributed for direct commercial advantage, the ACM copyright notice and the title of the publication and its date appear, and notice is given that copying is by permission of the Association for Computing Machinery. To copy otherwise, or to republish, requires a fee and/or specfic permission.

© 1988 ACM 0-89791-245-4/88/,001/0002 $1.50

With each new sample, s_i, the new SRTT is computed from the formula:

$$SRTT_{i+1} = (\alpha \times SRTT_i) + (1-\alpha) \times s_i$$

where $SRTT_i$ is the current estimate of the round-trip time, $SRTT_{i+1}$ is the new computed value, and α is a constant between 0 and 1 that controls how rapidly the SRTT adapts to change.

The retransmission time-out (RTO_i), the amount of time the sender will wait for a given packet to be acknowledged, is computed from $SRTT_i$. The formula is:

$$RTO_i = \beta \times SRTT_i$$

where β is a constant, greater than 1, chosen such that there is an acceptably small probability that the round-trip time for the packet will exceed RTO_i.

3.1. General Observations

There are several things to observe about the algorithm. First, it can be viewed as an attempt to approximate the next value from a function R, where $R(i)$ is the actual round-trip time for packet i. Given the sequence of measured round-trip times,

$$S = s_1, s_2, s_3, \ldots, s_{i-1}$$

which correspond to the values of R:

$$s_1 = R(1), s_2 = R(2), \ldots, s_{i-1} = R(i-1)$$

we hope that the RTO computed from those values will be a good upper bound on $R(i)$, the round-trip time for the next packet. Notice that if the measured round-trip times, S, are inaccurate then the RTO is probably incorrect; this problem is examined in the next section.

One should also observe that the values of the constants α and β have important effects on the behavior of the algorithm.

The value of α controls how rapidly the SRTT adjusts to changing round-trip times. Mills [11] has measured network round-trip times and recommends that there be two values for α, depending on the relative values of the sample, s_i, and $SRTT_i$. Mills observed that round-trip times are roughly Poisson distributed, but with brief periods of high delay. During these periods, he found that the standard way of computing SRTT and RTO often did not adapt swiftly enough, and the TCP sender would unnecessarily retransmit packets because the RTO was set too low. As a result, he suggested a nonlinear filter where α is smaller when $SRTT_i < s_i$, allowing the SRTT to adapt more swiftly to sudden increases in network delay.

Choosing a value for β is harder because it has important and conflicting effects on individual user throughput and overall network efficiency [15]. To achieve optimal throughput β should be only a little greater than 1. This keeps the RTO very close to the SRTT and ensures that packet loss will be quickly detected. Detecting lost packets quickly is important for good throughput, since the end-to-end flow control mechanisms in reliable protocols like TCP will cause the sender to stop transmitting new packets if a packet remains unacknowledged for much longer than the round-trip time.

Unfortunately, what is good for throughput is disastrous for efficient network utilization. If the RTO is nearly equal to the SRTT (i.e., if β is near unity) then a large number of packets will be retransmitted unnecessarily because the sender times out too soon. For example, consider the situation where $RTO = SRTT$, (i.e, $\beta=1$), and the SRTT is an accurate median of the round-trip times. In this case, roughly half of all packets will be timed out and retransmitted because their acknowledgement took too long, burdening the network with unnecessary retransmissions. To minimize retransmissions, β should be chosen such that the RTO will be a high upper limit on the round-trip times. The TCP specification [21] recommends a value of $\beta=2$ as a reasonable balance. Another possibility suggested by Van Jacobson [7,8] is to vary β based on the observed variance in measured round-trip times, although this is outside the immediate scope of this paper.

3.2. Back-off

Whenever a timeout occurs, virtually every TCP implementation increases the RTO by some factor before retransmitting the unacknowledged data. Should the new, larger RTO expire yet again before the retransmission is acknowledged, it is increased still further. This technique is known as *back-off*. (Back-off is performed independently of SRTT calculation, since without an acknowledgment there is no new timing information to be fed into the calculation). A variety of algorithms are used since the TCP specification does not prescribe one. Some (e.g., Berkeley UNIX[1]) step through a table of arbitrary back-off factors for each successive retransmission; others simply double the RTO (i.e., perform binary exponential back-off) for each consecutive attempt. Whatever the algorithm, TCP back-off is essential in keeping the network stable when sudden overloads cause packets to be dropped. When the overload condition disappears, packet loss stops and the TCPs reduce their RTO to their normal SRTT-based values.

---

[1] UNIX is a trademark of AT&T Bell Laboratories.

4. Sampling Round-Trip Times

A key assumption of the TCP algorithm is that the sequence of round-trip samples is an accurate measurement of the true network round-trip times (i.e., that $s_1=R(1), s_2=R(2)$, etc.). It has recently been shown that the two standard sampling methods, measuring from the first transmission and measuring from the most recent transmission, give inaccurate results [9,24].

This inaccuracy is caused by packet retransmission. The information carried in the packet headers of TCP and most other reliable protocols does not indicate if an acknowledgement is in response to the original transmission of a packet or a retransmission. As a result, a round-trip time measurement for a retransmitted packet is ambiguous. We will call this problem *retransmission ambiguity*.

4.1. Measuring From the First Transmission

Many TCP implementations measure round-trip times from the first transmission of a packet. Whenever an acknowledgement is received, the round-trip time is computed from the first time the packet was sent, regardless of how many times the acknowledged packet has been retransmitted.

Sampling from the first transmission may cause the SRTT to grow without bound when there is loss on the network. When there is loss, the TCP sender must retransmit lost packets. If we look at the sequence of samples, S_F, we discover that it contains samples of two types. If γ_i is a boolean function which is 0 if the acknowledgement for packet i is acknowledging a retransmission, S_F can be expressed as:

$$S_F = \begin{cases} s_i & \text{if } \gamma_i \neq 0 \\ \overline{s_i} & \text{if } \gamma_i = 0 \end{cases}$$

If we look at the values of $\overline{s_i}$, those samples which are derived from the acknowledgements of retransmissions, we find that they are a function of the true round-trip time, $R(i)$, the SRTT, and the particular retransmission of packet i, r_i, where $r_i > 0$, which is being acknowledged:

$$\overline{s_i} = R(i) + r_i \times RTO_i = R(i) + r_i \times \beta \times SRTT_i$$

$\overline{s_i}$ will be used to compute the new smoothed round-trip time, $SRTT_{i+1}$. Plugging $\overline{s_i}$ into the SRTT function gives:

$$SRTT_{i+1} = (\alpha \times SRTT_i) + (1-\alpha) \times (R(i) + r_i \times \beta \times SRTT_i)$$
$$= (\alpha \times SRTT_i) + (1-\alpha) \times R(i) + (\beta r_i - \alpha \beta r_i) \times SRTT_i$$

Since $0 < \alpha < 1$ the factor $(\beta r_i - \alpha \beta r_i)$ is greater than zero and distorts the function, causing it to inflate the value of the SRTT. Inflated round-trip time estimates may not be a problem if the original reason for the high loss rate was network congestion, because congestion tends to increase round-trip times anyway. It is also acceptable if the loss rate is very low since the accumulated error is so small that it will probably have no noticeable effect on the SRTT. However, if the path is lossy (e.g., a noisy packet radio channel operating without link level acknowledgements), the SRTT grows and throughput unnecessarily decreases to low levels.

4.2. Measuring From the Most Recent Transmission

Another popular method measures round-trip time from the most recent transmission of a packet. The implicit assumption in this method is that the RTO is accurate; if a packet has to be retransmitted then previous transmissions have almost certainly been lost.

Unfortunately, this assumption is often false. If the RTO is smaller than the true round-trip time, acknowledgements for previous transmissions may arrive after a retransmission. If τ_i is a boolean function which returns 0 if the acknowledgement is for a previous transmission, the sequence of sampled values, S_R is:

$$S_R = \begin{cases} s_i & \text{if } \tau_i \neq 0 \\ \overline{s_i} & \text{if } \tau_i = 0 \end{cases}$$

At first glance this doesn't look too bad. $\overline{s_i}$ is a value between 0 and the RTO, which might be expected to distort the SRTT a bit, but doesn't have the growth term caused by measuring from the first transmission.

But the picture is not quite so rosy. Recall that the RTO is intended as an estimate of the maximum possible round-trip time. If an acknowledgement arrives after the RTO has expired, it is highly likely to come very shortly afterwards. In other words, instead of being randomly distributed between 0 and the RTO, $\overline{s_i}$ is likely to be very close to 0 (recall that the sample timer was reset when the RTO had elapsed). This will cause the SRTT to decline, reducing the RTO, and increasing the likelihood that a packet will be acknowledged just after the RTO has expired. The SRTT stabilizes at an unreasonably low estimate. Unnecessary data retransmissions occur constantly, useful throughput drops sharply, and network bandwidth is wasted.

Observe that the problem of a declining SRTT could be avoided if the RTO were set extremely high, so high that no packet could survive that long unacknowledged. Recall however, that for high throughput, the RTO cannot be much larger than the SRTT. An algorithm which requires an extremely high RTO will give unacceptable performance across a lossy path.

4.3. Ignoring Round-Trip Times for Packets That Have Been Retransmitted

Some implementations simply ignore round-trip time samples tainted by retransmission.

This method works, provided the true round-trip time never grows faster than the algorithm can adapt. If there is a sudden increase in network round-trip time (e.g., when the failure of a primary path causes packets to be sent via a slower secondary path), and if the new path delay becomes larger than the RTO, all samples will be discarded, because every packet will be retransmitted before the acknowledgement comes back. Note that if the RTO is reasonable (i.e., if β is chosen well) then the chance of a dramatic surge is quite small. But the consequences of such a surge are truly disastrous — the sender is stuck with an unrealistically short RTO that it has little chance or no chance of correcting. Once again, there are numerous unnecessary retransmissions, throughput drops sharply and network capacity is wasted.

4.4. Karn's Algorithm

Very recently a new sampling method has been suggested by one of the authors. This method addresses the problems with ignoring round-trip times of retransmitted packets.

The fundamental notion of Karn's algorithm is to use RTO back-off to collect accurate round-trip time measurements uncontaminated by retransmission ambiguity. The rule is as follows:

> When an acknowledgement arrives for a packet that has been sent more than once (i.e., retransmitted at least once), ignore any round-trip measurement based on this packet, thus avoiding the retransmission ambiguity problem. *In addition, the backed-off RTO for this packet is kept for the next packet. Only when it (or a succeeding packet) is acknowledged without an intervening retransmission will the RTO be recalculated from SRTT.*

The last provision ensures that new and accurate round trip measurements will be taken and fed into the SRTT estimate regardless of any sudden increase in round-trip delay. If the increase is large, the RTO may oscillate between the backed-off value necessary to avoid an unnecessary retransmission and the value calculated from SRTT. However, the SRTT will converge to the correct value, and unnecessary retransmission will stop.

How quickly the SRTT converges to the new round-trip time depends on the back-off algorithm and the SRTT smoothing algorithm, but typically this convergence is quite fast. To prevent unnecessary retransmissions, the RTO must be greater than the new round-trip time. To achieve this new RTO value the SRTT must be at least as large as the new round-trip time, s, divided by β. (For simplicity in the proof, we assume that the new value for s does not vary). Reaching the new RTO takes n valid samples, where n is the minimum value for which the following equality in terms of the new RTT, s, and the old SRTT, z, is true:

$$\frac{s}{\beta} \leq (z \times \alpha^n) + \sum_{i=1}^{n}((s \times (1-\alpha)) \times \alpha^{(i-1)})$$

In the worst case $s-z$ is almost s (i.e., $s \gg z$), so the z term may be ignored. Dividing the remaining terms by s, we find that the upper limit on n is given by the solution to:

$$\frac{1}{\beta} \leq \sum_{i=1}^{n}(1-\alpha) \times \alpha^{(i-1)}$$

Using typical values of $\alpha = 0.875$ and $\beta = 2$, n is only 6. Since the number of required valid samples is small, convergence is usually swift.

A TCP implementation using Karn's algorithm and Mills' nonlinear filter has been in heavy use on perhaps the worst medium ever used to pass IP datagrams: amateur packet radio [10]. Despite packet loss rates often exceeding 50%, SRTT values remain quite stable, changing only in response to true changes in round-trip time. Packets lost due to noise leave the SRTT unaffected.

4.5. Sampling RTTs in Parallel

While Karn's algorithm is currently the best available solution to the sampling problem, it is worth taking a few paragraphs to discuss another class of sampling algorithms which have been developed recently. These algorithms depend on the fact that most transport protocols send more than one packet at a time, and as a result it is possible to take multiple round-trip time samples in parallel.

One such algorithm has recently been developed in an implementation of the Reliable Data Protocol (RDP), which uses the TCP algorithm to estimate round-trip times [4,17,22]. It relies on the fact that networks almost always preserve packet ordering. If two packets are sent close together it is likely that they will reach their destination in the order they were sent, and be acknowledged in the same order. So if an acknowledgement for packet i is received after the acknowledgement for packet j, where $j>i$, it is a strong hint that the acknowledgement is for a retransmission of packet i. We can check the retransmission count, r_i, for packet i, so this observation gives a sampling method.

Measuring from the first transmission, a sample for packet i, s_i, should be discarded if:

- An acknowledgement for some packet j, $j>i$, has already been received, *and*
- $r_i \neq 0$

The first test can only be applied if packets can be acknowledged when they are received out of order. Such acknowledgements are called *extended* or *selective acknowledgements*. RDP supports extended acknowledgements. TCP does not, although consideration is being given to adding this facility [1].

The performance of this sampling method is highly dependent on the number of parallel transmissions a protocol implementation will support. Observations suggest that the algorithm keeps accurate round-trip estimates at much higher loss rates than sampling from the first transmission.

Other estimation methods that use multiple samples taken in parallel have been explored in Mills' work on synchronizing network clocks [12,13,14]. Synchronizing clocks involves problems of handling a certain amount of bad data, caused by noisy links or faulty clocks. The techniques used to eliminate such bad values can also be applied to the problem of extracting good round-trip times from a set of several round-trip times collected at roughly the same time.

Parallel sampling methods tend to suffer from two problems. First, they can be adversely affected by the loss of an entire group of packets; all the samples become bad. Second, they often fail when a network is congested. When a network is congested, most protocols attempt to reduce the data they put on the network by limiting themselves to sending one packet at a time. Unfortunately, a network is most likely to drop packets when it is congested. Thus the ability to take parallel samples is lost at precisely the time we would most like to have an accurate sampling method. One could blur the notion of "parallel" and simply apply these techniques after every n samples, where n is chosen to equal the number packets that are normally in flight. But when the protocol is in one-packet-at-a-time mode, recomputing the SRTT must be delayed until n samples have been collected, which could be a long time, at minimum it is roughly $n \times SRTT$.

5. The Perfect Sampling Method

It is worth noting for a moment that most of the methods discussed in this section are attempts to achieve the sampling function γ discussed in section 3.2. Recall that γ was a boolean function which returned 0 if the sample was taken from the acknowledgement of a retransmission. The sampling methods want to use only those samples measuring the time between the first transmission of a packet and the acknowledgement of that first transmission, i.e., those samples for which $\gamma \neq 0$. The problem is that most sampling methods are inadequate approximations of γ, and either exclude too many good samples or include too many bad samples.

Karn's algorithm solves this problem by accepting only good samples and using the retransmission back-off strategy to ensure that good samples will eventually be available even if round-trip times increase dramatically.

6. Deficiencies in the TCP Algorithm

So far this paper has focussed on how to improve round-trip estimates by using better sampling methods. Before concluding we would like to touch briefly on some other ways that round-trip estimates can be improved.

One improvement is to sample more frequently. Some protocol implementations sample round-trips only once per sending window, leading to poor estimates because the estimator does not have enough recent samples to detect changes in the round-trip time.

Another possible improvement is to chose a new algorithm for estimating the RTO. The TCP algorithm assumes that a weighted average, the SRTT, adjusted by some estimate of variance, β, is a good approximation of the behavior of the network function, R. Recently, research by Jacobson has shown that R is a more complex function than a simple average can accurately model [6,8]. Encouragingly, however, Jacobson's work also suggests that it may be possible to predict the values generated by R with functions of roughly the same complexity as the functions presented in section 2.

7. Conclusion

Much attention has recently been paid to the question of whether one can accurately sample round-trip times over a transport protocol connection. The authors have shown that round-trip times can be accurately sampled and have presented a simple method that gives good round-trip time samples.

8. Acknowledgements

The authors would like to thank Will Leland and Chase Cotton for their useful comments on this paper.

Bibliography

1. Braden, Robert T., Selective Acknowledgments in TCP. Draft *ARPANET Working Group Requests for Comments*.
2. Clark, David D., Lambert, Mark L., and Zhang, Lixia. NETBLT: A Bulk Data Transfer Protocol; RFC998. In *ARPANET Working Group Requests for Comments*, no. 998. SRI International, Menlo Park, Calif., March 1987.
3. Edge, Stephen William. An Adaptive Timeout Algorithm for Retransmission Across a Packet Switching Network. In *Proceedings of SIGCOMM '83*, Association for Computing Machinery, 1983.
4. Hinden, Robert M. and Partridge, Craig. Version 2 of the Reliable Data Protocol. Draft *ARPANET Working Group Requests for Comments*.
5. International Organization for Standards, Information processing systems — Open Systems Interconnection — *Connection oriented transport protocol specification*. International Standard, no. 8073. ISO, Switzerland. 1986.
6. Jacobson, Van. Presentation to the Internet End-To-End Services Task Force. April 16, 1987.
7. Jacobson, Van. *Interpacket Arrival Variance and Mean*. Letter to the TCP-IP mailing list, 15 June 1987.
8. Jacobson, Van. *Retransmit Timers: Theory and Practice*, working title of draft paper.
9. Jain, Raj, Divergence of Timeout Algorithms for Packet Retransmissions. In *Proceedings Fifth Annual International Phoenix Conference on Computers and Communications*, Scottsdale, AZ, March 26-28, 1986.
10. Karn, P. R., Price, H., Diersing, R. Packet Radio in the Amateur Service. In *IEEE Journal on Selected Areas in Communications*, May 1985.
11. Mills, David. Internet Delay Experiments; RFC889. In *ARPANET Working Group Requests for Comments*, no. 889. SRI International, Menlo Park, Calif., Dec. 1983.
12. Mills, David. Algorithms for Synchronizing Network Clocks; RFC956. In *ARPANET Working Group Requests for Comments*, no. 956. SRI International, Menlo Park, Calif., Sep. 1985.
13. Mills, David. Experiments in Network Clock Synchronization; RFC957. In *ARPANET Working Group Requests for Comments*, no. 957. SRI International, Menlo Park, Calif., Sep. 1985.
14. Mills, David. Network Time Protocol; RFC958. In *ARPANET Working Group Requests for Comments*, no. 958. SRI International, Menlo Park, Calif., Sep. 1985.
15. Morris, Robert J.T. Fixing timeout intervals for lost packet detection in computer communication networks. In *AFIPS Conference Proceedings*, 1979 National Computer Conference. AFIPS Press, Montvale, Jew Jersey.
16. Nagle, John. Congestion Control in IP/TCP Networks; RFC896. In *ARPANET Working Group Requests for Comments*, no. 896. SRI International, Menlo Park, Calif., Jan. 1984.
17. Partridge, Craig. Implementing the Reliable Data Protocol (RDP). In *Proceedings of the 1987 Summer USENIX Conference*, Phoenix, Arizona.
18. Perry, Dennis G. *Congestion in the ARPANET*. Letter to the TCP-IP Mailing List, October 1, 1986.
19. Postel, J., ed. Internet Protocol; RFC791. In *ARPANET Working Group Requests for Comments*, no. 791. SRI International, Menlo Park, Calif., Sep. 1981.
20. Postel, J., ed. Internet Control Message Protocol; RFC792. In *ARPANET Working Group Requests for Comments*, no. 792. SRI International, Menlo Park, Calif., Sep. 1981.
21. Postel, Jon, ed. Transmission Control Protocol; RFC793. In *ARPANET Working Group Requests for Comments*, no. 793. SRI International, Menlo Park, Calif., Sep. 1981.
22. Velten, David, Hinden, Robert and Sax, Jack. Reliable Data Protocol; RFC908. In *ARPANET Working Group Requests for Comments*, no. 908. SRI International, Menlo Park, Calif., July 1984.
23. Watson, Richard W. *Timer-Based Mechanisms in Reliable Transport Protocol Connection Management*. Computer Networks 1981, North-Holland Publishing Company.
24. Zhang, Lixia. Why TCP Timers Don't Work Well. In *Proceedings of SIGCOMM '86*, Association for Computing Machinery.

INTERNET PROTOCOL IMPLEMENTATION EXPERIENCES IN PC-NFS™

Geoff Arnold
garnold@sun.com

Sun Microsystems Inc. – East Coast Division
Billerica, Massachusetts 01821

ABSTRACT

A team at Sun Microsystems East Coast Division has been engaged in developing and supporting a PC implementation of Sun's Network File System (NFS™) protocols. In the course of this work we were faced with the problem of implementing Internet protocol software within the PC environment. Our experiences revealed that there are some unique obstacles to be overcome in this kind of system, and indicate that further work is needed in the development of protocols to manage networks of low-end machines.

1. Introduction

In the summer of 1985 a team at Sun's newly-established East Coast Division began work on a PC implementation of Sun's Network File System (NFS) [1,2]. Today NFS is a well-established de facto industry standard, ported to a number of operating systems [3] and backed by licensees such as IBM, DEC, Data General, Wang, and Hewlett Packard. Back then, however, there were few licensees and even fewer implementations, all of which were derived from the original 4.2BSD Unix® version. We had some concerns about whether a real PC implementation was practicable, largely because of size and performance. A conventional NFS implementation on top of a full-blown TCP/UDP/IP protocol stack would, we estimated, occupy over 150KB, almost a quarter of the total memory of a fully loaded 640KB PC. A "smart" network adaptor with on-board TCP/IP would have reduced this somewhat, but we could not ignore the price advantage of "dumb" cards, nor the huge installed base. Since the conventional wisdom dictated that we had to allow 500KB PC applications to run, and recognizing that DOS would require 40-50KB, something had to give. One of the two themes of this paper is how we solved this problem.

As we proceeded with the development of PC-NFS, the question of software installation and configuration began to trouble us. We analyzed the process that people went through to add a Sun or a VAX™ to an Ethernet, compared this to the expectations of the average PC user, and saw a serious mismatch. The extent to which we were able to overcome this problem, and the issues which still need to be addressed in this area form the second theme.

It should be noted that this is not an NFS paper, although some references to the protocol-related aspects of NFS are inevitable. Readers seeking more information on NFS are referred to [list of references]; those who are interested in the way in which we overcame the differences between the NFS model and the MS™-DOS file system should read [4].

Our efforts do not represent the first attempt to provide Internet protocol services on the PC architecture. Quite apart from the extensive academic work in this area (much of which is touched on in [5]), there have been a number of commercially-developed products from vendors such as Excelan and Network Research Corp. All of these implementations have assumed that they could take over the complete PC for their own use; our work was characterized by the fact that we were implementing an extension to the native operating system services and therefore needed to leave as much PC memory as possible for the use of normal DOS applications.

2. Goals

Our first goal was to provide a mechanism for a PC to become an NFS client, and to map the server file systems into the DOS model to preserve the DOS semantics as faithfully as possible. This required an implementation of the lingua franca for NFS networking, which was (and remains) TCP/IP on Ethernet. We also recognized that simply offering file sharing would not make a useful product: we also needed to provide network printer redirection and spooling, remote login (if only so that the user could go in and fix problems arising from the differences between the Unix and DOS file system models), and (eventually) additional network services. Since we were committed to implementing a set of Internet protocols for NFS, we naturally thought in terms of providing standard Telnet and FTP capabilities. Where there was no Internet standard we followed 4.2BSD Unix (*rsh*, *rcp*), and where no adequate standard existed we chose to implement our own RPC-based [6] services (printing,

Permission to copy without fee all or part of this material is granted provided that the copies are not made or distributed for direct commercial advantage, the ACM copyright notice and the title of the publication and its date appear, and notice is given that copying is by permission of the Association for Computing Machinery. To copy otherwise, or to republish, requires a fee and/or specfic permission.

© 1988 ACM 0-89791-245-4/88/0001/0008 $1.50

authentication). Because all of this required the development of a networking toolkit library, we decided to make this available for people who wished to build or port network applications [7].

In addition to identifying deliverable functionality, we also established the criteria by which we could monitor the design and implementation process and judge the finished product: size, performance, ease of installation and use, breadth of hardware support, and conformance to standards (including the "standard" of DOS). As we quantified these, it became clear that they would have a major impact on the architecture.

3. Constraints

In working within the PC environment, one is faced with constraints in four areas: memory use, hardware limitations, software interaction, and user expectations. All of these arise from the nature of the PC: a small, cheap system with extremely primitive systems software and a highly competitive applications software market in which vendors are constantly competing in the areas of performance (even if it means bending the "rules") and presentation (user interface, documentation, installation, and so on).

3.1 Memory

The fact that DOS provides no support for multitasking means that PC users have to run applications in a serial fashion. This means that the size of any permanently resident software sets an upper bound on the size of application that can be run. Because many early PC lookalikes were limited to 512KB rather than the normal maximum of 640KB, many applications are designed to run in about 470KB (512KB less 40KB for DOS). This was one of the reasons for establishing our goal of being able to support 500KB applications in a 640KB PC.

There are other memory considerations, however. Many users rely on so-called Terminate-and-Stay-Resident (TSR) software which they can load and leave in the background until needed, and which can then be activated (even in the middle of another application) by the use of a "hot key" sequence. We decided that our Telnet should be capable of "TSR'ing" so that the user could switch between a DOS application and a remote session. Since TSR programs need to be small (otherwise you cannot do much useful work while they are in memory) this placed a limit on the size of Telnet.

DOS presented us with another small memory constraint. For a variety of technical reasons, we decided to implement the main PC-NFS and IP subsystem as a DOS device driver. It just so happens that DOS limits the size of drivers to 64KB. Those who have worked on PDP-11's will empathize.

3.2 Hardware

The main hardware issue was the choice of a first Ethernet adaptor. (Over time we planned to add support for various other designs, but we had to pick a first unit to support and OEM.) The large installed base and competitive price of 3Com's 3C501 made this a natural choice. It turned out to have far-reaching consequences for the Internet protocol implementation, due to two "features" of the design. First, the unit cannot receive a packet while a packet is being loaded into the transmit buffer. This led us to drop a few packets, but for a client employing a synchronous request-response protocol the situation is not too bad. More seriously, there is only one receive buffer so that it is impossible to receive closely-spaced ("back-to-back") packets. The consequences of this are discussed below in section 5.

3.3 Software

Some of the problems in writing systems software in the DOS environment arise from the attempt to do multitasking under DOS. Many applications – including those built on our network toolkit – need to implement some kind of private multitasking, usually by intercepting DOS clock interrupts. Unfortunately, certain programs, including a number of the more popular TSR's, can be rather careless when it comes to passing on clock interrupts to other applications. For most applications, this simply holds things up; for a TCP application it could lead to the session timing out.

3.4 Personal

Users of systems like Suns and VAXes have learned to expect that they, or some local guru, will have to learn about the care and feeding of the system. They may also have recourse to tools such as on-line manual pages, context-sensitive help, or interactive tutorials to help them when they get out of their depth. Software installation frequently requires the user to visit a machine room in order to use devices such as 9-track tape drives. Because few system configurations are 100% off-the-shelf, by-the-book affairs there is a certain acceptance (tinged with resignation) when it comes to complex customization and installation procedures. Finally, there is a reluctance to change historical methods (for example, moving from hand-editing a configuration file to using a visual configuration tool), particularly when there is a certain loss of flexibility. (There may also be a little bit of "guru job security" involved.)

PCs are intensely *personal* systems. Most PC users are focussed on the use of their system for one or two applications, and expect the application to take care of "everything." For example, instead of letting DOS report critical errors directly to the user, many applications install their own Critical Error Handler in place of the standard DOS service. This means that it is very important for system software layers such as PC-NFS to try to map all failures into something as DOS-like as possible and to use the DOS mechanisms for error reporting. On a Sun workstation, the failure of an NFS server to respond will cause the message:

```
NFS server name not replying...
```

to be displayed. In PC-NFS we report a

```
Drive not ready
```

condition, just as though the user had left the diskette drive door open. Applications such as Lotus 1-2-3 understand this error and can present the situation to the user in a appropriate fashion.

Installation of PC software *has* to be easy and non-threatening – after all, it is the first thing the user sees, and sets his or her expectations about the rest of the system.

Most PC applications ask about nothing more than the drive on which the software is to be installed, what kind of video and printer are being used, and (maybe) whether a mouse is present. In contrast, it is difficult to create an easy-to-use installation procedure which has to ask lots of hardware and network configuration questions, particularly if these involve unfamiliar concepts such as Internet addresses and Yellow Pages domains. We consider this further in section 7.

4. The Architecture of PC-NFS

In [8], David Clark suggests that there is an inevitable trade-off between good structure and good performance; that the "obvious" way of structuring a protocol implementation – along protocol boundaries – will usually not give the highest performance. In view of the fact that a PC is likely to be the slowest machine on the net with the most primitive network interface, it will come as no surprise that we concentrated on squeezing out every drop of performance and arrived at a design which was highly optimized for the most common network configurations. Following the ideas in [8], we found that the appropriate structuring strategy was along the boundaries involving demultiplexing. This allowed us to develop a design in which we could integrate both resident (OS level) and transient (application level) protocol components to give us the best usage of memory at a reasonable performance.

We cared passionately about not wasting cycles in processing packets which we were not interested in, and where possible we elected to have a server on the network worry about difficult issues. Despite the fact that most of us had backgrounds in C and Unix, we had no hesitation in deciding that to meet our goals we would have to use 8088 assembler language for the resident code, even though this meant that we would be unable to reuse any of the Unix NFS code.

4.1 Components

Figure 1 illustrates the functional components of PC-NFS. There are three resident subsystems, each organized as a DOS device driver. The first is pcnfs.sys which includes: the system call redirector; the NFS layer which maps each DOS function into the appropriate sequence of NFS operations; a tightly-integrated UDP/IP-based RPC/XDR subsystem which knows just enough to support NFS and lock manager calls; and a layer which includes IP, ICMP, ARP and RARP. This last layer is also accessible by application programs via a set of *ioctl*'s on the pcnfs "device." Much of the simplification which was necessary to meet the size, performance and ease-of-installation goals was carried out in this layer.

The second resident piece is the driver for the Ethernet adaptor, 3c501.sys. To transmit a packet, the IP layer calls the driver's send routine. When a packet is received, the driver reads its header and passes this to the input demultiplexing routine. This is logically part of the IP layer but is linked into the device driver for efficiency. The demultiplexing code determines which client "selector" should receive the packet and whether there is a buffer attached to the selector. (See figure 2.). If a selector is ready and waiting, the driver copies the data into the buffer and then upcalls the corresponding client so that it can schedule packet processing and allocate a new buffer. If no buffer is ready or if no client is listening for this packet, the driver is told to drop the packet; in the case of the 3C501 we don't even bother to read the data out of the adaptor.

The selectors are divided into two groups: those which correspond to entities within pcnfs.sys (for example NFS UDP/RPC or ARP), and those which are used by network applications. These applications need one additional piece of resident support: the driver socket.sys. This implements a set of socket devices, and thereby allows us to emulate the 4.2BSD Unix semantics of using regular *read()* and *write()* calls with sockets. The driver takes the *read* or *write* function and passes it back up to the application's network library where it can be mapped into a *send()* or *recv()*.

4.2 Network Library

The network library code itself is distantly related to MIT's PC/IP [9]. However in place of the tasking model developed by Saltzer et al we have adopted a pre-emptive, event-driven scheme which allows us to better emulate the 4.2BSD Unix environment while supporting multiple network applications. The library includes almost all of the socket, RPC (Remote Procedure Call), XDR (eXternal Data Representation), and YP (Yellow Pages) routines available in SunOS, together with the network environment routines such as gethostbyname which (like the SunOS version) uses Yellow Pages [10] if this is available. The only subsystem which is not supported is the set of RPC routines which support server operations: being an RPC server requires the presence of a portmapper daemon, and we decided that the complexity of implementing the necessary interprocess communication was not worth it.

5. Consequences of the Hardware

The principal problem which we had with the 3C501 board was its inability to receive back-to-back packets. This had two effects: we had to try to guarantee that no system ever tried to send back-to-back packets to us, and we had to cope with broadcasts.

5.1 Avoiding Fragmentation

Trying to ensure that nobody ever transmits back-to-back packets to you is surprisingly hard. In the TCP case we can limit MAX_SEG_SIZE to a value less than ETHERMTU, such as 1024, and refrain from opening our receive window any wider than that. The problem is with UDP-based services. For NFS operations we were careful to break up any large reads into 1KB chunks and never ask for more than 1KB of directory entries at a time. However, some services provide no way for the client to put an upper bound on the size of an RPC reply, with unpredictable results. For example, if you use the PC-NFS *showmnt* command to ask a server's mount daemon which systems are using its exported file systems, the daemon will blindly return a copy of its mount list, and if the latter is so large that causes the reply to exceed ETHERMTU the response will be lost and the RPC will time out. Diagnosis is tricky, because losing an IP fragment is something that the protocol suite is designed to handle, and if you were running on more sophisticated hardware you would want to let the higher levels handle it. In practice it is infrequent enough that we just

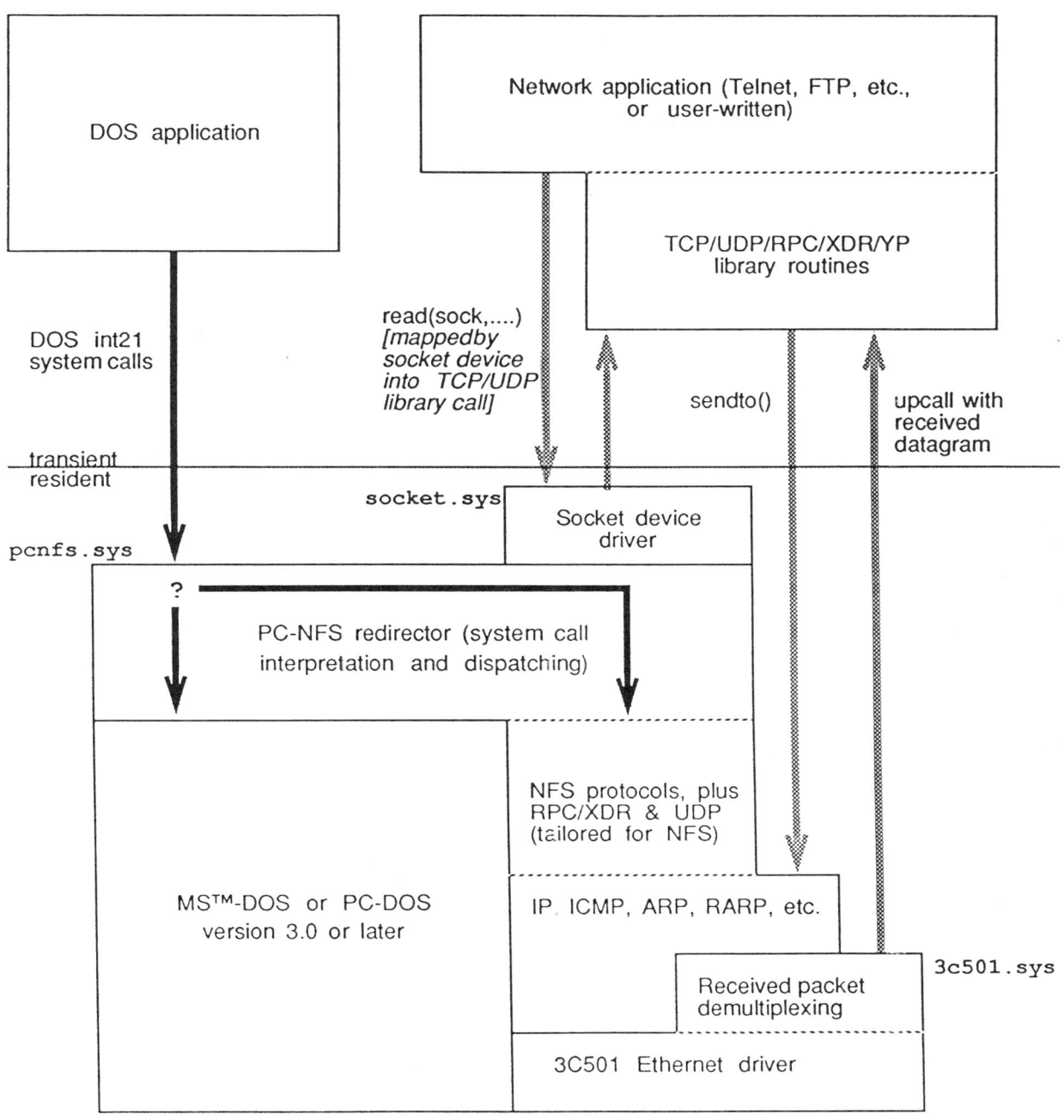

Figure 1. PC-NFS Architecture

put up with it.

One side effect of this hardware problem is that since all our incoming packets are supposed to be less than ETHERMTU bytes the only time that it is necessary to perform IP fragment reassembly is when our network is connected to another network with a smaller MTU. Since there are many small, isolated networks around, we added a feature to allow the user to eliminate the reassembly data structures and associated buffers, saving around 5KB.

5.2 Broadcasts

Two back-to-back packets don't have to come from the same machine, and the presence of a large number of broadcasts on a net guarantees that every so often you find yourself processing an unwanted broadcast while the packet you really wanted disappears into the ether. No good fix exists for this, other than trying to dump unwanted packets as quickly as possible. (In the future, the use of multicasts will

```
struct   sel_entry {
         void(far *     sel_routine)(short);
                                          /* upcall routine */
         char far *     sel_addr;         /* receive buffer */
         char           sel_busy;         /* 0: buffer is available for recv */
         short          sel_ds;           /* DS for upcall routine */
         short          sel_buffsize;     /* size of buffer */
         char           sel_proto;        /* protocol (0: free) */
         short          sel_localport;    /* our port number */
         short          sel_rmtport;      /* their port number */
         unsigned long  sel_rmt_addr;     /* IP addr of rmt host or 0 (don't */
                                          /* check) */
         short          sel_updata;       /* data passed to upcall */
};
```

Figure 2. Selector Structure

reduce the load for most systems, but dumb boards without multicast filtering will still wind up listening to everything.) The performance impact can be significant: for example, our peak FTP send rate is around 46KB/sec, but on our fairly noisy engineering net we get around 25-30KB/sec; using the Ungermann-Bass NIC board which has multiple receive buffers we experience almost no degradation in throughput.

6. Software Trade-Offs

6.1 Routing

Memory constraints clearly precluded the implementation of any kind of routing daemon, yet we needed to support gateways. Rather than having the user figure out the gateway to be used for each non-local net, we elected to support a single gateway. Whenever we need to resolve the address of a node which is not on our net (or subnet) we instead ARP for the gateway and construct an ARP table entry with the remote node's IP address and the gateway's Ethernet address. (We do not time out ARP entries – another simplification.) This scheme works well in any IP environment where a host is prepared to forward off-net traffic to the appropriate gateway without complaining unduly. It helps if you identify the right gateway, but it functions even if you do not.

6.2 TCP Issues

TCP acknowledgment strategy was – and is – a thorny question. Originally we wanted to use the deferred acknowledgment strategy described in [11]. Unfortunately our experiences with ill-behaved DOS applications convinced us that if we relied on getting clock interrupts we would wind up dropping Telnet connections. We therefore chose to acknowledge incoming TCP segments immediately, queuing the ACK transmit from the upcalled receiver. The double ACK which you would expect (once when you receive a segment, once when the application reads the data and releases buffer space so that the window can reopen) rarely occurs. We usually have more buffer space than we can advertise (because of the back-to-back packet problem) and so we can often slide the window up the buffer pool and keep things flowing.

When to retransmit is another problem. Computing the smoothed round-trip time in the environment we have described is fraught with problems, and we elected to go with a simple fixed time-out. In a future release we will at least detect whether the peer is local or remote and tune the time-out accordingly, but for now we have optimized for the local network situation.

6.3 Incompatibilities

Inevitably, we encountered incompatibilities with other NFS and TCP/IP implementations that made unwarranted assumptions about various protocol specifications. One NFS system insisted on sending us 2K chunks of directory information, assuming that the size field in the request was advisory (it isn't). At one stage before we had IP fragment reassembly working we turned on the "Don't Fragment" bit in all our IP packets to try to catch any inadvertent fragmentation, and ran into at least one IP implementation that broke when it saw this bit. Still another Telnet implementation absolutely refused to believe us when we replied "WON'T" to a number of option negotiations. In general we were pleased about the small number of protocol incompatibilities we had to resolve, particularly as we had in most cases implemented straight from the written specification without referring to existing code.

7. Ease of Use

As a group, we tend to be obsessive about ease-of-use issues. Every new member has to go through the ritual of watching Jim Henson's classic "Computer (How to Order a Pizza)" movie [12], an animated cri-de-coeur for end-user-oriented systems design. We looked at the way in which the majority of Internet networks are administered today, and decided that there had to be a better way than gurus muttering mysterious incantations over files like /etc/ethers and "pushing the YP maps."

7.1 Objectives

Although we didn't articulate them quite this clearly at the start of the project, we used three simple criteria to embody our idea of "easy to use." It is instructive to see how closely we have met them and what remains to be done. The criteria are:

(1) The installation and configuration of PC-NFS requires no network knowledge on the part of the user.
(2) No network configuration information (other than the PROM Ethernet address) is stored on the PC.
(3) No human intervention is required on the server; however, the system manager may choose a more restrictive mode of operation.

Let's look at the best we can do today. The user must first install an Ethernet controller, noting the Ethernet address on a form we provide. The server system manager must then be asked to assign a hostname and Internet address, edit the hosts and Reverse ARP databases, and fill out the rest of the form with a variety of information including the names of servers and file systems which the user can have access to. The user now runs the installation and configuration program, answering a minimal set of questions: what network services are available (from a menu), what time zone applies, the name of the local Yellow Pages domain, what gateway is to be used (if any), and the hosts and path names of any file systems or printers which are to be used. Finally the system must be rebooted; it uses RARP to find out who it is, locates a name server (via Yellow Pages in our case – *bind* would have worked just as well), and finds out its hostname. It then executes a series of commands stored in its `autoexec.bat` file which defines the gateway to be used, mounts drives and printers and allows the user to establish an identity via a login sequence.

Unfortunately, all of this is "best case". If, for instance, no name server was available the administrator would have had to add hostnames and IP addresses to the form, and the user would have had to type these in during the installation dialog.

Clearly we are a long way from meeting all of our objectives. In large part this is because we wanted to build only on standard protocols which we could reasonably expect to find implemented in the networks to which PC-NFS systems would be connected. In one area at least we are close: the only network configuration information we need on the PC is the Yellow Pages domain name. (Unfortunately there is at present no way for Yellow Pages servers to let clients know which domains exist. Maybe bind would have been better after all.) Subnets work automatically thanks to the ICMP subnet mask determination scheme [13] (although you can set the mask by hand if this feature is unavailable). However objectives (1) and (3) are far from being realized.

8. Future Work

Much of our current thinking is about ways of improving the ease-of-use situation. There are a number of obvious directions we can take. Rather than passing all of the NFS-related configuration information through two error-prone human links we can set up a data base on the server which the PC can access via Yellow Pages or a more specialized RPC service. We can work to ensure that all "subdomainized" services, such as Yellow Pages, provide a mechanism for determining the names of locally accessible service domains. And finally, we can work to develop a standard "new node" protocol (perhaps derived from RARP [14] or BOOTP [15]) which will detect a request from a new Ethernet address, automatically assign an IP address (and maybe a hostname), register the name-address mappings in the name and RARP server databases, and provide for local extensions to perform additional administrative task.

We are also looking at the feasibility of providing additional network services built on top of the toolkit. Among the various candidates are things like electronic mail (probably using POP [16] and SMTP [17] rather than anything as complex as PCMAIL [18] – there is that worry about size again), and network window servers. There are also a number of NFS-related developments which we will have to respond to, including the forthcoming NFS protocol revision.

9. Conclusions

but also for designers of the systems with which we interoperated.

We believe that our architectural approach to the implementation of the TCP/IP suite was correct, and allowed us to meet our goals. There were several areas where we took a somewhat paranoid view of the kinds of software we would have to coexist with; PC software is gradually becoming a little easier to get along with, and in some areas our implementation will benefit from relaxing certain of our worst-case assumptions, particularly in those situations where we have more capable network hardware.

This paper may have seemed to have implied severe criticism of the design of the 3Com 3C501. It was not meant to: this controller was one of the very first to be developed for the PC, and one should be impressed not by the number of problems that it had but by the fact that 3Com was able to squeeze the necessary functionality onto a PC card with the technology then available and turn it into a reliable product with many thousands of installations.

In addressing our ease-of-use objectives, we did better than we had feared but remain a long way from our goals. Various speakers at conferences over the last few years have emphasized how Unix needs to become user-friendly or lose the market to DOS and Macintosh systems. There is a parallel here: much of what we do today in networking is dominated by our experiences with Unix, Multics, Tenex, TOPS-20 and a few other systems, all of which have their own high priests, acolytes, folklore and arcana. Our goal should be to eliminate the guru as a species, or at least from the wild; we will always need to keep a few in captivity to remind us of the way things were.

Acknowledgments

I don't like acknowledgments that are just lists of names. Instead I'd like to recognize four groups of people: the PC-NFS team, past and present (in which I include the management who thought this was a neat way to start up a new division); the original designers of NFS who gave us our raison d'etre; the engineers from the various NFS licensees who helped make the NFS Multivendor Testing Sessions some of the most rewarding engineering experiences we've known; and last (but by no means least) our families and friends who somehow managed to put up with our obsession with the project.

References

[1] R. Sandberg et al, "Design and Implementation of the Sun Network File System", USENIX Conference Proceedings, Portland, Summer, 1985.

[2] R. Sandberg, "Sun Network File System Protocol Specification", Sun Microsystems Inc., Technical Report, 1985.

[3] M. Rosen, M. J. Wilde and B. Fraser-Campbell, "NFS Portability", USENIX Conference Proceedings, Atlanta, Summer, 1986.

[4] "PC-NFS User's Manual", Sun Microsystems Inc., April 1987

[5] L. Murch and D. Stoffel (ed.) "Proceedings for PC/IP MAC/IP Workshop", University of Maryland Computer Science Center, December, 1985.

[6] B. Lyon, "Sun Remote Procedure Call Protocol Specification", Sun Microsystems Inc., Technical Report, 1984.

[7] "PC-NFS Programmer's Toolkit Manual", Sun Microsystems Inc., April 1987

[8] D. Clark, "Modularity and Efficiency in Protocol Implementation", RFC 817, MIT LCS, July, 1982.

[9] J. Romkey et al, "MIT PC/IP User's Guide", MIT LCS, September 1985.

[10] P. Weiss, "Yellow Pages Protocol Specification", Sun Microsystems Inc., Technical Report, 1985.

[11] D. Clark, "Window and Acknowledgment Strategy in TCP", RFC 813, MIT LCS, July, 1982.

[12] J. Henson, "Muppet™ Side Splitter Film #2: Computer", Henson Associates Inc., 1982..

[13] J. Mogul and J. Postel, "Internet Standard Subnetting Procedure", RFC 950, August, 1985.

[14] R. Finlayson et al, "A Reverse Address Resolution Protocol", RFC 903, Stanford University CSD, June, 1984.

[15] B. Croft and J. Gilmore, "Bootstrap Protocol (BOOTP)", RFC 951, September, 1985.

[16] M. Butler et al, "Post Office Protocol – Version 2", RFC 937, USC ISI, February, 1985.

[17] J. Postel, "Simple Mail Transfer Protocol", RFC 821, USC ISI, August, 1982.

[18] D. Clark and M. Lambert, "PCMAIL: A Distributed Mail System for Personal Computers", RFC 993, MIT, December, 1986.

The Kiewit Network: A Large AppleTalk Internetwork

Richard E. Brown
Dartmouth College, Kiewit Computer Center, Hanover, NH 03755

Abstract: Dartmouth College's Kiewit Network connects nearly all of the computing resources on the campus: mainframes, minicomputers, personal computers, terminals, printers, and file servers. It is a large internetwork, based on the AppleTalk protocols. There are currently over 2900 AppleTalk outlets in 44 zones on campus. Over 90 minicomputers act as bridges between 177 AppleTalk twisted pair busses. This paper describes the extent and facilities of the current network; the extensions made to the AppleTalk protocols, including a stream protocol and an asynchronous link protocol; and current development projects, including an AppleTalk stream to TCP converter.

The Kiewit Network is a general purpose local data network. It serves as glue between all the host computers and nearly all the personal computers and terminals on campus. The network extends to the academic and administrative buildings, and the student residence halls, with network ports placed in almost all the offices and rooms. From these ports, users may access any of the host computers connected to the network. In addition, the hosts use network connections to communicate between themselves for electronic mail, file transfer, printer sharing, etc. The network also supports Apple Computer's AppleTalk® protocols. Departments and individuals can purchase standard devices which use AppleTalk (such as LaserWriters® and file servers), and connect them directly to the network.

The Kiewit Network is not part of the telephone, energy control, or security systems of the College. While there can be benefits from combining them, separating these systems has simplified our design in many ways. A network failure doesn't interrupt these other services. We can also schedule experimental time for testing new software at our convenience.

Dartmouth College started its campus network with General Electric Datanet 30 computers acting as front ends for the Dartmouth College Time Sharing (DCTS) system. In 1978, as the requirement for ports grew, Honeywell 716 minicomputers replaced the Datanet machines. In the same time period, two factors forced a change in perspective away from a front-end function toward a networked approach. New hosts began to arrive on campus. These new machines required enhancements to the network. Second, off-campus sites demanded more ports than the existing phone lines could supply. We served these remote users by using Prime P200 minicomputers as statistical multiplexors. In 1980, we implemented the DCTS terminal handling protocols on a less expensive minicomputer, and began to place these network nodes in the basements of buildings across the campus.

When the College recommended that the freshmen entering in the fall of 1984 purchase a Macintosh™ computer, funds were appropriated for three major network enhancements: installation of a network port for each undergraduate in the residence halls; conversion of the network to the AppleTalk protocols; and creation of a terminal emulation program to exploit the enhanced network capabilities.

Computers at Dartmouth

Dartmouth supports a variety of computing environments which include the Dartmouth College Time Sharing system (DCTS), Unix® (4.2 and 4.3 bsd), VAX/VMS, IBM VM/CMS, and Primos operating systems. The host computers which support these include two Honeywell DPS-8/49's, one VAX 8500, eight VAX 11/785 and 11/750's, six microVAX'es, one IBM 4381-1, a Convex C1 XP, and a Prime 650. The network also serves Sun and Xerox workstations, many IBM RT PC's, and the Telenet public data network.

Several services are accessible from the network without logging in: the library's on-line card catalog, a computer help system, the campus events calendar, and several student jobs databases.

Owners of Macintosh computers use DarTerminal, a locally-developed terminal emulation program, to connect to any of the host computers on campus. DarTerminal supports multiple simultaneous sessions, each in its own window; cut-and-paste transfer between sessions; VT100 emulation; TEK 4012 graphics; the ability to transfer arbitrary Macintosh documents to and from hosts; and a distributed screen editor called MacAvatar®. This screen editor works with a back-end editor on a host computer to give a Macintosh-style editing interface for each of the hosts. This gives us essentially the same screen editor on four of the popular operating systems on campus: Macintosh, DCTS, Unix, and VAX/VMS.

There are about 4000 Macintosh computers on campus. Over half are owned by students who live in residence halls. About 800 IBM PCs of various models use asynchronous ports to connect to the network. There are over 1200 known RS-232 terminals, including CRT's, dot-matrix printers, and letter-quality printers.

Why choose AppleTalk?

A number of factors led to our choice of AppleTalk as the base protocol within the Kiewit Network: the difficulty of maintaining the existing network; the desire to use higher bandwidth links; the existence of a coaxial cable around the campus; the low cost of an AppleTalk connection; and the College's decision to recommend Macintosh computers to the students.

In early 1984, the Kiewit Network comprised about 40 minicomputers which acted as packet switches and terminal concentrators. The network served about 1500 terminal ports (at 2400 bps) with a normal load of 200-250 simultaneous terminal sessions. Internally, the network was based on X.25 level 2 data links, with the DCTS terminal handling protocols as a transport layer. The links between buildings were 19.2 kbps local area data circuits.

The network met our user's demands, but was quite hard to maintain. The major problem was that all routing information had to be hard-configured: a network engineer had to enter an explicit path from each of the network hub nodes to each host computer. Furthermore, we had to balance traffic flows through the network manually, by reconfiguring these paths. As the number of hosts increased, it was becoming difficult to manage and configure the network.

In 1978, as part of a major project to install cable TV wire around the campus, Kiewit had several runs of coaxial cable laid to the major buildings on campus. We believed that the best way to exploit the coax was to have a datagram-oriented network. We had considered stripping down TCP and IP to make a protocol with adequate performance across the medium speed links on and off campus.

The decision, in 1984, to recommend that freshmen purchase personal computers gave us access to real networking, with enough computing power to support reasonable protocols. After studying Apple's network plans, we saw that AppleTalk gave adequate internetwork facilities, yet was simple enough to be reliable and implementable. In addition, AppleTalk was considerably more efficient than the other contender, the Internet protocols.

AppleTalk requires only a $50 connector to access the network. By using relatively inexpensive bridges, AppleTalk is very cost competitive with other networking schemes, even RS-232 async terminal ports.

All these reasons convinced us that AppleTalk would be a reasonable alternative. AppleTalk offered low-cost connections, with the dynamic configuration that we desired. We had great hope that it would succeed in the market, so that third party products could enhance the value of the campus network. Even if it failed, though, we were sure that AppleTalk would work here at Dartmouth. We began a major redesign of the network in May 1984. When the freshmen arrived in September, the network was providing AppleTalk services in the residence halls.

Inside the Network

The Kiewit Network is a large AppleTalk internet. The network nodes act as AppleTalk bridges, providing routing, naming and zone services. In addition, the bridges act as terminal servers and as controllers for networked line printers using an AppleTalk stream protocol. Any device which uses the Apple protocols can be connected to one of the 230.4 kbps ports and communicate with other AppleTalk devices anywhere on campus. As commercial products (networked printers, file servers, electronic mail, etc) have come to market, our users have a much wider choice of products than we could have developed internally.

We currently have 95 bridges active in the network. These support 82 AppleTalk busses (at 230.4 kbps). We give fictitious network numbers to the terminal servers, and thus have a total of 177 networks, divided over 44 zones. Typically, one zone serves a single building.

The network supports the full set of AppleTalk protocols including AppleTalk Link Access Protocol (ALAP), Datagram Delivery Protocol (DDP), Routing Table Maintenance Protocol (RTMP), Name Binding Protocol (NBP), and Zone Information Protocol (ZIP). ALAP sends packets between devices on a single bus. DDP is responsible for routing packets between devices on separate AppleTalk busses. RTMP defines how the network nodes keep track of the best route to all other nodes. NBP and ZIP define how a name of a service is converted to a (numeric) network address.

The Kiewit Network also supports the X.25 protocol, connecting us to host computers and public data networks. This X.25 package has been certified by Telenet, Tymnet, and Uninet.

The X.25 also provides terminal connections and file transfers to our VMS, Unix, and VM/CMS hosts.

In addition to the standard Apple-defined protocols, we designed and implemented two enhancements. An Async AppleTalk Link Access Protocol can replace the standard (230.4 kbps) ALAP. Async AppleTalk allows a Mac to connect into an AppleTalk network over an async (RS-232) link, even on a 1200 baud dial-up line. Async AppleTalk has been implemented as a Macintosh driver. We use Async AppleTalk for printing to LaserWriters, file serving, electronic mail, terminal access, and several of the public domain AppleTalk packages. Currently, Async AppleTalk only works with the terminal ports of the Kiewit Network; commercial products which convert between the async and 230.4 kbps links are beginning to come to market.

We also designed a data stream protocol (DSP) which we use for terminal access to host computers (see The Data Stream Protocol, below).

Network Hardware

The packet switching computers of the network are 16 bit minicomputers, manufactured by New England Digital (NED) of White River Junction, VT. These nodes act as terminal concentrators, and perform packet switching and resource naming. Nodes contain up to 128 Kb of RAM and a variety of interface boards.

All nodes contain a small ROM bootstrap. The program in the ROM establishes a connection to a central reload server and requests a reload. This ROM bootstrap loads in a larger RAM bootstrap program, which continues the reload procedure.

Each processor contains a 10 second watch dog timer which is reset by the software's main loop. If the software or hardware reaches an error condition and fails to reset the watch dog timer, the processor transfers into the ROM bootstrap.

Each node computer can support a combination of up to 56 asynchronous (RS-232) ports, or up to 12 HDLC interfaces which use X.25 (to 56 kbps) or the 230.4 kbps AppleTalk ALAP. We connect to our Honeywell hosts through disk channels on the I/O multiplexor. The NED nodes also support Centronics and Data Products printer interfaces.

Network Topology

The nodes of the network are connected to form a tree, rooted in the reloading machine located in the computing services building. There are multiple interconnections between the nodes within the computer center. Notable among these links is a cross-tree AppleTalk bus which joins a dozen nodes in the building.

These central nodes fan-out to other nodes which in turn connect to leaf nodes in the basements of buildings around campus. These leaf nodes contain asynchronous ports, AppleTalk interface boards, and printer interfaces.

Links between nodes are either medium speed synchronous (HDLC) lines or standard 230.4 kbps AppleTalk busses. The links between buildings are generally 19.2 kbps LADS (local area data set) circuits.

Within buildings, we place a four-prong telephone outlet (the old style square jack, not a modular jack) in each room or office and run four-conductor shielded station wire from the room to a central point on each floor. Additionally, we run a vertical backbone of 50-pair cable from the network node (generally in the basement) to each floor.

This wiring scheme has the advantage that it handles either asynchronous terminals with RS-232 signaling or AppleTalk devices with an RS-422 driver. We select asynchronous or Apple-Talk connections simply by cross-wiring the station wire to the appropriate pair(s) in the backbone cable.

In the residence halls, we have one outlet per bed, for a total of 2600 outlets. In the academic and administrative buildings, there are more than 1650 active asynchronous terminal ports. Currently, a project to convert these RS-232 outlets to AppleTalk has installed about 300 ports.

The Master Node

A single network node (the "master node") watches over the network. It runs standard network software with additional functions, and never carries production traffic; it only monitors the network and reloads nodes which have failed.

The master node is at the top of the network tree. It is the only machine which has mass storage. Its disks hold reload images and configuration information for all the nodes in the network. When a failure occurs, the master node receives a copy of the failed memory image (a "dump"), sends a fresh copy of the program and configuration information to the failed node, and forwards a copy of the dump to the DCTS mainframe for examination. To track down the cause of the failure, a program on DCTS displays a stack trace, identifies and formats packets in a human-readable form, and makes several automatic checks on the binary image.

Configuration and Startup

Configuration information for the network is stored in a (text) file on the master node. The configuration can be changed by editing the file and reloading the affected node (we cannot currently perform on-the-fly configuration). To reload a node, a technician either presses a front panel switch or forces a crash from a privileged terminal. Forcing a crash is simple: the node turns off interrupts, and enters a tight loop. The watch dog timer and ROM bootstrap do the rest. A front panel switch on the remote node, or on the master node, can force the master node to skip the dump procedure, saving time and storage.

New revisions of the software are installed the same way. We update the binary image of the program on the master node's disk, and then force a reload in the particular node. We can reload the entire network by asking the master node to pass a "death packet" to its children. Each recipient passes the packet to its children and then begins its reload procedure. Thus the reload request spreads outward through the network, and it reloads from the center. One node takes about two minutes to load (with a dump); the entire network reloads (without dumps) in 15 minutes.

Master Node Monitoring

The master node polls each of the other nodes, and prepares a display (called the "status display") which shows software response times, the round trip time from the master to the other node, number of connections in a node, errors on a link, and other performance statistics. Any terminal on the network may connect to the master and receive this display.

The status display has several views on the network's state. The default screen shows errors — nodes or links which are in an unusual state. The terminal bell sounds whenever an entity changes to a worse state. A technician can silence the bell by acknowledging the problem from a network privileged terminal; typically, the technician enters information about the trouble, with their actions and initials.

The status display can also show information about the entire network, a specific node or link, or a certain class of link.

Troubleshooting Capabilities

We have invested heavily in the control and monitoring functions for the network. In the standard network software, between 10 and 15 per cent of the total lines of code are devoted to testing and diagnostics.

Each network node has a "control process" which accepts connections (with password protection) from terminals. This process provides a user interface to the monitoring functions in the machine. Support personnel can connect to the control process and request information about the relevant aspects of a node's performance. This includes link information (bytes and packets per second, errors per minute), node information (free storage, per cent busy, per cent interrupt processing), routing tables, the current configuration, terminal port activity, the state of active connections, etc.

Each code module within the node has calls to routines which can produce error messages with detailed information about interesting events. Examples are CRC errors on a link, checksum errors, routing table changes, protocol violations, etc. The various protocol layers can produce lines containing relevant protocol information. A support person can cause these lines to be formatted and displayed by setting the appropriate monitoring flag. We are careful to keep monitoring flags turned off most of the time, since formatting the data is computationally expensive and often increases the node's response time.

Each node maintains a connection to one of our DCTS host computers for archival purposes. There, a log file for each node continually receives information about unusual events from the control process. We perform daily maintenance on these files, watching for files which have grown too much or which show unusual occurrences.

The Data Stream Protocol

In the summer of 1984, we designed and implemented a data stream protocol (DSP) as part of our DarTerminal terminal emulation program. We chose to design a new protocol, rather than use the industry-standard TCP family, for these reasons:

- At the time, none of our host computers used TCP (terminal connections were primarily over X.25 links); we would have had to integrate TCP/IP as well as the AppleTalk protocols into the existing network.

- There was no IP support within a Macintosh at the time.

- The links of the network were slow. Most of the links between buildings were medium speed (19.2 kbps) local area data circuits, we had several links to off-campus sites running at 2400 baud. With the overhead of TCP and IP headers, these links would have given poor service for many applications (most notably host character echoes).

The original design used a two-byte header. This has served well for the last three years. In the summer of 1987, we converted to a four-byte header because: a) The two-byte header had an eight-bit packet sequence number. This was too small to prevent wraparound over fast links. The new protocol has 16 bits in the sequence number; b) A cooperative effort with a third-party AppleTalk vendor required additional features that the two-byte protocol could not support. This commercial implementation will allow our users to use any Macintosh terminal emulator across an AppleTalk network. The rest of this document describes the four-byte header.

The DSP is a client of the AppleTalk Datagram Delivery Protocol (DDP) and Name Binding Protocol (NBP). A client may use DSP as its only interface to the AppleTalk network. The DSP establishes a connection between two entities on an AppleTalk network. The client may specify a name or the AppleTalk address of the peer for the connection.

A DSP connection provides full duplex, reliable, flow-controlled delivery of a stream of bytes. In addition to a raw stream of bytes, the DSP provides a record service whereby clients use an end of message (EOM) flag to indicate that one or more datagrams should be treated as a single transaction. A client may also create its own layered protocols, by using a protocol type field in the DSP header which is not interpreted by the DSP.

The sending side of the DSP accepts buffers of data from its client and sends that information across the connection. The DSP may fragment a buffer into several datagrams; each will contain a sequence number. Each of the datagrams is held in a retransmit queue, pending receipt of an acknowledge packet. The receiving side of the DSP checks the sequence number of the arriving datagrams, and sends back an acknowledge packet for any which are in-sequence. Acknowledge packets contain the sequence number of the next expected datagram and a receive window which indicates the number of additional maximum-length datagrams which may be sent. Datagrams which arrive ahead of sequence are stored in a short queue, pending arrival of the expected datagram(s).

If a block of data must be fragmented, each fragment retains the protocol type field, and all but the last have the EOM bit cleared. The last datagram has its EOM bit set to the value requested by the client. The receiver must observe the EOM bit and the protocol type field, and only reassemble packets into receive buffers which have the same type.

In addition to a reliable, sequenced stream of messages, DSP provides a means for its clients to exchange out-of-band information in the form of *attention* messages. Attention messages may be sent any time a connection is opened, even if the other end's receive window is closed. Delivery of these messages is best-effort; they are not sequenced, acknowledged or automatically retransmitted. Only one unread attention message will be held in a connection; subsequent attentions will be discarded.

The DSP Header

The DSP packets are sent as AppleTalk DDP datagrams. The DDP header carries several information fields, including the internet source and destination socket addresses. A DSP header follows the DDP header, using DDP protocol type $26 and contains information specific to the DSP protocol.

Sequence/Acknowledge Number (2 bytes)					
Connection ID (1 byte)	C T L	A C K	E O M	A T N	Modifiers (4 bits)
Data field (optional)					

The DSP Header

Byte ordering is assumed to have the most significant (high-order) byte first, conforming to the AppleTalk conventions.

Sequence/Acknowledge Number (16 bits)

> Generally, this field contains the sequence number of the packet. If ACK is set among the control bits, this field contains the sequence number of the packet the sender next expects to receive. If ATN is set, this field must be zero.

Connection ID (8 bits)

> The sender's identification of the connection. Coupled with the sender's internet address, this allows unique identification of the sender's client by the receiving DSP.

> The DSP uses a unique, incrementing connection ID number (ConnID) for each connection half, which must never be zero. The

connID is derived from a seed value maintained within each DSP implementation (initialized from a random source, such as the low order bits of a system clock); it is incremented at each connection attempt, and must be unique within the set of active connections.

Control bits (4 bits, mutually exclusive)

CTL: This packet transfers information between DSP peers; the CTL bit is not set by the client. The modifier field defines the control function. The data field may carry supplementary control information.

ACK: This is an acknowledge packet; the ACK bit is not set by the client. The modifier field contains the receive window. The sequence field specifies the next requested message. There is no data field.

EOM: This is the last data packet in a "record" message; the EOM bit is set by the client. The modifier field is user definable for implementing layered protocols.

ATN: This is a client supervisory control packet; the ATN bit is set by the client. The modifier and data fields carry user defined supplementary information. The value of the sequence field must be zero.

Modifier Bits (4 bits)

This field expands the meaning of the four control bits defined above (the default case, with no control bits, indicates a data packet).

If CTL is set, this field contains a control code which identifies the type of DSP control packet: note that the values marked as "processed immediately" will be processed even if ahead-of-sequence.

- $0 Connection Request (non-privileged)
- $1 Connection Request (privileged)
- $2 Reserved for future expansion
- $3 Connection Deny
- $4 Disconnect Request
- $5 Abort Advise *
- $6 Acknowledge Request *
- $7 Forward Reset Request *
- $8-$F Reserved for future expansion

    *- processed immediately

If ACK is set, this field contains the sender's receive window, i.e. the number of maximum-length packets, beginning with the one indicated in the sequence field, which the sender of this packet is willing to accept.

In all other cases (ATN, EOM, no control bits), this field is available for client-defined, higher-level layered protocols. Reserved protocol values are:

- $0 A data packet, requiring no special interpretation.
- $1 Kiewit Network terminal handling protocol (TCFACE).
- $2 Infosphere ComServe protocol.
- $F Extended modifier value – escape to next byte.

If the modifier field contains a value of $F, then the following byte (i.e. the first byte of the data field) contains the actual modifier value and the data field begins one byte later. This allows expansion to 256 modifier values. Extended modifier values of $00 to $0E have the same meanings as the basic value range.

Implementation recommendations

There is always a tradeoff between timely transmission of data and the desire to increase network efficiency by sending large packets. Optimal transmission strategies are an area of active research. The DSP specification offers recommendations which are simple (so they are likely to be implemented correctly) and safe (so they will work, with minimal impact, under all network conditions). Implementors may deviate from these recommendations, but must be sure that the differences will actually perform better than these recommendations.

Transmission Strategy

Whenever data is to be transmitted on an idle connection, the sender will foward a window-full of data. This is the number of packets specified in the receiver's receive window. Once a window-full has been sent, the sender will refrain from sending more packets until all outstanding packets have been acknowledged. This minimizes the number of packets that the network has to carry, while providing near-optimal response for the client.

If the sender receives more data from the client while packets are still outstanding, it may attempt to combine the new data with other packets waiting to be transmitted (if the DSP protocol type and EOM permit). This increases the network efficiency by increasing the amount of data carried in the packet.

If the sender cannot combine the new data, it will queue a separate message (with a new sequence number) to be sent when all outstanding packets have been acknowledged.

Retransmission Strategy

The sender retransmits packets which have not been acknowledged. To ensure that the network is not flooded with retransmissions, the DSP must dynamically adjust its retransmission rate. The algorithm must be robust, and take into account link speeds which can vary by three orders of magnitude (1200 baud to 10Mbps).

The DSP maintains two values: an estimate of the current round trip time (RTT) across the connection, and the current retransmit timeout (RTO). The DSP estimates the RTT by measuring the elapsed time between the transmission of a packet and receipt of its ack message. This estimate should only be used if the packet has been transmitted once. The RTT estimate should be a weighted average of recent samples, with a faster time constant for increasing RTT (to react quickly to congestion).

The DSP will a) set the RTO to twice the current RTT estimate for the initial transmission of a packet; b) only retransmit the packet with the lowest sequence number. Retransmitting all the messages in the retransmit queue generally won't improve performance, since only one packet is likely to have been lost. Subsequent packets would be waiting on the receiver's queue of ahead of sequence messages, and would not need to be retransmitted; c) double the RTO (but not the round trip time estimate) any time a packet is retransmitted. By backing off agressively, the DSP will not flood the network when load suddenly increases.

Window Management

The receiving DSP process sends acknowledge messages to update the sender's notion of the sequence number or receive window. The goal of the DSP is to minimize the number of acknowledge messages sent, and still give timely information about the receiver's state. The DSP will send an acknowledge when:

- An in-sequence message is received;
- The client empties the receive queue;
- The client drains the receive queue such that the receive window is twice the value sent in the previous acknowledge message;
- The 30 second "tickle" timer expires (without sending any other message).

The TCP to DSP Protocol Gateway Project

In parallel with the development of the AppleTalk network described above, local area nets using Ethernet have emerged in several key locations around campus. These include the engineering and computer science buildings and the Kiewit Computation Center. Whereas the typical AppleTalk device is a Macintosh, the devices on the Ethernet tend to be more powerful (and more expensive). They include the VMS and Unix VAX hosts mentioned above, Sun and Xerox workstations, and an increasing number of microVAX, IBM RT PC, and other small computers. All these devices can use the TCP/IP protocols to communicate over the Ethernet.

This division into two worlds, AppleTalk and Ethernet, has a major drawback: it is hard to communicate between the two networks. With AppleTalk wiring everywhere on the campus, and Ethernet connected to (nearly) all our host computers, we needed to find a general scheme for connecting an AppleTalk device with a computer on the Ethernet.

Currently, there are a few solutions which convert between AppleTalk DDP and IP datagrams. The most widespread are based on Stanford's SEAGATE technology, and its commercial implementation from Kinetics, Inc. While this hardware works, there are no off-the-shelf software packages which will support the terminal sessions we require. Rather than implement TCP/IP, we decided to design a converter between the stream and terminal protocols of the AppleTalk DSP and TCP/Telnet. There were several reasons:

- The links between buildings are still slow (19.2 kbps). Full TCP/IP headers would give poor performance. Async AppleTalk at 1200 baud would be unusable.

- The network nodes which perform terminal service have very little code space left. A new protocol family probably would not fit in the machine.

- We have three separate implementations of the DSP: the network terminal handlers, the DCTS host, and the Macintosh. All three implementations would have to be changed to a new protocol.

- A third-party AppleTalk vendor is developing an "AppleTalk serial driver" which will replace the current async RS-232 driver in the Macintosh. Any terminal emulator will then work across the AppleTalk network, simply by installing the new driver.

- The Internet protocols still cannot provide several of the services we get from AppleTalk: dynamic network address assignment; simple routing algorithms for a local network; naming algorithms which don't require a system administrator to update name tables.

The Gateway Implementation

We plan to use a Macintosh II computer running A/UX (Unix System V, Release 2) as the initial platform for this gateway. The advantages are: an Ethernet connection is available; the full set of IP protocols with all of the support functions (host name tables, name servers, etc) exist; and it has a strong development environment.

The Macintosh II has enough processor power to handle a large number of connections at once. It can be directly connected to the Ethernet, so that the communication link will not be a bottleneck. Also, the Mac II supports a large memory (up to 8 Mbyte) for message buffering and connection databases. The Mac II is a mass-produced machine; we will not have to build any hardware for this project.

The Mac II used for the gateway will be dedicated to this task. There is no need to share it for other functions, since it is a fairly low cost piece of network equipment. If price becomes an issue, we can reduce costs by porting the code to less expensive hardware after the gateway is functional.

Software

There are several major pieces of software within the gateway. They are: the stream conversion algorithm itself; conversions between the terminal handling modes; naming – how a service on one side becomes known to the other side of the converter; and finally, software to control, monitor, and troubleshoot the gateway.

Several complicating issues arise: the stream protocols are not identical, so some mapping must be made (perhaps losing some information); there needs to be flow control between the two connections; the terminal handling functions of the two protocols are distributed differently between the layers, and must also be mapped to (nearly) equivalent forms.

The conversion between the TCP and DSP is simple. The gateway simply "holds down" the ends of two connections: a DSP connection to an AppleTalk device, and a TCP connection to an Internet device. When a DSP message arrives, it will be converted to an equivalent TCP form, and sent to the ultimate destination. Similarly, an arriving TCP message will be translated and sent to the DSP device.

Telnet and TCFACE (the Kiewit Network terminal modes) are roughly equivalent terminal handling protocols. They specify forwarding conditions (when to send characters which have arrived), no/local/remote echoing, binary/ASCII transmission, and interrupts (breaks) to a process, among others. The conversion between them is relatively simple, since TCFACE terminal handlers have a small repertoire, and map to a simple Telnet device. Similarly, host computers on the TCFACE side of the network expect simple terminal handlers, and so a full Telnet handler should match these expectations.

Name conversions are difficult to do in full generality. Connecting from an AppleTalk device to an Internet service is straightforward. The protocol converter can contain a list of all the host names on the Ethernet side, and AppleTalk's NBP provides an escape hatch for connecting to other names. Connecting the other way, from an Internet host to a dynamically assigned AppleTalk network address, is not currently defined. (This is a current problem in the Internet, too. We plan to watch developments in this area, and will defer to others who are creating standards.)

The gateway will provide a mechanism to monitor and debug the data flowing through it. A monitoring process, accessible only from a network privileged terminal, will display operational modes and data streams within the converter.

Implementation

The initial implementation of the gateway will connect the DSP (and TCFACE) code to the Unix login process. This acts as a proof of concept, and allows us to test our conversion and naming algorithms, and provides a quick login service to the Mac II. Next, the DSP code will connect to an outgoing Telnet connection. It may suffer from low performance, since each packet could require multiple context switches on its way through the machine. The final implementation will probably process individual datagrams, translating and passing them on to the other protocol code on the fly.

A separate control process in the gateway will accept DSP (or Telnet) connections. This process can then display connection state, data streams, etc. within the operating gateway.

Naming will also progress through several stages. Names (and addresses) of services will initially be hard-configured in a file which is read at the gateway's startup. Later on, we can read the Internet host tables, and implement a scheme for registering an AppleTalk (DSP) service with the gateway.

Enhancements

Follow-on projects for the protocol converter, which haven't been well specified, include:

- Incorporation of the AppleTalk-to-Ethernet gateway functions currently performed by the Kinetics hardware;

- Conversions to new protocols (X.25 PAD and transparent service; DEC's LAT; and any other stream protocols which seem useful);

- A Mac-like user interface to the control process, to enhance the ease of use for debugging and troubleshooting;

- Booting from the master node. This draws the gateway closer to the existing network management system, and reduces the training required for network personnel. By reading configuration information from the master node, we get a single point of control.

Experience and Conclusions

AppleTalk has served our users well. We have had terminal service since the fall of 1984. Our users have also purchased a surprisingly wide variety of hardware and software which exploits the cabling that we installed.

Virtually the entire AppleTalk protocol suite has been implemented as specified. The only modification has to been a minor change to the routing algorithms to facilitate starting up a large network. AppleTalk bridges normally exchange routing tables every 10 seconds. This works in an environment where the network configuration is static, or where there are relatively few hops between networks. Our modification is to have a node send routing tables whenever a new network number appears (or an old network disappears). Thus, new routing information spreads quickly.

The dynamic configuration properties of AppleTalk have greatly simplified the network maintainer's life. We no longer worry about routing connections through the network; the routing algorithms take care of the work. Configuration of host names, network numbers, zones, etc. is easy to maintain. The values are entered in a single file, and installed at network initialization time.

The wiring scheme used in the residence halls (a star connection of the wires of a bus) did give us troubles during the initial installation. The reflections induced at the point where the wires tie together made communication erratic at various points on the bus. A 20 to 30 ohm resistor placed across the signal pair at the connection point solves the problem by absorbing much of the reflected energy. (Note that this problem only occurs with our wiring scheme, not with Apple's standard connectors.)

The 19.2 kbps links between buildings have not proven to be a bottleneck for terminal traffic. This will certainly change when people begin to demand file access as a normal service. By that time, we hope to have higher speed links between buildings, so that the network can support the offered load.

We have seen poor performance due to a large number of hops in the network. Worst case distances between an outlying building and a central server can be six hops. The initial release of Apple's file server issues many (up to 20) non-overlapped requests to the file server. With a normal afternoon network round trip time of 0.25 second, there is a built-in delay of five seconds before any result can be displayed on the user's screen. We hope that subsequent versions of the file server and workstation software will improve the situation.

The advantages of our network management scheme are manifold: we have widely dispersed network nodes, not only around the College, but at remote institutions across the East Coast. It is relatively easy to install new software (even if we must do it at 3:00 AM, to avoid interrupting users). A single machine (the master node) checks the health of the network. Consequently, troubleshooting can begin very quickly after a problem is detected. We avoid the expense and inconvenience of a data scope, since each node contains software which displays what we need to see (and if the software isn't good enough, we can fix it so that it is).

One disadvantage of using a network node to monitor itself is that the act of watching a data stream changes its characteristics. Although rare, the formatting of the display can slow the node down enough to mask a problem. A more frequent problem is loss of data, since the monitor cannot format the data fast enough to keep up with the real time data stream.

Dartmouth has invested the following amounts in the network: the hardware is approximately $1M, dispersed over the 95 nodes. There is close to another million dollars worth of wire in the walls, counting both materials and labor. (When we wire a building for data, we try to install an outlet per office, since the incremental cost is small compared to the cost of adding an outlet afterward.)

The effort to implement the AppleTalk protocols (including the DSP and Async AppleTalk) and the DarTerminal application was about 12 years. For on-going maintenance, an engineer acts as a user-services contact for problems and the electronics repair shop assigns one full-time technician.

Acknowledgments:

The DSP described in this document is a joint project of Dartmouth College and Infosphere Incorporated.

MacAvatar is a registered trademark of the Trustees of Dartmouth College. Macintosh is a trademark of, and AppleTalk and LaserWriter are registered trademarks of Apple Computer Inc. Unix is a registered trademark of AT&T Bell Laboratories.

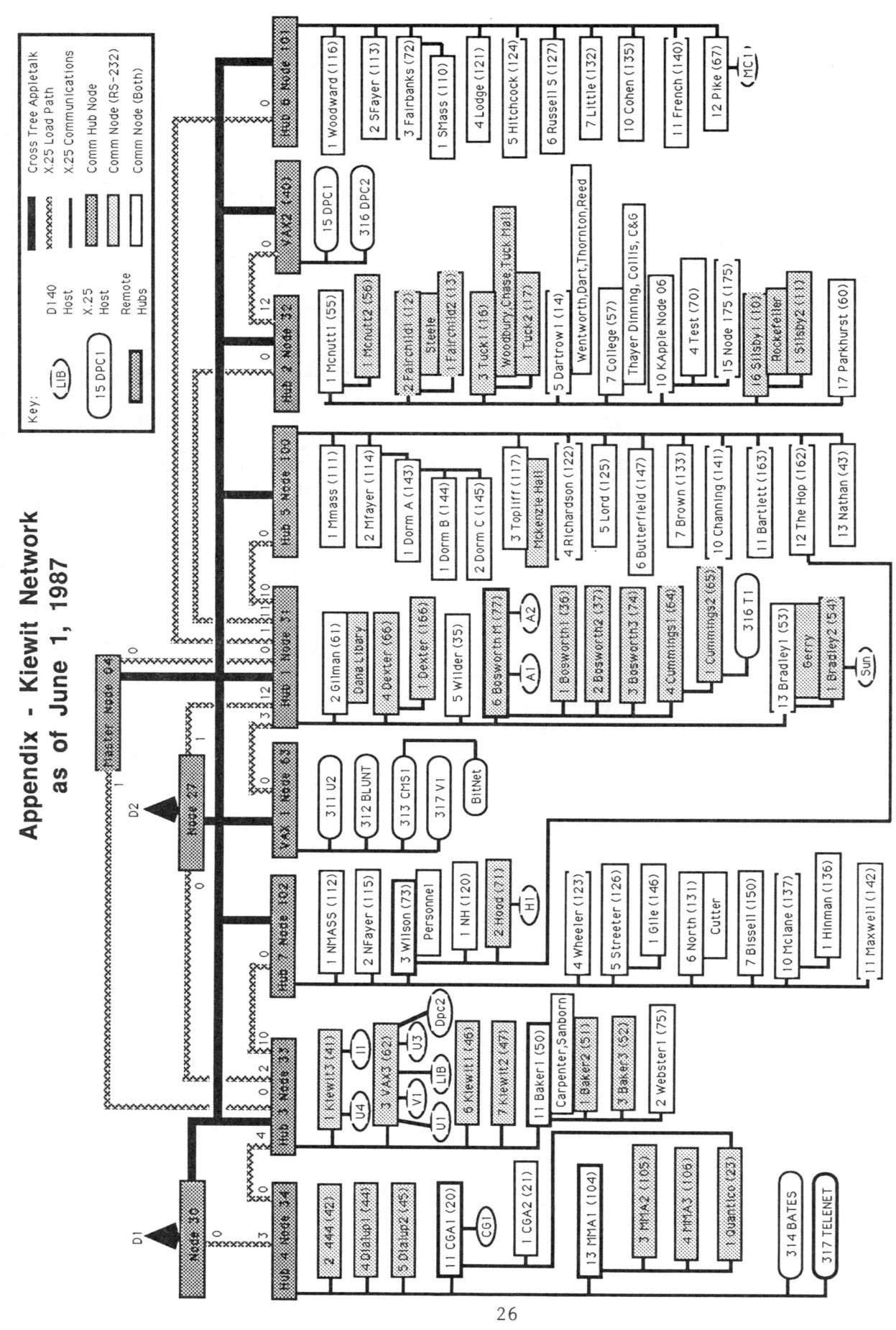

Appendix - Kiewit Network as of June 1, 1987

Supercomputers on the Internet:
A Case Study

Charley Kline

University of Illinois at Urbana-Champaign
1304 W. Springfield Avenue
Urbana, IL 61801

ABSTRACT

This paper will discuss the design of a TCP/IP implementation and its upper level protocols on the University of Illinois supercomputer. We will also discuss some of the issues peculiar to TCP communication with a supercomputer, and some of the special problems encountered while writing and debugging under CTSS, which is not an environment particularly conducive to network development.

1. Introduction.

In the planning stages of the National Center for Supercomputing Applications (NCSA) at the University of Illinois, it became clear that something was going to have to be done about the traditional ways of accessing supercomputers. The chosen operating system for the Cray, the Cray Timesharing System (CTSS), boasts of its networking facilities but in reality is quite poor at communication with heterogeneous systems. The protocols provided are not robust, not well defined, and certainly not widely known or implemented on many computers. What was desired was easy access to the supercomputer from everywhere.

Originally this goal was accomplished through the use of VAX/VMS front end computers which were equipped with as much networking connectivity as possible, from toll-free 9600 bps dialups to DECNET to TCP/IP. However, the somewhat arcane methods of communicating from the front ends to the Cray itself made access to the supercomputer difficult, even though it was easy to gain access to the front ends themselves. In addition, because input data and output results had to be staged on the front ends before being moved to the Cray, severe and peaky demands were made on the storage capacity of the front ends.

The solution was to implement a TCP/IP for CTSS itself, and to use the front ends as IP packet routers between the high speed Cray network and the many networks to which it was already connected. This was done over the course of about a year, and the NCSA Cray is now accessible via TCP/IP from the Internet at large.

1.1. Why TCP/IP?

The decision to implement TCP/IP natively on the Cray instead of using another protocol and gatewaying to the TCP services or implementing another protocol entirely was made primarily because of two other projects undertaken by the NCSA; namely, NSFNET and the Interdisciplinary Research Center.

NSFNET is a high-speed national network connecting the four NSF supercomputer centers. Its protocol is TCP/IP and thus it was felt that a direct connection to the NSFNET from the NCSA Cray would allow faster and more convenient access to the supercomputer facility.

The NCSA's Interdisciplinary Research Center provides users of the facility with graphics workstations for conducting their research. Most of the equipment at the IRC is TCP-based (Sun workstations, IBM PC's, DEC VAXstations), so direct access to the Cray from these workstations would be a great asset.

Because the VAX/VMS front end computers use DECNET as their networking protocol, we thought about a DECNET implementation for the Cray, but this proved to be far too much work in the time available to us, and probably would not have provided the necessary connectivity.

2. Initial Design Issues

The CTSS TCP/IP project underwent a careful design, since the hardware and operating system were very foreign to us, although we are perhaps only too intimate with them by now. Many factors were considered before a final design emerged.

2.1. Machine Awareness

Some attributes of the Cray X/MP turned out to be instructive in our design.

Permission to copy without fee all or part of this material is granted provided that the copies are not made or distributed for direct commercial advantage, the ACM copyright notice and the title of the publication and its date appear, and notice is given that copying is by permission of the Association for Computing Machinery. To copy otherwise, or to republish, requires a fee and/or specfic permission.

© 1988 ACM 0-89791-245-4/88/0001/0027 $1.50

First and most obvious, the Cray is a fast CPU. We realized that we wouldn't really have to concern ourselves with code optimization for the most part. Also, the vector registers make certain operations extremely fast, such as memory-to-memory copies and internet checksums. Thus, we assumed that we wouldn't worry about having to copy IP packets around in memory, because it could be done so quickly.

Although the Cray has a large (64 megabyte) memory, many of the programs it runs are very memory-intensive, so memory is at a premium. Therefore, it was to our advantage to make our TCP/IP as small as possible, since of course it would be in memory all the time. The entire address space, of course, is real; No model of Cray has virtual memory.

All I/O is performed by a separate I/O subsystem (IOS) which accepts small request packets from the CPU and transfers data in and out of main memory through a high speed channel. All the dirty details of device interfaces are handled by IOS software, so all the CPU needs to do is build the request packets.

2.2. Operating System Awareness

The most outstanding characteristic of any computer is its operating system. The NCSA Cray, running CTSS, is no exception.

We understood that it might not be easy to port an existing TCP/IP implementation to CTSS, and we were not wrong. With many of its concepts dating back to the 1960's and LTSS, its predecessor, CTSS lacks many tools which would normally be present in a program development environment. The kernel is written in LRLTRAN, a FORTRAN dialect, and there is little or no documentation on how it works.

We spent four months searching for a language in which to write TCP/IP. All that is really provided under CTSS is FORTRAN, and our language of choice was C. The one we settled on was a CTSS port of the Bell Labs portable C. Later on in the project we switched to Lawrence Livermore's vectorizing C compiler. Both compilers have bugs either in the code generator or the run-time library.

CTSS is a swapping-only system, of course. The memory scheduler is brutal. Memory is filled using a best-fit algorithm, and programs are loaded in strict order of priority. Programs at lower priorities often go many minutes without ever getting into execution. Since naturally we wanted TCP/IP to be in execution all the time, if it was to run in user mode it would have to run at a very high priority. This turned out to be easy to arrange. What also saved us was that programs cannot be swapped out while they have pending I/O. Since the device drivers always have network reads outstanding, CTSS has difficulty sending TCP/IP out to disk, which was fine by us.

CTSS blessed us with a rich set of system calls, but many of them are inconsistent with each other. For example, a program can request an interrupt on I/O completion or terminal input, but not on a timer or an incoming IPC message. Interrupt delivery does not wake up a program which is suspended. Some of these problems were circumvented with clever programming. Others we corrected by modifying the operating system.

CTSS does have its good points, however. Among them is that all I/O is asynchronous, which makes things like network device drivers easy to write.

2.3. Media Awareness

The Cray I/O Subsystem has a device driver for only one type of network hardware: Network Systems Hyperchannel. (Cray is testing an Ethernet interface internally.) Hyperchannel is a 50 megabit coaxial cable with high-speed device interfaces to various computer hardware.

Hyperchannel is an intriguing network architecture because each transmitted frame has two parts. The 64-byte Message Proper (MP) contains routing and control information but leaves about 50 bytes available for the datagram. The data associated with the MP (Associated Data or AD) can be arbitrarily long. Further, the transmission of AD causes both the transmitter to establish a virtual circuit between itself and the receiver during the exchange of the AD, thus locking out both units during this time. The conclusion therefore is that the use of AD is many times more expensive in terms of network bandwidth and throughput. Further, the host to Hyperchannel interaction involves several more commands in the transmission of an MP/AD frame as it does to transmit an MP frame alone. Thus, it's desirable to avoid sending AD unless necessary.

Since a large number of the packets flying around a network are simple acknowledgements and thus consist only of the 40-byte TCP and IP headers, they will all fit within the MP. Therefore, much TCP/IP traffic can be sent without using the more expensive AD frames.

There is no official standard for the encapsulation of IP packets into Hyperchannel messages. The *de facto* standard, originating at Tektronix in their TCP product (now being maintained by Carnegie-Mellon) and more recently modified and improved by NASA Ames Research Center, is implemented by almost all of the (few) sites using Hyperchannel for IP. This encapsulation is being formalized by Network Systems and should appear soon as an RFC. The CTSS TCP/IP Hyperchannel driver will be modified if necessary to fully conform with this official standard.

Very few operating systems have a working TCP/IP Hyperchannel driver. This posed a problem when the time came to connect the NCSA Cray to the Internet. The only machine at NCSA which can currently communicate IP on Hyperchannel is a 4.3bsd UNIX VAX. This VAX is the Cray's IP gateway to the world.

2.4. Which version to port?

When we began the design phase we decided to port an existing TCP/IP implementation instead of writing our own. The implementation most familiar to us was Berkeley's, and we took the 4.2 networking code and began the port to CTSS. Later we added most of the bug fixes incorporated into the 4.3 distribution.

The finished product bears little resemblance to Berkeley networking, although the TCP and IP modules went essentially unchanged. The socket code was heavily modified to operate in a user-mode environment with CTSS IPC. A dispatcher was written around the other modules to handle scheduling, timers, and interrupts. A user interface was added to accept configuration commands from a terminal instead of via *ioctl*. Finally, many structures and code segments had to be modified since Crays have a 64-bit word size and no byte addressability.

2.5. Kernel or User?

We recognized that placing TCP and IP within the CTSS nucleus would provide the greatest performance, for two main reasons. First, many interactions between TCP and its clients would mean many context switches between the two, which is an expensive operation. Second, nucleus code doesn't need to fight for CPU time or access to memory with other user jobs.

However, putting TCP/IP into the CTSS nucleus turned out to be a near-impossible task. First, TCP/IP was written in C, a stack-based language, while CTSS is written in FORTRAN, which is not stack-based. It would have been very hard to mate the two within the same operating system. Also, recall that CTSS is not well documented and not particularly well modularized. Making even small modifications to it would (as we discovered anyway) certainly introduce bugs which would take a prohibitively long time to correct. Finally, since the Cray is a production facility, the time available for testing operating system changes is very limited. This would have set the completion date of the project much further back.

So we went with a user-mode implementation, understanding that performance was probably going to suffer a bit, and decided to do whatever we could to improve throughput. One way was to play as many dirty tricks on the CTSS schedulers as we could in order to avoid being swapped out and to get CPU when we wanted it. Another way was to improve on the scheme by which TCP/IP would communicate with its clients.

2.6. Interprocess Communication

Since TCP/IP was doomed to reside in user space, uppermost in our minds was the issue of how to quickly and efficiently transfer data between TCP and clients such as FTP. The existing CTSS IPC system has several drawbacks. All messages sent with it are staged in a single 720-byte buffer in the CTSS nucleus, which introduces a very real possibility of deadlock because all messages which cannot be delivered to TCP from a client for lack of space are simply rejected. The small buffer size also seriously limits the amount of data which can be sent at a time between TCP and a client, which in turn causes more context switches to be performed and limits throughput. Finally, CTSS IPC is really a subset of an existing CTSS networking protocol, and as such all messages sent via it must have rather odd network headers prepended to them.

We decided that CTSS IPC would not be good enough to support the heavy traffic which TCP would present. We designed an alternate IPC system, CCC, which would operate by simple inter-address space copies of data from one program to another. We wanted it to be low-overhead, so transfer is done by a simple method of system calls:

The sender makes a system call giving the address and length of the data. The receiver is notified by a location in its address space being changed by CTSS. It then issues a system call giving the address where the data is to be placed, whereupon CTSS merely copies the data over using the vector registers. The sender is then notified by a location in its address space being changed by CTSS that the transfer is complete.

Data transfer rates with CCC show that throughput increases linearly with unit slope as buffer size increases. The conclusion is that the bottleneck in IPC under CTSS is in fact due to the number of context switches which must be performed, and not to overhead in copying data around in memory. TCP/IP and its clients communicate with CCC, using as large a buffer size as practical.

3. The Final Picture

This section gives a short overview of what the final implementation of TCP/IP and friends on CTSS looks like. Figure 2 shows schematically how the various pieces interact.

3.1. TCP and IP

As we hinted at above, TCP/IP is implemented in a single C program, running in user mode at a high priority. It occupies about 41,000 words of memory, plus dynamically allocated buffer space, for a total size of between 42,000 and 60,000 words depending on load. TCP/IP reads an initialization file on startup which gives interface addresses and routing information, and if a terminal is logged on to TCP/IP it will respond to commands typed to it in a similar fashion to Berkeley *netstat*.

Communication with TCP clients takes place via CCC. Clients identify themselves with a unique number provided by CCC, and TCP assigns each connection or socket a unique 16-bit connection id or *xid*. Each of the TCP requests (listen, open, send, receive, close, abort, and status) have a function code and parameters which are passed in a CCC message. User data, if any, follows the parameter list. All requests to TCP are acknowledged and all client interaction follows a strict request-response protocol.

Some idea of the code size of TCP/IP may be obtained by looking at the sizes of the modules in Figure 1.

3.2. The Hyperchannel Driver

The Hyperchannel interface in TCP simply encapsulates IP packets in MP's and AD's and passes them down to the CTSS nucleus via a pseudo-device driver which then passes them to the Cray I/O Subsystem which carries on the actual dialogue with the Hyperchannel hardware. The pseudo-device driver required a modification to the CTSS nucleus in the form of

Lines	Module Name	Function
136	tcpcks.s	Internet Checksummer (assembly)
458	tcpcmd.c	Terminal command processor
466	tcphi0.c	Hyperchannel driver
354	tcpicc.c	Interprocess communication services
254	tcpicm.c	ICMP
87	tcpif0.c	Common support for all network interfaces
94	tcpih0.s	Interrupt handlers (assembly)
210	tcpin0.c	Internet address space services
611	tcpipi.c	IP Input
187	tcpipo.c	IP Output
59	tcplo0.c	Loopback driver for testing
456	tcpmai.c	Initialization, dispatcher, timer and system services
452	tcpmbu.c	Dynamic memory management
31	tcpque.c	Emulation of two VAX machine instructions
251	tcpraw.c	Client request driver for raw IP
196	tcprou.c	IP routing services
822	tcptci.c	TCP Input
324	tcptco.c	TCP Output
365	tcptcs.c	Miscellaneous TCP things
204	tcptct.c	TCP Timers
606	tcptcu.c	Client request driver for TCP
175	tcptio.c	Terminal I/O services not provided by stdio
566	tcpusr.c	Client request handler; routes to tcpraw.c and tcptcu.c
1218		Include files
8582		Total lines

Figure 1. Lines of code for CTSS TCP/IP.

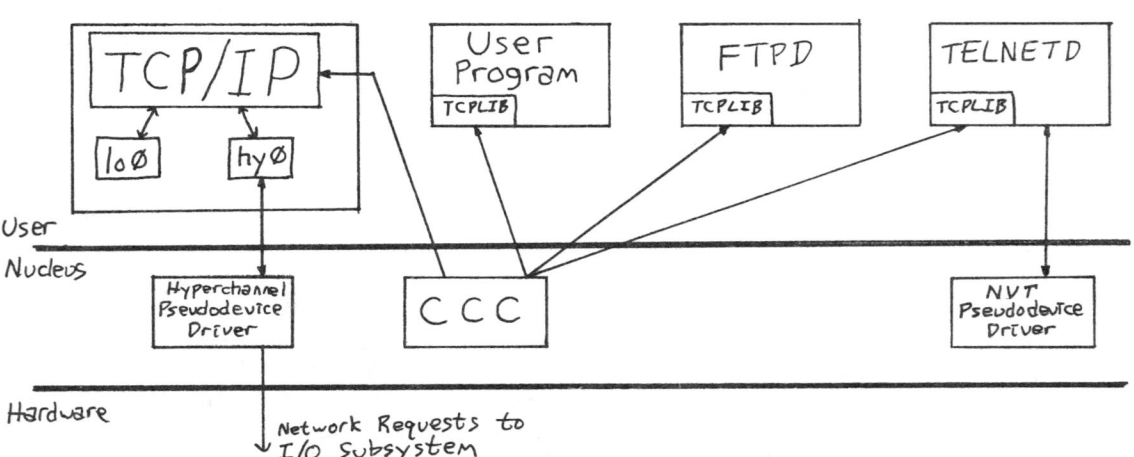

Figure 2. Block Diagram of CTSS Networking

added subroutines and a few other minor changes amounting to about 600 lines of LRLTRAN.

3.3. TCPLIB

To make TCP clients easier to write, we wanted to make it present itself to users much like Berkeley sockets. To this end, we wrote a C-callable library of functions called TCPLIB which provides access to TCP/IP. It handles local buffering of data, the building of CCC messages and TCP function requests, and allows either synchronous or asynchronous operation of TCP connections. Connections may be passed to other users, much like a socket file descriptor can be inherited by a child process under Berkeley UNIX.

All of the upper level protocols we implemented use TCPLIB to access TCP services.

3.4. The CTSS NVT Driver

In order to gain access to CTSS via TELNET, we needed a virtual terminal interface within CTSS. None existed. One was implemented through the use of another pseudo-device driver, this one pretending to be a network driver which would pass terminal messages to Hyperchannel but instead passes them up to a user program. This driver required another modification to CTSS in the form of added subroutines amounting to about 200 lines of LRLTRAN.

3.5. TELNET and FTP

The TELNET and FTP server processes were straightforward. Like TCP/IP, each took the form of C programs, linked with TCPLIB and communicating with TCP with CCC.

The TELNET demon handles all terminal sessions itself, matching TCP xid's with CTSS virtual terminal numbers. It implements only the basic half-duplex NVT of the TELNET spec, and refuses any additional options with DONT and WONT signals.

The FTP demon was based on the Berkeley 4.3 FTP server, and so behaves much like it. One problem, however, was that it is impossible to read and write other user's files under CTSS, so one demon running under one account could not access any other user directories. The solution to this was to split the demon into two parts. The first program accepts TCP connections and reads the accounting information, then spawns the second program which runs under the account of the given user, and passes the TCP connection to it. This second part handles all of the FTP file transfer functions. This scheme works well, but one side effect is that it is not possible to change user directories or reissue the USER command once logged in via FTP.

The FTP client was essentially a direct port of the Berkeley FTP client and so works exactly the same.

File transfer performance with FTP on the local campus network of Hyperchannel, Ethernet, and Proteon Pronet varies between about 5 thousand bytes per second and 60 thousand bytes per second, depending mostly on the load on the UNIX VAX which functions as an IP router to the Cray and to a lesser extent on the type of computer on the other end of the connection. Supposedly, a more recent version of the VAX UNIX Hyperchannel interface is more efficient, and we hope to improve file transfer data rates when it is installed.

3.6. Miscellaneous Pieces

Two miscellaneous programs were written in support of TCP/IP, TELNET, and FTP.

The first is INET, which is run as part of system initialization. It reads a file containing the names and account numbers of the other component programs such as TCP/IP, FTPD, TELNETD, and LOGS, and runs them in order to start everything up at system startup. It also wakes up every five minutes to make sure everything is still running, restarting any programs that may have aborted.

The other support program is LOGS, a distributed logging demon. Included in TCPLIB is a call to write a string to the logging demon. This string is sent via IPC to LOGS, which timestamps it and records it in a disk file. Thus all diagnostic output from the various other programs ends up in a single place, making it easy to track down problems and gather statistics.

4. Interoperability Lessons Learned

Once brought on-line and released to the users, TCP/IP and its friends gained wide use immediately. Almost as quickly, we began to realize what it was like to survive in the Internet (without killing it ourselves), and soon we were buried in a list of interoperability problems. Proudly, little of it was really our fault. Our experience with CTSS TCP/IP told us that there are many broken Internet modules out there, and the principle of robustness became very important.

4.1. Internet Friendliness

The first thing we discovered from many users FTPing large files to and from the NCSA Cray was that intermediate IP routers, particularly on the ARPANET, got bogged down on the flood of packets and would respond with floods of ICMP Source Quench packets. The initial implementation of TCP/IP ignored quenches, so we scrambled to teach IP to properly respond to them.

CTSS TCP/IP treats quenches as IP events rather than TCP events. Berkeley responds to quenches by reducing the size of the TCP window. We respond, as suggested by Postel in a draft RFC, by introducing a delay between the sending of IP packets to the host which is producing the quenches. The delay increases linearly as more quenches are received. If no quenches are received in a certain interval, the interval is decreased exponentially.

We thus learned a humble lesson. ICMP source quenches, nay, all ICMP messages, give valuable information about the Internet, particularly to a large, potentially dangerous host as a Cray. To ignore or misinterpret ICMP messages is a criminal abuse of Internet resources.

4.2. IP Routing

CTSS TCP/IP has very few facilities for dealing with IP packet routing. Because the typical supercomputer is connected through an expensive, high-speed network to a more apt networking machine, we reasoned that the typical routing algorithm would be "send all your traffic there." Apart from simple static routing tables and the ability to adjust these tables in response to an ICMP redirect message, CTSS TCP/IP has no special routing capability. In particular, the IP options for source routing and route recording are not implemented. We don't anticipate any difficulties will arise because these features are not present.

However, the issue of Type Of Service (TOS) routing may make source routing and better routing facilities desirable in the future, when hosts such as the Cray may be forced to make intelligent routing decisions based on knowledge about the entire Internet and not just the closest gateway.

4.3. A Hostile Crowd of Broken TCP's

The worst attack our project had to endure was the amazing number of telnet clients on the Internet which blatantly ignore the TELNET specification. Most ignore the requirement that, unless operating with remote echo, "as many characters as practical" must be buffered and sent as a single IP packet. As a result, there are many one-character TCP packets flying back and forth between TCP/IP and the TELNET server. Since each one results in three context switches (from TCP to TELNET and back to TCP), these broken TELNET clients have a deleterious effect on overall throughput. Berkeley 4.2 TELNET exhibits this brain-damage; the 4.3 TELNET behaves properly.

Perhaps worst of all, however, is a particular (unidentified) TELNET client on the Internet. Not only does it *ignore* the TELNET NVT, it *insists* that the server accept its request that the server to do character echoing. The result is an endless loop of DO! WON'T! DO! WON'T! commands between the broken client and the server. When this problem first appeared, it caused both TCP/IP and the TELNET server to begin making wild requests for more and more dynamic memory to handle the flood of tiny packets. Eventually CTSS crashed. The problem was eventually solved by bulletproofing the TELNET server option negotiotiation code so that such loops are detected. The offending connection is then aborted.

Other interesting war stories abound. There even seems to be disagreement among the implementors of TCP/IP modules as to whether or not checksums are required. The standards state that both the TCP checksum field and the IP checksum field are not optional; all messages must contain valid checksums. CTSS TCP routinely logs messages thrown out because the checksum field contains zero. The other TCP continues to send the zero-checksum packets, apparently in the hope that CTSS TCP will treat the zero as a "don't-care" and not examine the checksum.

On some of these interoperability problems, we have undertaken the effort to make our TCP and ULP's accept the way the broken peers work. For the most part we have been successful, at least at preventing disaster if not at actually allowing useful communication. On other problems, we have remained stubborn and insisted that other Internet modules follow the standards before we will consider any interoperability problems.

Someday perhaps all network modules on all computers will happily interoperate with no disasters such as the ones we have seen. But until then, we will stand watch and remember the principle of robustness.

4.4. TCP/IP is Widely Misunderstood

Surprisingly, although almost everyone has heard of TCP/IP and understands its connectivity, we discovered that a good many people, particularly scientists in non-computer science disciplines, do not fully grasp the power of the simple full-duplex TCP connection.

Even with TCP pipes available, users of the Cray still seem insistent upon running a job for many hours, producing many megabytes worth of graphic images, and then FTPing them one at a time to their workstation.

It would appear that the people who could most benefit from the interactivity to be gained by having TCP available directly on a supercomputer are unaware of that benefit. Perhaps what is needed is a TCP public relations task force.

4.5. Scientific Computing

It is interesting to see the differences in the use of TCP/IP facilities, particularly FTP, in the scientific computing environment.

On a typical day users will move perhaps five megabytes or so of data from other systems to the NCSA Cray, and over 150 megabytes of data from the Cray to other systems. Usually 90% or more of this outgoing data is many moderate-sized files, all the same size. These are graphics images forming frames of a movie, which usually in finished form shows a simulation of some physical process at work.

It appears that the typical application running on a supercomputer with a scientific mission is such a simulation. Little input data is required, but vast amounts of output are produced. Traditionally this output took the form of hundreds of pages of FORTRAN E-format numbers, but recently has begun to look more like images and movies of images.

Since this pattern of little data in, much data out seems to have a good explanation, we optimized the IPC paths from FTP to TCP and TCP's network writes more so than the reverse path, thinking that this would produce greater total throughput since so much traffic was in the outbound direction. This seems to have paid off.

TELNET connections to the Cray are usually short, lasting only a few minutes and producing about 5 thousand characters of output. Apparently most interactive use of the Cray via TELNET is simply to check on running jobs.

Network traffic generated by scientific computing is heavy and bursty, and accounting for more and more of the total network traffic on the national networks. It would be interesting to study how the scientific community could benefit by designing the networks and protocols it uses to better suit their needs and traffic behavior.

5. Work in Progress

Having TCP/IP available on CTSS allows many tools to be written. Besides FTP and TELNET, we are working on two others. Encouragingly, some NCSA users are writing their own TCP applications using TCPLIB to allow them to interact on their workstation with compute jobs on the Cray.

We are working on a printing demon which will run on an IBM system. It will listen for incoming connections and feed the data to the campus printing network. Users on the Cray can then get printouts anywhere on the University of Illinois campus quickly and easily.

A remote command execution demon is also being designed. We wanted to implement the Berkeley r-commands but since they do their authentication with UNIX uid's, they can't be used directly (CTSS has no concept of uid's and a user's password must be given in order to run a program under another user's account). Soon there should be a client program which will run on NCSA workstations that will allow short commands to be executed on the Cray without having to log in via TELNET.

6. Conclusions

In the course of a year, through TCP/IP, the supercomputer facility at NCSA has become accessible nationwide from the NSFNET and ARPANET. TCP/IP provided us with more connectivity and versatility than any other networking protocol we considered. In short, it is a great success.

Data transfer rates remain disappointingly slow, but for all but the most intensive of file transports, the advantage of convenience greatly outweighs the slower speed. And over long-haul networks, CTSS TCP/IP is quick enough to cause floods of ICMP source quenches from gateways.

Interoperability is surprisingly good, considering the hostile environment of the uncontrolled Internet. We are equally surprised at the number of malfunctioning, misfeatured, and otherwise broken TELNET's, TCP's, and IP's out there, and even more amazed that somehow it all works.

We feel that TCP/IP was a good choice for a networking protocol for NCSA, in light of its great robustness, versatility, and connectivity.

ACKNOWLEDGEMENT

The CTSS TCP/IP project would not have been possible without the efforts of Steve Dorner and Ed Krol. Also thanks to the networking group at the University of Illinois Computing Services Office for allowing another harebrained TCP onto the campus network. Finally, to the various wizened old Internet hands of the NSFNET mail reflector, who repeatedly pointed out errors and stray thinking and helped make a friendly TCP.

REFERENCES

Cray Research, Inc. *Cray X/MP-48 Mainframe Reference Manual*. HR-0097. August 1984.

Dorner, S. *CTSS TCPLIB Programmer's Manual*. NCSA Internal Document. May 1987.

Franta, W. R. and Heath, J. R. *Performance of Hyperchannel Networks*.

Kline, C. *CTSS TCP/IP Internals Manual*. NCSA Internal Document. June 1987.

Mills, D. *Internet Delay Experiments*. ARPA RFC-889. December 1983.

Postel, J. *TELNET Protocol Specification*. ARPA RFC-854. May 1983.

Postel, J. *DoD Standard Internet Protocol*. ARPA RFC-791. September 1981.

Postel, J. *Internet Control Message Protocol*. ARPA RFC-792. September 1981.

Postel, J. *DoD Standard Transmission Control Protocol*. ARPA RFC-793. September 1981.

Postel, J. *DoD Standard File Transport Protocol*. ARPA RFC-959. October 1985.

Postel, J. *Something a Host Could do with Source Quench*. Draft RFC. 1987.

PART 2. PERFORMANCE ANALYSIS

J.J. Garcia-Luna-Aceves

SRI International, USA

Performance Modelling of the Orwell Basic Access Mechanism

M. Zafirovic-Vukotic, I. G. Niemegeers
University of Twente,
P.O.B. 217, 7500AE Enschede, The Netherlands

Abstract : Orwell is a high speed slotted ring. Its protocol uses destination release of the slots. Because of this the carried load can be much larger than the transmission rate. A new analytical model of the Orwell basic access mechanism is presented in this paper. The model shows to be accurate and usable over a wide range of parameters. The performance analysis of the Orwell basic access mechanism is presented.

1. Introduction

Slotted ring protocols are suitable for high speed LANs (HSLANs) [ZANI'87]. Examples can be found in: the Cambridge Fast Ring [TEMP'84], Orwell [FAAD'85], Upperbus [GIBZ'84], IEEE P802.6 draft standard [SZE'85] and FXNET [CADG'86]. Orwell has the most efficient access protocol of all the slotted rings due to the destination release of the slots.

Orwell has been developed by British Telecom Laboratories for high transmission rates ranging up to 565 Mbit/s. It has been primarily designed as an interconnection structure within a telephone packet switch [FAAD'85]. Orwell torus has been proposed to be used within an ATD (asynchronous time divison) switch [ADAM'87]. The design of the Orwell protocol makes it suitable for a number of applications of HSLANs.

The performance of the basic access mechanism (i.e. the basic MAC layer protocol) of Orwell is studied in this paper. No special integrated synchronous/ asynchronous protocols are considered. The load is of the asynchronous type and transmission rates in excess of 100 Mbit/s are assumed.

A new approximative analytical model of the Orwell basic access mechanism (AM) and a stability condition are presented in this paper. The model considers the expected packet (i.e. LLC_PDU) delays. Only the queueing delays for access to the medium and the transfer delays are considered. Delays due to processing of the packets are not included.

The model has been tested by extensive and detailed simulations in a number of cases typical for HSLANs. On the basis of the results obtained from the model, a performance analysis of the Orwell basic AM has been done. Sensitivity to the number of stations, the number of slots, transmission rate, the expected packet length and the slot length has been evaluated.

The paper is organized as follows. The Orwell protocol is described first. The state of the art in analytical modelling of Orwell is given next. Notation is introduced and the workload model is presented. The stability condition is derived next. A M|G|1 with server breakdown model of the Orwell basic AM is then presented in detail. This model is tested by comparing to simulations. A performance analysis of the basic AM is done next. Finally, some conclusions regarding the model and the performance of the Orwell basic AM are presented.

2. The Orwell Basic Access Mechanism

The ring is partitioned into equal length slots. We assume that this is achieved by introducing a latency register at the monitor station to virtually lengthen the ring to a multiple of the slot length.

Slots circulate around the ring and can be empty or full. A full slot is occupied by a mini-packet, i.e. a MAC PDU. Stations are actively coupled to the ring. They repeat or modify the slots. An empty slot may be filled by a mini-packet, if there is

© 1988 ACM 0-89791-245-4/88/0001/0035 $1.50

one. A full slot circulating around the ring, reaches the destination station which reads it and passes it on to a higher layer. We assume that each station is capable of using every empty slot that arrives and of reading every slot destined to itself.

There are two classes of basic slotted ring AMs depending on which station empties a full slot: the source station, or the destination station. After emptying the slot there are two possibilities: the slot can be used by the station that empties it, or it must be passed to the next downstream station.

Orwell implements the following basic AM. The destination station releases a slot that was full and the next downstream station may use it (see Figure 2.). More than one slot at a time can be carrying mini-packets from the same source. This is the basic AM studied in this paper.

Precautions have to be taken to prevent a station from hogging the ring. We assume a symmetric load in which case the need for a fairer protocol is smaller than in an asymmetric case.

The Orwell protocol recognizes two service classes: class 1 for delay sensitive services, requiring a guaranteed bandwidth, e.g. synchronous traffic, and class 2 for the delay tolerant services, e.g. asynchronous data. Access is organized in intervals. Each station S_i on the ring has a counter, called the D_i counter, indicating the number of packets allowed to be sent during the interval. This way load control is provided. For a detailed description of the Orwell protocol the reader is referred to [FAAD'85].

In this paper we model the basic AM of Orwell. We consider a single traffic class.

3. State of the Art in Analytical Modelling of Orwell

As far as it is known to us there is only one model in the literature that considers the expected packet delay and which models a mechanism like the Orwell AM. That is the model of Hayes and Sherman [HASH'71].

The model of Hayes and Sherman assumes an interactive computer environment. The load is modelled by an interactive user model at each station. A user is modelled as a traffic source which alternates between a think time and a packet transmission time. Queueing at station S_i is modelled as a single server queue with server breakdown. Two variants of the model are developed which differ in the way the expected duration of server breakdown and waiting time are approximated. However, synchronous traffic sources and large bandwidth sources create most of the load in HSLANs [LLRS'85]. Such sources create a different type of load than the smaller bandwidth sources (e.g. interactive users). This makes the models of [HASH'71] inadequate for modelling HSLANs. Although the arrival processes are very different, our approch to the modelling is basicaly similar to the one of [HASH'71]. This will be explained later on.

Another analytical study of Orwell by Mitrani et al. [MIAF'86] addresses a different problem than the one we are considering. They give an approximation of the blocking probability of a telephone call due to overload. In this paper we consider the packet delay analysis.

For a state of the art overview and a shorter presentation of new models of the basic AMs of the slotted ring protocols the reader is referred to [ZANI'87a].

4. Notation

Let us introduce the following notation:

n - number of stations minus one,

S_i - i-th station in the ring, i=0,1,...,n, and for simplicity of notation we assume that station S_0 can also be denoted as S_{n+1},

w - transmission rate (bit/us or Mbit/s),

σ - duration of a slot (us),

ν - duration of an information field of a slot (us), such that $\nu<\sigma$,

λ_i - packet arrival rate at station S_i (packet/us), i=0,...,n,

Z_i - random variable denoting the bulk size of the arrival process at S_i, i.e. the number of mini-packets a packet is split into, i=0,...,n,

γ_i, EZ_i^2 - the first two moments of Z_i, i=0,...,n,

ρ - relative load, or the expected number of mini-packets arriving in the system during σ time units, such that

$$\rho = \sum_{i=0}^{n} \lambda_i \gamma_i \sigma , \qquad (1)$$

Y_i - random variable denoting a packet service time in the model (us), i=0,...,n,

EY_i, EY_i^2 - the first two moments of Y_i, i=0,...,n,

p_{ij} - an element of the packet communication source_to_destination matrix, $||p_{ij}||_{n+1 \times n+1}$ that represents the relative traffic intensity from source S_i to destination S_j, as observed by the network, and

$$0 \leq p_{ij} \leq 1 \quad \text{and} \quad \sum_{j=0}^{n} p_{ij} = 1, \quad i,j = 0,\ldots,n.$$

s — the number of slots in the ring,

τ_{ij} — propagation time from S_i to S_j including the latency at station S_j (us), $i,j=0,\ldots,n$,

τ — slot rotation time or τ_{ii} for all i (us), such that

$$\tau = \sum_{i=0}^{n} \tau_{i,i+1} \quad \text{and} \quad \tau = s\sigma. \quad (2)$$

τ_i — the expected propagation time from S_i to the destination of a packet or a mini-packet sent by S_i (us), $i=0,\ldots,n$,

EW_i — the expected packet waiting time at S_i (us), $i=0,\ldots,n$,

ET_i — the expected packet delay or the expected duration of MAC layer service per packet of S_i i.e. the expected packet delay from arrival at S_i till its complete delivery at the destination (us), $i=0,\ldots,n$.

5. Workload Model

Let us now specify the workload model. It includes the arrival process of packets and of mini-packets, the distribution of their lengths and the traffic pattern in the ring.

We assume that packets arrive at the MAC layer of station S_i according to a Poisson process with intensity λ_i. Packets (LLC_PDUs) are segmented and MAC protocol control information (PCI) is added to form a number of mini-packets (MAC_PDUs) of which the expected value is γ_i. So, the arrival process of mini-packets at S_i can be considered to be a bulk Poisson process.

Packet lengths are assumed to be i.i.d. distributed. Note that often when talking about packet lengths it is assumed that the length is expressed in time units, i.e. it represents the duration of packet transmission at rate w.

The information field of a MAC_PDU (mini-packet) in the slotted ring protocol has a constant length $v \times w$ (bits). The PCI of a mini-packet has a constant length too. So, the length of a mini-packet is also constant and equal to $\sigma \times w$ (bits) i.e. a slot length.

The random variable Z_i, denoting the number of mini-packets a packet is split into, has a distribution that is derived from the packet length distribution.

Since a symmetric load and traffic pattern are assumed:

$$\lambda_i = \lambda, \quad \gamma_i = \gamma, \quad i=0,\ldots,n, \quad (3)$$

and

$$p_{ij} = \begin{cases} \frac{1}{n}, & j <> i \\ 0, & j = i \end{cases}, \quad i,j=0,\ldots,n. \quad (4)$$

Note that we do not assume that the distance between adjacent stations is the same.

From (1), (3) and (4), the relative load ρ equals

$$\rho = (n+1)\lambda\gamma\sigma. \quad (5)$$

6. Stability Condition

The stability condition for this system in a symmetric case (see relations (3) and (4)) can be derived as follows.

The system can be looked at as a multiple cyclic servers multiqueue system with a limited service discipline where the queues are visited by the servers in a random order. Each slot corresponds to a cyclic server. Up to one mini-packet is sent per slot arrival at a station. This is why the limited service discipline is assumed. An overview of the single cyclic server models is given in [TAKL'85]. Some results for a multiple cyclic servers system are given in [MOWA'84].

In this multiple cyclic servers system a service unit is a mini-packet. The switchover time (H_i) is a constant and equals $\tau_{i,i+1}$. So,

$$P\{H_i = \tau_{i,i+1}\} = 1, \quad i=0,\ldots,n. \quad (6)$$

The mini-packet service time (X_i) in this model equals the propagation time from the source S_i to the first station downstream from the destination (S_{j+1}, which is the first station to be able to use the slot that was carrying that mini-packet) minus the propagation time from the source S_i to the first downstream station S_{i+1} since this time has already been included in the switchover time. So, $X_i = \tau_{i,j+1} - \tau_{i,i+1} = \tau_{i+1,j+1}$, where S_j is the destination station, $i,j=0,\ldots,n$. The random variable X_i has the following distribution

$$P\{X_i = x\} = \begin{cases} \frac{1}{n}, & x \in \{\tau_{i+1,j+1}, j=0,\ldots,n, j<>i\}, \\ 0, & \text{otherwise} \end{cases} \quad (7)$$

Note that

$$\frac{1}{n} \sum_{i=0}^{n} EX_i = \frac{\tau}{2}. \quad (8)$$

The servers intervisit time as observed by each queue (at S_i, $i=0,\ldots,n$), has a different distribution in the case of a random service order than in the case of a regular one. So, the expected waiting times at S_i are different for different order of queue service. However, when determining the stability condition, the random order of visiting the queues can be neglected. The reason is as follows. Due to the symmetry (relations (3) and (4)), the order of service of queues does not depend on the packet length nor on the class of the customers (i.e. queue) that has previously been served. The frequency of visiting a queue is the same for all the queues. Another order of visiting the queues may be assumed for determining the stability condition. The work conservation law can be used (see [KLEI'79], [WATS'84] and [BOGR'86]).

Let us assume a regular order of visiting the queues for determining the stability condition. Because of the work conservation law and according to the results for a multiple cyclic servers model (see also [MOWA'84]), we have that the expected duration of a cycle ER equals

$$ER = \frac{\sum_{i=0}^{n} EH_i}{1 - \frac{1}{s} \sum_{i=0}^{n} \lambda_i \gamma_i EX_i} . \qquad (9)$$

From (2), (3), (6), (8) and (9), we have

$$ER = \frac{\tau}{1 - \frac{1}{2}\rho} , \qquad (10)$$

with ρ given in (5).

For all the queues to be stable it is necessary that the denominator in (10) is positive i.e.

$$1 - \frac{1}{2}\rho > 0$$

wherefrom

$$\rho < 2 . \qquad (11)$$

For this limited cyclic servers system ([TAKL'85]) due to the work conservation law we have the following neccesary condition, in addition to (11):

$$\lambda \gamma ER < s . \qquad (12)$$

From (5), (10) and (12), we have

$$\frac{1}{n+1} \rho \cdot \frac{1}{\sigma} \cdot \frac{\tau}{1 - \frac{1}{2}\rho} < s$$

wherefrom

$$\rho < 2 - \frac{4}{n+3} , \qquad (13)$$

where ρ is given in (5).

Since (13) implies (11), the neccesary and sufficient condition for all queues to be stable is (13).

From (5) and (13) we get another form of the stability condition. Namely, we have

$$\lambda \gamma (n+1) < 2 - \frac{4}{n+3} \cdot \frac{1}{\sigma} . \qquad (14)$$

Note that no result concerning waiting times in a multiqueue multiple cyclic servers system with a random order of visits to the queues and a limited service discipline is available in the literature.

Let us now present the model itself.

7. Model Description

A station can use a number of consecutive slots. It is prevented from using a slot only when the slot is full. So, a station has to cease its transmission when a full slot or a sequence of full slots arrives, i.e. when it sees the ring is busy.

A queue at station S_i is modeled as a $M|G_1|1$ system with server breakdown. A packet is a service unit. The breakdown corresponds to the ring being busy because of activities of upstream stations. The duration of the server breakdown is determined using a $\Sigma M|G_2|1$ model. The expected packet waiting time and delay are obtained using a $\Sigma M, M|G_2, G_1|1$ model (notations are according to [CHTE'83]). Ring activities are illustrated in Figure 3. An illustration of the model is shown in Figure 4.

Let us now present the details of the model. First, the packet service time distribution at S_i is evaluated. The parameters of the $M|G_1|1$ queue and of the $\Sigma M|G_2|1$ queue are determined. The formulas for the expected packet waiting time and the packet delay are presented next.

The service time of a packet Y_i in the $M|G_1|1$ as well as in the $\Sigma M|G_2|1$ model is assumed to equal the packet transmission time. Let us determine the distribution of Y_i.

A packet is divided into Z_i mini-packets and the transmission time of a mini-packet is σ. Hence, the packet transmission time Y_i is given as follows

$$Y_i = Z_i \sigma . \qquad (15)$$

Y_i has a distribution of Z_i with time unit σ. So, we have from (15)

$$EY = \gamma \sigma \quad \text{and} \quad EY^2 = EZ^2 \sigma^2 . \qquad (16)$$

Index i has been omitted in (16) because of the symmetry. Indices will be omitted in some formulas. Sometimes we use them to improve the readability.

Let us now determine the characteristics of the $M|G_1|1$ queue with server breakdown that models queueing at S_i. The arrival process of packets is a

Poisson process with intensity λ_i. The packet service time is Y_i with the first two moments given by (16). The server is available at S_i only if an empty slot arrives at S_i. Otherwise, the server is blocked due to a ring busy period. A packet whose service has been interrupted by a server breakdown, is served after the server breakdown period, from the point where the service stopped i.e. the remaining mini-packets will be sent. So, we have a preemptive-resume service discipline.

We consider the activity of upstream stations as observed by S_i as a $\Sigma M|G_2|1$ queue. Customers in this model are packets that pass through S_i and cause a service break period.

The breakdown process, caused by activites of upstream stations, is assumed to be a regenerative process. In reality the process is not regenerative, because of the direct dependence between sending of mini-packets at upstream stations S_j and blocking of S_j by these and other mini-packets ($j<>i$) including packets sent by S_i.

Let us now determine the values of the parameters in the $\Sigma M|G_2|1$ queue. Let λ_i' be the intensity of the arrival process and EY_i' and $EY_i'^2$ the first and the second moments of the service time distribution at this queue.

Let us define a set $C_{k,i}$ of station indices j, such that a packet sent from S_k to S_j passes through S_i given k and i, $0 \leq i, k \leq n$. $C_{k,i}$ can be denoted as :

$C_{k,i}$ = { j|0≤j≤n and
 (if i≤k then i≤j≤k else (j≥i or j≤k)) }.

The intensity of the arrival process at $\Sigma M|G_2|1$ queue in this case is

$$\lambda_i' = \sum_{k=0}^{n} \lambda_k \sum_{j \varepsilon C_{k,i}} p_{kj}. \qquad (17)$$

Because of the symmetric load (see relation (3)) and a symmetric traffic pattern (see relation (4)), relation (17) reduces to

$$\lambda' = \lambda \frac{n}{2}. \qquad (18)$$

Since all of the packets in this queue have the same packet length distribution (relation (3)), we have that Y' has the same distribution as Y. So, we have

$$EY' = EY \quad \text{and} \quad EY'^2 = EY^2, \qquad (19)$$

where EY and EY^2 are given in (16).

The system can be modelled as an $\Sigma M,M|G_1,G_2|1$ model with two priority classes and a preemptive-resume service discipline. The higher priority class represents upstream activities, and the lower priority class represents activities at S_i. The delays of the lower priority customers are to be determined.

The expected packet waiting time EW_i at S_i is given by [COHE'82]:

$$EW_i = \frac{\lambda_i' EY_i'^2 + \lambda_i EY_i^2}{2(1-\lambda_i' EY_i')(1-\lambda_i' EY_i' - \lambda_i EY_i)}, \quad i=0,\ldots,n,$$

or, because of the symmetry from (16), (18) and (19), we have

$$EW = \frac{(n+2)\lambda \sigma EZ^2}{(2-n\lambda \gamma \sigma)(2-(n+2)\lambda \gamma \sigma)}. \qquad (20)$$

The expected packet delay ET_i consists of the following three components: the expected packet waiting time, the expected service completion time (the time between the beginning of service of a packet till its completion) and the expected packet transfer time. According to [COHE'82] the expected service completion time in this system is equal to

$$\frac{EY}{1-\lambda' EY'}, \quad \text{i.e.} \quad \frac{2\gamma\sigma}{2-n\lambda\gamma\sigma}.$$

So, we have

$$ET_i = EW + \frac{2\gamma\sigma}{2-n\lambda\gamma\sigma} + \tau_i, \quad i=0,\ldots,n. \quad (21)$$

where EW is given in relation (20).

8. Discussion of the Model

Note that basically the same idea of the server breakdown process observed by S_i has been used in [HASH'71]. However, because of the different arrival process that model uses different approximations.

Let us now discuss possible causes of inaccuracy. The correlation between the activities at S_i and the activities at other stations has not been taken into account. In addition to this the traffic that does not pass through S_i has been neglected. We will see that this causes both an overestimate and an underestimate of the delays at higher loads and in the case of a small number of stations.

Note that the approximation of the expected packet delay in (21) does not depend on the number of slots in the ring.

We expect that our model can easily be extended to handle a mixed synchronous and asynchronous traffic load, provided a Poisson arrival process is assumed for all types of traffic. Synchronous traffic influences the duration of the breakdown period through the moments of arrival and service time distributions which can easily be evaluated.

9. Testing and Analysis of the Model

The simulation model of the Orwell protocol is a detailed model. It is written in SIMULA and is documented in [VALK'87]. The analytical model has been tested by comparing the expected packet delays to the results of simulations. 90% confidence intervals have been obtained except for the runs where the correlation between the samples was too large. In those cases only a point estimate of the delay is shown in the figures.

Configurations, system parameters and workload models expected to be typical for HSLANs have been used. We present them here.

In all the examples an equal distance between the neighbouring stations has been assumed, i.e. $\tau_{i,i+1} = \tau_{j,j+1}$, $i,j=0,\ldots,n$. An exponential and a bimodal packet length distribution have been assumed.

We consider the following configurations, system parameters and workload: <u>configuration</u>: transmission rate = 140 Mbit/s, cable length = 5 and 1 km, number of stations = 40, 10 and 4; <u>system parameters:</u> slot information field = 512 bits, overhead in slot = 48 bits, latency register = 24 bits; and <u>workload:</u> expected packet length = 7100 and 3000 bits, a symmetric load, and a symmetric traffic pattern.

Note that in Orwell the slot information field length is 128 bits [FAAD'85]. We have taken another value of the length of the information field because of the following. We plan to do a comparative performance analysis of a number of slotted ring protocols. To be able to compare them a common information field length of 512 bits has been chosen. Such a choice does not change the qualitative behaviour of the protocol.

The expected packet delay of the Orwell basic access mechanism vs load is depicted in Figures 5. through 10. An exponential packet length distribution has been used except for the case of Figure 9. where the following bimodal distribution has been taken:

$$P\{Y = x\} = \begin{cases} 0.78, & x = 512 \text{ (bit)} \\ 0.22, & x = 30000 \text{ (bit)} \\ 0, & \text{otherwise} \end{cases}$$

This distribution was chosen because we would like to test the model using a distribution with the same expected value of 7100 bits and a second moment about twice as large as in the case of the exponential distribution. Moreover, a bimodal distribution was thought to be a realistic one for the packet lengths [VYDA'86]. Let us now analyse the accuracy of the model.

The M|G|1 with server breakdown model gives a good estimate of the delays except in the case of 4 stations in the ring (in Figure 10.) where an overestimate appears. In all other cases it shows a slight underestimate of the expected delays at low loads, an accurate estimate at moderate loads and an overestimate at high loads. The asymptote representing the maximum throughput is therefore underestimated. This is not the case when there are two slots in the ring (Figure 8.), then a slight underestimate of the delays appears over the whole range.

This effect can be explained as follows. The breakdown process is influenced by the activities of station S_i. So, S_i preempts the breakdown process by filling in the ring with its own packets. This effect is especially strong if there are a small number of stations in the ring (e.g. less than 5). Our model does not take this into account. Thus, the expected waiting time at S_i is overestimated. However, if the number of slots is small (e.g. 2) and the number of stations moderate or large (e.g. larger than 10) another effect appears. Namely, S_i is not able to preempt the breakdown process. Note that if there are e.g. 2 slots in the ring S_i has to reuse the same slot a few times to send a packet. Rather an effect of creating an extra load at the network appears. In this case the delays are underestimated in the model. These effects are the strongest under heavy load conditions. So, the main cause of inaccuracy is that the correlation between activities of S_i and of the other stations has not been modelled i.e. the breakdown process is assumed to be a regenerative one.

The model is more accurate for a larger number of stations (see Figures 5., 7. and 10.). The model is also more accurate when there are more slots in the ring (see Figures 7. and 8.). We attribute this to the smaller correlation between activities at S_i and other stations in these cases.

The accuracy of the model seems not to depend very much on the expected packet lengths, in the experiments conducted (see Figures 5. and 6.). The model is however, slightly more accurate with shorter packets. The accuracy of the model seems also not to depend strongly on the second moment of the packet length (see Figures 5. and 9.). Of course, the model is slightly more accurate in the case of a smaller second moment of the packet length.

10. Performance Analysis of the Orwell Basic AM

The experiments with the Orwell basic AM are depicted in Figures 5. through 16. The cases in Figures 5. through 10. have already been explained in the previous section. A sensitivity analysis of the Orwell basic AM is depicted in Figures 11. through 15. The expected packet delays with respect to the number of slots, the number of stations, transmission rate, the expected packet length and the slot information field length are shown, respectively. All the other parameters are kept unchanged and taken as in Figure 5. The load of 80 Mbit/s is used. The case in Figure 16. is the same as in Figure 5. except that the slot information field is 128 bits. Let us now evaluate the performance of the Orwell basic AM.

Stability Condition

The stability condition of the Orwell basic AM (see relations (13) and (14)) shows that the maximum carried load depends on the number of stations, the slot duration and the first moments of arrival process and bulk size. It does not depend on the number of slots. Hence, it also does not depend on the ring latency.

Let us now analyse the stability condition expressed in relation (14). For the system to be stable it is necessary and sufficient that the total arrival rate of mini-packets ($(n+1)\lambda\gamma$) is less than a value which is a function of the number of stations and the slot duration. The total arrival rate of mini-packets depends on the arrival rate of mini-packets at each station ($\lambda\gamma$). This arrival rate depends on the arrival rate of packets at each station (λ) and on the expected number of mini-packets included in a packet (γ) which depends on the slot information field length (ν) and on the packet length distribution. Let us now analyse the stability condition expressed in relation (13). If system is stable, the total arrival rate of mini-packets in σ time units (ρ) is bounded by a value which is a function of the number of stations. The larger the number of stations the larger the maximum carried load (i.e. the maximum number of packets that can be carried). However, ρ is bounded by 2 in the limit when the number of stations converges to infinity. In some other slotted ring protocols e.g. in the Cambridge ring ρ can never be greater than 1 if all the queues are stable. The difference appears due to the destination release of the slots in the Orwell basic AM, where a slot can be used more than once during a rotation.

Maximum Carried Load

The Orwell basic AM proves to be capable of carrying loads that are larger than the transmission rate e.g. about 220 Mbit/s in the case of Figure 5.

Number of Stations

The expected packet delays in the Orwell basic AM depend on the number of stations in the ring (see Figures 5., 7. and 12.). The delays decrease asymptotically, with the increase of the number of stations. The performance differs only for smaller number of stations (e.g. less than 15 in Figure 12.). The maximum carried load is also larger if the number of stations is larger (see the stability condition (13)). So, there is no sudden degradation of the performance when the number of stations increases or decreases (as is the case in some other slotted ring protocols e.g. the Cambridge ring).

Number of Slots

The Orwell basic AM shows a small change of performance with respect to the number of slots in the ring (see Figures 7., 8. and 11. and Table 1.). It performs worse if the number of slots is very small (e.g. 2) than if it is medium (e.g. 7), see Figures 7. and 8. This property could not be obtained from the analytical model (see section 8.) but only from the simulations. Because of the model properties (see again section 8.), the analytical model gives a more accurate estimate of the delays for a large number of slots (e.g. greater than 10 for the case depicted in Figure 11.). The delay increase shown in Figure 11. is linear and it is a consequence of a change of the ring latency. Note again, that the maximum carried load does not depend on the number of slots.

Moments of the Packet Length Distribution

The Orwell basic AM shows a small change of performance with respect to the different moments of the packet length distribution (see Figures 5., 6., 9. and 14.). The larger the moments the larger the packet delay. Note that when the expected packet length changes, the load on the network also changes. This happens because of the change in the expected number of mini-packets in a packet which causes a change in the expected number of mini-packets that are the last ones in a packet. These mini-packets are only partially filled in by data. Table 3. shows the relative load ρ vs the expected packet length (see relation (5)). When the expected packet length increases, the load on the network decreases. The increase of the delays in Figure 14. appears because of the longer packet transfer time, while the waiting times are smaller.

Transmission Rate

For the given load of 80 Mbit/s delays decrease as expected with increasing transmission rates e.g. up to 1 Gbit/s in the case of Figure 13. (see also Table 2. which shows the number of slots in the ring vs the transmission rate for the case of Figure 13.). Beyond that transmission rate, the delays slowly decrease to the propagation time from the source to the destination, at infinity. So, increasing the transmission rate beyond a certain limit does not contribute to a very large change in performance given a constant load. However, if the transmission rate is much larger than e.g. 1 Gbit/s it is to be expected that the load is larger than e.g. 80 Mbit/s. With a larger load an improvement of performance can be expected even if the transmission rate increases beyond 1 Gbit/s. So, the significant improvement of performance with the increase of transmission rate to a certain limit indicates that the Orwell basic AM could be successfully used at very high transmission rates as well.

Slot Information Field Length

A sensitivity analysis of the Orwell basic AM with respect to the slot information field length is depicted in Figure 15. (see also Figures 5. and 16.). The delay function is discontinuous because of the change in the number of slots with the increase of the information field length. Table 4. contains the number of slots in the ring vs the slot information field length for this case. The relative load ρ vs the slot information field length for this case is depicted in Table 5.

The AM performs the best with the information field length between 512 and 1024 bits. If the information field length decreases the performance sharply degrades since the overhead gets large in relation to the slot length. If the information field increases the performance also degrades. This happens because of the decrease of the expected number of mini-packets in a packet which causes the same effect as already explained in the case of a change in the expected packet length.

Note however, that the choice of the information field length in practice is much determined by the packet length distribution. Namely, if the most dominant traffic class has a constant packet length (e.g. voice with a packet length of 128 bits) the best performance of the protocol could be expected with a slot information field length equal to this one. The Orwell described in [FAAD'85] follows this reasoning. For the workload used here, the Orwell basic AM with 128 bits information field length has much worse performance than with 512 bits (see Figures 5. and 16.).

This analysis shows that the information field lengths between 256 bits and 2048 bits provide a good performance for the protocol. This also indicates that the implementation of a uniframe PCM like scheme over the Orwell protocol may significantly improve its performance.

Applications

Because of the properties of the Orwell basic AM, we can conclude that it can perform well over a wide range of applications.

11. Conclusions and Further Work

The basic AM of Orwell has been studied. A symmetrical load and a symmetrical traffic pattern have been assumed. A new analytical model of this AM has been developed and a performance analysis of this AM has been done.

The conclusions concerning the analytical model can be summarised as follows:

- the Orwell basic AM can be modelled as a multiple cyclic servers multiqueue system with limited service discipline where the queues are visited by the servers in a random order; however, no exact results for this model exist in the literature;

- the exact stability condition for the Orwell basic AM has been presented; it has been derived starting from the work conservation low;

- the M|G|1 with server breakdown model provides a good estimate of the expected packet delays over a wide range of parameters except when the number of stations is very small; it gives a good qualitative insight into the delays and at lower and medium loads an accurate delay estimate as well;

- the model is more accurate with more stations and more slots in the ring; and

- an extension of the model to take into account synchronous traffic is possible.

The conclusions concerning the performance of the Orwell basic AM can be summarised as follows:

- the Orwell basic AM shows to be able to carry loads that are larger than its transmission rate;

- the maximum carried load of the Orwell basic AM

does not depend on the number of slots in the ring (so neither on the ring latency);

- the packet delays in the Orwell basic AM show a small sensitivity to the number of slots and some sensitivity to the number of stations in the ring;

- the performance of the Orwell basic AM is also insensitive to both the first and second moment of the packet length distributions;

- the Orwell basic AM shows a good performance at higher transmission rates (e.g. up to 1 Gbit/s) as well;

- a slot information field length between 256 bits and 2048 bits provides good performance for representative system parameters and workloads; and

- the performance of the Orwell basic AM makes it interesting for a wide range of applications e.g. backbone network, multiprocessor interconnection structure, gathering office LAN, etc.

We plan to use this as well as the other developed analytical models [ZANI'87a] in the analysis of slotted ring protocols (e.g. CFR, Orwell, their variants and uniframe slotted ring) in particular applications. We plan to do a comparative performance analysis the slotted ring protocols implementing synchronous and asynchronous traffic. Analysis is to be conducted by means of simulation and analytical modelling. Further work will include the asymmetrical cases as well. In particular attention will be paid to the performance of the integrated Orwell protocol, where the D_i allocation will be studied.

Acknowledgement

The authors would like to thank Dr.M.Sposini for useful discussions and supplying literature concerning HSLANs. The authors would also like to thank Dr.E.van Dooren and Mr.B.van Arem for reading the manuscript and giving some usefull remarks. Finally, we are gratefull to Dr.O.J.Boxma for his interest in the work and for providing us with literature.

References

[ADAM'87] Adams J.L., *"The Orwell torus communication switch"*, GSLB -Seminar on Broadband Switching, Albufeira, Portugal, pp. 215 -224, January 1987.

[BOGR'86] Boxma O.J., Groenendijk W.P., *Pseudo-conservation Laws in Cyclic-service Systems*, Centre for Mathematics and Computer Science, Report OS-R8606, Amsterdam, June 1986.

[CADG'86] Casey L.M., Dittburner R.C., Gamage N.D., *"FXNET: a backbone ring for voice and data"*, IEEE Communications Magazine, Vol.24, No.12, pp. 23-28, December 1986.

[CHTE'83] Chaudhry M.L., Templeton J.G.C., *A First Course in Bulk Queues*, J.Wiley, 1983.

[COHE'82] Cohen J.W., *The Single Server Queue*, North Holland Pb.Co., 1969.

[GIBZ'84] Giloi W.K., Behr P., Zuber G., *"Upperbus: a high speed backbone for metropolitan area networks"*, Proceedings of EFOC/LAN, pp. 286-289, Amsterdam, June 1986.

[FAAD'85] Falconer R.M., Adams J.L., *"Orwell: a protocol for an integrated services local network"*, British Telecom Tech.J., Vol.3, No.4, pp. 27-35, October 1985.

[HASH'71] Hayes J.F., Sherman D.N., *"Traffic analysis of a ring switched data transmission"*, Bell System Techn.J., Vol.50, No.9, pp. 2947-2978, November 1971.

[KLEI'79] Kleinrock L., *Queueing Systems*, Vol.I, J.Wiley, 1975.

[LLRS'85] Lambarelli L., Luvison A., Roffinella D., Sposini M., *"Service integration in wideband local area networks: problems and system solutions"*, International Tirrena Workshop on Digital Communication, Tirrena (Pisa), North Holland, 1985.

[MIAF'86] Mitrani I., Adams J.L., Falconer R.M., *"A modelling study of the Orwell ring protocol"*, Teletrafic Analysis and Computer Performance Evaluation, O.Boxma, J.Cohen, H.Tijms (ed.), Elsviers Sc.Pb.B.V., pp. 429-438, 1986.

[MOWA'84] Morris R.J.I., Wang Y.I., *"Some results for multi-queue systems with multiple cyclic servers"*, Performance of Computer Communication Systems, H.Rudin and W.Bux (ed.), Elsvier Sc.Pb. pp. 4.2A-5-1 - 4.2A-5-7, 1985.

[SZE '85] Sze D.T.W., *"A metropolitan area network"*, IEEE Journal on Selected Areas in Communications, Vol. Sac-3, No.6, pp. 815-824, November 1985.

[TAKL'85] Takagi H., Kleinrock L., *Analysis of Polling Systems*, JSI Research Report TR87, IBM Japan Science Institute, August 1985.

[TEMP'84] Temple S., *"The design of the Cambridge Fast ring"*, Ring Technology Local Area Networks, Dallas I.N. and Spratt E.B.(ed.), Elsevier Sc.Pb.B.V., pp. 79-88, 1984.

[VALK'87] Valk D., *Performance Analysis of Integrated Services Slotted Ring Protocols in Gathering HSLANs*, Report no.080-87-08, University of Twente, The Netherlands, March 1987.

[VYDA'86]   Vyncke E., Danthine A., *"A realistic simulation of a wideband backbone network"*, Proceedings of ICCC'86, pp. 176-181, North Holand, 1986.

[WATS'84]   Watson K.S., *"Performance evaluation of cyclic service strategies - a survey"*, Performance'84, pp. 521-533, E. Gelenbe (ed.), Elsevier Science Publishers B.V. (North-Holland), 1984.

[ZANI'87]   Zafirovic-Vukotic M., Niemegeers I.G., *"An evaluation of high speed local area network access mechanisms"*, Proceedings of Communication in Distributed Systems, N.Gerner, O.Spaniol (ed.), Aachen, in Informatik -Fachbericht, Springer-Verlag, pp. 426 -440, February 1987.

[ZANI'87a]   Zafirovic-Vukotic M., Niemegeers I.G., *"Analytical models of the slotted ring protocols in HSLANs"*, IFIP WG 6.4 Workshop High Speed Local Area Networks, A.Danthine, O.Spaniol (ed.), Aachen, to be published by North Holland, 1987.

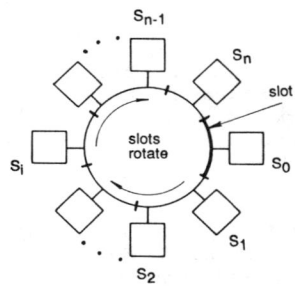

Figure 1.
The slotted ring structure.

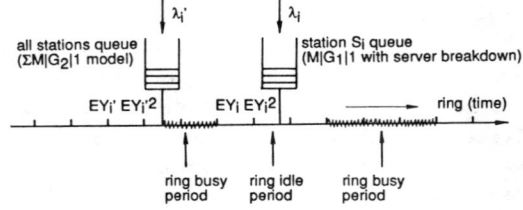

Figure 3.
Ring activities in the M|G|1 model with the server breakdown of the Orwell basic AM.

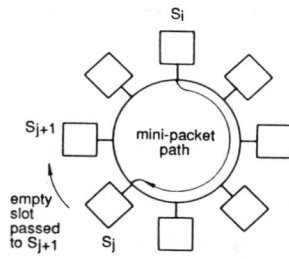

Figure 2.
Path of a mini-packet sent from S_i to S_j in Orwell.

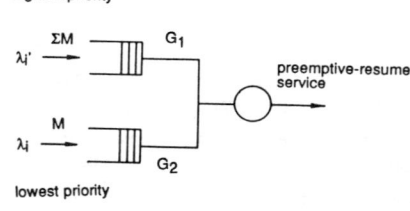

Figure 4.
A $\Sigma M, M|G_1, G_2|1$ model of the Orwell basic AM.

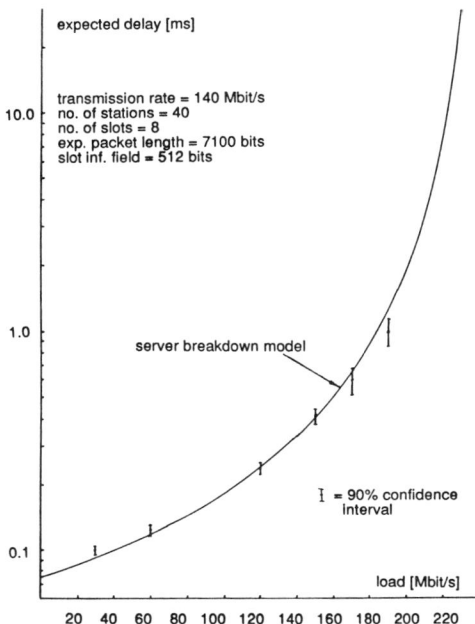

Figure 5.
Packet delay vs offered load with 40 stations, 8 slots, and an expected packet length of 7100 bits.

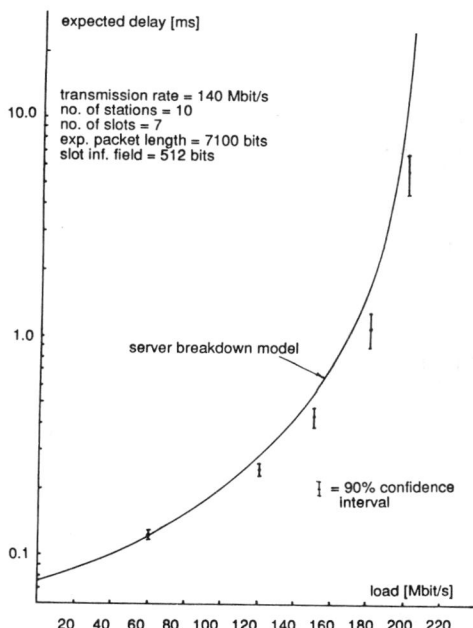

Figure 7.
Packet delay vs offered load with 10 stations, 7 slots, and an expected packet length of 7100 bits.

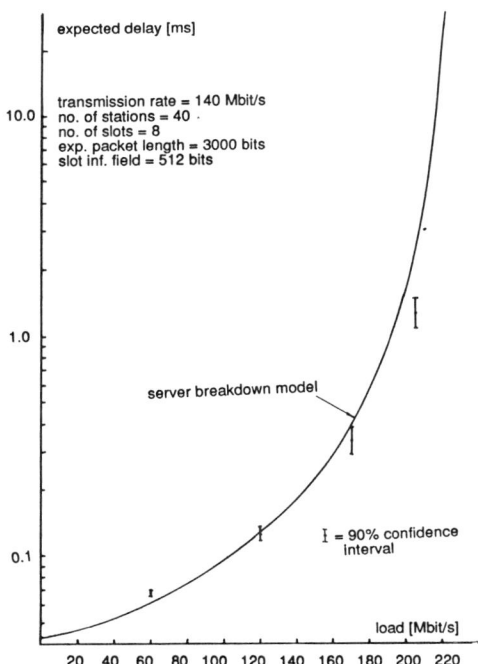

Figure 6.
Packet delay vs offered load with 40 stations, 8 slots, and an expected packet length of 3000 bits.

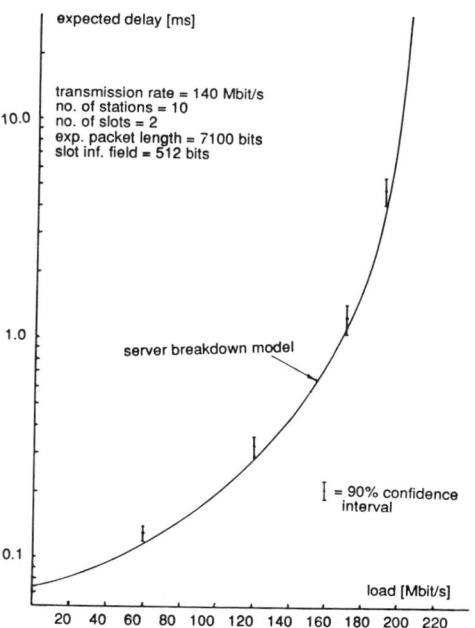

Figure 8.
Packet delay vs offered load with 10 stations, 2 slots, and an expected packet length of 7100 bits.

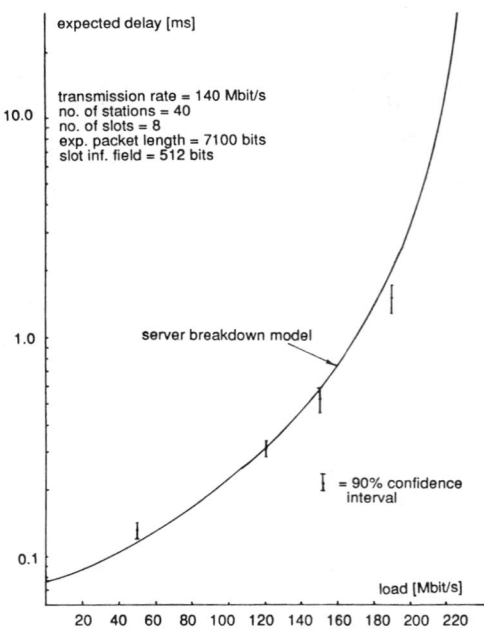

Figure 9.
Packet delay vs offered load with 40 stations, 8 slots, an expected packet length of 7100 bits and bimodal packet length distribution.

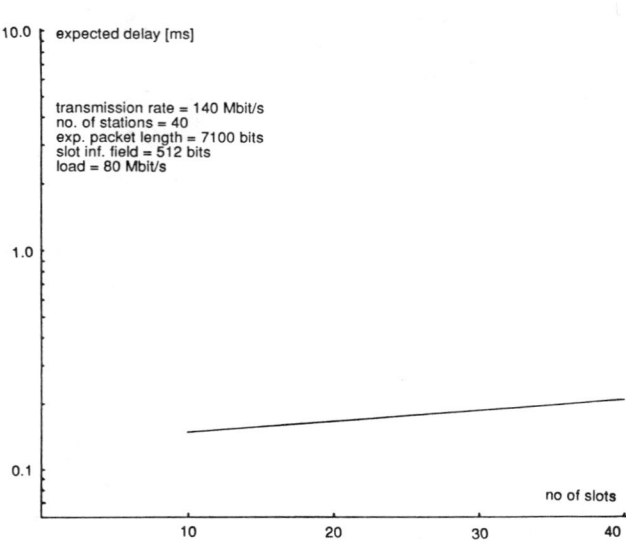

Figure 11.
Packet delay vs the number of slots.

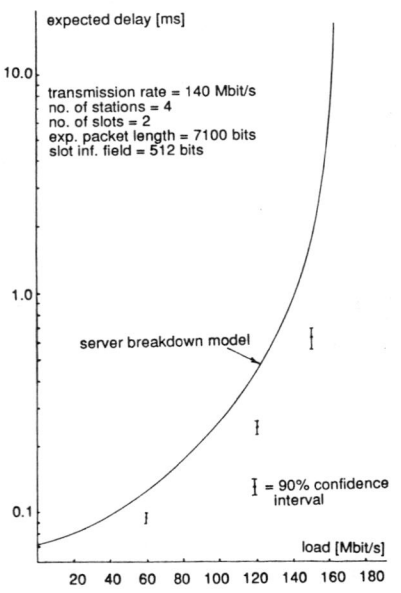

Figure 10.
Packet delay vs offered load with 4 stations, 2 slots, and an expected packet length of 7100 bits.

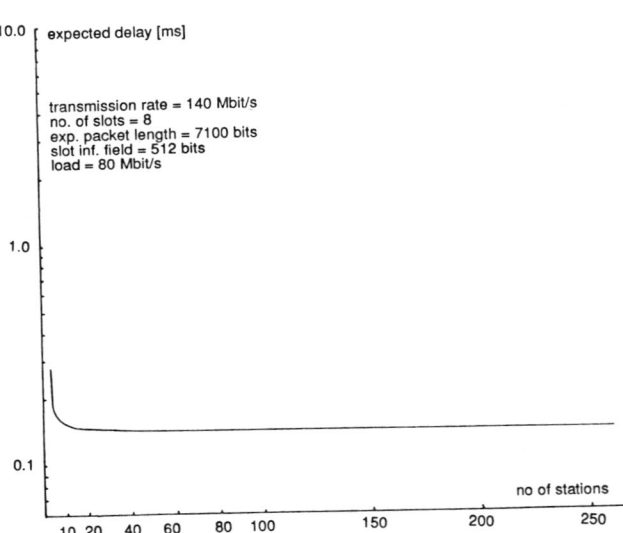

Figure 12.
Packet delay vs the number of stations.

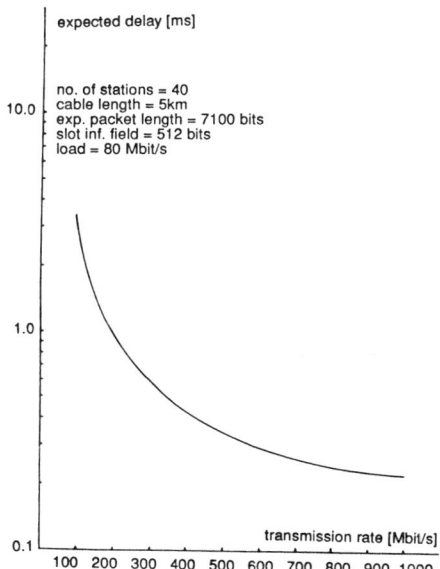

Figure 13.
Packet delay vs transmission rate.

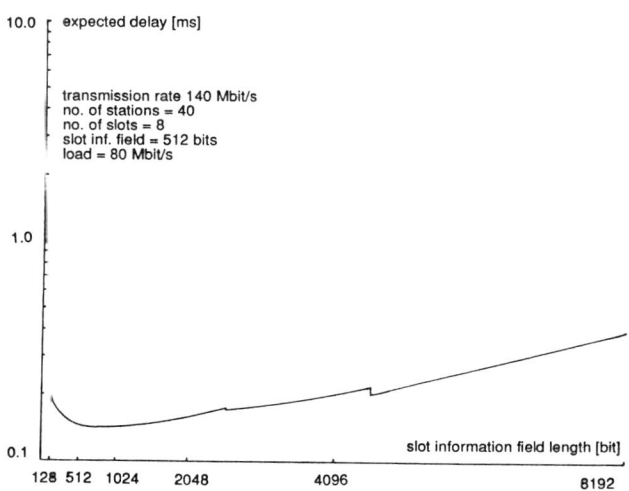

Figure 15.
Packet delay vs the slot information field length.

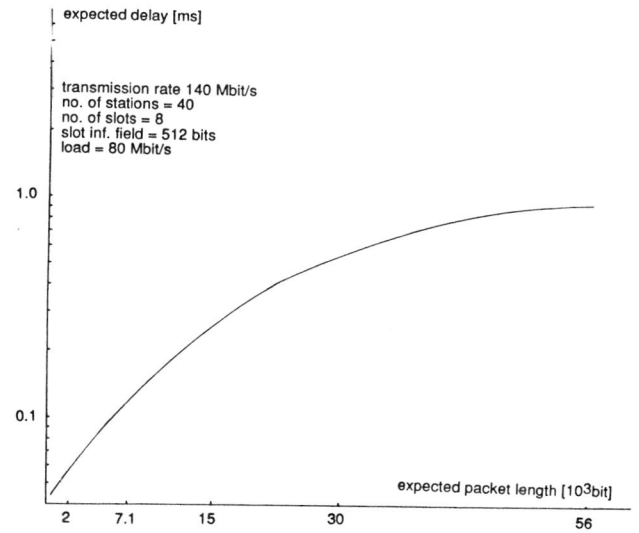

Figure 14.
Packet delay vs the expected packet length.

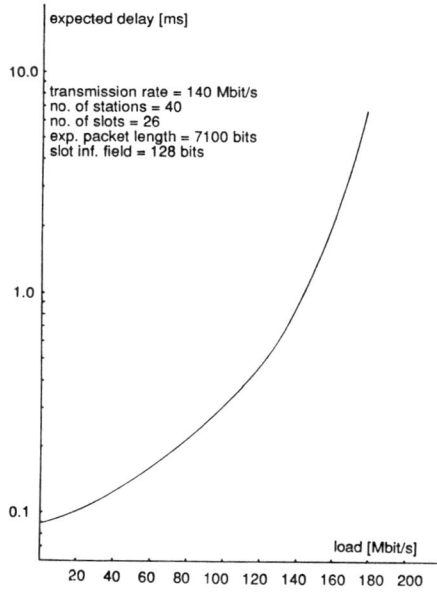

Figure 16.
Packet delay vs offered load with 40 stations, 26 slots, an expected packet length of 7100 bits and the slot information field of 128 bits.

no of slots	2	10	20	30	40
cable length (km)	0	6.63	14.63	22.63	30.63

Table 1.
The cable length vs the number of slots in the case of Figure 11.

transmission rate (Mbit/s)	100	140	565	800	848	896	1000
no of slots	7	8	27	38	40	42	47

Table 2.
The number of slots vs transmission rate in the case of Figure 13.

expected packet length (10^3 bit)	0.5	2	7.1	14	28	56
relative load	0.999	0.708	0.648	0.636	0.631	0.628

Table 3.
The relative load ρ vs the expected packet length in the case of Figure 14.

inform. field length (bit)	64	128	256	512	1024	2048	4096	8192
no of slots	33	32	16	8	5	3	2	1

Table 4.
The number of slots vs the slot information field length in the case of Figure 15.

inform. field length (bit)	64	128	256	512	1024	2048	4096	8192
relative load	1.01	0.73	0.69	0.65	0.64	0.67	0.76	0.97

Table 5.
The relative load ρ vs the slot information field length in the case of Figure 15.

Efficient Point–To–Point and Point–To–Multipoint Selective–Repeat ARQ Schemes with Multiple Retransmissions : A Throughput Analysis

Seshadri Mohan,   Jianguo Qian   and   Nagendra L. Rao

Dept. of Electrical and Computer Engineering

Clarkson University

Potsdam NY 13676

I Introduction

The most common method for handling transmission errors in computer networks is through the detection of errors and retransmission of the erroneous messages. This strategy has been called *Automatic Repeat Request* (ARQ). Various protocols have been established to achieve maximum possible utilization of avilable bandwidth in the most efficient manner possible. Previous works on ARQ schemes were done by Sastry [1], Towsley [2], Yu and Lin [3] - [4], Weldon [5], and Miller and Lin [6]. Yu and Lin [4] present a Selective Repeat ARQ scheme that assumes a limited receiver buffer size which makes the scheme a practical one to implement. Reference [4] also presents a lower bound on the throughput efficiency of this scheme. Here, the receiver buffer size has been considered to be N, where N is the number of packets that can be sent in one round trip delay period. In [5], Weldon presents an improved Selective Repeat ARQ strategy that is more efficient than Yu and Lin's scheme. The point–to–point selective repeat scheme proposed here proves to be more efficient than Yu and Lin's scheme and compares reasonably well with that of Weldon's. In [7], Ramchandran and Lin present a select-repeat ARQ scheme for point–to multipoint communications. We extend the point–to–point scheme we have proposed to point-to-multipoint communications and show that our scheme outperforms that in [7].

This paper uses the basic idea behind Yu and Lin's scheme. Section II proposes modifications to Yu and Lin's scheme that improve significantly the throughput efficiency for point–to–point communications. Simulation and analytical results presented in Section III indicate that this scheme is more efficient than the scheme in [4]. A lower bound on the efficiency of this scheme is derived in Section IV. Section V extends this scheme to point–to–multipoint communications and presents results for this scheme. Section VI provides a throughput analysis of the point–to–multipoint scheme. Finally, conclusions are presented in Section VII.

II The Point–To–Point ARQ Scheme

The description provided below is for the case where the size of the receiver buffer is N frames, the round trip delay. However the scheme can easily be modified for the case when the round trip delay is an integral multiple of N. Every frame that is transmitted has a frame number ranging from 1 to $3N$. These senquence numbers are reused in a cyclic manner. Metzner [8] has shown that when the receiver buffer is of size N and the range of sequence numbers is $3N$ or larger, the receiver will be able to determine whether a received block is a new one or one that was previously accepted correctly and delivered to the user. The explanation that follows is with respect to Fig. 1. Here, the roundtrip delay N is considered to be 5 and hence the frame numbers range from 1 to 15. Every frame that is ready for transmission is stored in the input queue. We assume for this discussion that a continuous supply of frames is available. Upon transmission of one frame, the transmitter picks the next one from the input queue and transmits it too. A copy of the transmitted frame is stored in the retransmission buffer. On receiving a frame, the receiver checks if the frame has been received without errors. If no errors are detected, an acknowledgement (ACK) frame is sent back to the transmitter. Otherwise a NACK (negative acknowledgement) is sent and a space is reserved for it in the receiver buffer. The receiver does not deliver any of the subsequently received frames, until the earliest improperly received frame is recovered. On receiving a NACK, the transmitter picks out the NACK'ed frame from the retransmission buffer and retransmits m copies of it. It must be pointed out here that in Yu and Lin's scheme, m is 1. In Fig. 1, m is taken to be two. The receiver now adopts the following strategy:

If the first retransmitted copy is received correctly, the receiver acknowledges it by sending an ACK and discards all the subsequent $(m-1)$ retransmissions and sends $(m-1)$ ACK's. If the first retransmitted copy is not received properly, then a NACK is sent for it. The receiver continues to send NACK's for subsequent frames received in error, till a copy is received correctly. It now acknowledges the correctly received frame by sending an ACK, discards all subsequent copies, and sends an ACK for each one of them. The transmitter considers that a frame has been successfully transmitted if at least one of the m frames is positively acknowledged by the receiver. If all the m copies are received in error, the transmitter retransmits m more copies of that frame. This process is repeated till that frame is successfully transmitted.

It is possible that a frame may be NACK'ed by the receiver though it is received correctly. Consider the case of frame 9 in Fig. 1. This frame is received properly by the receiver, but there is no space in the receiver buffer to store it. A buffer overflow is said to have occured in this case. The receiver discards this frame, and sends a NACK to the transmitter asking for a retransmission. The transmitter detects packets discarded due to buffer overflow at the receiver by checking the forward distance f_T, which is defined as $(y-x)$ mod $3N$, where y is the current frame number, x is the earliest unacknowledged frame and N, the round-trip delay. Note that if $f_T = 0$, then the data frames with sequence numbers $x+N, x+N+1, \ldots, x+2N-1$ have been rejected by the receiver due to buffer overflow. All these frames have $f_T \geq N$ and they are moved back to the input queue of the transmitter. So, it must be noted that if a frame is not received due to buffer overflow, only one copy of that frame is sent and not m. The receiver operates by alternating between two states, the *normal state* and the *blocked state*. In the normal state the receiver's buffer is empty and no space has been set aside for any NACK'ed block. While in the normal state, if any data block is received in error or out of sequence, the receiver enters the blocking state. While operating in the blocking state, the receiver returns to normal state by recovering the earliest NACK'ed block and by releasing all the data blocks so as to make the buffer empty again. While the receiver is in the normal state, define the forward distance f_{RN} of the currently received block y with respect to the last correctly received data block x as

$$f_{RN} = (y-x) \mod 3N$$

Note that $f_{RN} = 1$ if the receiver is receiving data error free and in proper sequence. While in the blocked state, the receiver makes decisions by computing the forward distance f_{RB} of the currently received block y with respect to the earliest NACK'ed block x, given by

$$f_{RB} = (y-x) \mod 3N$$

and the backward distance b_R with respect to the last stored or NACK'ed block z, given by

$$b_R = (z-y) \mod 3N$$

The details of the transmitter and receiver operations are given below in an algorithmic form. Ref. [4] describes transmitter and receiver operations for the case when $m = 1$. Here, we have extended it to arbitrary m.

An intuitive explanation for the better performance of this scheme as compared to Yu and Lin's scheme is as follows. If any frame is in error, it is retransmitted after a round-trip delay period. Assume that this retransmission also fails. Further assume that the second retransmission succeeds. In Yu and Lin's scheme, this would have caused some of the frames that followed the first retransmission to be discarded due to buffer overflow, initiating further retransmissions for each one of the frames that overflowed. In our scheme however, we retransmit m copies of the frame in error. Assuming the same scenario as above, the second copy of the m frames will be received correctly, thereby preventing overflow and resulting in increased throughput efficiency.

III Results for Point–To–Point ARQ

Following Yu and Lin [4], a regeneration point is defined as the instant at which a data frame is transmitted in error. After a time equal to the Round Trip Delay, the NACK is received for that frame. Call this frame the reference frame. Between the transmission of the reference frame and the reception of the NACK for that frame, $(N-1)$ new frames have been transmitted. Call the transmission of these N new frames starting from the regeneration point, as the transmission cycle. When the NACK for the reference frame is received, the transmitter begins the first retransmission cycle. During this cycle, for every NACK received, the transmitter retransmits m copies of the NACK'ed frame and for every ACK received, it transmits a new frame. A second retransmission cycle is initiated if any of the original N frames is still not correctly received by the receiver, i. e., all the m copies of a frame are received in error. The transmitter may enter subsequent retransmission cycles till all the original N frames transmitted during the transmission cycle are successfully retransmitted. After this, the transmitter continues transmitting new frames till a frame is transmitted in error, at which time it enters a regeneration point and begins a new cycle of transmission and retransmission cycles, all over again. Thus between every two adjacent regeneration points there is a transmission cycle and at least one retransmission cycle. Stochastically, the sequence of events between any pair of adjacent regeneration points is independent of that between any other pair. If X blocks are transmitted between any pair of regeneration points, and Y of these are received without errors and delivered to the host, the efficiency of the ARQ scheme is given by

$$\eta = \frac{E[Y]}{E[X]} \quad (1)$$

wher $E[X]$ and $E[Y]$ are the expectations of X and Y respectively. If every frame has n bits, the probability that a frame is successfully transmitted is given by

$$p = (1-\epsilon)^n \quad (2)$$

where n is the number of bits per transmitted frame and ϵ the bit error probability. As shown in Section IV, the throughput efficiency of this scheme is lower bounded by

$$\eta \geq T_1/(T_1+T_2) \quad (3)$$

where

$$\begin{aligned}T_1 &= (1-\alpha^3 q)K_3(N+\frac{1-q}{q}) \\ &\quad +\frac{1-\alpha^3-(1+(N-1)\alpha^3 q)K_3}{\alpha^3 q}\end{aligned} \quad (4)$$

$$\begin{aligned}T_2 &= (1-\alpha q)(1-K_1)mN + (1-\alpha^2 q)(1-K_2)mN \\ &\quad +m(1-\alpha)[K_1(\frac{1-q}{1-\alpha}+Nq) \\ &\quad +\alpha K_2(\frac{1-q}{1-\alpha^2}+Nq) + \alpha^2 K_3(\frac{1-q}{1-\alpha^3}+Nq)]\end{aligned} \quad (5)$$

where

$$\begin{aligned}K_1 &= (1-\alpha)(1-\alpha q)^{N-2} \\ K_2 &= (1-\alpha^2)(1-\alpha^2 q)^{N-2} \\ K_3 &= (1-\alpha^3)(1-\alpha^3 q)^{N-2}\end{aligned}$$

and
$$\alpha = (1-p)^m$$
$$q = 1-p$$

Figs. 2 and 3 compare the throughput efficiency of this scheme with that of the scheme proposed by Yu and Lin, as well as with the theoretical Selective Repeat scheme. Comparison has been made for different values of n and N. The curves clearly show that the new scheme outperforms that of Yu and Lin. Clearly Figs. 2 and 3 show that there is a one to one correspondence between the inferior scheme and the actual scheme (as represented by simulation). These figures show that the optimal m that maximizes throughput is a function of the bit-error rate. It is possible to conceive of an adaptive scheme in which the transmitter and receiver adapt to changing error conditions on the transmission link and use varying values of m depending on the prevailing bit-error rate, but such a discussion is beyond the scope of this paper.

IV Throughput Analysis of Point–To–Point ARQ Scheme

Now the lower bound on the throughput efficiency of the new ARQ scheme given in (3) will be derived. To do this, a new, inferior scheme is considered. This scheme operates with the assistance of a genie. A lower bound is derived on the throughput efficiency of the genie-aided inferior scheme which therefore serves as a lower bound to the original scheme as well. The following discussion is with reference to Fig. 4. RP_1 is a regeneration point, indicating that frame F_1 has been transmitted in error. In the proposed scheme, the NACK for F_1 is received after the completion of the round trip delay period. However, the inferior system is aware of the error at the instant of transmission itself, thanks to the genie. We consider the following four cases:

Case 1: All the erroneously transmitted frames are recovered in the first retransmission.

The probability that this occurs is given by
$$Q_1 = [1-(1-p)^m][1-(1-p)^{m+1}]^{N-1}$$

Substituting
$$\alpha = (1-p)^m$$
we can write this as
$$Q_1 = (1-\alpha)(1-\alpha q)^{N-1}, \quad (6)$$

where $q = 1-p$. During the first retransmission cycle of the original system, if any of the frames in the original transmission cycle are in error, m copies of the frame are transmitted. If the frame is properly transmitted, but an overflow occurs, the frame is transmitted only once in the retransmission cycle. So, the length of the retransmission cycle is $\leq mN$. During the first retransmission cycle of the inferior system, the transmitter retransmits m copies of each of the frames transmitted in error during the transmission cycle even before NACK's are received for them. This is possible due to the help of the genie which immediately informs the transmitter of any frame transmitted erroneously. The average number of retransmissions between two successive regeneration points of the inferior system is given by

$$E[L_1] = \frac{m}{Q_1} \sum_{k=0}^{N-1}(k+1)\binom{N-1}{k}p^{N-1-k}(1-p)^k \cdot [1-(1-p)^m]^{k+1}$$

This can be rewritten as
$$E[L_1] = \frac{m}{Q_1}(1-\alpha q)^{N-2}(1-\alpha)[N(1-\alpha q)-(N-1)p] \quad (7)$$

The average number of frames transmitted after the retransmissions and before the next regeneration point is given by
$$E[S] = \frac{p}{1-p} \quad (8)$$

Therefore the average number of successfully transmitted frames is given by
$$E[M_1] = N + E[S] \quad (9)$$

The average of the total number of blocks transmitted between two regeneration points is therefore
$$E[V_1] = N + E[S] + E[L_1] \quad (10)$$

Case 2: All the erroneously transmitted frames are recovered within the first or second retransmissions, but not all are recovered within the first:

The probability of occurance of this event is
$$Q_2 = [1-(1-p)^{2m}][1-(1-p)^{2m+1}]^{N-1} - Q_1$$

which can be rewritten as
$$Q_2 = [1-\alpha^2][1-\alpha^2 q]^{N-1} - Q_1 \quad (11)$$

The inferior scheme behaves as follows: If any of the transmitted frames is in error, m copies of the frame are dispatched. Also, during the first and the second retransmission cycles (of length $\leq mN$), no new frames are sent. As Fig. 5 shows, dummy blocks are sent instead. The average length of the second retransmission cycle, $E[L_2]$, is given by (after some manipulation)

$$E[L_2] = \frac{m}{Q_2}((1-\alpha^2 q)^{N-2}\alpha(1-\alpha)[(1-q) + (1-\alpha^2)Nq]) \quad (12)$$

Also,
$$E[M_2] = N + E[S] \quad (13)$$
and
$$E[V_2] \leq (m+1)N + E[S] + E[L_2] \quad (14)$$

The inequality in (14) is due to the fact that the first retransmission cycle is of length $\leq mN$. The equations above match the analysis in [4] when $m = 1$.

Case 3: All the erroneously transmitted frames are recovered within three retransmissions, but not all are recovered within the first two retransmissions:

The probability of the occurance of such an event is given by
$$Q_3 = [1-(1-p)^{3m}][1-(1-p)^{3m+1}]^{N-1} - Q_1 - Q_2$$

which can be rewritten as
$$Q_3 = [1-\alpha^3][1-\alpha^3 q]^{N-1} - Q_1 - Q_2 \quad (15)$$

The behaviour of the inferior scheme in this case is clearly illustrated in Fig. 6. In this case the average number of retransmissions during the third retransmission cycle, $E[L_3]$, is given by (after simplification)

$$E[L_3] = \frac{m\alpha^2(1-\alpha)(1-\alpha^3 q)^{N-2}}{Q_3}[Nq(1-\alpha^3) + 1 - q] \quad (16)$$

$$E[M_3] = N + E[S] \quad (17)$$

Also,

$$E[V_3] \leq (2m+1)N + E[S] + E[L_3] \quad (18)$$

The inequality and the factor $2mN$ in (18) are due to the fact that the first and second retransmission cycles together require $\leq 2mN$ frames.

Case 4: At least one of the blocks in the first transmission cycle has not been recovered by the third retransmission cycle:

If D_{T+1} is the earliest data frame that has not been recovered, T is a random variable with an expected value

$$\begin{aligned} E[T] &= \frac{1}{1-Q_1-Q_2-Q_3} \sum_{l=1}^{N-1} l[1-(1-p)^{3m+1}]^{l-1} \\ &\cdot (1-p)^{3m+1}[1-(1-p)^{3m}] \end{aligned} \quad (19)$$

This can be rewritten as

$$\begin{aligned} E[T] &= \frac{(1-\alpha^3)}{(1-Q_1-Q_2-Q_3)\alpha^3 q}(1-[1+(N-1)\alpha^3 q] \\ &\cdot (1-\alpha^3 q)^{N-1}) \end{aligned} \quad (20)$$

T_t is the regeneration point in this case. In this case the inferior system operates similiar to the original system until it reaches T_t. From this point onwards, it behaves as if a new cycle has started all over. The inferior system behaves worse than the normal system, because any of the frames from D_t onwards, that had been received error-free previously, are rejected by the receiver of the inferior system and therefore need to be retransmitted.

So, in this case

$$E[M_4] = E[T] \quad (21)$$

Also,

$$E[V_4] \leq (2m+1)N + E[T] \quad (22)$$

Substituting for

$$E[M] = Q_1 E[M_1] + Q_2 E[M_2] + Q_3 E[M_3] + Q_4[M_4] \quad (23)$$

and

$$E[V] = Q_1 E[V_1] + Q_2 E[V_2] + Q_3 E[V_3] + Q_4[V_4] \quad (24)$$

in the equation for the throughput efficiency of the inferior system

$$\eta_{inf} = \frac{E[M]}{E[V]} \quad (25)$$

simplifying, and realizing that

$$\eta \geq \eta_{inf}$$

we obtain the throughput efficiency of the system as in equations (3), (4), and (5).

It is clear, that for $m = 1$, our scheme reduces to that of Yu and Lin and hence equation(4) should yield the throughput efficiency of Yu and Lin's scheme for $m = 1$. This can be verified to be the case.

V Point–To–Multipoint ARQ Scheme and Its Results

We now extend the point–to–point selective repeat ARQ scheme described in Section II to point–to–multipoint communications. Variations of the go-back-N ARQ scheme have been proposed for point–to–multipoint communications by Sabnani [9], Mase et. al. [10], Gopal and Jaffe [11], and Towsley [12]. Ramchandran and Lin [7] have analyzed the selective-repeat ARQ scheme for point–to–multipoint communications where each receiver has a finite buffer size and have obtained a lower bound on the throughput efficiency of this scheme.

The scheme proposed here is similar to that in [7] and is a simple modification of the scheme described in Section II. We assume that the system consists of $R + 1$ stations with one transmitter broadcasting packets to R identical receivers. For each frame transmitted, the transmitter expects ACK's/NACK's from each of the R receivers. Each receiver checks the data frame received for errors and sends an ACK/NACK depending on whether the packet is received error free or not. After the transmission of a data frame, the transmitter stores that frame in the retransmission buffer. After a round trip delay of N frames, if the transmitter receives R ACK's, then that frame is discarded from the retransmission buffer. If one or more NACK's are received by the transmitter, then m copies of that frame are transmitted. If at least one of these m copies is ACK'ed by all the R receivers, then that frame is considered by the transmitter to have been successfully broadcast to all the R receivers. Otherwise m more copies of that frame are sent. The procedure is repeated until that frame is ACKed by all the R receivers. It is possible to provide a formal description of this protocol in a manner similar to that in Section II, but we leave out such a description here.

The efficiency of this scheme is given by (see Section VI)

$$\eta \geq \frac{N + E[S]}{N + E[S] + W1 + W2} \quad (26)$$

where $E[S], W1,$ and $W2$ are as given in Section VI.

It can be verified that when $R = 1$, the point–to–multipoint scheme reduces to the point–to–point scheme and that Equation (3) and (25) agree.

For the purposes of obtaining performance curves we choose the parameters as $n = 1024$ and $N = 1024$, where n is the total number of bits in one frame, and N is the total number of frames in one round trip delay. Fig. 7 plots the throughput versus the bit error rate for $R = 1, 2,$ and 4 and for $m = 1$. Clearly, as the number of receivers increases, the throughput decreases for a given bit error rate, for bit error rates less than 10^{-6}. Figures 8, 9, and 10 provide the relationship between the throughput and bit error rate for various values of $m = 1, 2, 3, 5,$ and 10 and for values of $R = 1, 2,$ and 4, respectively. Each of these figures provides us with an envelope of optimum performance that specifies the value of m to use for a given combination of R and bit error rate. Figures 11, 12, and 13 compare the throughput performance versus R of our scheme and that of Ramchandran and Lin for bit error rates of $10^{-5}, 10^{-6},$ and 10^{-7}, respectively and for $m = 1$. As can be seen, our scheme outperforms that of Ramchandran and Lin. This is due to the fact that Ramchandran and

Lin's scheme constrains the sequence number of a new frame to be transmitted to differ from the earliest unacknowledged frame to be less than or equal to N, the round trip delay. In our scheme this restriction is relaxed by allowing the range of sequence numbers to be $3N$. Figure 14 provides a scenario that illustrates why our scheme performes better than that of Ramchandran and Lin.

Fig. 15 shows that, if the scheme of Ramchandran and Lin is modified to include multiple retransmissions, due to the restriction their scheme imposes on the range of sequence numbers, their scheme is optimal for $m = 1$ and multiple retransmission will be inefficient. Figures 16 and 17 show the variation in throughput performance with respect to the number of receivers for bit error rates ϵ of 10^{-4} and 10^{-5}, respectively. From these figures we see that for $\epsilon = 10^{-4}$, when $R \leq 2$, $m = 5$ is optimal; when $2 < R \leq 6$, $m = 3$ is optimal; when $6 < R \leq 70$, $m = 2$ is optimal; and when $R > 70$, $m = 1$ is optimal. For $\epsilon = 10^{-5}$, $m = 2$ is optimal as long as $R \leq 70$; for $R > 70$, $m = 1$ becomes optimal. Figure 18 illustrates the behaviour of throughput performance versus R for $\epsilon = 10^{-6}$. It shows that at very small values of ϵ the multiple retransmissions strategy has no advantage and that $m = 1$ is optimal.

VI Throughput Analysis of Point-To-Multipoint Selective Repeat ARQ Scheme

The analysis is very similar to that in Section III and is therefore discussed very briefly and concisely. The analysis for $m = 1$ is to be found in [7].

Let f_0 be the probability that a data frame is successfully received by all R users in one transmission. Then

$$f_0 = p^R$$

Let $f_1, f_2, \ldots, f_j$ denote the probabilities of successful reception of a data frame by all R users within the 1st, 2nd, $\cdots$, j-th retransmission period, respectively. Then

$$f_1 = \sum_{i=0}^{R} \binom{R}{i} p^{R-i} [(1-p)(1-(1-p)^m)]^i$$
$$= [1-(1-p)^{m+1}]^R$$
$$f_2 = \sum_{i=0}^{R}\sum_{j=0}^{i} \binom{R}{i}\binom{i}{j} p^{R-i}(1-p)^i [1-(1-p)^m]^{i-j}$$
$$\cdot [(1-p)^m]^j [1-(1-p)^m]^j$$
$$= [1-(1-p)^{2m+1}]^R$$

Similarly, we get

$$f_j = [1-(1-p)^{jm+1}]^R$$

Let $f'_1, f'_2, \ldots, f'_j$ be the probabilities that the first data frame from regeneration point is successfully received by all R users within 1st, 2nd, $\cdots$, j-th retransmission period, respectively. Then it can easily be shown that

$$f'_1 = \frac{[1-(1-p)^{m+1}]^R - p^R}{1-p^R}$$
$$f'_2 = \frac{[1-(1-p)^{2m+1}]^R - p^R}{1-p^R}$$
$$\vdots$$
$$f'_j = \frac{[1-(1-p)^{jm+1}]^R - p^R}{1-p^R}$$

Let Q_j be the probability that all the N data frames following a regeneration point are successfully recovered by all R users during the j-th retransmission period, but not all recovered within the $(j-1)$-th retransmission period. Then

$$Q_1 = f_1^{N-1} f'_1$$
$$Q_2 = f_2^{N-1} f'_2 - Q_1$$
$$\vdots$$
$$Q_j = f_j^{N-1} f'_j - \sum_{i=1}^{j-1} Q_i$$

Let $E[L_j]$ be the average length of the j-th retransmission cycle for the inferior system. Then, it is possible to show that

$$E[L_1] = \frac{m}{Q_1} \sum_{k=0}^{N-1} (k+1)\binom{N-1}{k} f_0^{N-1-k}(f_1-f_0)^k f'_1$$
$$= \frac{m[(1-\alpha q)^R - p^R]}{Q_1(1-p^R)}[(1-\alpha q)^R]^{N-2}$$
$$\cdot [N(1-\alpha q)^R - (N-1)p^R]$$

$$E[L_2] = \frac{m}{Q_2}[\sum_{k=0}^{N-1}(k+1)\binom{N-1}{k}f_1^{N-1-k}(f_2-f_1)^k(f'_2-f'_1)$$
$$+ \sum_{k=1}^{N-1} k\binom{N-1}{k}f_1^{N-1-k}(f_2-f_1)^k f'_1]$$
$$= \frac{m}{Q_2(1-p^R)}[(1-\alpha^2 q)^R - (1-\alpha q)^R]$$
$$[(1-\alpha^2 q)^R]^{N-2}[N(1-\alpha^2 q)^R - (N-1)p^R]$$

$$\vdots$$

$$E[L_j] = \frac{m}{Q_j(1-p^R)}[(1-\alpha^j q)^R - (1-\alpha^{j-1} q)^R]$$
$$[(1-\alpha^j q)^R]^{N-2}[N(1-\alpha^j q)^R - (N-1)p^R]$$

The average number of frames successfully transmitted after the retransmissions and before next regeneration point is given by

$$E[S] = \frac{p^R}{1-p^R}$$

As in Section IV, we consider the following cases:

Case 1 : All the erroneously transmitted frames are recovered in the first retransmission period.
The average number of successfully transmitted frames is given by

$$E[M_1] = N + E[S]$$

The average of the total number of frames transmitted between two regeneration points is given by

$$E[V_1] = N + E[S] + E[L_1]$$

Case 2 : All the erroneously transmitted frames are recovered within the second retransmission period, but not all recovered within the first retransmission period.

$$E[M_2] = N + E[S]$$
$$E[V_2] \leq (m+1)N + E[S] + E[L_2]$$

Case j : All the erroneously transmitted frames are recovered within j-th retransmission period, but not all recovered within the first $(j-1)$-th retransmission period.

$$E[M_j] = N + E[S]$$
$$E[V_j] \leq [(j-1)m+1]N + E[S] + E[L_j]$$

Then

$$E[M] = \sum_{j=1}^{\infty} Q_j E[M_j]$$
$$E[V] = \sum_{j=1}^{\infty} Q_j E[V_j]$$

Hence, the throughput efficiency for the inferior system is given by

$$\begin{aligned}\eta_{inf} &= \frac{E[M]}{E[V]} \\ &= \frac{\sum_{j=1}^{\infty} Q_j E[M_j]}{\sum_{j=1}^{\infty} Q_j E[V_j]} \\ &\geq \frac{N + E[S]}{N + E[S] + W1 + W2}\end{aligned}$$

where

$$\begin{aligned}W1 =& \sum_{j=1}^{\infty}(j-1)mN\{[(1-(1-p)^{jm+1})^R]^{N-1} \\ &\cdot [\frac{(1-(1-p)^{jm+1})^R - p^R}{1-p^R}] \\ &- \sum_{i=1}^{j-1}[(1-(1-p)^{im+1})^R]^{N-1} \\ &\cdot [\frac{(1-(1-p)^{im+1})^R - p^R}{1-p^R}]\} \\ W2 =& \sum_{j=1}^{\infty}\frac{m}{1-p^R}[(1-\alpha^j q)^R]^{N-2}[(1-\alpha^j q)^R \\ &-(1-\alpha^{j-1}q)^R][N(1-\alpha^j q)^R - (N-1)p^R]\end{aligned}$$

VII Conclusions

We have described selective repeat ARQ schemes for point–to–point and point–to–multipoint communications. These schemes operate with finite receiver buffer and a range of sequence numbers of size $3N$. By transmitting multiple copies of a NACK'ed frame, the schemes achieve increased throughput, especially, when the channel is noisy. The analytical results show that the point–to–multipoint scheme proposed here outperforms the existing ones.

References

[1] A. R. K. Sastry, "Improving Automatic Repeat-Request(ARQ) performance on satellite channels under high error-rate conditions," *IEEE Trans. on Commun.*, Vol COM-23, pp. 436-439, Apr. 1975.

[2] D. Towsley, "The Stutter Go Back N ARQ Protocol," *IEEE Trans. on Commun.*, Vol COM-27, pp. 869-875, June 1979.

[3] S. Lin and P. S. Yu, "An effective Error-Control Scheme for Satellite Communications," *IEEE Trans. on Commun.*, Vol. COM-28 No. 3 pp. 395-401 Mar. 1980.

[4] P. S. Yu and S. Lin, "An Efficient Selective-Repeat ARQ Scheme for Satellite Channels and it's Throughput Analysis," *IEEE Trans. on Commun.*, vol. COM-29, pp. 353-363 Mar 1981.

[5] E. J. Weldon, Jr., "An improved selective-repeat ARQ strategy with finite receiver buffer," *IEEE Trans. on Commun.*, Vol. COM-30, pp. 480-486, Mar 1982.

[6] M. J. Miller and S. Lin, "The Analysis of some Selective Repeat Schemes with finite receiver Buffer," *IEEE Trans. on Commun.*, Vol. COM-29, pp. 1307-1315, Sept. 1981.

[7] S. Ramchandran and S. Lin, "A selective repeat ARQ scheme for point–to–multipoint communications and its throughput analysis," *Computer Communications Review*, Vol. 16, No. 3, pp. 292-301, Aug. 1986.

[8] J. J. Metzner, "A study of an efficient retransmission strategy for data links," in *NTC'77 Proc.*, pp. O3B: 1-1 – O3B: 1-5, 1977.

[9] K. K. Sabnani, "Multidestination protocols for satellite broadcast channels," Ph. D. dissertation, Columbia University, New York, NY, 1982.

[10] K. Mase, T. Takenaka, H. Yamamoto and M. Shinohara, "Go-Back- N ARQ scheme for point–to–multipoint satellite communications," *IEEE Trans. Commun.*, Vol. COM-31, No. 4, pp. 583-589, Apr. 1983.

[11] I. S. Gopal and J. M. Jaffe, "Point–to–multipoint communication over broadcast links," *IEEE Trans. Commun.*, Vol. COM-32, No. 9, Sept. 1984.

[12] D. Towsley, "An analysis of point–to–multipoint channel using a Go-Back-N error control protocol," *IEEE Trans. Commun.*, Vol. COM-33, No. 3, pp. 282-285, Mar. 1985.

Fig. 1 The new scheme

N represents NACK

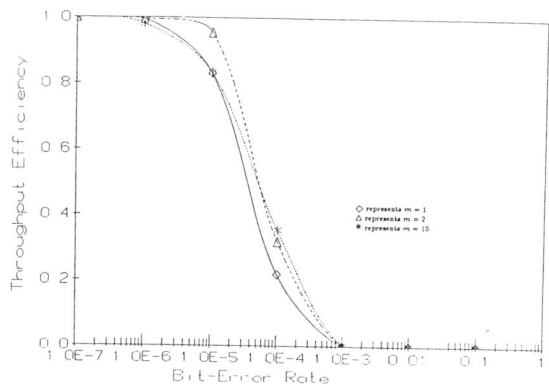

Fig. 2 Performance of the new scheme for $n=2024, N=512$ and $m=1,2,10$.
$m=1$ is also the efficiency of Yu and Lin's scheme.

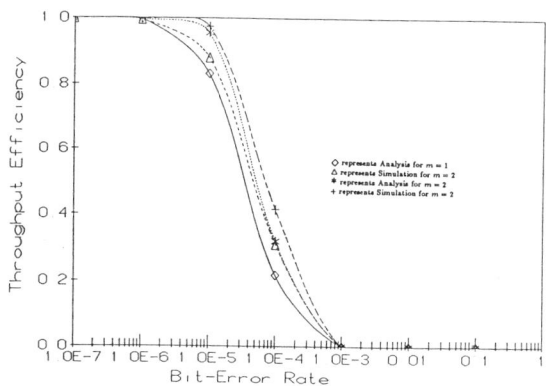

Fig. 3 Comparison of Analysis and Simulation for $n=2024$ and $N=512$ with $m=1,2$.

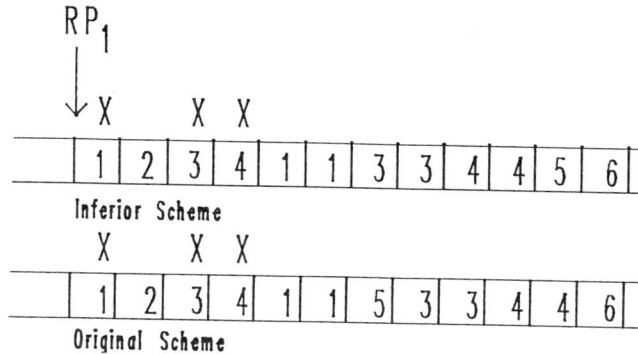

Fig. 4 Illustration for Case 1.

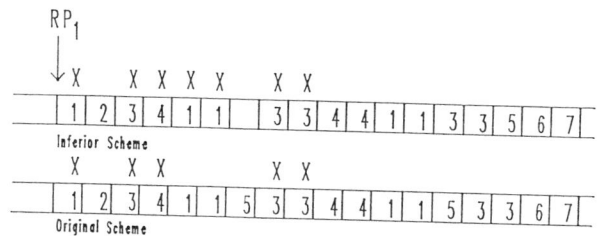

Fig. 5 Illustration for Case 2.

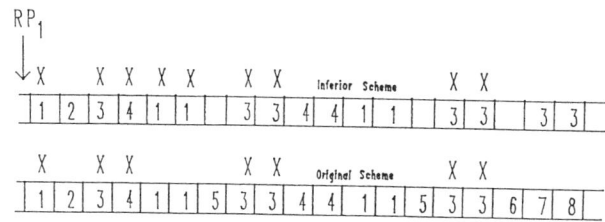

Fig. 6 Illustration for Case 3.

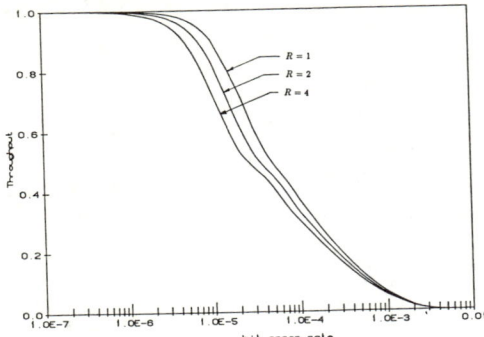

Fig. 7 Throughput η versus bit error rate ϵ for $n = 1024, N = 1024$ and $m = 1$ when $R = 1, 2, 4$.

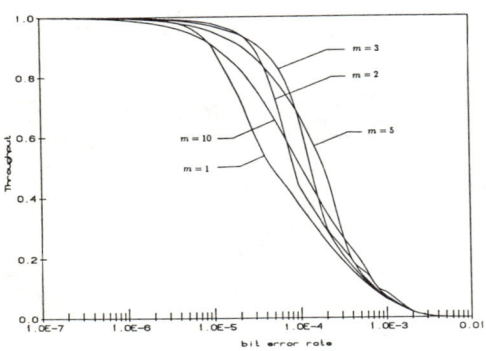

Fig. 8 Throughput η versus bit error rate ϵ for $n = 1024, N = 1024$ and $R = 1$, When $m = 1, 2, 3, 5,$ and 10.

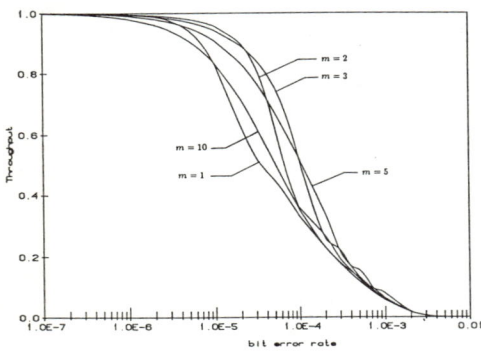

Fig. 9 Throughput η versus bit error rate ϵ for $n = 1024, N = 1024$ and $R = 2$, when $m = 1, 2, 3, 5,$ and 10.

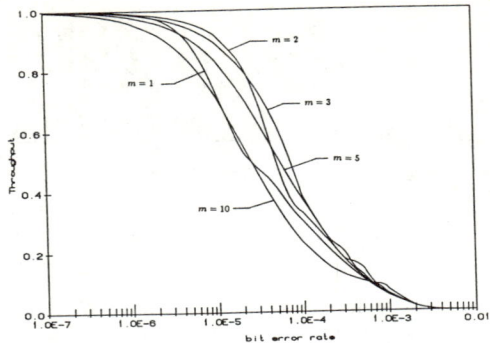

Fig. 10 Throughput η versus bit error rate ϵ for $n = 1024, N = 1024$ and $R = 4$, when $m = 1, 2, 3, 5,$ and 10.

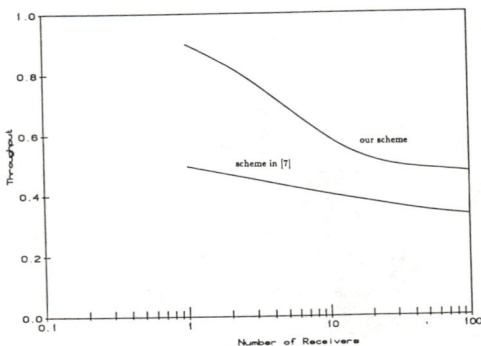

Fig. 11 Throughput η versus number of receivers R for $n = 1024, N = 1024$ and $m = 1$, when $\epsilon = 10^{-5}$ for both our proposed scheme and scheme in [7].

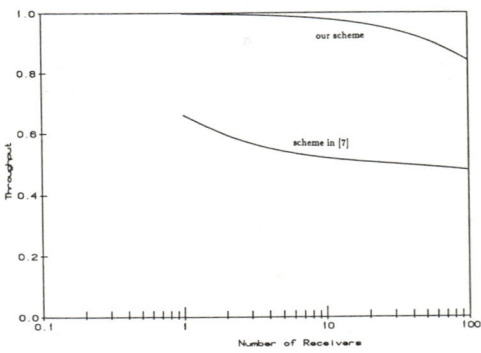

Fig. 12 Throughput η versus number of receivers R for $n = 1024, N = 1024$ and $m = 1$, when $\epsilon = 10^{-6}$ for both our proposed scheme and scheme in [7].

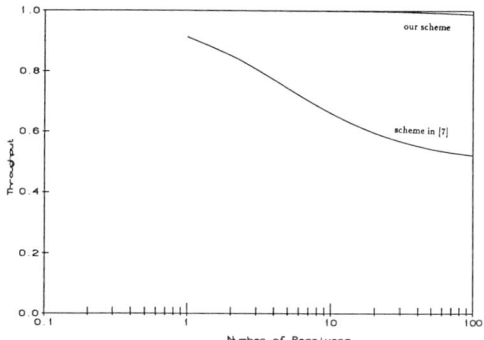

Fig. 13   Throughput η versus number of receivers R for $n = 1024, N = 1024$ and $m = 1$, when $\epsilon = 10^{-7}$ for both our proposed scheme and scheme in [7].

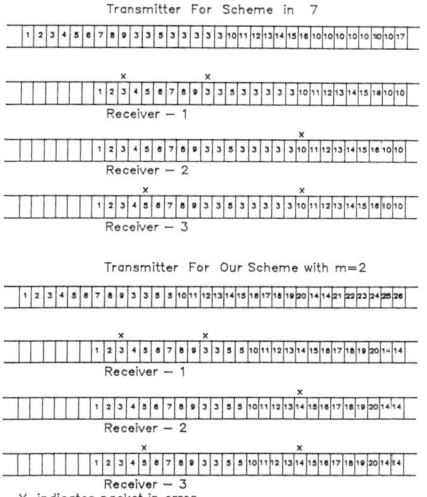

Fig. 14   Comparison of our scheme and scheme in [7].

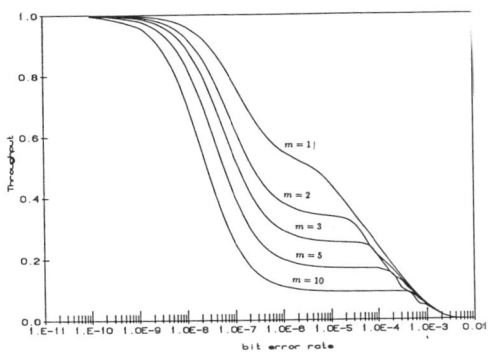

Fig. 15   Throughput η versus bit error rate ϵ for $n = 1024, N = 1024$ and $R = 4$, when $m = 1, 2, 3, 5,$ and 10. for extending the scheme in [7].

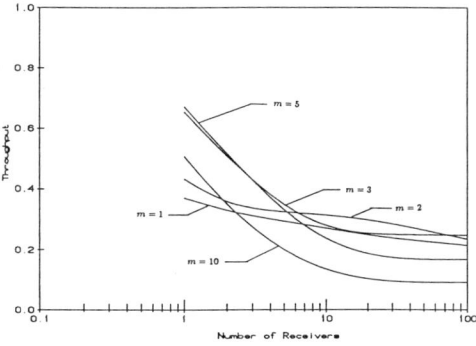

Fig. 16   Throughput η versus number of receivers R for $n = 1024, N = 1024$ and $\epsilon = 10^{-4}$, when $m = 1, 2, 3, 5,$ and 10.

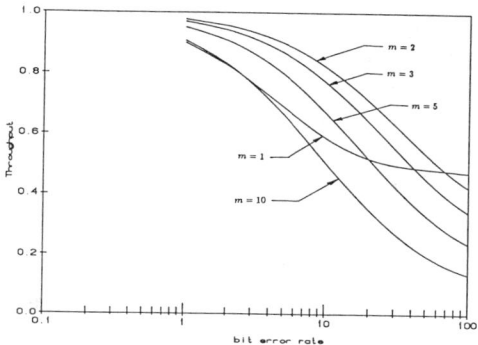

Fig. 17   Throughput η versus number of receivers R for $n = 1024, N = 1024$ and $\epsilon = 10^{-5}$, when $m = 1, 2, 3, 5,$ and 10.

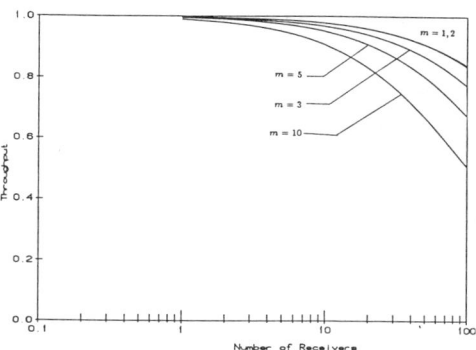

Fig. 18   Throughput η versus number of receivers R for $n = 1024, N = 1024$ and $\epsilon = 10^{-6}$, when $m = 1, 2, 3, 5,$ and 10.

Performance of Priorities on an 802.5 Token Ring

Jeffery H. Peden & Alfred C. Weaver
Department of Computer Science
Thornton Hall
University of Virginia
Charlottesville, Virginia 22903

Abstract — The IEEE 802.5 token ring allows the user to define multiple message priorities. The priority mechanism is implemented using a reservation scheme whereby packets attempt to reserve the token. We present an analytic model that predicts mean delay for each priority level. We show that operation of the priority mechanism is not free; that is, there is a well-defined cost (measured in terms of increased average message delay) associated with its implementation, and that in general there is minimal discrimination made between the various priority levels. We also show that the cost of the priority mechanism is an easily computable function of various network parameters. One of the circumstances where the priority mechanism results in a large discrimination between priorities is when service is limited to a single packet per received token. We show that single-packet-per-token service is necessary (but not sufficient) to gain maximum benefit from priority operation. Our main conclusion is that the network user will not, in general, receive much benefit from the priority mechanism since the priority mechanism can in fact *increase* slightly the delay for all priorities. The exception to this statement occurs when the network is operating under fairly extreme conditions which are well defined, and which we believe are unlikely in most installations.

1. Introduction

The IEEE 802.5 token ring protocol [5] provides multiple levels of packet priority by specifying a priority reservation scheme in which the token indicates the global ring priority level. The token contains a 3-bit field which indicates the lowest priority that may be currently transmitted; the protocol allows a maximum of eight priority levels.

A station may capture the token and transmit packets only if it has at least one enqueued packet whose priority is equal to or greater than the priority of the token. If all of a station's enqueued packets have priorities less than the token's priority, the station may bid for a token of lower priority by attempting to set a 3-bit reservation field in the token (if the reservation field already indicates a higher priority than the one desired, the attempted bid has no effect). Transmitting stations always emit the reservation field in packet headers with a zero value, thus ensuring that all stations have a chance to bid for the token.

Upon completion of its transmission, the transmitting station emits the token at the highest requested priority (the current token priority is also counted as a reservation request), saving the previous priority if it was lower. If a station raises the priority of the token from X to Y, and later receives a token of priority Y, with no reservations higher than X, it returns the priority of the token to X.

We present an analytic model which predicts mean delivery delay for packets on an 802.5 token ring. We assume a Poisson arrival process, and constant service times. We also assume that all stations on the network are members of the same class, that is, all stations exhibit homogeneous behavior. We do not assume that each priority has an equal share of the total offered load, but our model does assume that all stations divide their load among the priorities in an identical manner. We also assume that packets are long relative to ring latency, that is, the source address field in the packet header has returned to the transmitting station by the time the entire packet has been transmitted (the 802.5 protocol enforces a wait until this field has returned).

We present our model in three forms. The first is for single-packet-per-token (SPPT) service, the case where a maximum of one packet may be delivered per received token. The second form of our model is a generalization of the SPPT model to include multiple-packet-per-token (MPPT) service. We also show that our model reduces to the commonly known model for cyclic service when exhaustive (IPPT, or "infinite"-packets-per-token) service is assumed.

2. SPPT Analytic Model

2.1 Decomposing Total Delay

The total wait time experienced by a packet in a token ring is the sum of its queueing delay and the time it spends waiting for the token to arrive. It is possible to separate queueing delay and token wait delay into distinct components [4, p.413]. Separating queueing delay from token wait delay, the equation expressing the mean delay of a packet of priority i is

$$E[D_i] = E[Q] + E[W_i] + \left[1 + \frac{\alpha_i(1+\beta_i-\gamma_i)}{1-\gamma_i}\right] \times$$

$$\sum_{k=i}^{n}\left[\frac{\alpha_k(1+\beta_k-\gamma_k)}{1-\gamma_k}(E[Q]+E[W_k]+E[V]+\frac{1}{\mu})\right] +$$

$$\frac{1}{\mu} + \frac{L}{2}, \quad \Lambda E[C] < 1 \qquad (1)$$

where

- $\mu \equiv$ the constant service rate for all packets
- $L \equiv$ the total ring latency (propagation time plus latency buffers), also known as the empty ring walk time
- $\Lambda \equiv$ the sum of the arrival rates of packets of all priorities
- $\Phi \equiv$ the offered load contribution of a single station, $\Phi = \frac{\Lambda}{\mu}$
- $E[Q] \equiv$ the expected queueing delay
- $E[W_i] \equiv$ the expected token wait delay for priority i
- $N \equiv$ the number of ring stations
- $E[V] \equiv$ the expected token vacation time, that is, the elapsed time between the instant a station sends a token and the instant it receives that token, $E[V] = \frac{L(1-\Phi)}{1-N\Phi}$
- $E[C] \equiv$ the expected token cycle time, $E[C] = \frac{L}{1-N\Phi}$
- $\frac{\alpha_i(1+\beta_i-\gamma_i)}{1-\gamma_i} \equiv$ the expected number of times that a packet of priority i is preempted as service to priority i is reduced due to network load (defined later)

Note our labeling of the priority levels. The protocol allows eight priorities, numbered $0..n-1$, where a lower number indicates a lower priority. In our discussion, we are numbering the priorities $1..n$, the relative ordering being the same. We make this change only to simplify some of the terms in our derivations.

2.2 Queueing Delay

Queueing delay accounts for the time elapsed between a packet's arrival at a station and its bid for the token. Given the limitation $\Lambda E[C] < 1$ on equation (1), the expected number of packets enqueued at a station is less than one. Therefore, in the mean case, the token arrives to find zero or one packets in the queue. This has the result that service in FIFO order is equivalent to service in priority order, since the highest priority enqueued packet is (in the mean case) the one and only packet at the head of the queue.

From [1], the equation for the mean waiting time $E[T]$ for packets on a single priority token ring is the sum of the queueing delay and the token wait delay. This is given by

$$E[T] = E[Q] + E[W] \qquad (2)$$

The Pollaczek-Khinchine formula for the mean time $E[\Delta]$ a packet spends in an M/G/1 queue is

$$E[\Delta] = \frac{\frac{1}{m}}{1-\Phi}\left[1 - \frac{\Phi}{2}(1-m^2\tau^2)\right] \qquad (3)$$

where

- $m \equiv$ the mean service rate for packets
- $\tau^2 \equiv$ the variance of the service time distribution

Because of our assumption of constant service times, equation (3) reduces to

$$E[\Delta] = \frac{\frac{1}{\mu}}{1-\Phi}\left[1 - \frac{\Phi}{2}\right], \quad \Phi < 1 \qquad (4)$$

Since $E[Q] = E[\Delta] - \frac{1}{\mu}$, that is, the queueing *delay* does not include the service time, it follows that

$$E[Q] = \frac{\Lambda\frac{1}{\mu^2}}{2(1-\Phi)}, \quad \Phi < 1 \qquad (5)$$

which is also the result given in [4, p. 460].

2.3 Token Wait Delay

The token wait delay for a packet is the time elapsed between the packet's bid for the token and the reception of a usable token. Since the packet has bid for a token of its priority, token wait delay is dependent on the priority of the packet. We have from [1] that the token wait delay is given by $\frac{E[V^2]}{2E[V]}$. The variance of the token wait delay $Var[V]$ is given in [2], and using the fact that $Var[V] = E[V^2] - E^2[V]$, the token wait delay $E[W_i]$ for packets of priority i is given by equation (6):

$$E[W_i] = \frac{\alpha_i(1+\beta_i-\gamma_i)}{1-\gamma_i} \sum_{\underline{X}=1}^{R} (\underline{X} \cdot P(X=k) \cdot (E[V] + \frac{1}{\mu})) +$$

$$\frac{\sigma_i(N-1)\frac{1}{\mu} + L(1-\sigma_i)^2}{2(1-N\sigma_i)(1-\sigma_i)}, \quad \Lambda E[C] < 1 \qquad (6)$$

where

- $X \equiv$ the vector random variable which is the number of reservations attempted by the various priorities
- $\underline{X} \equiv$ the number of the X_i components of X which have non-zero values, which is equal to the number of *distinct* reserva-

The second term in equation (6) is the result of modifying the token wait delay for a single priority token ring to account for the actual load experienced by packets of the various priorities (equation (10) defines this load, and is explained below). The first term, $\frac{\alpha_i(1+\beta_i-\gamma_i)}{1-\gamma_i} \sum_{\underline{X}=1}^{R} (\underline{X} \cdot P(X=k) \cdot (E[V] + \frac{1}{\mu}))$, represents the time for the reservation mechanism to operate.

It requires an average of a token vacation time plus packet transmission time to lower the priority of the token from its present value to the value of the highest reservation since stations attempting reservations are competing with all the other stations on the ring. This is also dependent on the priority of the attempted reservation, hence the $\frac{\alpha_i(1+\beta_i-\gamma_i)}{1-\gamma_i}$ term (its use here is analogous to its use in equation (1), that is, it represents the effect of the network load on the expected number of attempts at lowering the token priority). Since the number of distinct reservations varies according to equation (8), with the mean number of reservations being given by equation (7), the first term of equation (6) is the direct result of the accumulation of all the possible ways of achieving distinct reservations multiplied by their probabilities.

We introduced several new terms in equation (6): R, $P(X=k)$, σ_i, and δ_i. The term R is the mean number of packets to arrive in one token cycle, which is also equivalent to the total number of (not necessarily distinct) reservations attempted in one token cycle. However, in order for stations to be making reservations (rather than simply capturing the token and transmitting), there must have been a transmission during the token cycle. Therefore, this particular token cycle is a token vacation time plus a transmission time. This then gives us

$$R = N(1 - \exp(-\Lambda(E[V] + \frac{1}{\mu}))) \qquad (7)$$

Equation (8) is the probability distribution for the number of distinct reservation requests made. A *distinct* reservation is one that is for a priority different from all other reservation requests, with several reservation requests for the same priority being counted as one. The term $R+1$ in equation (8) (rather than R) is due to the fact that, for a reservation to be distinct, the priority of the attempted reservation must be different not only from all other attempted reservations, but also from the priority of the token. Therefore, for R attempted reservations to be counted as R distinct reservations, $R+1$ priorities are involved: the priorities of the R reservations, plus the priority of the token. Note that equation (8) is an ordinary multinomial distribution, given by

$$P(X=k) = \binom{R+1}{k_1, k_2, \cdots, k_n} \prod_{i=1}^{n} \left(\frac{r_i}{n}\right)^{k_i} \qquad (8)$$

where

- $r_i \equiv$ the proportion of the total load of packets of priority i
- $n \equiv$ the number of priorities being offered to the network

Equation (9) is the formula for the minimum network load experienced by packets of priority i. A priority i packet cannot be blocked by packets of lower priority, but can be blocked by those of equal or greater priority. Therefore, the minimum load experienced by a priority i packet is the sum of the loads of the priorities greater than or equal to i, which is

$$\delta_i = \sum_{k=i}^{n} \rho_k \qquad (9)$$

where

- $\rho_i \equiv$ a station's offered load of priority i only

Equation (10) gives the actual load experienced by a packet of priority i, which we denote σ_i. The minimum possible load experienced by packets of priority i is δ_i. The maximum possible load experienced by priority i packets is $\Phi = \frac{\Lambda}{\mu}$, since packets cannot preempt others of higher priority (note that the lowest priority always experiences the maximum load on the network, since $\delta_1 = \Phi$).

However, packets of priority i do experience load contribution from packets of priorities less than or equal to i. Therefore, the *actual* load experienced by packets of any priority lies somewhere between these two limits, or $\Phi - k(\Phi - \delta_i)$, where k is some constant. To show that $k = \Phi$, consider the following. A load of Φ is equivalent to the station being busy $\Phi \cdot 100\%$ of the time. Therefore, only $\Phi \cdot 100\%$ of the time will the expected load reduction for a priority be in effect, resulting in a mean reduction of $\Phi(\Phi - \delta_i)$. Therefore, the actual load experienced by priority i packets is

$$\sigma_i = \Phi - \Phi(\Phi - \delta_i) \qquad (10)$$

2.4 Priority Blocking

The probability that a packet is blocked from transmission is of crucial importance, since this is what causes discrimination between the priority levels. A packet of priority i undergoes priority blocking when a packet of equal or higher priority prevents it from receiving service at the current token reception.

The mean number of packet arrivals of priority i at one station during one token cycle is $\lambda_i E[C]$. Arrivals are assumed to be Poisson, so the probability of an arrival any packet of any priority is $1 - \exp(-\Lambda E[C])$.

The probability that a packet of priority i is blocked from transmission at token reception, given that it has not been previously blocked, is equal to the probability that a packet of equal or greater priority is present at the station, which is

$$\alpha_i = 1 - \exp(-\sum_{k=i}^{n} \lambda_k E[C]) \qquad (11)$$

The probability that a packet is blocked is dependent on whether or not it was blocked on the previous token reception, due in part to the fact that the time frame during which more blocking packets could arrive is now $E[V] + \frac{1}{\mu}$. It is also necessary here to take "leftover" blocking packets into account.

Equation (12) gives the probability that a packet is blocked given that it has been blocked exactly once.

$$\beta_i = 1 - \exp(-\sum_{k=i+1}^{n} \lambda_k (E[V] + \frac{1}{\mu})) + 1 - \exp(-\sum_{k=i}^{n} \lambda_k E[C]) -$$

$$(1 - \exp(-\sum_{k=i+1}^{n} \lambda_k (E[V] + \frac{1}{\mu}))) \cdot (1 - \exp(-\sum_{k=i}^{n} \lambda_k E[C])) \qquad (12)$$

The probability that a packet is blocked given that it has been blocked two or more times is given by equation (13). The differences in these probabilities is due to two factors: the different time frame for arrivals, and the fact that new arrivals of the same priority as the blocked packet cannot block the previously blocked packet, since packets are served in strict FIFO order within each priority.

$$\gamma_i = 2(1 - \exp(-\sum_{k=i+1}^{n} \lambda_k (E[V] + \frac{1}{\mu}))) -$$

$$(1 - \exp(-\sum_{k=i+1}^{n} \lambda_k (E[V] + \frac{1}{\mu})))^2 \qquad (13)$$

The probability of a packet being blocked at a token reception given that it has been blocked depends on the current arrivals, and on arrivals during the previous token cycle only. Note that if we did not restrict our model such that $\Lambda E[C] < 1$, this would not be the case.

Equations (11), (12), and (13) are not sufficient, however, since they give the probabilities that packets are blocked for a single token cycle. A packet has probability α_i of being blocked at one token reception, a probability $\alpha_i \beta_i$ of being blocked on two token receptions, $\alpha_i \beta_i \gamma_i$ of being blocked on three, $\alpha_i \beta_i \gamma_i^2$ of being blocked on four, etc., leading to

$$\alpha_i + \alpha_i \beta_i + \alpha_i \beta_i \gamma_i + \alpha_i \beta_i \gamma_i^2 + \cdots = \frac{\alpha_i(1 + \beta_i - \gamma_i)}{1 - \gamma_i} \qquad (14)$$

which is the expected number of token cycles for which a packet of priority i will be blocked.

When a packet is blocked from transmission, it is requeued and must bid again for the token. Therefore, each time a packet is blocked, it experiences another round of queueing and token wait delay, plus the additional time to transmit a packet, plus a token vacation time. However, it must also wait for this same process to delay all higher priority packets for the expected number of times they will be blocked, thus resulting in the factor $\sum_{k=i}^{n} \left[\frac{\alpha_k(1 + \beta_k - \gamma_k)}{1 - \gamma_k} (E[Q] + E[W_k] + E[V] + \frac{1}{\mu}) \right]$ in equation (1).

The factor of $1 + \frac{\alpha_i(1 + \beta_i - \gamma_i)}{1 - \gamma_i}$ residing *outside* the summation in equation (1) is the expected number of times that a packet of priority i is preempted (and must begin the whole process over again) because of reduced service to its priority level due to network load.

Note that α_i is dependent on the load of all priorities greater than or equal to i. This is because the load for the highest priority may be so great that not only is service shut off to all lower priorities, but the highest priority is experiencing reduced service as well (i.e., the load contribution of the highest priority may be greater than the network capacity). Also note that as $\gamma_i \to 1$, the service to priority i approaches zero, since the expected number of preemptions of packets of that priority approaches infinity.

2.5 Transmission and Latency Delay

When a packet finally gains access to the network, it is necessary to add the transmission delay, $\frac{1}{\mu}$. Assuming that all packet destinations are equally likely, the latency to reach the destination will, on average, be half the ring latency or $\frac{L}{2}$. Adding the queueing delay and priority wait delay to the transmission and latency delay, and multiplying these terms by the expected number of times packets will be blocked and preempted results in equation (1).

2.6 Discussion

The above discussion was predicated on the assumption that a station may emit either zero or one packets upon token reception. The IEEE 802.5 token ring [5] allows multiple packets to be transmitted per token receipt, provided other restrictions on token rotation time and packet length are met.

SPPT service can be easily justified, however, on two grounds. The first is that the network manager may wish to restrict service to SPPT in order to reduce the variance of the token cycle time. This will have the effect of lowering the delay for the highest priority, thus giving better guaranteed service (at a cost of increased delay for the lower priorities).

The second justification for the SPPT restriction is the following. In a network of N stations, if Λ is the total arrival rate of all packets at a station, Φ is the total offered load contributed by a station, and L is the no-load latency of the ring (also called the empty ring walk time), then the expected length $E[Q_L]$ of a station's queue upon token arrival is

$$E[Q_L] = \frac{\Lambda L (1 - \Phi)}{1 - N \Phi}, \quad N\Phi < 1 \qquad (15)$$

The factors which would tend to make the queue grow are: large offered load, a small number of stations for a given offered load, short packets, and slow ring transmission speed (a ring latency that is long relative to packets would cause queues to grow large, but we are explicitly assuming that this is not the case). Assuming that $N\Phi = 0.95$, $N = 3$, $L = 30$ μsec, ring transmission speed is 1 Mbps, and frames are 32 octets in length, $E[Q_L] \approx 0.5$. In this example, the ring size of $N = 3$ is artificially small, and the frame size of 32 octets is considerable less than the maximum frame size (8192 octets) of IEEE 802.5. Also, the 1 Mbps ring transmission speed is slow when compared to the 4 Mbps capacity of the higher performance version of IEEE 802.5. Therefore, even for this extreme example, $\Lambda E[C] < 0.75$, which suggests that our model's restriction is quite realistic. Thus for "normal" configurations a token will arrive to find an expected queue length of significantly less than one.

3. MPPT Analytic Model

The analytic model for MPPT service is a generalization of the SPPT model. The calculation of the blocking probabilities changes, since it becomes a problem of expressing the number of ways in which a packet can be blocked, along with the associated probabilities. It is also necessary to take into account the fact that a packet may be delayed for less than one token cycle time (i.e., only a few packet transmission times). The actual load experienced by a packet of priority i changes, as well as the added delay incurred when a packet is blocked from transmission for at least one token cycle. In all, seven equations require modification in order to make our model applicable for MPPT service.

The first is equation (10), which is the actual load experienced by a packet of priority i. In order to present the modified version of equation (10), we now define ξ to be the maximum number of packets that may be delivered per received token. This is given by

$$\xi = \lfloor \Omega \mu \rfloor \qquad (16)$$

where

$\Omega \equiv$ the setting of the token holding timer in seconds

Since up to ξ packets may be delivered per received token, this means that up to ξ packets at or above the priority of the token may be delivered, which further increases the load relative to priority i packets, resulting in

$$\sigma_i = \Phi - \Phi \xi^{-\Phi(N-1)} (\Phi - \delta_i) \qquad (17)$$

The number of reservations made in a token cycle, R, also changes, necessitating a modification of equation (7) to yield equation (18). Since more packets may be transmitted per token, this results in a decrease of reservations made by non-transmitting stations.

$$R = N(1 - \exp(-\Lambda (E[V] \xi^{-\Phi(N-1)} + \frac{1}{\mu}))) \qquad (18)$$

Incorporating the changes to σ_i and R, the equation for the token wait delay, equation (6), becomes

$$E[W_i] = \frac{\alpha_i (1 + \beta_i - \gamma_i)}{1 - \gamma_i} \sum_{\underline{X}=1}^{R} (\underline{X} \cdot P(\underline{X} = \underline{k}) \cdot (E[V] + \frac{1}{\mu})) +$$

$$\sum_{k=1}^{\xi - 1} \left[1 - \exp(-\sum_{j=i}^{n} \lambda_j (E[C] + \frac{k-1}{\mu}) \right] \frac{k}{\mu} + \alpha_i -$$

$$\sum_{k=1}^{\xi - 1} \left[1 - \exp(-\sum_{j=i}^{n} \lambda_j (E[C] + \frac{k-1}{\mu}) \right] \frac{k}{\mu} \times \alpha_i +$$

$$\frac{\sigma_i (N-1) \frac{1}{\mu} + L(1 - \sigma_i)^2}{2(1 - N\sigma_i)(1 - \sigma_i)}, \quad \Lambda E[C] < 1 \qquad (19)$$

The new term in equation (19) is the result of the fact that a packet may be delayed only for a few transmission times. This new term is merely the summation of the probabilities of enough packets arriving ahead of the temporarily blocked packet to delay it for a few packet times.

The probability that a packet is blocked also changes since the blocking time frames are quite different. The change to α_i is

$$\alpha_i = 1 - \sum_{k=0}^{\xi} \frac{(\sum_{j=i}^{n} \lambda_j (E[C] + \frac{\xi}{\mu}))^k}{k!} \exp(-\sum_{j=i}^{n} \lambda_j (E[C] + \frac{\xi}{\mu})) \quad (20)$$

The change to β_i is

$$\beta_i = \alpha_{i+1} + 1 -$$

$$\sum_{k=0}^{\xi} \frac{(\sum_{j=i+1}^{n} \lambda_j (E[V] + \frac{\xi}{\mu}))^k}{k!} \exp(-\sum_{j=i+1}^{n} \lambda_j (E[V] + \frac{\xi}{\mu})) - \alpha_{i+1} \times$$

$$\left[1 - \sum_{k=0}^{\xi} \frac{(\sum_{j=i+1}^{n} \lambda_j (E[V] + \frac{\xi}{\mu}))^k}{k!} \exp(-\sum_{j=i+1}^{n} \lambda_j (E[V] + \frac{\xi}{\mu})) \right] \quad (21)$$

The change to γ_i is

$$\gamma_i = 2 \left[1 - \sum_{k=0}^{\xi} \frac{(\sum_{j=i+1}^{n} \lambda_j (E[V] + \frac{\xi}{\mu}))^k}{k!} \exp(-\sum_{j=i+1}^{n} \lambda_j (E[V] + \frac{\xi}{\mu})) \right] -$$

$$\left[1 - \sum_{k=0}^{\xi} \frac{(\sum_{j=i+1}^{n} \lambda_j (E[V] + \frac{\xi}{\mu}))^k}{k!} \exp(-\sum_{j=i+1}^{n} \lambda_j (E[V] + \frac{\xi}{\mu})) \right]^2 \quad (22)$$

The changes to α_i, β_i, and γ_i are adjusting for the change in the number of packets per token that may be delivered. Note that as more packets must arrive to block another packet from transmission, the probability of a packet being blocked decreases rapidly with the number of packets per token allowed.

Finally, equation (1) must be changed to reflect the change in the amount of time a packet must wait when it is blocked, since a packet is blocked for ξ packet transmission times rather than one.

$$E[D_i] = E[Q] + E[W_i] + \left[1 + \frac{\alpha_i(1 + \beta_i - \gamma_i)}{1 - \gamma_i} \right] \times$$

$$\sum_{k=i}^{n} \left[\frac{\alpha_i(1 + \beta_i - \gamma_i)}{1 - \gamma_k} (E[Q] + E[W_k] + E[V] + \frac{\xi}{\mu}) \right] +$$

$$\frac{1}{\mu} + \frac{L}{2}, \quad \Lambda E[C] < 1 \quad (23)$$

4. IPPT Analytic Model

The analytic model for exhaustive service is a special case of the priority model. Since blocking probabilities are zero when IPPT service is used, any term containing α_i becomes zero. Equation (1) therefore reduces to

$$E[D_i] = E[Q] + E[W_i] + \frac{1}{\mu} + \frac{L}{2} \quad (24)$$

The load experienced by a packet of priority i, σ_i, also approaches Φ, which is the total load contribution of a station. This is explained by expressing equation (17) as

$$\sigma_i = \Phi - \lim_{\xi \to \infty} \Phi \xi^{-\Phi(N-1)} (\Phi - \delta_i) \quad (25)$$

which results in $\sigma_i = \Phi$ for all priorities.

Equation (24) then becomes

$$E[D_1] = E[Q] + E[W_1] + \frac{1}{\mu} + \frac{L}{2} \quad (26)$$

Performing the addition of $E[Q]$ and $E[W_1]$, the final result $E[D_1] = E[D]$ is given by

$$E[D] = \frac{N \Phi \frac{1}{\mu} + L(1 - \Phi)}{2(1 - N\Phi)} + \frac{1}{\mu} + \frac{L}{2} \quad (27)$$

This is the result given in [4, p. 454], and has also been derived elsewhere.

5. Numerical Results

5.1 General Performance

Simulation results for a 1 Mbps IEEE 802.5 token ring in [3] show that for any particular offered load, achieved throughput for the token ring decreases as packet sizes become shorter, and that this loss of throughput is exaggerated when the number of ring stations is small. It was observed that the effect of MPPT service only had observable effect when the number of ring stations was less than 40; the maximum difference in delay recorded was a factor of two for a simulation of 3 stations. It was also shown that for a fixed offered load, delay is inversely proportional to packet size (i.e., small packets are less efficient than large packets). In this section we deal only with the "interesting" case where the number of stations is small, the packet length is short, and service is restricted to SPPT.

5.2 IPPT Model vs. Simulation Results

We simulated an IEEE 802.5 token ring with a transmission rate of 1 Mbps. The configuration used ring repeater latencies of 1 bit time per station and packet sizes of 32 octets. Offered loads were varied from 5% to 95% of capacity with arrivals following a Poisson distribution. Figure 1 compares the IPPT model prediction with simulation results for a 40 station network operating with only a single priority; the differences are negligible.

5.3 SPPT Model vs. Simulation Results

In the graphs showing results for SPPT (and MPPT) service, the load is equally distributed among all eight priorities. We do not show results for loads higher than 90% as the network becomes unstable. This is reflected in the fact that queue lengths are not stable over time. Figures 2, 3, and 4 compare the priority queueing model prediction with simulation results when using SPPT service for 3, 10 and 20 stations respectively. We also do not show results for low loads since, at low loads, there is virtually no difference in the delays for the various priorities.

At loads greater than 90%, the divergence between the analytic model and the simulations is as expected, that is, the model underestimates low priority delays, and overestimates high priority delays. This reflects the fact that at high loads, since queue lengths are no longer stable over time, low priority packets are blocked more often than is predicted for steady state network behavior, resulting in a reduction of load for higher priorities.

5.4 MPPT Model vs. Simulation Results

Figure 5 compares the analytic model to simulation results for a network configuration of 3 stations and MPPT service. The token hold timer (which controls the number of packets per token allowed) was set to the default value of 10 ms., which in this case results in 39 packets per token using 32 octet packets. All other parameters are the same as in the SPPT configurations.

Agreement between the simulation and the analytic model is quite close. Note that the ratio of the priority 0 delay to the priority 7 delay is less than 2. Also note that the agreement remains close even at 95% load. This is because the increased number of packets per token allowed increases the maximum throughput, which results in the network remaining stable through higher loads than when using an SPPT configuration.

This is the only figure showing results for MPPT service. When the number of stations is increased to only 10, the difference between the delays for the various priorities is too small to be noticed. Graphs of configurations consisting of higher numbers of stations would not be instructive.

5.5 Limitations

The applicability of this model is limited by two restrictions. First, the total offered load at a station is limited by $\Lambda E[C] < 1$. Second, we have not accounted for the special case where packets are short relative to ring latency; in this case a station delays until the packet header returns so that the new token will be issued at the highest reserved priority. We do not believe that either of these restrictions meaningfully inhibit the usefulness of the model.

6. Conclusions

We conclude that the analytic model presented here is a good predictor of delay for priority traffic on an 802.5 token ring. The model has been compared to simulations of an IEEE 802.5 token ring and agreement is close. We also conclude that the discrimination between the various priorities is not great unless the network is operating under conditions of either 1) overload, or 2) a combination of high load, a low number of stations, short packets, and short token hold times.

Acknowledgements

The authors gratefully acknowledge the financial support of the Institute of Information Technology of the Virginia Center for Innovative Technology.

References

[1] D. P. Heyman, "Data-transport Performance Analysis of Fasnet," *Bell System Technical Journal 62*, 8, Oct. 1983, pp. 2547-2560.

[2] A. G. Konheim and B. Meister, "Waiting Lines and Times in a System with Polling," *J. ACM 21*, 3, July 1974, pp. 470-490.

[3] J. H. Peden, "Performance Analysis of the IEEE 802.5 Token Ring," Master's Thesis, Department of Computer Science, University of Virginia, Jan. 1987.

[4] M. Schwartz, *Telecommunications Networks: Protocols, Modeling and Analysis*, Addison-Wesley, 1987.

[5] "Token Ring Access Method and Physical Layer Specifications," The Institute of Electrical and Electronics Engineers, Inc., 1985.

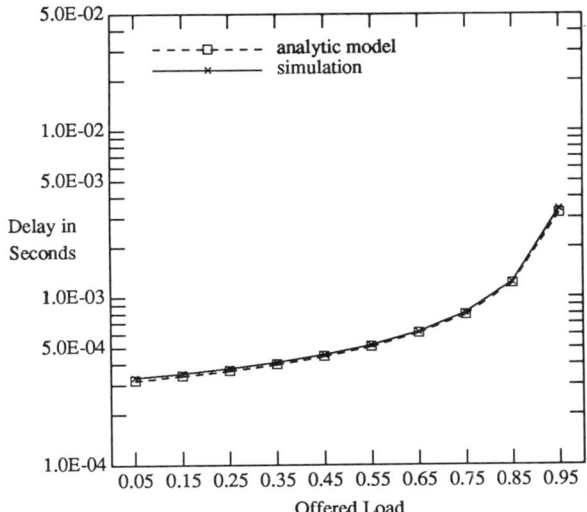

Figure 1
IPPT Model vs. Simulation
40 Stations
Single Priority

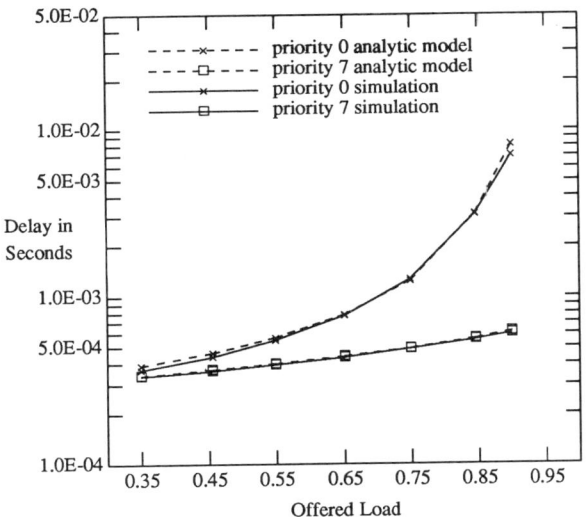

Figure 2
SPPT Model vs. Simulation
3 Stations

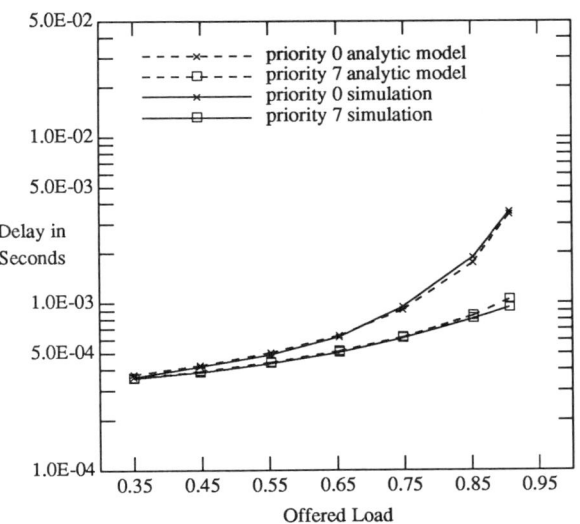

Figure 3
SPPT Model vs. Simulation
10 Stations

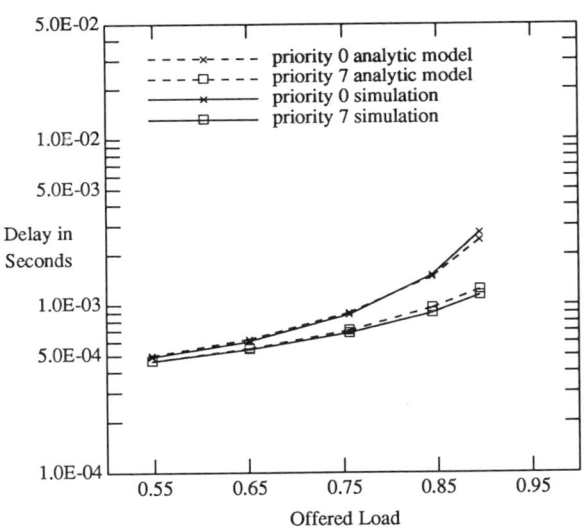

Figure 4
SPPT Model vs. Simulation
20 Stations

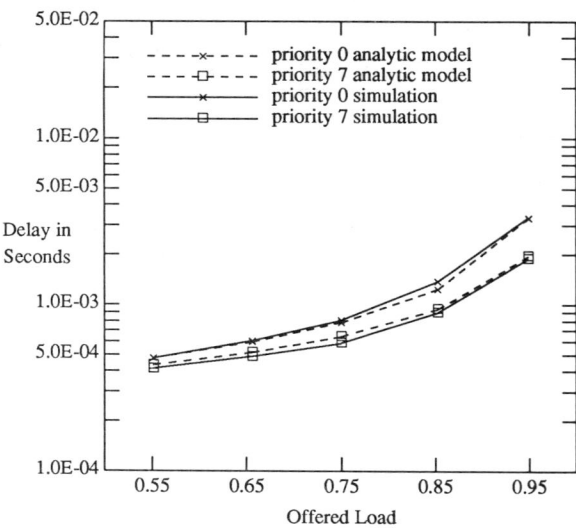

Figure 5
MPPT Model vs. Simulation
3 Stations

PART 3. COMPUTER NETWORKS IN JAPAN

Jun Murai

University of Tokyo, Japan

Researches in Network Developement of JUNET

Jun Murai[1]

Computer Center
University of Tokyo
2-11-16, Yayoi, Bunkyo
Tokyo, 113 JAPAN

Akira Kato[2]

Department of Computer Science
Faculty of Engineering
Tokyo Institute of Technology
2-12-1, Ookayama, Meguro
Tokyo, 152 JAPAN

Abstract

JUNET was developed in order to provide a testing environment for studies of computer networking and distributed processing by connecting a large number of computers and by providing actual services for the users. Research interests in development of the network have been focused on resource name managing, Japanese character handling and communication technologies.

For the name managements, the hierarchical domain concept is employed to construct a name space for the network, and a mechanism for text message exchange is implemented using the concept. An environment for text message exchange using Japanese characters is achieved as results of general discussions to handle 16-bit Kanji codes in computers. Efficient data transmissions with the high speed modems are achieved by a new UUCP protocol and the dial-up IP link mechanism developed with a tty driver which provides host-to-modem flow control mechanism.

As the result of researches described above, JUNET currently connects various types of organizations relating computer science which are 87 organizations with more than 250 computers in number. It connects universities and major research laboratories in Japan, and the protocols currently used are TCP/IP over leased lines as well as dial-up lines, and UUCP over dial-up lines. The services such as electronic mail and network news have been provided since the network was started, and special technologies for Japanese character handling, name servers, and multimedia mail supports have been developed.

In this paper, the current status of JUNET and its research results in development of the network are described.

[1]jun%u-tokyo.junet@relay.cs.net
[2]kato%cs.titech.junet@relay.cs.net

Permission to copy without fee all or part of this material is granted provided that the copies are not made or distributed for direct commercial advantage, the ACM copyright notice and the title of the publication and its date appear, and notice is given that copying is by permission of the Association for Computing Machinery. To copy otherwise, or to republish, requires a fee and/or specfic permission.

© 1988 ACM 0-89791-245-4/88/0001/0068 $1.50

1 Introduction

Since JUNET is the first and the only existing national wide computer network in Japan where user can exchange electronic mails and network news domestically and internationally, most of the experimental studies about wide-area computer networks, from physical communication technology to application design, have been done using the network. The purpose in the very first stage of the network, thus, was providing actual network services to researchers and put Japanese communities into world academic networks. And then, we started to work to solve problems existing on the network such as Japanese character handling, name handling for distributed resources, and communication technologies.

The history of JUNET started when University of Tokyo, Tokyo Institute of Technology, and Keio University started exchanging mails using UUCP on dial-up lines in October 1984. JUNET[10][13] connects local area networks at research institutes in Japan and it also provides users with the means of the worldwide communications via various international links.

There are some historical reasons which have prevented Japanese research and development communities from establishing a network for them. One of such a reason is that there have been not so many good computers for communication in the communities. Another example of such a reason may be that there used to be more restrictions in using the telephone lines than there are now. Since 1983, UNIX[3] has become popular in Japanese research and development communities, and this has encouraged the communities to start a simple network such as the one using UUCP[11] protocol over dial-up telephone lines. Applications used that time were electronic mails and electronic news.

At the time the three universities started the network, researches specially required in Japanese environment, such as Japanese language interface for communication applications, Japanese character code standard, and interconnection to existing research and development networks, were started to take place. The domain addressing over UUCP network was introduced in May 1985 with a system to gen-

[3]UNIX is a trademark of AT&T Bell Laboratories.

erate the address conversion software. High speed dial-up modems have been studied in order to increase the transmission rate of the communication. To achieve this purpose, UUCP enhancement with kernel driver development were done, and the efficiency using a dial-up line increased up to more than 13kbps. This encouraged us to migrate to TCP/IP protocol suite[3][4] even on dial-up lines as well as leased lines. As the result of the development, the dial-up IP link is providing as high as 7.5kbps in end-to-end transmission.

As for the internetworking between JUNET and other academic networks, two gateways are operated to exchanging electronic mails and news. One is Kokusai Denshin Denwa Co., Ltd. (KDD), an international telephone and telegraph company which serves a gateway between UUCP/USENET and JUNET, and University of Tokyo is providing a gateway function between CSNET[2] and JUNET.

One of the primary characteristics of JUNET is handling of Japanese characters in text messages. In order to provide the functions, a JUNET standard Kanji code was chosen and conversions between the network standard Kanji code and operating system Kanji codes are provided by the network application available in JUNET. The general computing environment for Japanese character handling are established as well in order to cooperate with the network environment. The statistics introduced in this paper shows drastic influences of Japanese character handling in computer network environment in Japan.

2 Current Status of JUNET

JUNET currently connects more than 250 hosts in 87 organizations. The geographic areas covered by the network expands from Hokkaido, the northern island, to Kyuushuu, the southern island, however, concentrations in Tokyo and Osaka areas are obvious as shown in Figure 1.

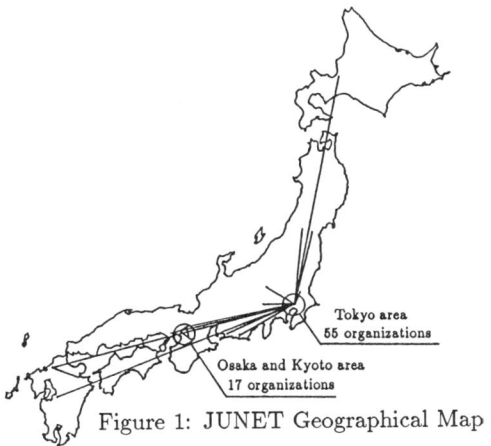

Figure 1: JUNET Geographical Map

Most of the links have been dial-up lines using 1200bps or 2400bps modems, although special mechanisms have developed for UNIX operating system and its communication software UUCP in order to use high speed dial-up modems with 9600bps or higher transmission rate. These mechanisms are also effective for TCP/IP protocols over dial-up telephone lines.

Organizations connecting to the network are universities, research laboratories of computer software/hardware companies, and research laboratories of telephone companies. All the functions are administrated by administrators at each of the institutes in totally volunteer basis.

2.1 Size of JUNET

Size of JUNET can be examined by various statistic values. The constant growth in number of organizations on the network is shown in Figure 2. One or two new organizations are being connected to JUNET every week.

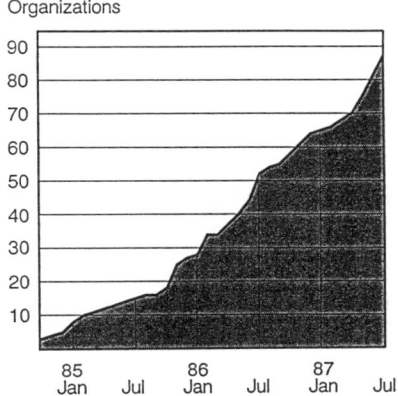

Figure 2: Number of domains

News articles are posted to the network constantly in the fj newsgroups which are currently distributed only within Japan. The number of articles posted has been growing as in Figure 3, and 1750 articles are posted in June 1987, as the latest example. Note that only about 10 percent of the articles are written in English alphabet including articles in ROMAJI, an alphabetical representation of Japanse language.

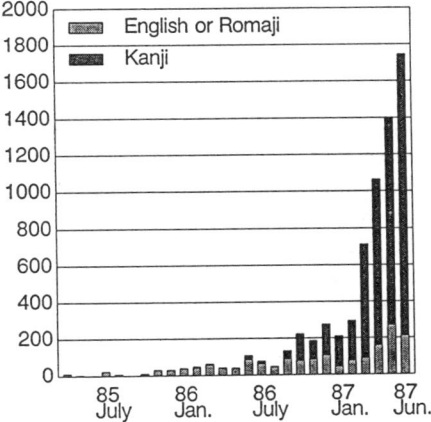

Figure 3: Number of Articles in fj newsgroups

Each of the JUNET gateways are handling 22 M bytes of articles in a month; 4 M bytes of `fj` newsgroups and 18 M bytes of USENET newsgroups.

One of the systems in the JUNET backbone handles about 200 M bytes of information in a month, and 85 percent of them are for the network news and 15 percent are for electronic mails. Since the network news are compressed to half of their size before the actual transmission, about 370 M bytes of text information is handled in one of the most busy systems in JUNET.

The international information exchanges are served by two gateways of JUNET; `ccut.cc.u-tokyo.junet` of University of Tokyo and `kddlab.kddlabs.junet` of KDD laboratories. The `ccut.cc.u-tokyo.junet` is on CSNET as `utokyo-relay` and is operated as the JUNET–CSNET gateway, on the other hand, the `kddlab.kddlabs.junet` is widely known in the UUCP network and is operated as the JUNET–UUCP network gateway.

The amount of international messages can be estimated by the total traffic at these two gateways. The example traffic of June 1987 are shown in Table 1.

Table 1: International Message Traffics

gateway	mail	news
`kddlabs.junet`	10MB	18MB
`u-tokyo.junet`	13MB	0
total	23MB	18MB

In summary, JUNET currently has approximately 41 M bytes of international traffic in a month, and it has been increasing about 3 M bytes per month in recent six months.

3 JUNET Domain Addressing

In the hierarchy of JUNET domain structure, a domain called 'junet' is the top domain, although we are now preparing to employ ISO's country code (ISO 3116)[7] for Japan 'jp' as the top domain name[12]. The second level domains are called sub-domains, and each of them represents a name of an institute or an organization. Lower level domains than the sub-domains may be determined at each of the sub-domains. In any cases, the lowest level domains are the names of hosts. The names of sub-domains usually are names well known to the society, but such names sometimes differ in intra/inter-national environment. Therefore, one or more names can be registered as synonyms for a sub-domain name to help users to address with general knowledge on the name of organizations. A name of a resource, thus, is defined in one of the domains.

There are one of the distributed name server in each of the domains which handles definitions and deletions of names using a database dedicated to that domain. A name server of a domain thus has a database to define names of lower level domains adjacent to the domain, or names of resources, such as names of mailboxes. The information held by each of the distributed name server is used in retrieving information of resource names and in accessing resources. By this concept, a resource can be defined in a logical domain; a mailbox can be defined even in the top domain, `junet`. This provides a name space which is well-matched to the naming concept of the real world yet providing consistency and efficiency of operations.

3.1 Design of JUNET message delivery system

There is one name server existing for a domain where a distributed resource name can be defined. In every host, at least one name server exits; a name server for a domain representing that host. Other than the one, name servers which represent domains located along a path from the root to this system in the domain tree can be existing in this system. Thus, name servers for the logical domains are managed by entities which are executed in a distributed manner.

A message delivery system using the above concept is implemented using sendmail[1] whose rule is generated by a rule generating system which plays a role of name servers of the JUNET naming concept.

Since the production rules of the sendmail system is differed site by site, the rules have to be generated at each site. To keep the consistency in the rules over JUNET sites, a configuration system to generate the necessary rules is designed and implemented. The configuration system to construct a name server receives information about domain names and about connections for communication among the name server. Then it generates sendmail rule as its output.

Information supplied to the configuration system are as follows:

Domain Names: List of domain names to be configured and names of domains defined in these domains.

Routing Information: Information about actual connections and name of mailers.

Mailer Definitions: Attributes of a mailer such as address formats and calling systax which the mailer is expecting.

The structure of the JUNET addressing system is illustrated in Figure 4.

In the input data, the following information about the system is described in the entries shown below:

name: A full name of this domain and its synonyms if any.

lower_level_name: A list of domain names defined in this domain.

neighbor: mailer (domain [cost])... *Neighbor* specifies a name of a system with which a direct connection is possible. A mailer used to transmit messages to the system is specified by *mailer*. A list of domain names defined in this domain are in *domain*. The optional *cost* field is used for each of the domains to represent a cost for sending a message to the domain. This is used to determine one route out of several possible routes.

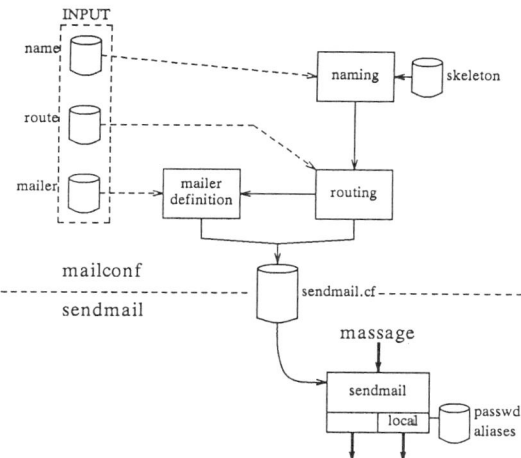

Figure 4: Structure of the Configuration System

The domain database contains relations between a physical link to a system and domain names which should be solved at that system. Other than the sendmail, the *rmail* command which receives messages through UUCP links was modified to handle JUNET addresses efficiently.

4 Japanese Character Handling

There always exist strong demands for Japanese character handling for computer software in Japan. Communication software can never be an exception: The statistics in Figure 3 shows most of the news articles are written in Japanese characters, or in *Kanji* codes. It is observed that the large amount of electronic mails are also exchanged using Kanji codes. Therefore, One of the remarkable characteristics of JUNET among academic networks in the worlds is Kanji message handling for text message exchanges. In order to discuss about this topic, some basic ideas about Japanese character handling have to be discussed beforehand.

4.1 Kanji code

The history of Kanji code handling in computers is rather short, and there still are several confusions about Kanji code itself. That is to say, there are some 'Kanji code standards' actually used in computer world. However, all the 'standards' refer to a single standard defined by JIS (Japanese Industrial Standard) X 0208 in their way of defining set of Kanji characters. JIS is always referred to because it can be introduced from any codes defined by International Standard Organization using ISO 2022 extension guidelines. It defines a Kanji code by two 7-bit bytes without using the most significant bits (MSBs). And there are several different Kanji codes exist for computer software because the switching method defined by ISO 2022 is not practical for random access to text messages.

The JIS X 0208 defines not only Kanji characters, but also English alphabets, digits, two types of 50 Kana characters (phonetic representation of Japanese language), and special characters. Among them, Kanji characters defined by JIS X 0208 are divided into two separated groups; one is called level one and another is called level two. The level one includes about 3500 Kanji characters and this set provides sufficient number of Kanji characters for most of ordinary texts such as technical writings. There although need more complicated Kanji characters for the advanced text applications such that text including names of persons, names of places, or text of literatures. For the purposes like these, JIS defines another set of Kanji characters called level two. In level two, there are about another 3400 characters.

In total, about 7 thousand Kanji characters are necessary for providing Japanese character capability in computer. Obviously, this requires more than one byte to represent, and representing a single character with two bytes is a standard concept. The important issue here is that we still need to use ASCII codes in computers as well as Kanji codes. This means we have to establish a way to handle a mixture of ASCII codes and Kanji codes. In order to solve the problem, there have to exists a way to distinguish ASCII codes sequences from Kanji code sequences.

In order to distinguish the Kanji sequences from sequences of ASCII representation of English alphabets and special characters, there are three major methods existing:

1. JIS X 0208 codes with JIS X 0202 (ISO 2022)
2. Extended Unix Code (EUC)
3. Microsoft Kanji Code (Shift-JIS)

By 1., a Kanji sequence is surrounded by a introducing escape sequence of Kanji characters (`ESC-$-@` or `ESC-$-B`) and introducing sequence of English alphabets (`ESC-(-J` or `ESC-(-B`).

2. is originally defined by AT&T UNIX Pacific to provide internationalized version of UNIX operating system[9] and is becoming to be a standard way to represent Kanji codes in UNIX operating system in Japan. In the EUC, the way to distinguish Kanji code sequences is somewhat different from the one of 1. By assumption that there never exists an ASCII code with its most significant bit on, a Kanji character can be distinguished by its significant bit; setting it on for every byte representing a half of a Kanji code.

3. was originally defined for CP/M on personal computers by a Japanese subsidiary of Microsoft Corporation. This is now a defacto standard for personal computers and is also supported in some of the Japanized UNIX environments. In the Microsoft Kanji codes, Kanji characters are mapped by some function so that first byte is in ranges of `0x81 - 0x9f` and `0xe0 - 0xff`.

In order to cooperate with the ISO standard method to handle character codes, and to utilize existing software which sometimes strips the MSBs off, we decided to use JIS X 0208 two 7 bit codes surrounded with escape sequences as the network standard. This decision requires conversion functions from JIS X 0208 to local operating system Kanji codes, namely EUC/JAPAN and Microsoft Kanji code.

4.1.1 Kanji code handling

In order to design network applications using Kanji codes, The following discussion have to be made regarding the average environments of existing JUNET systems.

1. There are several kinds of character codes including above three codes which are actually used in operating systems as internal codes to represent Japanese characters including Kanji characters. Among them, JIS X 0208 is not practical for internal code because of the complicated operations of switching modes when seeking a character in a byte sequence; random access to a sequence of byte is impossible. Thus, two 8 bit codes without escape sequence is preferable to two 7-bit codes with escape sequences as internal code for an operating system.

2. Since we have decided to use JIS X 0208 as the JUNET network standard Kanji code, we have to provide conversion mechanisms from JIS X 0208 to internal code of operating systems such as EUC and to Mircosoft Kanji code.

4.1.2 JUNET approaches

By assuming the above issues, we have developed the following environment for JUNET.

Kanji code: As we have described before, we are using JIS X 0208 with ISO 2022 / JIS X 0202 extension guide line as a network standard Kanji code. Escape sequence introducing JIS X 0208 can either be `ESC-$-@` or `ESC-$-B`. These are two definitions of two minor versions of JIS X 0208 and both are legal in a sense of standard definition. Escape sequence introducing ASCII code is `ESC-(-B` and introducing ROMAN character code of JIS is `ESC-(-J`. There are not much differences between ASCII and ROMAN character code, except that image representations for a few characters are different. We therefore treat both of them equally. Note that the default code set for JUNET text message is ASCII code; there is no introducing escape sequence necessary if a text starts with a ASCII code.

Control characters: According to the ISO 2022 / JIS X 0202, any control characters appear in both Kanji sequence and ASCII sequence, however, deep backtracking may be necessary to determine the character mode when a file is accessed randomly. So we decided not to allow control characters appeared within Kanji code sequence; they can only appear in ASCII code sequence. This rule contributes to make software which handles text messages to be simple and transparent in terms of internationalizing because a function to find a control character can transparently be defined.

Single byte Kana code: There are another code set for representing Japanse character in a single byte; JIS X 0201. In this code, only Kana characters are represented. This code set used to be used in mainframes because Japanizing of software was easy. Since we now have Kanji code set anyway and all the Kana representations are included in JIS X 0208 using 2 bytes, we eliminate usage of JIS X 0201 to avoid the complexity caused from handling of three different code sets at a time.

Network software: In order to provide an environment for Japanese text message capabilities in JUNET, we have modified the following software to adopt the above strategies:

- Bnews[5] was modified to pass the escape sequences which used to be stripped off in the original version. Conversion functions from JIS X 0208 to major internal Kanji codes are also added. Other network news interfaces such as rn and vn have been modified, too.

- MH[14] has been added the code conversion facility between the network standard code and the local code.

- GNU emacs and MICRO emacs were modified to handle Kanji codes so that we can edit Japanese mails and articles.

- X-window also was modified to represent Kanji characters. Level one Kanji fonts have been *handmade* and posted to JUNET[16] so that a user can read and write Kanji characters without a special Kanji terminals.

An example to picture example JUNET environment of Japanese character handling is shown in Figure 5.

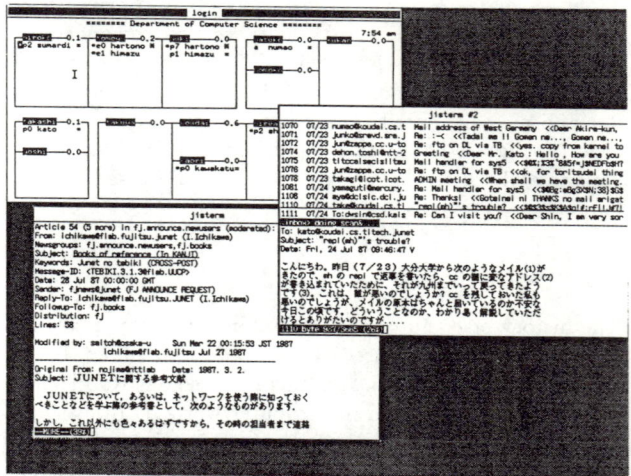

Figure 5: Example of JUNET Kanji Environment

5 Communication Software Technologies

The primary goal of the development of JUNET as the first step was to construct a network providing functions for text message exchange over research communities in Japan. Since JUNET project is a volunteer project to provide basis of researches on network communication, UUCP protocol over dial-up link was our choice to start the network because of the popular, easy to set-up and inexpensive features of UUCP technology. The dial-up modems used have been upgraded from V.21 300bps to V.22bis 2400bps and we have almost succeeded to eliminate the V.21 and V.22 1200bps modems.

However, as the size of the network has been grown and traffic has been increased as described in chapter 2. 2400bps communication is not practical at most of the major systems on the network, especially with limited resources of telephone lines at universities. In order to solve the problem, three major steps have been planned for the network; i) use of high speed dial-up modems, ii) dial-up IP links over the high speed dial-up modems, and iii) use of high-speed leased lines or X.25 packet switching network.

The purpose of the first step is to develop the most efficient usage of the high speed dial-up modems for UUCP usage; including protocol modification and kernel modification of UNIX operating system. This mechanism improves transmission efficiency at a system by 3~5 times compared with UUCP over V.22bis modems.

Utilizing technologies established by step i), major transport protocols such as TCP/IP over the dial-up link becomes practical. The step ii) thus designed and developed to provide better communication possibilities for network development as well as to provide better environment for users.

Step ii) above introduced us with technologies to construct an IP-based network; problems such as name serving, address managing and routing have to be studied and solved. This encouraged us to start working on developing a network based on permanent (virtual) circuits such as high speed leased line or X.25 based packet switching network.

5.1 UUCP modifications

The high speed dial-up modems in this paper means modems which have dial-up functions and realize error free and high speed data transmission by a modem-to-modem protocol. The actual transmission rate of these modems depends on size of the data transmitted because of the built-in protocol.

Since the host computers on JUNET varied in vendors and types of software and hardware including versions of UNIX operating system, the flow control mechanism in serial line communication are also varied. By experiences in JUNET, we found that we can hardly develop a general or portable communication mechanism by relying on flow control mechanism provided in vendor products especially for high-speed communication in serial ports.

Thus, we have employed DC1/DC3 flow control mechanism to achieve our purpose of efficient usage of the high-speed modems[15]. The basic strategies of the mechanism are; to develop a UUCP protocol which escapes DC1, DC3 and DLE ascii control characters, and to develop a *line discipline* module for UNIX tty driver in order to handle DC1/DC3 properly.

5.1.1 UUCP/j-protocol

There are some existing protocols for UUCP such as g, f, x, and t. The *j-protocol* developed for JUNET is similar to the f in purpose but has two primary characteristics: It allows 8 bit bytes and escapes DC1, DC3, and DLE ascii characters. Unlike *f-protocol* which was designed for communication using PADs, 7 bit encoding is not necessary for high-speed modem communications. DC1 and DC3 characters have to be escaped to make the link transparent as we use these characters for the flow control mechanism between the machine and the modem. The DLE was also escaped because this character is often treated specially in some serial communication path.

5.1.2 Utty — Line Discipline

UUCP normally sets UNIX tty driver to be in *raw* mode which provide transparent communication through serial ports. The *tandem* mode of tty driver exists where the driver suspend transmitting output characters by receiving a DC3 character. For the purpose of utilizing the high-speed modem with DC1/DC3 flow control, the driver have to generate a DC3 character when more than a certain amount of characters are in input queue to avoid overflow in the queue.

The line discipline developed for UUCP, *utty* (Uucp TTY), is a driver which has a 1024 bytes ring buffer for input data with a high water mark and a low water mark. When the input data in the buffer reaches the high water mark, the driver generate a DC3 onto the output queue, and a user process receives the data and the amount of the data in the buffer decreases less than the low water mark, it generates a DC1. Functions to control the output transmission is same as one of normal tty driver's.

5.1.3 Discussions

The UUCP communication using the *j-protocol* over *utty* line discipline has been working in JUNET for several months. The high-speed modems currently used are TrailBlazer of TELEBIT corporation and AX/9624c of Microcom corporation. The actual performance of the mechanisms for various data size of UUCP is shown in Figure 6.

This also shows the result of V.22bis 2400bps modem and V.22 1200bps modem. The statistics were collected from daily operations of a major JUNET system.

The maximum data transmission rate for the high-speed modems is 13kbps for TrailBlazer and 12kbps for AX/9624c. These performance could be achieved only for a large data transmission; the drastic increasing of the transmission rate for larger data is caused from built-in protocol

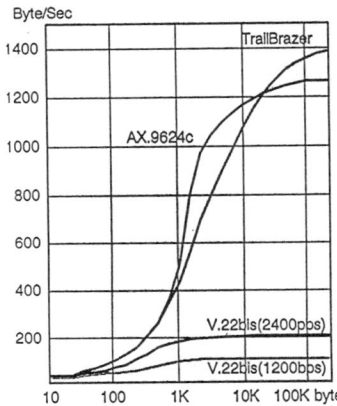

Figure 6: Performance using j-protocol UUCP/utty

mechanism. The port utilization time decreased to 25 percent of one by V.22bis modem. This is because most of the JUNET traffic is for transmission of news articles as described in chapter 2, and the news articles are spooled and concatenated (batched) into a large data which increases performance of the communication mechanism introduced in this chapter.

5.2 Dial-up IP Link

As the result of the high-speed dial-up modems described above, we could expect transmission rate of more than 10kbps on a dial-up link. This encouraged us of using a dial-up link for various transport protocols such as TCP/IP. IP connections over a dial-up link have been usually considered for personal computers at home[6] however, they are still effective for easy construction of an internetworking among universities, especially on the achieved performance with the high-speed modems.

The system for dial-up IP link thus was designed and developed[8]. The first version of the system was designed using the *utty* line discipline described in the previous section. And with the experiences from the first version, the second version was designed and developed which achieves improved performance by eliminating data movements between the user and the kernel space of UNIX operating system. Both of the systems are developed on SUN OS version 3.2 which is compatible with 4.2BSD UNIX.

5.2.1 The First Version

The first version of the system consists of 4 major modules and the *utty*. The *dldriver* resides in the kernel and receives and sends IP datagrams with the IP module which also exists in the kernel space. It has communication entities as a "special file" in the UNIX file space called /dev/dl*x*. The major portion of the system, *dldaemon*, is a permanent user process which reads/writes information from/to the *dldriver* and allocates *utty* driver. The character mappings to escape DC1/DC3 and other control characters are also performed by the *dldaemon*. Another module called *dlattach*, which is a user command, is invoked at login time to pass the information about the serial port to the *dldaemon*. Figure 7 shows the structure of the system.

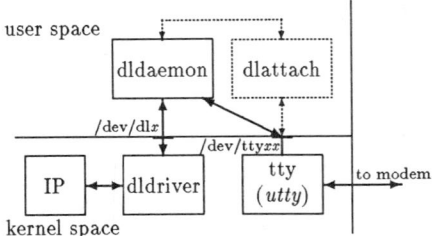

Figure 7: Structure of the Version one

A connection established with the system is a point-to-point connection between a master system which initiates the connection and a slave system. The following example of sequence shows an overview of the procedure and the functions of the system:

1. The *dldaemon* which is invoked at a boot time resides on the system permanently until the operating system goes down. As soon as the process is initiated, it registers a network interface (*if*) called dl*x* and sets up the routing information in the kernel space so that the IP module can pass IP fragments with addresses routed toward the link to the *dldriver*. This initiating procedure have to be done at both sides of the systems.

2. When an IP fragment is selected to the dl interface by the routing function in the IP module, the *dldriver* passes the fragment to the *dldaemon* running in the user space via a special device.

3. If no connection for the dial-up link is established, the *dldaemon* starts dialing to make a connection to the remote site. The dialing is done by a part of the public domain dial program.

4. According to the scenario description for dialing, the master *dldaemon* logs-in to the slave system and invokes the *dlattach* command.

5. The *dlattach* provides the running *dldaemon* on the slave system with the information about the serial line port and about the caller's system via Unix domain socket, as shown in the dotted line of Figure 7.

6. When the physical connection is established, each of the *dldaemons* at the both systems generates a system call to switch a line discipline to the *utty*. Finally, they complete establishment of an dial-up link ready for IP communication between the systems.

The resulted performance of the first version with two Trail-Blazers was approximately 3kbps for the end-to-end communication by ftp and the utilization of the line was fairly low. There are two reasons which decrease efficiency: The *dldaemon* waits for input both from *dldriver* and *utty* using the *select* system call and this is a bottle neck of the communication. Another reason is that the data movement between the kernel space and the user space obviously causes overheads.

5.2.2 The Second Version

The second version of the system eliminates the data movement between the kernel space and the user space by defining protocol interface between the *dldaemon* and the *dldriver*. The *dldriver* now includes a line discipline very similar to *utty*, but IP fragments are passed between the tty driver and the *dldaemon* directly using a character buffer called *clist*. The communication between the IP module and the *dldriver* is done via *mbuf*, a buffer control mechanism for network modules in the kernel. This also eliminates overhead of data movement. The structure of the second version of the system is illustrated in Figure 8.

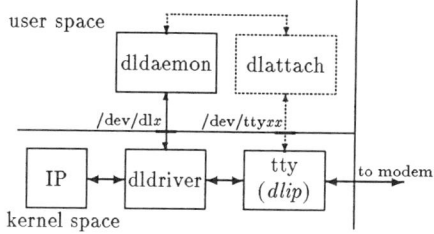

Figure 8: Structure of the Second Version

A connection is terminated by *dldaemon* when one of the following conditions is detected; i) 60 seconds passed without any IP fragment transmissions, or ii) missing of 'I am alive' control character from the remote system for 24 seconds. This character is generated every 8 seconds to indicate that the local *dldaemon* is active to the remote *dldaemon*.

Interactions between the *dldriver* and the *dldaemon* are performed by exchanging messages which defines protocol interface of *dldriver*. The actual data are no longer passed to *dldaemon*, however, some messages generated by *dldriver* are sent to *dldaemon* as follows:

DG_REC indicates arrival of an IP fragment from the remote site.

DG_SEND indicates that an IP fragment passed to the serial line.

IAA_REC indicates that the *dldriver* receives a control character of 'I am alive' from the remote site.

DIAL_REQ requires dialing to the remote site.

On the other hand, commands generated by the *dldaemon* for the *dldriver* are as follows:

OPEN_CONNECT indicates the establishment of physical connection by completion of the dialing.

SEND_IAA generates 'I am alive' control character to the remote site.

CLOSE_CONNECT forces termination of the connection and re-initialize the modules.

DIAL_FAIL indicates the dialing procedure fails and forces the queued fragments discarded as well as the re-initialization of the modules.

5.2.3 Discussions

The measured performance of the system with two TrailBlazers is about 7.5kbps for end-to-end data transmission by ftp, which achieves most efficient transmission rate for serial ports. Time consumed by the dialing sequence may be critical in terms of a timeout interval of upper layer protocol. By our experience, however, the dialing time has never exceeded the TCP's connection time out yet.

There is no dynamic routing control mechanism employed for this system. It is necessary for this system to develop intelligent routing functions with considerations of speed and availability of links.

6 International Information Exchange

As described in this paper, number of messages exchanged in JUNET has been increased rapidly, and number of messages exchanged internationally via the two gateways have also been increased as well. Users of other networks, however, sometimes complains about the insufficient information on world networks generated form JUNET. The primary reason for the complains is obviously caused by the preference of Japanese characters among JUNET users.

The development of general purpose software to handle Japanese characters in non-special hardware environment as well as development of the hand-made Kanji fonts encourages us to distribute JUNET Kanji messages to other countries. The experimental delivery of the domestic newsgroups to abroad has started in 1986 for some universities.

On the other hand, submission of news articles from USENET environment to JUNET can be achieved by adding a newsgroup called `fj.misc` to the newsgroup list of an article. This is efficient because all of the JUNET sites are subscribing `fj` newsgroups while some sites are not subscribing USENET newsgroups. The news article posted this way is handled as a JUNET news article inside Japan.

It is known that the addresses of JUNET are properly handled at both `relay.cs.net` and `seismo.css.gov`. Therefore,

- *user%domain*.`junet@relay.cs.net`
- *user%domain*.`junet@seismo.css.gov`

are the most popular style of addresses from the ARPA Internet name space. However, non university users in Japan can not use the link between `ccut.cc.u-tokyo.junet` and `relay.cs.net`. So mails to non university people should be routed to `kddlab.kddlabs.junet`. In order to contact JUNET administrators, `junet-admin@junet` is the address.

7 Conclusion

Development of JUNET started in October 1984 and various researches on computer networking and distributed environment have been actively done with the rapid growth in the size of the network. Among them, name management functions to construct a hierarchical domain name space, Japanese character handling, and communication technologies using the high-speed modems have been focused as primary research concerns.

The actual work for the addressing and routing of JUNET text messages is achieved by a name server concept and its implementation. This system receives control messages to specify the information about logical domain name, connections and methods to use to deliver messages, and generates a sendmail rule set. This software provides an environment where the logical naming definitions and physical routing issues are clearly separated so that reliability, efficiency, extensibility, and flexibility of communication in the network are simultaneously achieved.

Internationalization of computer software is one of the most important issues in computer science, and some works have been achieved in JUNET communication software. In JUNET, electronic mail and news software are designed to enable 16bit Japanese character handling, based on the studies and discussions on general computing environment using Japanese text. The clear separation of network Kanji code and internal operating system code employed in JUNET software provides a transparent environment on Japanese character handling in computer networks. Availability of Japanese messages obviously encourages users to exchanges messages over the network.

Requirements for higher transmission rate of the dial-up lines, which was chosen to start the network, have arisen and the use of the high-speed modems have been studied. A new UUCP protocol and tty driver enhancement are developed for the purpose. As the result, more than 13kbps UUCP data transmission rate is achieved. This encouraged us to migrate onto TCP/IP suite using dial-up lines as well as using leased lines. Performance of the implementation of the dial-up IP link is about 7.5kbps which is practical enough to construct a distributed environment over a widely interconnected network environment.

Progresses of JUNET technologies discussed in this paper lead us to many topics of future studies such as:

- Enhancement of name servers which handles general distributed resources.
- Establishment of gateway technologies such as optimal routing strategies based upon constructions of IP-based network using the dial-up IP link and IP over leased lines.
- Supports of multi-media message exchanges enhances the environment with multi-language supports currently achieved.

The technologies developed in JUNET can generally be used to construct a network interconnection with inexpensive cost.

Acknowledgment

The authors would like to express our gratitude to many researchers who have been contributing to establish the JUNET environment described in this paper. Among them, special appreciations go to Youichi Shinoda, Keisuke Tanaka, and Hiroshi Tachibana for their efforts in developing JUNET software. The dial-up IP link was achieved as a result of discussions with members of the JUNET project especially with Susumu Sano. Professor Haruhisa Ishida and Professor Yoshihiro Tohma for their valuable advices and encouragements. We would like to thank these people on behalf of the project.

References

[1] ALLMAN, E. Sendmail – An Interconnecting Mail Rerouter, Version 4.2. In *UNIX Programmer's Manual, 4.2 Berkeley Software Distribution*, Univ. of Califorma, Berkeley, 1983.

[2] COMER, D. The computer science research network CSNET: A history and status report. *CACM 26*, 10 (October 1983).

[3] (ED.), J. P. *Internet Protocol – DARPA Internet Program Protocol Specification*. Tech. Rep. RFC 791, USC/Information Sciences Institute, 1980.

[4] (ED.), J. P. *Transmission Control Protocol – DARPA Internet Program Protocol Specification*. Tech. Rep. RFC 793, USC/Information Sciences Institute, 1981.

[5] EMERSON, S. L. USENET: A bulletin board for UNIX users. *BYTE* (September 1983).

[6] FARBER, D. J., DELP, G. S., AND CONTE, T. M. *A Thinwire Protocol for connecting personal computers to the INETERNET*. Tech. Rep. RFC-914, Univ. of Delaware, 1984.

[7] ISO. *Codes for the Representation of Names of Countries*. Tech. Rep. ISO-3116, International Standard Organization, 1981.

[8] KATO, A. Network news system in JUNET. In *Proceedings of the 35th Annual Convention* (1987), IPSJ. (In Japanese).

[9] KOGURE, H., AND MCGOWAN, R. A UNIX System V STRAMS TTY Implimentation for Multiple Language

Processing. In *USENIX Summer Conference Processings* (1987), USENIX.

[10] MURAI, J., AND ASAMI, T. A network for research and developement communications in Japan — JUNET —. In *Proceedings of First Pacific Computer Communications Symposium* (1985).

[11] NOWITZ, D. A., AND LESK, M. E. *A Dial-Up Network of UNIX Systems.* Tech. Rep., Bell Telephone Laboratories, August 1978.

[12] POSTEL, J. *Domain Requirements.* Tech. Rep. RFC 920, Univ. of Southern California, 1984.

[13] QUATERMAN, J. S., AND HOSKINS, J. C. Notable Computer Networks. *CACM 29*, 10 (October 1986).

[14] S. BORDEN, R. S. G., AND SHAPIRO, N. Z. *The MH Message Handling System: User's Manual.* Rand Corporation, 1979.

[15] SHINODA, Y. Dialup network by high speed modems in JUNET. In *Proceedings of the 35th Annual Convention* (1987), IPSJ. (In Japanese).

[16] TACHIBANA, H. PD kanji font (tools and ascii fonts). Network news posted to JUNET newsgroup `fj.sources` as `<1676@rika.cs.titech.JUNET>`, July 1987.

Computer Networking for Large Computers in Universities

Jun Matsukata

Computer Centre
The University of Tokyo
2-11-16 Yayoi, Bunkyo-ku
Tokyo 113, JAPAN

Abstract

N-1 protocol was developed for construction of a computer network which connects universities in Japan. N-1 protocol has been adopted by Inter-University Computer Network and University Library Network.

NACSIS has started the construction of Science Information Network which will provide an infrastructure for digital communication for universities in Japan. High speed digital lines has been leased from NTT for that purpose.

A local area network was constructed at the Faculty of Engineering at the University of Tokyo. The network consists of an optical fiber backbone network and many IEEE802.3 10Mbps baseband networks connected to the backbone. Connection to large computers was one of the key issues in the planning of that network.

1. Introduction

In Japan, large computers, including main frames and supercomputers, have been very important computing resources for researchers in universities and colleges. Computer networks provide means for access to those large computers in a remote location.

N-1 protocol was developed for construction of a computer network which connects mainframes at computer centers in Japanese universities. *Inter-University Computer Network* which adopted N-1 protocol started its regular operation between seven inter-university computer centers in 1981. Many university computer centers have been connected to the network since then.

University Library Network which connects libraries in universities was established in 1984. Network Virtual Terminal Protocol of N-1 was revised to handle Japanese character codes to meet the requirement of that network.

National Center for Science Information System (NACSIS) has started the construction of *Science Information Network* which will provide an infrastructure for digital communication for universities in Japan. Connections between nodes located at four universities and NACSIS was established in 1987 and has been used as a subnetwork for Inter-University Computer Network and University Library Network.

As for local area networks, construction of campus-wide networks in national universities has started since 1986. A local area network was constructed at the Faculty of Engineering of the University of Tokyo in 1987. The network consists of a backbone network using optical fiber and seventeen IEEE802.3 10Mbps baseband networks connected to the backbone network. The function of the backbone network is that of a MAC bridge with switching capability. TCP/IP was adopted as the tentative standard transport protocol. Connection to large computers was one of the key issues in the planning of that network.

In Japan a volunteer based research network for researchers called JUNET[Murai87] is providing text message services for academic communities. Gateways to JUNET form mainframe network described in this paper are planned so that an environment for international message exchange can be provided.

This paper describes those experiences in computer networking related to large computers in universities in Japan.

2. Computer networks and large computers

Large computers for universities are important computing resources for researchers. Very large computers including supercomputers are usually shared among universities. Computer networks provide means for access to large computers in remote locations from local terminals and computers.

2.1. The advantage of computer networks

The general advantages of using computer networks compared with using telephone lines are (1) speed, (2) reliability, (3) transparency, and (4) versatility. Computer networks utilize a data communication line for many kinds of applications at the same time. It is inefficient to use a fast communication line for a single application. Furthermore, computer networks provide reliable and transparent end-to-end connection.

2.2. Data communication networks

Data communication networks serve as subnetworks for computer networks. Data communication networks are classified by distance in two categories, (1) local area networks (LAN) and (2) wide area networks (WAN).

LANs are networks usually within a site of an organization. The geographical distances is at most 2 or 3 kilometers. Typical transmission speed is 10Mbps for Ethernet and 48-56kbps for digital PBX. Network layer services tends to be of connectionless-mode except for X.25 packet switching of a digital PBX.

WANs provide data communication paths between sites, possibly of different organizations. Typical transmission speed is 48-56kbps for X.25 packet switching network. Higher speed is available for point-to-point links.

2.3. Requirements imposed on computer networks for access to large computers

Requirements imposed on computer networks which are peculiar to access to large computers are:

(1) it is necessary to consider connection to the intrinsic communication architechure of large computers, and

(2) broad data path corresponding to the computing power of large computers.

Large computers, especially main frames, have their own communication architecuture and there are a great amount of application programs depend on it.

The second requirement is important for file transfer. It have become possible to be sufficed to some extent in the local environment. It is not easy, however, to have broad data path in wide area network. The reason used to be the cost of fast communication lines. Public packet switching network service is expensive for transferring large amount of data and speed is slow compared with that of local area networks.

3. Computer networking for universities in Japan

The history of computer networking for universities in Japan begins with the development of *N-1 protocol*, which has been adopted as the protocol for *Inter-University Computer Network*, and *University Libarary Network*.

Inter-University Computer Network is a computer network which connects computer centers in universities, colleges and national inter-university research institute as well as inter-university computer centers.

The seven *inter-university* computer centers (*Oogata Keisanki centers*, in Japanese, which means "centers for large scale computers") have main frame computers and supercomputers and have made computing power of very fast computers available to researchers in universities and college in Japan. The first inter-university computer center, *Computer Centre, University of Tokyo* was established in 1965. Computers were precious facility in the country in those days. Today, most universities have their own computing facilities.

National Center for Science Information System (NACSIS)[NACSIS86] has started the construction of *Science Information Network* from 1986 fiscal year to provide an infrastructure for digital communication for universities in Japan. Connections between nodes located at four universities and NACSIS has been established in 1987 and has been used as a subnetwork for Inter-University Computer Network and University Library Network.

University Library Network is a network which connects libraries in universities, for which NACSIS plays a primary role.

As for LANs (local area networks), construction of campus-wide LANs in national universities has started in 1986 fiscal year. The construction of LAN at the Faculty of Engineering of the University of Tokyo, which was a pilot project for LAN construction in nation universities, has completed by March 1987. The constructions of LAN at Kyoto University, Tohoku University, and Shinshu University have started in 1987 fiscal year.

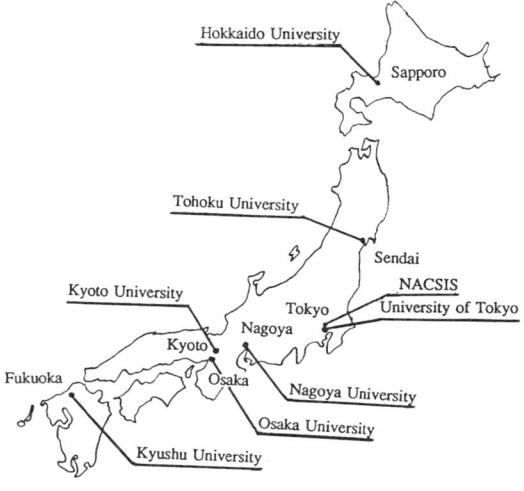

Fig. 1. Inter-university computer centers and NACSIS

3.1. Inter-University Computer Network

Inter-University Computer Network[Inose76, Inose78, Inose79, Inose80, Inose81] which is often called *N-1 Network* after the name of the protocol used is a computer network which connects computer centers in university in Japan. The network started its regular operation between the seven inter-university computer centers in 1981. The development of an experimental network for feasibility studies had started in 1974. The number of universities which is connected to the network has increased in number. The number of hosts as of March 1987 is sixty four.

Inter-University Network is a heterogeneous computer network which connects computers of different manufactures using a proprietary protocol, *N-1 Protocol*. N-1 protocol has been implemented on main frames of Hitachi, Fujitsu, NEC, Mitsubishi, and IBM. DDX-P (a public packet switching network operated by NTT) has been used as subnetwork. The packet switching service of Science Information Network is also used as subnetwork. N-1 protocol is also used for point-to-point connection using a dedicated line as subnetwork.

The structure of N-1 protocol is shown in Fig. 2. NVT protocol and RJE protocol are application level protocols. HOST-HOST protocol is the transport level protocol, and FEP-FEP protocol is the network level protocol. Two kinds of subnetworks are used as communication subsystem. One is a packet switching network. The other is a dedicated line for a point-to-point connection.

Though FEP-FEP protocol has a subnetwork independent address, no network layer routing is operated except for the cascade connection with dedicated line and routing between DDX-P and the packet switching service of Science Information Network.

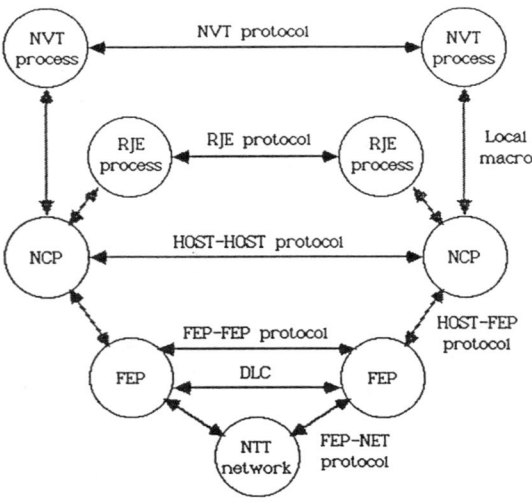

Fig. 2. The Structure of N-1 Protocol

Functions provided by Inter-University Computer Network are remote logon and remote job entry. Remote logon uses NVT (Network Virtual Terminal) protocol of N-1[Protocols85] Remote job entry uses RJE (Remote Job Entry) protocol of N-1. NVT protocol was revised to introduce Japanse character code set as a network virtual character code set.

The absense of electronic mail service has reduced the merit of the Inter-University Computer Network. Now, an electronic mail system on N-1 protocol is under development in a joint project between inter-university computer centers and NACSIS.[Sakata87] The protocol is based on MHS except that mechanism for data transfer is the revised version of N-1 NVT. NACSIS is undertaking development of an electronic mail system based on MOTIS besides that.

Although file transfer can be done with RJE or remote logon, one feels inconvenience when one transfers files frequently, or when the size of the file is large, or in case of binary file transfer. It would be more convenient, if file transfer facility using a file transfer protocol were available. File transfer protocol for N-1 has been defined but not implemented yet.

3.2. University Library Network

University Library Network is a computer network which connects computers in university libraries for which NACSIS plays a primary role. It has started operation in 1984 by the Center of Bibliographic Information, a department of the University of Tokyo, which is the predecessor of NACSIS. The protocol is N-1. NVT (Network Virtual Terminal) protocol was revised to handle Japanease character codes to meet the requirement of University Library Network.

3.3. Science Information Network

NACSIS (NAtional Center for Science Information System) has started the operation of a digital communication network, *Science Information Network* (*Gakujutsu Jouhou Network*, in Japanese) since January 1987, which will provide an infrastructure for digital communication between universities and colleges. High speed digital lines between the University of Tokyo, NACSIS, Nagoya University, Kyoto University, and Osaka University has been leased from NTT under budget from the government since January 1987 for that purpose.

Service available for the time being is X.25 packet switching service which is used as a subnetwork for Inter-University Computer Network and University Library Network. Data links on DDX-P for those network will be replace by those on Science Information Network.

Inter-university telephone service will be avaliable in the near future.

The current policy of operation is not to collect charge.

Fig. 3 shows the configuration of Science Information Network.

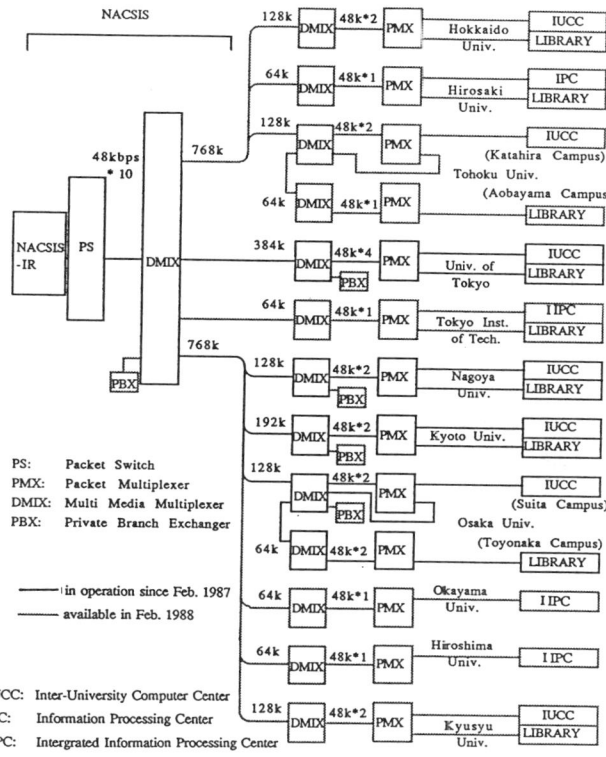

Fig. 3. Science Information Network (as of 1987)

DMIX (Multi Media Multiplexer) are installed at each node to allow communication in other modes than data. For example, PBX is connected to DMIX at some nodes (32kbps per line) to provide telephone service.

An X.25 packet switch is installed at NACSIS to provide packet switching service. Packet multiplexers are installed at each university and perform multiplexing and local switching of packets. These equipment are used to provide packet switching service. The interface for the packet switching service is made compatible to that of DDX-P to make easy to use as a subnetwork for N-1 in place of DDX-P.

NACSIS is developing a electronic mail system based on MOTIS.

3.4. Local area networks in Japanese universities

3.4.1. Kogaku-bu LAN at the University of Tokyo

A large scale local area network has been constructed at the Faculty of Engineering at the University of Tokyo by March 1987. The network, which is usually called Kogaku-bu LAN, is considered to be a part of the university-wide network which is under planning.

Kogaku-bu LAN consists of many branch networks which are IEEE802.3[IEEE83] 10Mbps baseband networks. All branch networks are connected to a backbone network which is a 100Mbps ring network. Since the backbone network is transparent to users, the whole network functions as if it were a very large *single* IEEE802.3 network.

The branch networks cover most of the building which belongs to the Faculty of Engineering. Users equipments, including personal computers, terminal servers, work stations, superminicomputers, and main frames, are connected to those branch networks. Some branches cover more than one building, in which case optical repeaters using optical fiber cable as physical media is used for connection between the buildings.

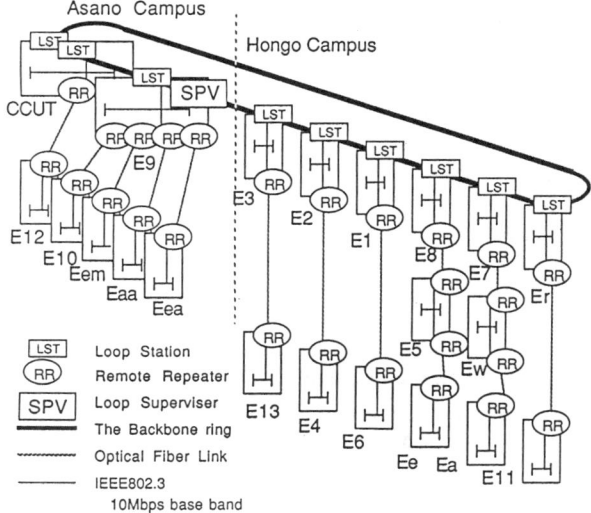

Fig. 4. The structure of Kogaku-bu LAN

The backbone network consists of node elements which are connected in a ring topology. It uses optical fiber cables as physical media with transmission rate of 100Mbps, which is divided into 10 channels of 10Mbps by time division multiplexing. To each backbone node is connected a branch network. Since four nodes are installed in a single cabinet, node elements are located in restricted number of buildings. Optical repeaters mentioned above are used for connection between the backbone node and the branch network in a remote building.

3.4.1.1. Increasing needs for LAN

As computers become more popular tools for researchers in the university, demands for connecting terminals with host computers in the *campus* have increased, which resulted in the shortage of telephone lines in the campus. The speed and quality required for those connection have also changed. In the early times, a 300bps modem was used on a dial up private branch telephone line. Today, many 1200bps and 2400bps modems are used, and 9600bps connections on 4-wire dedicated lines are preferred. The use of screen editor requires quality of a line as well as speed (endurable with 1200bps and satisfactory with at least 9600bps). Displaying graphics and images requires faster and more reliable lines, too.

The needs for fast and reliable file transfer have also increased, as personal computers gain popularity for computer terminals. The use of such program as Kermit meets such requirement to some extent, but the rate of data transfer limited by the line speed is slower by an order of magnitude than that of the slowest secondary storage, *i.e.* a floppy disk.

Since telephone line facility has been planned for voice communication, the number of lines tends to be insufficient to suffice the requirement for data communication. It is not so easy to increase lines especially in old buildings with thick and solid walls. If we have enough lines, however, the data transmission speed on the telephone line with conventional technology is slow.

On the other hand, computer networking on local area network with high transparency and coherency have become available on the market even for work stations and superminicomputers from different vendors which requires fast and reliable networks.

As mentioned above, Kogaku-bu LAN was planned in consideration of the situation mentioned above which will be summarized as follows.

(1) More data communication paths which are faster and more reliable are needed for data communication between terminals and computers.
(2) Faster and more reliable means for data communication between computers.

3.4.1.2. An IEEE802.3 baseband LAN with a backbone network

Kogaku-bu LAN consists of branches of IEEE802.3 10Mbps baseband networks and a backbone network which establish connection between branches.

3.4.1.3. Branches

The branch networks are IEEE802.3 (or ISO 8802/3) 10Mbps baseband networks. IEEE802.3 type LAN, which is a standard originates from Ethernet, is one of the most popular type of local area network for the time being. A wide range of products which can be connected directly to IEEE802.3 baseband networks are already on the market, including personal computers, terminal servers, work stations, superminicomputers, and main frames. It should be noted that IEEE802.3 10Mbps baseband network has enough bandwidth for such application as file sharing which requires fast data transmission rate.

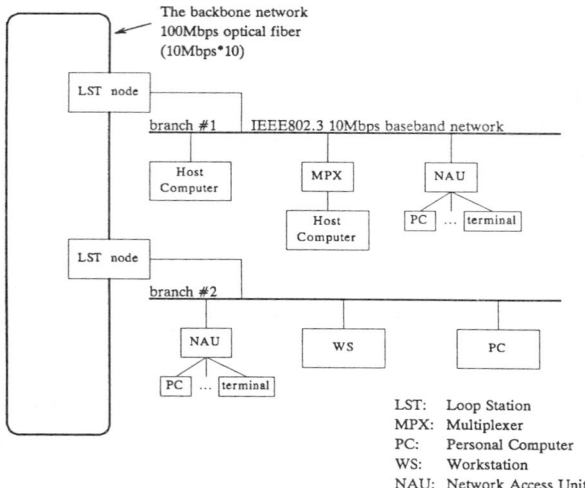

Fig. 5. IEEE802.3 baseband LAN with a backbone network

3.4.1.4. The role of the backbone network

The backbone network connects the branch IEEE802.3 networks together and plays the following roles.

(1) The backbone removes the restriction on the maximum distance between two devices connected to branches which is imposed by IEEE802.3 baseband standard, and makes it possible to implement a large scale network.
Dimensions of IEEE802.3 baseband networks are restricted as follows. The maximum length of a single segment of an IEEE802.3 baseband network is 500 meters. Segments can be connected together with repeaters, in which case the maximum distance along the cable between two devices should be less than 2.5 kilometers. If longer connection is needed, bridges and gateways are used to connect clusters of segments. The backbone network plays the role of MAC bridge with which has switching capability.

(2) The backbone localizes the traffic and improve the throughput of the whole network.
The backbone does not transfer any local packet on a branch network. Any packet submitted to any segment of a branch is propagated to all segments in the branch, Heavy traffic on an CSMA/CD network like IEEE802.3 baseband network extremely degrades the performance of the network. It is desirable to localize traffic within each branch, that is, to prevent packets destined for the same branch as originating from being transferred to other branches. Localization of traffic also improves security.

3.4.1.5. Requirements imposed on the backbone network

Taking into account that the network will be used in various ways, the functionality of the backbone is required to be transparent. The following requirements on the backbone network make the whole network seem as if it were a very large single IEEE802.3 network.

(1) The backbone imposes no restrictions on protocols of layers higher than MAC (Media Access Control) sublayer.

Since at least a few kinds of protocol families are used for the time being, and will be used in the future, it is inconvenient for a campus network to restrict high level protocols to a particular family of protocols, e.g. XNS, TCP/IP, OSI. The LLC (Logical Link Control) protocol may be either type 1 or type 2. Some bridges on the market is a gateway of network layer assuming a particular network layer protocol and does not suffice the requirement.

(2) The backbone imposes no restrictions on physical address.

To suffice the requirement (1), the routing of packets performed by the backbone should be based on the physical address, namely, MAC address. Since there are many IEEE802.3 LAN interface boards on which physical address is hard wired, it is not desirable to impose any restrictions on the physical address. If the address of the destination branch is encoded in the physical address, the routing of packets will be easier but the physical address will be restricted.

3.4.1.6. Implementation of the backbone.

The backbone network is implemented by Toshiba Corporation in a way which suffices our requirement aforementioned. The backbone network is implemented as a ring type network called TOTAL-LAN/RING†.[Kawabata79, Kawabata83] It uses optical fiber as physical media with the transmission rate of 100Mbps, which is divided into 10 channels of 10Mbps by time division multiplexing.

The backbone transfers MAC layer (IEEE802.3) packet between branches. It does not matter whatever kind of higher level protocol than MAC protocol may be used. Therefore, the LLC protocol may be either type 1 or type 2.

The routing of packets performed by the backbone is transparent to users in the sense that it imposes no restrictions on the physical address, i.e. IEEE802.3 address. The routing scheme is referred to as generic routing method,[Kuniyoshi87] in which each backbone node maintains a dynamic routing table monitoring packets on the branches and exchanging routing information with other nodes.

---
† TOTAL-LAN/RING is a product of Toshiba Corporation.

3.4.1.7. Application level interconnectivity

Though higher level protocols are not restricted to any protocol suite, it is desirable to have a *tentative standard* protocol suite in the view point of application level interconnectivity. OSI protocol family was a candidate but it was not practical to choose it for the time being. We chose TCP/IP as the tentative standard.

We took into account two kinds of applications, *remote logon* and *file transfer*. Electronic mail was not considered as an application for personal computers, because it was questionable to have a mailbox on personal computers currently available. Anyway, if file transfer is available, it will not be so difficult to make electronic mail available.

Fig. 6 shows the application level interconnectivity realized in Kogaku-bu LAN.

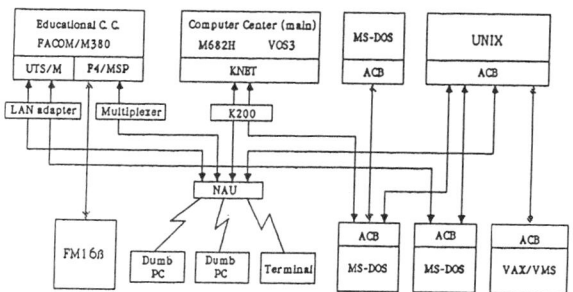

Fig. 6. Application Level Interconnectivity

As a result of having TCP/IP as a common protocol, most equipments of our concern from a MS/DOS PC to a main frame host computer can communicate in TCP/IP. Fast file transfer is available using *ftp* (file transfer protocol) between various kinds of computers.

Since the subnetwork is independent of higher level protocols, we can migrate to OSI protocols in the future.

3.4.1.8. Connecting host computers to LAN

The forms of the connection of host computers to LAN will be classified in three types.

(1) Connection with multiplexer
The host computer is connected to an equipment called multiplexer with serial lines. Each interactive session needs a single serial line. The typical line speed is 9600bps. File transfer is performed as an application on the interactive session.

(2) X.25 connection
The host computer is connected to an X.25 gateway with a single serial line. Terminals are connected as X.28 non-packet terminals. Line speed ranges from 9600bps to 1.544Mbps. File transfer is performed as an application on the interactive session.

(3) Direct connection (Ethernet-channel connection)
The host computer is connected to an Ethernet-

channel interface. Transport protocol such as TCP/IP is used. File transfer is performed by inter-process communication implemented on the transport protocol.

As for the CCUT main system, direct connection was realized using Fibronics K200 Ethernet-channel interface with TCP/IP protocol support by KNET software. Remote logon and file transfer are realized by telnet and ftp, respectively, which are standard application protocols of the TCP/IP protocol family.

3.4.2. Access to large computers

3.4.2.1. Networking features of large computers

The networking features of large computers such as main frames are somewhat different from local area network environment we have been discussed. Vendors of large computers have their proprietary network architecture, something like SNA but not necessarily fully compatible with SNA.

This section is mainly based on the experience at the Computer Centre at the University of Tokyo (CCUT) which is one of the inter-university computer center in Japan. The main system of CCUT is a loosely coupled multiprocessor system of three general purpose main frame computers and one supercomputer as shown in Fig. 7.

As the CCUT main system is one of the important computing resources for researchers in the Faculty of Engineering, the connection to Kogaku-bu LAN was carefully studied. An Ethernet-to-channel interface and TCP/IP support software were introduced to connect that system to Kogaku-bu LAN.

3.4.2.2. Style of terminal support

The vendor standard terminal for CCUT main system is a video display terminal called T560/20, which resembles 3270 in basic features. Screen oriented application programs including screen oriented editors are designed for that kind of terminals. As for CCUT, the vendor supported video display terminals only reside inside the CCUT building.

Dumb terminals are also supported but most screen oriented application programs do not work on them. CCUT has had a 'dumb terminal' policy for terminals located outside, and has made an effort to enrich the repertoire of dumb terminal support by application programs.

Therefore, the goal of implementation of remote logon to the CCUT main system was to provide dumb terminal access across the network. We did not adopt "protocol converter" approach by which dumb terminals are connected as a video display terminal, because (1) it is necessary to support dumb terminals in general, and (2) T560/20 is somewhat different from 3270 and there was not suitable terminal emulation program or protocol converter for it.

4. Aspects of access to large computers over computer networks

Application protocols affects the end user service of a computer network. It is not easy to distinguish issues of protocols from those of its implementation. In this section, the author would like to discuss aspects of application protocols and their implementations.

4.1. TCP/IP support at the CCUT main system

TCP/IP was supported at the main system of *CCUT (Computer Centre, University of Tokyo)* to provide access from the Kogaku-bu LAN mentioned above.

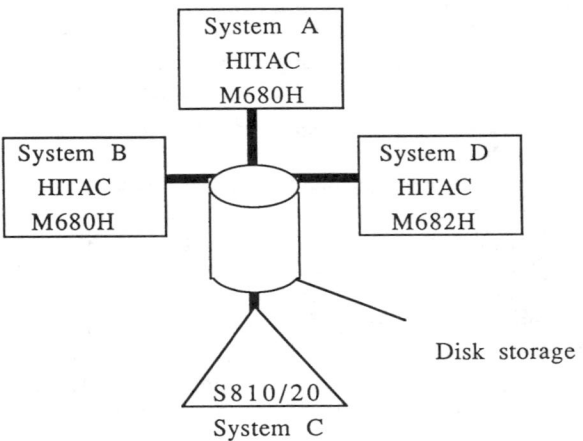

Fig. 7. The main system of CCUT

The main system of CCUT is a loosely coupled multiprocessor system consisting of three general purpose processors (two HITAC M680H and one HITAC M682H) and a supercomputer (HITAC S810/20).

System A and the supercomputer (System B) are used for processing only batch jobs. System C and System D are used for both TSS and batch job processing. TCP/IP was supported on System D. A batch job can be submitted from any of the four systems.

System D is a M682H which is a dual processor mode of M680H. The operating system is VOS3 which corresponds to MVS of IBM.

System D is connected to Kogaku-bu LAN with K200† Ethernet-to-channel interface attached to a block multiplexer channel. TCP/IP is supported by using KNET/TCP VOS3† software. Services provided for users are *telnet* client, *ftp* client, *telnet* server, and *ftp* server. *Smtp* is not delivered yet.

As a result of our request, *telnet* server was modified to generate attention to a task when it received a

---
† K200 and KNET/TCP VOS3 are products of Spartacus Inc., a Fibronics company.

telnet BREAK command.

VOS3

```
┌─────────────────────────┐
│  ┌───────────────────┐  │
│  │                   │  │
│  │       TSS         │  │
│  │   (Application)   │  │
│  │                   │  │
│  ├───────────────────┤  │
│  │       TIOP2       │  │
│  ├───────────────────┤  │
│  │   Telnet Server   │  │
│  ├───────────────────┤  │
│  │      TCP/IP       │  │
│  ├───────────────────┤  │
│  │  Ethernet Driver  │  │
│  └───────────────────┘  │
│  ┌───────────────────┐  │
│  │       K200        │  │
│  └─────────┬─────────┘  │
└────────────┼────────────┘
─────────────┴─────────────
                   Ethernet
```

Fig. 8. telnet server for VOS3

4.2. Application protocols of TCP/IP for large computer access

As for the TCP/IP interface installed in the main system of CCUT, only *telnet* and *ftp* are available for the time being, and *smtp* is coming. *Telnet* is the only general purpose NVT protocol, and that TCP/IP terminal servers usually supports telnet as a remote logon facility. *Rlogin* for UNIX† systems is inappropriate unless UNIX runs on the host computer. It is not that *telnet* is the best protocol for using TSS service of a large computer. Even *telnet* has various functions, there are cases which cannot be solved by *telnet* itself, which will be mentioned in detail in the following. As for *ftp*, there are some problems with the structure of files on large computers and problems with operation.

4.3. Considerations for Japanese character codes

As of now, considerations for Japanese character codes has been taken only for *telnet* client. Taking into account that *telnet* has no consideration for Japanese character codes, and that TIOP2 which is a versatile I/O program for TSS of VOS3 has powerful character code conversion facility, we decided to allocate code conversion

---
† UNIX is a trademark of Bell Laboratories.

to TIOP2 and nullify the code conversion performed by *telnet* server. This is also convenient for displaying graphics on terminals through the network.

As for file transfer with *ftp*, Japanese character codes are handled as binary data for the time being. *Ftp* does not take care of Japanese character codes, either.

Absense of network code for Japanese character is a problem in using TCP/IP application protocols in Japan.

4.4. An improved implementation of *telnet* client

Functions for operations across computer networks differs largely by implementations even if the same protocol is used. In the case of *telnet*, functions is determined by the implementations of both client and server.

Operation of *telnet* differs according to implementation of both client and server. In the case of accessing the CCUT main system from a telnet client on a terminal server or a computer, the features of operations will be:

(1) Attention interrupt to a task, which would be generated by pressing BREAK key on a dumb terminal connected by serial line, is gererated by sending *telnet* BREAK command. The operation of sending *telnet* BREAK command depends on the implementation of the *telnet* client.

(2) Erasing character or killing line is performed by TIOP2, by sending an appropriate control character.

(3) Character echo is performed, even in the case of typing a password. On a vendor supported terminal, echo is suppressed in that case.

The author made an attempt to improve the telnet client implementation of 4.3BSD UNIX as follows.

(1) Attention interrupt to a task will be generated by typing interrupt character of *tty* driver.
In *localchars* mode which is inconsistent with line-buffered mode, a *telnet* BREAK command could be sent by typing interrupt charcter.

(2) Line-buffered mode operation is selected to allow local line editing.
Telnet client can control the character echo in line-buffered mode to erase a character displayed on the screen if the character is cancelled. The author used the line editing facilities of the *new tty* driver of 4.2BSD or 4.3BSD UNIX. A word cancel is also available with new tty driver.

(3) Character echo is suppressed in case of typing a password.
Implementation of this facitility is indefinite. Current implementation is based upon such behavior of the server that a special code is sent in the case character echo would be suppressed on a vendor supported video display terminal. A noecho option for negotiation should be sent from the server for more general implementaion.

4.5. File transfer facilities

File transfer facilities which are provided as a command is inconvenient. *Remote file access* mechanism, which is a more transparent style of file transfer, should be introduced, while implementation of such mechanism will need some modification of the operation system.

5. Internetworking of local area networks and wide area networks

5.1. Categories of interconnections

Taking into account that large computers will be accessed from a terminal or a computer which is connected to a local area network, internetworking of local area networks and wide area networks is an important issue.

We assume that X.25 packet switching network is used for long haul connections. If the local area network is an X.25 packet switching network, internetworking between them will be accompished by CCITT X.75 approach.[Weir80] But, if the LAN protocol, or strictly speaking, if the network layer protocol of the LAN is connectionless, internetworking strategy with X.25 packet switching network becomes more complicated. The LAN protocol may be either TCP/IP, or a protocol based on OSI connectionless protocols, *e.g.* MAP, TOP.

Internetworking of networks with incompatible network architecuture involves a few categories of interconnection.[Zoline85] Here, we seek for the connection of subnetworks with different network layer protocol.

Interconnection of LAN and WAN will be classified in three categories. The first two categories belong to internetwork approach, and the last one to gatewaying approach.

(1) Connection between adjacent X.25 network layers

In this case, network layer protocol of the LAN is X.25, and CCITT X.75 approach is applicable for this case. Since LAN protocol standards are designed to allow coexistence of more than one protocols, it makes sense that both X.25 and another protocol, possibly connectionless, are used as network layer protocol of the LAN. There is another case that X.25 connection is realized on a higher layer of the LAN.

(2) Connection through networks including at least one network using connectionless network layer

It is assumed that an internetworking protocol is used as the network layer protocol through out the connection. The internetworking protocol may be either that of TCP/IP or OSI internetworking protocol (ISO DIS 8473). If the both ends of communication are LAN using the same connectionless network layer protocol, it is the case of using X.25 network as a data link between two LANs.

(3) Connection through a gateway between X.25 and the LAN protocol.

This is the case of realizeing interconneciton of networks in a higher layer than network layer. For example, if the LAN protocol is TCP/IP and connection between a non-packet terminal on X.25 packet switching network and a terminal on the LAN is realized by a gateway between X.28 (X.3 PAD) and telnet.

5.2. Wide area network based on internetwork protocol

A great deal of computing resources in universities will be connected to LANs. It would be useful, if all LANs are interconnected as a single computer network. Internetwork protocols are used to integrate networks with either connection-mode or connectionless-mode network layer services as subnetwork of an interconnected network. The category of connection is the second one of the classification above. *IP* (Internet Protocol) of TCP/IP protocol suite is such an internetwork protocol. Local area networks using TCP/IP protocol suite can be connected together using leased lines or X.25 packet switching networks.

The situation will remain the same if OSI protocols are introduced. LAN protocols based on OSI including TOP and MAP tend to have connectionless network layer services. OSI internetwork protocol (ISO DIS 8473) will be used instead of IP in that case.

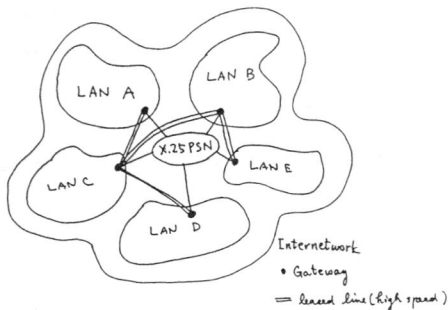

Fig. 9 Interconnection of LANs and WANs

Fig. 9 shows how LANs are interconnected with WANs which are either X.25 packet switching network or leased lines. Each gateway between WAN and LAN performs routing of datagrams. It will be necessary to use high speed digital lines for LAN to LAN connection to suffice the demands for higher data transfer rate. Since it is too expensive to establish a complete connection of high speed digital lines between all LANs, datagrams should be relayed by gateways reach the destination. Those gateways constitute a wide area packet switching network with datagram service. Routing of packets will be an important issue if the topology of the network become complex.

However, if X.25 packet switching network which suffice the requirement of higher speed were available, we could use it.

6. Conclusion

In Japan, Science Information Network will provide an nation-wide infrastructure for digital communication in universities. On the other hand, local area networks will be constructed in most universities. Large computers in universities will remain important computing resources for reseachers. Interconnection between wide area network and local area network will be one of the most important issues on computer networking in universities.

Acknowledgement

The author would like to appreciate people who helped preparation of the paper. Prof. Ishida supplied me helpful materials. Dr. J. Murai gave me useful advice for writing this paper. Mr. K. Tanaka helped me with preparing the camera ready.

References

IEEE83.
  IEEE, "Draft IEEE standarf IEEE 802.3: CSMA/CD Access Method," *Draft F*, IEEE Project 802 Local Area Network Standards, Jul. 1983.

Inose78.
  H. Inose, S. Asano, K. Hasebe, T. Sakai, H. Kitagawa, K. Tabata, and M. Kato, "User Level Protocols for and Field Trial on the Experimental Inter-University Computer Center Network in Japan," *Proceedings of Forth International Conference on Computer Communication (ICCC)*, pp. 507-512, Kyoto, 1978.

Inose80.
  H. Inose, "Development of Interuniversity Computer Network in Japan," *Research on Scientific Information Systems in Japan.*, University of Tokyo, 1980.

Inose79.
  H. Inose, *An Introduction to Digital Integrated Computer System*, University of Tokyo, 1979.

Inose81.
  H. Inose, "Researches on Experiments for Operation of the Inter-University Computer Network," *Technical Report*, University of Tokyo, 1981.

Inose76.
  H. Inose, T. Sakai, M. Kato, and S. Asano, "Networking for Inter-University Computer Centers in Japan," *Proceedings of Third International Conference on Computer Communication (ICCC)*, Toronto, 1976.

Kawabata83.
  T. Kawabata, Y. Sano, and H. Takimoto, "An Optical Ring Type Local Network which Connects Bus Type Networks," *NIKKEI ELECTRONICS*, vol. 12.5, 1983.

Kawabata79.
  T. Kawabata and H. Tanaka, "The Concept and Examples of a Distributed Computer System with a High-Speed Ring Data," *IFAC Workshop on DCCS*, Oct. 1979.

Kuniyoshi87.
  K. Kuniyoshi, K. Konishi, and N. Yazaki, "Generic Routing Method of TOTAL-LAN RING," *proceedings International Workshop on Industrial Automation Systems*, Tokyo, Feb. 1987.

Murai87.
  J. Murai and A. Kato, "Researched in Network Developement of JUNET," *Proceedings of ACM SIGCOMM Workshop 87*, Stowe, Vermont, Aug. 1987.

NACSIS86.
  NACSIS, *National Center for Science Information System*, Jul. 1986.

Protocols85.
  Research Group for Protocols, "Network Virtual Terminal Protocol," *Technical Report*, Apr. 1985.

Sakata87.
  M. Sakata and et. al., "Constitution of Interuniversity Electronic Mail System," *Proceedings of the 35th Annual Convention*, IPSJ, Sapporo, Sep. 1987.

Weir80.
  D. F. Weir, J. B. Holmblad, and A. C. Rothberg, "An X.75 Based Network Architecture," *Proceedings of the 5th International Conference on Computer Communication*, Atlanta, Georgia, Oct. 1980.

Zoline85.
  K. O. Zoline and W. P. Lidinsky, "An Approach for Interconnecting SNA and XNS Networks," *SIGCOMM 85*, pp. 184-198, 1985.

The SIGMA Network

Kimio Saito

SIGMA Project
Information-technology Promotion Agency, Japan

ABSTRACT

The Sigma network is one of the most important element of the Sigma system which is designed to improve productivity of a software.

The Sigma network has been developed in order to establish a infrastructure which acts as development environment provided by logically integrated Sigma workstations spread over various companies and inside the companies which approve the concept of the Sigma system. It is also included in the scope of its development to enrich application programs mainly for message communication required by network community.

The network supports IEEE802.3, digital packet exchange (X.25) and serial line under the TCP/IP layer and realizes end-to-end immediate communication.

Sigma network is a name oriented virtual network defined by hierarchical name space (domain) and named objects placed under the domains. Its key feature lies in the network management mechanism, i.e. Name Server.

1. Introduction

1.1. Overview of Sigma system

The Sigma network[1] is the basis for constructing the "infrastructure for software development" aimed at by the Sigma system. Before dealing with the network itself, an overview of the Sigma system, the parent of this network is introduced.

The Sigma system[2] is planned to improve software development productivity responding to the software crisis in Japan. Investment will be 25 billion yen ($165 million) for five years of development from 1985.

The Sigma project has been established in the Information-technology Promotion Agency, a quasi government organization. The project consists of more than 50 engineers from private companies, and manages planning, design, and development of the system.

There are over 175 companies participating in the Sigma Project. They are mainframe manufacturers, workstation manufacturers, common carrier, software houses and DP service companies, etc. This also includes more than 10 foreign based companies.

The Sigma system consists of four components: Sigma OS / Sigma WS, Sigma network, Sigma tools, and Sigma center.

Sigma OS/WS

Sigma OS[3] is an operating system based on UNIX† with the modifications for Japanese language processing capability, communication functions, multi-media windows, and graphics functions. Table 1.1.1 shows capabilities of the Sigma workstation (WS) which aims at one-man workstation.

Table 1.1.1 Hardware Requirement of Prototype Sigma WS

[Control mechanism]	
CPU	32-bit internal registers
Floating point	A floating point calculation mechanism is necessary, internal expression is IEEE format
Main memory	4MB(minimum)
Logical area	8MB(minimum)
[File mechanism]	
Hard disk	Minimum user area 20MB
Floppy disk	5" (2HD) and 8" (2D) for data transfer
For back-up	System must have back-up functions
[Display mechanism]	
CRT resolution	Graphics display: 1024 x 768 dots or more
	Text display (Kanji: 24 x 24 dots): 40 characters x 24 lines
Keyboard	Key layout is JIS standard
	10 function keys(minimum)
Mouse	Two or more buttons

† UNIX is a trademark of Bell Laboratories.

Printer interface   not specified by Sigma OS-V0
[External interfaces]
  Serial interface   Two RS232C (V. 24)(minimum)
  Parallel interface   Centronics interface (option)
  LAN interface   IEEE 802.3 standard
  Interface for DDX-P   V.28 (X. 21 bis) or V.11 (X.21)
  GPIB interface   For Sigma ICE interface (option)
[Copy prevention mechanism]
                         (Considering hardware mechanism)

Currently, prototype workstations are being developed by the major manufacturers, and approximately 200 Sigma workstations are already being used.

Sigma Network

The main role of the Sigma network is the basis for the distributed software development environment and also to promote the flow of information among industries and technical staffs.

Sigma Tools

The Sigma WS is equipped with many software tools for improving software development productivity and quality. The Sigma tools consist of "common tools" used widely for such tasks as text preparation, product management, project management, etc., and "application tools" used for the support of specific application areas such as business, science, and microcomputer field.

Sigma Center

This is the operation center for the Sigma system. It will offer a data base retrieval service and downloading of Sigma tools, etc., through the Sigma network.

The Sigma center will serve as a network information center for the Sigma network and will prepare the data needed for network operation such as user management information.

Development of the Sigma system is proceeding according to the schedule shown in Table 1.1.2. Design and programming of the system have already been completed and we are currently looking at the peak of comprehensive testing. From the fourth quarter of 1987 we will be recruiting monitors to evaluation and improve the system while test running it.

Table 1.1.2 Schedule

Fiscal year	1986			1987				88 and after	
	II	III	IV	I	II	III	IV	I	II
Product	Development of Sigma prototype system							Monitor testing	
Sigma Network	Function design	Production and testing		Comprehensive test I					
Sigma OS (Sigma WS)	Function design	Production and testing			Comprehensive test II			Upgrading and Modification	
Common tools		Function design	Production and testing		Comprehensive test I				
Application tools		Function design	Production and testing						
Sigma center		Function design	Production and testing		Comprehensive test I				

1.2. Overview of Sigma Network

The Sigma network has the configuration shown in Figure 1.2.1. The user companies are called the "user sites" and development environment is created which links many Sigma workstations by LAN or serial lines.

The various user sites are inter-connected by a wide network to provide communication between user sites and to construct a development environment which encompasses multiple user sites. The Sigma network is this amalgamation of many user sites and many networks.

The control mechanism for the network is also fully decentralized. Thus, the role of the Sigma Center is not network management but to participate in the Sigma network, and to provide its own services to users such as data base services and the downloading of tools.

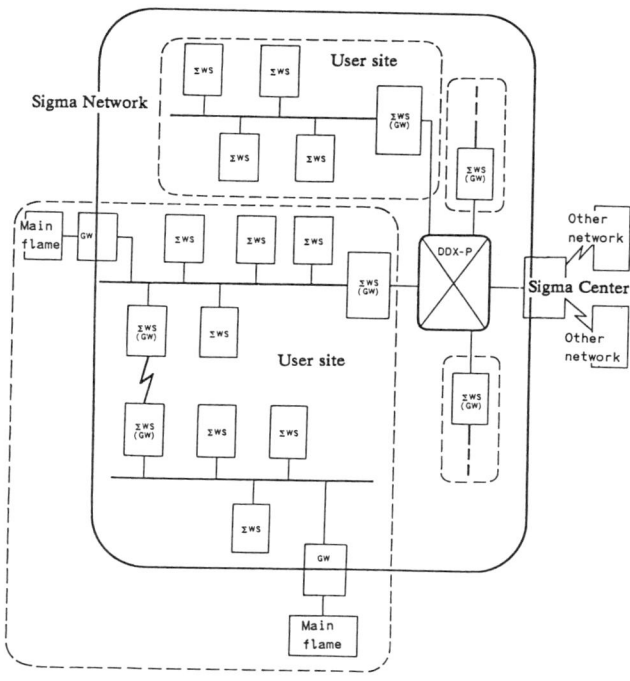

Figure 1.2.1 Network Configuration

The Sigma network is a non-volunteer network between companies and within companies, and the following concepts form the pillars of its realization.

The Sigma network consists of two "instruments": the "instrument" consisting of constituent materials such as workstations and gateways linked by communication protocols and communication lines, and the world of the network as seen by the users as an "instrument".

In order to realize the former, there is Sigma OS as the lower level of the network, the Sigma workstations, LAN and DDX networks, and TCP/IP and UDP/IP protocols.

The network world realized by Sigma is a virtual world close to the life environment of actual society, separate from physical components such as the workstations and communication lines. In this world, there are offices, there are organizations, and there are people, and these communication with each other, do work, and supply services (Figure 1.2.2).

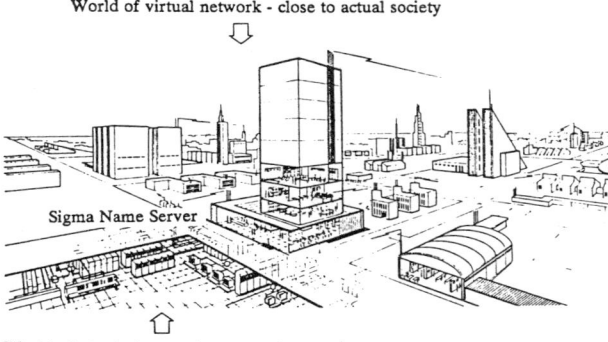

Figure 1.2.2 Image of Virtual Network

The world of this virtual network is based on the concept of hierarchical name space (domain) and name servers to manage the domain structures.[4] The basic concept of the Sigma Network, and in order to realize this, the Sigma name server[5] and network applications exist as the upper level of the network. The upper and lower levels of the network are connected by the socket interface as shown in Figure 1.2.3.

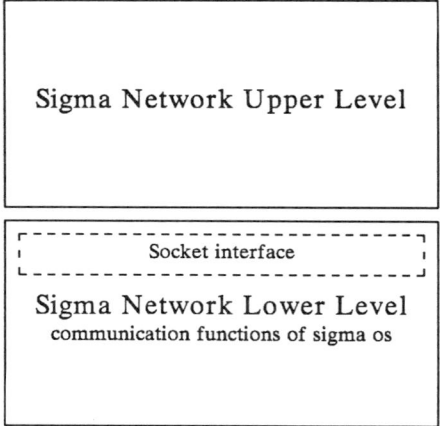

Figure 1.2.3 Upper and Lower Levels of Network

The world of the virtual network consists of two major elements. The first is similar to organizations such as companies, operation divisions, departments, sections, sub-sections, etc. These organizations are called "domains". A domain can be considered to be a single virtual computer. The uppermost domain in the hierarchical organization is the "user site", and this corresponds to a company in actual society. The Sigma Center and networks other than Sigma can be treated as special user sites lacking a Sigma Name Server.

The other constituent element is objects to be accessed. These are the three types of resources: "services", "users", and "files". These resources are established independently for each domain.

Rather than from a physical host, the user receives services supplied from the logical amalgamation of the domain, communicates with people (users), and uses files for totally natural use of the network.

Domains and services, users, and files within the domains are defined using the functions of the name server. The range which the user can access within the defined environment can be freely defined as only within a certain domain, only within the user site, or as public, etc.

The naming conventions in BNF format for domains, systems, users, files (including directories), and services are given below.

Table 1.2.1 The Naming Conventions

```
1:  <subspace_specification>       ::=  <domain_specification>
                                      | <system_specification>

2:  <domain_specification>         ::=  <domain_name> "." <domain_specification>
                                      | <domain_name>

3:  <system_specification>         ::=  <system_name> "." <domain_specification>

4:  <domain_name>                  ::=  <name>

5:  <system_name>                  ::=  <name>

6:  <service_name>                 ::=  <name>

7:  <network_user_specification>   ::=  <virtual_user_specification>
                                      | <local_user_specification>

8:  <virtual_user_specification>   ::=  <virtual_user_name> "@" <domain_specification>
                                      | <local_user_name> "@" <domain_specification>

9:  <local_user_specification>     ::=  <local_user_name> "@" <domain_specification>

10: <network_file_specification>   ::=  <virtual_file_specification>
                                      | <local_file_specification>

11: <virtual_file_specification>   ::=  <virtual_path_specification> "@" <domain_specification>

12: <local_file_specification>     ::=  <local_path_specification> "@" <domain_specification>

13: <virtual_path_specification>   ::=  <virtual_path_name> "/" <virtual_directory_name>
                                      | <virtual_path_name> "/" <virtual_file_name>
                                      | <virtual_path_name>

14: <virtual_path_name>            ::=  <virtual_path_name> "/" <virtual_directory_name>
                                      | <virtual_directory_name>

15: <virtual_directory_name>       ::=  <kanji_name>
                                      | NONE

16: <virtual_file_name>            ::=  <kanji_name>

17: <local_path_specification>     ::=  <local_path_name> "/" <local_directory_name>
                                      | <local_path_name> "/" <local_file_name>
                                      | <local_path_name>

18: <local_path_name>              ::=  <local_path_name> "/" <local_directory_name>
                                      | <local_directory_name>

19: <local_directory_name>         ::=  <kanji_name>
                                      | NONE

20: <local_file_name>              ::=  <kanji_name>

21: <kanji_name>                   ::=  <kanji_name> <ascii_character>
                                      | <kanji_name> <kanji_character>
                                      | <ascii_character>
                                      | <kanji_character>

22: <name>                         ::=  <name> <ascii_character>
                                      | <ascii_character>
```

2. Lower level of network

The lower level of the network is realized by the communication functions of the Sigma OS. The Sigma network uses TCP/IP and UDP/IP and these are on ETHERNET, NTT's X.25 packet network DDX-P, or a serial line. Communication with these is through the SOCKET interface. IP packet routing allows at least 10 hops. With X.25, connections are made using a virtual circuit.

Route selection and the data necessary for connection does not use /etc/hosts, networks, gateways, etc., but uses the RFC952[6] based inter-net routing data /etc/inet.txt and the DDX-P number table /etc/dteaddr.txt of the site information table described later.

The basic communication functions provided by Sigma OS-V0 are shown in Figure 2.1, and the supplied physical levels and data link levels are divided into the following three.

Serial line (SLIP)

Connection to telephone lines and dedicated lines is through a start-stop full-duplex V.24 (RS-232C) interface. The call procedure for automatic call conforms to V.52bis and provides a TTY interface the same as conventional UNIX. Furthermore, there is connection to IP modules through a packet module.

Local Area Network (LAN)[7,8]

Connection to a local area network (LAN) is by an IEEE 802.3 (CSMA/CD system) interface. Connection to IP modules is through a LAN address management module.

Digital packet exchange network (X.25)[9]

Connection to digital packet exchange networks is through X.21 and V.24 interfaces with the NTT's DDX-P digital packet exchange protocol uses (conforms to CCITT 1980 X.25 protocol). This connects with applications through the socket interface and to IP modules through the X.25 address management module.

A Sigma WS connected to a digital packet exchange network through the X.25 multi-link function is capable of being simultaneously connected to multiple Sigma WS through the network.

These connect the IP modules through packet module and address modules and to the UDP and TCP modules in the upper level. The UDP and TCP modules are connected to application programs and commands through the socket interface.

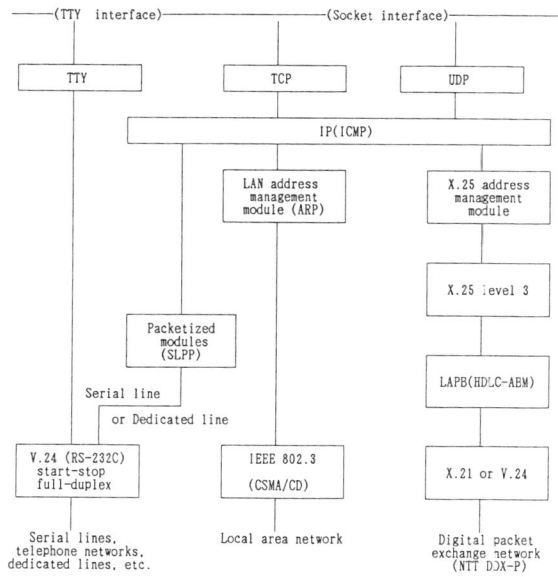

Figure 2.1 Lower level of network

3. Upper level of network

As shown in Figure 3.1, the upper level of the network consists of the network management mechanism[10] consisting of commands for network environment construction and environment inquiry and the name server, and the network application programs[11] making up the majority of the communication services.

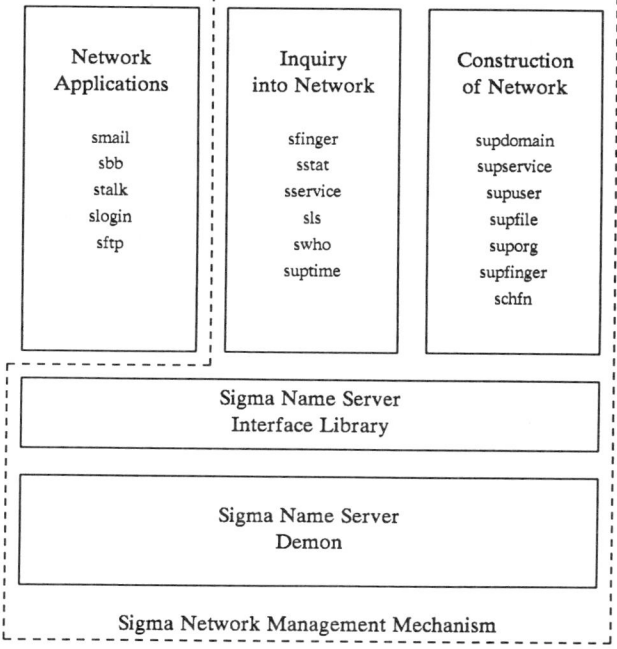

Figure 3.1 Upper Level of Network

3.1. Network management mechanism

The Sigma network is a virtual network based on the concept that there is a virtual computer in all domains and that the users use the services (applications) on this virtual computer.

Existing networks show that the major characteristics of a network are determined by its name server.[12,13,14,15,16,17,18]

The Sigma Name Server exists in all domains and has the following functions for constructing the virtual network.

1) Functions for constructing, maintaining, and managing the domain.

2) Functions for defining, maintaining, and managing services supplied by domain.

3) Functions for defining, maintaining, and managing the users (people) and files which are the virtual resources of the domain.

4) Security management functions for protecting these from unauthorized access.

5) Various inquiry and response functions for the virtual network.

6) Address determination and various interface functions with the name server needed for application programs to run in the virtual network environment.

3.1.1. Communications models

The services (distributed applications) in the Sigma System are realized through the so-called "client server model", and normally, communications are through the socket. However, for operation on the virtual network created by the Sigma Name Server, the communication model si as follows for selection of the connection destination.

The address (inter-net address and port number) of the server to be connected with is inquired to the Sigma Name Server by the cliant program using the designated domain name and service name as inquiry keys. This is the "basic communications model" (Figure 3.1.1.1).

For services which handle virtual resources (users and files), it is necessary to assume that the host for which the virtual resource is defined (Sigma workstation) is different from the host where the resource actually exists.

In other words, the client first makes a service request to the server of the target domain. When the domain server receives a request for virtual resources defined for it, checks the actual location of the resource. If it finds the resource does not exist in its host, it relays the service request to the proper host. Another option would be that the server notifies the client of the information it found and the client makes connection with the proper server based upon this information. These are referred to the "relay-type communication model" (Figure 3.1.1.2) and "re-connection communication model" (Figure 3.1.1.3) respectively.

In general, the relay-type communication model is appropriate for services which access multiple resources in a given domain one after the other.

The re-connection communication model is appropriate for services which can work only with the host having the actual resource once the actual location of the virtual resource has become known.

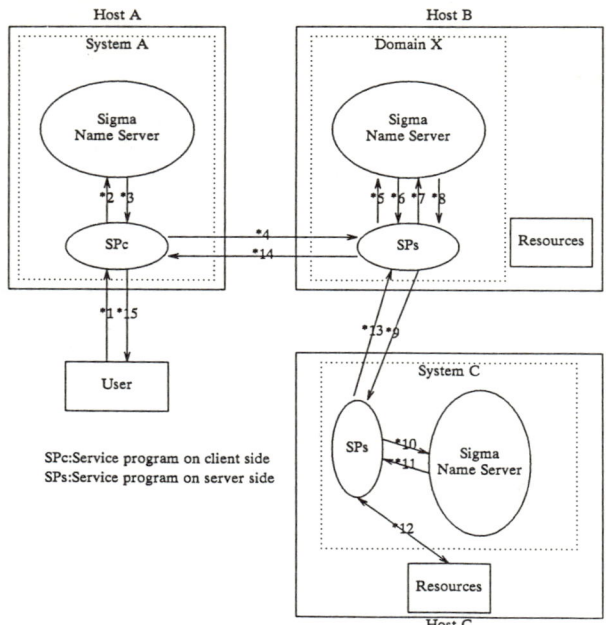

Figure 3.1.1.2 Relay-type communication model

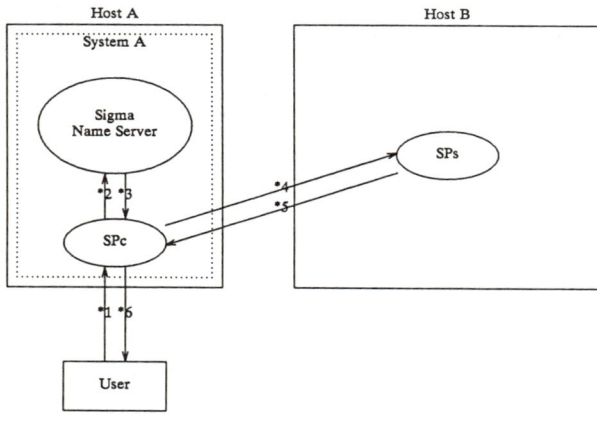

Figure 3.1.1.1 Basic communication model

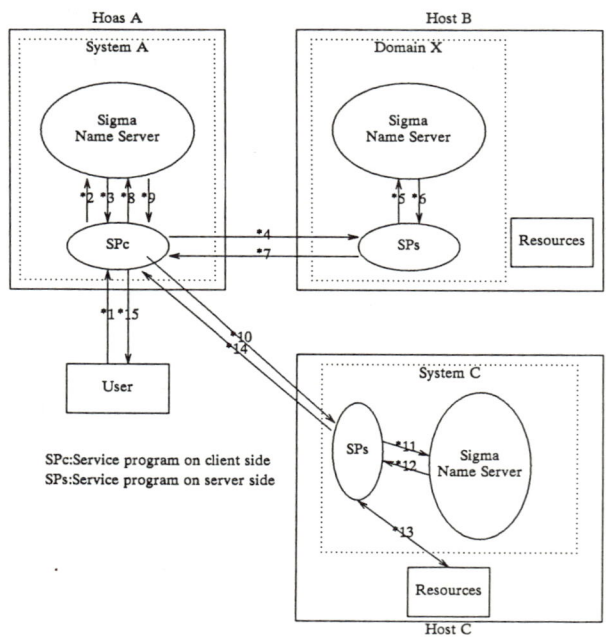

Figure 3.1.1.3 Re-connection communication model

3.1.2. Application Interface

The Sigma Name Server supplies an interface library between name server applications to make sure that the service programs (distributed applications) are properly connected between clients and servers.

Table 3.1.2.1 Sigma Name Server and Interface Functions

Inquiry into server address (sigma_inet_adr)
: Address of desired server is inquired with the target domain or names of system and service as key.

Create data for authentication (sigma_map_in)
: Data for authentication is created in the transmission buffer.

Inquiry into address for reception of service (sigma_servent)
: The address of the service to be received in the host is requested with the service name as key.

Development of data for authentication (sigma_map_out)
: Data for authentication is taken from reception buffer and developed.

Authentication between client and server (sigma_authent)
: An authentication check is requested for the name server based on the authentication data.

Copy authentication data (sigma_authcpy)
: The authentication data is copied.

Inquiry into name and address of own system (sigma_gethostname)
: The system name and address of own host are requested.

Inquiry into actual information on user (sigma_ustat)
: An inquiry is made from the virtual user name into the actual host where the user exists and the name within the host.

Inquiry into actual information on file (sigma_fstat)
: An inquiry is made from the virtual file name into the actual host where the file exists and the name within the host.

Inquiry into virtual files under virtual directory (sigma_flist)
: An inquiry is made from the virtual directory name into the list of files positioned under it.

Maintain connection with name server (sigma_open)
: A connection with the name server is established and this connection is maintained until sigma_close is called.

Release connection with name server (sigma_close)
: The connection with the name server established and maintained by sigma_open is released.

The following takes a situation appropriate to the basic communication model as an example and explains how services are realized by following the procedure from both the client program of the application and server program sides.

(1) Server program stand-by

The server operates as a demon process in order to receive requests from the Sigma workstations comprising the Sigma System. After the server is invoked by the "file for initial setting for boot", it asks the Sigma Name Server at what address (inter-net address and port number) it can receive services (sigma_servent). Then, it waits for connection requests from the client at that address.

(2) Establishment of connection between client and server

The client is invoked by user command input or from another program. After being invoked, the client asks the Sigma Name Server for the connection address taking the designated domain or system name and service name of the client itself as the key (sigma_inet_adr). Then, it makes a connection request for that address.

(3) Creation of service execution process

When the server receives the connection request from the client, it generates a process for execution of the process. This is for efficient processing when the service receives service requests from multiple clients. Subsequently, the newly generated process (service execution process) responds to the request and the original server process waits for a request for a new, separate client. In other words, after this service execution process is generated, the original server process and newly generated service execution process operate independently of each other.

(4) Authentication between client and server

Next, a check is made whether the client is actually connected to the desired service and that it has the security for connection. The procedure for this is authentication between the client and server.

In order to make this authentication, the client sends the authentication data received from the Sigma Name Server to the server (service execution process) immediately after establishment of the connection with the server (sigma_map_in).

The service execution process sets the authentication data received from the client to the Sigma Name Server to confirm that it is actually a request for itself (sigma_map_out, sigma_authent).

If the request from the client is correctly a request for the server, the service execution process accepts the request from the client and executes it, but if the connection is not correct or by mistake, this is indicated to the client and the connection is released.

When the client receives the report of the improper connection from the server, the client makes another server address inquiry to the Sigma Name Server without use of the cache information, clearly indicating that the search is based on new information, and tries to establish a connection.

(5) Service request and execution

After the client makes an actual service request after the client/server connection described above is established and there has been authentication between client and server. The service execution command accepts the service request from the client, executes the service, and answers the client.

(6) Releasing connection between client and server

After execution of the service, both the client and service execution process release the connection and the process is terminated.

For example, the procedure for inquiring into the address of the other server and making the connection is shown in Figure 3.1.2.1 and Figure 3.1.2.2.

3.1.3. Security

The Sigma Name Server has separate access lists for domains and their services, users, directories, and files for the protection of secrecy.

As protection of secrecy for these and information managed by the Sigma Name Server is realized in the interface functions with the Sigma Name Service, there is need for this awareness in distributed applications.

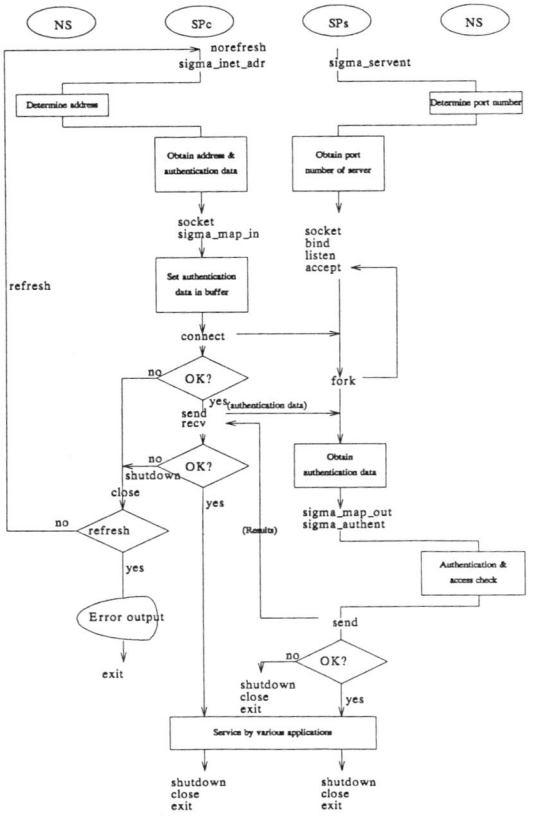

Figure 3.1.2.1 Example of Virtual Circuit Basic Communication Model

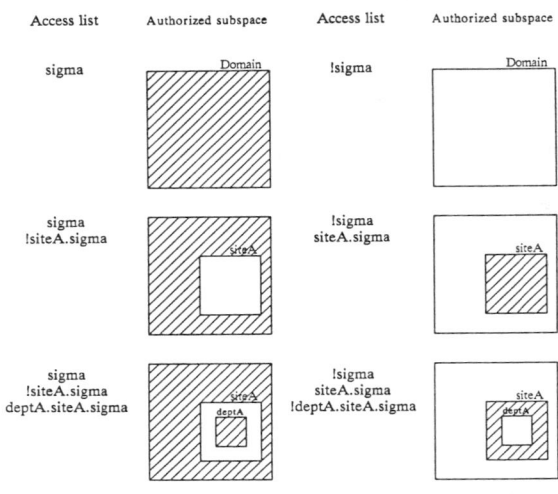

Figure 3.1.3.1 Examples of Access Lists

(1) Secrecy protection functions for domains

In these secrecy protection functions, there are limitations on access of a domain from other domains. That is, when access of a domain is not authorized, all services in that domain are refused.

(2) Secrecy protection functions for services

In these secrecy protection functions, there are limitations on access of services from other domains. That is, when access of a certain service of a certain domain is not authorized, the supply of that service refused.

(3) Secrecy protection functions for users and files

In these secrecy protection functions, access of the essential information on virtual users and virtual files of a designated domain is limited. That is, when access of certain information is not authorized, access of the user or file itself is refused.

```
refresh = NS_NOREFRESH;
for(;;) {
    ns_data = NULL;
    ns_inet = sigma_inet_adr(service, domain, refresh, &ns_data);
    if (ns_inet == NULL ) {
        fprintf(stderr, "sxxxx : sigma_inet_adr: %s¥n", ns_errlst[ns_errno]);
        exit(1);
    }
    s = socket(AF_INET, SOCK_STREAM, 0);
    if (s < 0 ) {
        perror("sxxxx : socket");
        exit(1);
    }
    if (connect(s, (char *)&(ns_inet->ad_addrin), sizeof(ns_inet->ad_addrin)) >= 0 )
        break;
    close(s);
    if ( ns_inet-> ad_cache != NS_USEDCACHE ) {
        perror("sxxxx : connect");
        exit(1);
    }
    refresh = NS_REFRESH;
      .
      .
```

Figure 3.1.2.2 Coding Example for Server Address Determination

3.2. Network services

In regards to network services, in addition to the five types of network applications, there are 13 environmental construction and inquiry commands available as the network management mechanism.

All of these network services are original services exclusively for the Sigma network, realized by TCP or UDP while interfacing with the Name Server.

Table 3.2.1 Network Services

[Network applications]
  Electronic mail (smail)
    Instant electronic mail service equipped with code and folder functions
  Electronic bulletin board (sbb)
    Equipped with folder functions and closed area services
  Electronic conversation (stalk)
    Equipped with multi-window group conferences and multi-user communication functions
  Virtual terminal (slogin)
    Remote log-in to other workstations
  File transfer (sftp)
    Can handle both virtual directories and virtual files in the domain

[Inquiry into virtual network environment]
  Individual/organization inquiry (sfinger)
    Who's who service for individuals and organizations
  Domain inquiry (sstat)
    Inquiry into subordinate domains
  Service inquiry (sservice)
    Inquiry into services registered in domain
  File inquiry (sls)
    Inquiry into virtual directories and virtual files in the domain
  User inquiry (swho)
    Network version of who
  Operation inquiry (suptime)
    Inquiry into operating status of workstation

[Construction of network environment]
  Domain definition (supdomain)
    Registration, update, or deletion of name area
  Service definition (supservice)
    Registration, update, or deletion of service entry
  Virtual user definition (supuser)
    Registration, update, or deletion of user in domain
  Virtual file definition (supfile)
    Registration, update, or deletion of file system in domain
  Organization information definition (suporg)
    Registration, update, or deletion of organization information
  Individual information definition (supfinger)
    Registration or deletion of individual information on user
  Individual information update (schfn)
    Update detailed individual information on user

The smail (electronic mail) has bi-directional compatibility with non-Sigma machines possessing SMTP[19] or UUCP. The slogin and sftp allow connection with non-Sigma machines equipped with TELNET[20] or FTP.[21] The smail can freely exchange electric mails with JUNET.[22]

Sigma Workstation		Non-Sigma
Electronic mail (smail)		
ssendmail	<—SMTP—>	semdmail
ssendmail —> uucp	—UUCP—>	rmail
ssendmail <— rmail	<—UUCP—	uucp
Remote login		
slogin	—TELNET—>	telnetd
(telnetd	<—TELNET—	telnet)
File transfer		
sftp	—FTP—>	ftpd
(ftpd	<—FTP—	ftp)

Figure 3.2.1 Inter-connection between Sigma and Non-Sigma

4. Network operation

4.1. Application procedure and site information table

When joining the Sigma network, the necessary items on the "Sigma System Application Form" are filled in and application procedure is carried out. The procedure establishes the user site name, network address, gateway address, DTE number in DDX, and representative name server address, etc.

In the Sigma Center, four types of "site information table"[23] needed for realizing communication between sites in the Sigma network, gateway routing, and connection with external networks, etc., are prepared based on the application information, and are batch transferred to all user sites as required. Delivery is by the following procedure.

* When there is a change in a table, the site is notified on the electronic bulletin board or by mail, etc.

* The site operator makes connection to the Sigma Center by FTP if required, and the table is transferred to the site.

* Data is distributed in full form (complete new tables); it is not distributed as partial data.

After the application procedure has been completed and table has been received, the network environment is created within the user site without the association of the Sigma Center and operation of a network within the site and between sites is possible.

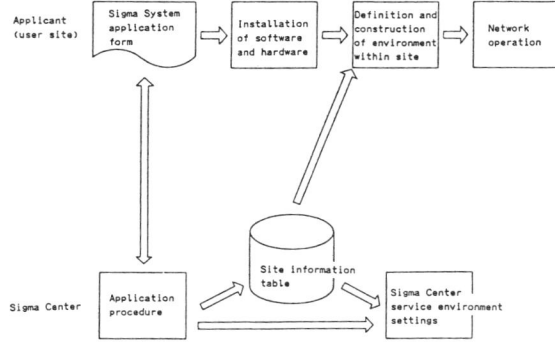

Figure 4.1.1 Application procedure

The site information tables consists of the following four.

Inter-net routing table (/etc/inet.txt)

This contains mainly the site inter-net address and gateway inter-net address, etc., information needed for routine, and the name of the networks, etc. This is essential for Sigma WS which are gateways.

Format
```
NET : inet-addr : net-name :
     :
GATEWAY : inet-addr, inet-addr,... : gateway-name : : : :
     :
```

DDX-P number table (/etc/dteaddr.txt)

This is the DDX subscriber number table. This is essential for Sigma WS connected to DDX.

Format
```
gateway-name : DDXP : dte_addr, dte_addr,... :
     :
```

Inter-net name server table (/usr/ns/inet_ns.txt)

This is the name server address table for the top domain of each user site. This is essential for Sigma WS positioned as top domain name servers.

Format
```
OURNET :: SIGMA :
SITE : inet_adr : site-name :
     :
```

External service table (/usr/ns/ext_services.txt)

This contains the service entry information for accessing networks lacking a Sigma name area and named resource system, ie. networks without a name server (Sigma Center, external networks, etc.). This is essential for Sigma WS positioned as top domain name servers.

Format
```
domain-pass-name, domain-pass-alias,... : service-name
                : inet_addr/port-no/protocol :
     :
```

4.2. Environment construction

The Name Server Install Menu is used to construct the network environment within the user site. Object information on domain attributes and subordinate services, users, and files are placed in a data base distributed to the various domains.

1. system install
2. create database
3. create site information
4. create top domain
5. create finger database
6. check environment
7. quit

Figure 4.2.1 Name Server Install Menu

Using the Install Menu, these database can be registered for each host in a single operation and the environment is created. Subsequent maintenance and management is performed using the individual network construction commands.

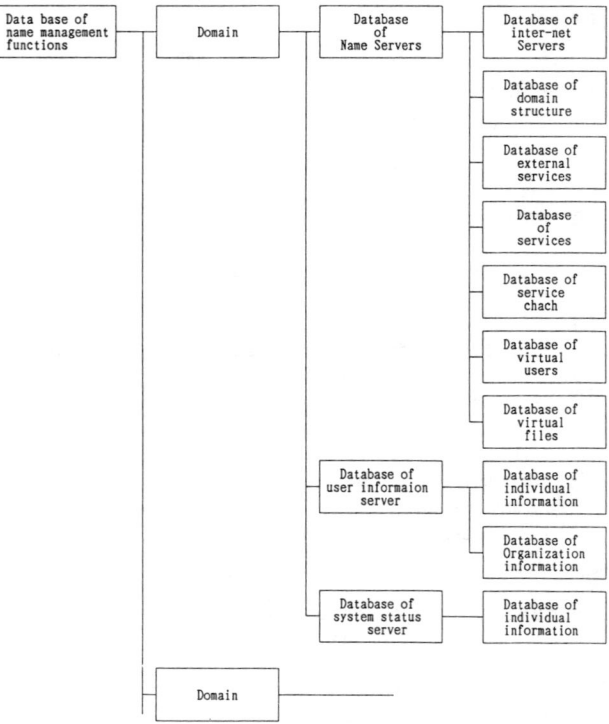

Figure 4.2.2 Domain Data Base System

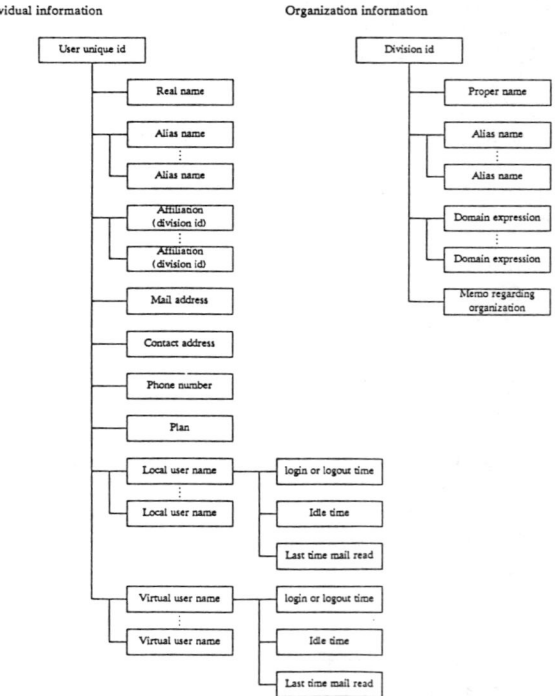

Figure 4.2.3 Outline of sfinger Database for Individual and Organization Information

5. Conclusion

Although the above concentrated mainly on the upper level of the network, the aim of the Sigma network is to establish the basis of a decentralized environment which will spread rapidly in the future, while of course spreading the message communications described in network applications.

The spread of a decentralized environment in the real world means that almost all software tools must be constructed in decentralized form rather than stand-alone. There was the need for a network structure which would allow users to easily produce distributed applications and provide services and yet would be flexible and easy to operate. In this meaning, I am sure that the Sigma network supported by the network management mechanisms described in this paper fully satisfies this role.

Acknowledgement

I would like to give my deepest thanks to Dr. J. Murai of Tokyo University for his enormous guidance and advice during the planning of the Sigma network.

I would also like to express my deepest regards to Nomura Computer Systems Co.,Ltd. which was responsible for the design and development of the network management mechanism and to Oki Electric Industry Co.,Ltd. which was responsible for the design and development of the network applications.

References

1. IPA, *Sigma System Network Plan (in Japanese)*, Information-technology Promotion Agency, Japan, March 1986.

2. IPA, *Sigma System Construction Basic Plan (in Japanese)*, Information-technology Promotion Agency, Japan, December 1985.

3. IPA, *Sigma Operating System Function Specifications (in Japanese)*, Information-technology Promotion Agency, Japan, July 1986.

4. Jun Murai, "Study on Network Software in Operating Systems for Distributed Environment," *Ph.D Dissertation*, Keio University, Japan, March 1987.

5. IPA, *Survey Report on Method for Realizing Sigma System Name Server (in Japanese)*, Information-technology Promotion Agency, Japan, February 1986.

6. K.Harrenstien, M.Stahl, E.Feinler, "RFC952 DoD Internet Host Table Specification," *DDN Protocol Handbook*, vol. Three, pp. 249-254, DDN Network Information Center, SRI International, CA, October 1985.

7. I.Winston, "RFC948 Transmission of IP Datagrams over IEEE802.3 Networks," *DDN Protocol Handbook*, vol. Three, pp. 601-605, DDN Network Information Center, SRI International, CA, June 1985.

8. C.Hornig, "RFC894 Transmission of IP Datagrams over Ethernet Networks," *DDN Protocol Handbook*, vol. Three, pp. 607-609, DDN Network Information Center, SRI International, CA, April 1984.

9. J.Korb, "RFC877 Internet Protocol on X.25 Networks," *DDN Protocol Handbook*, vol. Three, pp. 573-574, DDN Network Information Center, SRI International, CA, September 1983.

10. IPA, *Specifications of Sigma Name Server and Various Information Inquiry Functions (in Japanese)*, Information-technology Promotion Agency, Japan, February 1987.

11. IPA, *Sigma Network Application Function Specifications (in Japanese)*, Information-technology Promotion Agency, Japan, March 1987.

12. D.Oppen, Y.Dalal, "The Clearinghouse:A Decentralized Agent for Locating Named Objects in a Distributed Environment," *ACM Transaction on Office Information System*, vol. 1, July 1983.

13. M.Schroeder, A.Birrell, R.Needham, "Experience with Grapevine the Growth of a Distributed Systems," *ACM SIGOPS*, 1983.

14. A.Birrell, R.Levin, R.Needham, M.Schroeder, "Grapevine:An Exercise in Distributed Computing," *Communications of the ACM*, vol. 25, April 1982.

15. L.Landweber, M.Litzkow, D.Neuhengen, M.Solomon, *Architecture of The CSNET Name Server*, ACM, 1983.

16. J.Postel, "Internet Name Server," *IEN 116*, Informatin Sciences Institute, August 1979.

17. D.Terry, M.Painter, D.Riggle, S.Zhou, "The Berkeley Internet Name Domain Server," *Report No.UCB/CSD 84/182*, May 1984.

18. P.Mockapetris, J.Postel, P.Kirton, *Name Server Design for Distributed System*, 1984.

19. J.Postel, "RFC821 Simple Mail Transfer Protocol," *DDN Protocol Handbook*, vol. Two, pp. 809-880, DDN Network Information Center, SRI International, CA, August 1982.

20. J.Postel, J.Reynolds, "RFC854 Telnet Protocol Specification," *DDN Protocol Handbook*, vol. Two, pp. 575-589, DDN Network Information Center, SRI International, CA, May 1983.

21. J.Postel, J.Reynolds, "RFC959 File Transfer Protocol (FTP)," *DDN Protocol Handbook*, vol. Two, pp. 739-807, DDN Network Information Center, SRI International, CA, October 1985.

22. Jun Murai, "Researches on Network Development in JUNET," *Proceedings of SIGCOMM 87 Workshop on Frontiers in Computer Communications Technology*, ACM, August 1987.

23. IPA, *Site Information Table Specifications for Sigma Network (in Japanese)*, Information-technology Promotion Agency, Japan, September 1986.

PART 4. EXPRES: NEAR- AND LONG-TERM IMPLICATIONS OF THE NSF SPONSORED PROJECT ON EXPERIMENTAL RESEARCH IN ELECTRONIC PROPOSAL SUBMISSION.

Al Thaler

National Science Foundation, USA

An Overview of the Andrew Message System

A Portable, Distributed System for Multi-media Electronic Communication

Jonathan Rosenberg
Craig F. Everhart
Nathaniel S. Borenstein

Information Technology Center
Carnegie Mellon University
Pittsburgh, PA 15213

July 1987

1. Introduction

This paper provides an overview of the Andrew Message System, which is in operation within the Andrew project at Carnegie Mellon University. The Andrew environment currently consists of 300 high-function workstations (typified by the IBM RT-PC) each running Berkeley Unix and attached to a large campus-wide network. A central file system provides transparently the appearance of a large, monolithic Unix file system. In addition, there are approximately 600 IBM PC's and 300 (University-owned) Apple Macintoshes that may also participate in the network.

The Andrew Message System (often referred to in this paper as the *AMS*) is a suite of programs that provides powerful mechanisms for viewing, creating and manipulating multi-media mail and bulletin board messages. The AMS is usable from both high-function Andrew workstations and low-end workstations, such as IBM PC's and Macintoshes. This paper discusses our goals in designing the message system, the primary parts of the system, some of our design decisions and a number of the problems we encountered implementing such an ambitious system in our environment. In addition, we present some directions for future work and some statistics about our system.

2. Prior Work

Although space does not permit a complete survey of previous work on message systems, a few efforts influenced our design so strongly that they should be mentioned. The Grapevine system [21, 3] first demonstrated the feasibility and utility of truly distributed electronic message systems. Malone's work on the Information Lens [15] has stimulated our interest in mechanisms for dealing with information flood, and indeed we hope to implement some of Malone's ideas in future versions of the AMS (section 6.2).

Our ideas about user interfaces have been shaped by a succession of mail and bulletin board systems, most notably TOPS-10 RdMail [13], various Emacs-based message systems, earlier Andrew systems for mail and bulletin boards [4] and interfaces to the Unix Netnews system [22, 10]. Our passion for an integrated communication environment with a coherent and clean design can be traced in large part to personal experience with communication systems lacking in these aspects [6].

Other proposals have been made for distributed mail systems. Our design of a remote protocol for message system clients may seem similar to the Post Office Protocol [7]. The similarity is superficial, however, as the Post Office Protocol (POP2) server merely provides a method for retrieving and deleting mail from a remote host. POP2 contains no support for error recovery, bulletin boards, message transmission or message database manipulation. Our more complicated remote messaging protocol provides support for all of these functions and more (section 5.3.1). Pcmail [9], a distributed mail system done at MIT, defines a still higher-level protocol for communication between a user's agent and a remote mail repository. Pcmail allows considerable separation between the user agent and the repository, and is designed to provide reasonable service even when the user agent machine is only infrequently connected to the repository. This design requires user agents to maintain local state, though, and to be able to resynchronize their local state with the repository's state. The facilities available to the Pcmail user do not include multi-media mail or as comprehensive a set of information sources as are provided by the AMS

3. Andrew

The Andrew project is a joint venture of IBM and Carnegie Mellon University, the goal of which is to produce a suitable working environment for academic use of computers. The project is described in detail in the paper by Morris et. al. [16], but a few key points are noted here.

In Andrew, each user works on a high-function workstation (currently an IBM RT, Sun 2, Sun 3 or Dec MicroVAX with 2 to 4 MB of RAM, a 1 MegaPixel bitmap display, a mouse and 40-70 MB of fixed disk local storage. Each workstation is running Berkeley Unix (or its equivalent) and is connected to a campus-wide network over which it can talk to several dedicated file server machines. Running in this environment are two basic components that make up Andrew: VIRTUE and VICE.

VIRTUE is the user interface portion, which runs on the workstation, and includes a window manager and a multi-media editor subroutine library (known as the *base editor library*). Use of the base editor library provides an easy methodology for manipulating multi-media

Permission to copy without fee all or part of this material is granted provided that the copies are not made or distributed for direct commercial advantage, the ACM copyright notice and the title of the publication and its date appear, and notice is given that copying is by permission of the Association for Computing Machinery. To copy otherwise, or to republish, requires a fee and/or specfic permission.

© 1988 ACM 0-89791-245-4/88/0001/0099 $1.50

documents. In addition, VIRTUE provides a number of application programs (a text editor, for example) that exploit the facilities offered by the base editor library.

VICE (purported to be an acronym for Vast Integrated Computing Environment) is the central file system [20]; it emulates a Unix file system, so that as users move from one workstation to another, their picture of the file system remains consistent. In VICE a client process, called Venus, runs on each workstation and acts as the user's agent in making requests of the central file system. Small modifications to the Unix kernel allow it to route remote file requests to Venus. Venus then uses a remote procedure call protocol to make requests of a server process executing on a dedicated file server.

VICE works by performing *whole file transfer*: when a file is referenced from a workstation, Venus transfers the entire file from the remote file server into a cache on the workstation's local file system. From that point on, the file is treated as a local file by the workstation operating system. Venus may be told to invalidate the cached file in the event that the remote file system has changed the copy of the file stored there. For the purposes of writing, the client process treats the local disk as a write-through cache.

The use of whole file transfer has some advantages over the alternative scheme of executing remote file read and write operations. First, once the file is transferred, remaining accesses are as fast as using a local file system. In addition, whole file transfer means that the unit of granularity in VICE is the file. This allows VICE to notify clients efficiently of invalid cache entries; a client need only be notified when an entire file is stored, not when individual records change.

Of course, there are disadvantages to whole file transfer. The most glaring problem, and the one that affects people the most, is that an entire file is transferred even if only a small portion is going to be read. Studies have shown that this is not generally a problem because most applications read all the way through a file [19]. It is clear, however, that whole file transfer is entirely inappropriate for database applications. Many of the functions provided by the AMS are database applications, and discussions of how the design of VICE affected our work will be found throughout this paper.

To provide flexible security for files, VICE allows an *access list* to be attached to each directory. These lists allows selective access to be given or denied to individual users or groups of users. The access rights allowed are read, lookup (ability to see the file names in a directory), write, delete, insert, lock (ability to lock files in the directory) and administer access.

Both major parts of Andrew have strongly influenced the design of the Andrew Message System. Each has made some parts of the system easier and some parts more difficult. VIRTUE has, through the base editor library, made it almost trivial to deal with multi-media messages,[1] but has thus introduced serious complexities into the manner in which messages are sent and received to non-Andrew systems. VICE has made it easy to create a message database that is entirely location-independent, but has introduced, by its distributed nature, new failure conditions neither expected nor dealt with

---
[1]But, see section 6.1.

robustly by software written for typical, standalone systems. In particular, the file system conceptually simplified the mail delivery mechanism, but at the same time mandated a complete replacement of the existing mail delivery programs.

The stated objective of the Andrew project was to produce an effective working environment for high-function workstations. One of the goals of the Andrew Message System was to produce software that was usable from such lower-functionality machines as IBM PC's and Apple Macintoshes, and this required that our design be more general than Andrew's, and in particular that our communication mechanisms, though based on VICE, be more general and more portable than VICE.

4. Goals of The Andrew Message System

The Andrew Message System is an ongoing project with the goal of producing a production-quality electronic communication environment with several types of functionality that hitherto either have not been provided by electronic message systems or have been found only in experimental systems. To accomplish this, we set the following subgoals:

Reliability: As users grow to rely on electronic communication, they come to expect and demand that the underlying transport systems never lose their messages. Reliability is, therefore, of the utmost importance in an electronic messaging system. While there are many reliable message systems, the task of constructing such a system in the Andrew environment was especially challenging.

Machine and location independence: The AMS should allow users to read mail and bulletin boards from virtually any kind of workstation, transparently preserving user profile information to maintain a consistent message system state.

Integrated message database: The AMS should treat mail and bulletin boards uniformly as consisting of *messages*, allowing users to manipulate both with a single interface. Thus, we can provide a small set of tools that allow the manipulation of many kinds of information.

Separation of interface from functionality: The AMS architecture should make it easy to support multiple user interfaces while preserving for each the highest functionality.

Support for multi-media communication: The AMS should support messages that include formatted text, vector graphics, raster images, equations and other multi-media objects. Of course, some of these messages will look their best only when viewed on more powerful displays.

Support for coping with information flood: There should be mechanisms in the AMS for dealing with the flood of information that increasingly overwhelms users of large electronic communication systems. The AMS should avoid performance degradation in the face of a large volume of messages from diverse sites on various networks.

Flexible Architecture: The AMS should allow for easy expansion to include various kinds of functions not yet foreseen or implemented. We believe this is accomplished by having an open-ended architecture that provides high-level manipulations of the message database as one of its services.

Flexible addressing: The AMS should allow messages to be addressed using a variety of user-friendly address forms. A user should be able to specify a recipient by user id, by name, or even by making a best guess at the user's name.

5. Parts of the Message System

The Andrew Message System consists of several separable components: the message delivery system, the white pages, the message database and message server, and the user interface programs. The *delivery system* is responsible for accepting new messages for delivery and moving them through the various delivery queues and into users' in-boxes via a collection of daemons. The *white pages* is a database and access mechanism that provides sophisticated mappings from user-specified names to final mail destinations. The *message database* is the entire collection of public and private messages. The *message server* provides a high-level program interface to these underlying components: it is the procedural interface to the message database and also provides interfaces to the validation of mail destinations (via the white pages) and to sending and receiving mail (via the delivery system). The *user interface programs* are clients of the message server (which may execute on a different machine than the message server); their task is to present the capabilities of the message server to users in a way tailored to the capabilities of their environment.

5.1. The Delivery System

The delivery system is a set of programs responsible for many of the steps involved in delivering a message. The responsibilities of the delivery system include

- acceptance of messages for delivery to and from non-Andrew systems
- construction and return of error messages to originators of messages that were victims of failed delivery
- mapping from user-specified addresses to a list of recipients
- acceptance of messages for delivery from Andrew applications (via the *dropoff interface*)
- document format translation between Andrew and non-Andrew systems

It is our belief that the most important attribute of a delivery system is reliability. For the Andrew delivery system, we define reliability as the successful *disposition* of a message at the following points:
1. When a message is accepted from another system; and
2. When an invocation of the dropoff interface succeeds.

Furthermore, a message is successfully *disposed* of when, for each recipient: the message is successfully delivered or an appropriate error message has been constructed and delivered to the originator. For Andrew recipients, successful delivery of a message consists of storing a copy of the message into the recipient's mailbox. Successful delivery to a non-Andrew system consists of transferring the message to the remote system's mail transfer agent.

While there is nothing special about this definition of reliability, there are special design and implementation problems on Andrew due to the semantics of the VICE file system. The primary complication is the fact that a remote, distributed file system provides new error modes: in particular, *temporary errors*, which are errors that will eventually succeed if retried. On a standard timesharing system with a local file system, an application program, for all practical purposes cannot see a temporary error during a file operation. With VICE, however, these kinds of errors are relatively common. They may be caused by the temporary outage of a remote file server or a network error.

As a concrete example of this, consider the delivery of a message to a user's mailbox, which consists of creating a file in a designated directory. On a local file system an attempt to open a new file can result in success or in a one of a small number of permanent failure modes: permission denied, user over quota or hardware failure, for example. In the case of such a permanent failure, the appropriate response is to abort the delivery attempt and reject the message back to the originator. On Andrew, we have the additional possibility of a new failure mode: the file open failed because the remote server that would hold the file was down. In this case it is not appropriate to abort the delivery attempt; instead the message should be held and delivery attempted again.

Typically, code that performs reliable file system operations is riddled with assumptions about possible failure modes. The introduction of new modes by VICE has necessitated the creation of new delivery software for the Andrew environment. We have managed, however, to retain the use of sendmail [1] as our SMTP user and server by modifying it and restricting its execution environment.

Many messages constructed on Andrew take advantage of the multi-media capability afforded by the base editor library (section 3). The external representation of such messages contains ASCII encodings of fonts, structure information and multi-media objects. This datastream allows users of the advanced interface (section 5.4.2) to view all of the objects in the original message. When a formatted message is transmitted outside of Andrew, however, the datastream format may make the message unreadable. To avoid this problem, the delivery system formats the message for a "standard" display device: all font information is removed, lines are formatted to be 80 characters wide, text is centered as appropriate and other reasonable transformations are performed. Of course, attempting to format certain kinds of objects for an arbitrary display device--graphics, raster and equations, for example--is impractical. Although, we have not actually had to deal with these objects yet (section 6.1) we anticipate that such objects will simply be replaced by an "object omitted" marker.

Other sites are running Andrew and, thus, have the ability to recognize the base editor datastream. It would be nice if messages transmitted to these systems retained the formatting information. For this reason, the delivery system maintains a list of external sites that are running Andrew and transmits messages to these systems untouched. This is not a perfect solution: some users at the remote site may be using an interface without graphics capabilities, or the recipient may have his mail forwarded to a system not running Andrew. This is a difficult problem and the ideal solution depends on the widespread acceptance of mail and multi-media document standards [8, 11].

The delivery system supports some special addressing services by interpreting specially tagged address forms. These addresses have the syntax

+<keyword>+<args>

This is an open-ended notation that allows us to add keywords and new functionality as the need arises. Currently the delivery system supports two special services. The special form

+dist+<file name>

will cause the delivery system to treat the contents of <file name> as a distribution list. Besides a list of addresses, the file contains information specifying the address to which delivery errors should be sent. The address

+dir-insert+<directory name>

tells the delivery system to insert the message into the specified directory, just as if it were a mailbox directory.

5.2. The White Pages

The white pages facility contains both a database of recognized mail addresses and a library of procedures for mapping name probes to those addresses. This facility is used both by the delivery system (section 5.1) and by message composition (section 5.4). The delivery system uses the white pages to map the destination names given with a message to a list of mail addresses. During message composition an interface uses exactly the same facility to validate the destination names given by a user. The validation occurs interactively, so the user may correct addressing errors immediately rather than having to wait for a rejection notice. Using the same procedure in both places guarantees that a consistent interpretation is placed on all addresses.

The white pages facility supports one of the primary goals for the AMS: flexible naming of mail destinations. We wanted to allow people to address mail to Andrew users by specifying incomplete forms of users' names--their best guesses--as well as by specifying a unique user id. For example, we allow user "Jello Biafra," with user id "jb34", to be addressed in any of the following ways:

    jb34@andrew.cmu.edu
    Jello.Biafra@andrew.cmu.edu
    J.Biafra@andrew.cmu.edu

and even

    Gell.Byafro@andrew.cmu.edu

We assume that these addresses unambiguously identify Jello Biafra. The last form of addressing is permissible because we are currently installing heuristics for recognizing many accidental misspellings of user names.

The procedure that does the lookup in the white pages returns an indication of how many matches there were for a name and how flexible it needed to be in order to find the matches. Thus, when the delivery system uses the white pages to look up a name, if the name turns out to be ambiguous, the delivery system uses the white pages to compose an error message to the sender that lists the names that matched. Also, if a name turns out to be only a heuristic match, the delivery system can choose to send an advisory note back to the sender, or even to reject the delivery attempt completely and return an error message. Correspondingly, when an interface validates an address given by the user, the white pages may indicate that the address matches many possibilities, or is only a heuristic match for a mail destination. In such cases, the message composition system can ask the user either to choose from a list of possible matches to the given name or to confirm or reject the result of the heuristic match. This facility has proven to be quite useful with a large system such as Andrew (currently with over 4700 users); the support for sending to parts of names encourages people to attempt abbreviations of their correspondents' names. Immediate validation of mail destination addresses at message composition time grants users the freedom to experiment.

The white pages stores information about users and special mailboxes; the information includes users' names, possible aliases, user ids, home directories (used to find the mail in-box directory) and forwarding addresses. The information is gathered from many sources, including the list of accounts (/etc/passwd) and a list of special mailboxes.

Building the white pages database on VICE has been a challenge. While it might be reasonable to store the entire database as a single Unix file, it is not reasonable to store it as a single file in VICE. This is because VICE insists that an entire file be transferred to the workstation to read even a small piece. Secondly, we have supported the Unix convention wherein users establish a mail forwarding address by creating a file named ".forward" in their home directories. In order to keep the white pages up to date, a daemon must periodically look for changes to all users' .forward files, and must be able to distinguish and to tolerate temporary inabilities to examine users' home directories.

While the white pages database can grow to be very large, clients generally need to reference only a small portion. This locality of reference has allowed us to install a large database in VICE without requiring the transfer of large files to workstations. The B-tree discipline was designed to fit large amounts of data into a collection of fixed-size nodes, typically pages on a disk. We built a B-tree representation that uses a collection of VICE files as nodes, so that no file to be transferred need be larger than a reasonable size (currently up to 40,000 bytes). Our B-tree discipline supports concurrent reading and updating, using the B^{link}-tree variant described by Lehman and Yao [14], in which readers need do no locking.

We store records describing users and indices to those records in the same B-tree, so that locating a user generally requires fetching only one or two leaves of the tree. This representation of the white pages has recently replaced our initial, interim representation, which used an existing facility that stored the database as a single file. The size of that file had grown to over one megabyte, and it was taking so long for addresses to be validated that our users required ways to circumvent validation. With the new representation, performance is much better, and we are able to remove our circumvention mechanisms.

Every night a daemon verifies the white pages database, incorporating new accounts, removing deleted accounts and checking for changes to the mail forwarding addresses in users' .forward files. It has been crucial that this verification process be able to tolerate the temporary unavailability of a user's home directory and files, even though the verification process cannot then know whether the user had a .forward file, much less what its contents would be. If the verification process detects this temporary unavailability, it leaves the old mail forwarding information in place, with the expectation that having old information is better than having none. The initial state for a new account is to have a distinguished value **unknown** as its forwarding address. If the delivery system tries to deliver mail to an account whose forwarding address still has this distinguished value, it will attempt at that point to read the .forward file.

Eventually we will provide users with ways of updating parts of the white pages on-line. Users and administrators will send formatted messages to a designated address, and a daemon will carry out those requests, after verifying that the sender has appropriate permission. Once this mechanism is in place, we will no longer have to scan home directories looking for .forward files.

5.3. The Message Database

The *message database* is a hierarchical collection of all of the messages that may be manipulated by the AMS. The database is represented as a forest of directed acyclic graphs, similar in structure to the Unix file system. Each node is either a *message directory* or a message. A message directory may contain messages and other message directories. All of the nodes are stored in VICE so that although the database is distributed, it appears monolithic to users and application programs. Figure 5-1 presents a simplified view of the Andrew message database.

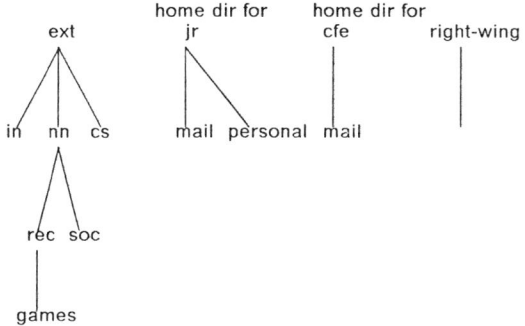

Figure 5-1: The Message Database

There are several interesting things to note about this picture. Some of the message directories are public and are stored in directories owned by Andrew administration. For example, the top-level message directories **ext** is public and centrally administered. Other directories are owned and administered by users: for example, personal mail directories and the **right-wing** directory.

Although the AMS is aware of the public message directories, and by convention can determine the location of personal mail directories, there is no root that can be used to find all the nodes of the message database. This means that the message database access routines (section 5.3.1) need not have a priori knowledge of the complete structure of the database. Users can create and maintain their own message directories without needing to register them in any manner with a central authority. For example, the **right-wing** message directory could have been created by a group of interested users without intervention by any Andrew administrators.

This ability provides great flexibility in the AMS by making it easy for any user to create and maintain a bulletin board. For convenience, a user may ask to have a bulletin board registered and its name will then be placed in a public, known location. Although this will make the name of the bulletin board publicly visible, it does not imply that anyone may read or post to this bulletin board. Because the bulletin board is stored as a VICE directory, the directory access list may be used to control access to the bulletin board.

A message directory is implemented as a VICE directory containing a distinguished file plus nested subdirectories and files containing the text of messages. This distinguished file contains administrative information as well as a structured record for each message in the directory. These records, known as *snapshots*, are of fixed size and allow rapid access to useful information about the messages. In particular, the snapshot for each message contains a time stamp and a condensed version of the header information from the message. The time stamp is used for ordering the messages and the condensed header information by user interfaces (section 5.4) to present summary information about a message. The user may then choose whether to view the entire message by inspecting this summary.

5.3.1. The Message Server

One particular goal we had for the AMS--to have the system available on the widest possible range of machines--has played a major role in its architecture. In order to make the system available on low-end machines, such as the IBM PC and Apple Macintosh, it was necessary to segment the functionality of the system into two major parts: the part that has access to the information in the database and the part that interacts with the user. The former, which we call the *message server* (MS), must run on a machine with full access to the message database as stored in the VICE file system. The latter, the user interface component, need only be able to talk to a message server via an agreed-upon mechanism.

The mechanism by which the message server and its clients communicate is called SNAP (for Simple Network Application Protocol). SNAP is a remote procedure call mechanism that was developed for the AMS and for use in connecting low-function workstations to the VICE file system [18]. SNAP runs on top of UDP [17] and supports sequencing, encryption and segmenting, thus providing a reliable packet protocol. The client code for SNAP (written in C) has been kept extremely simple to facilitate portability to multiple machines. To date, SNAP is running on the IBM RT-PC, Sun 2 and Sun 3 (under Berkeley Unix), the DEC MicroVAX (under Berkeley Unix and VMS), the IBM PC (under DOS) and the Macintosh.

The MS exports a subroutine interface that provide useful services for gaining access to and modifying the message database and for sending messages [5]. For example, the MS provides the following subroutines:

MS_SnapshotsSince
> This routine is used to retrieve a set of snapshots from a designated message directory. The snapshots for the messages in the designated directory that have been entered since a specified date are returned. The message associated with each snapshot is marked with a unique id.

MS_GetPartialBody This routine is used to retrieve the body of a specified message, identified by its unique id. The message may be retrieved in fixed-size chunks as specified by the client.

MS_CreateNewMessageDirectory
　　This routine is used to create a new message directory as a child of an existing message directory.

MS_SubmitMessage
　　This routine is used to submit a message for delivery to a list of specified addresses.

5.4. User Interfaces

The client-server design for access to the message database makes it relatively easy to create new user interfaces for the AMS to run on virtually any machine type. The implementor of an interface can program as if he were using a simple subroutine library. This allows him to ignore the intricacies of the message database regardless of the machine type on which the program will be executing. We provide a subroutine library, known as the CUILIB, that hides the complexities of the SNAP interface and allows the programmer to make local subroutine calls.

The ease of creating new interfaces is evidenced by the number of user interfaces that are available. The current interfaces of which we are aware are illustrated in figure 5-2.

	Andrew	VAX/VMS	PC
Messages	X		
CUI	X	X	X
PCmsgs	X		X
Batmail	X		

Figure 5-2: Current User Interfaces

In this figure, the first three interfaces were developed and are supported by the Andrew support and development staff. The *Batmail* interface is a popular, user developed and supported interface that runs within the EMACS text editor.

5.4.1. The CUI

The CUI (Common User Interface) is a simple, text-oriented interface that makes use of no graphics, screen or special input capabilities. The CUI is, thus, suitable to run on any terminal (even hard-copy) and in virtually any environment. The CUI has been ported to several machines (figure 5-2) and is, therefore, useful for the person wanting to learn only a single interface for use in many environments. An example of interaction with the CUI is shown in figure 5-3.

5.4.2. The Messages Program

Although the CUI provides full access to the AMS, it does not take advantage of the advanced features available on high-function Andrew workstations. For example, no use is made of the high-resolution graphics capabilities or of the mouse. For these reasons

```
CUI Version 3.30
CUI> update ext.nn.talk.origins
Checking ext.nn.talk.origins ...
1 7-Jul-87 Reality        gold@bbn.com (508)
2 7-Jul-87 Purpose        Bruce@sri (5558)

CUI READ> (Type '?' for help) [type]: type
From: jgold@cc6.bbn.com
Newsgroups: talk.origins
Subject: Re: The Nature of Reality
Date: 27 Jul 87 15:28:17 GMT
```
body omitted
```
CUI READ> (Type '?' for help) [next]: quit
CUI> quit
```
Figure 5-3: Using the CUI

we have implemented an interface that makes use of these features, known as **Messages**; an example of its display is shown in figure 5-4.

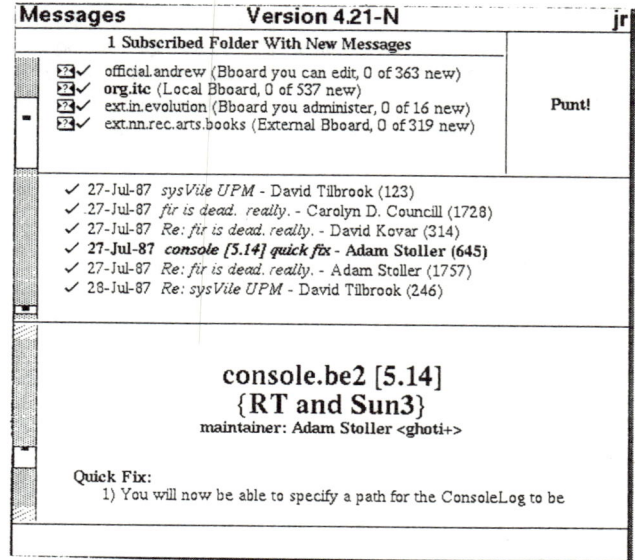

Figure 5-4: The Messages Interface

The Messages program is the interface of choice for most Andrew users. Considerable work has gone into the design of the interface that Messages presents; we have gone through several screen layouts and interaction styles before settling on one that seemed to please the widest number of users and styles of use. In fact, we currently offer two screen layouts, which differ in the placement of the message directory names, which appear in the top panel in figure 5-4. This technique of offering several alternative interfaces to users and collecting information on user reactions has been quite useful in the development of user interfaces on Andrew.

The Messages program is used to manipulate both mail and bulletin board messages. In fact, our initial design for the AMS included no distinction between personal mail and bulletin boards. While this may seem just plain wrong, consider that personal mail and bulletin boards are just two extreme points in a two-dimensional space of message directories. The axes are *the number of users who may read messages on this message directory* and *the number of users who may post messages on this directory*. Personal mail is a directory to which any user can post messages, but which only one user can read. On the other hand, a public bulletin board is a directory to which any user can post and which any user can read.

There are other reasonable, useful points in this space. Consider a message directory that is readable by any user but only postable by a small number of designated users. This corresponds to an "official" bulletin board: any user may read messages and be assured that they were posted by authorized users. Another useful message directory is one that is postable by any user but may only be read by a small number of users. This kind of message directory could be used by a manager for his personal mail as it allows his secretary to also read (and, possibly, manipulate) his mail. Figure 5-5 displays some of the directory types available in the AMS.

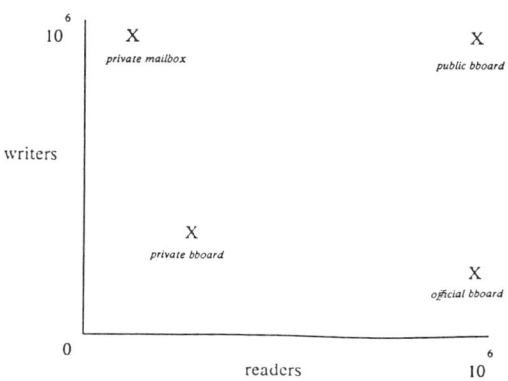

Figure 5-5: The Message Directory Space

The Messages program also supports an interface for composing and sending messages that uses the multi-media editing facilities of the base editor library (section 3). The user thus has access to a multi-media editor interface that is standardized across many Andrew applications.

The message composition interface takes full advantage of the flexible addressing afforded by the delivery system (section 5.1). In particular, the interface performs on-line validation of all forms of addresses. This provides immediate feedback to the user about local addressing errors and avoids the "send, receive error, correct error, resend" cycle.

In addition, the Messages composition interface provides two new forms of addresses: personal macros and bulletin board names. A user may maintain a list of personal macros in a designated file that is read by the Messages program. The appearance of one of these macros in an address list is expanded into the specified list of addresses. This is convenient for specifying commonly-used groups of users or for abbreviating long addresses. An example of such a personal file might be

```
group        cfe, ghoti, nsb, jr
mtg          group, mc35, KFS@vma.cc.cmu.edu
ams-folks    +dist+~postman/ams-folks.dl
```

The macro expansion may reference other macros, or any other form of address.

Posting a message to a bulletin board is done simply by using the name of the bulletin board as a destination. For example, a message may be posted to the Netnews message group **rec.arts.books** by addressing the message to **ext.nn.rec.arts.books** (the Andrew name of the bulletin board). This form of addressing works regardless of the method of redistribution for the bulletin board. For example, messages addressed to Netnews are automatically routed to a daemon that transmits the message via the Netnews protocol [12]. This form of addressing allows a message to be sent to both users and bulletin boards.

Section 5.3 discusses the fact that users can create new private message directory trees without the need for intervention from system programmers. In addition, at designated places in the public database hierarchy it is possible for users to create a new message directory as a child of an existing directory. For example, referring once again to figure 5-1, it is possible for a user to create a new message directory under the node **andrew.market**. This would be useful, for example, if many postings on this bboard were about the sale of cars. Any interested user could decide that cars for sale warranted a bulletin board of their own, so as not to clutter the market bulletin board. This user could then create the new bulletin board simply by addressing a message to **andrew.market.cars**.

5.5. The PCmsgs Program

Although the CUI is available on IBM PC's, another interface that takes advantage of the display capabilities is available. This interface is known as **PCmsgs** and, like the CUI uses the CUILIB (section 5.4). In the same manner as Messages, PCmsgs presents displays listing message directories and message snapshots. Unlike Messages, which uses the mouse for input, users of PCmsgs maneuver around the screen using keyboard commands. Figure 5-6 shows a PCmsgs screen that displays the snapshots of the user's new mail.

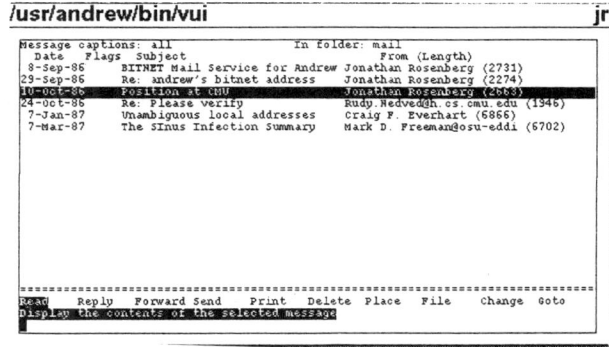

Figure 5-6: The PCmsgs Interface

Although PCmsgs was developed initially for the IBM PC (section 5.5), we have built a version of it that uses the Unix termcap interface [2] and, thus, runs on any display device that is supported by the user's particular Unix system. This version is especially useful when dialing in to Andrew.

6. Future Development

Although the Andrew Message System is already a rather sophisticated messaging system, it can be viewed as just the beginning. The delivery system, white pages, message database and the user interfaces can be thought of as the tools on which we might build an *information utility*. An information utility would provide users with access to a large number of diverse databases and access methods. Besides electronic bulletin boards and mail, there might be databases containing the full texts of popular newspapers dictionaries and encyclopedias.

Designing, integrating and implementing such databases and associated access mechanisms is a difficult task. The job is even more difficult in a distributed system like Andrew. The most serious problem on Andrew is that the VICE file system, with its whole file transfer paradigm (section 3), was not designed to support large databases. An efficient implementation for general database access on Andrew is an open question.

The proposed information utility contains a wide assortment of data with different timeliness constraints and modes of use. We would expect that there would be a corresponding need for different forms of user interfaces. While the bulletin board paradigm is appropriate for some databases, it is not clear that it is appropriate for viewing a newspaper. We need to investigate and experiment with new forms of interfaces.

Although we are looking forward to progressing towards this utopian information utility, more work remains to be done on the current AMS. The remainder of this section provides brief discussions of some of the most important tasks that we will undertake in the near future.

6.1. Integration of the Multi-media Editor

Several times in this paper we have mentioned the multi-media capabilities of the AMS. Any Andrew application can obtain these multi-media capabilities by using the base editor library. The base editor library is a suite of subroutines that provide an application with the ability to create, view, edit, print, read and write multi-media documents. These documents may contain text (including multiple fonts and complex structure, such as headings, chapters and paragraphs), vector graphics, raster images, equations and spread sheets. In fact, the base editor architecture is open ended and new multi-media objects may be added at any time. An example of a multi-media document, displayed using a base editor library application, is shown in figure 6-1.

While this picture is rosy, the truth is that the multi-media version of the base editor library is only just becoming available for use by applications. The current Messages interface uses an earlier version of the base editor library that supports only text (albeit with multiple fonts and complex structure). Integration of the Messages program with the new base editor library is underway. We expect to have a working multi-media version of Messages by October of this year.

6.2. Bulletin Board Reorganization--Real and Virtual

We have several plans for extending the services that the AMS provides for its users. We expect to complete a reorganization of our tree of bulletin boards this summer. The reorganization will not only

Figure 6-1: A Multi-media Document

clarify the position of the Andrew community on our campus and in the world at large, but will also allow departments and other organizations to publish their private bulletin boards in well-known locations. Also, we are implementing an extension language (FLAMES, the Filtering Language for the Andrew MEssage System) in which users will be able to compose calls to the message server without having to program in C. Perhaps our most novel extension will be an adaptation and extension of some of the work done in Malone's Information Lens system [15]--in particular, the work done by its "anyone server", in which users tell the system the kind of public messages that they would like to have sent to them. We expect to support a comparable service for a much larger user community by building on the services available in the extension language.

The goal of the message server extension language, FLAMES, is to allow message server clients to specify complex operations, including powerful database manipulations, that can be executed completely within the message server. Interface programs will have access to database manipulation primitives without having to re-code them for each new interface, and the database manipulations can take place in the message server rather than in the machine running the interface program. The advantage of moving complex computations to the message server host is that the message server is guaranteed to run on a high-function processor, connected over fast communication lines to VICE, whereas interface programs may execute on limited machines or over slow communications links.

The extension language is being built with a simple Lisp syntax, and we envision having two interpreters: a simple interpreter running FLAMES within the message server itself, and a full Lisp system running extended FLAMES (X-FLAMES). X-FLAMES will be available as a client of the message server. All interface programs will be able to ask a message server to execute a command in FLAMES. More complicated operations, such as we anticipate providing as a system service, can be handled by invoking the X-FLAMES interpreter directly.

It is this latter ability that we expect to exploit in building a massive information lens. A user of the information lens posts a predicate specifying the kinds of messages that are of interest. For example, someone might want to read all messages that are about automobiles or are from a specific message source and are about California wines. The user might post a predicate like

```
(union
    (word-search "automobile")
    (word-search "autos")
    (word-search "cars")
    (intersection
        (word-search "California")
        (word-search "wine")
        (bboard "rec.food.drink")))
```

This is a predicate that matches both messages that contain the words "automobile", "autos", or "cars", as well as messages from the bulletin board **rec.food.drink** containing both the word "wine" and the word "California".

In principle it would be possible for an interface program to find the set of all messages currently matching this predicate, then to subtract from that set the ones that the user has seen already, and finally to present to the user the new messages that match the predicate. This action would be too expensive to carry out today, but we hope to be able to support such actions by clever preprocessing performed by a special lens system application written in X-FLAMES. Our plan is to collect all the predicates posted by the lens users, to find common sub-expressions of these predicates (such as "(word-search "cars")") the results of which would accelerate the evaluation of later predicates. The lens system application would sift through all incoming messages and identify those messages that match the common sub-expressions. Suppose the Lens system application examined every incoming message destined for a public bulletin board and posted all messages that contained the word "automobiles" to a bulletin board named **lens.wordsearch.automobiles**. This preprocessing would make it more efficient to evaluate parts of predicates. If the first three word searches in the example above were maintained by the Lens system, evaluating the entire predicate would be fast indeed: a program would need to check for messages on only the three **lens.wordsearch** bulletin boards and the single bulletin board **rec.food.drink** before identifying the new messages of interest. With this kind of pre-indexing, in which the community of users influence the kinds of indices kept, we expect to be able to support the advanced information needs of a large community.

7. Statistics

This section contains a number of statistics related to Andrew and to the Andrew Message System. The figures are presented without commentary and are intended to give the reader a feel for the size of Andrew and its message system.

- 300 Andrew workstations
- 11,000 campus network access wall outlets
- 4700 Andrew accounts
- 17 gigabytes of storage available in VICE
- 1000 public bulletin boards
- 1 bulletin board post per minute (averaged over a 24 hour day)
    - 7 posts per hour received for ARPAnet bboards
    - 40 posts per hour received for Netnews bboards
    - 4 posts per hour received for local bboards
- 24 non-bboard messages per hour received from other sites
- 10 posts per day sent to Netnews bboards
- 34 messages per day sent to non-Andrew sites

Acknowledgements

Besides the authors, Adam Stoller is the fourth full-time member of the Andrew Message System group. Adam's primary job is to administer the AMS. This includes monitoring of the message system server machines (of which there are currently five), administration of the message database, answering users' requests and gripes (a never-ending and thankless task on Andrew) and other related problems that fall through the cracks. Without Adam, the Andrew Message System would not be as reliable, robust and responsive as it is today.

The message system would have been impossible to implement without the help of the entire Information Technology Center staff. In particular, we would like to thank the VICE file system group for being responsive to our needs and to the bugs we uncovered.

References

[1] Eric Allman.
SENDMAIL -- An Internetwork Mail Router.
In *UNIX System Manager's Manual*. University of California, Berkeley, 1986.

[2] Kenneth C. R. C. Arnold.
Screen Updating and Cursor Movement Optimization: A Library Package.
In *UNIX Programmer's Manual: Supplementary Documents*. University of California, Berkeley, 1984.

[3] Andrew D. Birrell, Roy Levin, Roger M. Needham and Michael D. Schroeder.
Grapevine: An Exercise in Distributed Computing.
Communications of the ACM 25(4):260-274, April, 1982.

[4] Sandra J. Bond.
Module 4: The Andrew Mail and News Systems.
Information Technology Center, Carnegie Mellon University, Pittsburgh, PA, 1986.

[5] Nathaniel S. Borenstein.
The Andrew Message System Server-Client Interface.
Internal documentation, Information Technology Center, Carnegie Mellon University, Pittsburgh, PA, November, 1986.

[6] Nathaniel S. Borenstein.
A House of Cards: A History of the Inorganic Evolution of the CMU Bboard System Software.
Technical Report CMU-CS-85-152, Computer Science Department, Carnegie Mellon University, Pittsburgh PA 15213, 1985.

[7] M. Butler, J. Postel, D. Chase, J. Goldberger and J. K. Reynolds.
RFC 937: Post Office Protocol - Version 2.
USC, Information Sciences Institute, 1985.

[8] Study Group VII.
Red Book, Volume VIII, Fascicle VIII.7: Data communication networks: message handling systems. Recommendations X.400-X.430.
CCITT, the International Telegraph and Telephone Consultative Committee, 1984.

[9] David D. Clark and Mark L. Lambert.
RFC 993: PCMAIL: A Distributed Mail System for Personal Computers.
Massachusetts Institute of Technology, 1986.

[10] Mark R. Horton.
RFC 850: Standard for Interchange of USENET Messages.
USC, Information Sciences Institute, 1983.

[11] ISO TC97/SC18.
Information Processing - Text and Office Systems Office Document Architecture (ODA) and Interchange Format.
Technical Report ISO/DIS8613, International Organization for Standardization, June, 1987.

[12] Brian Kantor and Phil Lapsley.
RFC 977: Network News Transfer Protocol.
UC San Diego, 1986.

[13] David Alex Lamb.
RdMail Message Management System: User's Guide and Reference
Seventh edition, CMU Computer Science Department, Pittsburgh, PA, 1982.

[14] Philip L. Lehman and S. Bing Yao.
Efficient Locking for Concurrent Operations on B-Trees.
ACM Transactions on Database Systems 6(4):650-670, December, 1981.

[15] Thomas W. Malone, Kenneth R. Grant, Franklyn A. Turbak, Stephen A. Brobst and Michael D. Cohen.
Intelligent Information-Sharing Systems.
Communications of the ACM 30(5):390-402, May, 1987.

[16] James H. Morris, Mahadev Satyanarayanan, Michael H. Conner, John H. Howard, David S. H. Rosenthal and F. Donelson Smith.
Andrew: A Distributed Personal Computing Environment.
Communications of the ACM 29(3):184-201, March, 1986.

[17] J. Postel.
RFC 768: User Datagram Protocol
USC, Information Sciences Institute, 1980.

[18] Larry K. Raper.
The CMU PC Server Project.
Technical Report CMU-ITC-051, Information Technology Center, Carnegie Mellon University, February, 1986.

[19] M. Satyanarayanan.
A study of file sizes and lifetimes.
In *Proceedings of the 8th Symposium on Operating Systems Principles.* Asilomar, CA, December, 1981.

[20] M. Satyanarayanan, John H. Howard, David A. Nichols, Robert N. Sidebotham, Alfred Z. Spector and Michael J. West.
The ITC Distributed File System: Principles and Design.
In *Proceedings of the 10th Symposium on Operating Systems Principles.* December, 1985.

[21] Michael D. Schroeder, Andrew D. Birrell and Roger M. Needham.
Experience with Grapevine: The Growth of a Distributed System.
ACM Transactions on Computer Systems 2(1):3-23, February, 1984.

[22] Larry Wall.
RN Manual Page.
1985.
RN is distributed via netnews; the author's mail address is lwall@sdcrdcf.UUCP.

PART 5. PROTOCOL VERIFICATION AND CONVERSION

S. Lam

University of Texas at Austin, USA

A VERIFIED CONNECTION MANAGEMENT PROTOCOL FOR THE TRANSPORT LAYER[1]

Sandra L. Murphy and A. Udaya Shankar
Department of Computer Science
University of Maryland
College Park, Maryland 20742

ABSTRACT

We specify and verify a connection management protocol for use between entities connected by channels that can lose, reorder, and duplicate messages. The protocol is symmetric. Each entity is in one of the following states: closed, listen, open, active opening, passive opening, or closing. The first three are stable states to be exited only by user request, while the last three are transient states. Each entity maintains a local incarnation number at all times, and a remote incarnation number only when opening, open, and closing. Our protocol employs the 3-way handshake used in TCP and ISO Transport Protocol (Class 4).

We verify the safety property that when an entity is open, its remote incarnation number matches the remote entity's local incarnation number. This ensures that data messages from past connection instances are not delivered to the user. We verify the following progress properties: an actively opening entity will eventually establish a connection, provided that the remote entity is willing to communicate or is itself actively opening; the states of active opening, passive opening, and closing are transient; if the entities remain closed, the channels will eventually become empty, assuming messages have a maximum lifetime.

This protocol specification can be immediately combined with the data transfer protocol specifications presented in [SHAN1, SHAN2, SHAN3] to provide a transport layer protocol with the functions of connection management and two-way data transfer. The verifications too can be immediately combined to provide a hierarchical verification of the multi-function protocol. The specifications and verifications can be combined because the connection management and data transfer protocols are images of the multi-function protocol. This illustrates the power of protocol projections in constructing multi-function protocols.

---

[1]Work supported by National Science Foundation Grant No. ECS 85-02113.

Permission to copy without fee all or part of this material is granted provided that the copies are not made or distributed for direct commercial advantage, the ACM copyright notice and the title of the publication and its date appear, and notice is given that copying is by permission of the Association for Computing Machinery. To copy otherwise, or to republish, requires a fee and/or specfic permission.

© 1988 ACM 0-89791-245-4/88/0001/0110 $1.50

1. INTRODUCTION

Connection management protocols [DoD, ISO, SUN] at the transport layer provide user processes with the services of establishing and terminating connections to remote user processes. Establishing a connection involves determining that the remote process is willing to accept the connection. For each connection instance, the connection management protocol must exchange incarnation numbers (i.e., initial sequence numbers in TCP [DoD], reference numbers in ISO TP [ISO]) between the entities. Incarnation numbers are used to distinguish data messages of the current connection instance from data messages of previous instances. This is necessary for reliable data transfer. The incarnation numbers are also used to distinguish connection management messages of current entity incarnations from those of old entity incarnations. This is necessary for reliable connection management.

We specify a connection management protocol for use between two entities connected by channels that can lose, reorder, and duplicate messages. See Figure 1. The protocol is *symmetric*. Each entity is in one of the following states: closed, listen, open, active opening, passive opening, or closing. Each entity maintains a *local incarnation number* at all times, and a *remote incarnation number* only when opening, open, and closing.

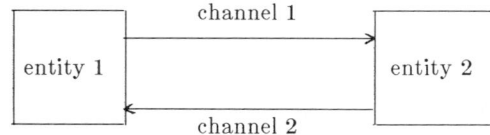

Figure 1. The protocol system

Connection establishment is achieved via a 3-way handshake similar to that described in [DoD, ISO, SUN]. A closed entity can become either active opening or listening. A listening entity becomes passive opening upon the receipt of any connection request. An opening (active or passive) entity *i* repeatedly sends connection requests until a response is received. The response can either terminate the connection attempt (the remote entity is closed), or result in connection establishment (entity *i* becomes open). At this point, if entity *i* was actively opening, it sends a final acknowledgement, completing the 3-way handshake. Our protocol allows for simultaneous connection attempts (balanced opening).

A passively opening entity that receives a response to a message that could not have been sent will request that the connection attempt be reset. In fact, it can send no other message to clear up the confusion. Actively opening entities do not have to request resets; they can send the connection request message to clear up the confusion.

Entity i increases its local incarnation number when it enters active opening from closed, when it enters passive opening from listening, and when it reenters passive opening from passive opening due to the reception of a connection request from a more recent incarnation of entity j.

Once entity i is open, it can send and receive data messages with the current incarnation numbers. This protocol has data send and receive events that are simple *images* [LAM] of the events of the data transfer protocols in [SHAN1, SHAN2, SHAN3]. Thus, the data send and receive events of this protocol can be replaced by the events of the data transfer protocols to provide a transport layer protocol with the functions of connection management and two-way flow-controlled data transfer. The protocol in this paper ensures that the invariants for the data transfer protocols hold whenever the connection is opened. Thus, the verifications of the data transfer protocols in [SHAN1, SHAN2, SHAN3] are valid for this multi-function protocol.

Connection termination is achieved via a 2-way handshake. The user process is responsible for determining that data transfer is complete before requesting termination, similar to the ISO TP. For the sake of brevity, we have not modeled the TCP connection termination here; i.e., where each entity independently closes its outgoing data connection.

Comparison to TCP

Our protocol has the functionality of TCP (other than the difference in connection termination mentioned above). However, we emphasize that there are internal differences between our protocol and TCP. In short, TCP and our protocol are different solutions to the same connection management problem. The logical behavior of our protocol (as represented by safety and progress properties) is simpler than that of TCP. Our protocol is verified. TCP is not, and in fact has numerous problems. Many of these problems do not show up often in practice because of the infrequent occurrence of events such as simultaneous opening (of the same socket pair), message duplication or reordering by the channels, etc. We have determined a set of changes to TCP that ensures logical correctness. However, the resulting TCP is still needlessly complicated in its logical behavior.

1.1. Safety properties of the protocol

For this protocol, we prove the following safety properties (formal specifications of these properties are in Section 3):

(A_0) If entity i is open, then its remote incarnation number equals the local incarnation number of entity j.

(A_1) If entity i is open, then entity j is not closed or listening.

When entity i is open, it only accepts received messages with sequence number fields that match the local and remote incarnation numbers. Thus, A_0 ensures that data messages from previous connection instances are not accepted.

To establish A_0 and A_1, we need to obtain additional assertions $A_2, \cdots, A_n$, which together with the protocol system specifications satisfy the proof rules. The difficult part of verification is to obtain these additional assertions. We have obtained the A_i's in incremental steps starting from A_0 and A_1, using a heuristic described in [SHAN0] and also applied in [SHAN2]. At each step, we do the following: take an A_i that is not preserved by some event of the protocol system; obtain a precondition [DIJK] of A_i with respect to the event; if this precondition is not implied by the existing A_i's, then let this precondition be a new A_i. The heuristic terminates when no new preconditions are generated. It is speeded up significantly by including at the outset obvious properties of the system variables.

The number of additional properties is considerable, indicative of the complex behavior of the protocol. Due to lack of space, we have not presented this derivation of the additional assertions. Instead, we list all the assertions at the outset, and prove in steps that they satisfy the safety proof rule. To some extent, the steps indicate the sequence in which the assertions were derived.

1.2. Progress properties of the protocol

For this protocol, we prove the following progress properties (formal specifications of these properties in Section 4):

(L_0) If entity i is active opening and entity j is listening or passive opening, then the entities eventually reach open states, provided that an open user does not prematurely issue a closing request, and a listening user at entity j does not become closed.

(L_1) If both entities are active opening, then the entities eventually reach open states, provided that an open user does not prematurely issue a closing request.

(L_2) If entity i is active opening, then it eventually becomes either closed or open.

(L_3) If entity i is passive opening, then it eventually becomes either closed or open.

(L_4) If entity i is closing, then it eventually becomes closed.

L_0 states that an actively opening entity will eventually establish a connection, provided the remote entity is willing to communicate. L_1 states that if both the entities are actively opening, a connection will be eventually established. L_2, L_3, and L_4 state that active opening, passive opening, and closing are indeed transient states.

The analysis of the liveness behavior of the protocol is simplified by dividing the messages into two types: primary and secondary. *Primary messages* are sent until a response message is received. *Secondary messages* are sent only in response to a received primary message. We have formulated two liveness proof rules to characterize this behavior, as a result of which our progress proofs are enormously simplified.

We have also established the following property:

(L_5) If the entities remain in closed states permanently, then the channels eventually become empty, provided messages have a maximum lifetime in the channels.

L_5 states that if the users are idle, activity in the protocol system dies out. The proof of L_5 requires a real-time system model (as in [SHAN2, SHAN3]), and is not presented here.

1.3. Related work

The literature contains many examples of specifications of connection management services and protocols for the transport layer. Only a few of these are concerned with verification [KUR, JUR1, JUR2, LIN, COUR]. Kurose and Yemini [KUR] and Lin[LIN] consider a connection establishment protocol with no connection termination and no data transfer, and with one active and one passive entity (no simultaneous connection attempts). They allow channels that can lose, reorder, and duplicate messages. They have incarnation numbers as in our protocol, and assume that the local incarnation number is unique. For this protocol they establish safety and liveness properties very similar to A_0 and L_0.

Jurgensen and Vuong [JUR1, JUR2] and Courtiat *et al* [COUR] consider Petri models of the ISO Transport protocol. In ISO TP [ISO], an entity establishes a new connection for each new reference number received; new reference numbers are assumed to be unique. Consequently, the issue of simultaneous opening is pushed to the upper layer. References [JUR1, JUR2, COUR] assume error-free channels, and specify connection establishment, data transfer, and connection termination. They verify general properties (bounded, safe, proper, live) of the Petri nets. However, the properties specific to connection management that they verify are limited: e.g., a request at one entity leads to a corresponding indication at the other entity; at most one TPDU is in a channel in each direction at any time.

1.4. Organization of the rest of this report

In Section 2, we summarize the distributed system model and specify the connection management protocol. In Section 3, we summarize the safety proof rules and verify the safety properties A_0 and A_1. In Section 4, we summarize the progress proof rules and verify the progress properties L_0 through L_4.

2. PROTOCOL SPECIFICATION

We first present our protocol system model. Each process of the protocol system (protocol entity or channel in Figure 1) is specified by a set of state variables along with their initial values, and a set of events. Each event is specified as a guarded command [DIJK]: **when** *enabling condition* **do** *action*. The event can occur only when its enabling condition is true. Its occurrence results in the execution of the action, which specifies an update to the state variables.

For each channel i, let $\mathbf{z}_i$ denote the sequence of messages in transit at any time. Initially, $\mathbf{z}_i$ is the empty sequence. The events of channel i can delete, duplicate, and reorder the entries in $\mathbf{z}_i$.

The messages sent by each entity are of the type (M, sn, rn), where M is a constant that indicates the type of the message, and sn, rn are the fields of the message. The sn field is referred to as the *send sequence number*. The rn field is referred to as the *receive sequence number*.

Let $\mathbf{v}_i$ denote the state variables of entity i. For each message type (M, sn, rn), entity i has the send event:

$SendM_i \equiv$ **when** B **do** $[S\,;\,Send_i(M, sn, rn)]$

where B is a boolean function of $\mathbf{v}_i$, S is a procedure that updates the value of $\mathbf{v}_i$ and assigns values to sn and rn, and $Send_i(M, sn, rn)$ appends the message (M, sn, rn) to the tail of $\mathbf{z}_i$. The variables sn and rn are local to the event.

For each message type (M, sn, rn), entity i has the receive event:

$RecM_i \equiv$ **when** $Rec_j(M, sn, rn)$ **do** S

where $Rec_j(M, sn, rn)$ is true only when a (M, sn, rn) message is at the head of $\mathbf{z}_j$, and S is a procedure that uses the values of sn and rn to update $\mathbf{v}_i$. The occurrence of the event removes the message (M, sn, rn) from the head of $\mathbf{z}_j$, in addition to executing S.

In some cases, the reception of the (M, sn, rn) message, results in the immediate transmission of a response message (N, sn_1, rn_1). Then, S will also contain the primitive $Send_i(N, sn_1, rn_1)$, where the values for sn_1 and rn_1 are computed using $\mathbf{v}_i$, sn, and rn. M is referred to as a *primary message type*, and N as a *secondary message type*.

An internal event of entity i has the form **when** B **do** S, where B is a boolean function of $\mathbf{v}_i$ and S is a procedure that updates $\mathbf{v}_i$. Internal events model user-driven activities such as initiating an active connection attempt, initiating a listening period, etc.

2.1. Entity state variables

Entity i, for $i = 1$ and 2, has the following state variables:

$State_i$: {*closed*, *listen*, *open*, *activeopening*, *passiveopening*, *closing*}

{$State_i$ equals *closed* means entity i is unwilling to communicate. *listen* means entity i is willing to accept a connection. *open* means entity i can send and receive data. *activeopening* means entity i wants to establish a connection. *passiveopening* means entity i is responding to a connection request from entity j. *closing* means entity i wants to terminate the connection. Initially, $State_i = closed$.}

$Lin_i : \{0, 1, \cdots\}$
{Local incarnation number. Identifies the latest incarnation of entity i. Lin_i is increased at each new connection attempt. Initially, $Lin_i = 0$.}

$Rin_i : \{null\} \cup \{0, 1, \cdots\}$
{Remote incarnation number. Rin_i is *null* if $State_i$ is *closed* or *listen*. Otherwise, Rin_i is entity i's perception of the remote entity's local incarnation number. Initially, $Rin_i = null$.}

2.2. Message types and entity events

We now describe each message sent by entity i, the values of entity i's state variables when the message is sent, and the effect of the message reception on the values of entity j's state variables. The entity events are formally specified in Table 1. We emphasize that the descriptions of receive events given below is incomplete. The complete description is given by Table 1.

Recall that each message sent by entity i is of the type (M, sn, rn). In this protocol, sn and rn take non-negative integer values; rn can also have the value *null*. When the message is sent, sn has the value of Lin_i, and rn usually has the value of Rin_i. Sometimes, rn has the value of a received message's send sequence number (see below). (Cyclic sequence numbers can be used in place of the unbounded incarnation numbers if we assume that messages in the channels have a maximum lifetime (as in [SHAN1, SHAN2]).)

If entity j receives a message (M, sn, rn) when it is not closed, Rin_j is set to $\max(Rin_j, sn)$. Typically, the message is ignored if $sn < Rin_j$; i.e., from an old incarnation. Sometimes, the message is ignored if $rn < Lin_j$; i.e., not intended for this incarnation.

In the following message types, the rn field has the value of Rin_i when the message is sent:

$(CRAO, sn, rn)$
{Connection request sent by an active opening entity i. Upon reception, entity j does the following: If it was listening, it becomes passive opening (start of a 3-way handshake for unbalanced opening). If it was active opening and $rn = Lin_j$, it becomes open and sends a $CRACK$ message (balanced opening). If it was open and $rn = Lin_j$, it sends a $CRACK$ message (balanced opening). If it was passive opening and $sn > Rin_j$, it increases Lin_j (it had been responding to a $CRAO$ from an old incarnation of entity i). If it was closing and $sn > Rin_j$, it becomes closed (it had been trying to close a connection with an old incarnation of entity i that had already closed).}

$(CRPO, sn, rn)$
{Connection request sent by a passive opening entity i. Upon reception, entity j does the following: If it was active opening and $rn = Lin_j$, it becomes open and sends a $CRACK$ message (start of the last handshake of unbalanced opening). If it was passive opening and $rn = Lin_j$, it sends a $RESET$ message and returns to listening (both entities had been responding to $CRAO$'s of old incarnations). If it was listening, it sends a $RESET$ message (entity i had responded to a $CRAO$ of an old incarnation of entity j). If it was closing and $sn > Rin_j$, it becomes closed.}

$(CRACK, sn, rn)$
{Sent by an active opening or open entity i, in response to a received $CRAO$ or $CRPO$. Entity i is then open. Upon reception, entity j becomes open if it was opening and $rn = Lin_j$.}

$(DATA, sn, rn)$
{Sent by an open entity i for data transfer purposes. We use $DATA$ to represent the image [LAM] of *all* the data transfer message types (data, acknowledgement, etc.) and their fields (data sequence number, data length, receive window size, etc.) [SHAN1]. Reception of a $DATA$ message is similar to the reception of a $CRACK$ message. Otherwise, transmissions and receptions of $DATA$ messages have no effect on the entity state variables defined in this report.}

(DR, sn, rn)
{Disconnect request sent by an closing entity i. Upon reception, entity j does the following if $rn = Lin_j$: If it was active opening, open or closing, it becomes closed and sends a $DRACK$ message. If passive opening, it becomes listening and sends a $DRACK$ message. If it was listening, it sends a $RESET$ message.}

$(DRACK, sn, rn)$
{Sent by opening, open, or closing entity i in response to a received DR message. Entity i then becomes closed. Upon reception, entity j becomes closed, if it was closing, $sn \geq Rin_j$, and $rn = Lin_j$.}

Recall that a message type can have the attribute of being primary or secondary. A message of a primary type is sent until a response is received. A message of a secondary type is sent only in response to the reception of a primary message. Of the above message types, $CRAO$, $CRPO$, and DR are primary types; $CRACK$ and $DRACK$ are secondary types.

The following are secondary message types. In these, the receive sequence number field is not set to the value of Rin_i, but rather to the sn value in the received primary message. For notational reasons, we shall denote the receive sequence number field in these messages by $recsn$, rather than rn.

$(REJ, sn, recsn)$
{Sent by a closed entity i in response to a received $CRAO$, $CRPO$, or DR message. Upon reception, entity j does the following if $sn \geq Rin_j$ and $recsn = Lin_j$: If it was active opening or closing, it becomes closed. If it was passive opening, it becomes listening.}

($RESET, sn, recsn$)
{Sent by a listening or passive opening entity i in response to a received $CRPO$ or DR message. Upon reception, entity j does the following if $sn \geq Rin_j$ and $recsn = Lin_j$: If it was passive opening, it becomes listening. If it was closing, it becomes closed.}

3. SAFETY VERIFICATION

A safety property of the protocol system states relationships between the current values of the state variables. It is represented by a predicate in the system state variables. A safety property is said to be *invariant* if it holds at every system state that is possibly reachable from an initial state. We now verify that the following safety properties are invariant:

$A_0 \equiv State_1 = open \Rightarrow Rin_1 = Lin_2 \wedge Rin_2 = Lin_1$

$A_{\bar{0}} \equiv State_2 = open \Rightarrow Rin_2 = Lin_1 \wedge Rin_1 = Lin_2$

$A_1 \equiv State_1 = open$
$\Rightarrow \neg(State_2 = closed \vee State_2 = listen)$

$A_{\bar{1}} \equiv State_2 = open$
$\Rightarrow \neg(State_1 = closed \vee State_1 = listen)$

For any assertion A_i, we use $A_{\bar{i}}$ to denote A_i with the variable subscripts 1 and 2 interchanged. Because our protocol is symmetric, for every assertion A_i, we also have the corresponding symmetric assertion $A_{\bar{i}}$. Henceforth, we will usually not explicitly write the assertion $A_{\bar{i}}$. We shall also use the notation $A_{i,j}$ to denote $A_i \wedge A_j$.

Given a sequential procedure S and predicates p, q, we use the well-known program verification notation $\{p\}S\{q\}$ to mean that the following can be proved (without any other assumptions): if S is executed from a state where p holds, then q will hold upon termination of S. For example, $\{y=3\}$ if $x \neq y$ then $x := y+1$ $\{x=3 \vee x=4\}$ holds, but $\{x=3\}$ $x := y+1$ $\{x=4\}$ does not hold. Given an event $e \equiv$ **when** b **do** S, we use the notation $\{p\}e\{q\}$ to denote $\{p \wedge b\}S\{q\}$; i.e., that if e is enabled at a state where p holds and occurs, then q will hold immediately after the occurrence.

We shall establish the invariance of $A_{0,1,\bar{0},\bar{1}}$ by presenting an assertion A that implies $A_{0,1,\bar{0},\bar{1}}$ and satisfies the following well-known inference rule:

Safety inference rule: Predicate A is invariant if it satisfies the following:
(a) *Initial* $\Rightarrow A$
(b) for each event e: $\{A\} e \{A\}$

where the predicate *Initial* specifies the initial values of the state variables, and $\Rightarrow$ denotes logical implication. Part (a) ensures that A holds initially. Part (b) ensures that A is preserved by any event occurrence.

The difficult part of verification is to obtain the assertion A. We have obtained a list of assertions $A_{0,\bar{0}}$, $A_{1,\bar{1}}$, $A_{2,\bar{2}}$, $\cdots$, which together constitute A. The list of assertions is presented in Table 2. As per convention, we have not indicated the $A_{\bar{i}}$'s. These assertions were obtained in incremental steps starting from A_0 and A_1, using a heuristic described in [SHAN0]. Due to lack of space, we will not present this derivation. Instead, we shall prove, in steps, that the assertions in Table 2 taken together satisfy the safety proof rule. To some extent, these steps (presented in detail in Appendix A) indicate the sequence in which the assertions were derived.

We say that an assertion A_i is *preserved* if $\{J\}e\{A_i\}$ holds for every event e, where J is a subset of the assertions from Table 2; i.e., given J, the occurrence of any event preserves A_i. Observe that this also preserves $A_{\bar{i}}$. The list of assertions J is referred to as a *sufficient precondition* of A_i.

At each step in the proof below, we choose an unpreserved assertion A_i, specify a list of assertions J to be a sufficient precondition for A_i, and provide a proof that $\{J\}e\{A_i\}$ holds for every event e. We also list the set of assertions that have been preserved thus far. The proof ends when all the assertions in Table 2 are preserved.

It is obvious that every assertion in Table 2 is satisfied by the initial conditions

$$\begin{aligned} Initial \equiv\ & State_1 = State_2 = closed \\ & \wedge\ Lin_1 = Lin_2 = 0 \wedge Rin_1 = Rin_2 = null \\ & \wedge\ \mathbf{z}_1 = \mathbf{z}_2 = empty \end{aligned}$$

3.1. Preserving A_0

Consider the events that may violate A_0: an event of entity 1 that sets $State_1$ to $open$, changes Lin_1, or changes Rin_1; an event of entity 2 that changes Lin_2 or Rin_2. We now prove that (a subset of) the assertions in Table 2 ensure that A_0 cannot be thus violated.

From entity 1 events, we see that just before $State_1$ becomes $open$, it must have been either *activeopening* or *passiveopening*. If *activeopening*, it must have received a $CRAO$, $CRPO$, $CRACK$, or $DATA$ message with $rn = Lin_1$. In this case, from C_0 we have that $sn = Lin_2$ and $Rin_2 = Lin_1$. Thus, the reception of $CRAO$ or $CRPO$ message will establish the consequent of A_0. In the case of receiving $CRACK$ or $DATA$, from $C_{0,3}$, we see that the consequent of A_0 already held prior to the reception. If *passiveopening*, it must have received a $CRACK$ or $DATA$ message with $rn = Lin_1$. In this case, $C_0 \wedge D_1$ establishes the consequent of A_0. Thus, A_0 must hold when $State_1$ becomes $open$.

From entity 1 events, we see that if $State_1 = open$ neither Lin_1 nor Rin_1 can be changed.

We now prove that no entity 2 event can change Lin_2. We assume $State_1 = open$; otherwise, $State_1 \neq open$ will continue to be true after the event occurrence, and A_0 will be vacuously true. From $State_1 = open$ and A_0, we have $Rin_1 = Lin_2$ and $Rin_2 = Lin_1$ before the event occurrence. From this and A_3, we have that every (X, sn, rn) in $\mathbf{z}_1$ satisfies $sn \leq Rin_2$ and $rn \leq Lin_2$. Thus, the only way that Lin_2 can be incremented is if $State_2$ goes from closed or listening to opening. But this

114

cannot be, because from $State_1=open$ and A_1, we have $State_2 \notin \{closed, listen\}$ before the event occurrence.

We now prove that no entity 2 event can change Rin_2. As in the previous paragraph, the following hold before the event occurrence: $Rin_1=Lin_2$, $Rin_2=Lin_1$, and every $(X,sn,rn) \in \mathbf{z}_1$ satisfies $sn \leq Rin_2$ and $rn \leq Lin_2$. Thus, Rin_2 cannot be changed by the reception of a message with $sn > Rin_2$. All that is left is to show that Rin_2 is not set to $null$ by the reception of a REJ, RESET, CRPO, or DRACK message with $sn=Rin_2$ and $rn=Lin_2$, or a DR message with $rn=Lin_2$.

We first prove that a DR message with $rn=Lin_2$ also has $sn=Rin_2$. Recall that $State_2 \notin \{closed, listen\}$. For the other values of $State_2$, from $C_{\overline{0}}$, $E_{\overline{1}}$ and $F_{\overline{1}}$, we have $sn=Rin_2$.

From $Rin_2=Lin_1$, $State_1=open$, and B_2, we have that the only messages in $\mathbf{z}_1$ with $sn=Rin_2$ are CRAO, CRPO, CRACK, DATA. Consequently, a REJ, RESET, DR, or DRACK message cannot be received.

All that is left now is to ensure that the reception of a $(CRPO,Rin_2,Lin_2)$ in $\mathbf{z}_1$ does not result in Rin_2 being set to $null$. From B_4 and $Rin_2=Lin_1$, we have that $State_2 \neq passiveopening$. Thus, $State_2$ is either $activeopening$, $open$, or $closing$. From the event $Rec\ CRPO_2$, we see that the reception of $(CRPO,Rin_2,Lin_2)$ with these values of $State_2$ does not result in Rin_2 being set to $null$.

We have now proved that A_0 is preserved by the sufficient precondition $A_{0,1,3} \wedge B_{2,4} \wedge C_0$. At this point, we have the following for every event e (a formal proof is in Appendix A):

$$\{A_{0,1,3} \wedge B_{2,4} \wedge C_{0,\overline{0},3} \wedge D_1 \wedge E_{\overline{1}} \wedge F_{\overline{1}}\}\ e\ \{A_0\}$$

At this point, we have

$$\text{PRESERVED ASSERTIONS} = \{A_0\}$$

3.2. Preserving $A_{1\text{-}5}$ and $B_{0\text{-}3}$

Unlike the other properties, A_1 is directly implied by $A_0 \wedge A_{\overline{2}}$. Assume $State_1=open$. From A_0, we have $Rin_2=Lin_1 \neq null$. Thus, from $A_{\overline{2}}$, we have $State_2 \notin \{closed, listen\}$. Therefore, if we preserve A_0 and A_2, then A_1 is automatically preserved.

It is easily proved that the following hold for every event e (a formal proof of A_2 and A_4 is in Appendix A):

$$\{A_2\}\ e\ \{A_2\}$$
$$\{A_4 \wedge A_{\overline{3}}\}\ e\ \{A_3\}$$
$$\{A_4 \wedge A_{\overline{3}}\}\ e\ \{A_4\}$$
$$\{A_{0,\overline{0},5}\}\ e\ \{A_5\}$$

At this point, we have

$$\text{PRESERVED ASSERTIONS} = \{A_{0\text{-}5}\}$$

It is easily proved that the following hold for every event e:

$$\{A_3 \wedge B_0\}\ e\ \{B_0\}$$
$$\{B_1 \wedge A_3\}\ e\ \{B_1\}$$
$$\{B_{0\text{-}2}\}\ e\ \{B_2\}$$
$$\{B_{2,3}\}\ e\ \{B_3\}$$

At this point, we have

$$\text{PRESERVED ASSERTIONS} = \{A_{0\text{-}5}, B_{0\text{-}3}\}$$

3.3. Preserving C_0

We have already seen the usefulness of C_0 in preserving A_0. More generally, C_0 states the following: Let entity 1 be attempting to establish a connection. Let channel 2 contain a message M intended for the current incarnation of entity 1, and whose reception would either establish or normally terminate the connection. Then, M has been sent by the current incarnation of entity 2; i.e., entity 2 has not restarted the connection attempt after sending M. Furthermore, entity 2 knows of the current incarnation of entity 1.

Consider the events that may violate C_0: entity 1 event sets $State_1$ to $activeopening$ or $passiveopening$, or increments Lin_1; entity 2 sends a message, or changes Lin_2 or Rin_2. Any entity 1 event that makes $State_1$ enter $activeopening$ or $passiveopening$ also increments Lin_1. From $A_{\overline{3}}$, we know that channel 2 cannot contain (X,sn,Lin_1) messages after this increment to Lin_1. So C_0 is vacuously true after this event. When entity 1 goes from opening to open, C_0 held nonvacuously before the event occurrence, and therefore continues to hold after the event occurrence. An entity 2 event sends a message satisfying the antecedent of C_0 only if $Rin_2=Lin_1$; this automatically satisfies the consequent of C_0. The other possibilities are disproved as in A_0. We have the following for every event e (formal proof in Appendix A):

$$\{A_{3,\overline{3}} \wedge B_{0,1} \wedge C_{0\text{-}4} \wedge D_{1,2} \wedge E_{\overline{1}} \wedge F_{\overline{1}}\}\ e\ \{C_0\}$$
$$\text{PRESERVED ASSERTIONS} = \{A_{0\text{-}5}, B_{0\text{-}3}, C_0\}$$

3.4. Preserving the remaining assertions

We next have the following for every event e:

$$\{A_{3,\overline{3}} \wedge B_0 \wedge C_{0,1} \wedge E_{\overline{1}} \wedge F_{\overline{1}}\}\ e\ \{C_1\}$$
$$\{A_{3,\overline{3}} \wedge B_0 \wedge C_{0,\overline{0},2}\}\ e\ \{C_2\}$$
$$\{A_{\overline{0},3,\overline{3}} \wedge B_0 \wedge C_{0,\overline{0},3} \wedge E_{\overline{1}} \wedge F_{\overline{1}}\}\ e\ \{C_3\}$$
$$\{A_{3,\overline{3}} \wedge B_0 \wedge C_{0,4} \wedge F_{\overline{1}}\}\ e\ \{C_4\}$$
$$\text{PRESERVED ASSERTIONS} = \{A_{0\text{-}5}, B_{0\text{-}3}, C_{0\text{-}4}\}$$

We next have the following for every event e (a formal proof of B_4 is in Appendix A):

$$\{A_1 \wedge B_{0,4} \wedge D_1\} \; e \; \{B_4\}$$
$$\{A_{\overline{0,3},\overline{3}} \wedge B_1 \wedge C_{\overline{0}} \wedge D_1 \wedge E_{\overline{1}} \wedge F_{\overline{1}}\} \; e \; \{D_1\}$$
$$\{A_{3,\overline{3}} \wedge B_1 \wedge C_0 \wedge D_2 \wedge F_{\overline{1}}\} \; e \; \{D_2\}$$
$$\{A_{0,3} \wedge B_2 \wedge C_4 \wedge D_2 \wedge E_1 \wedge F_{\overline{1}}\} \; e \; \{E_1\}$$
$$\{A_{0,5} \wedge B_{\overline{0,1}} \wedge C_{\overline{0}} \wedge E_1 \wedge F_1\} \; e \; \{F_1\}$$
PRESERVED ASSERTIONS
$$= \{A_{0-5}, B_{0-4}, C_{0-4}, D_{1,2}, E_1, F_1\}$$

Note that B_4 implies that two *passiveopening* entities will not reach *open*.

At this point, all the assertions in Table 2 are preserved. The safety verification is complete.

4. PROGRESS VERIFICATION

A progress property states how the values of the state variables evolve. We shall consider progress properties of the form A *leads–to* B, where A and B are predicates in the system state variables. A *leads–to* B means that if the system state variables satisfy A, then the system will eventually enter a state where B holds, assuming a fair implementation. A *fair implementation* is defined as follows: every entity send or receive event that is continuously enabled will eventually occur; a message sent repeatedly into a channel will eventually be delivered to the remote entity.

Before stating the progress properties formally, we need to clarify what is meant by an entity being willing to communicate. For example, the desired progress property L_0 states: if entity 1 is active opening and entity 2 is willing to communicate, then the entities eventually reach open states. The following sequence of events can happen: at time t_1, the local user requests entity 1 to go from closed to active opening; entity 1 sends a $(CRAO, Lin_1, null)$ which arrives when entity 2 is closed; entity 2 thus responds with a (REJ, Rin_2, Lin_1); at time t_2, entity 2 becomes listening; at time t_3, entity 1 receives the REJ and becomes closed, even though at this time entity 2 is willing to communicate.

The same phenomenon can occur in balanced opening. This is appears especially undesirable in the case of balanced opening if $t_1 \approx t_2 \ll t_3$. We then have a situation where the entities do not establish a connection even though both are attempting to establish one for the major proportion of the time! It is important to realize that this is not a fault of the connection management protocol, but is a result of the behavior of the users of the protocol. The protocol can however minimize the likelihood of this happening by retrying an active opening attempt that is rejected. With this motivation, we add the following state variable at entity i:

$Remtry_i$: $\{0,1, \cdots, MaxCount\}$

{Remaining try count number. When entity i goes from closed to active opening due to user request, $Remtry_i$ is set to $MaxCount$. If $Remtry_i > 0$ when a (REJ, sn, Lin_i) message is received and $State_i$ = *activeopening*, entity i merely increments Lin_i and decrements $Remtry_i$, rather than becoming closed.}

The *Rec REJ* event in Table 1 is modified as follows: in the *then* clause of the action following the *activeopening* guard, replace $[State_i \leftarrow closed \; ; Rin_i \leftarrow null]$ by

if $Remtry_i > 0$
  then $[Lin_i \leftarrow Lin_i + 1; Remtry_i \leftarrow Remtry_i - 1]$
  else $[State_i \leftarrow closed \; ; Rin_i \leftarrow null].$

Observe that exactly the same effect can be achieved with the event specifications in Table 1 by requiring that *ActiveOpen* be executed immediately after reception of a (REJ, sn, Lin_i) when $State_i = activeopening$. (More formally, the modified protocol is a *refinement* [SHAN2] of the original protocol.) Consequently, all the safety properties in Table 2 continue to hold for this modified protocol.

Increasing the value of *MaxCount* reduces the likelihood of the undesirable phenomenon described above. We can now formally state and verify the desired progress properties:

$L_0 \equiv State_1 = activeopening \; \wedge \; Remtry_1 > 0$
  $\wedge \; State_2 \in \{passiveopening, listen\} \wedge Lin_1 = k$
  leads–to $State_1 = State_2 = open$

provided $InitClosing_1$, $InitClosing_2$, and $EndListening_2$ are inhibited from occurring. $InitClosing_i$ is inhibited to prevent entity i from closing the connection as soon as it becomes open. Otherwise, entity j may receive a DR before it can become *open*. $EndListening_2$ is inhibited to prevent entity 2 going from listening to closed before the $CRAO$ from entity 1 can reach it.

$L_1 \equiv State_1 = activeopening \; \wedge \; Remtry_1 > 0 \wedge Lin_1 = k$
  $\wedge \; State_2 = activeopening \; \wedge \; Remtry_2 > 0 \wedge Lin_2 = j$
  leads–to $State_1 = State_2 = open$

provided $InitClosing_1$ and $InitClosing_2$ are inhibited (for the same reason as in L_0).

$L_2 \equiv State_1 = activeopening$
  leads–to $State_1 = closed \; \vee \; State_1 = open$

$L_3 \equiv State_1 = passiveopening$
  leads–to $State_1 = listen \; \vee \; State_1 = open$

$L_4 \equiv State_1 = closing$ *leads–to* $State_1 = closed$

4.1. Primary and secondary message liveness axioms

The progress behavior of the protocol is determined almost entirely by interactions between corresponding primary and secondary message types. We now formulate two liveness proof rules that characterize this interaction. As a result of these rules, our proofs are enormously simplified.

Our first rule deals with a property that is established by entity i repeatedly sending a primary message of type PM until it is received by entity j. Given an assertion A, we use the notation $A[x/y]$ to denote A with every free occurrence of y replaced by x. Below, let *Rec PM* at entity j have the form **when** $Rec_j(PM, sn, rn)$ **do** S.

Liveness rule for primary messages: Let I be an invariant assertion. We can infer A $leads$-to B via primary message PM_i, if the following hold:

(a) for each event e: $\{A \wedge I\}\ e\ \{A \vee B\}$

(b) $A \wedge I \Rightarrow enabled\,(Send\,PM_i)$

(c) $\{I \wedge A \wedge A\,[sn/Lin_i,\ rn/Rin_i]\}\ S\ \{B\}$

We now present a justification for the rule. Assume that the system satisfies A. Part (a) ensures that any event occurrence that violates A will establish B. As long as A holds, we have the following. Part (b) ensures that $Send\,PM$ is continuously enabled. Thus, if $Send\,PM$ is fairly implemented, entity i will repeatedly send (PM, sn, rn) messages with sn and rn equaling the current Lin_i and Rin_i. More precisely, these sn and rn values will satisfy $A\,[sn/Lin_i,\ rn/Rin_i]$. From the fairness property of channels, one of these PM messages is eventually delivered to entity j. The message will be processed by entity j because $Rec\,PM$ is always enabled to receive a message in our model. Part (c) ensures that this reception establishes B.

Our second rule deals with a property that is established by entity i repeatedly sending a primary message PM until a responding secondary message SM_k is received at entity i. Below, let the $Rec\,PM$ event at entity j have the form

when $Rec_i(PM, sn, rn)$ **do**
$\quad$[**if** G_1 **then** $[S_1;\ Send_j(SM_1, sn_1, rn_1)]$ **else**
$\quad$ **if** G_2 **then** $[S_2;\ Send_j(SM_2, sn_2, rn_2)]$ **else**
$\quad\quad \cdots$
$\quad$ **if** G_n **then** $[S_n;\ Send_j(SM_n, sn_n, rn_n)]]$

Note that sn_k equals Lin_j, and rn_k equals either Rin_j (if SM_k is $CRACK$ or $DRACK$) or sn (if SM_k is REJ or $RESET$). At entity i, let the event $Rec\,SM_k$ be of the form **when** $Rec_j(SM_k, sn, rn)$ **do** T_k, where rn is replaced by $recsn$ if SM_k is REJ or $RESET$.

Liveness rule for secondary messages: Let I be an invariant assertion. We can infer A $leads$-to B via primary message PM_i and secondary messages $\{SM_1, SM_2, \cdots, SM_n\}$, if the following hold:

(a) for each event e: $\{A \wedge I\}\ e\ \{A \vee B\}$

(b) $I \wedge A \Rightarrow enabled\,(Send\,PM_i)$

(c) $I \wedge A \wedge A\,[sn/Lin_i,\ rn/Rin_i] \Rightarrow G_1 \vee \cdots \vee G_n$

(d) For $k=1, \cdots, n$:
$\quad \{I \wedge A \wedge A\,[sn/Lin_j,\ rn/Rin_j,\ recsn/Lin_i]\}\,T_k\,\{B\}$

Assume that the system satisfies A. Part (a) ensures that any event occurrence that violates A will establish B. As long as A holds, we have the following. Part (b) ensures that $Send\,PM$ is continuously enabled. So entity i will repeatedly send (PM, sn, rn) messages with sn and rn values satisfying $A\,[sn/Lin_i,\ rn/Rin_i]$. From the fairness property of channels, these PM messages will be repeatedly delivered to entity j. Part (c) ensures that each reception of such a PM message results in the transmission of some SM message. The sn and rn (or $recsn$) fields of this message will satisfy $A\,[sn/Lin_j,\ rn/Rin_j,\ recsn/Lin_i]$. Because the PM messages are repeatedly delivered to entity j, one of these SM messages will be eventually delivered to entity i. Part (d) ensures that the reception of such a message establishes B.

We use $leads$-to to denote the closure of the $leads$-to-via relation [CHAN, SHAN0]; e.g., A $leads$-to D if A $leads$-to $B \vee C$, B $leads$-to D and C $leads$-to D.

4.2. Proof of L_0

We define the following predicates:

$Y_0 \equiv State_1 = activeopening \wedge Remtry_1 > 0$
$\quad\quad \wedge State_2 \in \{passiveopening,\ listen\}$
$\quad\quad \wedge Lin_1 = k$

$Y_1 \equiv State_1 = activeopening \wedge Lin_1 = k \wedge Remtry_1 > 0 \wedge State_2 = passiveopening \wedge Rin_2 = k$

$Y_2 \equiv State_1 = activeopening \wedge Lin_1 = k+1$
$\quad\quad \wedge (X, sn, Lin_1) \notin z_2$
$\quad\quad \wedge State_2 \in \{passiveopening,\ listen\}$
$\quad\quad \wedge Rin_2 < k+1.$

$Y_3 \equiv State_1 = open \wedge Lin_1 = k$
$\quad\quad \wedge State_2 = passiveopening$

$Y_4 \equiv State_1 = activeopening \wedge Lin_1 = k+1$
$\quad\quad \wedge State_2 = passiveopening \wedge Rin_2 = k+1$
$\quad\quad \wedge (REJ, sn, k+1) \notin z_2$

$Y_5 \equiv State_1 = State_2 = open \wedge Lin_1 = k$

The following $leads$-to properties are proved in Appendix B:

$P_0 \equiv Y_0$ $leads$-to $Y_1 \vee Y_2 \vee Y_3$ via primary message $CRAO_1$

$P_1 \equiv Y_1$ $leads$-to $Y_2 \vee Y_3$ via primary message $CRPO_2$

$P_2 \equiv Y_2$ $leads$-to Y_4 via primary message $CRAO_1$

$P_3 \equiv Y_3$ $leads$-to Y_5 via primary message $CRPO_2$ and secondary messages $\{CRACK, DATA\}$

$P_4 \equiv Y_4$ $leads$-to $Y_3[k+1/k]$ via primary message $CRPO_2$

Applying the closure property of $leads$-to relations to Y_0 through Y_4 results in Y_0 $leads$-to Y_5, which is L_0.

4.3. Proof of L_1

We define the following predicates:

$Z_0 \equiv State_1 = activeopening \wedge Lin_1 = k_1 \wedge Remtry_1 > 0 \wedge State_2 = activeopening \wedge Lin_2 = k_2$
$\quad\quad \wedge Remtry_2 > 0$

$Z_1 \equiv State_1 = activeopening \wedge Lin_1 = k_1+1$
$\quad\quad \wedge State_2 = activeopening \wedge Remtry_2 > 0$
$\quad\quad \wedge Lin_2 = k_2 \wedge (REJ, sn, Lin_1) \notin z_2$

$Z_2 \equiv State_1 = activeopening \wedge Lin_1 = k_1 \wedge Rin_1 = k_2$
$\quad\quad \wedge State_2 = activeopening \wedge Lin_2 = k_2 \wedge Remtry_2 > 0$

$Z_3 \equiv State_1 = open \wedge Lin_1 = k_1$
$\quad\quad \wedge State_2 = activeopening \wedge Lin_2 = k_2$

$Z_4 \equiv State_1=activeopening \land Lin_1=k_1+1$
$\quad \land State_2=activeopening \land Lin_2=k_2$
$\quad \land Rin_2=k_1+1 \land (REJ,sn,Lin_1) \notin z_2$

$Z_5 \equiv State_1=activeopening \land Lin_1=k_1+1$
$\quad \land State_2=activeopening \land Lin_2=k_2+1$
$\quad \land (REJ,sn,Lin_1) \notin z_2 \land (REJ,sn,Lin_2) \notin z_1$

$Z_6 \equiv State_1=activeopening \land Lin_1=k_1 \land Rin_1=k_2$
$\quad \land State_2=activeopening \land Lin_2=k_2+1$
$\quad \land (REJ,sn,Lin_2) \notin z_1 \land (REJ,k_2,rn) \notin z_2$

$Z_7 \equiv State_1=activeopening \land Lin_1=k_1 \land Rin_1=k_2$
$\quad \land State_2=activeopening \land Lin_2=k_2$
$\quad \land Rin_2=k_1$

$Z_8 \equiv State_1=activeopening \land Lin_1=k_1 \land Rin_1=k_2$
$\quad \land State_2=activeopening \land Lin_2=k_2+1$
$\quad \land Rin_2=k_1 \land (REJ,k_2,rn) \notin z_2$

$Z_9 \equiv State_1=open \land State_2=open$

The following *leads-to* properties can be proved (similar to Y_{0-4}):

$Q_0 \equiv Z_0$ leads-to $Z_1 \lor Z_{\bar{1}} \lor Z_2 \lor Z_{\bar{2}} \lor Z_3 \lor Z_{\bar{3}}$ via primary message $CRAO_2$

$Q_1 \equiv Z_1$ leads-to $Z_2[k_1+1/k_1] \lor Z_3[k_1+1/k_1]$
$\quad \lor Z_{\bar{3}}[k_1+1/k_1] \lor Z_4 \lor Z_5$ via primary message $CRAO_2$

$Q_2 \equiv Z_2$ leads-to $Z_3 \lor Z_{\bar{3}} \lor Z_6 \lor Z_7$ via primary message $CRAO_2$

$Q_3 \equiv Z_3$ leads-to Z_9 via primary message $CRAO_2$ and secondary messages $\{CRACK, DATA\}$.

$Q_4 \equiv Z_4$ leads-to $Z_7[k_1+1/k_1] \lor Z_3[k_1+1/k_1]$
$\quad \lor Z_{\bar{3}}[k_1+1/k_1]$ via primary message $CRAO_2$

$Q_5 \equiv Z_5$ leads-to $Z_{\bar{4}}[k_1+1/k_1] \lor Z_4[k_2+1/k_2]$
$\quad \lor Z_3[k_1+1/k_1, k_2+1/k_2]$
$\quad \lor Z_{\bar{3}}[k_1+1/k_1, k_2+1/k_2]$ via primary message $CRAO_2$

$Q_6 \equiv Z_6$ leads-to $Z_3[k_2+1/k_2] \lor Z_{\bar{4}} \lor Z_8$ via primary message $CRAO_2$

$Q_7 \equiv Z_7$ leads-to $Z_3 \lor Z_{\bar{3}}$ via primary message $CRAO_2$

$Q_8 \equiv Z_8$ leads-to $Z_3[k_2+1/k_2] \lor Z_7[k_2+1/k_2]$ via primary message $CRAO_2$

Applying the closure property of *leads-to* relations to Q_0 through Q_8 results in Q_0 leads-to Q_8, which is L_1.

4.4. Proof of L_2

We define the following predicates:

$W_1 \equiv State_1=open \lor State_1=closed$

$W_2 \equiv State_1=activeopening \land Remtry_1>0$
$\quad \land Lin_1=k \land (State_2 \in \{closed, listen\}$
$\quad \quad \lor (State_2=passiveopening \land Rin_2<Lin_1))$
$\quad \land Lin_2=j$

$W_3 \equiv State_1=activeopening \land Remtry_1=0$
$\quad \land Lin_1=k+1 \land (State_2 \in \{closed, listen\}$
$\quad \quad \lor (State_2=passiveopening \land Rin_2<Lin_1))$
$\quad \land Lin_2=j$

$W_4 \equiv State_1=activeopening \land Remtry_1=0$
$\quad \land Lin_1=k+1 \land Rin_1<j+1$
$\quad \land State_2=activeopening \land (X,sn,Lin_2) \notin z_1$
$\quad \land Lin_2=j+1$

$W_5 \equiv State_1=activeopening \land Remtry_1=0$
$\quad \land Lin_1=k+1 \land Lin_2=j+1$
$\quad \land State_2=passiveopening \land Rin_2=k+1$

$W_6 \equiv State_1=activeopening \land Remtry_1=0$
$\quad \land Lin_1=k+1 \land Rin_1<j+1$
$\quad \land State_1=activeopening \land Lin_2=j+1$
$\quad \land Rin_2=k+1$

$W_7 \equiv State_1=activeopening \land Remtry_1>0 \land Lin_1=k$
$\quad \land State_2=closing \land Lin_2=j \land Rin_2<Lin_1$

$W_8 \equiv State_1=activeopening \land Lin_1=k$
$\quad \land State_2=closing \land Lin_2=j \land Rin_2=Lin_1$

$V_0 \equiv State_1 \in \{open, closed\} \land State_2=closing$

$V_1 \equiv State_1=activeopening \land State_2=closed$

The following *leads-to* properties hold:

$R_1 \equiv W_2$ leads-to $W_3 \lor Y_1 \lor Z_0[k/k_1, j/k_2]$ via primary message $CRAO_1$

$R_2 \equiv W_3$ leads-to $W_1 \lor W_4 \lor W_5$ via primary message $CRAO_1$

$R_3 \equiv W_4$ leads-to $Z_{\bar{4}}[k+1/k_1, j/k_2] \lor W_6 \lor W_1$ via primary message $CRAO_1$

$R_4 \equiv W_5$ leads-to $Y_3[k+1/k] \lor W_1$ via primary message $CRPO_2$

$R_5 \equiv W_6$ leads-to $Z_7[k+1/k_1, j+1/k_2]$
$\quad \lor Z_3[k+1/k_1, j+1/k_2] \lor W_1$ via primary message $CRAO_2$

$R_6 \equiv W_7$ leads-to V_1 via primary message $CRAO_1$

$R_7 \equiv W_8$ leads-to V_0 via primary message DR_2

$R_8 \equiv Z_{\bar{3}}[k/k_1, j/k_2]$ leads-to $W_1 \lor W_8$ via primary message $CRAO_1$ and secondary messages $\{CRACK, DATA\}$.

L_2 is $W_2 \lor Y_1 \lor Z_0 \lor Z_{\bar{3}} \lor W_7 \lor W_8$ leads-to W_1. By closure of R_1 through R_5, W_2 leads-to $W_1 \lor Y_1 \lor Y_3 \lor Z_0 \lor Z_3 \lor Z_{\bar{4}} \lor Z_7$. We have Y_1 leads-to Y_3 as in L_0 (closure of P_1, P_2 and P_4). We also have Z_0 leads-to $Z_{\bar{3}} \lor Z_3$ as in L_1 (closure of Q_0 through Q_2 and Q_4 through Q_8). From Q_4 and Q_7, we have $Z_{\bar{4}}$ leads-to $Z_3 \lor Z_{\bar{3}} \lor Z_{\bar{7}}$ and Z_7 leads-to $Z_3 \lor Z_{\bar{3}}$. Thus, by closure of these rules with R_7 and R_8, W_2 leads-to $W_1 \lor Y_3 \lor Z_3 \lor V_0$. Since $V_1 \Rightarrow W_2$, from R_6 we have W_7 leads-to $W_1 \lor Y_3 \lor Z_3 \lor V_0$.

We can now see that $W_2 \lor Y_1 \lor Z_0 \lor Z_{\bar{3}} \lor W_7 \lor W_8$ leads-to $V_0 \lor W_1 \lor Y_3 \lor Z_3$. Since $V_0 \Rightarrow W_1$, $Y_3 \Rightarrow W_1$, and $Z_3 \Rightarrow W_1$, we have established L_2.

4.5. Proof of L_3

$W_9 \equiv State_1 = listen \lor State_1 = open$

$W_{10} \equiv State_1 = passiveopening \land Lin_1 = k$
$\land State_2 \in \{closed, listen, passiveopening\}$
$\land Lin_2 = j$

$W_{11} \equiv State_1 = passiveopening \land Lin_1 = k$
$\land State_2 = closing \land Lin_2 = j \land Rin_2 = Lin_1$

$W_{12} \equiv State_1 = passiveopening \land Lin_1 = k$
$\land State_2 = closing \land Lin_2 = j \land Rin_2 < Lin_1$

$W_{13} \equiv State_1 = passiveopening \land Lin_1 = k$
$\land State_2 = activeopening$
$\land Lin_2 = j \land Remtry_2 > 0$

The following *leads-to* properties hold:

$R_9 \equiv W_{10}$ leads-to $W_9 \lor W_{13}$ via primary message $CRPO_1$ and secondary messages $\{RESET, REJ\}$.

$R_{10} \equiv W_{11}$ leads-to W_9 via primary message DR_2.

$R_{11} \equiv W_{12}$ leads-to W_{10} via primary message $CRPO_1$.

$R_{12} \equiv Y_{\overline{3}}$ leads-to $Y_{\overline{5}} \lor W_{11}$ via primary message $CRPO_2$ and secondary messages $\{CRACK, DATA\}$.

L_3 is $W_{10} \lor W_{11} \lor W_{12} \lor W_{13} \lor Y_{\overline{3}}[j/k]$ leads-to W_9. $W_{13} \Rightarrow Y_0[j/k]$ and $Y_{\overline{5}}$ leads-to $Y_{\overline{3}}$ as in L_0. From the closure of R_9 through R_{12} and P_0, P_1, P_2, and P_4, we have that $W_{10} \lor W_{11} \lor W_{12} \lor W_{13} \lor Y_{\overline{3}}[j/k]$ leads-to $W_9 \lor Y_{\overline{5}}$. Since $Y_{\overline{5}} \Rightarrow W_9$, this establishes L_3.

4.6. Proof of L_4

$W_{14} \equiv State_1 = closing$
$\land (State_2 \in \{closed, listen, open, closing\}$
$\lor State_2 = passiveopening \land Rin_1 < Lin_2)$

$W_{15} \equiv State_1 = closing \land State_2 = passiveopening$
$\land Rin_1 = Lin_2$

$W_{16} \equiv State_1 = closed$

The following lead to properties hold:

$R_{13} \equiv W_{14}$ leads-to $W_{16} \lor W_{\overline{7}}$ via primary message DR_1 and secondary messages $\{REJ, RESET, DRACK\}$.

$R_{14} \equiv W_{15}$ leads-to W_{16} via primary message $CRPO_2$.

L_4 is $W_{\overline{7}} \lor W_{\overline{8}} \lor W_{14} \lor W_{15}$ leads-to W_{16}. From $R_{\overline{7}}$ we have $W_{\overline{8}}$ leads-to $V_{\overline{0}}$. Because $V_{\overline{0}} \Rightarrow W_{14}$, we have $W_{\overline{8}}$ leads-to $W_{16} \lor W_{\overline{7}}$. From $R_{\overline{6}}$, we have $W_{\overline{7}}$ leads-to $V_{\overline{1}}$. From the closure of R_{13} through R_{14}, and R_6 through R_7, we have $W_{\overline{7}} \lor W_{\overline{8}} \lor W_{14} \lor W_{15}$ leads-to $V_{\overline{1}} \lor W_{16}$. Since $V_{\overline{1}} \Rightarrow W_{16}$, we have established L_4.

REFERENCES

[COUR] J. P. Courtiat, J. M. Ayache, and B. Algayres, "Petri Nets are Good for Protocols", *Proc. ACM SIGCOMM '84*, June 1984.

[CHAN] K. M. Chandy and J. Misra. "An Example of Stepwise Refinement of Distributed Programs," *ACM Trans. on Prog. Lang. and Syst.*, Vol. 8, No. 3, July 1986.

[DIJK] E. W. Dijkstra, *A Discipline of Programming*, Prentice Hall, 1975.

[DoD] *Transmission Control Protocol*, DDN Protocol Handbook: DoD Military Standard Protocols, DDN Network Information Center, SRI, MILSTD1778, Aug 1983.

[ISO] International Organization for Standardization, *Information Processing Systems* – Open Systems Interconnection – Transport Protocol Specification, ISO DIS 8073, 1985.

[JUR1] W. Jurgensen and S. T. Vuong, "Formal Specification and Validation of ISO Transport Protocol Components, Using Petri Nets", *Proc. ACM SIGCOMM '84*, Jun 1984.

[JUR2] W. Jurgensen and S. T. Vuong, "CSP and CSP Nets: A Dual Model for Protocol Specification and Verification", *Protocol Specification, Testing, and Verification IV*, ed. Y. Yemini, R. Strom, and S. Yemini, 1984.

[KUR] J. F. Kurose and Y. Yemini, "The Specification and Verification of a Connection Establishment Protocol Using Temporal Logic," *Protocol Specification, Testing and Verification II*, ed. C. A. Sunshine, 1982.

[LAM] S. S. Lam and A. U. Shankar, "Protocol verification via projections," *IEEE Trans. on Soft. Eng.*, Vol. SE-10, No. 4, July 1984, pp. 325-342.

[LIN] H. P. Lin, "Modeling a Transport Layer Protocol Using First-Order Logic", *Proc. ACM SIGCOMM '86*, Aug 1986.

[SHAN0] A. U. Shankar and S. S. Lam, "Time-dependent distributed systems: proving safety, liveness and real-time properties," Tech. Rep. CS-TR-1586, Computer Science Dept., Univ. of Maryland, also TR-85-24, Computer Science Dept., Univ. of Texas, October 1985, revised October 1986, to appear in *Distributed Computing*.

[SHAN1] A. U. Shankar, "A Verified Sliding Window Protocol with Variable Flow Control", *Proc. ACM SIGCOMM '86*, Aug 1986.

[SHAN2] A. U. Shankar, "Verified data transfer protocols with variable flow control", CS-TR-1746, Dept. of Computer Science, University of Maryland, Mar 1987.

[SHAN3] A. U. Shankar and S. S.. Lam, "A Stepwise Refinement Heuristic for Protocol Construction", CS-TR-1812, Dept. of Computer Science, University of Maryland, Mar 1987.

[SUN] C. A. Sunshine and Y. K. Dalal, "Connection Management in Transport Protocols", *Computer Networks*, Vol.2(6), Dec 1978.

Table 1: Events of entity i

$ActiveOpen_i \equiv$
    when $State_i = closed$ **do** $[State_i \leftarrow activeopening\,;\ Lin_i \leftarrow Lin_i +1]$

$PassiveOpen_i \equiv$
    when $State_i = closed$ **do** $State_i \leftarrow listen$

$EndListening_i \equiv$
    when $State_i = listen$ **do** $State_i \leftarrow closed$

$Send\ CRAO_i \equiv$
    when $State_i = activeopening$ **do** $Send_i(CRAO, Lin_i, Rin_i)$

$Rec\ CRAO_i \equiv$
    when $Rec_j(CRAO, sn, rn)$ **do**
      case $State_i$ **is**
        $closed \rightarrow Send_i(REJ, Lin_i, sn)$
        $listen \rightarrow [State_i \leftarrow passiveopening\,;\ Rin_i \leftarrow sn\,;\ Lin_i \leftarrow Lin_i +1]$
        $activeopening \rightarrow$
          $[\textbf{if}\ sn > Rin_i\ \textbf{then}\ Rin_i \leftarrow sn\,;$
            $\textbf{if}\ rn = Lin_i\ \textbf{then}\ [State_i \leftarrow open\,;\ Send_i(CRACK, Lin_i, Rin_i)]]$
        $passiveopening \rightarrow \textbf{if}\ sn > Rin_i\ \textbf{then}\ [Rin_i \leftarrow sn\,;\ Lin_i \leftarrow Lin_i +1]$
        $open \rightarrow \textbf{if}\ rn = Lin_i\ \textbf{then}\ Send_i(CRACK, Lin_i, Rin_i)$
        $closing \rightarrow \textbf{if}\ sn > Rin_i\ \textbf{then}\ [State_i \leftarrow closed\,;\ Rin_i \leftarrow null]$

$Send\ CRPO_i \equiv$
    when $State_i = passiveopening$ **do** $Send_i(CRPO, Lin_i, Rin_i)$

$Rec\ CRPO_i \equiv$
    when $Rec_j(CRPO, sn, rn)$ **do**
      case $State_i$ **is**
        $closed \rightarrow Send_i(REJ, Lin_i, sn)$
        $listen \rightarrow Send_i(RESET, Lin_i, sn)$
        $passiveopening \rightarrow$
          $\textbf{if}\ sn \geq Rin_i\ \textbf{then}$
            $[Rin_i \leftarrow sn\,;$
            $\textbf{if}\ rn = Lin_i\ \textbf{then}$
              $[Send_i(RESET, Lin_i, sn)\,;\ State_i \leftarrow listen\,;\ Rin_i \leftarrow null]]$
        $activeopening \rightarrow$
          $[\textbf{if}\ sn > Rin_i\ \textbf{then}\ Rin_i \leftarrow sn\,;$
            $\textbf{if}\ rn = Lin_i\ \textbf{then}\ [State_i \leftarrow open\,;\ Send_i(CRACK, Lin_i, Rin_i)]]$
        $open \rightarrow \textbf{if}\ rn = Lin_i\ \textbf{then}\ Send_i(CRACK, Lin_i, Rin_i)$
        $closing \rightarrow \textbf{if}\ sn > Rin_i\ \textbf{then}\ [State_i \leftarrow closed\,;\ Rin_i \leftarrow null]$

$Rec\ CRACK_i \equiv$
    when $Rec_j(CRACK, sn, rn)$ **do**
      case $State_i$ **is**
        $closed, listen, open, closing \rightarrow$ no action;
        $passiveopening, activeopening \rightarrow \textbf{if}\ rn = Lin_i\ \textbf{then}\ State_i \leftarrow open\,;$

$Rec\ RESET_i \equiv$
    when $Rec_j(RESET, sn, recsn)$ **do**
      case $State_i$ **is**
        $closed, listen, activeopening, open \rightarrow$ no action
        $passiveopening \rightarrow \textbf{if}\ sn \geq Rin_i\ \wedge\ recsn = Lin_i$
              $\textbf{then}\ [State_i \leftarrow listen\,;\ Rin_i \leftarrow null]$
        $closing \rightarrow \textbf{if}\ sn \geq Rin_i\ \wedge\ recsn = Lin_i$
              $\textbf{then}\ [State_i \leftarrow closed\,;\ Rin_i \leftarrow null]$

Table 1 (continued): Events of entity i

$Rec\ REJ_i\ \equiv$
    when $Rec_j(REJ, sn, recsn)$ **do**
        case $State_i$ **is**
            $closed, listen, open \rightarrow$ no action
            $passive opening \rightarrow$ **if** $sn \geq Rin_i \land recsn = Lin_i$
                      then $[State_i \leftarrow listen\ ;\ Rin_i \leftarrow null]$
            $active opening \rightarrow$ **if** $sn \geq Rin_i \land recsn = Lin_i$
                      then $[State_i \leftarrow closed\ ;\ Rin_i \leftarrow null]$
            $closing \rightarrow$ **if** $sn = Rin_i \land recsn = Lin_i$
                      then $[State_i \leftarrow closed\ ;\ Rin_i \leftarrow null]$

$Rec\ DATA_i\ \equiv$
    when $Rec_j(DATA, sn, rn)$ **do**
        case $State_i$ **is**
            $closed, listen, closing \rightarrow$ no action
            $active opening, passive opening \rightarrow$
                if $rn = Lin_i$ **then** $[State_i \leftarrow open\ ;\ \{\text{Sink data if in window}\}]$
            $open \rightarrow$ **if** $rn = Lin_i$ **then** $\{\text{Sink data if in window}\}$

$Send\ DATA_i\ \equiv$
    when $State_i = open$ **do** $Send_i(DATA, Lin_i, Rin_i)$

$InitClosing_i\ \equiv$
    when $State_i = open$ **do** $State_i = closing$

$Send\ DR_i\ \equiv$
    when $State_i = closing$ **do** $Send_i(DR, Lin_i, Rin_i)$

$Rec\ DR_i\ \equiv$
    when $Rec_j(DR, sn, rn)$ **do**
        case $State_i$ **is**
            $closed \rightarrow Send_i(REJ, Lin_i, sn)$
            $listen \rightarrow Send_i(RESET, Lin_i, sn)$
            $passive opening \rightarrow$
                if $rn = Lin_i$ **then**
                      $[State_i \leftarrow listen\ ;\ Rin_i \leftarrow null\ ;\ Send_i(DRACK, Lin_i, Rin_i)]$
            $active opening, open, closing \rightarrow$
                if $rn = Lin_i$ **then**
                      $[State_i \leftarrow closed\ ;\ Rin_i \leftarrow null\ ;\ Send_i(DRACK, Lin_i, Rin_i)]$

$Rec\ DRACK_i\ \equiv$
    when $Rec_j(DRACK, sn, rn)$ **do**
        case $State_i$ **is**
            $closed, listen, active opening, passive opening, open \rightarrow$ no action
            $closing \rightarrow$ **if** $sn \geq Rin_i \land rn = Lin_i$
                then $[State_i \leftarrow closed\ ;\ Rin_i \leftarrow null]$

Table 2: Invariant properties of the protocol

{Desired properties relating entity state variables}

$A_0 \equiv State_1 = open \Rightarrow Rin_1 = Lin_2 \wedge Lin_1 = Rin_2$

$A_1 \equiv State_1 = open \Rightarrow State_2 \in \{passiveopening, activeopening, open, closing\}$

{Properties relating entity state variables and sequence numbers in z_1, z_2}

$A_2 \equiv State_1 \in \{closed, listen\} \Rightarrow Rin_1 = null$

$A_3 \equiv (X, sn, rn) \in z_1 \Rightarrow sn \leq Lin_1 \wedge rn \leq Lin_2$ {note that $rn \leq Lin_2$ includes $rn = null$}

$A_4 \equiv Rin_1 \leq Lin_2$

$A_5 \equiv closing_1 \wedge closing_2 \Rightarrow Rin_1 = Lin_2$

{Properties relating $State_1$ and message types sent by current incarnation}

$B_0 \equiv State_1 = activeopening \wedge (X, Lin_1, rn) \in z_1 \Rightarrow X = CRAO$

$B_1 \equiv State_1 = passiveopening \wedge (X, Lin_1, rn) \in z_1 \Rightarrow X = CRPO$

$B_2 \equiv State_1 = open \wedge (X, Lin_1, rn) \in z_1 \Rightarrow X \in \{CRAO, CRPO, CRACK, DATA\}$

$B_3 \equiv State_1 = closing \wedge (X, Lin_1, rn) \in z_1 \Rightarrow X \in \{CRAO, CRPO, CRACK, DATA, DR\}$

$B_4 \equiv State_1 = open \wedge (CRPO, Lin_1, rn) \in z_1 \Rightarrow State_2 \neq passiveopening$

{Properties relating $State_1$, messages in z_2, and $State_2$}

$C_0 \equiv (State_1 = activeopening \wedge (X, sn, Lin_1) \in z_2$
$\qquad \wedge X \in \{CRAO, CRPO, CRACK, DATA, DR\})$
$\quad \vee (State_1 = passiveopening \wedge (Y, sn, Lin_1) \in z_2 \wedge Y \in \{CRACK, DATA, DR\})$
$\quad \Rightarrow sn = Lin_2 \wedge Rin_2 = Lin_1$

$C_1 \equiv State_1 = activeopening \wedge (CRAO, sn, Lin_1) \in z_2 \Rightarrow State_2 \in \{activeopening, open, closing\}$

$C_2 \equiv State_1 = activeopening \wedge (CRPO, sn, Lin_1) \in z_2 \Rightarrow State_2 = passiveopening$

$C_3 \equiv State_1 = activeopening \wedge (X, sn, Lin_1) \in z_2 \wedge X \in \{CRACK, DATA\}$
$\quad \Rightarrow Rin_1 = Lin_2 \wedge State_2 \in \{open, closing\}$

$C_4 \equiv State_1 = activeopening \wedge (DR, sn, Lin_1) \in z_2 \Rightarrow sn = Lin_2 \wedge State_2 = closing$

$D_1 \equiv State_1 = passiveopening \wedge (X, sn, Lin_1) \in z_2 \wedge X \in \{CRACK, DATA\}$
$\quad \Rightarrow Rin_1 = Lin_2 \wedge State_2 \in \{open, closing\}$

$D_2 \equiv State_1 = passiveopening \wedge (DR, sn, Lin_1) \in z_2 \Rightarrow sn = Lin_2 \wedge State_2 = closing$

$E_1 \equiv State_1 = open \wedge (DR, sn, Lin_1) \in z_2 \Rightarrow sn = Lin_2 \wedge State_2 = closing$

$F_1 \equiv State_1 = closing \wedge (DR, sn, Lin_1) \in z_2$
$\quad \Rightarrow sn = Rin_1 \wedge State_2 \in \{activeopening, passiveopening, closing, closed, listen\}$

APPENDIX A

We say that q is *not affected* by event e, if the occurrence of e does not update any of the variables in q. We say that q is *disables* event e, if q is of the form $A \Rightarrow B$ where A implies that e is not enabled. In either case, $\{q\} e \{q\}$ holds automatically.

We use $(M_1 \mid M_2, sn, rn) \in z_i$ to denote $(X, sn, rn) \in z_i \wedge X \in \{M_1, M_2\}$. We sometimes use comma to denote conjunction: e.g., $\{p, q\} e \{r\}$ to denote $\{p \wedge q\} e \{r\}$.

We will often need to refer to *subevents* "e_i when p". A subevent is an event e_i occurring when the condition p holds. We use the notation $Rec(X, n, m)_i$ to denote the event $RecX_i$ when $(Rec_j(X, sn, rn) \wedge sn = n \wedge rn = m)$.

We will find it convenient to refer to the following sets of subevents.

$UpdateLin_i \equiv$
$\{ActiveOpen_i; Rec(CRAO, sn_1, rn)_i$ when $State_i = passiveopening$ and $sn_1 > Rin_i;$
$Rec(CRAO, sn_2, rn)_i$ when $State_i = listen\}$.
$UpdateLin_i$ refers to events of entity i under conditions when Lin_i will be updated.

$UpdateRin_i \equiv$
$\{Rec(CRAO, sn_1, rn)_i$ when $State_i = listen$ or $(State_i \in \{activeopening, passiveopening\}$ and $sn_1 > Rin_i); Rec(CRPO, sn_2, rn)_i$ when $State_i \in \{activeopening, passiveopening\}$ and $sn_2 > Rin_i\}$. $UpdateRin_i$ refers to events and conditions under which Rin_i will be updated to a non *null* value.

$NullPO_i \equiv$
$\{$when $State_i = passiveopening$:
$Rec(REJ, sn_1, Lin_i)_i$ and $sn_1 \geq Rin_i;$

$Rec\ (RESET, sn_2, Lin_i)_i$ and $sn_2 \geq Rin_i$;
$Rec\ (CRPO, sn_3, Lin_i)_i$ and $sn_3 \geq Rin_i$;
$Rec\ (DR, sn_4, Lin_i)_i\ \}$.

$NullAO_i \equiv$
{when $State_i = activeopening$: $Rec\ (REJ, sn_1, Lin_i)_i$ when $sn_1 \geq Rin_i$; $Rec\ (DR, sn_2, Lin_i)_i\ \}$.

$NullClosing_i \equiv$
{when $State_i = closing$: $Rec\ (CRAO, sn_1, rn)_i$ when $sn_1 > Rin_i$; $Rec\ (CRPO, sn_2, rn)_i$ when $sn_2 > Rin_i$; $Rec\ (RESET, sn_3, Lin_i)_i$ when $sn_3 \geq Rin_i$; $Rec\ (REJ, sn_4, Lin_i)_i$ when $sn_4 = Rin_i$; $Rec\ (DR, sn_5, Lin_i)_i$; $Rec\ (DRACK, sn_6, Lin_i)_i$ and $sn_6 = Rin_i\ \}$.

$NullRin_i \equiv$
$NullPO \cup NullAO \cup NullClosing \cup$
{$Rec\ (DR, sn, Lin_i)_i$ when $State_i = open$}.
$NullRin_i$ refers to events and conditions under which Rin_i will be set to null. These are also the same as the events and conditions under which $State_i$ is set back to closed or listen.

$CRACKsent_i \equiv$
{$Rec\ (CRAO, sn, Lin_i)_i$ when $State_i \in \{activeopening, open\}$; $Rec\ (CRPO, sn, Lin_i)_i$ when $State_i \in \{activeopening, open\}\}$. $CRACKsent_i$ refers to the events and conditions under which a $CRACK$ will be sent.

$BecomeOpen_i \equiv$
{$Rec\ (CRAO, sn_1, Lin_i)_i$ when $State_i = activeopening$; $Rec\ (CRPO, sn_2, Lin_i)_i$ when $State_i = activeopening$; $Rec\ (CRACK\ |\ DATA, sn_3, Lin_i)_i$ when $State_i \in \{activeopening, passiveopening\}$}.
$BecomeOpen_i$ refers to events and conditions under which an entity will become open.

$\{p\}\ S\ \{q\}$, where S is one of these sets of subevents, will mean $\{p\}\ e\ \{q\}$ for each subevent in S.

Proof of preservation of A_0

$A_0 \equiv State_1 = open \Rightarrow Rin_1 = Lin_2 \land Rin_2 = Lin_1$.
The events that affect A_0 are $BecomeOpen_1$, $InitClosing_1$, $UpdateRin_1$, $UpdateRin_2$, $UpdateLin_1$, $UpdateLin_2$, $NullRin_1$, $NullRin_2$. We have the following:

$\{C_0 \land C_3 \land D_1\}\ BecomeOpen\ \{A_0\}$. To become $open$, entity 1 must be $activeopening$ or $passiveopening$. $C_0 \land C_3 \land D_1$ states that the consequent of A_0 holds when the conditions of $BecomeOpen$ are met.

$\{A_0\}\ InitClosing\ \{A_0\}$. After the event, A_0 is vacuously true because $State_1 = closing$.

We now assume $State_1 = open$; otherwise, $State_1 \neq open$ will continue to be true after the following events occur and A_0 will be vacuously true.

$\{A_0\}\ UpdateRin_1\ \{A_0\}$ because none of the conditions of $UpdateRin_1$ are satisfied when $State_i = open$.

$\{A_{0,1,3}\}\ UpdateRin_2\ \{A_0\}$. From A_0 we know $Rin_2 = Lin_1$. From A_1, we know $State_2 \neq listen$, so we need only consider the conditions of $UpdateRin_2$ when $State_1 = activeopening$ or $passiveopening$. Those include $sn_1, sn_2 > Rin_2$. From A_3 we know $sn_1, sn_2 \leq Lin_1$. So the conditions cannot be met, Rin_2 is not changed, and A_0 holds after the events.

$\{A_0\}\ UpdateLin_1\ \{A_0\}$ because none of the conditions of $UpdateLin_1$ are met when $State_i = open$.

$\{A_{0,1,3}\}\ UpdateLin_2\ \{A_0\}$. From A_1 we know $State_2 \notin \{closed, listen\}$, so the only condition of $UpdateLin_2$ to be considered is when $State_1 = passiveopening$. From A_0 we know $Rin_2 = Lin_1$ and from A_3, $sn_1 \leq Lin_1$. Thus, the condition $sn_1 > Rin_2$ cannot be met, Lin_2 is not changed, and A_0 holds after the events.

$\{A_0 \land A_3 \land B_2 \land B_4 \land C_{\bar{0}}\}\ NullPO_2\ \{A_0\}$. From A_0 we know $Rin_2 = Lin_1$. The conditions in $NullPO_2$ state $sn_1, sn_2, sn_3 \geq Rin_2$. From A_3 we know $sn_1, sn_2, sn_3 \leq Lin_1$. Therefore, $sn_1, sn_2, sn_3 = Lin_1$. From $C_{\bar{0}}$ we know $sn_4 = Lin_1$. But $(REJ\ |\ RESET\ |\ DR, Lin_1, Lin_2) \notin \mathbf{z}_1$ by B_2, and $(CRPO, Lin_1, Lin_2) \notin \mathbf{z}_1$ by B_4. So A_0 holds after the events.

$\{A_0 \land A_3 \land C_{\bar{0}} \land B_2\}\ NullAO_2\ \{A_0\}$. From A_0 we know $Rin_2 = Lin_1$. The condition $sn_1 \geq Rin_2$ in $NullAO_2$ with A_3 implies $sn_1 = Lin_1$. From $C_{\bar{0}}$ we know $sn_2 = Lin_1$. But B_2 says $(REJ\ |\ DR, Lin_1, Lin_2) \notin \mathbf{z}_1$. So A_0 holds after the events.

$\{A_0 \land A_3 \land B_2 \land F_{\bar{1}}\}\ NullClosing_2\ \{A_0\}$. From A_0, we know $Rin_2 = Lin_1$. From A_3, we know $sn_1, sn_2, sn_3, sn_4, sn_6 \leq Lin_1$. The conditions $sn_1 > Rin_2$ and $sn_2 > Rin_2$ are therefore impossible to satisfy. The condition $sn_3 \geq Rin_2$ with A_3 implies $sn_3 = Lin_1$. From $F_{\bar{1}}$, we know $sn_5 = Lin_1$. But B_2 says $(RESET\ |\ REJ\ |\ DR\ |\ DRACK, Lin_1, Lin_2) \notin \mathbf{z}_1$. So A_0 holds after the events.

$\{A_0 \land E_{\bar{1}} \land B_2\}\ Rec\ DR_2$ when $State_1 = open\ \{A_0\}$. From A_0 we know $Rin_2 = Lin_1$. This event will set Rin_2 to null if $(DR, sn_1, Lin_2) \in \mathbf{z}_1$. But $E_{\bar{1}}$ says $sn_1 = Lin_1$, and B_2 says $(DR, Lin_1, Lin_2) \notin \mathbf{z}_1$. So A_0 holds after the event.

$\{A_{0,3} \land B_{2,4} \land C_{0,\bar{0}} \land E_1 \land F_1\}\ NullRin_2\ \{A_0\}$. From the proof above of $NullAO$, $NullPO$, $NullClosing$, and $Rec\ DR$.

$\{A_0\}\ NullRin_1\ \{A_0\}$. Because $State_1 = open$, the only event of $NullRin_1$ to consider is the $Rec\ DR$ event which makes $State_i = closed$, leaving A_0 vacuously true after the event.

For all other events e, A_0 is either not affected by e, disables e, or is made vacuously true by e. Since the events of entities 1 and 2 are symmetric, and we have considered events at both entities 1 and 2 that might affect A_0, we now consider both A_0 and $A_{\bar{0}}$ to be marked as PRESERVED.

$$\boxed{\{A_{0,1,3} \land B_{2,4} \land C_{0,\bar{0},3} \land D_1 \land E_{\bar{1}} \land F_{\bar{1}}\}\ e\ \{A_0\}}$$
PRESERVED = $\{A_0\}$

Proof of preservation of C_0

$C_0 \equiv (State_1 = activeopening \wedge$
$\quad (CRAO \mid CRPO \mid CRACK \mid DATA \mid DR, sn, Lin_1) \in \mathbf{z}_2$
$\quad \vee (State_1 = passiveopening$
$\quad \wedge (CRACK \mid DATA \mid DR, sn, Lin_1) \in \mathbf{z}_2)$
$\Rightarrow sn = Lin_2 \wedge Rin_2 = Lin_1.$

Case 1. $State_1 = activeopening \wedge$
$\quad (CRAO \mid CRPO \mid CRACK \mid DATA \mid DR, sn, Lin_1) \in \mathbf{z}_2$
$\Rightarrow sn = Lin_2 \wedge Rin_2 = Lin_1.$

The events that affect C_0 are $ActiveOpen_1$, $SendCR_2$, $Send\ CRPO_2$, $Send\ DATA_2$, $Send\ DR_2$, $CRACKsent_2$, $UpdateLin_2$, $UpdateRin_2$, $NullRin_2$. Note that the only event of $UpdateLin_1$ enabled is $ActiveOpen$, which is already being considered.

$\{A_{\overline{3}} \wedge C_0\}\ ActiveOpen_1\ \{C_0\}$. By $A_{\overline{3}}$, for all messages $(X, sn, rn) \in \mathbf{z}_2$, $rn \leq Lin_1$. This event increases Lin_1 and sends no new messages. Therefore, after the event, there are no messages $(X, sn, Lin_1) \in \mathbf{z}_2$, and C_0 becomes vacuously true.

$\{C_0\}$ (all listed send events of entity 2) $\{C_0\}$ because all these events send a message of the form (X, Lin_2, Rin_2).

We now assume the antecedent of C_0; otherwise, the antecedent will continue to be false after the following events occur and C_0 will be vacuously true.

$\{C_{0-4} \wedge A_3\}\ UpdateLin_2\ \{C_0\}$. Given the antecedent of C_0, C_{1-4} implies that $State_2 \notin \{closed, listen\}$. Thus, the only part of $UpdateLin_2$ to be considered is when $State_2 = passiveopening$. From C_0, $Rin_2 = Lin_1$. The argument proceeds as in A_0, using C_{1-4} instead of A_1 and C_0 instead of A_0.

$\{A_3 \wedge C_{0-4}\}\ UpdateRin_2\ \{C_0\}$. From C_{1-4}, we know $State_2 \neq listen$, so we need only consider the conditions of $UpdateRin_2$ when $State_1 = activeopening$ or $passiveopening$. From C_0, we know $Rin_2 = Lin_1$. From A_3, we know $sn_1, sn_2 \leq Lin_1$. So the conditions $sn_1 > Rin_2$ and $sn_2 > Rin_2$ in $UpdateRin_2$ cannot be satisfied. Thus C_0 holds after the event.

$\{A_3 \wedge B_0 \wedge C_4\}\ NullRin_2\ \{C_0\}$. From C_0 we know $Rin_2 = Lin_1$. The argument proceeds as in marking A_0 for $NullRin_2$, using C_0 instead of A_0 and B_0 instead of B_2 and B_4.

Case 2. $State_1 = passiveopening$
$\quad \wedge (CRACK \mid DATA \mid DR, sn, Lin_1) \in \mathbf{z}_2$
$\Rightarrow sn = Lin_2 \wedge Rin_2 = Lin_1.$

The events that affect C_0 in this case are $Rec\ CRAO_1$ when $State_1 = listen$, $CRACKsent_2$, $Send\ DATA_2$, $Send\ DR_2$, $UpdateLin_1$, $UpdateLin_2$, $UpdateRin_2$, $NullRin_2$.

$\{A_3 \wedge C_0\}\ Rec\ CRAO_1$ when $State_1 = listen\ \{C_0\}$ because Lin_1 increases, as before.

$\{C_0\}$ all the listed send events $\{C_0\}$ because in all cases the message sent is (X, Lin_2, Rin_2).

We now assume the antecedent of C_0; otherwise, the antecedent will continue to be false after the following events occur and C_0 will be vacuously true.

$\{A_{\overline{3}} \wedge C_0\}\ UpdateLin_1\ \{C_0\}$ since Lin_1 increases, as before.

$\{D_1 \wedge D_2\}\ UpdateLin_2\ \{C_0\}$. We know from D_1, D_2 that $State_2 \notin \{passiveopening, closed, listen\}$, so none of these events are enabled.

$\{A_3 \wedge C_0 \wedge D_{1,2}\}\ UpdateRin_2\ \{C_0\}$. From $D_{1,2}$ we know $State_2 \neq listen$, so we need only consider the conditions of $UpdateRin_2$ when $State_1 = activeopening$ or $passiveopening$. From C_0, we know $Rin_2 = Lin_1$. From A_3, we know $sn_1, sn_2 \leq Lin_1$. So the conditions $sn_1 > Rin_2$ and $sn_2 > Rin_2$ in $UpdateRin_2$ cannot be satisfied. Thus, C_0 holds after the events.

$\{A_3 \wedge B_1 \wedge C_0 \wedge D_{1,2} \wedge E_{\overline{1}} \wedge F_{\overline{1}}\}\ NullRin_2\ \{C_0\}$. From C_0 we know $Rin_2 = Lin_1$, and from D_1, D_2 we know $State_2 \neq passiveopening$, so we need not consider the $NullPO$ events. Otherwise, the argument proceeds just as in marking A_0 for $NullRin_2$, using C_0 instead of A_0 and B_1 instead of B_2.

For all other events e, the assertion C_0 are either not affected by e, disable e, or are made vacuously true by e. Since the events of entities 1 and 2 are symmetric, and we have considered events at both entities 1 and 2 that might affect C_0, we now consider both C_0 and $C_{\overline{0}}$ to be marked as PRESERVED.

---
for all events e
$\{A_{3,\overline{3}} \wedge B_{0,1} \wedge C_{0-4} \wedge D_{1,2} \wedge E_{\overline{1}} \wedge F_{\overline{1}}\}\ e\ \{C_0\}$
PRESERVED = $\{A_0, C_0\}$

Proof of preservation of A_2, A_4, B_4.

$A_2 \equiv State_1 \in \{closed, listen\} \Rightarrow Rin_1 = null.$

The events that affect A_2 are $NullRin_1$, $UpdateRin_1$.

$\{A_2\}\ NullRin_1\ \{A_2\}$. These events make $State_1 \in \{closed, listen\}$, but they also make $Rin_1 = null$ in each case, so A_2 holds after the event.

We now assume the antecedent of A_2; otherwise, the antecedent will continue to be false after the following events occur and A_2 will be vacuously true.

$\{A_2\}\ UpdateRin_1\ \{A_2\}$. None of the conditions of $UpdateRin_1$ are satisfied when $State_1 = closed$. When $State_1 = listen$, Rin_1 may be made non-null, but only if $State_1$ is changed to $passiveopening$. In either case, A_2 holds after the event.

$A_4 \equiv Rin_1 \leq Lin_2.$

The events that affect A_4 are $UpdateRin_1$, $NullRin_1$, and $UpdateLin_2$. The $UpdateLin_2$ events only increment Lin_2, so A_4 holds after the events. The $NullRin_1$ events make $Rin_1 = null$ and $null \leq Lin_2$, so A_4 holds after the events. The $UpdateRin_1$ events make $Rin_1 = sn$ for $(X, sn, rn) \in \mathbf{z}_2$. From $A_{\overline{3}}$, we know $sn \leq Lin_2$. Thus, $Rin_1 \leq Lin_2$ after the events and A_4 holds.

$B_4 \equiv State_1 = open \wedge (CRPO, Lin_1, rn) \in \mathbf{z}_1$
$\quad \Rightarrow State_2 \neq passiveopening$

The events that affect B_4 are $BecomeOpen_1$ and

$Rec\ CRAO_2$ when $State_2 = listen$. Notice that $Send\ CRPO_1$ and $UpdateLin_1$ are not enabled when $State_1 = open$.

$\{B_4 \wedge B_0 \wedge D_1\}\ BecomeOpen_1\ \{B_4\}$. To satisfy the conditions of $BecomeOpen$, $State_1$ must be $activeopening$ or $passiveopening$. From B_0, $State_1 = activeopening$ implies $(CRPO, Lin_1, rn) \notin \mathbf{z}_1$. In that case, B_4 holds after the event trivially. The only other condition of $BecomeOpen$ that could be met is $State_1 = passiveopening \wedge$ $(CRACK \mid DATA, sn_3, Lin_1) \in \mathbf{z}_2$. In that case, D_1 states $State_2 \in \{open, closing\}$. Thus, B_4 holds after the event.

We now assume the antecedent of B_4; otherwise, the antecedent will continue to be false after the following events occur and B_4 will be vacuously true.

$\{A_1 \wedge B_4\}\ Rec\ CRAO_2$ when $State_2 = listen\ \{B_4\}$. When $State_1 = open$, we know from A_1 that $State_2 \neq listen$, so this event is not enabled.

For all other events e, the assertions $A_{2,4}, B_4$ are either not affected by e, disable e, or are made vacuously true by e. Since the events of entities 1 and 2 are symmetric, and we have considered events at both entities 1 and 2 that might affect $A_{2,4}, B_4$, we now consider both $A_{2,4}, B_4$ and $A_{\overline{2},\overline{4}}, B_{\overline{4}}$ to be marked as PRESERVED.

```
for all events e :
  {A_2} e {A_2}
  {A_4 ∧ A_3̄} e {A_4}
  {A_1 ∧ B_{0,4} ∧ D_1} e {B_4}
  PRESERVED = {A_{0,2,4}, B_4, C_0}
```

APPENDIX B

In the following, the event $Rec\ REJ_i$ is modified as in Section 4.

Proof of P_0

Recall $P_0 \equiv Y_0\ leads\text{-}to\ Y_1 \vee Y_2 \vee Y_3$ via primary message $CRAO_1$. We have the following application of the primary message liveness axiom:

$\{Y_0\}\ Rec\ CRAO_2\ \{Y_1 \vee Y_0\}$
$\{Y_0\}\ Rec\ REJ_1\ \{Y_2 \vee Y_0\}$
$\{Y_0\}\ Rec\ CRPO_1\ \{Y_3 \vee Y_0\}$
$\{Y_0\}\ e\ \{Y_0\}$ all other events e.

In particular, C_1, C_3, and C_4 guarantee that $CRAO$, $CRACK$, $DATA$, or DR will not be accepted at entity 1 to change $State_1$. $D_{\overline{1}}$ guarantees that $CRACK$ or $DATA$ will not be accepted at entity 2 to change $State_2$. All other receive events preserve Y_0. The send events at entities 1 and 2 do not affect Y_0.

$Y_0 \Rightarrow Send\ CRAO_1$ enabled.
$\{Y_0 \wedge Y_0[sn/Lin_1, rn/Rin_1]\}\ Rec\ CRAO_2\ \{Y_1\}$
End of proof.

Proof of P_1

Recall $P_1 \equiv Y_1\ leads\text{-}to\ Y_2 \vee Y_3$ via primary message $CRPO_2$. We have the following application of the primary message liveness axiom:

$\{Y_1\}\ Rec\ CRPO_1\ \{Y_3 \vee Y_1\}$
$\{Y_1\}\ Rec\ REJ_1\ \{Y_2 \vee Y_1\}$
$\{Y_1\}\ e\ \{Y_1\}$ by $A_3, B_0, B_4, C_1, C_3, C_4, D_{\overline{1}}, D_{\overline{2}}$
$Y_1 \Rightarrow Send\ CRPO_2$ enabled
$\{Y_1 \wedge Y_1[sn/Lin_2, rn/Rin_2]\}\ Rec\ CRPO_1\ \{Y_3\}$
End of proof.

Proof of P_2

Recall $P_2 \equiv Y_2\ leads\text{-}to\ Y_4$ via primary message $CRAO_1$. We have the following application of the primary message liveness axiom:

$\{Y_2\}\ Rec\ CRAO_2\ \{Y_2 \vee Y_4\}$
$\{Y_2\}\ e\ \{Y_2\}$ by $A_3, B_0, D_{\overline{1}}, D_{\overline{2}}$
$Y_2 \Rightarrow Send\ CRAO_1$ enabled
$\{Y_1 \wedge Y_1[sn/Lin_1, rn/Rin_1]\}\ Rec\ CRAO_2\ \{Y_4\}$
End of proof.

Proof of P_3

Recall $P_3 \equiv Y_3\ leads\text{-}to\ Y_5$ via primary message $CRPO_2$ and secondary messages $\{CRACK_1, DATA_1\}$. We have the following application of the secondary message liveness axiom:

$\{Y_3\}\ Rec\ CRACK_2\ \{Y_3 \vee Y_5\}$
$\{Y_3\}\ Rec\ DATA_2\ \{Y_3 \vee Y_5\}$
$\{Y_3\}\ e\ \{Y_3\}$ by $A_0, A_3, B_2, D_{\overline{2}}, E_1$
$Y_3 \Rightarrow Send\ CRPO_2$ enabled
$\{Y_3 \wedge Y_3[sn/Lin_2, rn/Rin_2]\} \Rightarrow Send\ CRACK_1$ enabled
$Y_4 \wedge Y_4[sn/Lin_1, rn/Rin_1]\}\ Rec\ CRACK_2\ \{Y_5\}$
End of proof.

Proof of P_4

Recall $P_4 \equiv Y_4\ leads\text{-}to\ Y_3[k+1/k]$ via primary message $CRPO_2$. We have the following application of the primary message liveness axiom:

$\{Y_4\}\ Rec\ CRPO_1\ \{Y_3[k+1/k] \vee Y_4\}$
$\{Y_4\}\ e\ \{Y_4\}$ by $A_3, B_0, C_1, C_3, C_4, D_{\overline{1}}, D_{\overline{2}}$
$Y_4 \Rightarrow Send\ CRPO_2$ enabled
$\{Y_4 \wedge Y_4[sn/Lin_1, rn/Rin_1]\}\ Rec\ CRPO_1\ \{Y_3[k+1/k]\}$
End of proof.

Protocol Verification Using Reachability Analysis: The State Space Explosion Problem and Relief Strategies*

F. J. Lin, P. M. Chu, and M. T. Liu

Department of Computer and Information Science
The Ohio State University
Columbus, OH 43210

ABSTRACT

Reachability analysis has proved to be one of the most effective methods in verifying correctness of communication protocols based on the state transition model. Consequently, many protocol verification tools have been built based on the method of reachability analysis. Nevertheless, it is also well known that state space explosion is the most severe limitation to the applicability of this method. Although researchers in the field have proposed various strategies to relieve this intricate problem when building the tools, a survey and evaluation of these strategies has not been done in the literature. In searching for an appropriate approach to tackling such a problem for a grammar-based validation tool, we have collected and evaluated these relief strategies, and have decided to develop our own from yet another but more systematic approach. The results of our research are now reported in this paper. Essentially, the paper is to serve two purposes: first, to give a survey and evaluation of existing relief strategies; second, to propose a new strategy, called PROVAT (PROtocol VAlidation Testing), which is inspired by the heuristic search techniques in Artificial Intelligence. Preliminary results of incorporating the PROVAT strategy into our validation tool are reviewed in the paper. These results show the empirical evidence of the effectiveness of the PROVAT strategy.

---

*Research reported herein was supported by U. S. Army CECOM, Ft. Monmouth, NJ, under Contract No. DAAB07-87-K-A005. The views, opinions, and/or findings contained in this paper are those of the authors and should not be construed as an official Department of Defense of the Army position, policy or decision.

1. Introduction

Reachability analysis has proved to be one of the most effective methods in verifying correctness of communication protocols based on the state transition model. Both general properties and functional properties of protocols can be verified using reachability analysis. Techniques for the former are often called protocol validation; and those for the latter protocol verification. Nevertheless, as far as reachability analysis algorithms are concerned, we will make no distinction between validation and verification in this paper.

Due to its effectiveness and ease of mechanization, many protocol verification tools have been built based on the method of reachability analysis. However, the applicability of this method is severely restricted by the so-called *state space explosion* problem. Although researchers in the field have proposed various strategies to relieve this intricate problem when building the tools, a survey and evaluation of these strategies, to the best of our knowledge, has not been done in the literature. In searching for an appropriate approach to tackling this problem for a grammar-based validation tool [16, 20, 21], we have collected and evaluated these relief strategies, and have decided to develop our own from yet another but more systematic approach.

Thus this paper is written to serve two purposes: to survey and evaluate various relief strategies and to propose a new relief strategy. The readers are assumed to have the basic knowledge of protocol verification via reachability analysis such as those in [12] and [25].

The relief strategy proposed in this paper, called PROVAT (PROtocol Validation Testing), is inspired by the heuristic search techniques in Artificial Intelligence. Preliminary results of incorporating the PROVAT strategy into the grammar-based validation tool have shown its effectiveness in dealing with the state explosion problem.

Permission to copy without fee all or part of this material is granted provided that the copies are not made or distributed for direct commercial advantage, the ACM copyright notice and the title of the publication and its date appear, and notice is given that copying is by permission of the Association for Computing Machinery. To copy otherwise, or to republish, requires a fee and/or specfic permission.

© 1988 ACM 0-89791-245-4/88/0001/0126 $1.50

The rest of the paper is organized as follows. Section 2 gives a survey and classification of existing relief strategies. Section 3 evaluates these strategies and summarizes the features that are essential to an effective relief strategy. In Section 4, we propose the PROVAT strategy based on the observations in previous sections. Section 5 gives the preliminary results of incorporating PROVAT into the validation tool. Finally, we give concluding remarks in Section 6.

2. A Survey and Classification of Existing Relief Strategies

The relief strategies surveyed in this section can be classified into three categories according to when they should be applied. The strategies in the first category are those applied in protocol modeling, i.e., in the stage of formally specifying protocols. The second category of relief strategies are applied after the protocol modeling is done but before the actual verification is performed. The third category of strategies are those incorporated into the verification (and thus reachability analysis) algorithms. In this paper, emphasis will be placed on the third category of strategies.

Relief strategy proposed by West [25] in 1982

The relief strategy proposed by West in 1982 falls into the first category. The major techniques proposed by him are:

1) Restricting the use of many-valued parameters such as sequence numbers in the specification,
2) Limiting the number of messages underway in the message queues,
3) Limiting the classes of transmission errors under consideration.

Relief strategies proposed by Vuong and Cowan [22], Choi and Miller [5], and Chow, Gouda, and Lam [6]

Though different terms such as decomposition, partition, and multi-phase are used by these groups of researchers, the relief strategies they proposed basically follow the same direction. They observe that certain classes of protocols can be decomposed/partitioned into components (or multiple phases), which then can be separately verified to ensure the correctness of the original protocol. This relieves the complexity of verification problem since protocol components are always smaller in the numbers of states and transitions than the original protocol. They are relief strategies of the second category as classified at the beginning of this section.

Relief strategy proposed by Lam and Shankar [14]

The strategy proposed by Lam and Shankar also belongs to the second category. Unlike the strategies of decomposition/partition, Lam and Shankar proposed the *projection* approach, which, instead of partitioning a protocol into multiple phases, constructs from the given protocol an image protocol for each of the functions that is intended to be verified. The states, messages, and events of entities in an image protocol are obtained by aggregating groups of states, messages, and events of corresponding entities in the original protocol. The resulting protocol therefore is smaller than the original protocol and the complexity of the problem is reduced.

The following relief strategies all belong to the third category which are of our major concern in this paper.

Relief strategy proposed by Blumer and Sidhu [3]

The Finite State Machine (FSM) analyzer, built as one of the tools in the protocol development system by Blumer and Sidhu, is based on the model of the extended finite state machine. A mechanism called *transition choice rule* is provided, which is associated with each of the transitions. The choice rule is a Boolean condition whose value decides whether or not the associated transition of the FSM is to be executed during the reachability analysis. For example, a rule may specify that no transition may be executed twice in the same path, or that no transition may be executed to bring a state to itself. As a result, the scope of the state exploration is controlled by the choice rules. For instance, infinite loops that may occur in the analysis can be eliminated with appropriate choice rules.

Relief strategy proposed by Ansart [1]

LISE is also a tool based on the model of the extended finite state machine. It can be operated in two modes: validation mode and *simulation* mode. When the system is operated in validation mode, it fires all the possible transitions in every global state. On the other hand, if the system is in simulation mode, only one transition out of a global state is selected to fire. The simulation mode is adopted whenever it turns out that a complete validation is infeasible due to the state explosion. Selection in simulation mode is accomplished in two ways. In the first way, the selection is simply done on a random basis; in the second way, a priority is assigned to each of the transitions and the transition with the highest priority is always the one being chosen.

Relief strategies proposed by Rubin and West [19], Gouda and Han [8], Zhao and Bochmann [28]

This group of strategies have their foundation on the *fair progress state exploration*. It is first proposed by Rubin and West, then extended by other researchers. The idea is to explore only those global states which are reachable, provided that two protocol entities proceed at the same speed. Protocol design errors such as deadlocks and unspecified receptions can still be completely detected though the exploration is not exhaustive. The limitation of this strategy is that it only applies to two-entity protocols.

Relief strategy proposed by Gouda and Yu [7]

This strategy is called the *maximal progress state exploration*. The idea is similar to that of the fair progress state exploration and its applicability is also limited to two-entity protocols. Basically, it says that the global states of a two-entity protocol can be generated in two separate explorations, during each of which a different entity is forced to proceed at its maximal speed whenever possible. The state space thus explored is not exhaustive. Nevertheless, protocol design errors such as deadlocks, unspecified receptions, and channel overflows can still be detected. In addition, this method has another advantage over others in that it can be structured to run as two processes on two processors to further speed up the validation process.

Relief strategy proposed by Itoh and Ichikawa [12]

The relief strategy proposed by Itoh and Ichikawa is applicable to protocols whose entity FSM's do not contain any cycle not passing the initial states. In each global state, the admissible events of different entities are executed simultaneously to derive the next global state. Moreover, if there is some potentially admissible event in the current state of an entity E, additional global state derivations by inhibiting the execution of all the admissible events of E should also be performed. The purpose is to force entity E to wait in order that any of its potentially admissible events may become executable later. Following this algorithm, only part of the global state graph is explored. The interaction sequences thus explored are called the *reduced implementation sequences* and are used to verify the protocol against the given requirement specification.

Relief strategies proposed by Brand and Zfiropulo [4], Kakuda, Wakahara, and Norigoe [13]

This group of strategies are called the *tree (or acyclic form) protocol validation*. Instead of exploring the global states of a protocol, this strategy grows each entity of the protocol into a tree or an acyclic form. During the growing process, protocol design errors such as unspecified receptions, deadlocks, and channel overflows can be detected. The algorithm of this strategy is much more complicated than the traditional "global states" reachability analysis. Nevertheless, the validation speed is improved.

Relief strategy proposed by Holzmann [9, 10]

Holzmann designed a tool called *Trace*, which also works under two modes, either as a fast debugging tool or as a slower correctness prover. The main emphasis is that the user can control the scope of each search. When used as a debugging tool, *Trace* uses a search strategy called *scatter search* to explore the global states graph, which basically is a depth first search guided by some simple heuristics and restricted by a depth limit. Examples of the heuristics proposed by Holzmann are:

1) Restrict the amount of nondeterminism: There are two types of nondeterminism in protocols, those due to concurrency and those due to local behavior. It is the nondeterminism of the former type that can be hopefully removed.

2) Assign priorities among concurrent events: For example, internal actions > receive actions > send actions > channel timeouts, where ">" means "having priority over".

3) Limit queue sizes.

4) Discard all the states after the depth first exploration except those that are *loop states*. Here loop states are global states in which at least one of the interacting entities is at the start of a local execution loop.

5) Keep a limited size of cache for storing global states. Discard states by a simple round robin selection when the cache is full.

6) Minimize the FSM models of protocol entities before verification.

Relief strategy proposed by West [26] in 1986

This strategy is called the *random-walk state exploration*. From his experience in validating the OSI session layer protocol, West observed that the majority of errors detected are found many times in different global states for a complex protocol. This suggests that an analysis of a subset of the reachable global states may be sufficient to identify a significant fraction of errors. The random-walk strategy is thus proposed as a way to partially explore the global states graph. The strategy says that:

1) If there is any event which may cause message collision when executed, such an event is fired first; otherwise arbitrarily choose any event to fire.

2) The state exploration is stretched out continuously along a single path without backtracking. As a result, none of the previous states needs to be remembered and the states that have already been explored may be explored again.

Relief strategy proposed by Vuong, Hui, and Cowan [23]

Vuong et al. proposed a new global state representation based on which the reachability algorithm developed can generate "finite graphs" for all non-FIFO and for a certain class of FIFO protocols even though these protocols may produce an unbounded number of messages in the transmission media. This approach thus solves a class of problems which the conventional reachability analysis fails to deal with due to the infinity of the reachable global states induced by unbounded accumulation of messages in the media.

3. The Key Features of an Effective Relief Strategy

Hereafter the paper will concentrate only on the third category of relief strategies, which are directly related to the reachability analysis. This section briefly evaluates these strategies, then concludes with the features that are essential to an effective one.

The survey in the last section leads to the following observations:

1) None of the relief strategies as surveyed above can totally supersede the others or even the exhaustive reachability analysis. For example, although the tree protocol validation [4] is faster than the conventional reachability analysis, it lacks the ability of detecting properties such as *tempo blockings* or *livelocks* and still has an exponential behavior in the worst case. On the other hand, partial state explorations such as random-walk [26], scatter search [9, 10], transition choice rules [3], and simulation [1] may be able to identify design errors quickly; but they cannot guarantee that the protocol is free from any errors even though none is ever found during the exploration. Finally, although verifications based on the fair progress [19], the maximal progress [7], the reduced implementation sequences [12], and the special global state representation [23] can completely validate a protocol faster, they are only applicable to some restricted classes of protocols.

2) To verify *a wide variety* of protocols, an ideal tool based on reachability analysis should operate in two modes. One mode is to exhaustively explore the global states such that protocol properties can be completely verified. The other mode is to explore only partial state space to locate as large set of errors as possible in a limited amount of time/space. The latter is especially important when speed rather than completeness is the major concern to the user or when thorough exploration of global states turns out to be infeasible.

3) The success of the dual mode tools lies in the strategies employed to perform the partial state exploration. Random-walk, scatter search, state transition rules, and simulation are these types of strategies. Basically, they are search techniques guided by some heuristics. For example, random-walk uses collision-first heuristics; state transition rules are heuristics based on state variables; simulation is guided by heuristics of priorities. On the other hand, the heuristics employed by scatter search are more sophisticated than others, which include priorities, depth limit, state space cache, noninterleaved actions, and some others.

4) The techniques of heuristic search has been extensively studied in the field of Artificial Intelligence (AI) [2, 17]. As quoted from [2], there are three points at which heuristic information can be applied in a search:

   a) deciding which node to expand next, instead of doing the expansions in a strictly breadth-first or depth-first order,

   b) in the course of expanding a node, deciding which successor or successors to generate -- instead of blindly generating all possible successors at one time, and

   c) deciding that certain nodes should be discarded, or pruned, from the search tree.

In fact, random-walk, choice rules, scatter search, and simulation did their search by utilizing the heuristics at the second point only.

As a conclusion, it is believed that an effective relief strategy for wide range and general protocol verification using reachability analysis should have the following key features:

1) It is a strategy incorporated into the tool of exhaustive analysis as a last resort. The tool thus "armed" is capable of switching to the strategy whenever needed by the tool user.

2) The core of the strategy is a set of heuristics which are capable of guiding the search to discover protocol design errors effectively without incurring too much overhead.

The relief strategies utilizing the heuristic information, as proposed in the literature [1, 3, 9, 26], has been ad hoc. We believe that the problem should be attacked more systematically by borrowing some idea from the search strategies developed in the field of AI. Therefore, instead of adopting any of the existing strategies in our validation tool, we have decided to develop our own from a new approach.

4. The PROVAT Strategy

Based on the observations in Section 3 and inspired by the heuristic search techniques in AI, the PROVAT strategy is derived. We call the strategy PROVAT (PROtocol VAlidation Testing) due to the following two reasons:

1) It is a strategy incorporated into a validation tool.

2) When the tool resorts to the PROVAT strategy, it is performing a task of *design testing* instead of *design validation* since only part of reachable global states will be explored. The purpose is to show the existence, *not* the absence of protocol design errors.

Compared to general search problems, the search done on the state space of a protocol has the following distinguished features:

1) Rather than searching for an optimum or satisfactory solution, Validation Testing searches for protocol design errors of unspecified receptions, deadlock states, and channel overflows.

2) The quality of search strategy is judged by the discovered percentage of the total number of errors in a limited amount of time and space. Better strategies will have higher percentages in the same amount of time and space.

3) When searching into the protocol state space, pruning can be done based on how likely a subtree of states can be exercised by the protocol operation. In case that an exhaustive analysis is infeasible, those states which are more frequently exercised by the protocol should be validated first.

4) An effective search will primarily target at one type of errors at a time because the heuristics required in locating different types of errors may contradict with each other.

Like the *best first search* developed in the AI field, an ideal search in the domain of protocol validation is called the *error first search*. PROVAT is a first attempt to characterize such an error first search.

As pointed out in the last section, heuristics can be applied at three points in a search process, namely, the points to decide which global states to expand next, to decide which transitions to fire next, and to decide which global states to discard. PROVAT is designed to employ heuristics at all three points.

Following the definitions in [17], global states are said to be *generated* when its data representation is computed from that of its parent. When this occurs, the parent state is said to be *expanded*. A state is *fully expanded* if all of its children are generated; otherwise, it is *partially expanded*. At some point, each generated state has to be inspected to see whether it reveals any of the protocol design errors. A state is said being *explored* if it has been inspected. In addition, during the validation process, the states generated are dynamically partitioned into two sets: CLOSED and OPEN. In the search algorithm of PROVAT, the generated states that are never or partially expanded are placed in OPEN, and those that have been fully expanded are moved to CLOSED. Since a state may remain in OPEN for a long time before it is expanded, it is reasonable to explore the state immediately after it is generated.

In the following, the heuristics used by PROVAT are explained. We assume that the only available protocol operations are "send" and "receive".

1) <u>Heuristics in Deciding Which Global States to Expand Next</u>: The purpose is to expand those global states in OPEN which are closer to errors. The heuristics are mainly concerned with the status of queues and entities. For each type of protocol errors, different heuristics are derived.

   a) <u>Unspecified Reception</u>: We count the number of queues which satisfy the following conditions: (1) the queue is nonempty, and (2) its destination entity is willing to receive the message at the head of the queue. Global states having the largest number of this type of queues will be expanded first.

   b) <u>Deadlock</u>: Examine all the empty queues in a global state, and call the number of empty queues whose destination entities are in receiving states (states without any outgoing "send" transitions), N_1; and the number of empty queues whose destination entities are not, N_2. Global states then are scored according to the weighted sum of N_1 and N_2. The states that receive the highest score will obtain the attention first.

c) <u>Channel Overflow</u>: Global states are compared based on the length of their longest queues. If a tie occurs, the comparison continues on the length of the second longest queue. States win in this contest will be explored first.

2) <u>Heuristics in Deciding Which Transitions to Fire Next</u>: The purpose is to perform those actions that are more likely leading to the error from a selected state. The heuristics are concerned with either action types or queue lengths. Different heuristics are developed for each type of errors.

a) <u>Unspecified Reception</u>: We choose a "receive" operation if that operation is able to receive a message from the shortest queue which contains at least two messages; otherwise, choose to "send" a message to an empty queue. For other operations, consider "receive" before "send". These heuristics tends to sustain the decision made by the heuristics of choosing the next expanded global state.

b) <u>Deadlock</u>: "Receive" operations are always considered first. Among "receive" operations, we choose those which extract from the shortest queue.

c) <u>Channel Overflow</u>: "Send" operations are always considered first. Among "sends", those which add to the longest queue have the highest priorities. If there is no send operation, "receives" which extract messages from the shortest queue are chosen. The heuristics for the above two types of errors are also derived to be compatible with those in deciding which global states to expand next.

3) <u>Heuristics in Deciding Which Global States to Discard</u>: The purpose is to decide which global states should not be generated during the global state expansion, which in fact prunes the subtree rooted by any state thus inhibited. To bring in meaningful heuristics in making this decision, we enhance the original formal model (TG) [16], on which the validation tool is based, to include probability specifications. Then a simple method is developed to approximately estimate how likely each of the global states will be reached in terms of probabilities (similar work is done on CCS by [18] for a different purpose). Global states being assigned smaller probabilities are less probable to be reached by the protocol operation. Consequently, if speed is the major concern to the protocol verifier, she can ask PROVAT only to explore those states with probabilities of reachability higher than a specified threshold.

All the heuristics informally defined above are quantified by the *evaluation functions*, which play major roles in guiding the reachability analysis.

Another problem left out in the above discussion is when to terminate the partial state exploration. In PROVAT, this is decided by two criteria:

1) <u>Specifying a probability threshold to explore only the states which are more likely to be exercised by the protocol</u>: Those global states with probabilities of reachability dropped below the threshold value will never be generated.

2) <u>Specifying an upper bound on the number of expansion steps</u>: When a state is expanded, some new or existing states will be generated. Each step of generating a state, whether the resulting state is new or already existing, is called an expansion step. When the number of expansion steps exceeds the specified value, the analysis terminates.

The first criterion essentially is supported by the third kind of heuristics discussed above. On the other hand, the second criterion gives an approximate estimate on how much time will be taken by the analysis. In PROVAT, the first criterion is used to tailor the state space to contain only those states which are more likely to be exercised by the protocol, then the second criterion is applied to obtain a desirable response time.

5. Preliminary Results of the Tool Incorporating PROVAT Strategy

The PROVAT strategy has been built into an exhaustive validation tool based on the formal model of *transmission grammar* (TG) [16, 20, 21]. In order to incorporate PROVAT into the TG validation tool, the model is first enhanced to include probability specifications and is named PTG (Probabilistic Transmission Grammar) [15]. Then a part of the tool is recoded to encompass the PROVAT strategy based on the new model.

The original TG validation tool runs under 4.3BSD UNIX and contains about 3800 lines of C language code. The resulting PTG tool contains about 4500 lines of C code. Several real life protocols have been extensively validated/tested to evaluate the effectiveness of PROVAT. Here only the tests performed on the call establishment procedure of the CCITT X.21 as specified in [24] are reported. Though the X.21 interface is designed to operate in a physical environment where no more than one message can be outstanding in the channel of either direction, as an exercise to compare PROVAT with the other search strategies in a large state space, the behaviors of X.21 with other channel sizes are also tried. Also, when testing the power of the heuristics for deadlock detection, we delete some of the transitions from the X.21 specification in [24] to create deadlock states uniformly scattered in the global state space.

Five search strategies are tested to compare their performance in locating different types of design errors: (1) D-search [11] (DS for short), (2) depth-first search (DFS for short), (3) heuristic search based on state heuristics only (abbreviated SBHS: State-Based Heuristic Search), (4) heuristic search based on transition heuristics only (abbreviated TBHS: Transition-Based Heuristic Search), and (5) heuristic search based on both state and transition heuristics. Notice that PROVAT adopts the fifth search strategy, whereas the TG validation tool used the first strategy. Also, the second, third, and fourth strategies are special cases of the fifth.

The results of the X.21 testing are shown in Figures 1 to 3 and Tables 1 to 4. In these results, state pruning is not considered though it is also part of PROVAT. Figure 1 compares the results of detecting unspecified receptions via five search strategies when the channel size of X.21 is set to be 1, which clearly shows the power of heuristics in guiding the "error first" search. Then, in Figure 2, the results of the PROVAT search and the D-search in detecting unspecified receptions for X.21 with channel size 3 are compared, which exhibits the improvement of PROVAT over D-search. Finally, Figure 3 shows the superiority of the PROVAT search over all the other strategies in quickly locating the first 20% of reception errors when the channel size is also 3.

Tables 1 to 4 compare the results of detecting deadlocks via five search strategies under the assumption of different channel sizes. Each table entry gives the expansion steps needed to discover one more deadlock error. It is interesting to note that when the channel size is 4, PROVAT only exercised 3.4% of total expansion steps needed for a exhaustive search in order to locate all the deadlock states. These results give a strong evidence that with PROVAT incorporated, the validation tool is much more effective than blindly performing the D-search.

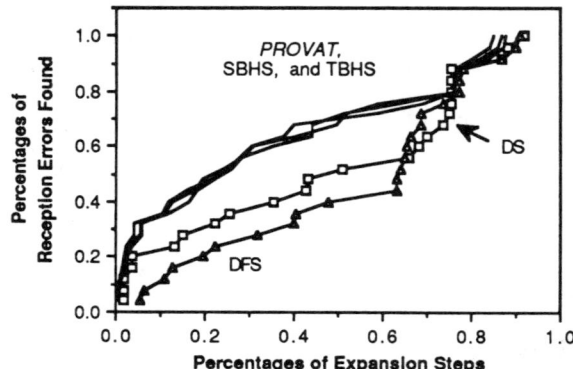

Figure 1: Detection of Unspecified Reception Errors with Channel Size 1

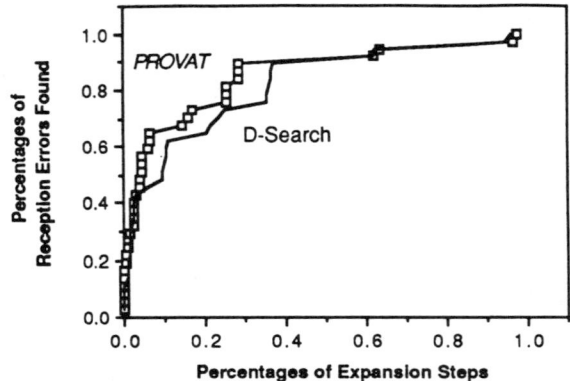

Figure 2: Comparison of PROVAT vs. D-Search in Detecting Reception Errors

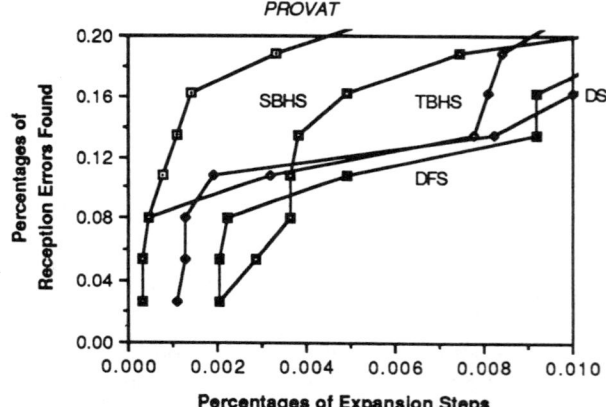

Figure 3: Detection of the First 20% of Unspecified Reception Errors

Search strategy deadlock error	Channel Size = 1				
	DS	DFS	TBHS	SBHS	PROVAT
1	20	18	16	6	4
2	23	118	118	17	16
3	212	119	119	159	155
4	382	301	299	259	259
Percentage of Steps Exercised	94.3%	74.3%	73.8%	64%	64%

Table 1: The Detection of Deadlock State Errors with a Total Space of 280 States

Search strategy deadlock error	Channel Size = 2				
	DS	DFS	TBHS	SBHS	PROVAT
1	20	18	16	6	4
2	23	221	221	19	16
3	336	222	222	220	212
4	1408	767	764	394	389
Percentage of Steps Exercised	98%	53.4%	53.2%	27.4%	27%

Table 2: The Detection of Deadlock State Errors with a Total Space of 946 States

Search strategy deadlock error	Channel Size = 3				
	DS	DFS	TBHS	SBHS	PROVAT
1	20	18	16	6	4
2	23	271	271	19	16
3	4930	272	272	260	248
4	5178	1374	1370	513	508
Percentage of Steps Exercised	99.6%	26.4%	26.4%	9.8%	9.8%

Table 3: The Detection of Deadlock State Errors with a Total Space of 3237 States

Search strategy deadlock error	Channel Size = 4				
	DS	DFS	TBHS	SBHS	PROVAT
1	20	18	16	6	4
2	23	290	290	19	16
3	17953	291	291	280	268
4	18275	2027	2023	624	619
Percentage of Steps Exercised	99.8%	11%	11.1%	3.4%	3.4%

Table 4: The Detection of Deadlock State Errors with a Total Space of 11054 States

The experimental results from these tests are optimistic in that when we resort to PROVAT, it does help locate the errors in fewer steps than the other strategies. Though these results are still insufficient to conclude that PROVAT will also perform superiorly in validating other protocols, it indicates that with good heuristics the verification tool may do a better job when state explosion prohibits a thorough analysis of protocol behavior.

The heuristics employed by PROVAT are based on the local information of a global state. Thus only a little overhead is incurred to the reachability algorithm. Though it seems not easy, if not impossible, to capture the characteristics of the interactions leading to a protocol design error by some heuristics, PROVAT has shown its effectiveness through our experimentation.

It is also worthy noting that among heuristics of locating unspecified receptions, deadlock states, and channel overflows, those for unspecified receptions are the most difficult to capture. This seems to match with the research efforts in protocol synthesis where incompleteness of receptions is always the major issue [27].

6. Concluding Remarks

State explosion is always and will continue to be the major problem in techniques of protocol verification via reachability analysis. In this paper, relief strategies from various approaches are surveyed and evaluated. First, the strategies collected from the literature are classified into three categories depending on when they should be applied. Then the effort is focused on the relief strategy for the reachability algorithm per se. As a result, PROVAT is proposed as a search strategy incorporated into the conventional exhaustive state exploration. It has been built into a grammar-based validation tool to make the enhanced tool operated in dual mode. The tool user thus can decide to perform an exhaustive analysis or as a final resort, to use PROVAT as a relief strategy when state explosion arises. The preliminary empirical results has shown the effectiveness of PROVAT in error search.

Though it is difficult to compare the effectiveness of PROVAT strategy with that of the other approaches due to the lacking of a common ground, the advantage of PROVAT lies in its simplicity and systematic approach. Its drawback is common to any heuristics-based approach in the lacking of theoretic support and predictability. Our experience shows that to perform protocol verification via reachability analysis, care must be taken from the beginning. As the classification we made on the relief strategies indicates, serious attention should be paid to the early stages of verification such as modeling and function abstraction/decomposition. Only through these combined efforts, the unbeaten state explosion problem can be resolved more effectively.

References

[1] J. -P. Ansart.
Issues and Tools for Protocol Specification.
The Advanced Course on Distributed Systems - Methods and Tools for Specification.
Springer-Verlag, 1985, pages 481-538.

[2] A. Gardner.
Search.
The Handbook of Artificial Intelligence.
William Kaufman, 1981, Chapter II.

[3] T. P. Blumer and D. P. Sidhu.
Mechanical Verification and Automatic Implementation of Communication Protocols.
IEEE Trans. on Software Engineering
SE-12(8):827-843, August, 1986.

[4] D. Brand and P. Zafiropulo.
On Communicating Finite-State Machines.
Journal of ACM 30(2):323-342, April, 1983.

[5] T. Y. Choi and R. E. Miller.
A Decomposition Method for the Analysis and Design of Finite State Protocols.
In *Proc. Data Communication Symposium*, pages 167-176. ACM SIGCOMM, 1983.

[6] C. Chow, M. G. Gouda, and S. S. Lam.
A Discipline for Constructing Multiphase Communication Protocols.
ACM Trans. on Computer Systems 3(4):315-343, November, 1985.

[7] M. G. Gouda and Y. T. Yu.
Protocol Validation by Maximal Progress State Exploration.
IEEE Trans. on Communications
COM-32(1):94-97, Janunary, 1984.

[8] M. G. Gouda and J. -Y. Han.
Protocol Validation by Fair Progress State Exploration.
Computer Networks and ISDN Systems
9:353-361, 1985.

[9] G. J. Holzmann.
Tracing Protocol.
AT&T Technical Journal 64(10):2413-2433, December, 1985.

[10] G. J. Holzmann.
Automatic Protocol Validation in Argos: Assertion Proving and Scatter Searching.
IEEE Trans. on Software Engineering
SE-13(6):683-696, June, 1987.

[11] E. Horowitz and S. Sahni.
Chapter 6.
Fundamentals of Computer Algorithms.
Computer Science Press, 1978, pages 318.

[12] M. Itoh and H. Ichikawa.
Protocol Verification Algorithm Using Reduced Reachability Analysis.
The Trans. on the IECE of Japan E66(2):88-93, February, 1983.

[13] Y. Kakuda, Y. Wakahara, and M. Norigoe.
A New Algorithm for Fast Protocol Validation.
In *Proc. COMPSAC*, pages 228-236. IEEE, 1986.

[14] S. S. Lam and A. U. Shanker.
Protocol Verification via Projections.
IEEEE Trans. on Software Engineering
SE-10(4):325-342, July, 1984.

[15] F. J. Lin, P. M. Chu, and M. T. Liu.
Probabilistic Transmission Grammmar.
1987
Unpublished Notes.

[16] C. S. Lu.
Automated Validation of Communication Protocols.
PhD thesis, The Ohio State Univ., 1986.

[17] J. Peral.
Heuristics -- Intelligent Search Strategies for Computer Problem Solving.
Addison-Wesley, 1984.

[18] S. Purushothaman and P. A. Subrahmanyam.
Reasoning About Probabilistic Behavior in Concurrent Systems.
IEEEE Trans. on Software Engineering
SE-13(6):740-745, June, 1987.

[19] J. Rubin and C. H. West.
An Improved Protocol Validation Technique.
Computer Networks 6:65-73, 1982.

[20] A. Y. Teng and M. T. Liu.
The Transmission Grammar Model for Protocol Construction.
In *Proc. Trends and Applications Symposium*, pages 110-120. NBS, 1980.

[21] L. D. Umbaugh.
Automated Techniques for Specification and Validation of Communication Protocols.
PhD thesis, The Ohio Sate Univ., 1983.

[22] S. T. Vuong and D. D. Cowan.
A Decomposition Method for the Validation of Structured Protocols.
In *Proc. INFOCOM*, pages 209-220. IEEE, 1982.

[23] S. T. Vuong, D. D. Hui, and D. D. Cowan.
VALIRA - A Tool for Protocol Validation Via Reachability Analysis.
Protocol Specification, Testing, and Verification, VI.
North-Holland, 1987, pages 35-41.

[24] C. H. West and P. Zafiropulo.
Automated Validation of a Communication Protocol: the CCITT X.21 Recommendation.
IBM Journal of Research and Development 22(1):60-71, 1978.

[25] C. H. West.
Applications and Limitations of Automated Protocol Validation.
Protocol Specification, Testing, and Verification, II.
North-Holland, 1982, pages 361-371.

[26] C. H. West.
Protocol Validation by Random State Exploration.
Protocol Specification, Testing, and Verification, VI.
North-Holland, 1987, pages 233-242.

[27] P. Zafiropulo, C. H. West, H. Rudin,
D. D. Cowan, and D. Brand.
Towards Analyzing and Synthesizing Protocols.
IEEE Trans. on Communication 28(4):651-660, April, 1980.

[28] J. -R. Zhao and G. V. Bochmann.
Reduced Reachability Analysis of Communicaiton Protocols : A New Approach.
Protocol Specification, Testing, and Verification, VI.
North-Holland, 1987, pages 243-254.

NEW COMMUNICATION PROTOCOLS FROM OLD[1]

Zamir Bavel
Jerzy W. Grzymala-Busse
Yen-Teh Hsia
Rodolfo Mancisidor-Landa

Department of Computer Science
University of Kansas
Lawrence, Kansas 66045

ABSTRACT

The **power tier automaton (PTA)** is introduced as a model of preference for representing and manipulating systems in general, computer architectures and, in particular, communication networks and their protocols. The PTA is superior to Petri nets, both in computing power (Turing machine power) and in ease and selectivity of representation. The **tier automaton**, a species of the PTA, is used to represent networks and protocols to a greater advantage than other existing models. Homomorphisms and reachable-domain (r.d.) homomorphisms on tier automata are introduced and used to *manipulate* two distinct protocols for reliable full-duplex transmission over half-duplex lines, both of whose images are the same familiar alternating-bit protocol.

1. Introduction

The representation of communication networks and their protocols by a theoretical model has been of interest for some time. With varying degrees of success, a number of models and treatments have been proposed. (See, for example, [1], [6 - 12], and others.) Of note among these is a treatment of networks as communicating finite-state machines, with [9] as a recent example. Such representation facilitates the investigation of various properties of networks and protocols, such as safeness and liveness. It also permits formal statements, and their proofs, concerning the represented protocols.

In [5], we introduced the **tier automaton**, first used in [3] in a more general setting, as a model for an *entire* network, including the communications among its nodes and the transmission medium. We further presented a scheme for the tier-automaton representation of networks and protocols, illustrated on a restricted class, and cited some of the more obvious advantages of such a representation.

---

[1] Supported by System Development Foundation Grant No. 565.

In the present article we go one step further. We use the tier automaton to provide one of the means, *homomorphisms*, for *manipulating* networks and protocols. We show how to get new protocols from old, while preserving desired properties of the old ones and discarding the undesired ones. (We also briefly discuss other types of manipulation that are beyond the scope of this article.)

Although homomorphisms on conventional automata have been thoroughly explored, and algorithms for their acquisition constructed (Bavel, [2]), only minor attempts have been made to apply a very restricted subclass of them to models for communication protocols, and even then they were not recognized as homomorphisms. (See, for example, [11].)

Here, we use homomorphisms on the tier automaton representation of one protocol to obtain an improved protocol.

Such manipulation is made possible by the structure of the tier automaton, by the fact that it represents the entire system of communication including in particular *communication among components of the system*, and by the fact that it is a single monolithic structure amenable to manipulation.

We chose small, simple and (partly) familiar cases (of full-duplex transmission over half-duplex telephone lines) with which to make our point. Many of the common concerns are left unattended here, in the first view of the process. However, all the ingredients for dealing with such concerns are within the tier automaton model and, in fact, present a choice of handling methods.

Of particular interest is the ability of the model to account for *continuous time*—a concern of many researchers. However, this topic is left out of the scope of the present article for lack of space.

We reproduce from [5] only enough to make the present article self-contained: a block diagram for the representation of the alternating-bit protocol and a diagram of the details of the core of that representation, with some of the communications displayed. (The reason is that the protocol is shown, later in the present article, as a homomorphic image of each of two other network protocols.)

The scheme we use for representing network protocols by the model is detailed in [5]. It should be fairly transparent from its use here.

The point of advocacy is the following. With the techniques exhibited below, it is a simple matter to construct a straightforward algorithm which yields all abstract homomorphic images of a network protocol under specified constraints, such as mapping component automata one-to-one, removing certain requirements of the network, and the like. Such constraints represent the differences between design requirements of the source protocol and those of the desired outcome.

With the use of such an algorithm, all homomorphic images which obey the new requirements may be obtained and the most useful among them may be used. It should be expected, though, that a number of resulting protocols may be unsuitable, perhaps because some of the necessary constraints were unstated.

Starting with Section 4, then, we present two network requirements and accompanying protocols, and show on each a homomorphism that yields the one of Bartlett *et al.* from [1]. We make no claims about the two newly presented protocols. In fact, the less suitable these protocols are, the stronger our point is: we may get even *better* new protocols from the old ones.

2. The Power Tier Automaton—An Intuitive View

The PTA (power tier automaton) may be easier to perceive from a few examples than from its definition. (For the sake of simplicity, we take some liberties here in refering to parts of the PTA.)

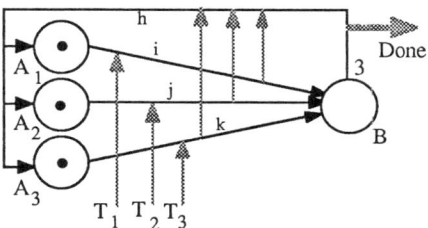

A 3-operation synchronizer PTA
Figure 1

In the 3-operation synchronizer of Figure 1, there are four "**states**," A_1, A_2, A_3 and B. (Formally, they are called "pairs" for reasons seen later, but in this section, we use "states" for simplicity.) Each state has a **power**, which is an index of the "activeness" of the state. The initial power of each of A_1, A_2 and A_3 is 1 and that of B is 0.

There is one **transition** from each of A_1, A_2 and A_3 to B and one transition from B to all of A_1, A_2 and A_3. Each transition is labeled by an **input**. (The input labels may be omitted from small diagrams, as we do below in Figure 4.)

Each transition has a **threshold**, a positive integer which indicates the power the origin state must have for the transition to fire. The threshold is shown at the shank of the transition arrow, if it is greater than 1. Each of transitions i, j and k to B has threshold 1 and the transition h from B has threshold 3. Consequently, any combination of the transitions from A_1, A_2 and A_3 to B may fire, since the states each has power 1 —sufficient for each of the three transitions. On the other hand, the transition h cannot fire now since it requires B to have power 3 and currently the power of B is 0.

Each transition has a **yield** for each of its arrowheads. The yield is a nonnegative integer which appears by the arrowhead if it is different from 1.

The PTA in Figure 1 has three **external incoming signals**, labeled by T_1, T_2, and T_3. Each of these signals becomes **active** when the corresponding operation has terminated. When operation T_1 terminates, the gray arrow into transition i becomes **active** and it then **stimulates** the transition **to fire** (alt., **enables** the transition). Since the power (1) of A_1 is not smaller than the threshold (1) of i, the transition fires and the **power distribution** changes to: $m(A_1) = 0$, $m(A_2) = m(A_3) = m(B) = 1$ (where m denotes the power of the state). The diagram in Figure 2 shows the current situation.

Note that the PTA displayed has full concurrency, in that the three operations T_1, T_2, and T_3 may terminate independently of each other and thus the transition i, j and k may fire independently of each other.

The PTA also has three **trunk elements**, one from each of the *transitions* i, j, and k to the *transition* h. When i fires, it **activates** the trunk element from transition i to transition h

which, in turn, **enables** h (**stimulates h to fire**). But, since the threshold of h is 3 and the power of B is 1, h **does not fire**.

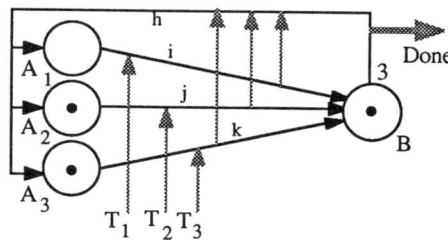

The synchronizer, view 2
Figure 2

Now, let operation T_3 terminate. Then transition k fires, "moving" the "token" from A_3 to B (since both the threshold of k and its yield at B are 1), but the trunk element from k to h, just activated by the firing of k, still cannot cause h to fire, since the power of B is 2 and the threshold of h is 3.

When T_2 terminates, j fires, causing the power distribution to be as is shown in Figure 3.

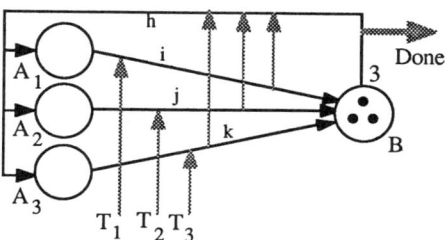

The synchronizer, view 3
Figure 3

In the process of j firing, the trunk element from j to h is activated and it, in turn, stimulates h to fire. Finally, the power 3 of B is not smaller than the threshold of h and thus h fires. In consequence, since the threshold of h is 3, the new power of B becomes (old power of B) - (threshold of h) = 3 - 3 = 0. Likewise, since the yield of h at each of A_1, A_2 and A_3 is 1, the new power of each of A_1, A_2 and A_3 is $0 + 1 = 1$ and the PTA is restored to its original form.

At this point, a signal may be extracted from transition a (shown by the "Done" arrow) to signify that all three operations have terminated[2].

Another simple example is the exclusive-OR PTA of Figure 4.

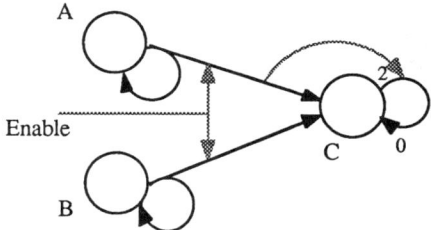

A Boolean exclusive-OR PTA
Figure 4

---

[2]The case shown here assumes no simultaneity in the firing of transitions and thus no multiple stimulation of transitions a by the trunk elements. If simultaneity is permitted, the difficulty is easily overcome with the use of the signal refresher of Figure 5.

A and B may each have power 0 or 1. The external signal "Enable" causes C eventually to have the power 1 iff $A \oplus B = 1$, and otherwise C has the power 0.

The reader may find it helpful to trace the succession of external signal, firing or nonfiring of the transitions from A and B to C, activating or not activating the only trunk element of the PTA, and then the firing or nonfiring of the transition from C to itself, under the four possible power distributions of A and B.

A fact worth noting is that, when the trunk element is activated and the power of C is 2, the transition at C fires and the resulting power of C is 0.

Another fact worth noting is that the transition from A has two destinations, A and C. Thus, if $m(A) = 1$, the result of firing of the transition is that $m(A)$ is decreased by 1 but then both $m(A)$ and $m(C)$ are increased by 1, restoring A to its original power and asserting its presence at C. The same is true for the transition from B.

The third and last illustration is a signal refresher, shown in Figure 5. One of the advantages of the PTA as a model for systems is that it provides the option to keep a delivered signal persistent when the power of a state is too small for the transition to fire, the other option being the "death" of the signal. (The benefit from such an option should be easily evident in systems in general and in communication protocols in particular.)

The signal refresher of Figure 5 requires little comment at this point.

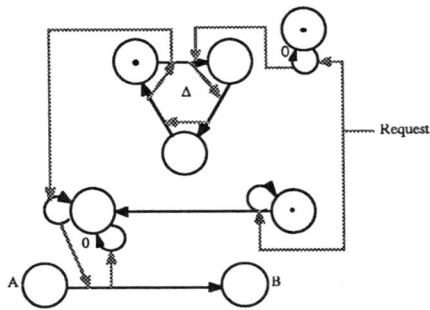

A signal refresher PTA
Figure 5

The states with dots in them have power 1 and the others have power 0, except that A may be given positive power at any time.

The signal to be refreshed is delivered to the transition from A to B, as a result of the activation of the "Request" external signal. (The first such request starts the self-sustaining operation of the triangle Δ.)

As long as $m(A) = 0$, the trunk element ending at the transition from A to B is repeatedly activated and the transition is repeatedly stimulated. However, once A has positive power, the transition fires, causing one of the "requested" signals to be used up.

Any number of "requests" may be accumulated, with the potential of firing from A to B the requested number of times.

The power of the PTA has been shown in [4] to be that of a Turing machine by showing a canonical PTA representation of arbitrary Petri nets and, in addition, showing a "zero tester" (branch-on-zero mechanism).

The full power of the PTA, however, is not needed for the present application. We obtain a **tier automaton** from the power tier automaton (for definition, see the Appendix) by allowing the power of each state to be either 0 or 1, by making all thresholds and yields 1, and by imposing on the activation, firing and changes of power the arithmetic $0 + 1 = 1 + 0 = 1 + 1 = 1$ and $0 + 0 = 0$; i.e. we have only active and inactive "states" and once a transition fires, the origin state becomes inactive (unless replenished).

The strength of the tier automaton remains in the ability to stimulate *selected* transitions and in the ability to achieve *autonomous* operation, with trunk elements causing the firing of transitions which, in turn, activate trunk elements able to cause the further firing of transitions, etc.

For the present application, we divide the tier automaton, minus the trunk elements and the external signals, into **tag automata** (the seven "boxes" of Figure 6), which are input-ouput connected by trunks.

In the tag automaton, rather than states, the beginning and end of each transition is a state-tag pair, whose use is obvious from the diagrams of Figure 7 and beyond. (The tags do not increase the computing power of the model, but they make for a very convenient representational scheme and solve, in many cases, the state-explosion problem.)

We denote the **trunk from** tag automaton A **to** tag automaton B by $K_{A,B}$. We refer to a state-tag unit (we used "state" above) as a **pair** and thus to a (pair, input) couple as a **triple**, which is the argument of the transition function of the tag automaton.

There are a few disagreements between the notation used in the definitions in the Appendix and the notation we use in the sections to follow. The latter is employed in order to conform to the notation in [5], which emphasizes the separation of a "pair" into a (state, tag) couple.

(a) We use here the 5-tuple $(S, \Sigma, \delta, T, P)$ for a tag automaton, while in the Appendix we discard S and T and denote a tag automaton by (P, Σ, δ).

(b) We call δ here the **action function** and in the Appendix the **transition function**. Consistent with the difference in (a), we denote the action on the pair $p = (s, t)$ by the input i as $\delta(s, t, i)$, while the corresponding transition in the Appendix is denoted by $\delta(p, i)$.

(c) We denote a **tier automaton** here by $Z = (\mathbb{R}, \mathbb{K})$, where $\mathbb{R}$ is the tag automaton of Z and $\mathbb{K}$ is the trunk of Z; in the Appendix we denote a tier **automaton** by $Z = (P, \Sigma, \delta, K, H, J)$, with (P, Σ, δ) the tag automaton of Z, K the trunk of Z, H and J the sets of external signals of Z. [$\mathbb{R}$ is the union of the blocks of Z and $\mathbb{K}$ is the union of the trunks of all the 2-deck tier automata. We indicate the external signal in H as the "initial input," since that is its sole use here.]

(d) The "**initial conditions**" of Z here correspond to the **initial power distribution** of Z in the Appendix, with one pair in each block being **active**, i.e. with positive power.

The remainder of the terminology should be evident from its use.

3. A Partial View of $Z_{Bartlett}$—A Tier Automaton Representation of the Alternating-Bit Protocol

A reminder of some of the terms we use. By a **pair** is meant a (state, tag) pair of the deterministic tag automaton. A **trunk** on a component A to a component B is a collection of 4-tuples of the form (p_1, i_1, p_2, i_2), where p_1 is a pair of A, i_1 is an input of A, p_2 is a pair of B, and i_2 is an input of B. We assume a MERGE function for each component whose purpose is to merge several inputs into one, as dictated by the application. EXT is the set of all components receiving external inputs and INT is the set of the remaining components of the tier-automaton representation.

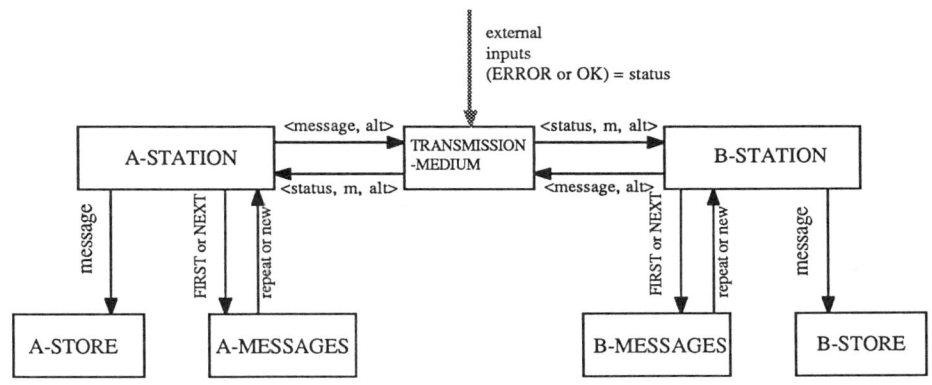

A tier-automaton block diagram for the alternating bit protocol
Figure 6

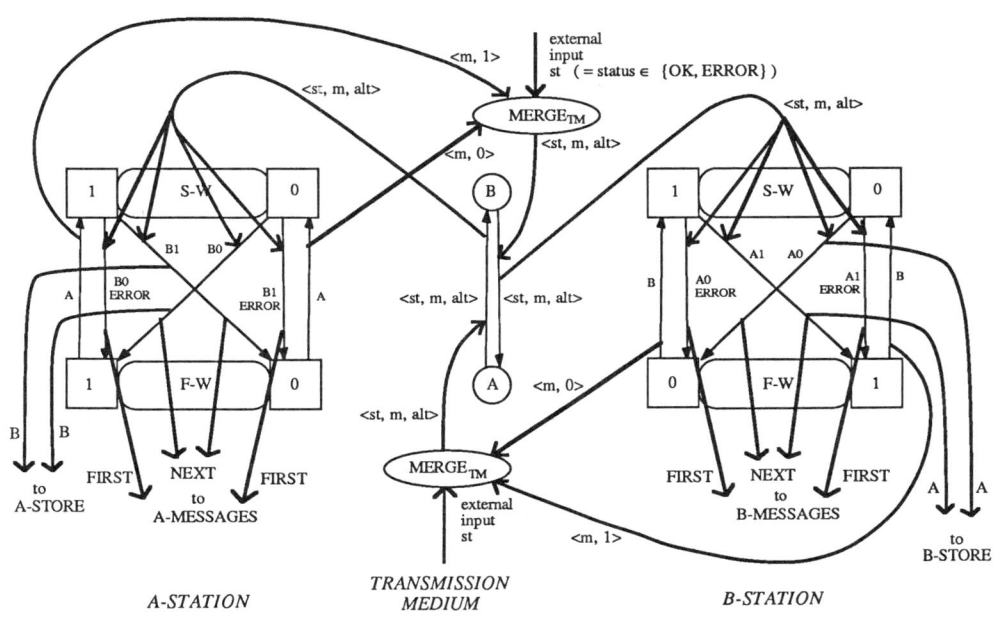

Transmission of messages between stations through TRANSMISSION-MEDIUM.
Figure 7

subsections of B use one node in the network: B-STATION for control, B-MESSAGES for messages going to headquarters A-STATION, and B-STORE for receiving and storing messages from A-STATION.

However, if no interruption in sequencing occurs, the messages to branch B should be sequenced in the order: to B_{11}, B_{21}, B_{12}, B_{22} to distribute the load evenly. Once the messages arrive at B-STORE, they can be called from, or channeled to, each subsection by the control information attached to each message.

One more requirement. In the event the receiving apparatus for B_{11} is inaccessible (malfunction, planned vacation for B_{11} personnel, or what-have-you), it should be possible to manually interfere with the sequencing (switch, hard wire, etc.) and send the B_{11}-bound messages to B_{12}. The same relationship should occur in reverse, from B_{12} to B_{11}, and between B_{21} and B_{22}, as well.

Figure 7 describes all communications between the stations and TRANSMISSION-MEDIUM, and most of the remaining ones.

4. Network #1

4.1 The Requirements

A network is needed for communications between company headquarters A and one of its branches B in the field. Branch B has two locations, B_1 and B_2, city-blocks apart. B_1 has two parts, B_{11} and B_{12}, in two nonadjacent rooms; B_2 is split in a likewise manner into B_{21} and B_{22}.

Both the expected traffic and the limited capacity of computing equipment in branch B dictate that all four

Any unplanned interruption in the sequencing should be automatically corrected by the protocol. However, an error in a message reception should cause retransmission of the message and, if it is B-bound, its destination among the four possible subsections should be preserved. Thus, A should be designed to be self-adjusting in the event of such manual intervention in B.

4.2 The Protocol—Protocol #1

[We employ the scheme and settings from [5] for the tier automaton representation. We assume perfect error detection and no loss of message]

A-STATION and B-STATION use the two-bit Gray code ($00 \rightarrow 01 \rightarrow 11 \rightarrow 10 \rightarrow 00$) to keep track of the position in the sequence.

When no disruption in transmission sequence occurs, after the reception of an errorless message from B with the proper control bits, or at the beginning of transmission, A-STATION transmits a message to B with control bits starting with 00 for the first message (destined for B_{11}) and following the two-bit Gray code for the ensuing transmissions.

Whenever B-STATION receives an errorless message from A (without sequence interruption), it stores the message with its control bits in B-STORE and transmits a message to A with the same control bits just received from A. For instance, with m and n denoting messages from A and B, respectively, A sends $<m_1, 00>$ to B, which stores it and sends $<n_1, 00>$ to A. A stores n_1 and sends $<m_2, 01>$ to B, which stores it and sends $<n_2, 01>$ to A; and so on through the control-bit sequence 11, 10 and 00 again.

Suppose A receives a flawed message (status = ERROR) when it expects the control bits with the message from B to have the value t (the pair (S-W, t) is active in A-STATION). Since A cannot know whether B has received A's last message, A retransmits it with control bits = t, the same value as with the previous message to B. (Of course, A does not store the flawed message.)

Suppose B receives a flawed message (status = ERROR) when it expects the control bits with the message from A to have the value t (the pair (S-W, t) is active in B-STATION). It then retransmits the previous message with control bits = t - 1 in the Gray code sequence (as detailed below, just preceding the formal definition of the components in Section 4.3), since that was the control information accompanying the previous message. Thus, if B expects 11 with the message from A, a bad transmission will cause B to retransmit 01 with the previous message.

The codes (addresses) for the subsections are 00 for B_{11}, 01 for B_{21}, 11 for B_{12} and 10 for B_{22}.

If B receives an errorless message but the control information, "bits", is not the expected one, if bits = address of the adjacent subsection (B_{11} and B_{12} are adjacent, and so are B_{21} and B_{22}) B will accept and store it and will resume the Gray code sequence starting with the new address as the value of the control bit. For example, if B expects $<m, 01>$ but receives $<m, 10>$, it will store $<m, 10>$ and then transmit to A $<n, 10>$ (even though it was about to transmit $<n, 01>$ before the sequence interruption).

On the other hand, if the control bits value is an address of a subsection blocks away, B will not store it and treat the event like a message with an ERROR.

In the event the Gray code sequence in the reception at A is interrupted, if the bits value is that of the subsection adjacent to the one expected, then the message will be accepted and the transmission sequence will continue unchanged.

On the other hand, A treats either of the two remaining values of the control bits (the ones for nonadjacent subsections to the one A expects) as an error.

4.3 Z_1—Tier-Automaton Representation of Protocol #1

The STATIONs of Z_1 are shown in Figure 8.

$Z_1 = (\mathbb{R}_1, \mathbb{K}_1)$, where $\mathbb{R}_1, \mathbb{K}_1$ and EXT are as in $Z_{Bartlett}$ from [1] and their members are defined below. We divide the possibly continuous operation of the net into sessions of equal duration such as each of three shifts in a 24-hour period. As a consequence all sets in the following are finite. We use the following notation generically:
ST is the status set (ST = {OK, ERROR}),
SEQ is the set of all 2-bit binary sequences
   (SEQ = {00, 01, 11, 10}),
COM = {FIRST, NEXT},
M is the (finite) set of all legal messages,
Q is the (finite) set of all legal message queues (bounded by session-length),
M′ = {m′ = <m, seq>: m ∈ M, seq ∈ SEQ},
Q′ is the set of all legal queues of members of M′ (likewise bounded by session-length),
SMS = {<st, m, seq>: st ∈ ST, m ∈ M, seq ∈ SEQ}.

Each appearance of the following is assumed to be universally quantified over the stated set.

st ∈ ST, seq, bits ∈ SEQ, $bit_1, bit_2, seq_1, seq_2 \in \{0, 1\}$,
m ∈ M, q ∈ Q, m′ ∈ M′, q′ ∈ Q′ and sms ∈ SMS.

We also use the following notation:
seq + 1 [alt., seq - 1] is the successor [alt., predecessor] to seq in the two-bit Gray code, and $\oplus$ denotes the (Boolean) exclusive OR.

seq	seq + 1	seq - 1
00	01	10
01	11	00
11	10	01
10	00	11

Components:

A-STATION = (S, Σ, δ_A, T, P);
S = {S-W, F-W};
Σ = M ∪ SMS;
T = SEQ;
P = S × T;
δ_A(S-W, bit_1bit_2, <OK, m, seq_1seq_2>) =
   (F-W, bit_1bit_2 + 1), if $bit_1 \oplus bit_2 = seq_1 \oplus seq_2$,
   and (F-W, bit_1bit_2), otherwise,
δ_A(S-W, bits, <ERROR, m, seq>) = (F-W, bits),
δ_A(F-W, bits, m) = (S-W, bits).

B-STATION = (S, Σ, δ_B, T, P);
δ_B(S-W, bit_1bit_2, <OK, m, seq>) =
   (F-W, seq_1seq_2), if $bit_1 \oplus bit_2 = seq_1 \oplus seq_2$,
   and (F-W, bit_1bit_2 - 1), otherwise,
δ_B(S-W, bits, <ERROR, m, seq>) = (F-W, bits-1),
δ_B(F-W, bits, m) = (S-W, bits + 1).

TRANSMISSON-MEDIUM = ($S_{TM}, \Sigma_{TM}, \delta_{TM}$);
S_{TM} = {A, B};
Σ_{TM} = ST ∪ {<m, seq>} ∪ SMS;
δ_{TM}(A, <st, m, seq>) = B, δ_{TM}(B, <st, m, seq>) = A;
MERGE$_{TM}$(st, <m, seq>) = <st, m, seq>.

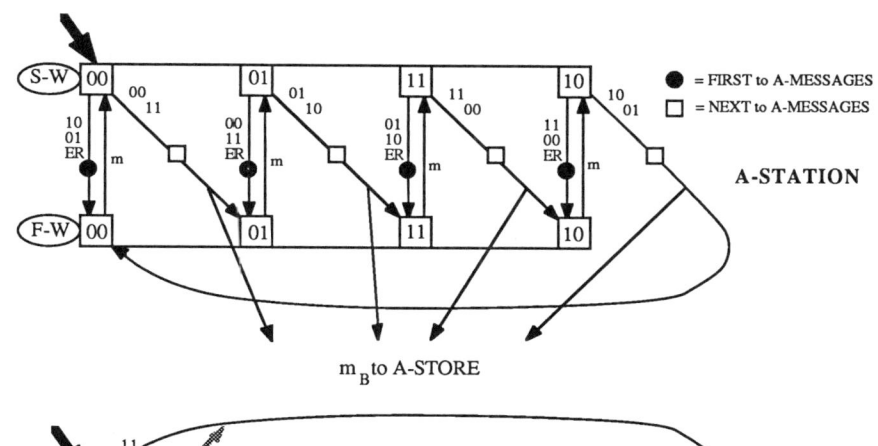

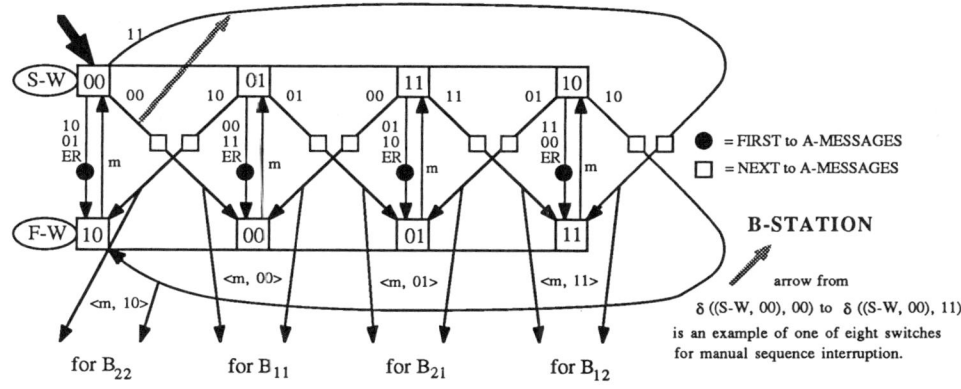

The STATIONs of Z_1
Figure 8

A-STORE = (Q, M, δ_{AS});
  $\delta_{AS}(q, m) = qm = $ (APPEND q (LIST m)).

B-STORE = (Q', M', δ_{BS});
  $\delta_{BS}(q', m') = q'm' = $ (APPEND q' (LIST m')).

A-MESSAGES = (Q, COM, δ_M);
  $\delta_M(q, FIRST) = q$,
  $\delta_M(q, NEXT) = $ (TAIL q).

B-MESSAGES = (Q, COM, δ_M).

Trunks:

$K_{TM,A}(A, sms, (S\text{-}W, bits)) = sms$.
$K_{TM,B}(B, sms, (S\text{-}W, bits)) = sms$.
$K_{A,TM}((F\text{-}W, bits), m, B) = \langle m, bits \rangle$.
$K_{B,TM}((F\text{-}W, bits), m, A) = \langle m, bits \rangle$.
$K_{A,AS}((S\text{-}W, bit_1 bit_2), \langle OK, m, seq_1 seq_2 \rangle, q) = m$,
    if $bit_1 \oplus bit_2 = seq_1 \oplus seq_2$.
$K_{B,BS}((S\text{-}W, bit_1 bit_2), \langle OK, m, seq_1 seq_2 \rangle, q') = $
    $\langle m, seq_1 seq_2 \rangle$, if $bit_1 \oplus bit_2 = seq_1 \oplus seq_2$.
$K_{A,AM}((S\text{-}W, bit_1 bit_2), \langle st, m, seq_1 seq_2 \rangle, q) = $
    FIRST, if st = ERROR or $bit_1 \oplus bit_2 \neq seq_1 \oplus seq_2$,
    and NEXT, otherwise.

$K_{B,BM}((S\text{-}W, bit_1 bit_2), \langle st, m, seq_1 seq_2 \rangle, q) = $
    FIRST, if st = ERROR or $bit_1 \oplus bit_2 \neq seq_1 \oplus seq_2$,
    and NEXT, otherwise.
$K_{AM,A}(q, i, (F\text{-}W, bits)) = $ (HEAD q), if i = FIRST,
                and (HEAD (TAIL q)), if i = NEXT.
$K_{BM,B}(q, i, (F\text{-}W, bits)) = $ (HEAD q), if i = FIRST,
                and (HEAD (TAIL q)), if i = NEXT.

Initial Conditions:

Component	Initial pair	Initial input
A-STATION	(F-W, 00)	
B-STATION	(S-W, 00)	
TRANSMISSION-MEDIUM	B	
A-STORE	ε	
B-STORE	ε	
A-MESSAGES	$q_A \in Q$	FIRST
B-MESSAGES[3]	$q_B \in Q$	

In the terms of [5], it is easy to see that there are no circular chains in Z_1 and hence there is no unending internal communication in it, since an external input is needed to continue. Consequently, the reachability tree of Z_1 (between applications of external inputs) is finite (actually quite small) and hence the reliability of the protocol represented by Z_1, as well as other protocol properties, are easy to verify.

---

[3]The first message of q_b is a dummy message.

The addition of sequence interruption to the basic part of the protocol amounts to the introduction of additional initial conditions and the changing of several actions and trunks in B-STATION.

For example, if B_{11}'s messages are to have B_{12}'s address, i.e. 11 instead of 00, we change (for the duration)

δ_B(S-W, 00, <OK, m, 00>) =

(F-W, 11) instead of (F-W, 00), and

$K_{B,BS}$(S-W, 00, <OK, m, 00>, q) =

<m, 11> instead of <m, 00>.

The light arrow in the diagram of B-STATION of Figure 8 represents such a change. The change in any of the remaining three cases of planned manual sequence interruptions is similar. In each of these cases, the preceding remarks concerning the absence of circular chains and the ease of checking the reachability tree apply.

4.4 Network #1 Modified

It is desired to construct a protocol similar to Protocol #1 for communication between A and its new branch C, which is similar in operational characteristics to A and thus does not require four separate addresses for the A-to-B messages.

The technique we use to obtain such a protocol is that of finding a homomorphic image of Z_1 with the following major properties:

(a) The seven components (two STATIONs, two STOREs, two MESSAGES, TRANSMISSION-MEDIUM) are mapped intact and separate from each other.

(b) The control information to determine the four addresses in B is superfluous and can be eliminated from B-STORE-received messages.

(c) Thus, there is no need for sequencing the A to B messages and hence the four tags in each of the states in the STATIONS may be reduced in number.

(d) The members of such important role-pairs as (FIRST,NEXT)—inputs to MESSAGEs, (S-W, F-W)—states of STATIONs, ("store", "do not store")—trunk-actions from STATIONs to STOREs, must retain their meanings and their separate identities in the homomorphic image.

4.5 The Function and Its Outcome

We exhibit the function first, and follow it in the next section by a description of a homomorphism on the tier automaton.

The function α consists of seven component functions, each on the respective component of Z_1 to that of Z_B. Each is a homomorphism, as explained in the next section. The subscript 1 identifies a component of Z_1, while the subscript B identifies it as a component of $Z_{Bartlett}$.

Each appearance of the following is assumed to be universally quantified over the stated set.

st ∈ ST, seq, bits ∈ SEQ, bit_1, bit_2, seq_1, seq_2 ∈ {0, 1},
m ∈ M, q ∈ Q, m' ∈ M', q' ∈ Q' and sms ∈ SMS.

Component Homomorphisms:

On A-STATION$_1$ to A-STATION$_B$:

$\alpha_S(s) = s, \forall s \in S$;
$\alpha_T(bit_1 bit_2) = bit_1 \oplus bit_2$;
$\alpha_\Sigma(m) = m$,
$\alpha_\Sigma(<st, m, seq_1 seq_2>) = <st, m, seq_1 \oplus seq_2>$.

[Note: In general, α_D is defined on (state, tag) pairs and may not be decomposable into α_S on the states and α_T on the tags.]

On B-STATION$_1$ to B-STATION$_B$:

$\alpha_S(s) = s, \forall s \in S$;
$\alpha_T(bit_1 bit_2) = bit_1 \oplus bit_2$;
$\alpha_\Sigma(m) = m$,
$\alpha_\Sigma(<st, m, seq_1 seq_2>) = <st, m, seq_1 \oplus seq_2>$.

On TRANSMISSION-MEDIUM$_1$ to TRANSMISSION-MEDIUM$_B$:

$\alpha_S(s) = s, \forall s \in S_{TM}$;
$\alpha_\Sigma(st) = st, \alpha_\Sigma(<m, seq_1 seq_2>) = <m, seq_1 \oplus seq_2>$,
$\alpha_\Sigma(<st, m, seq_1 seq_2>) = <st, m, seq_1 \oplus seq_2>$.

On A-STORE$_1$ to A-STORE$_B$:

$\alpha_S(s) = s, \forall s \in S_{AS}$;
$\alpha_\Sigma(i) = i, \forall i \in \Sigma_{AS}$.

On B-STORE$_1$ to B-STORE$_B$:

$\alpha_\Sigma(m') = m$, where m' = <m, seq>, for some seq ∈ SEQ.
$\alpha_S(q') = q$, where, if q' =
<m_1, seq_1><m_2, seq_2>...<m_k, seq_k>, then
q = $m_1 m_2 ... m_k$, m_i ∈ M and seq_i ∈ SEQ,
$\forall i \in \{1, 2, ..., k\}$.

On A-MESSAGES$_1$ to A-MESSAGES$_B$:

$\alpha_S(s) = s, \forall s \in S_{AM}$;
$\alpha_\Sigma(i) = i, \forall i \in \Sigma_{AM}$.

On B-MESSAGES$_1$ to B-MESSAGES$_B$:

$\alpha_S(s) = s, \forall s \in S_{BM}$;
$\alpha_\Sigma(i) = i, \forall i \in \Sigma_{BM}$.

A comparison with the specifications in [5] shows that $\alpha(Z_1) = Z_{Bartlett}$, including all trunk elements.

As remarked, other homomorphisms may exist with less desirable images, for a number of reasons (perhaps because we failed to detail all that was desired of the new protocol). Nevertheless, we *did* obtain $Z_{Bartlett}$ as a homomorphic image of Z_1. At least in 1968, Lynch conjectured (in [12]) against the existence of $Z_{Bartlett}$, making the "automatic" discovery of the latter a nontrivial event.

5. Homomorphisms on a Tier Automaton

In order to interrupt the flow as little as possible, we relegate the formal definitions to the Appendix. Here, we give a brief description of a homomorphism on Z_1 to Z_2, for two tier automata Z_1 and Z_2.

The basic building block is a function on a component to a component, say A-STATION$_1$ of Z_1 to A-STATION$_2$ of Z_2. (A less accommodating function could map A-STATION$_1$ of Z_1 to B-STATION$_2$ of Z_2, or worse—to TRANSMISSION-MEDIUM.)

Such a function, call it α_A, need not in general have the special properties we require of a homomorphism. It need only have an image—any (state, tag) pair of A-STATION$_2$—for every (state, tag) pair of A-STATION$_1$, and an image—any input of A-STATION$_2$—for every input of A-STATION$_1$. As a result, suppose that the input i acts on the pair (s, t) in A-STATION$_1$ to produce the action $\delta_{A1}((s, t), i) = (s', t')$. The function α_A must have images $\alpha_A(s, t) = (p, q)$, $\alpha_A(s', t') = (u, v)$, and $\alpha_A(i) = j$. There need not be a connection between (p, q) and j. In fact, $\delta_{A2}((p, q), j)$ may be undefined in A-STATION$_2$; and even if it is defined, it need not be (u, v).

On the other hand, if α_A is a **homomorphism**, $\delta_{A2}((p, q), j)$ must not only be defined, but it must equal (u, v). In symbols,

$$\alpha_A(\delta_{A1}((s, t), i)) = \delta_{A2}(\alpha_A(s, t), \alpha_A(i)) \text{ so that}$$

$$(u, v) = \delta_{A2}((p, q), j).$$

We call this **preservation of action** or **action preservation**, and we say that α_A preserves the action of i on (s, t).

In this manner, if α_A is a homomorphism, it must preserve *all* actions of A-STATION$_1$.

A **homomorphism** on Z_1 to Z_2 has such component homomorphisms α_C for each component tag automaton of Z_1. However, a function on Z_1 to Z_2 may have such component homomorphisms and still not be a *homomorphism* on Z_1 to Z_2. The additional property it must possess is that of **preservation of trunk action**.

To illustrate, consider the trunk in Z_1 from A-STATION$_1$ to A-MESSAGES$_1$. Say that one of the trunk elements is $(s_1, t_1, i_1, s'_1, t'_1, i'_1)$, where (s_1, t_1, i_1) is a triple of A-STATION$_1$ and (s'_1, t'_1, i'_1) is a triple of A-MESSAGES$_1$. [In our examples, (s_1, t_1, i_1) may look like (S-W, 00, <OK, m, 11>) while (s'_1, t'_1, i'_1) may look like (q, NEXT), since A-MESSAGES$_1$ is a conventional automaton— i.e. a tag automaton with just one tag.]

The added burden of the homomorphism on the entire Z_1 to Z_2 is that the image of the first triple, that of A-STATION$_1$, by the component homomorphism α_A on A-STATION$_1$ to A-STATION$_2$, must occupy the left position in an element of a trunk in Z_2 from A-STATION$_2$ to A-MESSAGES$_2$ and, likewise, the image of the second triple, that of A-MESSAGES$_1$, by the component homomorphism α_M on A-MESSAGES$_1$ to A-MESSAGES$_2$, must occupy the right position *of the very same trunk element* in Z_2 from A-STATION$_2$ to A-MESSAGES$_2$. In symbols,

$$(\alpha_A(s_1, t_1), \alpha_A(i_1), \alpha_M(s'_1, t'_1), \alpha_M(i'_1))$$

must be an element of the trunk in Z_2 from A-STATION$_2$ to A-MESSAGES$_2$.

The verification that the function described in Section 4.5 is indeed a homomorphism is straightforward, and thus we omit it.

6. Remark on Z_1; Network #2

"So why not provide four different STOREs to branch B of Z_1, create a new Protocol #2 and call its representation Z_2?" is a natural question.

The answer is that a difficulty arises in trying to map homomorphically several queues into a merged queue while preserving actions (transitions). This difficulty is magnified when no synchronizing information and no sequencing information is available.

In all such cases, a preprocessing transformation of protocols is needed, one we call a **clutch mapping**, with whose help we do obtain the same desired outcome as a homomorphic image. But that is beyond the scope of this paper, as it touches a wider spectrum of concerns.

7. Some of Z_1 Is (Almost) Superfluous

Suppose that Protocol #1 did not include the requirements that the network operate properly even under resequencing. The exhibited homomorphism on Z_1 would still yield $Z_{Bartlett}$, but we observe that a number of conditions of Z_1 are not reachable from the initial condition of Z_1.

For example, neither δ(S-W, 00, <OK, m, 11>) nor δ(S-W, 00, <OK, m, 01>) is reachable in A-STATION and in B-STATION of Z_1; the same is true for six other triples in each of the two STATIONs. Consequently, a function on Z_1 to some Z_2 that preserves actions and trunk actions, but only on the reachable arguments, is all that a practical application requires.

In Z_1, above, the function we described on A-STATION$_1$ to A-STATION$_{Bartlett}$ need not therefore be checked for action preservation on δ_A(S-W, 00, <OK, m, 11>) or on any of the remaining seven unreachable triples of A-STATION of Z_1.

Moreover, although (S-W, 00, <OK, m, 11>, q, m) is a member of the trunk $K_{A, A-STORE}$ of Z_1, for any state q and any message m $\in$ M, the unreachable triple (S-W, 00, <OK, m, 11>) of A-STATION cannot be active and thus cannot transmit m to q of A-STORE. This trunk element is one of several in Z_1 which, under the changed requirements, cannot be activated from the initial conditions of Z_1.

When we seek to define a function on Z_1 that preserves the actions of components and trunk action, we need to check such preservation only on those arguments that are reachable from the initial condition of Z_1.

A cautionary note: a given triple (s, t, i) may be reachable in a component tag automaton C from the initial condition of C, and yet, when the entire network representation Z_1 is considered, that triple may never be reached, since there may be no configuration of Z_1 that is reachable simultaneously in *all* components from the initial condition of Z_1, which also has (s, t, i) as its triple in C.

[In the following, again, we relegate the formal definitions to the Appendix. Here, we only describe the concepts intuitively.] We call the set of those triples of all components of an initialized tier automaton Z, which are reachable from the initial condition of Z, the **reachable domain** of Z. We call the set of those triples of an initialized tag automaton R, which are the component's share of the reachable domain of Z, the **reachable domain** of R. Where R_i and R_j are initialized tag automata, we call a function $\alpha^i: R_i \to R_j$ on R_i to R_j a **reachable-domain (r.d.) homomorphism** if and only if it preserves actions on the reachable domain of R_i. Where Z_1 and Z_2 are two initialized tier automata, we call a function $\alpha: Z_1 \to Z_2$ a **reachable-domain (r.d.) homomorphism** if and only if each of the constituent functions $\alpha^1, ..., \alpha^m$ of α on the respective components $R_1, ..., R_m$ of Z_1 is an r.d. homomorphism and, in addition, trunk actions are preserved for all elements of all trunks of Z_1 whose arguments are in the reachable domain of Z_1. Thus, an r.d. homomorphism is a less demanding construct than a homomorphism.

In the process of designing a protocol, as in constructing its tier automaton representation, it is often easier to state (and to think of) the behavior of the respective construct under a *cluster of conditions* (e.g., "if any of the remaining values of the control bits arrive with an error-free message"), than to do so for each single condition. Consequently, the reachable domain of a tier automaton representation Z_1 of a protocol is often smaller than the entire set of triples of all components of Z_1. In such a case, an r.d. homomorphism on Z_1 to some tier automaton Z_2 may exist, while a homomorphism on Z_1 to Z_2 may not.

In the following section, we show such an example.

8. Network #3

8.1 The Requirements

In 1968 W. C. Lynch discussed (in [12]) schemes for achieving reliable full-duplex transmission over half-duplex lines by alternating messages in either direction. Lynch used two control bits, one **alternation** bit (a message is accepted only when its alternation bit differs from that of the previous accepted message) and one **verification** bit (indicating "error-free reception independently of the acceptance of the error-free reception").

We quote from [12]. "To each message sent from A to B we attach an extra bit called the alternation bit. This bit is of course subject to the error checking. After B receives the message it decides if the message had no errors (is error-free). It sends back to A a verification message (*verify bit*) indicating to A whether or not the immediately preceding A $\to$ B message was error-free. After A receives this verification one of three possibilities holds: (1) the A $\to$ B message was good, (2) the A $\to$ B message was bad, (3) the verification was in error so that A does not know whether the A $\to$ B message was good or bad. In cases (2) and (3) A simply resends the same A $\to$ B message as before. In case (1), A *fetches* the next message to be sent, and sends it, *inverting the setting of the alternation bit* with respect to the previous A $\to$ B message.

Whenever B receives a message that is not in error it compares the alternation bit of this new message to the alternation bit of the most recent error-free reception. If the alternation bits are equal the new message is not accepted. If they differ the new message is accepted. The verify from B to A indicates error-free reception independently of the acceptance of the error-free reception." At this point, Lynch presents a reliability argument.

The following sequence of events is possible:
A sends message m_1 to B, which is received error-free; m_1 is <u>accepted</u>.
B sends message n_1 to A with verify = 1, but n_1 is received with an error.
A retransmits m_1 to B, but this time m_1 is received with an error.
Thus, B retransmits n_1 to A with verify = 0, error-free, and A <u>accepts</u>.

According to the Lynch protocol, A should retransmit m_1 (with verify = 1). But this inhibits progress, since information exists in the network to conclude that B has received m_1 without error. True, B did not indicate so in its transmission to A, but it could have—by telling which value it expects the alternation bit from A to have next time. Then A can send the next message m_2 rather than retransmit m_1.

This may be sufficient motivation to modify the Lynch protocol by adding a bit x to the existing two, ver and alt, in the control information sent with each message. The value of x is *the value of alt this station expects to receive next time*.

Now, when a station, say A, receives an error-free message from B with ver = 0, A checks the value of x. If the value of x from B now differs from the last value of the alternating bit A sent to B, then B has accepted the old message and A can transmit a new one; otherwise (if x from B equals the last alt from A), B still expects the old message and A should retransmit it.

The remainder of the protocol can be retained from the Lynch protocol. We call the result Protocol #3. The argument for the reliability of Protocol #3 is the same as Lynch's argument, with the obvious modification.

As it turns out, now the verification bit is unnecessary, but this may or may not be discovered. One may be content with what appears to be an improvement over Lynch's protocol. However, since a 3-bit protocol seems a bit bulky, an attempt at improvement with an r.d. homomorphism seems in order. The (surprising?) result is that only one bit is needed, since the r.d. homomorphic image of Z_3 (the tier-automaton representation of Protocol #3) is none other than $Z_{Bartlett}$.

8.2 The Details of Z_3 and of an R.D. Homomorphism on Z_3 onto $Z_{Bartlett}$

Z_3 : the specification

$Z_3 = (\mathbb{R}_3, \mathbb{K}_3)$ where $\mathbb{R}_3, \mathbb{K}_3$ and EXT are as in $Z_{Bartlett}$ from [1] and their members are defined below. We use the following notation generically:
ST is the status set (ST = {OK, ERROR}),
COM is the command set (COM = {FIRST, NEXT}),
M is the (finite) set all legal messages,
Q is the finite set of all legal bounded message queues (as in Section 4.3),
SMB =
  {<st, m, v, x, alt>: st $\in$ ST, m $\in$ M, v, x, alt $\in$ {1, 0}}.
[B of SMB denotes the control-bit triple <v, x, alt>.
x = the expectation bit accompanying a message.]
Each appearance of the following is assumed to be universally quantified over the stated set.
st $\in$ ST; m $\in$ M; q $\in$ Q; smb $\in$ SMB;
v, x, alt, e, ls $\in$ {0, 1}.
[e = the value this station expects alt to be.]

Components:

A-STATION = (S, Σ, δ, T, P);
S = {S-W, F-W};
Σ = M $\cup$ SMB;
T = {<e,ls>, <v, e, alt>} =
  {<"expect", "last-sent value of alt">,
  <"verification", "expectation", "alternation">};
P = ({S-W} $\times$ {<e, ls>}) $\cup$ ({F-W} $\times$ {<v, e, alt>});
δ(F-W, <v, e, alt>, m) = (S-W, <e, alt>),
δ(S-W, <e, ls>, <ERROR, m, v, x, alt>) =
  (F-W, <0, e, ls>),
δ(S-W, <e, ls>, <OK, m, v, x, alt>) =
  (F-W, <1, 1 - e, 1 - ls>), if e = alt and v = 1,
δ(S-W, <e, ls>, <OK, m, v, x, alt>) =
  (F-W, <1, 1 - e, x>), if e = alt and v $\neq$ 1,
δ(S-W, <e, ls>, <OK, m, v, x, alt>) =
  (F-W, <1, e, 1 - ls>), if e $\neq$ alt and v = 1,
δ(S-W, <e, ls>, <OK, m, v, x, alt>) =
  (F-W, <1, e, x>), if e $\neq$ alt and v $\neq$ 1.

B-STATION = A-STATION.
TRANSMISSION-MEDIUM = (S_{TM}, Σ_{TM}, δ_{TM});
S_{TM} = {A, B};
Σ_{TM} = ST $\cup$ {<m, v, x, alt>} $\cup$ SMB;
δ_{TM}(A, smb) = B,
δ_{TM}(B, smb) = A;
MERGE$_{TM}$ (st, <m, v, x, alt>) = <st, m, v, x, alt>.

A-STORE = (Q, M, δ_S),
  δ_S(q, m) = qm = (APPEND q (LIST m)).
B-STORE = (Q, M, δ_S),

A-MESSAGES = (Q, COM, δ_M),
 δ_M(q, FIRST) = q,
 δ_M(q, NEXT) = (TAIL q).
B-MESSAGES = (Q, COM, δ_M).

Trunks:

$K_{TM,A}$(A, smb, (S-W, <e, ls>)) = smb.
$K_{TM,B}$(B, smb, (S-W, <e, ls>)) = smb.
$K_{A,TM}$((F-W, <v, e, alt>), m, B) = <m, v, e, alt>.
$K_{B,TM}$((F-W, <v, e, alt>), m, A) = <m, v, e, alt>.
$K_{A,AS}$((S-W, <e, ls>),<OK, m, v, x, alt>, q) = m, if e = alt.
$K_{B,BS}$ = $K_{A,AS}$.
$K_{A,AM}$((S-W, <e, ls>),<ERROR, m, v, x, alt>, q) = FIRST,
$K_{A,AM}$((S-W, <e, ls>),<OK, m, 1, x, alt>, q) = NEXT,
$K_{A,AM}$((S-W, <e, ls>),<OK, m, 0, x, alt>, q) = FIRST,
 if x = ls,
$K_{A,AM}$((S-W, <e, ls>),<OK, m, 0, x, alt>, q) = NEXT,
 if x ≠ ls.
$K_{B,BM}$ = $K_{A,AM}$.
$K_{AM,A}$(q, FIRST, (F-W, <v, e, alt>)) = (HEAD q),
$K_{AM,A}$(q, NEXT, (F-W, <v, e, alt>)) = (HEAD (TAIL q)).
$K_{BM,B}$ = $K_{AM,A}$.

Initial Conditions:

Component	Initial State	Initial input
A-STORE	ε	
B-STORE	ε	
TRANSMISSION-MEDIUM	B	
A-STATION	(F-W, <1, 1, 1>)*	
B-STATION	(S-W, <1, 0>)*	
A-MESSAGES	$q_1 \in Q$	FIRST
B-MESSAGES**	$q_2 \in Q$	

* Three alternative couples of initial pairs exist:

A-STATION				B-STATION		
state	v	e	alt	state	e	ls
F-W	1	0	0	S-W	0	1
F-W	1	1	0	S-W	0	0
F-W	1	0	1	S-W	1	1

** The first message in q_2 is a "dummy" message.

An R.D. Homomorphic Image of Z_3

We allow either of only two of the four possible initial pairs of A and B;

 A: (F-W, <1, 1, 1>) B: (S-W, <1, 0>);
 A: (F-W, <1, 0, 0>) B: (S-W, <0, 1>).

The Result of Reachability Analysis on Z_3:

The reachable domain of A-STATION is

{ ((S-W, <1, 1>), <st, m, 1, 0, 1>),
 ((S-W, <1, 1>), <st, m, 0, 1, 0>),
 ((S-W, <0, 0>), <st, m, 1, 1, 0>),
 ((S-W, <0, 0>), <st, m, 0, 0, 1>),
 ((F-W, <0, 1, 1>), m), ((F-W, <0, 0, 0>), m),
 ((F-W, <1, 1, 1>), m),
 ((F-W, <1, 0, 0>), m): m ∈ M, st ∈ ST}.

The reachable domain of B-STATION is

{ ((S-W, <1, 0>), <st, m, 1, 1, 1>),
 ((S-W, <1, 0>), <st, m, 0, 0, 0>),
 ((S-W, <0, 1>), <st, m, 1, 0, 0>),
 ((S-W, <0, 1>), <st, m, 0, 1, 1>),
 ((F-W, <0, 0, 1>), m), ((F-W, <0, 1, 0>), m),
 ((F-W, <1, 0, 1>), m),
 ((F-W, <1, 1, 0>), m): m ∈ M, st ∈ ST}.

For any other component automaton C, the reachable domain is all of $P_C \times \Sigma_C$.

Component Homomorphisms:

On A-STATION$_3$ to A-STATION$_B$:

 ∀e, ls, ne, v, alt ∈ {0, 1},
 α_P(S-W, <e, ls>) = (S-W, e), α_P(F-W, <v, ne, alt>) = (F-W, alt).
 ∀st ∈ {OK, ERROR}, ∀m ∈ M, ∀v, x, alt ∈ {0, 1},
 α_Σ(<st, m, v, x, alt>) = <st, m, alt>, α_Σ(m) = m.

On B-STATION$_3$ to B-STATION$_B$:
 same as the component homomorphism on A-STATION$_3$ to A-STATION$_B$.

On TRANSMISSION-MEDIUM$_3$ to TRANSMISSION-MEDIUM$_B$:

 ∀s ∈ {A, B}, α_S(s) = s.
 ∀st ∈ {OK, ERROR}, ∀m ∈ M, ∀v, x, alt ∈ {0, 1},
 α_Σ(<st, m, v, x, alt>) = <st, m, alt>, α_Σ(st) = st,
 α_Σ(<m, v, x, alt>) = <m, alt>.

On A-STORE$_3$ to A-STORE$_B$:
 α_Σ and α_S are identity functions.

On B-STORE$_3$ to B-STORE$_B$:
 α_Σ and α_S are identity functions.

On A-MESSAGES$_3$ to A-MESSAGES$_B$:
 α_Σ and α_S are identity functions.

On B-MESSAGES$_3$ to B-MESSAGES$_B$:
 α_Σ and α_S are identity functions.

Another R.D. Homomorphic Image

If we employ either of the other two of possible initial pairs of A and B, i.e.

 A: (F-W, <1, 0, 1>) and B: (S-W, <1, 1>) or
 A: (F-W, <1, 1, 0>) and B: (S-W, <0, 0>),

we obtain a different r.d. homomorphism, but with almost the same r.d. homomorphic image.

9. Retrospective

As some readers must have suspected by now, we first looked for the simplest illustration of homomorphisms—mapping the Lynch protocol onto the Bartlett *et al.* protocol homomorphically. Unfortunately, the latter is just not a homomorphic image (not even with an r.d. homomorphism) of the former, as is likely to be the case often when an analogy is pushed beyond its limitations.

We then had to manufacture a second protocol in order to make our point. Nevertheless, the point is made, and perhaps more so if the manufactured protocols are less than satisfying.

10. Conclusion

Using our representation scheme of a protocol as a tier automaton Z, from [5], we introduced the reachable domain homomorphism and its use to *manipulate* the representation of one protocol to obtain another with desired features retained and others discarded. We illustrated the procedure on two protocols to obtain a familiar one.

11. Appendix: Definitions

I. UNINITIALIZED STRUCTURES

Definition 1.

Let S be a set (of **states**) and T be a set (of **tags**). We call a subcollection $C(T) \subseteq 2^T$ (of subsets of T) **complete** iff, $\forall t \in T, \exists b \in C(T)$ such that $t \in b$.[4]

Let $C(T) \subseteq 2^T$ be complete, and let $P \subseteq S \times C(T)$. Then P is a set of **pairs** over S and T iff, $\forall s \in S, \exists b \in C(T)$ such that $(s, b) \in P$, and $\forall b \in C(T), \exists s \in S$ such that $(s, b) \in P$.

A **power tier automaton (PTA)** is a 6-tuple $Z = (P, \Sigma, \delta, K, H, J)$, where

P is a set (of **pairs** over some S and T);

Σ is a finite nonempty set (of **inputs**);

$\delta: P \times \Sigma \to \mathbb{N}^+ \times \mathbb{N}^P$ is a partial function (the **transition function**)[5];

$K \subseteq \text{dom}(\delta) \times \text{dom}(\delta)$ is a relation (the **trunk** of Z), where $\text{dom}(\delta)$ is the domain of δ;

$H \subseteq \text{dom}(\delta)$ is the set of **incoming external signals**; and

$J \subseteq \text{dom}(\delta)$ is the set of **outgoing external signals**.

[We permit (p_1, i_1, p_2, i_2) for $((p_1, i_1), (p_2, i_2))$ and thus we permit both $K \subseteq P \times \Sigma \times P \times \Sigma$ and $K \subseteq (P \times \Sigma) \times (P \times \Sigma)$, as no confusion results.]

Each $(p, i, n, y) \in \delta$ is a **transition** of Z. We say that (p, i, n, y) is the **transition from** (or **at**) p **by** i and we call p the **origin** of the transition.

Let $t = (p, i, n, y)$ be a transition of Z. Then n is the **threshold** of t; $\forall p' \in P, y(p')$ is the **yield of** t **at** p'; and each $p' \in P$ such that $y(p') > 0$ is a **destination** of t. Each destination of t is an **i-successor** of p. The **set of i-successors** of p is the set of destinations of t, i.e. $\delta_i(p) = \{p' \in P: y(p') > 0\}$.

Let $i \in \Sigma$. Then the **set of i-successors** of Z is the union of the sets of i-successors of p over all $p \in P$, i.e. $\delta_i(Z) = \bigcup_{p \in P} \delta_i(p)$.

A power tier automaton $Z = (P, \Sigma, \delta, K, H, J)$ is **finite** iff P is finite.

Definition 2.

A **power tag automaton** is a triple $R = (P, \Sigma, \delta)$, where

P is a set (of **pairs** over some S and T);

Σ is a finite nonempty set (of **inputs**); and

$\delta: P \times \Sigma \to \mathbb{N}^+ \times \mathbb{N}^P$ is a partial function (the **transition function**).

Let $Z = (P, \Sigma, \delta, K, H, J)$ be a PTA. Then the **power tag automaton** of Z is the triple $R = (P, \Sigma, \delta)$.

All pertinent components of the PTA, such as **transition**, **origin**, **threshold**, **yield**, **destination** and **successor**, are named and defined identically in the power tag automaton.

Definition 3.

Let $R = (P, \Sigma, \delta)$ be a power tag automaton. A triple $R' = (Q, \Sigma, \delta')$ is a **power tag subautomaton** of R, written $R' \triangleleft R$, iff

(i) $Q \subseteq P$;

(ii) $\delta' = \delta|_{Q \times \Sigma}$ (the restriction of δ to $Q \times \Sigma$); and

(iii) $\forall (q, i, n, y) \in \delta', \forall p' \in P, y(p') > 0 \Rightarrow p' \in Q$.

[We permit $\delta': Q \times \Sigma \to \mathbb{N}^+ \times \mathbb{N}^Q$ for convenience, since no confusion results. Thus, each power tag subautomaton may be regarded as a power tag automaton in its own right. We also permit the use of δ for δ' where no confusion arises.]

R' is a **proper** power tag subautomaton of R iff $R' \triangleleft R$ and Q is a proper subset of P.

Let $R = (P, \Sigma, \delta)$ be a power tag automaton and let $R' = (Q, \Sigma, \delta') \triangleleft R$. Then R' is **separated** iff, $\forall (p, i, n, y) \in \delta$ such that $p \notin Q, \forall p' \in P, y(p') > 0 \Rightarrow p' \notin Q$.

R' is a **block** of R iff it is minimal separated; i.e., R' is separated and no proper power tag subautomaton R'' of R' is separated.

A power tag automaton $R = (P, \Sigma, \delta)$ is **connected** iff it has no separated proper power tag subautomaton. [Note that R' is a block of R iff R' is both separated and connected, iff R' is maximal connected.]

Definition 4.

Let $Z = (P, \Sigma, \delta, K, H, J)$ be a power tier automaton, let $R = (P, \Sigma, \delta)$ be the power tag automaton of Z and let $R_1 = (P_1, \Sigma, \delta_1)$ and $R_2 = (P_2, \Sigma, \delta_2)$ be blocks of R.

The **2-deck power tier automaton** $Z(R_1 \to R_2)$ is the 6-tuple $(P_1 \cup P_2, \Sigma, \delta', K', H', J')$, where

$\delta' = \delta_1 \cup \delta_2$;

$K' = K \cap (\text{dom}(\delta_1) \times \text{dom}(\delta_2))$;

we denote K' by K_{R_1, R_2} and call it the **trunk** from R_1 to R_2.

Let the **set of incoming internal signals** of $Z(R_1 \to R_2)$ be denoted by IIS_{12} and defined by,

$IIS_{12} = \{(q, j) \in \text{dom}(\delta_1): \exists k = (p, i, q, j) \in K\}$.

(Intuitively, IIS_{12} is the set of second halves of trunk elements ending in transitions of R_1.)

Then $H' = (H \cap \text{dom}(\delta_1)) \cup IIS_{12}$.

Let the **set of outgoing internal signals** of $Z(R_1 \to R_2)$ be denoted by OIS_{12} and defined by,

$OIS_{12} = \{(p, i) \in \text{dom}(\delta_2): \exists k = (p, i, q, j) \in K\}$.

(Intuitively, OIS_{12} is the set of first halves of trunk elements beginning in transitions of R_2.)

Then $J' = (J \cap \text{dom}(\delta_2)) \cup OIS_{12}$.

Definition 5.

Let $Z_1 = (P_1, \Sigma_1, \delta_1, K_1, H_1, J_1)$ and $Z_2 = (P_2, \Sigma_2, \delta_2, K_2, H_2, J_2)$ be PTAs.

Let $F_{12} \subseteq J_1 \times H_2$, let $F_{21} \subseteq J_2 \times H_1$ and let $F = F_{12} \cup F_{21}$. We call F a **fusion of** Z_1 **and** Z_2.

We use $F_{12}|_{H_2}, F_{21}|_{H_1}, F_{12}|_{J_1}$ and $F_{21}|_{J_2}$ to mean,

---

[4] Such a subcollection is a **cover** (or **covering**) of T.

[5] $\mathbb{N}$ is the set of nonnegative integers, $\mathbb{N}^+$ is the set of positive integers, and $\mathbb{N}^P$ is the set of all functions on P to $\mathbb{N}$.

respectively,

$F_{12}|_{H_2} = \{(q, j) \in H_2: \exists (p, i, q, j) \in F_{12}\}$,
$F_{21}|_{H_1} = \{(q, j) \in H_1: \exists (p, i, q, j) \in F_{21}\}$,
$F_{12}|_{J_1} = \{(p, i) \in J_1: \exists (p, i, q, j) \in F_{12}\}$, and
$F_{21}|_{J_2} = \{(p, i) \in J_2: \exists (p, i, q, j) \in F_{21}\}$.

The **connection of Z_1 and Z_2 by** F (alt., the F-**connection of Z_1 and Z_2**) is denoted by $Z_1 \;\textcircled{F}\; Z_2$ and is defined by,

$Z_1 \;\textcircled{F}\; Z_2 = (P, \Sigma, \delta, K, H, J)$, where
$P = P_1 \cup P_2$;
$\Sigma = \Sigma_1 \cup \Sigma_2$;
$\delta = \delta_1 \cup \delta_2$;
$K = K_1 \cup K_2 \cup F$;
$H = (H_1 \cup H_2) - (F_{12}|_{H_2} \cup F_{21}|_{H_1})$; and
$J = (J_1 \cup J_2) - (F_{12}|_{J_1} \cup F_{21}|_{J_2})$.

A PTA Z is a **connection** of two PTAs Z_1 and Z_2, written $Z = Z_1 \bigcirc Z_2$, iff there exists a set F such that $Z_1 \;\textcircled{F}\; Z_2$. When $F = \emptyset$, $Z_1 \;\textcircled{\emptyset}\; Z_2$ is said to be the **trivial connection of Z_1 and Z_2**.

Definition 6.

Let $Z = (P, \Sigma, \delta, K, H, J)$ be a PTA, let $R = (P, \Sigma, \delta)$ be the power tag automaton of Z and let $R_i = (P_i, \Sigma_i, \delta_i)$ be the blocks of R, where $i \in A$ and A is an indexing set.

The 6-tuple $Z' = (P', \Sigma, \delta', K', H', J')$ is a **full sub PTA** of Z iff $\exists B \subseteq A$ such that

$P' = \bigcup_{i \in B} P_i$;

$\delta' = \bigcup_{i \in B} \delta_i$;

$K' = \bigcup_{i,j \in B} K_{R_i, R_j}$;

$H' = (H \cap \text{dom}(\delta')) \cup$
  $\{(q, j) \in \text{dom}(\delta'): \exists k \in K - K' \text{ with } k = (p, i, q, j)\}$; and
$J' = (J \cap \text{dom}(\delta')) \cup$
  $\{(p, i) \in \text{dom}(\delta'): \exists k \in K - K' \text{ with } k = (p, i, q, j)\}$.

II. INITIALIZED STRUCTURES AND FIRING RULES

Definition 7.

An **initialized power tier automaton** (IPTA) is a triple $Z^0 = (Z, m_0, H_0)$, where

$Z = (P, \Sigma, \delta, K, H, J)$ is a power tier automaton;

$m_0: P \to \mathbb{N}$ is the **initial power distribution** of Z^0; and

$H_0 \subseteq H$ is the set of **initial incoming (external) signals** of Z^0.

An **initialized J-power tier automaton** (IJPTA) is a quadruple $Z^0 = (Z, m_0, H_0, J_0)$, where Z, m_0, H_0 are as in the definition of the IPTA and $J_0 \subseteq J$ is the set of **initial outgoing (external) signals** of Z^0.

[**Remark 1.** For convenience of reference, we denote by Z^0 both the IPTA and the IJPTA. No confusion should result as the context indicates which variety is used.

Remark 2. The initial incoming (external) signals are regarded intuitively as the "external" inputs to the Z^0 which cause the start of its operation. These incoming signals are "active" at time $t = 0$.

Remark 3. The initial outgoing (external) signals are regarded intuitively as the outputs to the external environment of the IJPTA Z^0 before the start of its operation.

In many applications such "initial outputs" have no counterpart in the modeled entity. For such applications, the IPTA is sufficient and J need not be carried as an unused component.

However, it becomes desirable at a later point in the development of the PTA to map homomorphically one initialized PTA at time $t = 0$ to an IPTA at $t = r \neq 0$, i.e. that is already in operation. In fact, mapping an initialized PTA into, or onto, *its own future*, may yield interesting and useful results on liveness, safety and other properties of the PTA.

An active "initial output" may be needed for such purposes and hence the definition of the IJPTA. The IPTA may then be regarded as an IJPTA with $J_0 = \emptyset$.]

A **power distribution** of Z^0 is any function $m: P \to \mathbb{N}$.

An **interpretation** *I* (of the timing and firing behavior) of Z^0 is any rule which completely describes the transformation of a power distribution of Z^0 to a (resulting) power distribution of Z^0. [See Definitions 9, 10 and 11 for the interpretation which we employ for the specific application of this article.]

Given an interpretation *I* of the timing and firing behavior of the initialized power tier automaton $Z^0 = (Z, m_0, H_0)$, a **power distribution under** *I* of Z^0 is any function $m_r: P \to \mathbb{N}$ which may be reached from $Z^0 = (Z, m_0, H_0)$ by a finite number r of steps under *I*.[6] We call $m_r(p)$ the **power** of $p, \forall p \in P$.

Let $t = (p, i, n, y) \in \delta$ and let m be a power distribution under *I* of Z^0. Then t is **ready** (alt., a **ready transition**) **under** m iff the threshold of does not exceed the power of p, i.e. iff $n \leq m(p)$.

We denote the set of **active pairs** of Z^0 **under** m by $m^+(P)$ and define it by, $\forall q \in P, q \in m^+(P)$ iff there exists a ready transition $(p, i, n, y) \in \delta$ with $p = q$.

Definition 8.

An **initialized power tag automaton** is a pair $R^0 = (R, m_0)$, where

$R = (P, \Sigma, \delta)$ is a power tag automaton, and

$m_0: P \to \mathbb{N}$ is the initial power distribution of R^0.

All pertinent components of the IPTA, such as (**initial**) **power distribution**, **power of a pair**, **ready transitions**, **set of active pairs**, are named and defined identically in the initialized power tag automaton.

Let $Z^0 = (Z, m_0, H_0)$ be an IPTA, where $Z = (P, \Sigma, \delta, K, H, J)$. Then the **initialized power tag automaton of** Z^0 is $R^0 = (R, m_0)$, where $R = (P, \Sigma, \delta)$.

---

[6] See Definition 10.

Definition 9 (The Firing Rule for Transitions).[7]

Let $Z^0 = (Z, m_0, H_0)$ be an IPTA (initialized power tier automaton) and let $h \in H$. Then the incoming external signal h is **activated (made active) initially** iff $h \in H_0$. Z^0 is **operational** iff $H_0 \neq \emptyset$. An incoming external signal that is activated initially is **activated (made active)**. An incoming external signal $(p, i) \in H$ may also be **activated** at any time during the operation of Z^0.

Let $\tau_0 \subseteq \delta$ and let $t = (p, i, n, y) \in \tau_0$ iff $(p, i) \in H_0$. Then, initially, each $t \in \tau_0$ is **enabled** (alt., **stimulated to fire**) by the corresponding active initial incoming signal $t|_{P \times \Sigma} \in H_0$. (Whether a transition $t = (p, i, n, y)$ actually fires depends also on the power $m(p)$ of p and the threshold n of t, as is seen below.)

At any time, a transition $t = (p, i, n, y)$ of Z^0 is **enabled** (or **stimulated to fire**) iff either an incoming external signal (p, i) of Z is activated or a trunk element $k = (q, j, p, i) \in K$ is activated. (For activation of trunk elements, see Definition 11.) [We regard (p, i) of $k = (q, j, p, i) \in K$ as an **incoming internal signal**, and the collection of incoming external signals and incoming internal signals as the **set of incoming signals** of Z. We likewise regard (q, j) of $k = (q, j, p, i) \in K$ as an **outgoing internal signal** and the collection of outgoing external signals and outgoing internal signals as the **set of outgoing signals** of Z.]

Let the current power distribution of Z^0 be $m: P \to \mathbb{N}$, and let $\Sigma = \{i_1, ..., i_r\}$.

For each $p \in P$, define $m^*(p)$ by the following. For each $i_j \in \Sigma$, if $\delta(p, i_j)$ is not defined, let $x_j = 0$, and if $\exists (p, i_j, n_j, y_j) \in \delta$, let x_j be the sum of the total number of activations of the trunk elements enabling $(p, i_j, n_j, y_j) \in \delta$ (see Definition 11, below) and the total number of activations of the incoming external signals (p, i_j). If $m(p) \geq \sum_{j=1}^{r} x_j n_j$, then exactly those transitions t_j at p with positive x_j **fire**. In that case, $m^*(p) = m(p) - \sum_{j=1}^{r} x_j n_j$. Otherwise, (if $m(p) < \sum_{j=1}^{r} x_j n_j$), no transition at p fires and $m^*(p) = m(p)$, unless otherwise specified by the **modified firing rule (m.f.r.)**.

Let $D \subseteq \delta$ be the set of all transitions of Z^0 enabled and actually firing when the power distribution of Z^0 is $m: P \to \mathbb{N}$. For each $t_c = (q_c, j_c, h_c, y_c) \in D$, let x_c be the sum of the total number of activations of the trunk elements and the total number of activations of the external incoming signals enabling t_c. Then m is transformed into the **resulting power distribution** $m': P \to \mathbb{N}$ defined by:

$$\forall p \in P, m'(p) = m^*(p) + \sum_{t_c \in D} x_c y_c(p).$$

Definition 10 (Modified Firing Rule).

Let the conditions of Definition 9 hold and let $m^*(p) = m(p) - \sum_{j=1}^{r} x_j n_j$, if $m(p) \geq \sum_{j=1}^{r} x_j n_j$, as in Definition 9. However, if $m(p) < \sum_{j=1}^{r} x_j n_j$, define $m^*(p)$ by the following **modified firing rule (m.f.r.)**. For each transition t_j, where $j \in \{1, ..., r\}$, t_j may be made to **fire** x_j' times (i.e. with multiplicity x_j') provided $0 \leq x_j' \leq x_j$ and provided $m(p) \geq \sum_{j=1}^{r} x_j' n_j$ (where n_j is the threshold of t_j). In that case, $m^*(p) = m(p) - \sum_{j=1}^{r} x_j' n_j$.

The **resulting power distribution** $m': P \to \mathbb{N}$ is defined, as in Definition 9, by:

$$\forall p \in P, m'(p) = m^*(p) + \sum_{t_c \in D} x_c y_c(p).$$

Definition 11.

Let $Z^0 = (Z, m_0, H_0)$ be an initialized power tier automaton and let $k = (p, i, q, j) \in K$. Then k is **activated (made active)** iff the transition $t = (p, i, n, y)$ of Z fires. (The trunk element k is activated immediately after t fires.)

If t fires with multiplicity x as a result of a multiple stimulation of t, then k is **activated** x times and it **enables (stimulates to fire)** the transition $t' = (q, j, n', y')$ x times, i.e. with multiplicity x, regarded as simultaneous action (or sequential action in sufficiently close succession to be regarded as simultaneous).

[Note that the multiplicity of activation of k by the transition $t = (p, i, n, y)$ may be redefined by the m.f.r.]

Definition 12.

Let $Z = (P, \Sigma, \delta, K, H, J)$ be a power tier automaton. Then Z is a **tier automaton** iff, $\forall (p, i, n, y) \in \delta$, $n = 1$ and $y(p') \in \{0, 1\}$, $\forall p' \in P$.

Let $Z^0 = (Z, m_0, H_0)$ be an initialized power tier automaton, where Z is a tier automaton. Then Z^0 is an **initialized tier automaton (ITA)** iff $m_0: P \to \{0, 1\}$ and the arithmetic which determines the resulting power distribution m' from the current power distribution is:

$n \cdot 1 = 1$, $\forall n \in \mathbb{N}^+$; $0 + 0 = 0$, $0 + 1 = 1 + 0 = 1 + 1 = 1$.

III. MAPPINGS

Definition 13 (Homomorphism on Initialized Tier Automata).

Let $Z_1^0 = (Z_1, m_{10}, H_{10})$ and $Z_2^0 = (Z_2, m_{20}, H_{20})$ be two initialized tier automata, with $Z_1 = (P_1, \Sigma_1, \delta_1, K_1, H_1, J_1)$ and $Z_2 = (P_2, \Sigma_2, \delta_2, K_2, H_2, J_2)$.

A **function** $\alpha: Z_1 \to Z_2$ is a pair $\alpha = (\alpha_P, \alpha_\Sigma)$ of functions, with $\alpha_P: P_1 \to P_2$ and $\alpha_\Sigma: \Sigma_1 \to \Sigma_2$.

---

[7]**Remark on Timing and Firing**

Other than in a very restricted species of the initialized power tier automaton, it is possible for two, or more, pairs to be engaged in transitions concurrently. For such cases, and others in which more than one pair may be "active" at one time, an assumption must be made concerning the timing of various transitions.

The simple assumption of uniform time for all transitions is most suitable for the synchronous case. However, in the general case each transition may be assigned a real value as its duration—the amount of time from initiation to termination (including negative values of time for such cases as time-warp architectures and other virtual-time instances in some distributed mail systems). It is thus possible to model *continuous time*. When such timing assumptions are made, it may become necessary to augment the model by a time-keeping variable in order to determine for each enabled transition whether and when it will fire.

Here we assume uniform duration for all transitions and uniform duration for all trunk elements to "stimulate" transitions. (Trunk-element activation occurs immediately after transition firing; see Definition 11.)

The formalism admits a wide variety of interpretations of the timing and firing behavior of Z^0. The class of interpretations we use for the application in this paper is detailed in Definitions 9, 10 and 11.

A function $\alpha: Z_1 \to Z_2$ is **transition preserving** iff, $\forall (p, i, n, y) \in \delta_1, \exists (q, j, n', z) \in \delta_2$ such that $q = \alpha_P(p)$, $j = \alpha_\Sigma(i)$ and $\forall s \in P_1, y(s) = z(\alpha_P(s))$.

A transition preserving function $\alpha: Z_1 \to Z_2$ is a **homomorphism** iff,

(i) $\forall (p_1, i_1, p_2, i_2) \in K_1, (\alpha_P(p_1), \alpha_\Sigma(i_1), \alpha_P(p_2), \alpha_\Sigma(i_2)) \in K_2$,

(ii) $\forall (p_1, i_1) \in H_1, (\alpha_P(p_1), \alpha_\Sigma(i_1)) \in H_2$, and

(iii) $\forall (p_1, i_1) \in J_1, (\alpha_P(p_1), \alpha_\Sigma(i_1)) \in J_2$.

Let Z_1^0 and Z_2^0 operate under the interpretations I_1 and I_2, respectively, each with uniform time for its own transitions.[8] For each power distribution $m_j: P_j \to \mathbb{N}$ of Z_j under I_j, we let the resulting power distribution $m_j': P_j \to \mathbb{N}$ of Z_j be defined from m_j by the firing rule for transitions in Definitions 9 and 10, $\forall j \in \{1, 2\}$.

A homomorphism $\alpha: Z_1 \to Z_2$ is a **homomorphism on** Z_1^0 **to** Z_2^0 (an **ITA homomorphism**) iff, it satisfies the two conditions:

(iv) $\forall (p_1, i_1) \in H_{10}, (\alpha_P(p_1), \alpha_\Sigma(i_1)) \in H_{20}$ [we may write $\alpha(H_{10}) \subseteq H_{20}$, for brevity];

(v) $\forall r \in \mathbb{N}, \alpha_P(m_{1r}^+(P_1)) \subseteq m_{2r}^+(P_2)$;[9]

[In case Z_1^0 and Z_2^0 are IJPTAs, the following condition must also hold:

(vi) $\forall (p_1, i_1) \in J_{10}, (\alpha_P(p_1), \alpha_\Sigma(i_1)) \in J_{20}$; and we may write $\alpha(J_{10}) \subseteq \alpha(J_{20})$, for brevity.]

Z_2^0 is the homomorphic image of Z_1^0 under α iff each inclusion ($\subseteq$) in (iv) and (v) above is an equality. (In the case of IJPTAs, the inclusion in (vi), too, must be an equality.)

Definition 14.

Let Z_1^0 and Z_2^0 be as in Definition 13, let I be the interpretation for both Z_1^0 and Z_2^0, and let the durations be uniform, as in footnote 4, and synchronized for Z_1^0 and Z_2^0.

An ITA homomorphism $\alpha: Z_1^0 \to Z_2^0$ is an **m-homomorphism** on Z_1^0 to Z_2^0 iff it satisfies:

(*) $\forall s \in P_1, \forall r \in \mathbb{N}, m_{1r}(s) = m_{2r}(\alpha_P(s))$.

Definition 15 (Reachable Domain (R.D.) Homomorphism on ITA).

Let $Z^0 = (Z, m_0, H_0)$, where $Z = (P, \Sigma, \delta, K, H, J)$, be an ITA and let Z^0 operate under an interpretation I. A pair $p \in P$ is **reachable** in Z^0 (under the interpretation I) iff there exists a power distribution m under I of Z^0 such that $\exists t = (q, i, n, y) \in \delta$ that is ready under m such that $y(p) > 0$ and (q, i) is an active incoming signal (an active member of the set of incoming signals) under m. (See Definition 7.).

The **reachable domain** $rd(Z^0)$ of Z^0 is a subset of δ defined by:

$t = (p, i, n, y) \in rd(Z^0)$ iff there exists a power distribution m under I of Z^0 such that p is reachable and t is ready.

Let Z_1^0 and Z_2^0 be as in Definition 13. A function $\alpha: Z_1 \to Z_2$ is **r.d. transition preserving (r.d.t.p.)** iff,

$\forall (p, i, n, y) \in rd(Z_1^0), \exists (q, j, n', z) \in \delta_2$ such that $q = \alpha_P(p), j = \alpha_\Sigma(i)$ and $\forall s \in P_1, y(s) = z(\alpha_P(s))$.

An r.d.t.p. function $\alpha: Z_1 \to Z_2$ is an **r.d. homomorphism** iff,

$\forall (p_1, i_1, p_2, i_2) \in K_1$ such that $(p_1, i_1, n, y) \in rd(Z_1^0)$ for some $(n, y) \in \mathbb{N}^+ \times \mathbb{N}^P$,

$(\alpha_P(p_1), \alpha_\Sigma(i_1), \alpha_P(p_2), \alpha_\Sigma(i_2)) \in K_2$.

An r.d. homomorphism $\alpha: Z_1 \to Z_2$ is an **r.d. ITA homomorphism on** Z_1^0 **to** Z_2^0 iff it satisfies conditions (iv), (v) [and (vi) in case of IJPTA] of Definition 13.

Z_2^0 is the r.d. homomorphic image of Z_1^0 under α iff each inclusion ($\subseteq$) in (iv), (v) [and (vi)] of Definition 13 is an equality.

[The fact should not be overlooked that each ITA homomorphism is an r.d. ITA homomorphism, but not every r.d. ITA homomorphism is an ITA homomorphism.]

An r.d. homomorphism $\alpha: Z_1 \to Z_2$ is an **r.d. m-homomorphism on** Z_1^0 **to** Z_2 iff it satisfies the condition (*) of Definition 14.

ACKNOWLEDGEMENT

We wish to acknowledge the help and participation of our associates William Simpson, Thomas Magliery and Karen Barnes in the construction of the PTA illustrations, and of Karen Barnes and Chien-Chung Chan in readying this paper for publication.

REFERENCES

[1] Bartlett, K.A., R.A. Scantlebury, and P.T. Wilkinson, "A Note on Reliable Full-Duplex Transmission over Half-Duplex Lines." *Comm. ACM* 12, 5, (May 1969), 260-261.

[2] Bavel, Z., *Introduction to the Theory of Automata*, Reston Publishing Company, Inc., Reston, Virginia 1983.

[3] _____, "Manipulable Computer Architecture." First Annual Report to the System Development Foundation" (May 1985).

[4] _____, "The Computing Power of the Power Tier Automaton." System Development Foundation Technical Report SDF-565-86-11.

[5] Bavel, Z., Grzymala-Busse, J.W., Hsia, Y.T. and Mancisidor-Landa, R., "Tier Automaton Representation of Communication Protocols." *ACM Sigcomm '86 Symposium on Communications Architectures and Protocols* (Aug. 1986). (pp138-147)

[6] Bochmann, G.V., "Finite State Description of Communication Protocols." *Computer Networks*, vol. 2 (Oct. 1978), 361-372.

[7] Brand, D., and Zafiropulo, P., "On Communicating Finite-State Machines." *J. ACM* 30, 2 (Apr. 1983), 323-342.

[8] Chang, C.K., Gouda, M.G., and Rosier, L.E., "Deciding Liveness for Special Classes of Communicating Finite State Machines." *Proceedings 22nd Annual Allerton Conference on Communication, Control, and Computing* (Oct. 1984), 931-939.

---

[8] The uniform duration for the transitions of Z_1 need not equal the uniform duration of the transitions of Z_2.

[9] See Definition 7.

[9] Gouda, M.G. and Chang, C.K., "Proving Liveness for Networks of Communicating Finite State Machines." *ACM Transactions on Programming Languages and Systems* 8, 1 (Jan. 1986), 154-182.

[10] Gouda, M.G., Manning, E.G., and Yu, Y.T., "On the Progress of Communication between Two Finite State Machines." *Inf. Control* 63, 3 (Dec. 1984).

[11] Lam, S.S. and Shankar, A.U., "Protocol Verification via Projections." *IEEE Transactions on Software Engineering* SE-10, 4 (July 1984), 474-491.

[12] Lynch, W.C., "Reliable Full-Duplex Transmission over Half-Duplex Telephone Lines." *Comm. ACM* 11, 6 (June 1968), 361-371.

An Exercise in Deriving a Protocol Conversion*

Kenneth L. Calvert
Simon S. Lam

Department of Computer Sciences
The University of Texas at Austin
Austin, Texas 78712-1188

Abstract

This paper demonstrates formal techniques useful in solving and reasoning about protocol conversion problems. A simple example problem is solved and the resulting conversion system is shown to have certain desired properties, using the *projection paradigm*. The example problem is representative of some real-world problems in that the protocols involved are similar in function, and even in structure, but have fundamental differences that render them incompatible in the absence of an active translation entity (protocol converter). The use of mappings, as well as images and inverse images of properties, in comparing semantics of protocols is discussed and illustrated.

1 Introduction

A wide variety of formal methods for verifying and modeling protocols have been developed [8]. However, these methods generally are intended to deal with the correctness of individual protocols, more or less in isolation. The problem of enabling productive interoperation among entities that were *not* designed to operate together, i.e., the *protocol conversion* problem, has recently begun to receive some attention. Several recent papers have dealt with protocol conversion from various perspectives [1,2,4,7]; there is general agreement that protocol conversion is and will remain an important problem, and that formal methods for reasoning about the problem are a necessity.

In the general protocol conversion problem, two *processes*, A_1 and A_2, perform some useful function in a network environment by exchanging messages over channels according to a protocol, A; while two other processes, B_1 and B_2, have been designed to accomplish a similar func-

---
*work supported by the National Science Foundation under grant no. ECS-8304734 and under grant no. NCR-8613338

tion using a different protocol, B (Figure 1). The classical example of such a function is ensuring reliable transmission of data messages over unreliable channels.

Now, suppose we need to use A_1 and B_2 (or B_1 and A_2) to provide some or all of the service normally implemented by protocols A and B. To accomplish this we must consider *what* services are implemented by each protocol, and *how* the processes interoperate in each case to provide those services. In other words, we must understand the *semantics* of each of the protocols. Then we must relate the semantics of the two in order to understand what service can reasonably be provided by the conversion system, and use that relationship to specify a transformation between the *syntaxes* of the protocols. We can then implement this transformation via an intermediary, a *protocol converter* (Figure 3). The converter maps messages or sequences of messages from one protocol into messages or sequences of messages in the other protocol.

We consider the processes in isolation, as they are depicted in Figure 2. This is an abstraction from the general case, in which A and B may be part of some layered architecture; the channels connecting A_1 and B_2 in the figure imply the existence of any conversion necessary at lower levels to be able to provide a transmission path between the processes.

In this paper, we illustrate the approach described in [4,5] for reasoning about conversion systems and their correctness. The approach makes use of *protocol projection* [3], an abstraction technique for verifying properties of complex protocols. The basis of the projection paradigm is the idea that a property of a complex system can be proved by finding a property-preserving transformation to a simpler system, and then proving the property of the simpler system. The rest of the paper is organized as follows. The next section explains the model of protocol systems used for the examples, and briefly describes protocol projection. Then we introduce our example problem, a conversion between the Alternating Bit protocol and a version of the Bisync protocol. A converter is constructed, and the use of protocol projection to prove that the conversion system has certain properties is demonstrated. We conclude with some discussion about the general applicability of these ideas.

Permission to copy without fee all or part of this material is granted provided that the copies are not made or distributed for direct commercial advantage, the ACM copyright notice and the title of the publication and its date appear, and notice is given that copying is by permission of the Association for Computing Machinery. To copy otherwise, or to republish, requires a fee and/or specfic permission.

© 1988 ACM 0-89791-245-4/88/0001/0151 $1.50

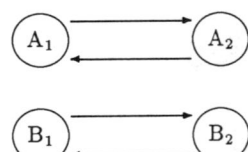

Figure 1: Protocols A and B

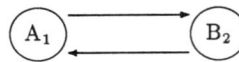

Figure 2: Conversion Configuration

Figure 3: Conversion between A and B

2 Background

We have stated that we wish to use A_1 and B_2 to provide "some or all" of the function of the original protocols, and that the conversion system is to be proved correct somehow. Intuitively, we want the conversion system involving A_1, B_2, and possibly a converter process, to have certain *properties*, somehow related to those of the protocols A and B. In order to reason formally about the conversion, we must have a formalism for expressing such properties. In this section, we describe a simple model for protocol systems and its semantics. Then we discuss methods of relating the semantics of one protocol to those of another, including the method of protocol projection.

The Model

The protocols of our example problem are modelled using a simple *communicating finite-state machines* (cfsm) model. In this model a protocol consists of a set of *processes* connected by *channels*. Each process is defined by a finite *process state space*, a finite set of *events*, and an *initial state*, and may be represented conceptually as a directed graph with nodes corresponding to process states and labeled arcs corresponding to events. The processes of the protocols for the example are depicted using this representation in Figures 4 and 5. A channel is a means of transmission of *messages* from one process to another, and is represented by an infinite-capacity FIFO queue, to which one process may add messages while another process may remove enqueued messages from the other end. Thus communication in this model is completely asynchronous.

The *events* represent activity, or change in the state of the system. In our model, every event involves exactly one process, and directly affects only the state of that process and/or the channels connected to it. Events are considered to be indivisible: only one event may occur at a time, and events considered concurrent may occur in any order. A process event may be one of three types: a send event (represented by a label "–m"), involving the addition of the message m to the tail of a channel and a change in the state of the process; a receive event, (label "+n"), involving removal of a particular message n from the head of a channel and a state change, or an *internal* event, which involves a process state change but no messages; an internal event can be an abstraction of interactions with other entities that are not modeled. In the text, we denote events by triples: an event that changes the state of the process from a to b, and removes the message m from a channel coming from process P, is denoted $(a, b, +m/P)$. When there is only one incoming and outgoing channel per process, the channel designation is omitted: $(a, b, +m)$.

The state of a channel is the ordered sequence of messages sent on the channel but not yet received on it. The set of possible states of a channel is determined by the set of all messages that may be sent on it, and is the set of all finite sequences of messages in that set. If the set of messages that may be sent on a channel is M, the set of all finite sequences of messages in M (i.e., the channel state space) is denoted by M^*.

The global state of the protocol is defined by the states of all the processes and channels; the global state space of protocol A is denoted A and is the cartesian product of the state spaces of all the processes and channels. For example, if protocol A has two processes with state spaces S_1 and S_2, and two channels with message sets M_1 and M_2, its global state space is defined by:

$$S_1 \times S_2 \times M_1^* \times M_2^*$$

and a global state $g \in A$ may be specified by a 4-tuple:

$$g = [s_1, s_2, U_1, U_2],$$

where

$$s_1 \in S_1, s_2 \in S_2, U_1 \in M_1^*, U_2 \in M_2^*.$$

The *initial global state* is defined as the global state in which all processes are in their initial process states and the channels are empty.

A receive event $(a, b, +m/P)$ of a process is said to be *enabled* in any global state in which the state of the process is a and the head message of the channel from P is m. An internal or send event (a, b, e) of a process is enabled in any global state in which the state of that process is a. Thus, an event defines a set of transitions between global states; we say an event e *takes* the system from global state g to global state h, and write $g \xrightarrow{e} h$, if e is enabled in g and the state changes associated with e change g to h. For example, the event $(a, b, -m)$ of process 1 in protocol A takes the state $[a, x, U, V]$ to state $[b, x, Um, V]$ (where "Um" represents the appending of message m to sequence U), for any x, U, and V.

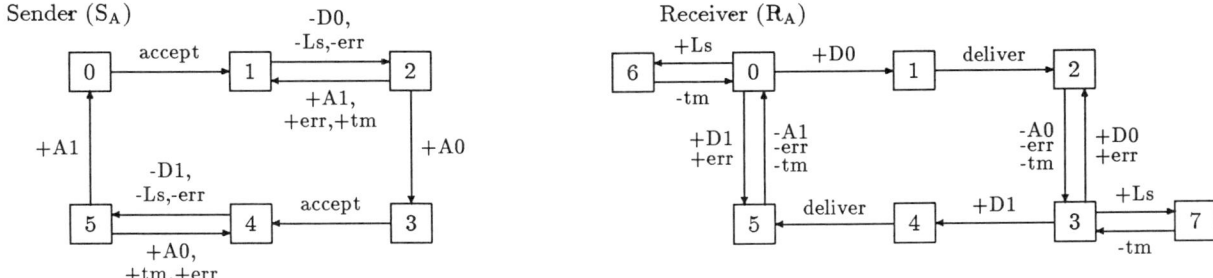

Figure 4: Alternating-Bit Protocol

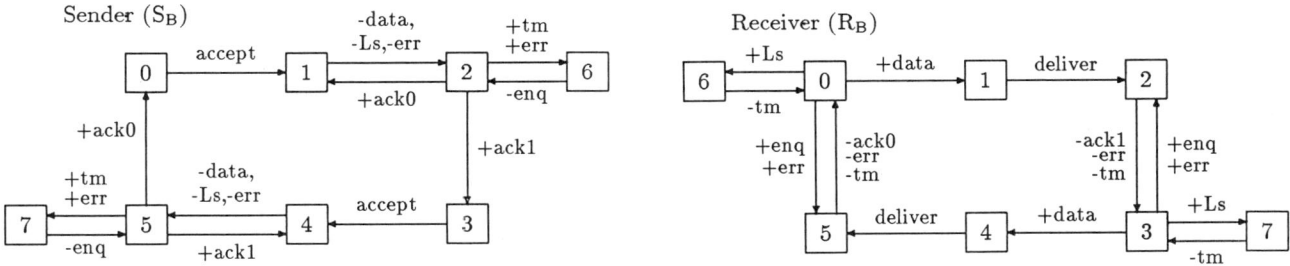

Figure 5: A version of Bisync Protocol

The behavior of the protocol over time is represented by a sequence of global states $g_0, g_1, g_2, \ldots$, such that each pair of successive states in the sequence are related by some event; that is, there exist $e_0, e_1, \ldots$ such that

$$g_0 \xrightarrow{e_0} g_1 \xrightarrow{e_1} g_2 \xrightarrow{e_2} \ldots$$

We call such a (finite or infinite) sequence of states (which may also be considered a sequence of events) a *path*. We say a path is a *computation* if and only if (i) g_0 is the initial global state and (ii) either the path is infinite or no event is enabled in its terminal state. Note that at any state in a sequence there may be several events enabled, while only one occurs to take the system to the next state.

We say a path is *fair* if and only if no event that is enabled infinitely many times in the path occurs only a finite number of times. (This definition is sometimes called "strong fairness," and reflects one criterion for deciding whether an infinite behavior is in some sense "realistic." There are others — fairness is a topic of study in itself.) Note that all finite paths are fair. It can be shown that *any finite path from the initial state can be extended to a fair computation*. That is, if there is a sequence of states and events $g_0 \xrightarrow{e_0} \ldots \xrightarrow{e_{k-1}} g_k$, where g_0 is the initial state, then there is a fair computation, the first $k-1$ states of which are $g_0, \ldots, g_k$. This fair computation may be finite if and only if no event is enabled in its final state. (The proof, which we omit in the interest of brevity, involves showing that there is a path from any global state in which the number of times any event may be enabled between occurrences is bounded.)

The set of all fair computations of a protocol is denoted R. (When we refer to a particular protocol A we write R_A.) The set R embodies the *semantics* of the protocol in the following sense: any possible behavior of the system is represented by some computation in R.

Properties of Protocols

In the model we have just described, the semantics of a protocol is defined *operationally*, by specifying a set of transitions in the global state space that determine the set R of fair computations. The behavior of a system may also be described *functionally* by characterizing the set R by means of logical assertions. We now introduce a language for simple logical assertions about the set R; such assertions can be used to specify certain basic *properties* of a protocol. A full system for stating and proving assertions about the set R is beyond the scope of this paper; we define just what is necessary to specify the properties relevant to our example protocols and the conversion. (The language introduced here is essentially a small piece of *temporal logic*; for a full treatment, see [6].) Our approach to the example will allow us to avoid proving properties of the conversion system from its operational definition. Instead, we find a relation between the conversion system and the original protocols such that it has properties corresponding to their (known) properties.

For any protocol A, a *global state predicate* is a mapping of the global state space A into the set $\{true, false\}$.

We say "p holds at g" or "p is true for g", if and only if $p(g) = true$. A predicate may be considered equivalent to a particular subset of A, namely the set of all states g for which $p(g) = true$. Conversely, any set of states in A may be considered as a predicate; the predicate is true for a state if and only if the state is in the set. In what follows, we use the concepts "subset of A" and "predicate on A" interchangeably.

The expression "P **at** s," where P is a process of protocol A and s is a process state of P, denotes a predicate that is true for all global states in which the state of P is s. For example, if we represent a global state of protocol A (as in Figure 1) by $[a_1, a_2, U_1, U_2]$, then the set of states denoted by "A_1 **at** s" contains exactly those states in which $a_1 = s$. If S is a *set* of process states of P, "P **at** S" denotes the set of global states in which process P is at one of the process states in S. Because the process P is at *exactly one* process state in every global state, if S is the entire process state space of P, then P **at** $S = true$.

If the expressions p and q denote sets on A, then $p \wedge q$ denotes their intersection, and $p \vee q$ denotes their union. The expression $\neg p$ denotes the set complement of the set denoted by p, so $\neg p(g) = true$ if and only if $p(g) = false$. Thus, a boolean combination of **at** expressions defines a predicate. Two such expressions are equivalent if and only if they define the same predicate. From the above definitions, it follows that "P **at** $x \vee P$ **at** y" is equivalent to "P **at** $\{x, y\}$."

We define two types of properties of protocols. A *safety property* expresses the fact that "the system is always in a good state," where "goodness" is defined by a predicate. If p is an expression defining a state predicate, we define the assertion "p is a safety property of A" to be equivalent to "for every state g in every computation in R_A, $p(g) = true$." In other words, every state of every fair computation of A is in the set denoted by p. Since every fair computation is a path from the initial state, if p holds at every state of every path from the initial state of A, then p is a safety property. Also, since any finite path from the initial state can be extended to a fair computation, if $\neg p$ holds at some state on some path from the initial state, then p cannot be a safety property. Thus, "p is a safety property of A" is also equivalent to "p holds at every state of every path from the initial state of A."

A liveness property is an assertion that "something good will eventually happen" in any possible behavior of the system. If p and q are predicates, then "$p \leadsto q$ (read 'p leads to q') is a liveness property of A" is equivalent to "in any fair computation in R_A, every state at which p holds is followed by some state at which q holds." This expresses the characteristic that, at any point in a computation, if p is true, q will eventually become true.

Mappings and Images

In this section, we consider how the properties of one protocol may be related to those of another by relating the global state spaces of the two protocols through a *functional mapping*; such a mapping associates each global state of one protocol with a unique global state of the other. Such a mapping may be considered to define a semantic equivalence between a global state and the state to which it maps.

Suppose we have two protocol systems, A and B, defined operationally as described above. Let A represent the global state space of A, and B the global state space of B. Now consider any functional mapping, $F : A \mapsto B$. For any global state g in A, $F(g)$ is a (unique) global state in B, called the *image of g under the mapping* F. (Note that F may be many-to-one, so that we may have $F(g) = F(h)$ for some $g \neq h$.) The image of a subset $p \subseteq A$ under the mapping is the set of all the $F(g)$'s such that $g \in p$. In what follows, the image of a quantity x under the mapping F will be denoted by x'. So for example $g' = F(g)$ and $p' = \{g' : g \in p\}$.

If t is a state in B, the *inverse image* of t is the *set* of states g in A such that $F(g) = t$. We denote the inverse image of a quantity x by $\hat{x}$. The inverse image of a subset q of B is a subset $\hat{q} = \{x : x' \in q\}$. From these definitions and the fact that each $g \in A$ has a unique image, it follows that the *inverse image* of the intersection of two sets in B is the same as the intersection of their inverse images:

$$\begin{aligned}\widehat{(p \cap q)} &= \{g : g' \in p \cap q\} \\ &= \{g : g' \in p \wedge g' \in q\} \\ &= \{g : g' \in p\} \cap \{g : g' \in q\} \\ &= (\hat{p} \cap \hat{q})\end{aligned}$$

Similar properties hold for union and complementation: the inverse image of $p \cup q$ is $\hat{p} \cup \hat{q}$, and $\widehat{\neg p} = \neg \hat{p}$.

The image of a computation $g_0 \xrightarrow{e_0} g_1 \xrightarrow{e_1} \ldots$ is defined to be the sequence of image states $g'_0, g'_1, \ldots$, with adjacent occurrences of the same image state consolidated into one image state, so that the same state does not occur twice in succession. Thus the image of an infinite computation of protocol A might be a finite sequence of states in B, if all states beyond a certain point in the computation have the same image under the mapping F. Note that the image of a computation of A is a sequence that is *not necessarily a computation* of B, because there might be some point in the image sequence where for no event e of B is it the case that $g'_k \xrightarrow{e} g'_{k+1}$; or, the image of the computation might be finite, with some event enabled in the terminal state.

The inverse image of a computation of B (or any sequence of global states in B) is the set of sequences of states having that computation as image. That is, if α is any sequence of global states of B, $\alpha = \alpha_0, \alpha_1, \ldots$, the inverse image of α, denoted by $\hat{\alpha}$, is the set of sequences of states, given by (with "$\times$" denoting cartesian product)

$$\hat{\alpha} = \hat{\alpha}_0 \times \hat{\alpha}_1 \times \ldots = \{\sigma : \sigma' = \alpha\}.$$

A sequence of states of A in the inverse image of a computation of B is not necessarily a computation.

Now, suppose we want to relate the properties of some protocol B to another protocol A; we would like to find assertions about A that correspond to the assertions of properties of B. In our simple assertion language, properties are defined by **at** expressions relating the states of the processes in the protocol. If we want to obtain assertions about A from assertions about B, we must define a correspondence between the process states of A and those of B. *Protocol projection* is one way of defining such a correspondence.

Protocol Projection

Protocol projection [3] is an abstraction technique that can be used to prove properties of a complex protocol by mapping it onto a simpler *image protocol*. The image protocol and the mapping are both derived from the given protocol. While projection is applicable to distributed systems with more general structure, we shall describe it in terms of the simple cfsm model used for the example. The following discussion is necessarily brief; for a complete discussion the reader is referred to [3].

Given a protocol A, a protocol projection is defined by partitioning the state spaces of each of A's processes. The idea is that process states which are to be functionally indistinguishable in the image protocol are *aggregated* into the same partition, and map to the same *image process state*. The (unique) image of any process state a is defined by this state aggregation, and is denoted by a'. The set of process states corresponding to the image process state b is denoted by $\hat{b}$. Because of the structure of a protocol, a partitioning of the process state spaces defines a corresponding partitioning of the message and event sets of the protocol. Every message (and event) maps to a message (event) in the image protocol or has a *null image*. The messages and events of the image protocol are exactly those that are the image of some message or event in the original protocol.

The image of a message is determined by the effect of its reception in the image of the receiving process' state space: messages that cause the same state changes have the same image, while any message that does not cause any state change in its receiver is said to have a null image. For example, suppose a, b, c and d are process states of some process, and m and n are messages that may be received by the process. If $(a, b, +m)$ and $(c, d, +m)$ are the only receive events involving the message m, and $a' = b'$ and $c' = d'$, then the message m has a *null image*. If $a' = c'$ and $b' = d'$ for any two events $(a, b, +m)$ and $(c, d, +n)$, then m and n have the same image. In the former case, the projection has abstracted away completely the function served by the message m, while in the latter case, the functional distinction between m and n has been removed.

The image of a process event (a, b, e) is determined by the images of a, b, and any messages involved in e. If $a' = b'$, and e is the label of an internal event or involves a message with a null image, then the event has a null image; otherwise its image is the event (a', b', e').

Thus, a projection yields a specification of image processes, which define the image protocol. The image protocol has a process and channel corresponding to each process and channel of the original protocol. The image process corresponding to P is denoted P'. Because the partitioning of the process state space defines an image for every process state and message, the projection also defines a mapping from the global state space of A to the global state space of of the image protocol: the image of a global state $g = [a_1, a_2, U_1, U_2]$ is $g' = [a_1', a_2', U_1', U_2']$; the image of a sequence of messages U is the sequence of (non-null) images of the messages in U. The initial global state of the image is the image of the initial global state.

For any event e and global states g and h in A such that $g \xrightarrow{e} h$, either $g' = h'$, or there is some image event e', such that $g' \xrightarrow{e'} h'$ in the image protocol. From this it follows ([3]) that the image of any computation of A is a path of the image protocol beginning at the initial global state. If the projection meets some additional structural conditions, then the image is said to be *well-formed*, and the image of any fair computation is a fair computation of the image protocol.

Now suppose B is an image protocol of A, and let $F : A \mapsto B$ be the functional mapping of global states defined by the projection. Then F has the following characteristic: any global state of A in which the state of process P is x maps to a global state in which the state of process P' is x'. Conversely, the only global states with images in which the state of P' is y, are those in which the state of P is one of the process states whose image is y, i.e., those in the set denoted by P **at** $\hat{y}$. Thus, the inverse image of the predicate defined by P' **at** y is defined by P **at** $\hat{y}$.

From the correspondence between boolean combinations of **at** expressions and set operations described earlier, and the fact that $\widehat{p \cap q} = \hat{p} \cap \hat{q}$, $\widehat{p \cup q} = \hat{p} \cup \hat{q}$, and $\widehat{\neg p} = \neg \hat{p}$, it follows that the inverse image of any predicate defined by a boolean combination of **at** expressions is defined by the same boolean combination of **at** expressions with each process P' replaced by P, and each process state y replaced by $\hat{y}$. For example, suppose protocol B in Figure 1 is an image of protocol A, and processes A_1 and A_2 correspond to processes B_1 and B_2, respectively. Then the inverse image of the predicate on B defined by B_1 **at** $x \Rightarrow B_2$ **at** y is defined by the predicate A_1 **at** $\hat{x} \Rightarrow A_2$ **at** $\hat{y}$. From now on we use $\hat{p}$ to represent the expression defining the inverse image of the predicate defined by p.

Now we can relate properties of one protocol to those of another. Suppose B is an image protocol of A, and p is a safety property of protocol B. Then p holds for every state in any path from the initial state of B. As noted above, the image of any computation α of A under the mapping defined by the projection is a path α' from the initial state of B. Since p holds at every state of α', it follows that $\hat{p}$ holds at every state of α. (Suppose not. Then for some α, α' is a path from the initial state of B, and there is a state g in α for which $\hat{p}(g) = \mathit{false}$. But by the definition of $\hat{p}$, we have $p(g') = \mathit{false}$. Since g' is a state in a path from the initial state of B, p cannot be a safety property of B, a contradiction.) Thus, $\hat{p}$ is a safety property of A.

If the image protocol B is well-formed, then the image of any fair computation α of A is α', a fair computation of B. If $p \rightsquigarrow q$ is a property of B, then every state in α' at which p holds is followed by some state at which q holds. But this means that every state in α at which $\hat{p}$ holds is followed by a state where $\hat{q}$ holds, so $\hat{p} \rightsquigarrow \hat{q}$ is a property of A.

If two protocols can be projected onto the same image protocol, then they share the inverse images of the safety properties of that image. Furthermore, if the images are well-formed, then they have its safety and liveness properties in common. This suggests the following approach to solving a conversion problem such as that described in the first section. We first specify the properties required of the conversion; then we look for a projection of the two protocols onto a common image with the properties we desire. If one is found, we are done, for the two projections define a correspondence between the messages of the two protocols: those with the same image are semantically equivalent.

If the protocols do not have a common image with the desired properties, a protocol converter must be obtained by considering the properties required and the structure of the processes involved in the conversion. Given a candidate converter, if the conversion system can be projected onto each of the two original protocols, the inverse images of their properties are properties of the conversion system. We illustrate these concepts in the next section with our example.

3 The Example Problem

The protocols in our example problem are the venerable Alternating-Bit (AB) protocol and a simplified version of the data transfer portion of the Bisync protocol. Each protocol provides reliable, sequenced transmission of data messages from the Sender to the Receiver over unreliable channels that may lose or corrupt messages. The protocols are represented in Figures 4 and 5. In those figures, the transitions labeled "accept" and "deliver" are internal events denoting interaction with some (higher-level) user entity. They represent acceptance of a message (e.g., higher-level protocol data) for transmission, and the delivery of a correctly received message to the receiver-side user, respectively. We are not concerned with the contents of the data messages themselves, as the service provided is a "transparent" transmission service. Thus we consider all data messages to be equivalent; in AB, the "D0" and "D1" messages represent the presence of a one-bit sequence number attached to the data message.

Modeling Lossy Channels

The example protocols are designed to function with unreliable channels; each Sender detects lost messages by means of a timeout mechanism. However, the channels in our cfsm model are perfectly reliable. To model channels that may lose or corrupt messages using ideal channels, we use "pseudo-messages" that represent loss, timeout, and corruption events. Receipt of a "tm" message represents a timeout event at the process receiving the message; receipt of an "err" message represents reception of a message corrupted in transit. "Ls" represents a message lost on its way to the receiver.

The pseudo-messages model losses as follows: each send event has two parallel "error" events, one representing the loss and one the corruption of the message sent. For example, in Figure 4, whenever the "–D0" event is enabled at the Sender, the "–Ls" and "–err" events are enabled as well. If a message is being sent *to* the process where a timeout may occur, the "tm" message may (non-deterministically) be sent instead of the intended message. If the timeout is located at the sending process, the "Ls" message may be sent instead of the intended message. Whenever a "Ls" message is received by a process, a "tm" message is returned to the sender. Thus, receipt of a "tm" message indicates loss of *either* a message or its acknowledgement. This mechanism models only non-premature timeouts, so that a timeout pseudo-message is received *if and only if* a loss has occurred.

The "err" pseudo-message carries no information other than that some message was sent and corrupted. It is not hard to see that if there is a path to a global state g, in which a message m is in some channel, then there is a path to a state h, identical to g except for the "loss" or "corruption" of m, represented by the presence of "Ls" or "err" in the channel in place of m. For example, if $[s, r, U, V]$ is a global state in some computation, where U is a sequence of messages containing m, then there is a computation in which $[s, r, U_{\text{err}}^m, V]$ is a state, where U_{err}^m is U with err substituted for m. Our fairness requirement ensures that in any fair computation, no message may be lost or corrupted infinitely many times without being correctly sent.

Properties of the Protocols

Our problem is to enable reliable transmission of data messages from the Sender of one protocol to the Receiver of the other. There are actually two different problems: enabling S_A and R_B to interoperate, and enabling S_B and R_A to interoperate. In general these problems must be solved separately; if an active intermediary (converter) is required it may be different for the two cases. However, if the two protocols have a well-formed common image protocol, the characteristics of either converter may be determined from the two projections. In the exposition that follows, we focus on the S_B-R_A conversion, the converter for which we denote by C_0. The S_A-R_B problem (with converter C_1) has an analogous solution.

Before constructing any converter, we must specify the properties required of the conversion system. Before considering those required properties, we first state the properties of the AB and Bisync protocols. The properties that we give can be proved by any of several means; we shall simply accept them as given.

Each of the following is a safety property of both AB and Bisync. ("S" represents the Sender process of either protocol, "R" the Receiver):

$$S \text{ at } 0 \Rightarrow R \text{ at } 0$$
$$S \text{ at } 3 \Rightarrow R \text{ at } 3$$
$$R \text{ at } 1 \Rightarrow S \text{ at } 2$$
$$R \text{ at } 4 \Rightarrow S \text{ at } 5$$

These safety properties together assert that the protocol maintains synchronization; in particular, together they imply that no message is accepted for transmission unless the previous message has been delivered and acknowledged.

The following liveness properties are common to both protocols:

$$(S \text{ at } 1 \lor S \text{ at } 2) \leadsto (S \text{ at } 3)$$
$$(S \text{ at } 4 \lor S \text{ at } 5) \leadsto (S \text{ at } 0)$$

These properties indicate that every message accepted for transmission will eventually be delivered and acknowledged.

The above properties may be considered to specify the "service" provided by the protocol. Since the same assertions are used to express the properties of both protocols, it is clear that state 0 of S_A corresponds (with respect to these properties) to state 0 of S_B, state 1 of R_A corresponds to state 3 of R_B, etc. Therefore it makes sense to consider the above properties to specify the service of the conversion system. We shall require that the above (with "S" representing "S_B" and "R" representing "R_A") be safety and liveness properties of the S_B-R_A conversion system.

Deriving the Conversion

The obvious and essential difference between the protocols is that AB includes a sequence number attached to each data message, while the Bisync protocol does not. This means that the AB Sender may safely transmit a data message to the Receiver after the Receiver has already delivered that message to the user; the sequence number attached to the message ensures that the duplicate is detected, and prevents the Receiver from delivering multiple copies of the same message. The Bisync Sender, however, may not retransmit a message unless the state of the Receiver is known; this is because the Receiver has no means to distinguish between old and new messages, and would otherwise deliver the retransmitted message as a new message. Thus, in AB, the responsibility for maintaining synchronization and ensuring correctly-sequenced delivery is essentially the Receiver's; in Bisync it resides with the Sender.

Since these two protocols seem to be so similar in structure, we first consider whether it might be possible to project one onto the other, or both onto a common image. We have already noted that the state spaces are substantially equivalent. By aggregating S_B's states 1 and 6 into a state equivalent to S_A's state 1, and similarly with 4 and 7, we can project the Bisync protocol onto an image protocol identical to AB, *except* for its messages. The image thus obtained still has only one "data" message, while AB has two semantically different ones, "D0" and "D1." In other words, the AB message set has a *higher resolution* than Bisync's.

On the other hand if we try to project AB onto Bisync, R_A can be projected onto R_B by a simple mapping of messages, but we cannot project S_A onto S_B, because S_B has a larger state space. That is, Bisync's state space has a *higher resolution* than AB's. So neither protocol is an image of the other. Although it is always possible to come up with a common image for any two protocols, it is not hard to see that in this case the common image (obtained by projecting out the semantic difference between the data messages in AB, i.e., by "folding" the state space in half) does not have the properties desired of the conversion.

When the protocols do not have a common image with the desired properties, an active converter (a finite state machine) is required. We therefore consider the necessary characteristics of such a converter. Now, we would like to be able to use the properties of the original protocols to prove that the conversion system involving our converter has the desired properties. We may do this using projection as described in [5] by making the combined function of the converter and S_B correspond to the behavior of S_A (with respect to communications with R_A), while similarly the interactions of C_0 with S_B correspond to what R_B would do. Figure 6 illustrates half of the idea: the communications between C_0 and R_A are projected onto the AB system.

So C_0 should "emulate" R_B when interacting with S_B, and S_A when interacting with R_A; the question is how to relate those two behaviors in a single machine. Obviously, data messages received from S_B will have a sequence number attached and be forwarded to R_A. But when should an acknowledgement be sent to S_B? How should retransmissions be handled?

Observe that a message may be lost or corrupted *after* being correctly received by C_0 but *before* being received by R_A. In this case it must be retransmitted. But if the communications between S_B and C_0 are to be projected onto those of Bisync, C_0 *must* send a *positive* acknowledgement after correctly receiving a data message; therefore, if a data message must be retransmitted to R_A, it must be retransmitted by C_0 without interaction with S_B. In other words, C_0 must "accept responsibility" for delivery of a message to R_A, once it is received from S_B. So C_0's behavior should repeat the pattern:

emulate R_B until receiving a message correctly; then

emulate S_A until the message is acknowledged by R_A; then

resume emulation of R_B by acknowledging message

The stop-and-wait nature of our two protocols makes it a simple matter to construct a converter with the above

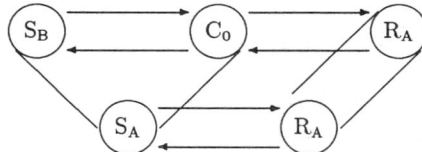

Figure 6: Projection of 3-process system onto 2-process system

structure; it is illustrated in Figure 7. In order to emulate S_A, it is necessary for C_0 to have a timeout mechanism of its own. To distinguish the pseudo-messages for the two timeout events, S_A's is designated "tm0" and C_0's "tm1." Note also that receipt of a correct data message from S_B corresponds to the "accept" event of S_A, while receipt of a positive ack from R_A corresponds to the "deliver" event of R_B. The converter for the S_A-R_B system is similar and is shown in Figure 8.

Correctness of the Conversion System

We have constructed C_0 so that AB and Bisync will be images of the conversion system. We now show that this is so, and also that the Bisync projection has *well-formed events*. If no message can remain in a channel forever in the original system (as is the case for the conversion system), then the well-formedness of the events in a projection is a sufficient condition for the image of any fair computation of the original system to be a fair computation of the image system.

We project the three-process system (S_B,C_0,R_A) onto each of the two-process original systems by considering two processes, and the channels between them, as a single machine, as shown in Figure 6. In order to project (S_B,C_0,R_A) onto (S_B,R_B), we define an aggregation of the states of the subsystem (C_0,R_A). Then we show that the image machine defined by the aggregation is R_B, so that the image of $(S_B,(C_0,R_A))$ is (S_B,R_B). A similar approach applies to AB: we project states of (S_B,C_0) onto those of S_A, and the image system is (S_A,R_A).

In what follows, we represent an arbitrary global state of the conversion system by $g = [s, U, V, c, X, Y, r]$, where s, c, and r are the states of S_B, C_0, and R_B respectively, and U, V, X, and Y are the states of the channels. Thus when we mention c, we refer to the state of the converter, r refers to the state of R_A, etc. In the projection onto Bisync, the image of g is a global state $g'_B = [s, U, V, r']$, where r' is a state of R_B, the image of the subsystem state $[c, X, Y, r]$. The image of g under the projection onto AB is $g'_A = [s', X, Y, r]$, where s' is the image of $[s, U, V, c]$.

To define the projection, we define the correspondence between the subsystem states $[s, U, V, c]$ and the process states of S_A, and between $[c, X, Y, r]$ and the states of R_B. These subsystem states are to be aggregated according to the state of C_0. The image of $[s, U, V, c]$ in the Bisync projection (or $[c, X, Y, r]$ in the AB projection) will be a function of c, and all subsystem states with the same value of c are aggregated together and have the same image. We

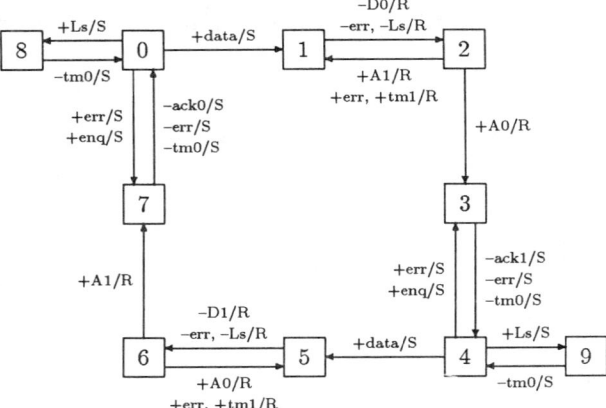

Figure 7: S_B-R_A Converter (C_0)

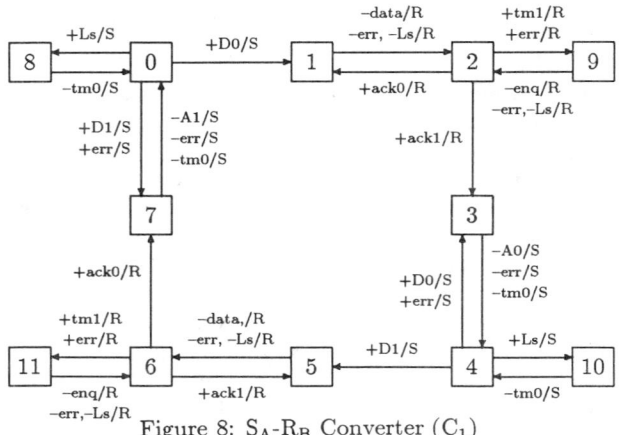

Figure 8: S_A-R_B Converter (C_1)

also aggregate further the subsystem states, by combining some states of C_0 in each projection, as shown in Figures 9 and 10. Comparison of Figures 5 and 9 shows that state 0 of C_0 corresponds to state 0 of R_B, the aggregated states 1 and 2 correspond to state 1 of R_B, etc. Each event of C_0 that involves sending or receiving a message to or from S_B corresponds exactly to an event of R_B, and for each event of R_B there is a corresponding event of C_0. Events of C_0 that involve interaction with R_A do not cross image state boundaries, and therefore have null images; the exceptions are the events $(2, 3, +A0/R)$ and $(6, 7, +A1/R)$, which correspond to the two "deliver" internal events of R_B.

Now, events of R_A can change the state of the (C_0,R_A) subsystem, but do not involve sending messages to the rest of the system; they are considered "internal" events of the composite process. Furthermore, since they do not change the state of C_0, they cannot affect the image process state of the subsystem, and therefore have null images. Since the image of S_B is itself, it follows that (S_B,R_B) is an image of $(S_B,(C_0,R_A))$; by a similar argument, (S_A,R_A) is the image of $((S_B,C_0),R_A)$. Table 1 shows how the image process states s' and r' under the two projections correspond to c.

We now proceed to show that the Bisync image has

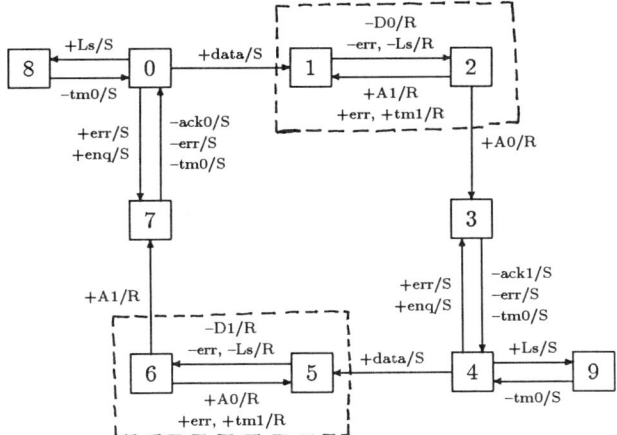

Figure 9: C_0 state aggregation in projection onto Bisync

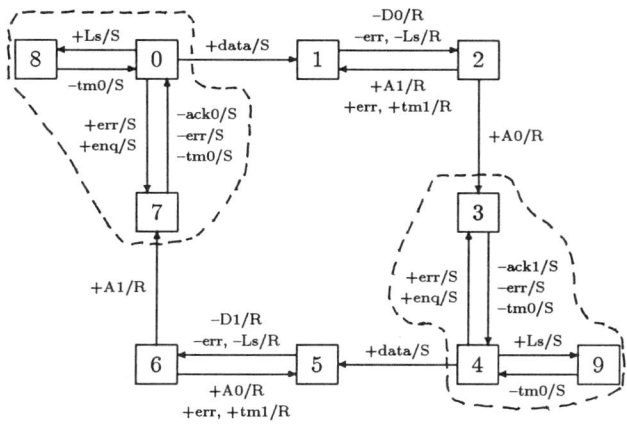

Figure 10: C_0 state aggregation in AB projection

well-formed events. An image process event e is well-formed if, for any global states g and h such that $g \xrightarrow{e} h$, and any r in $\hat{g}$, there is a path from r to some state in $\hat{h}$, such that the last event is e', and all other events are internal or send events (involving null-image messages) of that process. In a projection defined by an aggregation of process states, this condition may be checked simply by inspection of the processes' state spaces. In this case, because we are considering subsystem states as process states, we must show that the well-formedness condition is satisfied for the *subsystem's* state space, which we so far have not made explicit. However, thanks to the characteristics of C_0 (and the liveness property of AB), we can show the well-formedness of the image without having to explore the complete state space of the (C_0,R_A) subsystem.

Because no aggregation of process states of S_B is involved in the projection onto Bisync, and all messages project onto themselves, the events of S_B in the Bisync projection are clearly well-formed. Whenever an event of S_B is enabled in g'_B, the same event of S_B must be enabled in g; similarly for g'_A and events of R_A. So we just need to show the well-formedness of events of R_B in the Bisync image.

Let $g = [s, U, V, c, X, Y, r]$ be the state of the conversion system and $g'_B = [s, U, V, r']$ be its image under the projection onto Bisync. We shall show that if an event of R_B is enabled in g'_B, then a sequence of events not affecting s, U, or V can occur and take the subsystem to a state where an event whose image is the R_B event is enabled. Consider the events of R_B that might be enabled in a state $[s, U, V, r']$ when r' is 0. Figure 5 shows that these include $(0,1,+\text{data})$, $(0,6,+\text{Ls})$, $(0,5,+\text{err})$, and $(0,5,+\text{enq})$. Table 1 shows that when r' is 0, c is 0. Figure 9 shows if one of these events can occur in the image state $[s, U, V, 0]$, then the event with that image can occur in the state $[s, U, V, 0, X, Y, r]$. So all the events enabled when r' is 0 are well-formed. A similar argument applies to any events enabled when r' is 2, 3, 5, 6 or 7:

only a single state of C_0 corresponds to each of these states of R_B, and the corresponding events of C_0 are enabled in each.

If r' is 1, the event $(1, 2, \text{deliver})$ is enabled. We shall show that for any g in any fair computation such that $g'_B = [s, U, V, 1]$, there is a sequence of events that takes the (C_0, R_A) subsystem to a state in which $(2, 3, +A0/R)$ is enabled (the image of that event is $(1, 2, \text{deliver})$). Table 1 shows that $c = 1$ or $c = 2$ in any such g. Consider $g'_A = [s', X, Y, r]$, the image of g under the projection onto AB: from Table 1 we have $s' = 1$ in g'_A if $c = 1$ in g, and $s' = 2$ in g'_A if $c = 2$ in g. Now, the image, under the projection onto AB, of the path in the conversion system from the initial global state to g is a path from the initial state of AB to g'_A. As we noted earlier, this path can be extended to a fair computation of AB. In that fair computation, the global state g'_A must be followed by some global state in which the state of S_A is 3, by AB's liveness property. Consider the sequence of events leading from g'_A to this state. From Figure 4, the only events of S_A that may occur in the sequence are those that correspond to events of C_0 that are enabled when c is 1 or 2. Furthermore, the last event in the sequence must be $(2, 3, +A0)$. So corresponding to the sequence of events beginning in $[s', X, Y, r]$ and culminating in a state where the event $(2, 3, +A0)$ of S_A is enabled, is a sequence of events of C_0 and R_A beginning in $g = [s, U, V, c, X, Y, r]$ and culminating in a state where the event $(2, 3, +A0/R)$ of C_0 is enabled. All events in this sequence have null images in the Bisync projection. Thus we have shown there is a sequence of events with null images that takes the system to a state where the event whose image is $(1, 2, \text{deliver})$ is

C_0 state	0	1	2	3	4	5	6	7	8	9
Image R_B state	0	1	1	2	3	4	4	5	6	7
Image S_A state	0	1	2	3	3	4	5	0	0	3

Table 1: Mapping from converter to image process state spaces

enabled, from any state g of the conversion system such that $(1, 2, \text{deliver})$ is enabled in g'_B; that event is therefore well formed. A symmetric argument applies to the other "deliver" event. Thus all the events of the image Bisync protocol are well formed.

Properties

Because AB and Bisync are both images of the conversion system, the inverse images of their safety properties hold in it. Since the Bisync image has well-formed events, the inverse image of its liveness property holds in the conversion system.

The global state predicate "R_B at x" defines the set of states $[s, U, V, r]$ of Bisync for which $r = x$. The inverse image of this set under the projection onto Bisync contains exactly those states g of the conversion system such that $r' = x$ in g'_B. Table 1 associates with each such x a state or states of C_0, so that we can make explicit the inverse image of the predicate "R_B at x" for any particular x. The inverse image of the predicate "S_B at x" is of course itself under this projection. Thus we have the following inverse images of the properties given earlier.

From the projection onto Bisync:
S_B at $0 \Rightarrow C_0$ at 0
S_B at $3 \Rightarrow C_0$ at 4
$(C_0$ at $1 \lor C_0$ at $2) \Rightarrow S_B$ at 2
$(C_0$ at $5 \lor C_0$ at $6) \Rightarrow S_B$ at 5

From the projection onto AB:
$(C_0$ at $0 \lor C_0$ at $7 \lor C_0$ at $8) \Rightarrow R_A$ at 0
$(C_0$ at $3 \lor C_0$ at $4 \lor C_0$ at $9) \Rightarrow R_A$ at 3
R_A at $1 \Rightarrow C_0$ at 2
R_A at $4 \Rightarrow C_0$ at 6

The safety properties desired of the conversion system follow immediately from the properties above:

S_B at $0 \Rightarrow R_A$ at 0
S_B at $3 \Rightarrow R_A$ at 3
R_A at $1 \Rightarrow S_B$ at 2
R_A at $4 \Rightarrow S_B$ at 5

The inverse image of the Bisync liveness property is

$(S_B$ at $1 \lor S_B$ at $2) \leadsto S_B$ at 3,

which is the desired property.

4 Summary and Conclusions

We have illustrated the use of the projection paradigm both in reasoning about protocol conversions and proving them correct. The notion of the inverse image of a predicate and of simple properties was formalized, and used in obtaining properties of an example conversion system from those of the two original protocols. The importance of formal specifications in solving problems of this kind is clear.

The example problem illustrates that even when protocols provide identical service and have substantially equivalent state spaces, a simple, stateless message mapping may not be sufficient. In this case, the essential difference between the two protocols took the form of additional messages in one protocol, and additional process states in the other. Work is continuing on understanding and formalizing the requirements for protocol conversion.

References

[1] P. E. Green, Jr., "Protocol Conversion," *IEEE Transactions on Communications*, March 1986.

[2] I. Groenbak, "Conversion between TCP and ISO Transport Protocols as a means of achieving interoperability," *IEEE Journal on Selected Areas in Communications*, March 1986.

[3] S. S. Lam & A. U. Shankar, "Protocol Verification via Projections," *IEEE Transactions on Software Engineering*, July 1984.

[4] S. S. Lam, "Protocol Conversion: Correctness Problems" *Proceedings ACM SigComm '86 Symposium*, Stowe, VT, August 1986.

[5] S. S. Lam, "Protocol Conversion," University of Texas Computer Sciences Department Technical Report TR-87-05, February 1987; to appear in *IEEE Transactions on Software Engineering*, 1987.

[6] Z. Manna & A. Pnueli, "Adequate Proof Principles for Invariance and Liveness Properties of Concurrent Programs," *Science of Computer Programming* 4, North-Holland, 1984.

[7] K. Okumura, "A Formal Protocol Conversion Method," *Proceedings ACM SigComm '86 Symposium*, Stowe, VT, August 1986.

[8] C. S. Sunshine, ed., "Communications Protocol Modeling," Artech House, 1981

PART 6. ROUTING IN LARGE NETWORKS

L. Chapin

Data General, USA

Modeling, Analysis, and Optimal Routing of Flow-Controlled Communication Networks[1]

Simon S. Lam and Ching-Tarng Hsieh[2]

Department of Computer Sciences
The University of Texas at Austin
Austin, Texas 78712-1188

Abstract

Closed queueing networks have been advocated by several authors to be a more desirable model than open queueing networks (Kleinrock's model) for network design. We compare open and closed network models and demonstrate the accuracy of a particular closed network model with experimental results. The proportional approximation method (PAM) is presented for evaluating performance measures of closed queueing networks. PAM algorithms have computational time and space requirements of $O(KM)$, where M denotes the number of queues and K denotes the number of virtual channels in the network. Thus, PAM is the first (and only) method that can be used for solving industrial-strength network design problems using a closed network model.

We formulate the following optimal routing problem: Find a route for a new virtual channel to be added to a network with existing flow-controlled virtual channels. A fast heuristic algorithm is presented. The algorithm uses PAM and exploits the following empirical observation: The route that maximizes the individual throughput of a virtual channel coincides in most cases with the route that maximizes the total network throughput (this is not true in general). We present statistical results from studies of 100 randomly generated networks to demonstrate the accuracy of PAM algorithms and the effectiveness of the optimal routing algorithm. (Exact solutions obtained by the tree convolution algorithm were used as benchmarks in our statistical studies.)

1. Introduction

Consider a store-and-forward communication network which accepts data packets from host computers and terminals for delivery to other host computers and terminals. (See Figure 1.) As

---

[1]Work supported by National Science Foundation under grant no. ECS-8304734 and grant no. NCR-8613338.

[2]AT&T Bell Laboratories, Naperville, Illinois 60566.

Permission to copy without fee all or part of this material is granted provided that the copies are not made or distributed for direct commercial advantage, the ACM copyright notice and the title of the publication and its date appear, and notice is given that copying is by permission of the Association for Computing Machinery. To copy otherwise, or to republish, requires a fee and/or specfic permission.

© 1988 ACM 0-89791-245-4/88/0001/0162 $1.50

each packet is routed through the network, from its source to its destination, it joins queues inside network switching nodes for transmission over communication links. A queueing network model is most appropriate for the analysis and design of such communication networks.

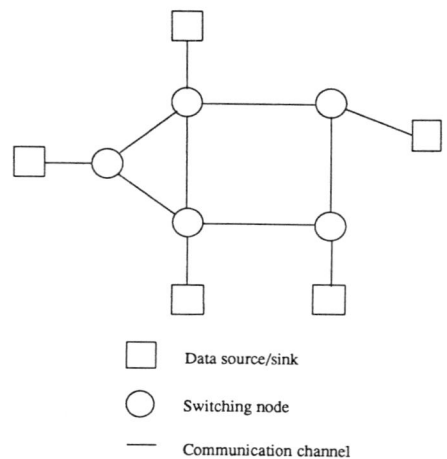

Figure 1. A store-and-forward communication network.

Analytic tools for the design of packet networks have been based primarily on the model of Kleinrock [6, 7], which is an open network of M/M/1 queues. Kleinrock's model will be referred to as the open network model. It is *open* because sources are assumed to generate new packets according to Poisson processes at constant rates and *all* such Poisson arrivals are assumed to be accepted by the communication network without any input control. In practice, most packet networks implement window protocols for flow control across logical connections between pairs of communicating sources and destinations [1, 2, 18]. In this paper, we shall refer to such logical connections as *virtual channels*.[3] A window protocol limits the number of packets, belonging to a virtual channel, that can be traversing the network at the same time. Such a limit is called the *window size* of the flow-controlled virtual channel.

---

[3]In practice, such flow-controlled logical connections can also be identified in the so-called datagram networks.

Flow-controlled packet networks can be more accurately modeled by a *closed* queueing network model than by an open queueing network model. Consider the implementation of a window protocol with window size N_k by placing N_k permits initially at the source of virtual channel k. Whenever the number of permits at the source is nonzero, each packet generated is given a permit and accepted into the network. When the packet reaches its destination, its permit is then carried back to the source by an ack message from the destination to the source. Thus, the N_k permits circulate in the network, carried alternately by data packets and by acks, just like the circulating customers of a closed routing chain in a queueing network [13]. Whenever there is no permit at the source, it is assumed that the source is blocked from generating new packets. (Equivalently, new packets are generated by Poisson processes at constant rates but any new packet that finds no permit at the source is dropped.)

Use of a closed network model for the analysis and design of flow-controlled packet networks has been advocated by Reiser [15], Kobayashi and Gerla [8], Schwartz [18], Lam and Lien [10, 14], and Lam and Hsieh [9], and others. The open network model is accurate for networks that are lightly utilized (when flow control mechanisms have little or no effect on network performance). As a network's offered load increases, the open network model cannot be used to predict the throughputs of virtual channels since it does not model flow control; it also significantly overestimates network delays. In Section 2, we present experimental results to illustrate these observations about the open network model and to demonstrate the accuracy of some closed network models.

A serious drawback of closed network models has been the large computational time and space needed for calculating network performance measures, i.e., throughputs and mean delays of virtual channels. Consider a model of a network with M queues and K virtual channels. Let N_k be the window size of virtual channel k. Both the convolution and MVA computational algorithms have a time requirement of $MK\prod_{k=1}^{K}(N_k+1)$ [16, 17]. Thus the time complexity grows exponentially with K, the number of virtual channels.[4] (The space complexity also grows exponentially with K.) For example, if the window size is 8 for all virtual channels, these algorithms are not applicable to the analysis of networks with more 6 or 7 virtual channels. The tree convolution algorithm was designed to exploit routing information and the sparseness of routes in a communication network and it has been used to solve numerically many network examples with 32 to 50 virtual channels [12]. (The number of virtual channels that can be handled for a specific network depends upon window sizes and the sparseness of routes in the network.) However, it is still not applicable to the analysis of many real-life wide area networks which can be quite large. Even for those networks that can be analyzed, the algorithm is too slow for use in network design and optimization procedures.

We present in Section 3 the *proportional approximation method* (PAM) for analyzing closed multichain queueing networks [5]. PAM is based upon the MVA algorithm and the idea used in the derivation of proportional bounds [4]. Two PAM algorithms are presented. They have time requirements of $(3M+1)K$ and $(5M+2)K$ multiplications (we count multiplications and divisions only and refer to them both as multiplications.) Given these time requirements, networks with thousands of queues and thousands of virtual channels can be analyzed. The accuracy of the PAM algorithms was investigated by randomly generating 100 networks which were solved exactly by the tree convolution algorithm. We found the PAM algorithms to be very accurate (see Section 3). Additional experimental studies of the accuracy of PAM as well as a comparison of PAM algorithms with other approximate solution methods can be found in [5]. We note that all other approximate solution methods of closed queueing networks perform an iterative solution of some modified MVA equations. Many iterations may be needed for a solution to converge. PAM algorithms are non-iterative.

In Section 4, the following optimal routing problem is formulated. Consider a network with a fixed topology, known channel capacities, and a set of existing virtual channels; the routes and flow-control window sizes of the virtual channels are also known. Find a route for a new virtual channel to be added to the network between a given pair of source and destination. The objective is to maximize the total throughput of the network including the new virtual channel. We present a fast heuristic algorithm for the above optimal routing problem. The network throughput and virtual channel throughputs are evaluated using a PAM algorithm. The key idea used in the design of the heuristic is the following: The route that maximizes the individual throughput of a virtual channel coincides in most cases with the route that maximizes the total network throughput (even though this is not true in general for *all* cases). The effectiveness of the heuristic algorithm was examined using the 100 randomly generated networks and exact solutions provided by the tree convolution algorithm. Statistics from our experimental study show that the heuristic algorithm either found an optimal route or a route with a throughput close to the maximum almost all the time.

2. Comparison of Open and Closed Network Models

In a queueing network model of packet networks, communication channels and nodal processors are modeled as FIFO servers with exponentially distributed service times.[5] We assume that the packet network has adequate buffers so that buffer overflow at a node has negligible probability. The *independence assumption* of Kleinrock [6] is needed for both open and closed network models.

Let M denote the number of servers and K the number of virtual channels. For simplicity, we assume that each virtual channel has a loop-free fixed route from its source to its destination. (Actually, the routing behavior of a class of customers in queueing networks is specified by a Markov chain, which can be used to specify probabilistic bifurcated routing, i.e., the actual route of a packet is chosen probabilistically from a set of routes [13].)

In the open network model, new packets arrive to the source node of virtual channel k according to a Poisson process at a constant rate of γ_k packets per second. It is assumed that all arrivals to a virtual channel are accepted into the network without any input control.

---

[4]Time requirements are counted in number of multiplications and divisions only.

[5]In our examples, nodal processors are not modeled because processor delays are typically very much smaller than the communication channel delays in these examples.

Consider the closed network model in Figure 2. The route of each virtual channel is *closed* by the addition of two servers outside the communication network boundary. The generation of external arrivals to a virtual channel is modeled with a FIFO server with exponentially distributed service times, called the *source server* of the virtual channel. The service rate of the source server for virtual channel k is γ_k. Imagine that the N_k permits for flow control to be N_k customers circulating in the closed queueing network. The source generates new packets at the rate of γ_k only when the source has permits (i.e., the source server works only when its queue is nonempty). When there is no permit at the source, generation of new packets is blocked (i.e., the source server does not work when its queue is empty).

We model the delay of a permit's return from the sink to the source by a delay server (also called an infinite-server service center in the queueing networks literature). The mean service times of a delay server can be different for different virtual channels. The delay server is an abstraction of end-to-end acks that are sent in a real packet network. It is not important to model the storing and forwarding of end-to-end acks explicitly because these acks are either encoded in data packets or, if they are sent separately, are very short. Thus they consume relatively small amounts of channel capacities, which can be neglected or accounted for separately.

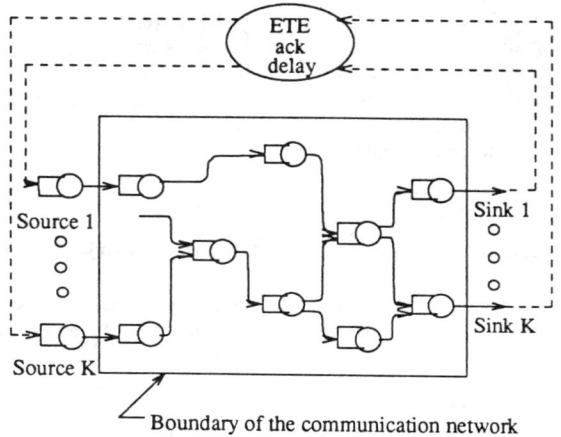

Figure 2. A closed queueing network model of a store-and-forward communication network.

The mean delays of end-to-end acks are not known and can only be estimated. In the experimental study to be presented next, we modeled the end-to-end ack delay of a virtual channel by

(*number of channels in route*)τ

where τ is the average packet transmission time. We found that performance measures of this network example are rather insensitive to the mean end-to-end ack delays. Increasing them all by 50%, or decreasing them all by 50%, varies the performance measures by a maximum of 10%.

We next compare performance predictions of the open network model and the closed network model (described above) with predictions given by a network simulator. The simulator implements most of the important elements of a real network [11]. (See Table 1.) In particular, it implements a data link protocol (similar to Arpanet's). The storing and forwarding of end-to-end acks, both standalone and piggybacked, are explicitly simulated. Virtual channels have a window mechanism for flow control. The length of a packet is sampled from a general probability distribution and remains constant for the entire journey of the packet through the network, i.e., no independence assumption. Key differences between the models are summarized in Table 1. Note that the closed network model, like the open network model, requires the independence assumption and the assumption of exponentially distributed service times. As was observed by Kleinrock many years ago for the open network model [6], we found that the accuracy of throughputs and mean delays of virtual channels predicted by the closed network model does not depend strongly on these two assumptions.

	Simulator	Closed Model	Open Model
Link-level acks	yes	no	no
End-to-end acks	yes	abstraction	no
Window flow control	yes	yes	no
Independence assumption	no	yes	yes
Packet length distribution	Exponential or General	Exponential	Exponential

Table 1. Comparison of model features.

The network used for the comparison of models has 8 switching nodes and 20 full-duplex links. It has 18 virtual channels, in 9 symmetric pairs, randomly chosen between node pairs. The window size of each virtual channel is equal to the number of links in its route. The capacity of each communication link is 10,000 bits/second and the average packet length is 1,000 bits.[6]

The performance predictions of seven models are compared in Figures 3-6. The open network model is labeled OPEN. The closed network model described above is labeled FIXED. The closed network model labeled ITERATIVE employs an iterative solution method; it is described in [9]. The four sets of simulation results correspond to four packet length distributions used by the simulator. EXP denotes the exponential distribution. The other three distributions are specified below:

HYPER   a hyperexponential distribution with coefficient of variation equal to 1.40

BURST1   a distribution with 0.3 probability at 100 bits, 0.3 probability at 1900 bits, and 0.4 probability uniformly distributed between 100 bits and 1900 bits; the coefficient of variation is equal to 0.77

BURST2   a distribution with 0.4 probability at 50 bits, 0.4 probability at 1950 bits, and 0.2 probability uniformly distributed between 50 bits and 1905 bits; the coefficient of variation is equal to 0.88

Note that the exponential distribution has a coefficient of variation equal to 1. Each virtual channel in the network example has the same packet arrival rate of γ at the source. Thus each source server in closed network models has a mean service time of $1/\gamma$. The exponential distribution was used in the simulator to generate interarrival times of packets to sources, the same as what is assumed in the queueing network models (i.e., Poisson arrivals).

---

[6]The reader is referred to Chapter 3 of [3] for a full description of the network, for numerical values of performance measures shown in Figures 3-6, as well as for a study of confidence intervals of the simulator's predictions.

Figure 3 shows the network throughput as a function of γ. The closed network models and the four simulation models give predictions that are very close to each other. The open network model assumes that the throughput of each virtual channel is γ. At γ=4, one of the servers in the network saturates, i.e., its packet arrival rate exceeds its service rate. In plotting the throughput curve labeled OPEN, we have assumed that γ can still be increased for those virtual channels that do not visit a saturated server.

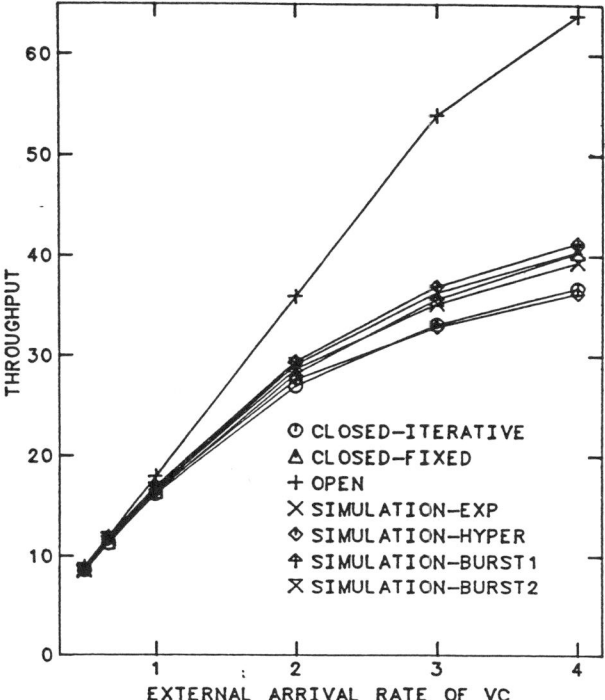

Figure 3. Network throughput versus γ for different models.

Figure 4 shows the average network delay as a function of γ. Again, the predictions of the closed network models and simulation models are very close to each other. The open network model gives predictions that are substantially higher than those of other models as γ increases. At γ=4, it predicts infinite average delay since one of the servers is saturated. Have we treated the open network model unfairly since its average delay is calculated using virtual channel throughputs that are too high as shown in Figure 3 ? To be fair, we have plotted an additional delay curve in Figure 4 labeled OPEN-IDEAL. The delay values of this curve are calculated by the open network model using virtual channel throughputs obtained by the best available closed network model (FIXED). In practice, these virtual channel throughputs may be measured in a real network. Figure 4 shows that the IDEAL open network model gives delay predictions that are still higher than all of the simulation predictions for γ≥3. The model is said to be ideal because it requires another model to supply it with virtual channel throughputs.

Figures 5 and 6 show the throughputs and average delays of individual virtual channels predicted by the seven models for γ=3 packets/second.

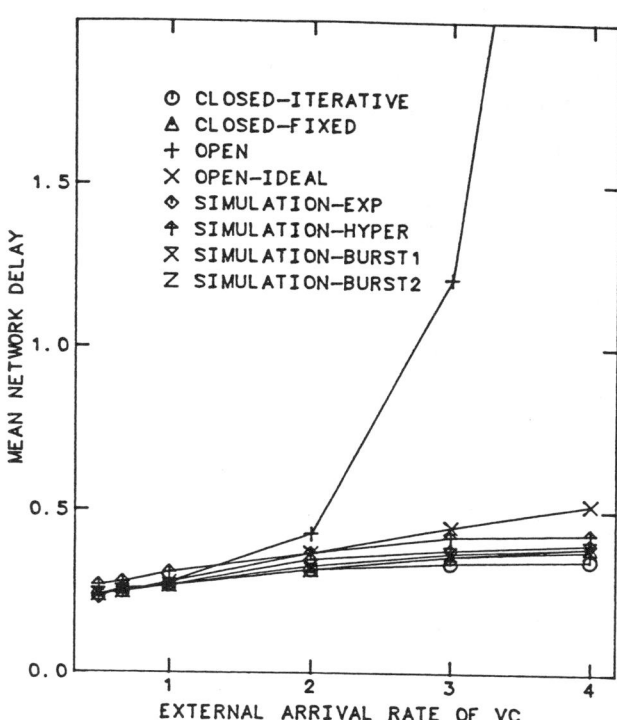

Figure 4. Mean end-to-end delays versus γ for different models.

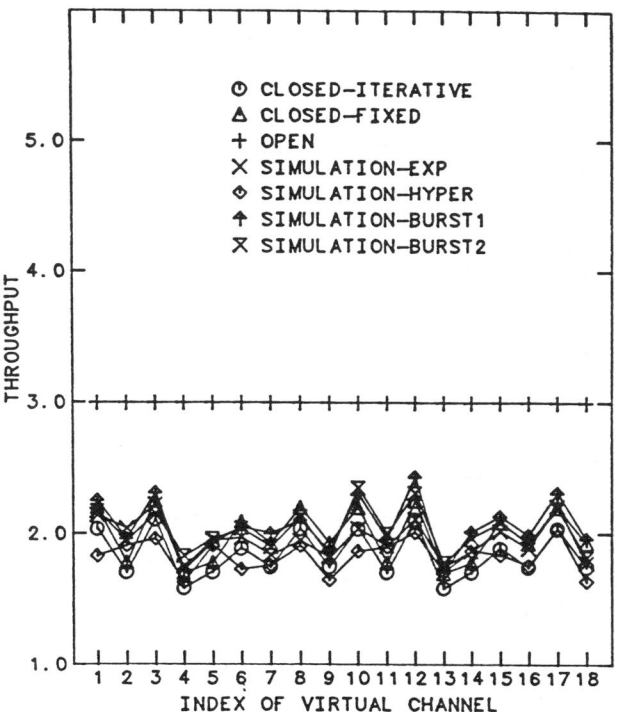

Figure 5. Virtual channel throughputs given by different models at γ=3 packets/second.

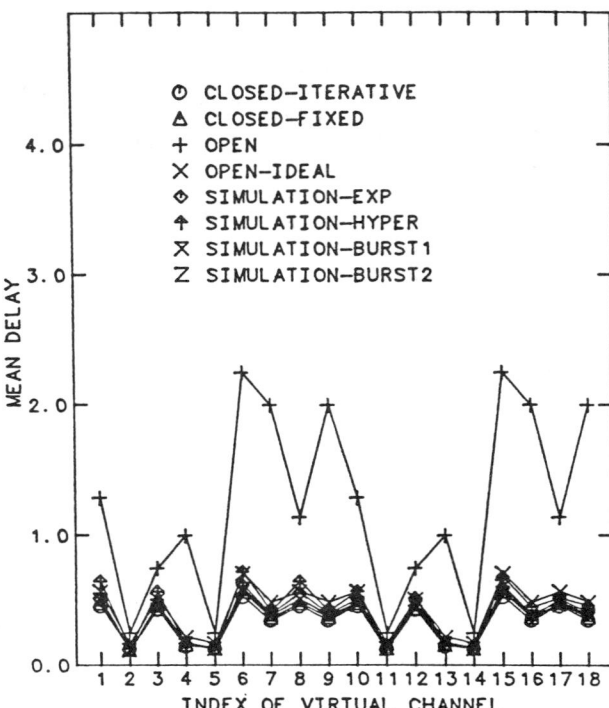

Figure 6. Mean delays of virtual channels given by different models at $\gamma=3$ packets/second.

The simulation results indicate that throughput and average delay predictions of the closed network model are quite accurate despite the independence assumption and the delay-server abstraction of end-to-end acks. Examining the numerical values of throughputs and average delays given by the four simulation models, we found that these performance measures do depend to some extent on the coefficient of variation of the packet length distribution. Not surprisingly, network performance is generally better (i.e., larger throughputs and smaller average delays) for packet lengths with a small coefficient of variation than for packet lengths with a large coefficient of variation. For the range of coefficients considered, 0.77 to 1.40, we conclude that the closed network model (FIXED) is quite robust. Its predictions for *individual* virtual channels differ from simulation results (for all four packet length distributions) by less than 10 percent in most cases and by less than 15 percent with only a few exceptions.

Using the EXP curves obtained from simulations as benchmarks, we found that, between the two closed network models, the FIXED model is more accurate than the ITERATIVE model, in addition to being computationally faster.

3. Algorithms for Analyzing Closed Queueing Networks

Consider a closed queueing network with k customer classes (or chains). We refer to $\underline{N}=(N_1, N_2, \ldots, N_K)$ as the *population vector* of the queueing network, where N_k denotes the population of the kth chain. If N_k in $\underline{N}$ is greater than or equal to 1, then $\underline{N}-\underline{1}_k$ refers to the population vector $\underline{N}$ with a chain k customer removed. Let τ_{mk} denote the mean service time of chain k customers at server m, for $k=1, \ldots, K$ and $m=1, \ldots, M$. There are two kinds of servers: delay servers with no queueing and fixed-rate servers with queueing. We use $D_{mk}(\underline{n})$ to denote the approximate mean delay of chain k customers at server m, $q'_{mk}(\underline{n})$ to denote the approximate mean queue length of chain k customers at server m, and $T_k(\underline{n})$ to denote the approximate throughput of chain k customers, in a network whose population vector is $\underline{n}$.

PAM algorithms are based upon MVA formulas [17]. However, the iterations from population vector $\underline{0}$ to population vector $\underline{N}-\underline{1}_k$ in the MVA algorithm are skipped. Instead, mean queue length approximations $q'_{mh}(\underline{N}-\underline{1}_k)$ at population vector $\underline{N}-\underline{1}_k$ are obtained by distributing the population N_h of chain h, over the servers on its route, proportional to τ_{mh}. This approach was the basis of proportional upper bounds for single-chain networks in [4]. In multichain networks, this approach leads to approximations rather than upper bounds. We refer to it as the proportional approximation method.

We present below two algorithms based upon the proportional approximation method [5]. The first algorithm, PAM_BASIC, calculates throughputs of individual chains. The second algorithm, PAM_IMPROVED, calculates throughputs of all chains and the utilizations of all servers. The algorithm then checks server utilizations to see if any utilization exceeds 1. (This is possible because the chain throughputs are approximations.) The throughputs of those chains that visit a server whose utilization exceeds 1 are then scaled down.

Algorithm PAM_BASIC

Step 1: Calculate proportional approximations of mean queue lengths from

$$q'_{mh}(\underline{N}-\underline{1}_k) = \begin{cases} \dfrac{\tau_{mh} N_h}{\sum_{i=1}^{M} \tau_{ih}} & \text{if } h \neq k \\[2ex] \dfrac{\tau_{mh}(N_h - 1)}{\sum_{i=1}^{M} \tau_{ih}} & \text{if } h = k. \end{cases}$$

for $m=1,2,\ldots,M$, $k=1,2,\ldots,K$, and $h=1,2,\ldots,K$.

Step 2: Calculate approximate mean delay of chain k at server m and approximate throughput of chain k from the following MVA formulas:

$$D_{mk}(\underline{N}) = \begin{cases} \tau_{mk}\left(1 + \sum_{h=1}^{K} q'_{mh}(\underline{N}-\underline{1}_k)\right) & \text{if } m \text{ is a fixed-rate server} \\[2ex] \tau_{mk} & \text{if } m \text{ is a delay server} \end{cases}$$

for $m = 1,2,\ldots,M$ and $k = 1,2,\ldots,K$, and

$$T_k(\underline{N}) = \dfrac{N_k}{\sum_{m=1}^{M} D_{mk}(\underline{N})} \quad \text{for } k = 1,2,\ldots,K.$$

Total throughput of the network, if needed, is equal to the summation of the chain throughputs. (Note that Step 1 can be implemented with MK multiplications and MK divisions.)

Algorithm PAM_IMPROVED

The first two steps of this algorithm are the same as those of Algorithm PAM_BASIC.

Step 3: Calculate server utilizations from the following formula:

$$U_m(\underline{N}) = \sum_{k=1}^{K} \tau_{mk} T_k(\underline{N})$$

for $m = 1, 2, \ldots, M$, where $U_m(\underline{N})$ is the utilization of server m at population vector $\underline{N}$.

Step 4: Find the largest utilization S_k among the fixed-rate servers visited by chain k,

$$S_k = \max_{\substack{m \text{ in} \\ \text{chain } k \text{ and} \\ m \text{ is a fixed-rate server}}} U_m(\underline{N})$$

for $k = 1, 2, \ldots, K$.

Step 5: (Scale down throughputs of individual chains if necessary.)
If $S_k > 1$ then $T_k(\underline{N}) := T_k(\underline{N}) / S_k$.

Step 6: Calculate total throughput, and recalculate server utilizations if the throughput of any chain has been scaled down,

$$T(\underline{N}) = \sum_{k=1}^{K} T_k(\underline{N})$$

and

$$U_m(\underline{N}) = \sum_{k=1}^{K} \tau_{mk} T_k(\underline{N}), \text{ for } m = 1, 2, \ldots, M.$$

Because of the additional steps, the approximate throughputs calculated by PAM_IMPROVED are, in general, more accurate than those calculated by PAM_BASIC. Another algorithm, PAM_TWO, is presented in [5]. It is more accurate than PAM_IMPROVED but it has a computational time requirement of $O(MK^2)$ instead of $O(MK)$ for the two algorithms presented above; the space requirement is $O(MK)$ for all three PAM algorithms.

In the above algorithms, we have assumed that the virtual channels in a communication network have loop-free fixed routes. If the routing behavior of a closed chain is specified by a first-order Markov chain, then τ_{mk} in the above algorithms should be interpreted as the load, or traffic intensity, of chain k at server m rather than as the mean service time [17].

We have conducted two sets of experiments to examine the accuracy of PAM algorithms [5]. In the first, 100 networks with characteristics of models of communication networks were generated randomly; these networks have fixed-rate servers only.[7] The accuracy of PAM_BASIC and PAM_IMPROVED was studied by comparing their approximate results with exact results given by the tree convolution algorithm (TCA). In the second set of experiments, 500 networks with characteristics of models of computer systems were generated and the accuracy of PAM_IMPROVED and PAM_TWO was studied by comparisons with exact results given by the MVA algorithm and approximate results given by three iterative approximate solution methods. These networks have delay servers and fixed-rate servers.

We shall present some statistical data from the 100-network experiment. Before doing so, we consider a network example with 30 fixed-rate servers and 20 chains and compare the approximate throughputs computed by PAM_BASIC and PAM_IMPROVED with the exact throughputs computed by TCA. (The network example is completely specified in [5].) The network is fairly heavily utilized. The maximum server utilization, computed by TCA, is 0.990. The average server utilization, among those with nonzero traffic, is 0.398. The accuracy of PAM_BASIC is illustrated in Figure 7. The accuracy of PAM_IMPROVED is illustrated in Figure 8. Chain throughputs computed by PAM_IMPROVED are very accurate for this example. The maximum percentage error is 6% for chain 10. Throughputs computed by PAM_BASIC and PAM_IMPROVED are the same for those chains that do not visit a highly utilized server. For those chains that visit a highly utilized server (chains 3, 7, 14, 18), throughputs computed by PAM_BASIC have much larger percentage errors than PAM_IMPROVED. The proportional approximation tends to underestimate mean queue lengths at bottleneck servers. Thus PAM_BASIC overestimates the throughputs of chains that visit such bottlenecks. While PAM_IMPROVED checks server utilizations and compensates for these errors, PAM_BASIC does not.

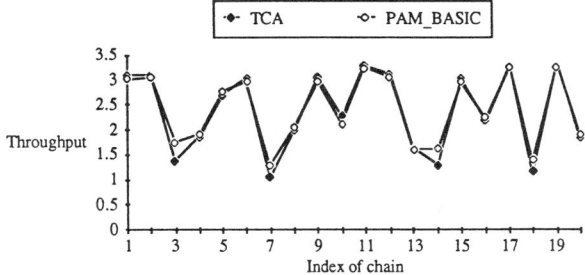

Figure 7. Throughputs of chains calculated by TCA and PAM_BASIC.

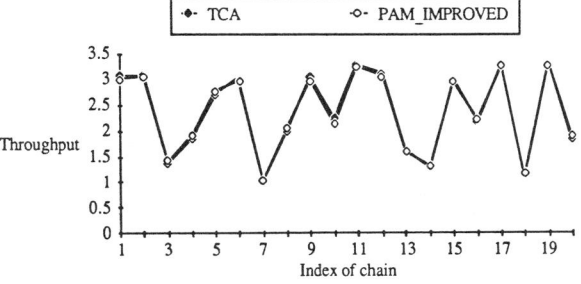

Figure 8. Throughputs of chains calculated by TCA and PAM_IMPROVED.

---

[7] In other words, mean end-to-end ack delays are assumed to be zero.

We next present some results of the 100-network experiment. The 100 networks were generated randomly (see [3, 5] for details). Statistics on the parameters of the 100 networks are shown in Table 2. In Table 2, #packets denotes the summation of all chain populations. In Figures 9-11, we show distributions of percentage errors of total network throughput, chain throughputs, server utilizations calculated by PAM_IMPROVED compared to exact solutions of TCA. A summary of the error statistics is shown in Table 3. Note that the maximum percentage error of total network throughput calculated by PAM_IMPROVED is 3.55% for the 100 networks. The average percentage error of chain throughput is 2.67%. Given its modest computational time requirement, we consider PAM_IMPROVED to be highly accurate.

	Maximum	Minimum	Average
1. # nodes	25	7	15
2. # links	37	9	20
3. # queues	74	18	40
4. # chains	43	8	23
5. # packets	107	19	57
6. Ave. queue util.	0.546	0.291	0.419

Table 2. Statistics of 100 test networks.

	Statistics of percentage errors				
	#samples	Minimum	Maximum	Mean	Variance
Total throughput	100	0.009	3.554	0.824	0.002
Throughput of chain	2255	0.000	20.503	2.667	7.167
Utilization of queue	3104	0.000	14.769	2.064	4.263

Table 3. Statistics of approximation errors of total throughput, chain throughputs, and server utilizations calculated by PAM_IMPROVED for the 100 networks.

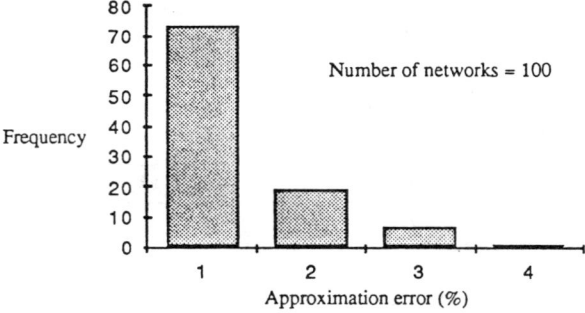

Figure 9. Distribution of approximation errors of total throughputs calculated by PAM_IMPROVED for the 100 networks.

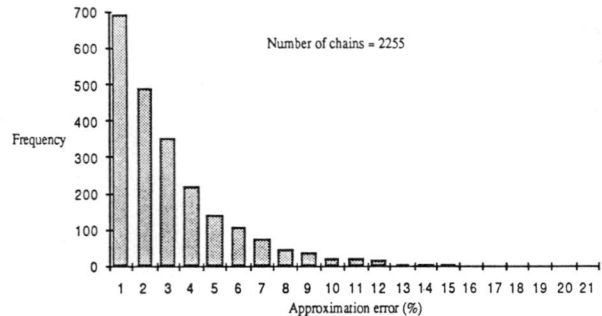

Figure 10. Distribution of approximation errors of throughputs of individual chains calculated by PAM_IMPROVED for the 100 networks.

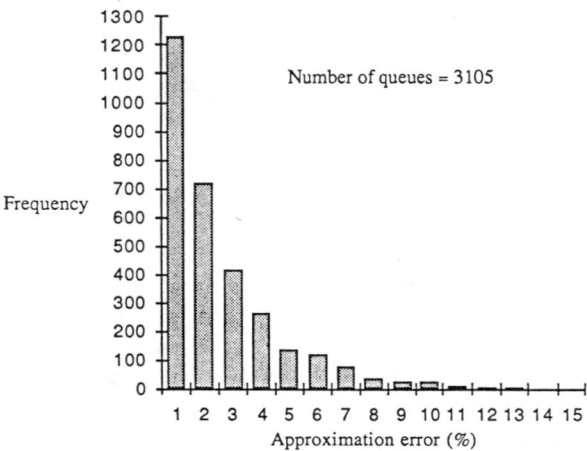

Figure 11. Distribution of approximation errors of server utilizations calculated by PAM_IMPROVED for the 100 networks.

We also studied the correlation between the percentage error of the throughput of a chain calculated by PAM_BASIC and the maximum utilization among servers visited by the chain. We selected one chain from each of the 100 networks in the above experiment and calculated its throughput with PAM_BASIC. The percentage error in throughput and the corresponding maximum server utilization are plotted in Figure 12. Note that throughput errors of PAM_BASIC and maximum server utilizations are highly correlated. Percentage errors are large only for chains that visit servers with utilizations very close to 1. This is a very useful observation! It suggests that PAM_BASIC, being the fastest of the three PAM algorithms, can be used in many network design procedures. The general objective of optimal routing, for example, is to route traffic in such a way that no bottleneck exists in the network. While PAM_BASIC has relatively large errors for those chains that visit bottlenecks during an intermediate step of an optimal routing procedure, it can still be effectively used to select good routes which generally do not include bottlenecks. And after bottlenecks have been eliminated from a network, PAM_BASIC provides accurate throughputs.

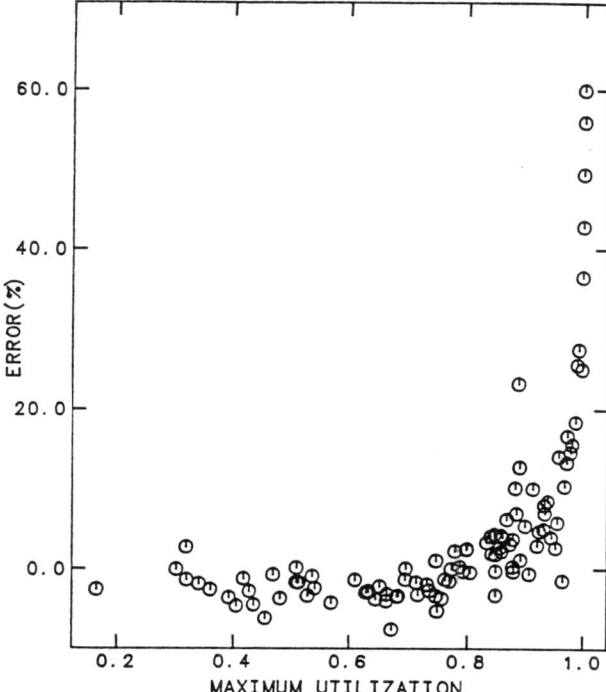

Figure 12. Correlation between percentage error of chain throughput calculated by PAM_BASIC and the maximum utilization of the servers visited by the chain.

4. Optimal Routing

Optimal routing plays a central role in network design problems. In the process of designing a network, numerous modifications are usually made before a satisfactory network is obtained. After each modification, optimal routing has to be performed to adapt to any change in network topology or traffic. An optimal routing algorithm to be used in network design should be as fast as possible. Also the algorithm that is used for evaluating network performance within the optimal routing algorithm has to be very fast.

We present an algorithm to solve the following problem for the closed network model: Given a network with a set of flow-controlled virtual channels, find the optimal route for a virtual channel to be added to the network to maximize the total throughput of the network including the new virtual channel. This algorithm can be used to add virtual channels to a network one at a time until all virtual channels have been included in the network. If further improvement in the network throughput is desired, then some virtual channels can be selected for rerouting.

Most optimal routing algorithms are based upon finding the shortest path between a pair of source and destination; they differ primarily in their link metrics. When a closed network model is used for network design, however, a link metric is not easily defined. The two basic steps of our optimal routing algorithm are the following:

(1) Find a set of routes with the smallest end-to-end mean delays for the virtual channel being added to the network.

(2) Use PAM_BASIC to find a route, from the set in step (1), that gives the highest network throughput.

The mean delays in step (1) are calculated using the proportional approximation. However, the mean queue lengths of the virtual channel for which a route is to be found, say virtual channel k, are not included since virtual channel k does not yet have a route. This is equivalent to treating virtual channel k as having a window size of one so that $q'_{mk}(\underline{N}-1_k)=0$ for all m. This is the key assumption that makes possible the use of mean delay as a link metric and transforms step (1) into a shortest path problem that can be solved very efficiently.

A route selected in step (1) with the smallest end-to-end mean delay for the new virtual channel does not necessarily maximize the total throughput of the network in a closed queueing network. Thus in step (1) we employ one metric to select a set of good candidates and in step (2) employ a better metric to pick the best route from the set of candidates. Note that the metric in step (2) cannot be evaluated efficiently because each possible route has to be evaluated separately by solving a closed network model. By using different performance metrics at different stages of our search heuristic we reduce computational time very substantially.

The effectiveness of our algorithm to find an optimal or suboptimal route depends upon the accuracy of the proportional approximation as well as the following empirical observation: The route that maximizes the individual throughput of the new virtual channel coincides frequently with the route that maximizes the total network throughput (this is not true in general). Note that the route that maximizes the throughput of a closed chain in a queueing network also minimizes its mean delay according to Little's formula. In fact, only an approximation of the new virtual channel's mean delay is evaluated in step (1). Nevertheless, statistics from our 100-network experiment show the following heuristic optimal routing algorithm to be very effective.

Algorithm HRA1 (*To find an optimal route for chain k*)

Step 1: Calculate approximate mean queue length $q_{mh}(\underline{N}^k)$ by the following formula:

$$q_{mh}(\underline{N}^k) = \frac{\tau_{mh}}{\sum_{i=1}^{M} \tau_{ih}} N_h$$

for $m=1,2,\ldots,M, h=1,2,\ldots,K$ and $h \neq k$

where $\underline{N}^k$ is the population vector of the network with chain k removed.

Step 2: Compute the approximate delay using the MVA formula,

$$D_{mk}(\underline{N}) = \tau_{mk}(1 + \sum_{\substack{h=1 \\ h \neq k}}^{K} q_{mh}(\underline{N}^k)) \quad \text{for } m=1,2,\ldots,M$$

Step 3: Create a routing tree for chain k. The root node of the tree is the source and the leaf nodes are the destination of chain k. Select a set R of shortest delay routes from the routing tree using the approximate delays calculated in Step 2 as metric.

Step 4: Use algorithm PAM_BASIC to calculate the total network throughput for each route in R. Select the route in R that yields the largest network throughput.

With a slight modification, Algorithm HRA1 can be used to find a route to maximize the individual throughput of chain k. The algorithm, to be called HRA2, is given below.

Algorithm HRA2

The first three steps of the algorithm are the same as those of Algorithm HRA1.

Step 4: Use algorithm PAM_BASIC to calculate the throughput of chain k for each route in R. Select a route from R that yields the largest throughput of chain k.

The key to a successful application of these algorithms is to find a small set R which includes the optimal route or a near-optimal route. The following three choices of R were used in our experimental study.
  I. Only the shortest delay route among all possible routes is selected.
  II. Up to three shortest delay routes are chosen.
  III. Up to ten shortest delay routes are chosen.

The *Branch-and-Bound* paradigm was used to find the |R| shortest routes for a chain.

Experimental results

The algorithms were tested on the 100 randomly generated networks used for testing the accuracy of PAM. For each network, the source node and destination node of a new chain, for which an optimal route is to be found, were randomly generated. (If the source node and the destination node are adjacent to each other then another node pair is generated.) The parameter values of the new chain were selected in the same way as those of existing chains in the network by the network generator as described in [3, 5]. To be practical, we introduce the following maximum-hop constraint: Each chain can visit up to 9 nodes, or 80 percent of the nodes in the network (including the source and destination nodes), whichever is smaller. Each heuristic routing algorithm was applied to the test networks to find the best routes for the new chains. Exact throughputs for all feasible routes satisfying the maximum-hop constraint were also computed by the tree convolution algorithm as benchmarks. Statistics of results from our experiment using Algorithm HRA1 with different choices of R are given in Table 4. In this table, $\Delta = |T^o - T^h|$, where T^o is the largest exact total throughput that can be achieved among all feasible routes satisfying the maximum-hop constraint and T^h is the exact total throughput achieved by the route chosen by Algorithm HRA1. Both T^o and T^h were calculated using TCA.

	Statistics of deviations from optimal total throughput					
|R|	1		3		10	
	Δ	$\frac{\Delta \times 100\%}{T^o}$	Δ	$\frac{\Delta \times 100\%}{T^o}$	Δ	$\frac{\Delta \times 100\%}{T^o}$
Minimum	0.0	0.0	0.0	0.0	0.0	0.0
Maximum	0.839	1.072	0.838	1.071	0.412	0.547
Average	0.056	0.062	0.026	0.032	0.018	0.022
Std. dev.	0.161	0.185	0.106	0.134	0.068	0.084

Table 4. Statistics of deviations from optimal total throughput for Algorithm HRA1.

A distribution of the percentage differences (with respect to T^o) between T^o and T^h for the routes selected by Algorithm HRA1 is shown in Figure 13. In this experiment, Algorithm HRA1 examined only the shortest delay route for the new chain (|R|=1). Table 4 and Figure 13 show that the heuristic algorithm HRA1 found the optimal route most of the time! Even when it failed to find the optimal route, the exact total throughput of the network for the route chosen by HRA1 is very close to the optimal total throughput. Table 4 also shows that increasing the number of routes examined by HRA1 does improve its performance, though not by very much.

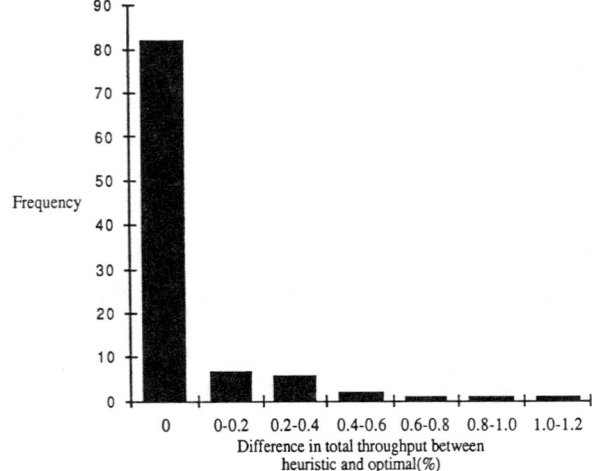

Figure 13. Distribution of percentage difference between the optimal total throughput and the total throughput achieved by the heuristic algorithm.

We also applied Algorithm HRA2 to the 100 networks used to test Algorithm HRA1. Again, the value of |R| was one. In Table 5, Δ is $|T_k^o - T_k^h|$, where T_k^o is the largest throughput of chain k (calculated by TCA) among all feasible routes satisfying the maximum-hop constraint, and T_k^h is the exact throughput of chain k (calculated by TCA) whose route was chosen by Algorithm HRA2.

	Maximum	Minimum	Average	Std. dev.
Δ	0.202	0.0	0.003	0.022
$\frac{\Delta \times 100\%}{T_k^o}$	13.732	0.0	0.214	1.442

Table 5. Statistics of results from the heuristic routing algorithm HRA2.

Of the 100 networks tested, Algorithm HRA2 actually found a route maximizing the throughput of chain k in 95 networks. Among these 95 networks, 80 of them also have the largest total throughputs that can be achieved among all feasible routes of chain k (subject to the maximum-hop constraint).

The network used in the next example has 21 nodes, 30 links (60 queues), and 30 virtual channels. (See Tables 6 and 7.) The optimal route for a new virtual channel from node 20 to node 3 is to be selected. We found that both heuristic algorithms gave the same ten shortest delay routes for the new chain (because the first three steps of the algorithms are the same). Exact throughputs and approximate throughputs of the new chain for these ten routes, calculated by TCA and PAM_BASIC respectively, are shown in

Figure 14. In this figure, the order of the best seven routes is the same whether the routes are ordered by exact chain throughput or approximate chain throughput. The exact total throughput and approximate total throughput of the network resulting from assigning each of the ten routes to the new chain are shown in Figure 15. In this figure, the two curves have the same trend for all ten routes.

Link	Capacity (bits/second)
(1,19)	2400
(14,6)	2400
(17,12)	9600
(20,12)	2400
(1,5)	4800
(7,10)	2400
(14,9)	9600
(17,20)	9600
(18,15)	4800
(1,11)	9600
(2,21)	2400
(3,18)	2400
(4,13)	2400
(5,16)	2400
(7,13)	4800
(8,9)	2400
(10,4)	2400
(14,8)	2400
(17,11)	4800
(19,5)	4800
(20,6)	9600
(1,16)	9600
(2,10)	9600
(3,14)	2400
(7,18)	9600
(12,19)	2400
(15,21)	4800
(17,8)	2400
(20,19)	2400
(21,16)	2400

Table 6. Links and their capacities in network example.

Chain	Population	Mean service time at source server	Route (in node sequence)
1	2	0.1	11 1 16
2	3	0.3	17 20 6 14
3	3	0.3	17 20 19 5
4	2	0.2	3 14 8
5	2	0.2	14 6 20 19
6	2	0.3	16 1
7	2	0.3	9 14 3
8	2	0.3	8 17 12 19
9	2	0.3	4 10 7
10	3	0.2	7 10
11	3	0.3	13 7 10 2
12	2	0.2	9 14 6 20 17 12
13	2	0.3	18 3 14 8
14	3	0.3	17 11 1 5
15	2	0.3	17 12 19 5
16	2	0.2	3 18 7 10
17	3	0.2	21 15 18 7 13
18	3	0.1	3 18 7 13 4
19	2	0.1	20 17 11 1 16
20	2	0.2	13 4
21	3	0.3	2 21 15
22	2	0.3	4 10 2 21
23	2	0.2	13 4
24	4	0.3	17 8 9
25	2	0.2	18 15 21
26	4	0.1	15 21 2 10 4
27	2	0.1	4 13 7 18 15
28	2	0.1	18 3
29	2	0.3	9 8 17 12
30	2	0.3	18 15 21 2

Table 7. Chain populations, mean service times at source servers, and routes of chains in network example.

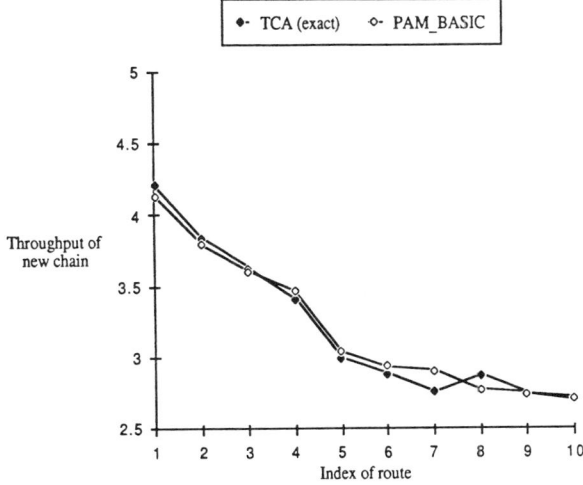

Figure 14. Exact and approximate throughputs of a chain using different routes.

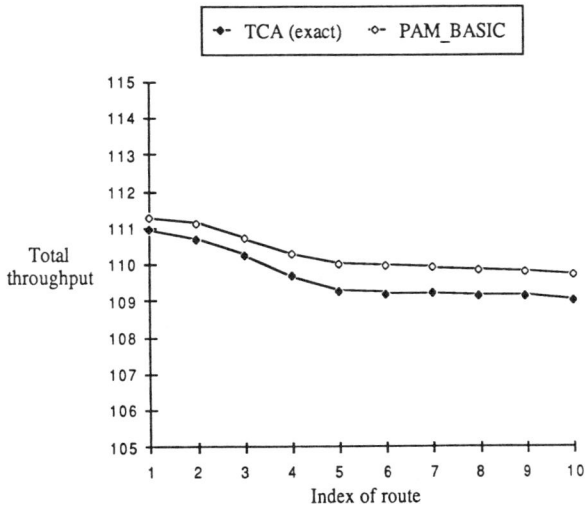

Figure 15. Exact and approximate total network throughputs for different routes of a particular chain.

What we have demonstrated using the above example is that approximate throughputs calculated by PAM_BASIC are adequate as a metric for comparing routes. This is because bottleneck queues are usually not visited by an optimal route (or a near-optimal route). We have shown in Section 3 that the approximate throughputs of individual chains calculated by PAM_BASIC are very accurate if they do not visit bottleneck queues. Note also, from Figures 14 and 15, that the first seven routes that yield the largest throughputs for the new chain also yield the largest total throughputs for the network. This gives further evidence that it is effective to search for a route maximizing total throughput from among a set of routes that maximize the throughput of the new chain.

5. Conclusions

We have described a closed queueing network model for the analysis and design of flow-controlled communication networks and demonstrated its accuracy and robustness with experimental results. It gives a network designer more information about the performance of a flow-controlled communication network than an open queueing network model which cannot be used to predict throughputs of flow-controlled virtual channels.

In applying the closed network model to network analysis and design, some engineering judgment is needed to determine the "effective window sizes" of virtual channels. There are two sources of uncertainty. First, the implementations of some sliding window protocols are more complicated than the one described in Section 2, e.g., SNA pacing [1, 18]. Second, the mean delays of acks travelling from destinations to sources need to be estimated. Suppose we let the end-to-end ack delay of each virtual channel be zero in the closed network model. In order for a virtual channel in the communication network being modeled to achieve the throughput predicted by the closed network model, its window size should be larger than the chain population N_k in the model by $\alpha_k T_k$, where T_k is the chain throughput predicted by the model and α_k is virtual channel's average end-to-end delay of acks. By Little's formula [7], $\alpha_k T_k$ is the average number of permits that are en route from the destination to the source. Alternatively, one might estimate this number directly instead of estimating α_k first and then rounding off $\alpha_k T_k$ to an integer.

We have presented two algorithms based upon the *proportional approximation method (PAM)* for evaluating performance measures of closed queueing networks. These PAM algorithms have computational time and space requirements of $O(KM)$, where K denotes the number of virtual channels and M the number of queues; they can be used to solve models of large communication networks. Statistical studies comparing the predictions of PAM algorithms with exact solutions calculated by the tree convolution algorithms show that the PAM algorithms are very accurate.

We have also illustrated the use of the closed queueing network model and the PAM algorithms for network design by solving the following optimal routing problem: Find a route for a new virtual channel to be added to a network with existing flow-controlled virtual channels. The total network throughput is to be maximized. (Note that this problem cannot be solved using an open queueing network model.) A fast heuristic solution algorithm based upon PAM is presented. Routes obtained by the heuristic algorithm were compared with optimal routes obtained by an exhaustive search using exact results calculated by the tree convolution algorithm. The heuristic algorithm was very effective in finding an optimal route or a near-optimal route almost all the time.

References

[1] F. D. George and G. E. Young, "SNA Flow Control: Architecture and Implementation," *IBM Systems Journal*, Vol. 21, No. 2, 1982, pp. 179-210.

[2] M. Gerla and L. Kleinrock, "Flow Control: A Comparative Survey," *IEEE Trans. on Commun.*, Vol. COM-28, No. 4, April 1980, pp. 553-574.

[3] C.-T. Hsieh, *Models and Algorithms for the Design of Store-and-Forward Communication Networks*, Ph.D. Dissertation, Department of Computer Sciences, University of Texas at Austin, May 1987.

[4] C.-T. Hsieh and S. S. Lam, "Two Classes of Performance Bounds for Closed Queueing Networks," *Performance Evaluation*, Vol. 7, No. 1, 1987, pp. 3-30.

[5] C.-T. Hsieh and S. S. Lam, "PAM — A Noniterative Approximate Solution Method for Closed Multichain Queueing Networks," Technical Report TR-87-28, Department of Computer Sciences, University of Texas at Austin, July 1987.

[6] L. Kleinrock, *Communication Nets: Stochastic Message Flow and Delay*, McGraw-Hill, New York, 1964.

[7] L. Kleinrock, *Queueing Systems, Vol. 2: Computer Applications*, John Wiley, New York, 1976.

[8] H. Kobayashi and M. Gerla, "Optimal Routing in Closed Queueing Networks," *ACM Transactions on Computer Systems*, Vol. 1, No. 4, Nov. 1983, pp. 294-310.

[9] S. S. Lam and C.-T. Hsieh, "Models and Algorithms for the Design of Store-and-Forward Communication Networks, *Conf. Record International Conf. on Communications*, Chicago, June 1985, pp. 43.1.1-43.1.6.

[10] S. S. Lam and Y. L. Lien, "Modeling and Analysis of Flow Controlled Packet Switching Networks," *Proc. 7th Data Communications Symposium*, Mexico City, October 1981.

[11] S. S. Lam and Y. L. Lien, "Congestion Control of Packet Communication Networks by Input Buffer Limits—A Simulation Study," *IEEE Trans. on Computers*, Vol. C-30, No. 10, October 1981, pp. 733-742.

[12] S. S. Lam and Y. L. Lien, "A Tree Convolution Algorithm for the Solution of Queueing Networks," *Comm. ACM*, Vol. 26, No. 3, March 1983, pp. 203-215.

[13] S. S. Lam and J. W. Wong, "Queueing Network Models of Packet Switching Networks, Part 2: Networks with Population Size Constraints," *Performance Evaluation*, Vol. 2, No. 3, October 1982, pp. 161-180.

[14] Y. L. Lien, *Modeling and Analysis of Flow Controlled Computer Communication Networks*, Ph.D. Dissertation, Department of Computer Sciences, University of Texas at Austin, 1981.

[15] M. Reiser, "A Queueing Network Analysis of Computer Communication Networks with Window Flow Control," *IEEE Trans. on Communication*, Vol. COM-27, pp. 1199-1209, 1979.

[16] M. Reiser and H. Kobayashi, "Queueing Networks with Multiple Closed Chains: Theory and Computational Algorithms," *IBM J. Res. Develop.*, Vol. 21, pp. 283-294, 1975.

[17] M. Reiser and S. Lavenberg, "Mean Value Analysis of Closed Multichain Queueing Networks," *Journal of ACM*, Vol. 27, No. 2, pp. 313-322, April 1980.

[18] M. Schwartz, *Telecommunication Networks: Protocols, Modeling and Analysis*, Addison-Wesley, Reading, Mass., 1987.

ADAPTIVE ROUTING IN BURROUGHS NETWORK ARCHITECTURE

Jeffrey L. Rosenberg, Steven A. Gruchevsky,
and David M. Piscitello

Devon Engineering Offices
Unisys Corporation
P.O. Box 1874
Southeastern, PA 19398-1874

ABSTRACT

The routing function used for Burroughs Network Architecture (BNA) to determine the best routes for traffic through the network is known as the *Burroughs Integrated Adaptive Routing System*, or BIAS™.[1]

Based on the algorithm devised for the MERIT Computer Network [3], BIAS™ is a decentralized, deterministic system which adapts to changes in network topology automatically. The current BIAS™ routing architecture incorporates improvements [1] in the original algorithm which significantly reduce the recovery time from failures of nodes or links and is virtually loop-free, even during recovery from those failures.

BIAS™ automatically re-determines the best routes for traffic throughout the network in response to the following changes to the network topology:

- a node (an end system or intermediate system) is added to the network;

- a node is removed from the network;

- the cost of transiting a node is changed;

- a logical link (LAN, leased or switched circuit, X.25 virtual circuit) is added to the network;

- a link is removed from the network; and/or

- the cost of transiting a link is changed.

---

[1] BIAS is a trademark of Unisys Corporation.

1.0 INTRODUCTION

Burroughs Network Architecture (BNA) is a model which defines the functional requirements necessary for implementations to participate in an association known as a network. Like many other network architectures, BNA can be best described as a hierarchical arrangement of layers of functionality, each of which provides a specific service, or services, to the layer immediately above. Where OSI defines seven layers of protocols and services, BNA defines four (see Figure 1). The BNA Link Layer provides functions which correspond to the Physical and Data Link Layers of OSI. BNA's Network Layer provides a connectionless ("datagram") data transfer service (using ISO 8473 [5]) to the Port Level, which provides the services and functionality similar to that provided by the upper four layers of OSI. BNA Host Services are Unisys-supplied application-level services such as file transfer, job transfer, and remote file and terminal access.

The *Burroughs Integrated Adaptive Routing System* (BIAS™) routing function is one of the principal functions of the Network Layer of BNA. BIAS™ is a decentralized, deterministic routing function which adapts to changes in network topology automatically. The routing function may be applied to network topologies employing any combination of BNA supported Link Layer protocols, which include leased lines, dial-up lines, PDNs and LANs. BIAS™ provides logical connectivity to all nodes in the BNA Network, making use of whatever combination or succession of communication facilities is made available to it by the Link Layer in order to provide communication paths for network users.

2.0 HISTORY

The original BIAS™ routing algorithm was developed for Burroughs Network Architecture, Version 1 (BNAv1) in the late 1970s. It was based on the routing algorithm developed for the MERIT Computer Network [3], and was used in a number of private networks. During the development of Version 2 of BNA, a number of improvements were incorporated into the original BIAS™ algorithm to reduce the recovery time from failures of network components [1]. A hierarchical addressing scheme based on the Kamoun and Kleinrock clustering technique [2] was introduced to expand the number of possible systems (nodes) in the network. Facilities for load splitting and congestion avoidance[2] were introduced.

Simulation studies performed on BNAv2 BIAS™ indicate that BIAS™ performs well in configurations of several hundred nodes per cluster. Considerably more can be accommodated if all the nodes in a cluster are connected by a single LAN or a single PDN, or if the topology is otherwise constrained. Additional levels of the hierarchy allow for hundreds or thousands of such clusters in a single BNAv2 subnetwork.[3]

BNAv2 is a recently released product, which incorporates numerous improvements in addition to those to BIAS™ described in this article. A Unisys internal corporate network utilizing BNAv1 currently has over 125 nodes, and is expected to double in size by mid-1988. Conversion to BNAv2 is anticipated. The largest and most notable private network currently utilizing BNAv2 is the financial transfer network of S.W.I.F.T., the Society for Worldwide Interbank Financial Telecommunication, which is expected to have 80 - 100 nodes within the near future. Other networks are currently planned to have up to 1000 nodes.

3.0 OVERVIEW

BIAS™ is a distance-vector routing method; that is, each node which participates in the routing process maintains a vector of its own distance to each destination. Each node begins with the knowledge that it is zero (0) from itself, and adds the distance to neighbors it discovers during network initialization to determine its distance to every other node/cluster in the network. The routing update function uses a set of router control frames which indicate the cost of using specific links between neighboring (logically adjacent) nodes and the reachability and distances of destinations from each neighbor node.

BIAS™ takes into account the capacities of nodes and links in a network by assigning each a "cost" called a "resistance factor". Resistance factor is basically a measure of distance and is typically based on anticipated delay for a packet of given (average) length. Where throughput is more critical, and a mix of terrestrial and satellite links is in use, the resistance factor is usually based on the inverse of throughput. The calculation used to determine resistance factor yields a positive integer in order to facilitate the summation of distances between nodes. BIAS™ automatically assigns default resistances to each node and to each link, based on capacity.

Default link resistances are defined for each link, and default node resistances are defined for each node. These default values are based on bandwidth (for links) and relative processing power committed to transiting traffic (for nodes). The default resistance approximates the time (in milliseconds) for a frame (PDU) to transit a link or be processed and forwarded by a node.

4.0 CONCEPTS AND DEFINITIONS

The following concepts and terms are useful in understanding the BIAS™ routing function.

4.1 Node

In BNA, the term used to refer to an element in the network is node. For the purpose of routing, a node in BNA terminology corresponds to an Intermediate System in OSI terminology. However, in BNAv2, each system is both an End System and an Intermediate System.

4.2 Cluster

A collection of nodes that share a common position at a certain level of the BNAv2 addressing hierarchy is referred to as a cluster. The nodes in a cluster are expected to be mutually and efficiently reachable from each other, without going outside the cluster, under normal conditions. A single node is, itself, a special case of a cluster.

4.3 Link

For the purpose of routing, the point-to-point connections or logical associations made available to the Network Layer by the Link Layer are generically referred to as links. In BNAv2, links are usually supported by such means as LANs, leased or switched HDLC-based circuits, and X.25 VCs or PVCs.[4]

---

[2] The congestion avoidance features of BNAv2 involve close cooperation between the router and the Port Level; they are not described further in this paper.

[3] Since subnetworks are treated like an additional level of cluster, BNAv2 is expected to perform well in multi-domain configurations involving many thousands of nodes.

[4] Additional link types are available for the connection of terminal devices, which are not visible to the BIAS™ routing function.

4.4 Neighbor

A node connected to the local node by a single link, or by a set of single links in parallel, is termed a neighbor of the local node.

4.5 Destination

A cluster to which the router is directing, or might have to direct, data units is referred to as a destination. A data unit is always addressed to a specific node, but routing is often done toward a destination which is a cluster containing that addressed node.

4.6 Path

A path is the sequence of individual nodes and links traversed in order to reach some destination. Complete paths are not generally known by any single node.

4.7 Routing

A routing is the local node's view of a path to a particular destination; this view primarily identifies the neighbor node to which messages for that destination are to be sent. Neighbor node identification takes the form of the neighbor's Node Address (described in the *Addressing* section). Additional information about the path through the network to the destination includes:

- the number of consecutive links in the path (hop count);

- the (total) resistance factor of the path; i.e., the sum of the costs of the links and nodes in the path, excluding the source node and destination cluster themselves; and

- the maximum segment size (i.e., maximum router frame size) that can be sent along the path.

The actual topology of a path is not known to any node.

4.8 In-Use Routing

An In-Use Routing is the current best path (paths, if load-splitting is used) to a destination from the local node.

4.9 Load-Splitting

The routing mechanism provides a means of distributing traffic over multiple paths which exist between two nodes. This technique is called load-splitting and has the effect of spreading message traffic more evenly throughout the network which results in the paths between nodes being less susceptible to overloading.

Load-splitting is accomplished by modifying the procedure for determining the best path to a node (constructing the In-Use Routings), and by providing a mechanism to distribute data traffic over all the in-use paths.

Load-splitting is only performed over equally-good routings.

4.10 Good News

GOOD NEWS is information which notifies the local node of the addition of a node or link, a change of the maximum segment size, a change in hop count, or the lowering of a resistance factor. The process for the distribution of good news is called the *Independent Update Procedure (IUP)*.

4.11 Bad News

BAD NEWS is information which notifies the local node of the removal of a node or a link, or the increase of a resistance factor. The process for the distribution of bad news is called the *Coordinated Update Procedure (CUP)*.

4.12 Spanning Tree

For a given destination, an arc is directed from every node to the neighbor on the best path to the destination. These arcs form a directed tree rooted at the destination, called a "spanning tree". The spanning tree is directed towards the destination, as illustrated in Figure 2. Each spanning tree defines a partial order among all the nodes of the network, relative to the associated destination, and is used by the CUP. (The nodes closer to the destination, under this ordering, are called *downtree* nodes; those further away, *uptree*.)

4.13 Confirmation

A Confirmation is a type of message used in the CUP to indicate the completion of BAD NEWS processing (in the sending node and all nodes uptree of that node).

4.14 Frame

"Frame" is the BNAv2 term for a BIAS™ protocol data unit (PDU).

4.15 Router Control Unit

A Router Control Unit (RCU) is a frame exchanged between BIAS™ routers containing control or routing information, but not user data.

4.16 Resistance Factor

BIAS™ uses two mutually additive metrics, known as Link Resistance Factor (*linkrf*) and Node Resistance Factor (*noderf*), in determining the cost or the relative desirability of transiting a link or node. The cost/distance to a destination is the Resistance Factor (*RF*) of the path, which is the sum of the linkrfs and noderfs along the path to the destination (excluding the source and destination noderfs). In general, paths of high resistance are less desirable than paths of low resistance.

The highest resistance factor value supported by the router update protocol is 65535.

A maximum resistance factor (*MAXRF*) is assigned at each node for the entire network that limits the acceptable cost from that node to any destination. No traffic is routed over a path whose resistance factor is greater than or equal to MAXRF. Any unusable path is assigned a Resistance Factor of MAXRF. (No larger value is ever assigned.)

4.17 Hop Count

The hop count of a path is the number of consecutive links in the path. This value is maintained in the router tables for each routing to every known destination.

A maximum hop count (*MAXHC*) is defined at each node for the entire network. No traffic is routed to a destination whose hop count is greater than or equal to MAXHC.

4.18 Fully Connected Network

A Fully Connected Network (*FCN*) is a grouping of nodes and links such that there is full interconnectivity under all anticipated conditions. Link Layer connections (or connectionless associations) are assigned to an FCN by an operator. A Public Data Network (PDN) or a Local Area Network (LAN), together with the nodes attached to it, normally may constitute an FCN. The FCN concept is used in an optimization of the routing update algorithm.

4.19 Max Seg Size

The maximum segment size (*Max Seg Size*) is a number calculated for each link and path.

For a link, the *Working Link Max Seg Size* represents the maximum size (in octets) of a frame that can be handled on the link. It is the minimum of the corresponding values specified for each endpoint of the link. These values are exchanged when the neighboring routers discover the link(s) between them.

The *Path Max Seg Size* of a routing is the minimum of the Max Seg Size values of all the links in the path. Thus, it represents the largest frame size that can be guaranteed to be supported across the path, from end to end.

There is a defined value, *Infinite Max Seg Size*, used in the routing update protocol, that corresponds to the largest segment size supported by BNAv2. (The value is 65535 octets, which is also the largest value representable in the protocol.)

5.0 ADDRESSING

The BIAS™ routing function uses hierarchical addressing based on the Kamoun/Kleinrock "cluster" addressing scheme for large networks [2]. Each address component, or *Id*, identifies a unit called a *Cluster*. BIAS™ employs four levels of cluster: subnetwork, super-cluster, simple-cluster and node. The subnetwork-id is the highest level of the addressing scheme followed by the super-cluster-id, simple-cluster-id, and node-id, respectively. A *Node Address* consists of all four levels of -ids. An *N-Cluster Address* contains all except the *N* lowest levels, for *N* between zero and three. Thus a Node Address is identical to a *0-Cluster Address*, and every Node is also a (*0-*)Cluster.[5]

If X is an *M*-Cluster, and Y is an *N*-Cluster, then we say "X is in Y", or "Y contains X", if $M<N$ and the (4-*N*) high order components of X's address are identical to (the components of) Y's address.

The *elements* of an *N*-Cluster Z are all the (*N-1*)-Clusters in Z.

The format for a Node Address in a BIAS™ frame header fits conveniently in the Domain Specific Part (DSP) of the ISO Network Service Access Point Address [6].

Node-ids must be unique within simple-clusters, simple-cluster-ids must be unique within super-clusters, and super-cluster-ids must be unique within subnetworks. As a result, the Node Addresses of all BNAv2 nodes are unique (if properly administered).

---

[5] The format for a Node Address in a BIAS™ frame header was intentionally designed to fit conveniently in the Domain Specific Part (DSP) of the ISO Network Service Access Point Address [6].

6.0 GUARANTEED DELIVERY OF RCUs

All Router Control Units (RCUs) for a given neighbor are sent over a single Link Layer connection to ensure that they are received in order. BIAS™ provides a guarantee of delivery of its own RCUs by using an acknowledgment procedure fashioned after the IEEE 802.2 Type 3 LLC class of service [4]. This type of operation may be summarized as "send one message, wait for the acknowledgment, retransmit on time out".

With such a protocol, there is a possibility that messages may be duplicated. Therefore, a one-bit sequence space is employed to guarantee that such a possibility does not result in the loss of a message (e.g., so that a duplicate message is not acknowledged instead of the next message).

7.0 ROUTING TABLES

BIAS™ uses three routing tables: *Routing-Table-Info* (*RTI*), *Routing-Table-Current* (*RTC*), and *Routing-Neighbor-Table* (*RNT*)[6].

The RTI is the table of all known routings from the local node to each reachable destination cluster/node. The following information is maintained in the RTI for each known destination:

- Destination Cluster Address
  (may be a node address)
- Total Confirmations Required
- Confirmations To Send
- List Of Routings, each containing:
  - Neighbor Node Address
  - Hop Count
  - Resistance Factor
  - Path Max Seg Size
  - Outstanding Confirmations

The RTC contains the current or in-use routing(s) for each known destination. The RTC is an abstract table that contains a list of best paths to a given destination. (Implementations may find it more desirable to use a single table, RTI.) The following information is maintained in the RTC for each known destination:

- Destination Cluster Address
- Hop Count

---
[6] The representation of the router tables in this article does not indicate all the information maintained by the BIAS™ Router. Some of that information has been left out because it is not germane to the router protocol.

- Resistance Factor
- Path Max Seg Size
- FCN Name (if any)
- Coordinated Update Procedure (CUP) State
  (FROZEN, UNFROZEN)
- FREEZE timer
- Destination Temporarily Unreachable
  (Boolean)
- TEMPORARY-UNREACHABLE timer
- List Of Neighbor Node Addresses
  (one for each In-Use Routing)

The ability to maintain a list of neighbor node addresses supports the load-splitting mechanism. The Resistance Factor and Path Max Seg Size are each required to be equal for all In-Use Routings.

The RNT contains information about the logical link to each neighbor node. The following is maintained in the RNT:

- Neighbor Node Address
- Working RF (see *Initialization* section)
- Working Link Max Seg Size (see *Initialization*)
- FCN Name (if any)

If a neighbor belongs to multiple FCNs (as determined by the corresponding link attributes), then a single FCN is picked for this table entry, using a deterministic algorithm that preference-orders the FCNs in the same way at all nodes. The FCN Name in this table (and in the RTC) is used to drive the FCN Optimization described later in this article.

8.0 LINKCHANGES AND NETCHANGES

LINKCHANGE and NETCHANGE messages are RCUs passed between neighbors to update their routing topology information.

LINKCHANGE messages are RCUs exchanged between neighbors when the status of the link(s) directly connecting the two nodes changes.

NETCHANGE messages are sent to neighbors to inform them of the status of destinations within the network and at what cost they may be reached (if their status indicates they are Reachable). The information in a NETCHANGE is obtained from the RTC. If there are no In-Use Routings to a destination, or if the Resistance Factor in the RTC is MAXRF, or if the Hop Count is MAXHC, then the destination is marked as Unreachable (in the NETCHANGE) and the Resistance Factor (in the NETCHANGE) is set to MAXRF. Otherwise, the destination is marked as Reachable; the Resistance Factor is set to the RTC value plus the local (sending) node's noderf; the Hop Count is set to the RTC value; and the Max Seg Size is set to the Path Max Seg Size value in the RTC.

Each NETCHANGE is marked as GOOD NEWS, BAD NEWS, or a Confirmation, with respect to an indicated destination.[7] The determination of whether a NETCHANGE is GOOD or BAD NEWS is made by the *Update RTI* and *Select Best Routing* Functions described later in this article.

9.0 BNAv2 NETWORK LAYER

In OSI terminology, the BNAv2 Network Layer is composed of a connectionless protocol machine, a layer management process, and a routing process. BNAv2 uses the *Protocol for Providing the Connectionless-mode Network Service* (ISO 8473) for data frames. However, since BNA performs its frame segmentation/reassembly in the Transport Layer (Port Level), the non-segmenting subset is currently always selected, i.e., the Don't Segment Flag is set and the segmentation part is not included in the frame header. The layer management process interacts with a system management process and other layer managers to coordinate system operation. The layer management process controls initialization and termination of the protocol machine and routing process, and supervises their operating phase.

MAXRF, MAXHC, average segment size, and the node addresses are the only items which need to be predefined on a network-wide basis for the routing function. Defaults exist for all of these except the node addresses. Each node address is predefined at its local node; all other (destination) addresses can be automatically discovered.

The routing process is BIAS™, and is described in the following sections.

10.0 BIAS™ ROUTING FUNCTION

The primary functions of BIAS™ include

- routing locally-originated data traffic from the Port Level to some destination;

- routing locally-destined data traffic to the Port Level; and

- routing transit traffic (data generated at some remote originating node for some other remote destination node using a path through the local node).

Additional functions include responding and adapting to changes in the network topology, allowing operator control of the routing function, determining the compatibility of the neighbor (i.e., negotiating a common router protocol version, checking the validity of the neighbor's address, and verifying the password supplied by the neighbor, if any), and providing operational analysis tools.

As used within BNAv2 networks, the BIAS™ routing function can be performed using any combination or sequence of connection-oriented services from the Link Layer. In particular, the connections involved need not guarantee delivery or even maintain order. They must, however, guarantee the integrity of individual data units and must report failure of the connection. This is due to the facts that the Router provides its own guarantees of delivery for the control frames used to exchange routing information, and that it depends on the Link Layer to inform it when links to neighbor nodes have failed.

The remaining sections deal directly with the functional capabilities of the router.

11.0 INITIALIZATION

After link layer connectivity (reachability) has been established between two (neighbor) nodes, a series of GREETING messages are exchanged. GREETINGs are performed to verify compatibility between the nodes. If the nodes are incompatible GREETINGs fail, and the Link Layer connection is terminated.

Upon successful completion of the GREETINGs process, LINKCHANGE messages are exchanged between the two nodes. The LINKCHANGE message indicates the sending node's view of the link between it and its neighbor. LINKCHANGE messages may also be sent at any time subsequent to the GREETING process if the local node detects a change in the link's status.

Each of the two neighbor nodes calculates the resistance factor (the Working RF) of the link between them; that is, each node averages its own view of the linkrf and its neighbor's view of the linkrf. This calculation guarantees that the two neighbors have the same perception of the linkrf of the link that connects them.

The Working Link Max Seg Size is also calculated by the two neighbors, in this case using the minimum of the two views.

Multiple links can exist in parallel between two neighbors. These links are collectively referred to as a *link bundle*. In this case, the linkrf value in each LINKCHANGE reflects the combined capacity of all the links, and a single Working RF is calculated for the link bundle. Similar-

---

[7] The BIAS™ protocol (and BNAv2 implementations) support the blocking of multiple NETCHANGEs into a single RCU.

ly, the Working Link Max Seg Size of the link bundle is set to the minimum of the values for the various component links. A link bundle is treated as a single link by the routing update mechanism.

Once the Working Linkrf and the Working Link Max Seg Size are calculated, the local node sends NETCHANGE messages to the neighbor node about the local node itself as (an entry point to) an N-Cluster, for each value of N such that the neighbor is not in the same N-Cluster as the local node. This, of course, always includes the local Node itself, as a 0-Cluster. The Resistance Factor and Hop Count in these NETCHANGEs is always zero (0). The Max Seg Size value in these NETCHANGEs is the local node's N-Cluster Max Seg Size. This is zero (0) for the local node itself (the 0-Cluster). For each other (non-zero) value of N, it is defined as the minimum Path Max Seg Size of all RTC entries for destinations within the local node's own N-Cluster.

After receiving the initial NETCHANGE messages from all of its known neighbors, the local node sends NETCHANGE messages to each of its neighbors about other remote destinations that it can reach, and their associated costs.[8]

12.0 ROUTING UPDATE ALGORITHM

The purpose of the Routing Update Algorithm is to maintain in each node in the network the best routings to each known destination. A destination is defined to be a cluster and is identified by a cluster address. The best routing(s) is(are) defined to be the path(s) with the lowest Resistance Factor, and, among those, the one(s) with the largest Path Max Seg Size.

The results of the Routing Update Algorithm, including the identification of the In-Use routings, are stored in the Router Tables.

The update mechanism is performed (logically) independently for each destination cluster. The action taken in response to an event depends on what type of news is to be distributed to neighbors.

After the results of a change are stored in the RTI, the local node determines whether the impact constitutes GOOD or BAD NEWS, or, perhaps, no news at all (i.e., no change in the local node's routing metrics to the destination). This is done by the *Update RTI* and, where appropriate, *Select Best Routing* Functions, as described below.

If the change has no impact on the routing metrics to the destination, then no further action is required. Otherwise, the change must be distributed to the node's neighbors by means of NETCHANGE messages.

Two different procedures are required for the distribution of NETCHANGE messages. The Independent Update Procedure (IUP) is used for sending GOOD NEWS. This procedure has been demonstrated [3] to be efficient and loop free when the NETCHANGE message is distributed relative to non-increasing costs, but has proven to be inefficient and subject to loops for increasing costs. Therefore, a Coordinated Update Procedure (CUP) has been developed for the distribution of BAD NEWS [1]. Both of these procedures are further described later in this section.

12.1 Rules for Sending NETCHANGE Messages

The clustering scheme of BNAv2 network addressing allows a reduction in the table space and message traffic used to store and exchange routing information. To do this, only the following information is included in NETCHANGE messages from the local node to a neighbor:[9]

- information relating to other subnetworks (3-Clusters);

- information about N-Clusters within either the neighbor's or the local node's own $(N+1)$-Cluster, except for the neighbor's own N-Cluster (for each N between 0 and 2).

When several NETCHANGEs must be sent at the same time to a neighbor, they may be blocked into one message (RCU).

Additional optimization may be performed to reduce the amount of information exchanged between neighbors, based on the FCN concept. This is described in the *FCN Optimization* section.

For any given destination, the set of neighbors that the local node will send NETCHANGEs to (about that destination) are referred to as the *relevant* neighbors of the local node (with respect to the subject destination).

---

[8] In addition, current implementations of BIAS™ exchange a complete set of NETCHANGEs (about all reachable destinations) whenever a later LINKCHANGE exchange is completed.

[9] The early releases of BNAv2 do not support communication between different subnetworks.

12.2 Changes to the Local Noderf

Whenever the local node's noderf changes (for example, due to operator input), NETCHANGEs must be sent about every reachable destination. If the noderf decreased, these will be GOOD NEWS; if it increased, they will be BAD NEWS and the local node initiates the CUP and enters the FROZEN state for each destination after sending the NETCHANGEs. The NETCHANGEs are sent to all of the relevant neighbors for each respective destination.

Note that this process involves no changes to the local node's routing tables, other than those required for CUP bookkeeping (in the BAD NEWS case).

12.3 Update RTI Function

The local node updates its RTI whenever it receives information about changes to links or paths. In each such case, the node performs all the updates to the RTI that it can. This function can be performed with respect to a given destination or a particular neighbor.

Improvement of the RTI, relative to a routing to a particular destination, is caused by:

1) Receipt of a NETCHANGE message containing GOOD NEWS about the destination (unless the Hop Count to the destination in the NETCHANGE is greater than or equal to MAXHC minus one). In this case, the RTI entry for the path to that destination via the source neighbor is created (if not already present) and then updated to reflect: a Resistance Factor equal to the value received in the NETCHANGE plus the Working RF in the RNT for the source neighbor (up to a limit of MAXRF); a Hop Count equal to the value in the NETCHANGE plus one (up to a limit of MAXHC); and a Path Max Seg Size equal to the minimum of the value received in the NETCHANGE and the Working Link Max Seg Size in the RNT for the source neighbor.

2) A decrease in the Working RF of a link bundle. In this case, the RTI entry for each destination reachable via the neighbor has its Resistance Factor reduced by an amount equal to the decrease in the Working RF.

3) A change in the Working Link Max Seg Size of a link bundle to a neighbor; changes; in this case, the RTI entry for each destination reachable via the neighbor has its Path Max Seg Size set to the minimum of the previous value in the entry and the new value for the link bundle.

Deterioration of the RTI, relative to a routing to a particular destination, is caused by:

1) Receipt of a NETCHANGE about the destination, containing BAD NEWS or containing GOOD NEWS with a Hop Count greater than or equal to MAXHC minus one. The RTI update in this case is identical to that performed in *Improvement* case (1) above.

2) An increase in the Working RF of a link bundle to a neighbor. In this case, the RTI entry for each destination reachable via the neighbor has its Resistance Factor increased (up to a limit of MAXRF) by an amount equal to the increase in the Working RF.

3) The failure or removal of the (last) link to a neighbor. In this case, all RTI entries for paths to any destination via the neighbor are removed (or, equivalently, have their Resistance Factors set to MAXRF).

After updating its RTI, the local node then performs the *Select Best Routing* function (as described below) for the destination if the RTI update constituted an Improvement. *Select Best Routing* is also performed if the RTI update constituted a Deterioration for one, but not all, of the (multiple) In-Use Routings for the destination.

If the RTI update is a Deterioration of the last (or only) In-Use Routing for the subject destinations, the local node makes a corresponding update to the metrics of the RTC entry for the destination, changes its update state to FROZEN, and then sends a (BAD NEWS) NETCHANGE to each of its relevant neighbors about the destination (without invoking *Select Best Routing*).

If the RTI update is a Deterioration, but does not affect an In-Use Routing, then no action is taken after updating the RTI.

12.4 Select Best Routing Function

The *Select Best Routing* function is performed whenever it is necessary to derive a new set of routings for a destination about which routing metrics have been modified.

In examining entries in the RTI (or RTC), the complete lack of entries for a given destination is equivalent to an indication that the subject destination is unreachable, which is in turn equivalent to the "path" to that destination having a resistance factor of MAXRF.

The router examines the RTI entries for the subject destination which have Hop Count values less than MAXHC and Resistance Factor values less than MAXRF, and finds those among them that have the smallest Resistance Factor. Among those it chooses the one(s) with the largest Path Max Seg Size. These entries constitute the set of New Routings-to-Use, and define a set of associated routing metrics: Resistance Factor, Path Max Seg Size, and Hop Count. (If the Hop Count differs among the selected entries, the metric used is the minimum of the values represented.) If the set of New Routings-to-Use is null, this indicates that the destination is now unreachable; in this case, the Resistance Factor is considered to be MAXRF and the other metrics are undefined.

Having determined a set of New Routings-to-Use for a subject destination, the metrics associated with that set of new routings are compared against the metrics currently in the RTC for the destination. This comparison results in a classification of the update result as either Unchanged, Good, or Bad, as follows:

Unchanged: All routing metrics remain the same (although the set of routings may have changed), and the set of routings either were and remain non-null, or were and remain null.

Good: The Resistance Factor has decreased, or the Resistance Factor is unchanged and either Hop Count or Path Max Seg Size (or both) have changed, or the set of routings was previously null but is now non-null.

Bad: The Resistance Factor has increased, or the set of routings was previously non-null and is now null.

If the update result is either Unchanged or Good, the In-Use Routings (and metrics) for the destination (in the RTC) are now replaced by the New Routings-to-Use (and their associated metrics).

If the update result is Bad, the current entry for this destination (in the RTC) is altered to reflect the metrics associated with the corresponding routings (those via the **same** neighbors) in the RTI. If the metrics of these RTI entries now differ, those chosen are those of an entry (from this set) with the minimum value of Resistance Factor and, if several such exist, one of those with the maximum value of Path Max Seg Size. However, the In-Use Routings continue to designate the same neighbor(s) as before. The CUP state is then set to FROZEN.

For either a Good or Bad result, the local node now sends an appropriate NETCHANGE to all of its relevant neighbors.

12.5 Independent Update Procedure

When a local node has GOOD NEWS to distribute, it sends a NETCHANGE message containing the GOOD NEWS to each of its relevant neighbors. The neighbor interprets the NETCHANGE message to mean that the originator's best path (least resistance) to the destination has the new (better) resistance factor indicated in the NETCHANGE message. The NETCHANGE recipient performs the *Update RTI* function, using the information provided in the message, and selects its best routing(s) to the destination, as described above.

If the NETCHANGE recipient's best routing to the destination changes as a result of processing the NETCHANGE message, it updates its RTC and sends a NETCHANGE to each of its relevant neighbors. If the network topology remains constant, then, after a finite number of exchanges, every node in the network will have recorded its new best routing to the destination.

12.6 Coordinated Update Procedure

BAD NEWS is distributed independently for each destination. When a linkrf increases (which includes the case of a link failing within a link bundle while other good links remain in that bundle), or when (the last link in) a link bundle fails, the local node performs the *Update RTI* Function. Note that the loss of a link bundle means that all destinations are unreachable via the neighbor involved. If the result of the RTI update is a Deterioration of the route to some destination, the node then initiates the CUP, as described below. (For completeness, the sequence below includes some actions taken by the *Update RTI* Function.)

The node first updates its tables (RTI and RTC) for the affected routing, but does not change its In-Use Routing(s) to the destination. The local node then enters the FROZEN state for that destination. While in the FROZEN state, a node may update its RTI with respect to the destination, but does not change its In-Use Routing(s) to the destination in its RTC at this time. This prevents a loop from forming due to an uptree node having a lower resistance while in the FROZEN state.

The local node next notifies all of its relevant neighbors of the BAD NEWS via a NETCHANGE message.

When a node receives a BAD NEWS NETCHANGE, it performs the *Update RTI* Function. If that function determines that the local impact of the change is (again) a Deterioration - because the local node is uptree of the source of the BAD

NEWS - then the recipient node enters the FROZEN state, and, in turn, notifies all of its relevant neighbors about the BAD NEWS. This process continues until all of the neighbors receiving BAD NEWS from a FROZEN node are themselves "unaffected nodes" relative to this BAD NEWS. An "unaffected node" is one for which the best path to the destination is not through the neighbor from which it receives the BAD NEWS (i.e., it is not uptree of that neighbor). If the recipient node is load-splitting (has multiple In-Use Routings for the destination), it is always unaffected. (A Deterioration on one of several In-Use Routings does not generate BAD NEWS, although the Routing involved is removed from the set of In-Use Routings.)

Each node that is FROZEN and has sent out BAD NEWS waits until all of its relevant neighbors have informed it that they have updated their RTIs and (if appropriate) RTCs. They do this by returning CUP Confirmations.

When an unaffected node receives BAD NEWS, it immediately returns a Confirmation to the neighbor that sent the BAD NEWS, and then performs the *Update RTI* Function, using the information in the NETCHANGE.

Only after receiving Confirmations from all of its relevant neighbors can the FROZEN node itself unfreeze and, if necessary, send out its own Confirmation. The Confirmations thus proceed downtree towards the original source of the BAD NEWS.[10]

Once a node leaves the FROZEN state, it selects the best routing to the destination from its updated RTI, and updates its RTC, using the *Select Best Routing* Function. Each node then performs the IUP, as it recognizes from its RTC that new best routings exist to the destination, and disseminates the corresponding GOOD NEWS.

12.7 Handling Data for Unreachable Destinations during the Coordinated Update Procedure

The CUP has the property that, during the distribution of BAD NEWS, some destination(s) may be temporarily unreachable from some of the nodes in the network.

The reason for this is that, during the CUP, a node in the FROZEN state is not permitted to use information maintained in its RTI for the subject destination. This restriction is imposed because the knowledge of the topology maintained in the RTI during the CUP may be obsolete; i.e., it is based on the information about the state of the network before the update. Thus, some of the paths may be incorrect. In the RTI, for example, all neighbors offer potential paths to a given destination, but many simply offer a path which sends a frame out to the neighbor only to have it returned by the neighbor on the same link. This is called a "loop-back" path. If a destination is unreachable from a node, and the node is allowed to use a "loop-back" path from its RTI, the node may cause frames to loop during the time of the routing update mechanism, unless it is specifically prohibited from doing so.

In order to avoid this "loop-back" situation, a node that is participating in the update must wait until it is sure that the paths maintained in its RTI for the destination are correct; that is, until it can evaluate all possible paths (and build a new RTC) before handling information frames. Hence, it must wait until it is taken out of the FROZEN state.

When a destination is temporarily unreachable, the Network Layer attempts to avoid losing any frames received (either from the local Port Level or as transit frames) for that destination. The node will attempt to tank such frames (e.g., by queueing them in a temporary queue) for as long as system resources allow it to do so. If resources are exhausted, these frames are discarded[11].

12.8 Handling Update State Transitions

Each time a node enters the FROZEN state for any destination, it starts a FREEZE timer. This timer bounds the amount of time the node waits before it assumes that CUP Confirmations will not arrive. The Router in the node may be tanking Router Information Units in transit to the destination, for all or a part of this time.

If the update state for the destination remains FROZEN when the FREEZE timer expires, the frames temporarily queued are discarded. The router acts as if it has received all of the outstanding

---

[10] The BIAS™ CUP protocol (and BNAv2 implementations) allow for the simultaneous occurrence of multiple BAD NEWS updates affecting a common destination. In such cases, a node remains FROZEN until Confirmations have been received for all such updates, and then sends the appropriate number of Confirmations to its downtree neighbor.

[11] BNA treats the lifetime of a RIU as a strict hop count; hence, to avoid introducing excessive duplicate frames into the network, the Port Level acknowledgment timeout should be set to a value longer than the sum of the time limits on the FREEZE timer and the TEMPORARY-UNREACHABLE timer (described in the next section).

CUP Confirmations it is expecting; that is, it forces a transition to the UNFROZEN state, sends Confirmation(s) to its downtree neighbor (if necessary), and disseminates the GOOD NEWS. If Confirmations arrive at some later time, the router discards them.

When the state of the update for a destination changes from FROZEN to UNFROZEN, and if the destination remains unreachable, the TEMPORARY-UNREACHABLE timer is set. This timer bounds the amount of time that the node continues to wait in anticipation of receipt of a NETCHANGE message describing the reachability of the destination via the IUP. If system resources exist, the node continues to tank in-transit frames.

If a destination becomes reachable (due to an Improvement in the RTI during the *Update RTI* Function), then the TEMPORARY-UNREACHABLE timer is reset, the RTC is recomputed and the GOOD NEWS disseminated (using the *Select Best Routing* Function), and the frames are requeued to the neighbor through which the destination can now be reached (possibly the same neighbor as before).

If the TEMPORARY-UNREACHABLE timer expires, the *Select Best Routing* Function is used to recompute the RTC. If the destination remains unreachable, any in-transit frames being held for this destination are discarded.

13.0 FCN OPTIMIZATION

A Fully Connected Network (FCN) is a set of BNA nodes and links where each node has a direct connection to every other node in the set, using a link in the set. Membership in an FCN is specified by a network or system operator or administrator as a Link Layer attribute. The FCN attribute is exchanged by neighbor routers during the GREETINGS process. FCNs are useful during the update process for reducing the number of update messages that need to be distributed.

When FCN optimization is used, the rules for sending NETCHANGEs are altered as follows:

NETCHANGEs are not sent via an FCN when the best path to the subject destination is via the same FCN. If a destination's best path changes to be via an FCN, the local node sends a NETCHANGE to each of its neighbors in the same FCN, informing them that the destination is unreachable through the local node. If an existing neighbor of the local node becomes a neighbor via an FCN (but was not previously a neighbor via that FCN), the local node sends NETCHANGEs to this new (FCN) neighbor informing it that all the destinations for which the local node's best path is via the same FCN are unreachable via the local node.

The FCN optimization is especially useful for LANs and PDNs. It may also be useful for sets of nodes fully connected by mixed media, providing they satisfy the appropriate constraints and assumptions. The network operator or administrator has control over the grouping of sets of nodes (and links) into FCNs.

14.0 HANDLING CLUSTER PARTITIONS

14.1 Normal Routing Path Constraints

The visibility of routing information, based on the rules described in this article, is such that paths within a particular cluster X are restricted to sequences of nodes in X, possibly including one or more bridges. A *bridge* for a cluster X is a sequence of three nodes on a path such that the first and last nodes are both members of cluster X, and the middle node is not a member of cluster X.

14.2 Partition Handling

When links (or nodes) within a cluster fail or are removed in such a way that some of the destinations within the cluster become unreachable from some node(s) within the cluster, under the normal routing path constraints, that cluster is said to have become *partitioned*. In the case that no such path exists, but a physical path is available, within the subnetwork as a whole, there are ways to make use of the path outside the normal routing path constraints. This is known as the *partition handling* mechanism.

The basic notion used in the partition handling mechanism is the classification of the connectivity of any given cluster into two states: *connected* and *non-connected*. The connected state is the normal operational state of a cluster, defined by every cluster element being reachable from every other cluster element, using paths that obey the normal routing constraints.

The non-connected state implies one of two substates: *partitioned* and *isolated*. Partitioned indicates that some of the elements of the cluster X cannot be reached via paths that obey the normal routing constraints, but are reachable via other paths within the subnetwork. Isolated indicates that some element(s) of the cluster X cannot be reached from other element(s) of the subnetwork via any possible path.[12]

---

[12] A set of elements of a cluster which can maintain connectivity among themselves but which are isolated from all other elements in a subnetwork may continue to act as a separate subnetwork.

Partitions are hidden through the use of cocooning. *Cocooning* is a method of providing paths that violate the normal routing path constraints, at the cost of additional network (and application) protocol overhead and routing table space. While cocooning, data frames are encapsulated with an additional router header. A cocoon is woven around a partitioned cluster X by means of Port Level connections among the routers in a set of nodes that are neighbors to X. Further details are beyond the scope of this article.

15.0 CONCLUSION

With the substantial improvements introduced into Version 2, BIAS™ provides a highly resilient and responsive routing function while imposing considerably less processing and memory overhead than its Version 1 and MERIT ancestors. We believe that BIAS™ compares favorably with other routing schemes used in many private and multi-vendor networks today.

16.0 ACKNOWLEDGMENTS

The authors would like to acknowledge Robert Donecker, James Hopkins, Jerzy Sliwinski, and Scott Stein, with whom we had the privilege of developing the BIAS™ Routing Function.

17.0 REFERENCES

[1] J. Jaffe and M. Moss, "A Responsive Distributed Routing Algorithm for Computer Networks," *IEEE Transactions on Communications*, vol. COM-30, pp. 1758-1762, July 1982.

[2] F. Kamoun and L. Kleinrock, "Hierarchical Routing for Large Networks," *Computer Networks*, vol. 1, pp. 155-174, 1977.

[3] W. Tajibnapis, "A Correctness Proof of a Topology Information Maintenance Protocol for Distributed Computer Networks," *Communications of the Association for Computing Machinery*, vol. 20, pp. 477-485, July 1977.

[4] ANSI/IEEE Standard 802.2. IEEE Standards for Local Area Networks: Logical Link Control.

[5] ISO 8473, Information Processing Systems - Data Communications - Protocol for Providing the Connectionless-mode Network Service (DIS version, May 1984).

[6] ISO 8348/DAD2, Information Processing Systems - Data Communications - Addendum to the Network Service Definition Covering Network Layer Addressing.

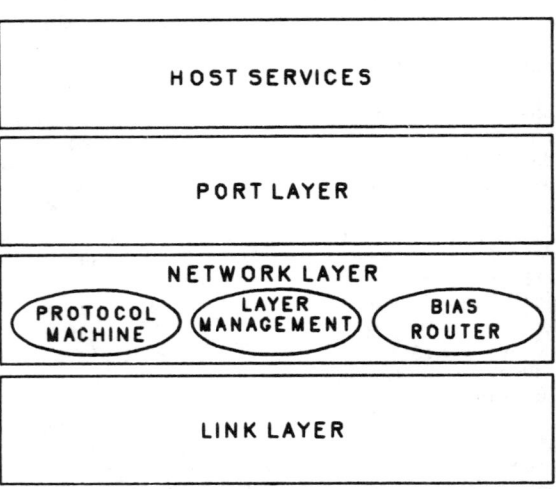

FIGURE 1: BNA OVERVIEW

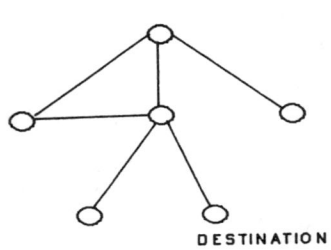

A: NETWORK CONFIGURATION

B: SPANNING TREE OF THE NETWORK CONFIGURATION

FIGURE 2: SPANNING TREE TO A DESTINATION

AN ARCHITECTURE FOR NETWORK-LAYER ROUTING IN OSI

Paul F. Tsuchiya
The MITRE Corporation

ABSTRACT

Work on the standardization of routing protocols for OSI is in progress. The envisioned set of routing protocols is expected to work in nearly all of the environments which constitute OSI networks. Behind these routing protocols is an architecture which outlines problems and goals, establishes a framework upon which to base the development of protocols, and provides a conceptual baseline for continued work on unsolved problems. This architecture defines routing in the OSI network layer, functionally partitions the problem into its components, defines a routing hierarchy and an address hierarchy and discusses their relationship, and discusses arms-length routing relationships between differently administered networks. This paper presents that architecture, and discusses problems which remain to be solved as work progresses towards a global OSI network.

1. INTRODUCTION

In the International Organization for Standardization (ISO) Open Systems Interconnection (OSI) suite of data communications protocols, mature point-to-point communications standards exist for all seven layers of the reference model. Missing, however, are the various management standards (including routing standards) required to facilitate the operation of open systems. This paper concerns itself with the problem of routing in OSI, and the ongoing effort to define network layer routing standards for OSI.

In ISO, the primary motivation for network layer routing work has come from the American National Standards Institute (ANSI) Accredited Standards Committee (ASC) X3S3.3, Network and Transport Layer. In X3S3.3, work has been going on for several years to develop routing protocols for the network layer. This work has spawned the relatively mature DIS 9542, "End System to Intermediate System Routing Exchange Protocol for use in conjunction with the Protocol for the Provision of the Connectionless-mode Network Service (ISO 8473)" (ES-IS). A parallel effort for an ES-IS for use with ISO 8208 (ISO's X.25) is also underway. Further, solid and complete proposals for Intermediate System to Intermediate System (IS-IS) Routing within a single administrative domain have been submitted to X3S3.3 for consideration. (I apologize for this early barrage of alphabet soup. These concepts will be explained later in the paper.)

Behind these efforts is a set of architectural principles which are guiding the protocol developments. These architectural principles are continuously evolving as the problem of global routing in OSI is contemplated and solutions are put forth. They are based on X3S3.3's understanding of 1) the OSI environment, 2) the problems associated with that environment, 3) routing architectures, and 4) routing techniques.

This paper, then, describes the set of architectural principles which is guiding the development of routing protocols in ISO. The purpose of this paper is both to distribute information and to solicit comments. It represents not the final word on routing in the global OSI environment—rather, it represents the current position in an evolving process. Input to this process from as many communities as possible is requested.

2. DEFINITION OF ROUTING

When we say "routing", we refer to all of the procedures involved in building a routing table and relaying individual Protocol Data Units (PDUs). Routing consists of several component parts, which are illustrated in Figure 1.

In Figure 1 we see two kinds of flow—data flow and information flow. Data flow is flow that enters and leaves a System through PDUs. Information flow is internal to the System. (System is short for End System and/or Intermediate System.)

There are two types of data flows which invoke routing procedures: Routing PDUs and Data PDUs. Routing PDUs are those PDUs which are exchanged between systems to collect or distribute routing information such as link status, reachable Systems, and so on. Data PDUs are those PDUs, such as ISO 8473 packets, upon which a routing action must be made. We call this relaying, and it is decomposed into three functions: the Locate Function, the Route Function, and the Forward Function.

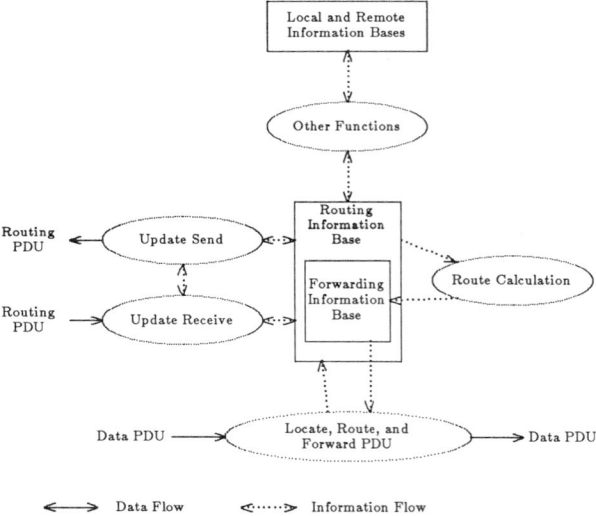

Figure 1

The Locate Function examines the destination Network Address—specifically, the Network Service Access Point (NSAP) Address in the case of ESs, and the Network Entity Title (NET) in the case of ISs—of the PDU and determines where (in the routing hierarchy) the destination ES is. This may be a simple masking operation on the address itself to extract the so called "routing information", or it may be a table or directory lookup function if the address contains no routing information. Relaying data PDUs is much simpler when the hierarchy location information is embedded in the Network Address in the data PDU. However, getting the hierarchy location information into the Network Address in the first place is not trivial.

The Route Function is what is often thought of as "routing". It is the function which returns the Network Address of the next hop when given the location of the destination ES derived from the Locate Function.

The Forwarding Function returns the Subnetwork Point of Attachment (SNPA) when given the Network Address of the next hop. An Ethernet address or an X.121 address are examples of SNPAs.

In addition, we define a data base called the Routing Information Base (RIB). This data base contains all information pertinent to routing, such as local link status, a network topology map, and so on. A subset of the RIB is the Forwarding Information Base (FIB). This data base contains the information which is directly accessed when the relaying functions are performed. It is what is often thought of as a "routing table"—that is, a list of destinations and the next hop to those destinations. The Route Calculation Function derives the FIB from information in the RIB.

Finally, we show Other Functions and the Local and Remote Information Bases in Figure 1. This is "everything else" routing procedures might require, such as directory service access, authentication information, and so on.

2.1. OSI Environment

In this following paragraphs, we describe the environment within which routing is expected to take place.

There will be a virtually unlimited number of ESs and ISs. An ES is the source or destination of data traffic. An IS relays traffic between ESs and/or other ISs. In particular, there will be many more ESs than ISs.

There will be collections of interconnected Systems which are administered by a single entity (a corporation, for instance). These collections of Systems, called Administrative Domains, will be routing traffic to and through other Administrative Domains. These Administrative Domains may not trust each other, however, and will require autonomy from each other and protection from each other's failures.

There will be very diverse means of transmission between Systems. These include direct links ranging in capacity from dial-up modems to fiber optic, Local Area Networks (LANs), satellites, packet switched data networks, and so on. These transmissions may be interconnected in any arbitrary fashion.

Systems in the OSI environment fall under a global addressing structure (ISO 8348/AD 2, "Network Service Definition - Addendum 2: Network Layer Addressing") which by definition allows addresses to be structured differently by different communities. In particular, it frees the assignment of addresses from necessarily being constrained by routing considerations.

The routing should be as automatic as possible. In particular, the routing protocols should to the extent possible automatically discover the appearance or disappearance of Systems and links, and to modify routes accordingly.

3. NETWORK LAYER ROUTING ARCHITECTURE

In this section, we develop the different but related components of the routing architecture—the routing hierarchy and its relation to the addressing hierarchy; the four functional tiers of routing; and the nature of routing and routing agreements between different Administrative Domains.

3.1. The Routing Hierarchy

As soon as one recognizes that a set of Systems (this Administrative Domain) wishes to distinguish itself from another set of Systems (that Administrative Domain) *for the purposes of routing*, one has embraced the notion of a routing hierarchy (as opposed to an addressing hierarchy, which is an entirely different thing). Any time a set of entities have been grouped such that they can be treated externally as a single entity, a hierarchy has been formed. If only one such level of grouping exists, then a two-level hierarchy results. If groups are recursively grouped, then a multiple level hierarchy results. (We avoid the temptation to provide a figure here. A drawing of the hierarchy must necessarily be simple, and invariably seems to mislead more than it enlightens.)

The address of a System may or may not correspond to the System's group memberships—that is, the address hierarchy may or may not correspond to the routing hierarchy. We say that an address corresponds to a grouping when all of the members of the group can be identified as belonging to the group, and all non-members of the group can be identified as not belonging to the group, by merely examining the address of the member or non-member. In addition, there must be paths between all group members—that is, it must be possible to get from one group member to another group member without going through a non-member (this is true for a routing hierarchy, not for an address hierarchy).

In this architecture, we have three reasons for grouping Systems, or for grouping groups of Systems. Each grouping has an impact on how routing is done. We therefore have three different names for groups.

The first reason for grouping is simply to reduce the amount of routing information which must be spread around, thus achieving greater efficiency. This sort of grouping has been thoroughly studied in many contexts, but in particular by Kleinrock and Kamoun, and by Hagouel, in the context of data networks. We call this type of group a Cluster. Within Clusters and between Clusters, there is full trust, full agreement on routing procedures (algorithms, metrics, and so on)—in other words, no autonomy—and a high correspondence between clustering and addressing. This is not to say that there isn't a difference between intra-Cluster routing procedures and inter-Cluster routing procedures. For instance, handling cluster partitions (the situation where a message between two members of a Cluster cannot, in fact, be delivered without leaving the cluster) requires different intra-cluster and inter-cluster procedures. It is worth noting that many of the efficiencies achieved by clustering are lost if there is not a high correspondence between the clusters and the addresses.

The second reason for grouping Systems is because one group of Systems has different routing procedures than another group of Systems—in other words, the two groups are largely autonomous. We call this group a Routing Domain. We assume full trust between Routing Domains, and a maximum of autonomy. We say maximum (as opposed to full) here because full autonomy is not achievable in practice. For instance, if the efficiency benefits of consistent addressing are desired, then the Routing Domains do not have complete autonomy for choosing addresses. A better example, however, is that the two Routing Domains must use common routing procedures to talk to each other. These *exterior* routing procedures may have an impact on how the *interior* routing procedures must behave, thus limiting autonomy.

For instance, assume three Routing Domains A, B, and C, with A and B connected, and B and C connected, but with A and C not connected. Assume further that the border ISs (those which share a link with ISs in other Routing Domains) participate in the exterior routing procedures, and that all ISs participate in their respective interior routing procedures. Now, for traffic to pass from A to C, traffic must be forwarded from B's border IS with A to B's border IS with C. For this to happen, either 1) the interior ISs of B must have an awareness of the world outside of Routing Domain B, 2) or the border ISs of B must have some way of getting traffic to each other without requiring that the interior ISs have a notion of the world outside—the border ISs must either be directly connected, or they must tunnel through the interior ISs, either by enveloping the original packet, or by partial source routing (a feature of ISO 8473). In any event, the internal operation of Routing Domain B is effected by B's relationship with other Routing Domains, thus limiting true autonomy.

The third reason for grouping Systems is administrative commonality among those Systems—or, more to the point, a lack of administrative commonality between different groups of Systems. We call these groups Administrative Domains. In particular, there is a maximum of autonomy between Administrative Domains, there is a lack of trust, and there are very specific notions about where traffic may and may not go. Because of this, there is the notion of contractual agreements between Administrative Domains which determine whether the Administrative Domains will accept traffic from each other, and determine for which (if any) other Administrative Domains they will forward traffic. In particular, only routing information which is valid according to a set of agreements should be exchanged. This allows an Administrative Domain to protect itself from learning about routes which it does not wish to use (for security or legal reasons, for instance). It also limits the amount of potentially incorrect routing information an Administrative Domain can receive by limiting the set of other Administrative Domains which can pass third party information. However, it does so at the expense of dynamic and automatic configuration.

3.1.1. Structure of the Routing Hierarchy

In general, Clusters can consist of Systems and/or lower level Clusters. Routing Domains can consist of Systems and/or Clusters. Administrative Domains can consist of Routing Domains and lower level Administrative Domains. Beyond this, the architecture does not specify how groups may be arranged. For instance, they may overlap in arbitrary ways. The complexity of the arrangement of the hierarchies will be determined by the routing protocols, not by the architecture.

There will not be one global monolithic routing hierarchy. Instead, there will many separate routing hierarchies. Each of these separate routing hierarchies can be viewed as an Administrative Domain, and the global routing structure will consist of a flat (non-hierarchical) super-network of Administrative Domains, tightly or loosely coupled according to agreements made between Administrative Domains.

3.2. Addressing Hierarchy

The NSAP addressing hierarchy, on the other hand, is a global monolithic structure in that it is defined by ISO (ISO 8348/AD 2, "Network Service Definition - Addendum 2: Network Layer Addressing"), which specifies portions of the NSAP address space. The maximum NSAP address is 20 octets long. ISO 8348/AD 2 is designed to facilitate the assignment of globally unique NSAP addresses while accommodating (or more appropriately, subsuming) all existing standardized ISO and CCITT addresses. The technique for guaranteeing globally unique addresses is to recursively assign portions of the address to lower addressing authorities who are instructed to further parse the address as necessary. For instance, ISO has assigned a certain range of addresses to ANSI (specifically, all addresses where the first octet is hex 38 or 39, and the next octet and a half are hex 840). ANSI, as an address authority, then will break that space up into smaller chunks to be handed to different organizations. These organizations may take their space and further divide it among sub-organizations, and so on. This recursive assignment essentially defines the address hierarchy.

After some number of recursions (hopefully not too many), some address authority will receive an address space which it hopes to parse in accordance with a routing hierarchy. It is not necessarily the case that at this point the remaining portion of the address must be parsed the same way by all Systems within this routing hierarchy. For instance, the address/routing authority may further assign the address by giving ranges to each of several regional networks, which may operate independently but communicate with each other extensively. Each of the regional networks may be quite different in composition, and may wish to parse their address spaces differently. This will work, however, because it is not necessary for Systems in Region A to understand how Systems in Region B parse their addresses. It is only necessary for Systems in Region A to recognize that an address is, in fact, in Region B, and to route it to a Region B System. The Region B System will then further parse the address for routing within its region.

It is not even necessary for the address/routing authority to assign the same size ranges to the regions. As long as one region (group) has a method to tell the other region which range (or ranges) of addresses are in its region, routing can take place. A typical method for doing this is to use a mask to indicate where the significant bits of address are, and an address to indicate the value of those bits. This technique is used both in the Internet Control Message Protocol (ICMP) Subnet Mask, and in ISO 9542.

3.3. Four Functional Tiers of Routing

Having defined a hierarchy for routing, we must consider the development of one or more routing protocols for use in that hierarchy. One option might be to define one standard which accomplished routing at all hierarchical levels. This, however, is not an appropriate approach for several reasons. First, we know how to do routing at only some levels of the hierarchy. If we try to delay any routing standards until we know how to do all routing, the development of useful routing protocols which can be of use in a limited environment will be unnecessarily delayed. Second, we can partition routing into several component parts because of functional differences between those parts. By partitioning the problem, we can work on individual parts without necessarily sacrificing the whole.

The first component part is routing between ESs and ISs, called ES-IS routing. The second is routing between ISs which fall under a single routing authority, share a common set of routing procedures, and which fully trust each other. This is called Intra-Domain IS-IS routing. The third is routing between ISs which fall under a single routing authority and which fully trust each other, but which have different routing procedures. This is called Inter-Domain IS-IS routing. The fourth is routing between ISs which fall under different routing authorities and which don't necessarily trust each other. This is called Inter-Administration IS-IS routing.

The creation of the first component, ES-IS routing, results from the observation that routing functions involving Systems which cannot relay traffic (ESs) are fundamentally different than those involving Systems which do relay traffic (ISs). In particular, since ESs cannot relay traffic, they have no reason to propagate routing updates *about other Systems*. This greatly simplifies the tasks that an ES must perform. An ES need only discover one or more ISs which will then perform relaying for the ES. The ISs can tell the ES which IS is the best choice for a given set of destinations. An ES, however, does not need to involve itself in a complex n-party routing algorithm. A side benefit of separating ES-IS routing from any IS-IS routing is that ESs can be as simple as possible—saving the complexity, and therefore expense, for the less numerous ISs.

In the second component, Intra-Domain IS-IS routing, a great deal of coordination between ISs is possible. Within the bounds of correct operation, an IS can accept information another IS gives it without question. Therefore, any discovered routes can be fully advertised (within the boundaries of the Domain). ISs can agree on routing metrics (such as delay, bandwidth, hops, etc.), a necessary requirement for the discovery and prevention of loops. The assignment of addresses can be controlled to reflect the hierarchical clustering which may exist within a Routing Domain.

The first two components are clear-cut and well understood. This is supported by an ES-IS protocol in ISO (DIS 9542), and two proposed Intra-Domain routing protocols in X3S3.3.

The last two components, Inter-Domain and Inter-Administration routing, are less clear-cut. It is not obvious what should be standardized with respect to these two components of routing. For example, for Inter-Domain routing, what can be expected from the Domains? By asking Domains to provide some kind of external behavior, we limit their autonomy. If we expect nothing of their external behavior, then routing functionality will be minimal.

Across administrations, it is not known how much trust there will be. In fact, the definition of trust itself can only be determined by the two or more administrations involved.

Fundamentally, the problem with Inter-Domain and Inter-Administration routing is that autonomy and mistrust are both antithetical to routing. Accomplishing either will involve a number of trade-offs which will require more knowledge about the environments within which they will operate.

4. EXAMPLE

The following example/problem gives perspective to some of the above discussion. Consider two corporations, A and B, each of which has research centers in several continents around the world. The research centers of their respective corporations communicate with each other through their corporate network—that is, the research centers do not have direct links with each other. Assume that the two corporations embark on a joint research project and Corporation A contributes one of its research centers in Continent 1 (called joint research center A), and Corporation B contributes one of its research centers in Continent 2 (called joint research center B). Let us assume that both Corporations parse their addresses in the format *Corporation.Continent.Region*, and that the address of joint research center A is *A.1.1* and the address of joint research center B is *B.2.1*. It is necessary that the two joint research centers exchange data, but because the two corporations are competitors, they do wish to exchange data otherwise.

Assume it is determined that the most cost-effective way to allow the two joint research centers to communicate is by adding a link between the two corporate networks which connects locations which are not near either research center. This is depicted in Figure 2. If this link goes down, we assume that the two joint research centers wish to communicate alternatively via the more expensive public data networks. In Figure 2 we see a connection between an IS in Corporation A which is in a different region from Joint Research Center A to an IS in Corporation B which is in a different continent from Joint Research Center B. Because only communications between *A.1.1* and *B.2.1* can cross this link, it is necessary to constrain routing updates which cross that link to only mention *A.1.1* or *B.2.1*. It is also necessary to impose access control mechanisms on both ends of that link to prevent other data from crossing. While this may appear straight-forward enough, it is not a typical function of existing routing protocols.

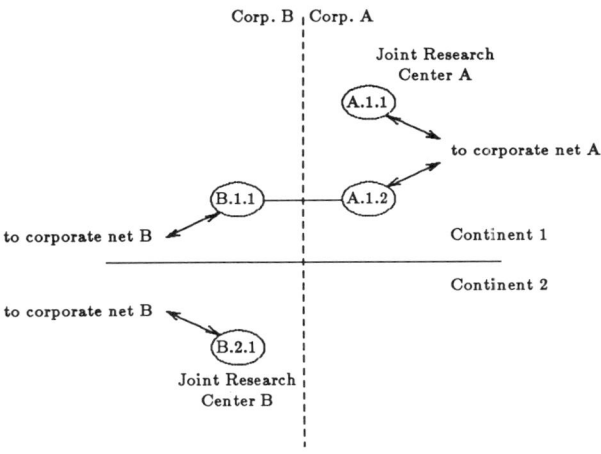

Figure 2

This kind of scenario can be made arbitrarily complex. For instance, what if a third corporation C had also contributed a research center, but this center was only connected to Corporation B, not Corporation A? Then the restrictions on the links between A and B and between B and C become still more complex. The amount of information required to describe complex restrictions on links and Systems, and the techniques for exchanging (or not exchanging) that information has not been studied.

5. DISCUSSION

We have outlined some approaches to the problems of routing in the global OSI data communications network. In spite of the extensive research in dynamic routing for data networks over the last twenty years (a modest bibliography is included), it seems that we still have more questions than answers. This is largely because most of the work has centered on routing in a non-hierarchical, singly-administered network. Some of the recent work has focused on hierarchical, singly-administered networks, but there is little work on hierarchical, multiply-administered networks.

With regard to multiply-administered networks, there are questions about what kinds of routing agreements can be made, how those agreements can be modeled, how they translate into restrictions on routing information and data traffic, and how they can be enforced.

There are questions concerning the nature of global networks. How much of the global connectivity will be provided by public domain networks, how much by private? How will routing algorithms in public domain networks interact with those in private networks? In many respects, good routing translates into power—power to circumvent public data networks, power to construct global networks without a central point of administration or control. How will this power be handled, legally and economically?

There are questions concerning faulty routing. How will faulty routers be isolated and fixed? This is hard enough to do in a singly administered network. How will it be done when routing takes place across arbitrarily complex topologies and agreements? How can the collapse of the global network due to faulty routing be prevented?

What is the relationship between routing at the network layer and routing at the application layer, for instance, mail handling systems? Should they be completely separate, or can information from one make the other more efficient?

6. SUMMARY

This paper gives a progress report on network layer routing architecture work in ANSI X3S3.3 for ISO. Some of the problems encountered in network layer routing are discussed, and an architectural basis for modeling and solving some of those problems is presented. In particular, a functional partition of the routing problem into four tiers (ES-IS routing, IS-IS routing within a single Routing Domain, IS-IS routing between different Domains but within an Administrative Domain, and IS-IS routing between Administrative Domains) is presented. A routing hierarchy, an address hierarchy, and the relationship between the two, are discussed. An example of a routing agreement between different administrations, and the constraints that are placed on routing as a result, is given. Finally, questions concerning outstanding problems in routing in the global OSI network are posed. It is hoped that these questions will help motivate discussion and research.

BIBLIOGRAPHY

American National Standards Institute ANSI X3S3.3, 3.3/86-215R2, *Draft Routing Architecture*, April, 1987.

Callon, R. and Lauer, G., *Hierarchical Routing for Packet Radio Networks*, Report No. 5945, SRNTN No. 31, BBN Laboratories Incorporated, June, 1985.

T. Cegrell, *A Routing Procedure for the Tidas Message-Switching Network*, IEEE Trans. on Communications, Vol. COM-23, No. 6, June 1975, pp. 575-585.

M. Gerla, *Controlling Routes, Traffic Rates, and Buffer Allocation in Packet Networks* IEEE Communications Magazine, Vol. 22, No.11, November 1984, pp. 11-23.

S. Gruchevsky, D. Piscitello, *The Burroughs Integrated Adaptive Routing System (BIAS)*, ACM Computer Communication Review, Volume 17, Nos. 1 and 2, January/April 1987

J. Hagouel, *Issues in Routing for Large and Dynamic Networks,* PhD. Thesis, Columbia University, 1983.

J. M. Jaffe, F. H. Moss, *A Responsive Distributed Routing Algorithm for Computer Networks,* IEEE Trans. on Communications, COM-30, No. 7, July 1982, pp. 1758-1762.

Kamoun, F. and Kleinrock, L., *Hierarchical Routing for Large Networks: Performance Evaluation and Optimization, Computer Networks,* Vol. 1, pp. 155-174, 1977.

Kamoun, F. and Kleinrock, L., *Stochastic Performance Evaluation of Hierarchical Routing for Large Networks, Computer Networks,* Vol. 3, No. 5, pp. 387-353, November, 1979.

Kamoun, F. and Kleinrock, L., *Optimal Clustering Structures for Hierarchical Topological Design of Large Computer Networks, Computer Networks,* Vol. 10, No. 3, pp. 221-248, 1980.

Khanna, A. and Seeger, J., *Large Network Routing Study Design Document,* Report No. 6119, BBN Communications Corporation, January, 1986.

J. M. McQuillan, I. Richer, E. C. Rosen, *The New Routing Algorithm for the ARPANET,* IEEE Trans. on Communications, Vol. COM-28, No. 5, May 1980, pp. 711-719.

J. Mogul, J. Postel, *Internet Standard Subnetting Procedure,* RFC950, SRI International, Network Information Center, Menlo Park, CA, August 1985.

R. Perlman, *Hierarchical Networks and the Subnetwork Partition Problem,* Computer Networks and ISDN Systems 9, North-Holland, 1985, pp. 297-303.

R. Perlman, *Fault Tolerant Broadcast of Routing Information,* Computer Networks, Vol. 7, 1983, pp. 395-405

Saltzer, J., Reed, D., and Clark, D., *Source Routing for Campus-wide Internet Transport, Proceedings of the IFIP WG 6.4 Workshop on Local Networks,* August, 1980.

M. Schwartz and T.E. Stern, *Routing Techniques used in Computer Communication Networks,* IEEE Trans. on Communications, Vol. COM-28, No. 4, April 1980, 539-552

Shacham, N., *Hierarchical Routing in Large, Dynamic Ground Radio Networks,* SRI International, November, 1985.

Sparta Incorporated, *Design and Analysis for Area Routing in Large Networks,* McLean, VA, April, 1986.

Sunshine, C., *Addressing Problems in Multi-network Systems, Internet Engineering Note (IEN) 178,* April, 1981.

Zakon, S., *An Architecture for Routing in the ISO Connectionless Internet, Computer Communication Review,* Vol. 15, No. 5, pp. 10-39, October, 1985.

The NSFNET Backbone Network

David L. Mills
University of Delaware

Hans-Werner Braun
University of Michigan

Abstract

The NSFNET Backbone Network interconnects six supercomputer sites, several regional networks and ARPANET. It supports the DARPA Internet protocol suite and DCN subnet protocols, which provide delay-based routing and very accurate time-synchronization services. This paper describes the design and implementation of this network, with special emphasis on robustness issues and congestion-control mechanisms.

1. Introduction and Background

The NSFNET is a loosely organized community of networks funded by the National Science Foundation to support the sharing of national scientific computing resources, data and information [JEN86]. NSFNET consists of a large number of industry and academic campus and experimental networks, many of which are interconnected by a smaller number of regional and consortium networks. The NSFNET Backbone Network is a primary means of interconnection between the regional networks and is the subject of this report.

The NSFNET Backbone Network, called simply the Backbone in the following, includes switching nodes located at six supercomputer sites: San Diego Supercomputer Center (SDSC), National Center for Supercomputer Applications (NCSA) at the University of Illinois, Cornell National Supercomputer Facility (CNSF), Pittsburgh Supercomputer Center (PSC), John von Neumann Center (JVNC) and the National Center for Atmospheric Research (NCAR). The six nodes are interconnected by 56-Kbps internode trunks (see Figure 1). The Backbone is extended for regional interconnects (not shown) to the University of Michigan and the University of Maryland, with a further one planned at Rice University. Additional nodes (not shown) are used for program development and testing, bringing the total to about thirteen.

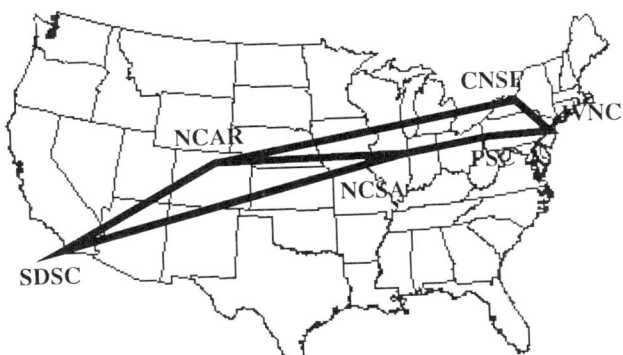

Figure 1. The NSFNET Backbone Network

Permission to copy without fee all or part of this material is granted provided that the copies are not made or distributed for direct commercial advantage, the ACM copyright notice and the title of the publication and its date appear, and notice is given that copying is by permission of the Association for Computing Machinery. To copy otherwise, or to republish, requires a fee and/or specfic permission.

© 1988 ACM 0-89791-245-4/88/0001/0191 $1.50

Each Backbone node is connected to an onsite Ethernet, which serves as the attachment point for supercomputers and other local hosts. Most sites have an extensive system of local networks and gateways, including high-speed bus, ring and point-to-point links, which serve to concentrate traffic from throughout the site. Other gateways connect to regional and consortium networks, which in some cases span large regions of the country. Some sites are connected to other backbone networks such as ARPANET and public data networks as well.

The Backbone uses the DARPA Internet architecture, which is based on the IP and TCP protocols [LEI85]. Most of the regional and consortium networks, as well as the campus networks they connect also use these protocols. There are several thousand service hosts and gateways connected to the Internet, as well as many more personal computers and workstations. In late July, 1987, there were 4625 hosts on 676 networks interconnected by 184 gateways listed at the Department of Defense Network Information Center alone, which by itself is only a small fraction of the overall Internet. There are presently about 63 networks either directly connected to the Backbone or by means of gateways and other regional and consortium networks, while over 250 networks are in regular operation on the Internet system as a whole.

In following sections the Backbone subnet architecture and protocols are described along with its hardware and software components. Its design features are summarized, including factors related to robustness, congestion control and services. Operation and maintenance issues are described, including system control, monitoring and performance measurement. Finally, plans for further expansion are summarized.

2. Network Architecture

The Backbone, as well as the onsite local-net complexes, regional networks and the campus networks they connect, are part of the Internet System developed by the Defense Advanced Research Agency (DARPA) over the last several years and conform to its architecture and protocols. The Internet operates in connectionless mode using the Internet Protocol (IP) [POS81a] as the basic internetworking mechanism. End-to-end reliability is maintained using the Transmission Control Protocol (TCP) [POS81c], which assembles and reorders datagrams (protocol data units) received over possibly diverse and unreliable paths using retransmissions as necessary. The User Datagram Protocol (UDP) [POS80] provides direct IP datagram access for transaction services, including routing and network control in some cases.

Since the basic service expected of the Backbone is connectionless, no provision for end-to-end reassembly, reordering or retransmission is necessary. The network does not support end-to-end virtual circuits and has no implicit connection-setup or other resource-binding mechanisms as does, for example the ARPANET. However, in order to improve overall service, reliable (retransmission) services are provided on selected internode trunks, in particular the 56-Kbps trunks interconnecting the Backbone sites, which use the DEC Digital Data Communications Message Protocol (DDCMP) for the pragmatic reason that the hardware interfaces happen to support this protocol.

The Backbone subnet protocols are based on the Distributed Computer Network (DCN), which uses Internet technology and an implementation of PDP11-based software called the Fuzzball. DCN networks of hosts and gateways are now in regular service in the INTELPOST facsimile-mail system, which was built by COMSAT Laboratories and operated by the U.S. Post Office and international affiliates, as well as the Backbone and about a dozen campus networks in the U.S. and Europe, including the Universities of Maryland, Michigan and Delaware, Ford Scientific Research Laboratories and M/A-COM Linkabit.

The DCN architecture is intended to provide connectivity, routing and timekeeping functions for a set of gateways, service hosts and personal workstations using a specialized protocol called HELLO [MIL83], which is based on IP. HELLO services include delay-based routing and clock-synchronization functions in an arbitrary topology including point-to-point links and multipoint bus systems. However, the DCN architecture is not intended for use in very large networks such as ARPANET, since it does not include load-adaptive routing algorithms and comprehensive congestion controls.

A brief description of the process and addressing structure used in the DCN may be useful in the following. A physical host is a PDP11-compatible processor which supports a number of cooperating sequential processes, each of which is given a unique identifier called its port ID. Every physical host contains one or more designated internet processes, each of which supports a virtual host assigned a unique identifier called its host ID. Virtual hosts can migrate among the physical hosts at will, as long as their host IDs remain unchanged, since the routing tables are automatically updated by the HELLO protocol.

The physical host also supports other processes for input/output devices (disks, terminals and network-interface devices), as well as spooling systems, various network daemons and users, which are provided with separate virtual address spaces. The physical host is identified by a host ID for the purpose of detecting loops in routing updates, which establish the minimum-delay paths between the virtual hosts. Additional host IDs are assigned dynamically by the operations of other routing and address-binding protocols such as the Internet Control Message Protocol (ICMP) [POS81b], Address Resolution Protocol (ARP) [PLU82], Exterior Gateway Protocol (EGP) [MIL84] and related protocols.

Each virtual host can support multiple transport protocols, connections and, in addition, a virtual clock. Selected virtual hosts can act as gateways to other networks as well. Each physical host contains a physical clock which can operate at an arbitrary rate and, in addition, a 32-bit logical clock which operates at 1000 Hz and is assumed to be reset each day at 0000 hours UT. Not all physical hosts implement the full 32-bit precision; however, in such cases the resolution of the logical clock may be somewhat less.

DCN networks are self-configuring for all hosts and networks; that is, the routing algorithm will automatically construct entries in the various tables, find minimum-delay paths and synchronize logical clocks among all virtual hosts and gateways supporting the DCN protocols. For routing beyond the span of the DCN routing algorithm, the tables can be pre-configured or dynamically updated using the ICMP, ARP and EGP protocols. In addition, a special entry can be configured in the tables which specifies the gateway for all address ranges not explicitly designated in the tables.

2.2. Subnet Addressing and Routing

The correspondence between IP addresses and host IDs is determined by two tables, the Local Mapping Table and the Global Mapping Table, which are structured in the same way. Each entry in these tables defines a range of IP addresses which map onto a specified host ID and thus a virtual host. There is no restriction on the particular range or ranges assigned a virtual host, so that these hosts can be multi-homed at will and in possibly exotic ways. The mapping function also supports the subnetting and filtering functions outlined in [BRA87]. By convention, one of the addresses assigned to a virtual host in each physical host is declared the base address of the physical host itself. Entries in these tables can be pre-configured or dynamically updated using the HELLO, ICMP, ARP and EGP protocols.

Datagram routing is determined entirely by IP address - there is no subnet address as in the ARPANET. Each physical host contains a table called the Host Table, which is used to determine the port ID of the network-output process on the minimum-delay path to to each virtual host. This table also contains estimates of roundtrip delay and logical-clock offset for all virtual hosts indexed by host ID. For the purpose of computing these estimates the delay and offset of each virtual host relative to the physical host in which it resides is assumed zero. The single exception to this is a special virtual host associated with an NBS radio time-code receiver, where the offset is computed relative to the broadcast time.

Host Table entries are updated by HELLO messages exchanged frequently over the links connecting physical-host neighbors. At present, the overhead of these messages is controlled at about 3.4 percent of the aggregate network traffic. They include data providing an accurate measurement of delay and offset between the neighbors on the link itself, as well as a list of the delay and offset entries in the Host Table for all virtual hosts. There are two list formats, a short format with indexed entries used when the neighbors share the same subnet and a long format including the IP address used in other cases.

The routing algorithm is a member of the Bellman-Ford class [BER87], which includes those formerly used in the ARPANET and presently used in several Internet gateway systems. The measured roundtrip delay to the neighbor is added to each of the delay estimates in its HELLO message and compared with the corresponding delay estimates in the Host Table. If the sum is less than the value already in the Host Table or if the HELLO message is received on the next-hop interface, as previously computed by the routing algorithm, the sum replaces the value and the routing to the corresponding virtual host is changed accordingly. In other cases the value in the Host Table remains unchanged.

Each entry in the Host Table is associated with a time-to-live counter, which is reset upon arrival of an update for the entry and decrements to zero otherwise. If this counter reaches zero, or if an update specifying infinite distance is received on the next-hop interface, the entry is placed in a hold-down condition where updates are ignored for a designated interval, in the Backbone case two minutes. The hold-down interval is necessary for old routing data, which might cause loops to form, to be purged from all Host Tables in the system. In order to further reduce the incidence of loops, the delay estimate is set at infinity for all hosts for which the next-hop interface is the one on which the HELLO message is sent, regardless of the value in the Host Table.

3. Switching Nodes

A Backbone node consists of a Digital Equipment Corporation LSI-11/73 system with 512K bytes of memory, dual-diskette drive, Ethernet interface and serial interfaces. One or two low-speed asynchronous interfaces are provided, as well as one to three high-speed synchronous interfaces. All Backbone nodes include crystal-stabilized time bases. One node (NCAR) is equipped with a WWVB radio time-code receiver providing a network time reference accurate to the order of a millisecond.

Other nodes connected to the Backbone and running DCN protocols use LSI-11 and other PDP11-compatible systems with from 256K to 2048K bytes of memory, plus various hard disks and serial interfaces, including ARPANET interfaces, X.25 interfaces and terminal multiplexors. Most of these nodes also include crystal-stabilized time bases, while two are equipped with WWVB time-code receivers and one with a GOES time-code receiver. Some of these systems are used for general-purpose network access for mail, word-processing and file staging, as well as packet-switching and gateway functions.

The software system used in the Backbone nodes, called the Fuzzball, includes a fast, compact operating system, comprehensive network-support system and a large suite of application programs for network protocol development, testing and evaluation. The Fuzzball software has been rebuilt, modified, tinkered and evolved over several generations spanning a twenty-year period [MIL76]. It has characteristics similar to many other operating systems, in some cases shamelessly borrowing their features and in others incorporating innovative features well before other systems made these features popular.

Originally, the Fuzzball was designed primarily as an investigative tool and prototyping workbench. Many Fuzzballs have been deployed for that purpose at various locations in the U.S. and Europe, including Norway, United Kingdom, Germany, Holland and Italy. Various organizations use Fuzzballs as terminal concentrators, electronic-mail and word-processing hosts, network monitoring and control devices and general-purpose packet-switches and gateways. For the Backbone the Fuzzball is used primarily as a packet switch/gateway, while the application programs are used for network monitoring and control.

The Fuzzball implementation incorporates complete functionality in every host, which can serve as a packet switch, gateway and service host all at the same time. The system includes host and gateway software for the complete DARPA Internet protocol suite with network, transport and applications-level support for virtual-terminal and file-transfer services, along with several mail systems with text, voice and image capabilities. In order to provide a comprehensive user interface and platform for program development and testing, a multiple-user, virtual-machine emulator supports the Digital Equipment Corporation RT-11 operating system for the PDP11 family, so that RT-11 program-development utilities and user programs can be run along with network-application programs in the Fuzzball environment.

4. Robustness Issues

When the Internet was small and growing rapidly there was great concern about its potential vulnerability to destructive routing loops or black holes that could form when more than one routing algorithm was used or when an protocol misbehaved because of algorithmic instability or defective implementation. The solution to this problem was to partition the Internet into multiple, independent systems of gateways, called autonomous systems, where each system could adopt any routing algorithm it chose, but exchange routing information with other systems using the Exterior Gateway Protocol (EGP).

The expectation was that the Internet would evolve into a relatively small, centrally managed set of backbone gateways called the core system, together with a larger set of unmanaged gateways grouped into stub systems with single-point attachments to the core system. In this model the stub systems would normally not be interconnected to each other, except via the core system, with exceptions handled on an ad-hoc, engineered basis.

As the Internet evolved into a richly interconnected, multiple-backbone topology with large numbers of regional and campus networks, the stub-system model became less and less relevant. Requirements now exist in NSFNET where gateways within and between autonomous systems need to interoperate with different routing algorithms and metrics and with different trust models. Backbones now connect to backbones, while regional systems now connect wily-nilly to each other and to multiple backbones at multiple points, so that the very concept of a core system as effective management tool has become obsolete.

As specified, EGP by is designed primarily to provide routing information between the core system and stub systems. In fact, only the core system can provide routing information for systems not directly connected to each other. The enhancements to EGP described in [MIL86] suggest restructuring the Internet as a number of autonomous-system confederations, as well as an outline for a universal metric. Neither the baseline or enhanced EGP model is adequate to cope with the evolving requirements of NSFNET.

A great deal of study was given these issues during the design phase of the Backbone. One issue is the vulnerability of NSFNET as a whole to routing loops, either due to adventurous, unstable configurations or defective implementations. Another is the robustness of the various metrics (e.g. hop-count based and delay based) with respect to the various transformations required between them. Still another is protection from false or misleading addressing information received from or transmitted to neighboring systems. Each of these issues will be discussed in following sections.

4.1. Metric Transformations

Since it is not possible for the Backbone routing algorithm to have unlimited scope, there exist demarcations where the algorithm must interoperate with other routing algorithms, protocols and metrics. In order to support multiple routing algorithms in a single autonomous system or confederation, it is necessary to explore how they can safely interoperate without forming destructive routing loops.

Consider two Bellman-Ford algorithms one with metric R, which might for example represent hop count, and the other with metric H, which might represent measured delay. Nodes using each metric send periodic updates to their neighbors, some of which may use a different metric. Each node receiving an update in a different metric must be able to transform that metric into its own. Suppose there are two functions: Fh, which maps R to H, and Fr, which maps H to R. In order to preserve the non-negative character of the metrics, both Fh and Fr must be positive and monotone-increasing functions of their arguments.

It is not difficult to show [MIL87b] that loops will not occur if both of the following conditions are satisfied:

$$x <= F_r(F_h(x)) \qquad \text{and} \qquad x <= F_h(F_r(x)).$$

As long as these conditions are satisfied and both the domains and ranges are restricted to non-negative values, mutually inverse functions for F_h and F_r can readily be found, such as linear transformations $Ax + B$, powers x^n and exponentials $\exp(x)$, together with their inverses. Note that these conditions require careful analysis of the finite-precision arithmetic involved and the errors inevitably introduced.

Several of the Backbone nodes are connected to extensive regional networks, some of which use a routing protocol called the Routing Information Protocol (RIP) [HED87]. In some cases a regional network is connected to more than one Backbone node. A typical case involves the translation between RIP and HELLO at both sites, in which case the above conditions come into play. Note that these conditions do not guarantee the shortest path relative to either metric, just that whatever path is chosen, no loops will form.

4.2. Fallback Routing

Ordinary routing algorithms compute shortest paths on a directed, labeled graph. If there are multiple paths between given endpoints, the algorithm will select the one with minimum total distance, but will make an arbitrary choice when more than one path exists with that distance. A reachability algorithm is defined as a routing algorithm in which all paths between given endpoints have the same distance; therefore, the algorithm will select one of them arbitrarily. In practice such algorithms are useful mainly in tree-structured topologies where autonomous systems with only a few reachable networks are interconnected by one or at most a few gateways, such as the stub-system model commonly associated with EGP.

Cases exist in NSFNET where several autonomous systems with many reachable networks are haphazardly interconnected by multiple gateways. In order to insure stability, it is desirable to hide the internal routing details of each system; however, for reasons of load balancing it is desirable to control which gateway is to be used for normal traffic in to and out of the system and which is to be used as backup should the normal gateway fail. A fallback algorithm is defined as a routing algorithm in which two sets of paths exist between given endpoints, one intended as primary paths and the other as fallback paths should all primary paths fail. However, in both the primary or fallback set, the algorithm will select one of them arbitrarily.

In reachability algorithms it is not necessary to know the distance along the path selected, only that it exists (i.e. the distance is less than infinity); therefore, the metric has only two values: zero and infinity. In fallback algorithms a finer distinction is necessary in order to determine whether a primary or fallback path is in use; therefore, the metric has three values: zero, one and infinity. It is not difficult to invent metric transformations which preserve this distinction without introducing loops [MIL87b].

Fallback routing is now used by the EGP-speaking gateways between the various Backbone site networks and the core system. For each Backbone network one of these gateways is designated primary and uses an EGP metric of zero, while the remaining gateways are designated fallback and use a nonzero metric. The primary gateway is assigned on the basis of pre-engineered configurations and traffic forecasts. As a special experimental feature, the core-system EGP implementation incorporates an ad-hoc form of fallback routing. The effect is that, if the primary gateway for a particular network fails, the load is nondeterministically shared among the fallback gateways.

4.3. Routing Agents

Since the Backbone nodes are connected directly to Ethernets serving a general population of potentially defective hosts and gateways, the Backbone design includes a special routing agent which filters information sent between the switching nodes and other gateways in the local autonomous system. In order to conserve resources in the node itself, the agent is implemented as a daemon in a trusted Unix-based host attached to the same Ethernet. The agent, now installed at all Backbone sites, mitigates routes computed by other routing systems, such as RIP and/or EGP, and communicates with the Backbone node using the HELLO protocol. It consists of a portable C-language program for the Berkeley 4.3 Unix system distribution [FED87].

Among the features implemented in the routing agent are exclusion lists, which delete selected networks known to the local routing algorithm from HELLO messages sent to the Backbone node. Others include calculation of the metric transformations, when required, and management of the various data bases involved. At present, the resources necessary to operate the routing agent are provided by the sites themselves, while configuration control of the data bases is maintained by the network operations center.

5. Congestion Control

Like many networks designed for connectionless-mode service, the Backbone does not bind resources to end-to-end flows or virtual circuits. In order to deal with traffic surges, the Internet architecture specifies the ICMP Source Quench message, which is in effect a choke packet sent to the originating host when a downstream gateway experiences congestion. While the choke packet can be an effective mechanism to control long-term flows; that is, when the flow intensities are relatively stable over periods longer then the nominal transit time of the network, it is usually not an effective mechanism in other cases.

Therefore, when a short-term traffic surge occurs, the only defense possible is to either drop arriving packets or selectively preempt ones already queued for transmission. Previous designs drop arriving packets when the buffer pool becomes congested, which has unfortunate consequences for fairness and end-to-end performance. Simply increasing the size of the buffer pool does not help [NAG85]. In addition, it has long been suspected that a major cause of Internet traffic surges is defective transport-level implementations or antisocial queueing policies, resulting in large, uncontrolled bursts of packets. Thus, an effective preemption strategy must take fairness into account in order to avoid capture of excessive network resources by reckless customers.

Extensive experience in the design, implementation and experimental evaluation of connectionless-mode networks suggests an interesting preemption strategy which has been implemented in the Fuzzball system. It is based on two fairness principles:

1. Every customer (IP source host) has equal claim on buffer resources, so that new arrivals can preempt other customers until the space claimed by all customers is equalized.

2. When a preemption is necessary for a customer with buffers on multiple queues, the preemption rates for each of these queues are equalized.

The intent of the first rule is to identify the customer capturing the most buffer space, since this customer is most likely a major contributor to the congestion. The intent of the second rule is to spread the preemptions evenly over the output queues in case of ties.

It is not possible without a heavy performance penalty to implement the above rules in their purest form. In the Fuzzball implementation an input buffer is almost always available for an arriving packet. Upon arrival and inspection for correct format and IP checksum, the (sometimes considerable) unused space at the end of the buffer is returned to the buffer pool and the packet inserted on the correct output queue, as determined by the routing algorithm. A preemption is necessary when an input buffer must be allocated for the next following packet.

When preemption is necessary, each output queue is scanned separately to find the customer with the largest number of 512-octet blocks. Then the queue with the largest number of such blocks is determined and the last buffer for the associated customer is preempted, even if the buffer preempted was the one just filled. In case of ties, the queue with the most packets transmitted since the last preemption is chosen. The entire process is repeated until sufficient buffer space is available for the input buffer request.

The experience with the Fuzzball implementation has been very satisfying, as shown below and in Section 7. Table 1 illustrates the performance of the policy over a typical period of several days. There are sixteen internode trunks in the Backbone (including the SURA regional network). The Rate column shows the mean packets per second sent on the trunk, while the Timeout and Preempted columns show the percentage of packets deleted from the trunk queue due these causes.

Line	Rate	Timeout	Preempted	Total
1	.32	.767	0	.767
2	.62	.504	0	.504
3	1.56	.058	0	.058
4	1.91	.020	0	.020
5	.30	.059	0	.059
6	.58	.141	0	.141
7	2.23	.018	.025	.044
8	3.02	.045	.018	.063
9	1.82	.110	.026	.137
10	1.61	.056	0	.056
11	2.20	.021	.162	.184
12	3.41	.059	.071	.130
13	3.79	.034	.027	.061
14	3.98	.027	0	.027
15	2.79	.033	0	.033
16	1.39	.052	.004	.056
Totals	31.52	.060	.028	.088

Table 1. Dropped Packet Rates

These data should be compared with the weekly statistics collected for the seven ARPANET/MILNET gateways operated by Bolt Beranek Newman for the Defense Communication Agency [CHA87]. These gateways, which operate in an environment similar to the Backbone, drop an arriving packet when the output queue for an ARPANET/MILNET destination subnet address exceeds eight packets. On a typical week in late July 1987 these gateways carried an aggregate of 56.74 packets per second for an equivalent of 14 lines, with a mean drop rate of 7.035 percent, almost two orders of magnitude greater than the Backbone. The busiest gateway carried an estimated 6.44 packets per second per line and dropped 12.5 percent of these packets.

6. Network Services

The Backbone nodes are intended primarily to serve as IP packet switches and gateways for NSFNET client networks. However, There are several other services available, some for the general user population and others for monitoring and control purposes. These include some applications based on TCP and some on UDP (see [DCA85] for service descriptions and protocols, unless indicated otherwise):

1. TCP-based virtual-terminal (TELNET), file-transfer (FTP) and mail (SMTP) services intended for system monitoring and control purposes.

2. UDP-based name-lookup (NAME and DOMAIN-NAME), file-transfer (TFTP) and time (TIME, NTP) services, as well as a special statistics (NETSPY) service [MIL87a] intended for network monitoring.

3. IP-based utilities (ECHO, TIMESTAMP), primarily intended for system monitoring and fault isolation.

The UDP-based time services TIME and NTP are unique features of the Fuzzball. The physical-clock hardware and Fuzzball software, as well as the DCN protocols, have been specially designed to maintain network time synchronization to an unusual precision, usually less than a few milliseconds relative to NBS broadcast standards. The Network Time Protocol (NTP) [MIL85b] implemented by every Fuzzball provides accurate timestamps in response to external requests, as well as providing internal synchronization and backup for a network of NTP servers spanning the entire Internet.

There are presently five Fuzzball systems with WWVB or GOES time-code receivers on the Internet, with at least one attached via high-speed lines to the Backbone, ARPANET and MILNET. A conforming NTP daemon program has been written for the Berkely 4.3 Unix system distribution. A discussion of the synchronization algorithms used can be found in [MIL85a].

7. Network Operations

The NSFNET Backbone Network Project is presently managed by the University of Illinois. Network operations, including configuration control and monitoring functions, are managed by Cornell University. Additional technical support is provided by the Information Sciences Institute of the University of Southern California, and the Universities of Michigan, Delaware and Maryland. The NSFNET Network Services Center (NNSC), operated by Bolt Beranek Newman, provides end-user information and support.

The NSF Information and Services Center (NISC) at Cornell University is presently responsible for the day-to-day operations and maintenance functions of the Backbone. They are assisted by staff at the various sites and regional operating centers for hardware maintenance, as well as the resolution of node and trunk problems. Most of the software maintenance, including bugfixes, version updates and general control and monitoring functions, are performed remotely from Cornell.

The Fuzzball includes event-logging features which record exception events in a log file suitable for periodic retrieval using the standard Internet file-transfer protocols FTP and TFTP. In addition, a special UDP-based server has been implemented [MIL87a] so that cumulative statistics can be gathered from all nodes with minimum impact on ongoing service. At present, statistics are gathered on an hourly basis from every node and incorporated in a data base suitable for later analysis. About nine months of history data are now available in the data base, which is used to produce periodic management reports with performance statistics similar to those shown in this report.

A great deal of additional information is available from the Backbone nodes, the Unix-resident routing agent (gated) and various other sources. This information, which is available via remote login (TCP/TELNET), includes the contents of various routing tables, the state of system resources such as the buffer pool, state variables for the various protocols in operation and so forth. An interesting sidelight is that the time-synchronization function, which requires precise measurement of network delays and logical-clock offsets, serves as a delicate indicator of network stability. If the network becomes congested or routing loops form, the delays and offsets usually become unstable and are readily noticed by an experienced operator. In fact, the precision of the system is so exquisite that the temperature of the machine room can be estimated from the drift-compensation term of the logical-clock corrections computed by each node.

The growth in traffic carried by the Backbone over the nine-month period since October 1986 is clearly apparent in Figure 2, which shows the number of packets delivered to the destination Ethernets per week. Figure 3 shows the preemption rate (percentage of packets preempted per packet delivered) per week. The dramatic reduction in preemption rate at about week 27 was due to an expansion in buffer space together with adjustments to system parameters such as retransmission limits. A second dramatic drop in preemption rate at about week 33 was due to the introduction of the new preemption policy described previously. The effectiveness of this policy is evident by the fact that, during a period in which the packets delivered rose by 50 percent, there was a six-fold decrease in the number of packets preempted.

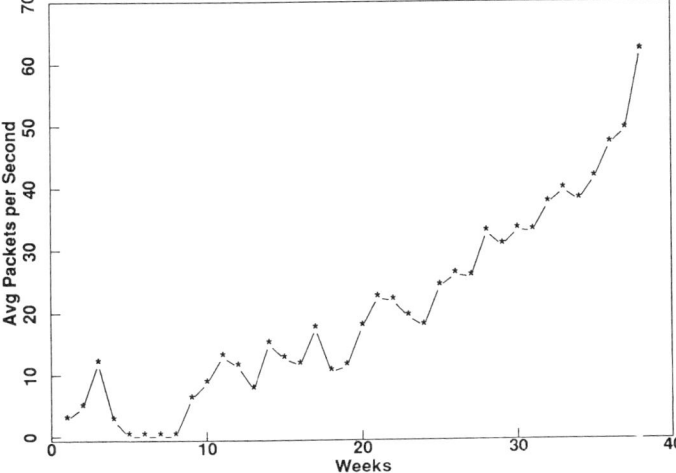

Figure 2. Packets Delivered, Averaged by Week

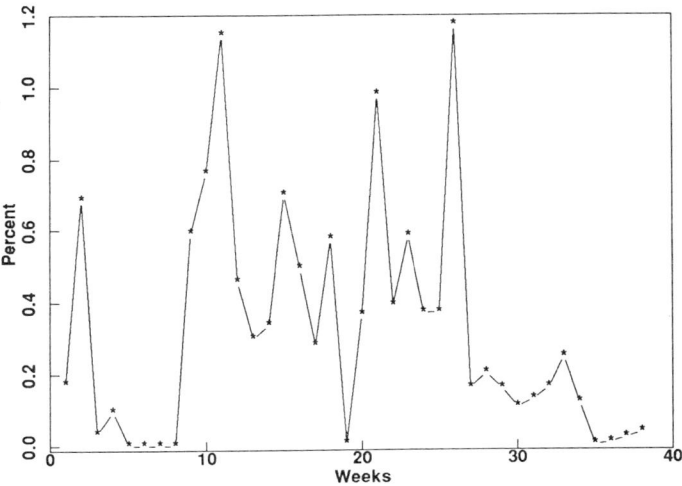

Figure 3. Percentage of Packets Dropped, Averaged by Week

8. Future Plans

Today the Backbone is an integral part of the Internet system; in fact, over one-fourth of all Internet networks are reachable via this network. As evident from the previous section, the aggregate traffic carried by the Backbone is currently approaching that of the ARPANET/MILNET gateways, which are overloaded and soon to be replaced. Moreover, although the preemption policy is working well and suggests that additional node and trunk capacity remains, the alarming rate of growth indicates the current Backbone configuration will be inevitably overwhelmed within a short time.

Current plans are to augment Backbone service by the addition of high-speed nodes and additional trunking capacity. While no decision has been made on the node configuration or trunk speeds, it is likely that T1 speeds (1.544 Mbps) and new high-speed packet switches will become available in 1988. The migration path from the existing Backbone to a new one using this technology is now under review.

It is anticipated that the current interim network-management structure will be replaced by a permanent one. The National Science Foundation has solicited a Cooperative Agreement for "Project Solicitation for Management and Operation of the NSFNET Backbone Network," with award expected by November of 1987. The awardee will have primary responsibility for designing, installing and operating upgrades to the Backbone. The emerging OSI protocols will become a very important factor for the future evolution of the NSFNET. The migration of NSFNET to an OSI connectionless-mode environment will become imperative as the OSI protocols mature and implementations become widely available. A most likely migration strategy will be to support both Internet IP and OSI connectionless-mode (CNLS) protocols in all NSFNET gateways, including the Backbone. This will allow hosts supporting either or both protocol suites to coexist in the same internetwork. Changes in subnet protocols and addressing mechanisms necessary to implement this strategy are already in progress. In addition, it is likely that application-level gateways may be installed at strategic points in order to support essential services such as mail during the migration period.

9. Acknowledgments

Doug Elias of Cornell University and Mike Minnich of the University of Delaware provided invaluable assistance in the generation, analysis and presentation of the performance data in this report.

10. References

[BRA87] Braden, R. Requirements for Internet gateways. DARPA Network Working Group Report RFC-1009, USC Information Sciences Institute, June 1987.

[BER87] Bertsekas, D., and R. Gallager. Data Networks. Prentice-Hall, Englewood Cliffs, N.J., 1987.

[CHA87] Chao, J. Weekly Throughput Summary for the BBN LSI-11 Gateways. Report distributed via electronic mail by Bolt Beranek Newman.

[DCA85] Defense Communications Agency. DDN Protocol Handbook. NIC-50004, NIC-50005, NIC-50006, (three volumes), SRI International, December 1985.

[FED87] Fedor, M. Gated - network routing daemon. Unix manual description pages, Cornell University, 1987.

[HED87] Hedrick, C. Routing Information Protocol. DARPA Network Working Group Report (number to be assigned), Rutgers University, July 1987.

[JEN86] Jennings, D.M., L.H. Landweber, I.H. Fuchs, D.J. Farber and W.R. Adrion. Computer networks for scientists. Science 231 (28 February 1986), 943-950.

[LEI85] Leiner, B., J. Postel, R. Cole and D. Mills. The DARPA Internet protocol suite. Proceedings INFOCOM 85, Washington DC, March 1985. Also in: IEEE Communications Magazine, March 1985.

[MIL76] Mills, D.L. An overview of the Distributed Computer Network. Proc. AFIPS 1976 NCC, New York, N.Y., June 1976.

[MIL83] Mills, D.L. DCN local-network protocols. DARPA Network Working Group Report RFC-891, M/A-COM Linkabit, December 1983.

[MIL84] Mills, D.L. Exterior Gateway Protocol formal specification. DARPA Network Working Group Report RFC-904, M/A-COM Linkabit, April 1984.

[MIL85a] Mills, D.L. Algorithms for synchronizing network clocks. DARPA Network Working Group Report RFC-957, M/A-COM Linkabit, September 1985.

[MIL85b] Mills, D.L. Network Time Protocol (NTP). DARPA Network Working Group Report RFC-958, M/A-COM Linkabit, September 1985.

[MIL86] Mills, D.L. Autonomous confederations. DARPA Network Working Group Report RFC-975, M/A-COM Linkabit, February 1986.

[MIL87a] Mills, D.L. Statistics server. DARPA Network Working Group Report RFC-996. University of Delaware, February 1987.

[MIL87b] Mills, D.L. Metric Transformations. Memorandum distributed to the Internet Activities Board, Internet Architecture Task Force and Internet Engineering Task Force, June 1987.

[NAG85] Nagle, J. On packet switches with infinite storage. DARPA Network Working Group Report RFC-970, Ford Aerospace, December 1985.

[PLU82] Plummer, D. An Ethernet address resolution protocol. DARPA Network Working Group Report RFC-826, Symbolics, September 1982.

[POS80] Postel, J. User datagram protocol. DARPA Network Working Group Report RFC-768, USC Information Sciences Institute, August 1980.

[POS81a] Postel, J. Internet Protocol. DARPA Network Working Group Report RFC-791, USC Information Sciences Institute, September 1981.

[POS81b] Postel, J. Internet control message protocol. DARPA Network Working Group Report RFC-792, USC Information Sciences Institute, September 1981.

[POS81c] Postel, J. Transmission control protocol. DARPA Network Working Group Report RFC-793, USC Information Sciences Institute, September 1981.

PART 7. PROTOCOL DEVELOPMENT AND PERFORMANCE

W. Kosinsky

Norwich University, USA

Algorithms For The Reduction Of Timed Finite State Graphs

G. H. Masapati and George M. White
Computer Science Dept.
University of Ottawa,
Ottawa, Ont. K1N 9B4
Canada

ABSTRACT

A set of algorithms to reduce the size of timed finite state graphs are presented. In particular, we develop a more general algorithm for vertex folding than those presently existing. It is based on the law of conservation of transition time. We demonstrate the application of these reduction algorithms to a version of the stop-and-wait protocol.

We have also developed a graph reduction software package incorporating all these algorithms which can be used in automated performance prediction. Graph reduction software tools such as these are important and form an integral part of automated protocol performance prediction tools[RUD 83].

1 Introduction

It is known that computer communication protocols used in real life can be described by various kinds of finite state graphs and that these graphs are very large. The size of these descriptions reflects the underlying complexity of the protocol being specified.

Large graphs however are difficult to analyse and difficult to understand. The more states present in the graph being analysed, the more difficult it is to demonstrate the correctness of the protocol and to compute its efficiency and delay or throughput. In this paper we present a series of algorithms which permit the systematic reduction of the states of a timed finite state graph to any size desired. The target size of the reduced system is determined by the semantics attached to each node of the graph. A series of nodes with low semantic content can be coalesced with little reduction in useful information. Nodes with large semantic content, i.e. those which are important for some reason, can be preserved. In any case the reduction of the graph may be stopped at any time to preserve useful states and eliminate redundant ones while keeping the temporal relationships between nodes and the probabilities of path traversal.

In the past ([BEI 70],[GRA 73],[ZUB 86a]), attempts have been made to derive general reduction rules. Beizer[BEI 70] and Graham[GRA 73] employed reduction rules to calculate the running time of computer programs. Zuberek[ZUB 86a] employed similar reduction rules for protocol performance evaluation.

In the next section, we present a set of reduction rules, namely, vertex reduction, junction removal, decision removal, multi-in multi-out vertex removal, parallel self-loop merge, parallel edge merge and self-loop removal. The vertex folding rule is more general than any presently existing and extends Zuberek's definition[ZUB 86a] which is valid only for equal transition times. In the following section, we demonstrate the application of these rules to a version of the stop-and-wait protocol.

All these rules are incorporated into a graph reduction software package which can be used in automatic performance prediction. Graph reduction software tools such as these are important and form an integral part of automated protocol performance prediction tools[RUD 83].

2 Graph Reduction Rules

The graphs which are discussed here are generated from models of communication protocols obtained using the timed Petri-net formalism[PET 81] [ZUB 86a]. In this method, elements of the communication sub-net are modeled using D-timed Petri-nets and the resulting probabilistic transition graphs contain the states of the receiver, transmitter and channel. The notation used is tabled below:

TABLE OF NOTATIONS:

$G(G', G''; G_m)$	(reduced;modified) probabilistic transtion graph
$V(V', V''; V_m)$	The set of vertices in $G(G', G''; G_m)$
$D(D', D''; D_m)$	The set of directed edges in $G(G', G''; G_m)$
$p(p', p''; p_m)$	The set of probabilites associated with each element of $D(D', D''; D_m)$
$I(X)(O(X))$	The set of input(output) vertices of vertex X
$\#I(X)$	The number of elements in I(X)
$v_i, v_j, v_k, v_l, v_m, v_+$	The elements of V or V' or V'' or V_m
$v_-, v_{k+1}, \ldots, v_{k+n}$	The elements of V or V' or V'' or V_m
$E(v_i, v_j)$	The set of directed edges from v_i to v_j
$L(v_j)$	The set of self-loops of v_j
t_{ij}^k	The transition time associated with the kth directed edge from v_i to v_j
p_{ij}^k	The probability associated with the kth directed edge from v_i to v_j

$p(e), p'(e), p''(e), p_m(e)$	The probability assocaited with the directed edge e
LCTT	Law of Conservation of Transition Time
T1,T2,T3,T3-A,T3-B	Transformations
$\emptyset$	empty set
$\wedge(\vee)$	AND(OR)
f(t)	false(true)

Definition 1
A *probabilistic transition graph*, $G = (V, D, p)$, is a directed graph where

- V is a set of vertices,

- D is a set of directed edges; each directed edge is a 3-tuple (v_i, v_j, t_{ij}) where v_i is the source vertex, v_j is the destination vertex and t_{ij} is the transtion time, and

- p is a set of probabilities associated with each directed edge in D.

Interpretation of t_{ij}^k and p_{ij}^k

If there exists more than one directed edge from v_i to v_j then we denote these directed edges by (v_i, v_j, t_{ij}^k) where $k=1,2,\ldots$,number of directed edges from v_i to v_j. When there is only one directed edge from v_i to v_j, we omit k and denote this directed edge by (v_i, v_j, t_{ij}). A similar interpretation holds for p_{ij}.

Definition 2
A *reduced probabilistic transition graph* $G' = (V', D', p')$ or $G'' = (V'', D'', p'')$ is a probabilistic transition graph obtained by applying any one of the reduction rules presented in this chapter.

Definition 3
A *modified probabilistic transition graph* $G_m = (V_m, D_m, p_m)$ is a probabilistic transition graph obtained by either adding a vertex or by relocating the incoming directed edges of a vertex to some other vertex.

Definition 4
Vertex v_j is a *junction vertex* if $\#I(v_j) > 1 \wedge \#O(v_j) = 1$

Definition 5
Vertex v_j is a *decision vertex* if $\#I(v_j) = 1 \wedge \#O(v_j) > 1$

Definition 6
Vertex v_j is a *multi-in multi-out vertex* if $\#I(v_j) > 1 \wedge \#O(v_j) > 1$

Definition 7
Let v_i and v_j be two vertices. Then, we denote the set of all the directed edges from v_i to v_j by $E(v_i, v_j)$. That is,

$$E(v_i, v_j) = \{(v_l, v_m, t_{lm}^k) \in D : l = i \wedge m = j\}$$

If $\#E(v_i, v_j) > 1$ then we say that v_i has *parallel edges* to v_j.

Definition 8

Vertex v_j has a *self-loop* if $v_j \in I(v_j)$. We denote the set of all the self-loops of v_j by $L(v_j)$. That is,

$$L(v_j) = \{(v_l, v_m, t_{lm}^k) \in D : l = j \wedge m = j\}$$

We occasionally refer to probabilistic transition graphs as simply graphs.

Rule 1: Vertex Reduction

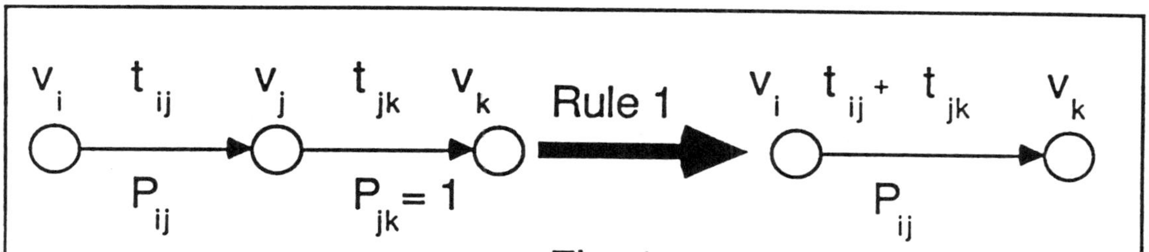

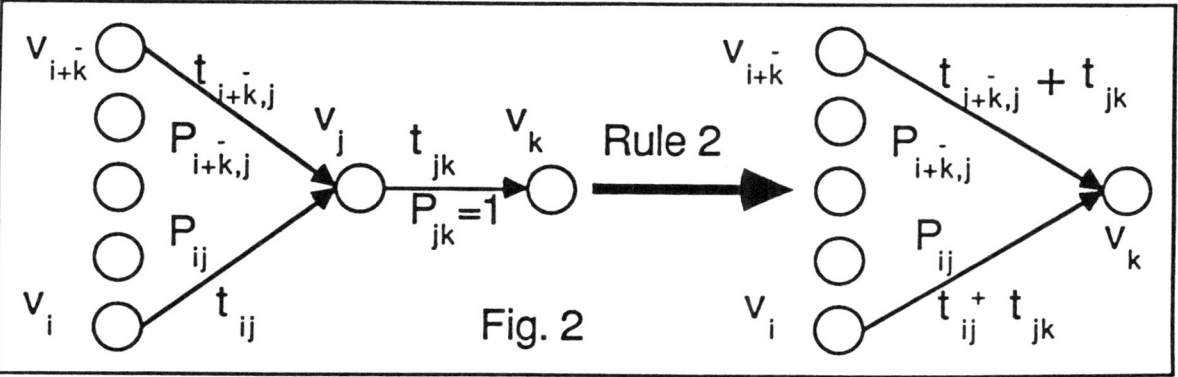

Fig. 1

If $\quad I(v_j) = v_i \wedge O(v_j) = v_k$
Then $\quad V' \leftarrow V - v_j$
$\quad\quad\quad D' \leftarrow D - (v_i, v_j, t_{ij}) - (v_j, v_k, t_{jk}) + (v_i, v_k, t_{ij} + t_{jk})$

$$p'(v_l, v_m, t_{lm}) \leftarrow \begin{cases} p(v_i, v_j, t_{ij}) & \text{if } l = i \wedge m = k \\ p(v_l, v_m, t_{lm}) & \text{otherwise} \end{cases}$$
$$\forall (v_l, v_m, t_{lm}) \in D'$$

Rule 2: Junction removal

Fig. 2

If $\#I(v_j) = n \wedge O(v_j) = v_k \wedge n > 1$
Then $V' \leftarrow V - v_j;$
$D' \leftarrow D - (v_j, v_k, t_{jk}) - (v_l, v_j, v_{lj}) + (v_l, v_k, t_{lj} + t_{jk}) \qquad \forall v_l \in I(v_j)$

$$p'(v_l, v_m, t_{lm}) \leftarrow \begin{cases} p(v_l, v_j, t_{lj}) & \text{if } v_l \in I(v_j) \wedge m = k \\ p(v_l, v_m, t_{lm}) & \text{otherwise} \end{cases}$$
$$\forall (v_l, v_m, t_{lm}) \in D'$$

Note: When $n = 1$, this rule becomes Rule 1 : Vertex reduction.

Rule 3: Decision removal

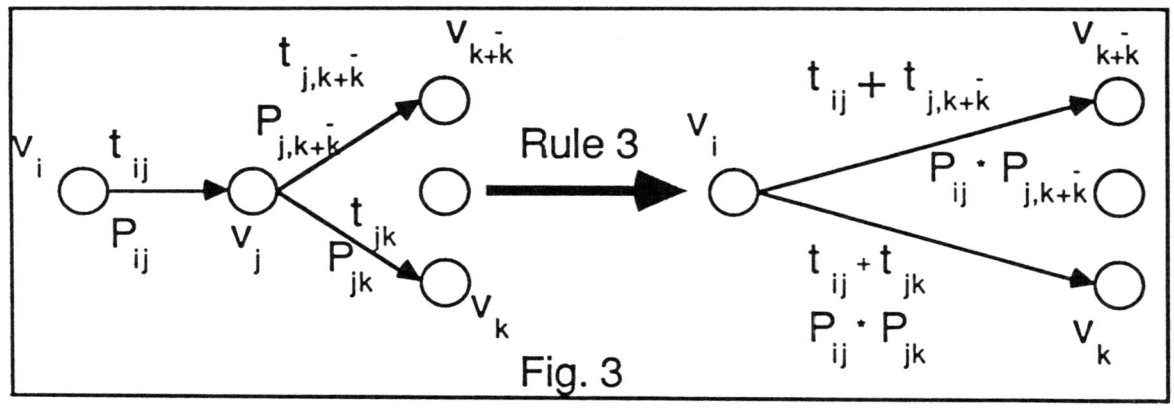

Fig. 3

If $I(v_j) = v_i \wedge \#O(v_j) = n \wedge n > 1$
Then $V' \leftarrow V - v_j;$
$D' \leftarrow D - (v_i, v_j, t_{ij}) - (v_j, v_m, t_{jm}) + (v_i, v_m, t_{ij} + t_{jm}) \qquad \forall v_m \in O(v_j)$

$$p'(v_l, v_m, t_{lm}) \leftarrow \begin{cases} p(v_i, v_j, t_{ij}) * p(v_j, v_m, t_{jm}) & \text{if } l = i \wedge v_m \in O(v_j) \\ p(v_l, v_m, t_{lm}) & \text{otherwise} \end{cases}$$
$$\forall (v_l, v_m, t_{lm}) \in D'$$

Note: When $n = 1$, this rule becomes Rule 1 : Vertex reduction.

Rule 4: Multi-in Multi-out Vertex removal

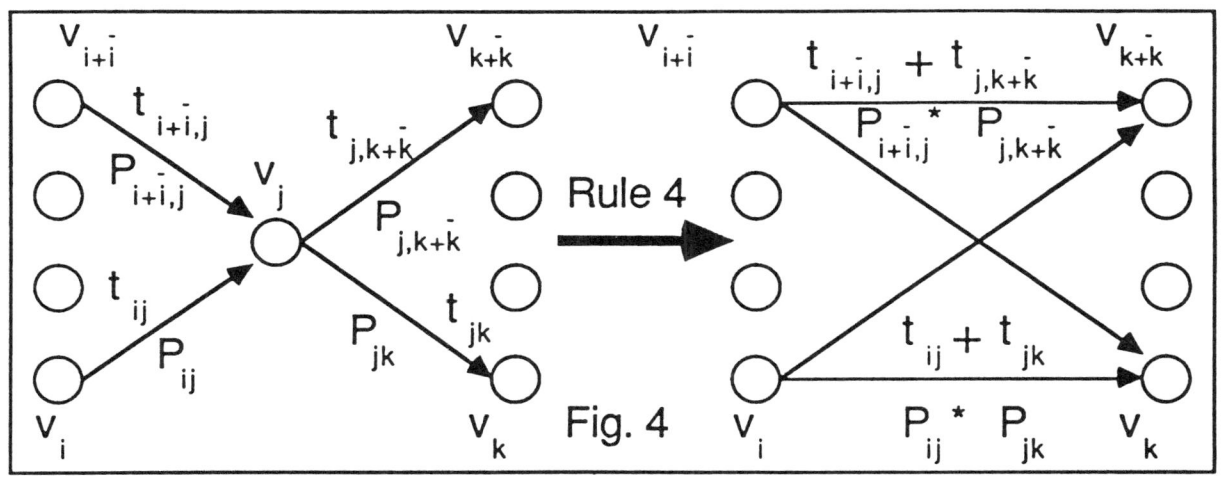

Fig. 4

If $\quad \#I(v_j) = m \wedge \#O(v_j) = n \wedge m > 1 \wedge n > 1$
Then $\quad V' \leftarrow V - v_j$
$\quad\quad D' \leftarrow D - (v_l, v_j, t_{lj}) - (v_j, v_m, t_{jm}) + (v_l, v_m, t_{lj} + t_{jm})$
$\quad\quad \forall v_l \in I(v_j) \wedge \forall v_m \in O(v_j) \wedge \forall v_l \in I(v_j)[\forall v_m \in O(v_j)]$

$$p'(v_l, v_m, t_{lm}) \leftarrow \begin{cases} p(v_l, v_j, t_{lj}) * p(v_j, v_m, t_{jm}) & \text{if } v_l \in I(v_j) \wedge v_m \in O(v_j) \\ p(v_l, v_m, t_{lm}) & \text{otherwise} \end{cases}$$
$$\forall (v_l, v_m, t_{lm}) \in D'$$

Note: When $m = 0, n = 0$ Rule 4 becomes Rule 1.
When $m > 0, n = 0$ Rule 4 becomes Rule 2.
When $m = 0, n > 0$ Rule 4 becomes Rule 3.

Rule 5: Merging parallel self-loops

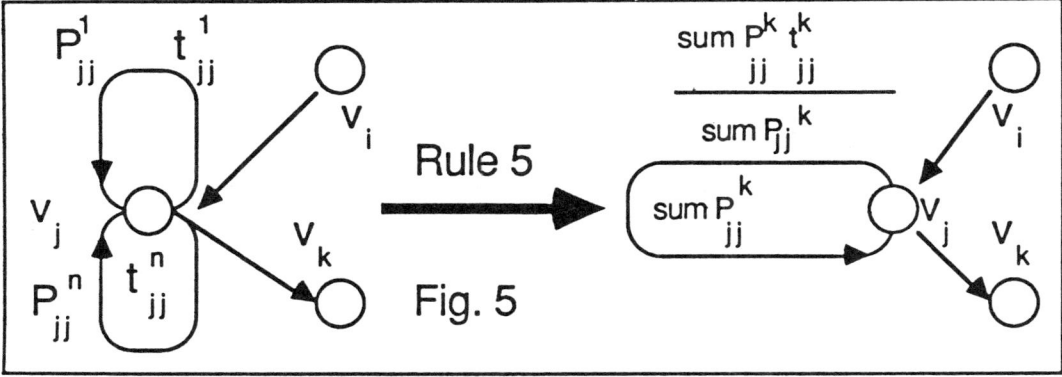

Fig. 5

If $\#L(v_j) = n \wedge n \geq 2$
Then $V' \leftarrow V$
$D' \leftarrow D - L(v_j) + (v_j, v_j, \frac{\sum_{k=1}^{n} p_{jj}^k t_{jj}^k}{\sum_{k=1}^{n} p_{jj}^k})$

$$p'(v_l, v_m, t_{lm}) \leftarrow \begin{cases} \sum_{k=1}^{n} p_{jj}^k & \text{if } l = m = j \\ p(v_l, v_m, t_{lm}) & \text{otherwise} \end{cases}$$
$$\forall (v_l, v_m, t_{lm}) \in D'$$

Rule 6: Merging parallel edges

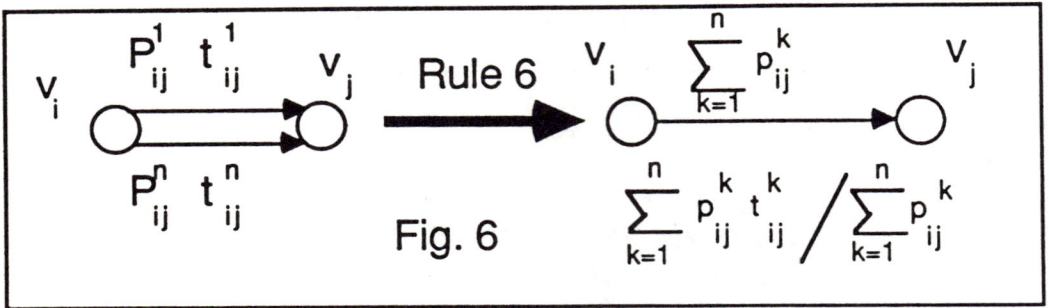

Fig. 6

If $\#E(v_i, v_j) = n \wedge n \geq 2$
Then $V' \leftarrow V$
$D' \leftarrow D - E(v_i, v_j) + (v_i, v_j, \frac{\sum_{k=1}^{n} p_{ij}^k t_{ij}^k}{\sum_{k=1}^{n} p_{ij}^k})$

$$p'(v_l, v_m, t_{lm}) \leftarrow \begin{cases} \sum_{k=1}^{n} p_{ij}^k & \text{if } l = i \wedge m = j \\ p(v_l, v_m, t_{lm}) & \text{otherwise} \end{cases}$$
$$\forall (v_l, v_m, t_{lm}) \in D'$$

Rule 7: Self-loop removal

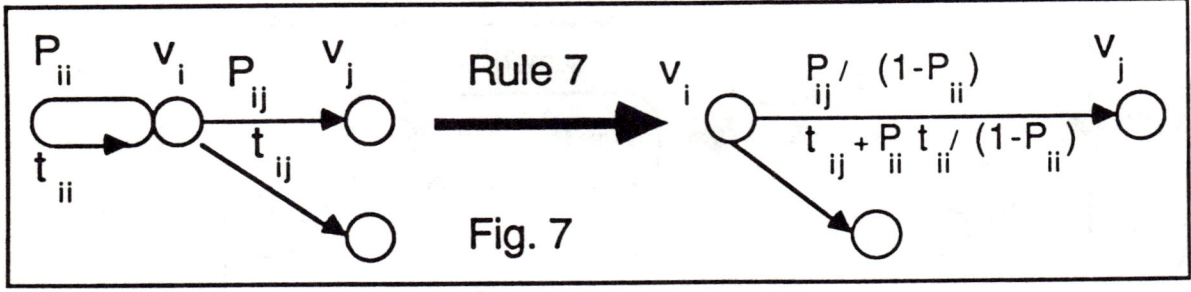

Fig. 7

If $\#L(v_i) = 1 \wedge \exists v_j : v_j \neq v_i \wedge v_j \in O(v_i)$
Then $V' \leftarrow V$
           $D' \leftarrow D - L(v_i) - (v_i, v_j, t_{ij}) + (v_i, v_j, t_{ij} + p_{ii} * t_{ii}/(1 - p_{ii}))$

$$p'(v_l, v_m, t_{lm}) \leftarrow \begin{cases} p_{ij}/(1 - p_{ii}) & \text{if } l = i \wedge m = j \\ p(v_l, v_m, t_{lm}) & \text{otherwise} \end{cases}$$
$$\forall (v_l, v_m, t_{lm}) \in D'$$

Note: Modified probabilities and transition times must be calculated for all other remaining edges with v_i as a source vertex.

Derivation of vertex folding rule

We now present the derivation of vertex folding rule. It is based on the law of conservation of transition time(LCTT).

Law of Conservation of Transition Time(LCTT)

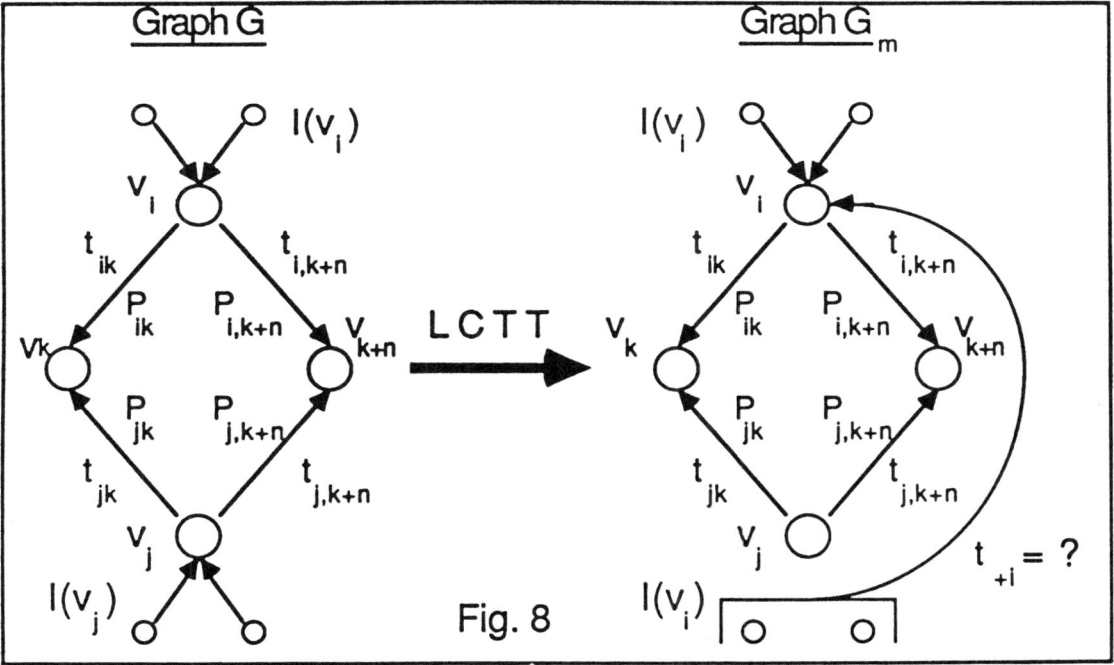

Fig. 8

1.	$v_i \neq v_j$
2.	$\#O(v_i) > 1 \wedge \#O(v_j) > 1$
3.	$O(v_i) = O(v_j)$
4.	$p_{i,k+\bar{k}} = p_{j,k+\bar{k}} \quad \forall \bar{k} = 0, 1, \ldots, \#O(v_i) - 1$
5.	$t_{i-} \quad \forall v_- \in O(v_i) \quad$ are equal
6.	$t_{j-} \quad \forall v_- \in O(v_j) \quad$ are equal
7.	$v_i \notin O(v_i) \wedge v_j \notin O(v_j)$

Table 1: Conditions of LCTT

Let $v_i, v_j \in V$ (Fig.8) and satisfy the conditions in Table 1. Condition 7 will be relaxed later(Transformation T3). Let $t_{i-} \neq t_{j-}$. The case, $t_{i-} = t_{j-}$ is trivial and is treated in Procedure EQUAL(section 3.2). It is interesting to note that Zuberek's[ZUB 86a] definition of vertex folding is valid only for the case, $t_{i-} = t_{j-}$. The analysis presented here includes the case, $t_{i-} \neq t_{j-}$. We present the complete algorithm for vertex folding in the latter part of this section(Rule 8 : Vertex folding). To the best of our knowledge, this is the first general vertex folding algorithm.

Objective: To delete vertex v_j (that is, to fold v_j onto v_i)

Case i. Let $I(v_j) \neq \emptyset$

The steps needed to be taken before deleting vertex v_j are:

1. Delete directed edges $(v_+, v_j, t_{+j}) \quad \forall v_+ \in I(v_j)$

2. For every deleted directed edge in step 1, add a new directed edge (v_+, v_i, t_{+i})

3. Calculate p_{+i} and t_{+i} for every new directed edge as described below

Hence, the modified probabilistic transition graph G_m(Fig.8) can be obtained from graph G(Fig.8) if

$$V_m \leftarrow V$$

$$D_m \leftarrow D - (v_+, v_j, t_{+j}) + (v_+, v_i, t_{+i}) \quad \forall v_+ \in I(v_j)$$

$$p_m(v_l, v_m, t_{lm}) \leftarrow \begin{cases} p(v_+, v_j, t_{+j}) & \text{if } v_l = v_+ \in I(v_j) \wedge m = i \\ p(v_l, v_m, t_{lm}) & \text{otherwise} \end{cases}$$

$$\forall (v_l, v_m, t_{lm}) \in D_m$$

and t_{+i} is given by the following equation:

$$\boxed{t_{+i} = t_{+j} + t_{j-} - t_{i-}} \qquad \forall v_+ \in I(v_j) \tag{1}$$

Case ii. Let $I(v_j) = \emptyset$

Let $I(v_i) \neq \emptyset$. The case, $I(v_i) = \emptyset$ is trivial and is considered in the later part of this section(Algorithm for vertex folding).

The only step needed to be taken before deleting vertex v_j is to adjust t_{+i} and $t_{i-}\ \forall v_+ \in I(v_i), v_- \in O(v_i)$ as described below.

Hence, the modified probabilistic transition graph G_m can be obtained from graph G if

$$V_m \leftarrow V$$

$$D_m \leftarrow D(\text{modified } t_{+i}, t_{i-} \forall v_+ \in I(v_i), v_- \in O(v_i) \text{ as given below})$$

$$p_m(v_l, v_m, t_{lm}) \leftarrow p(v_l, v_m, t_{lm}) \qquad \forall (v_l, v_m, t_{lm}) \in D_m$$

$$\boxed{t_{i-_{new}} = t_{j-}} \qquad \forall v_- \in O(v_i) \tag{2}$$

$$\boxed{t_{+i_{new}} = t_{+i_{old}} + t_{i-} - t_{j-}} \qquad \forall v_+ \in I(v_i) \tag{3}$$

Equations (1) and (2)-(3) are called the *Laws of Conservation of Transition Time* (LCTT).

We have now established the basis for deleting vertex v_j from G, a process called the vertex folding. The only restriction is that t_{+i} and $t_{+i_{new}}$, calculated using equations (1) and (3) respectively must be non-negative. Hence, the transformations for deleting vertex v_j(that is, folding v_j onto v_i) for cases(i) and (ii) respectively are as follows:

Transformation T1:

$$V' \leftarrow V - v_j$$

$$D' \leftarrow D - (v_j, v_-, t_{j-}) - (v_+, v_j, t_{+j}) + (v_+, v_i, t_{+i}) \qquad \forall v_- \in O(v_j), v_+ \in I(v_j)$$

and p', t_{+i} are same as p_m and t_{+i} respectively given in case(i).

Transformation T2:

$$V' \leftarrow V - v_j$$

$$D' \leftarrow D - (v_j, v_-, t_{j-}) \qquad \forall v_- \in O(v_j)$$

and $p', t_{+i_{new}}, t_{i-_{new}}$ are same as p_m, $t_{+i_{new}}$ and $t_{i-_{new}}$ respectively given in case(ii).

Example 1

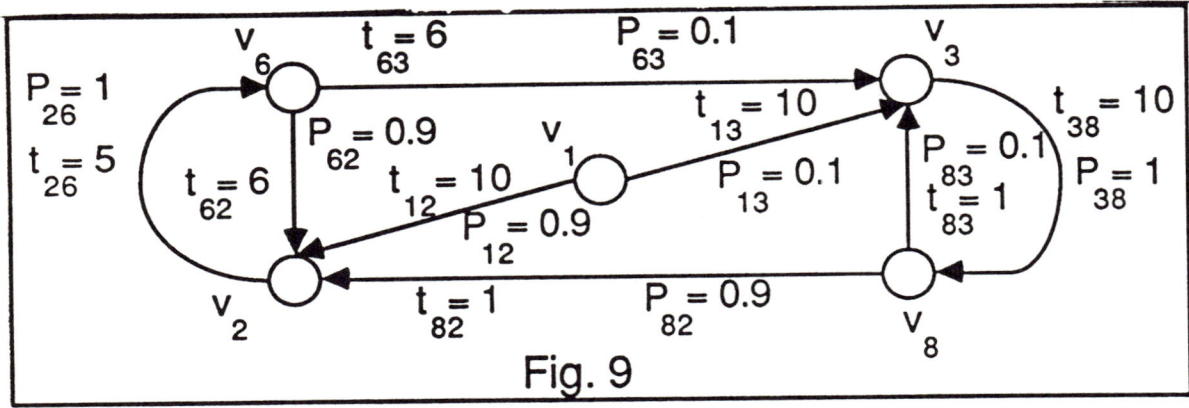

Fig. 9

$V = \{v_1, v_2, v_3, v_6, v_8\}$

$D = \left\{ \begin{array}{l} (v_1, v_2, 10), (v_1, v_3, 10), (v_2, v_6, 5), (v_3, v_8, 10) \\ (v_6, v_2, 6), (v_6, v_3, 6), (v_8, v_2, 1), (v_8, v_3, 1) \end{array} \right\}$

$p = \{0.9, 0.1, 1.0, 1.0, 0.9, 0.1, 0.9, 0.1\}$

The probabilistic transition graph shown in Fig.9 is taken from [ZUB 86b] (after applying Rule 1 : Vertex reduction) to demonstrate LCTT, Transformation T1 and Transformation T2.

Let $v_i = v_6, v_j = v_8, v_k = v_2, v_{k+1} = v_3$

Referring to Fig.9, we obtain:

$O(v_6) = O(v_8) = \{v_2, v_3\}$

$p_{6,2} = p_{8,2} = 0.9 \quad \wedge \quad p_{6,3} = p_{8,3} = 0.1$

$t_{6,2} = t_{6,3} = 6 = t_{i-} \quad \wedge \quad t_{8,2} = t_{8,3} = 1 = t_{j-}$

$v_6 \notin O(v_6), v_8 \notin O(v_8) \quad \wedge \quad I(v_8) = \{v_3\} \neq \emptyset$

Hence, all the conditions in Table 1 are satisfied. Now, we can obtain the modified probabilistic transition graph as shown in Fig.10 using LCTT. That is,

$$\begin{aligned}
V_m &= V = \{v_1, v_2, v_3, v_6, v_8\} \\
D_m &= D - (v_3, v_8, 10) + (v_3, v_6, t_{3,6}) \\
&= \left\{ \begin{array}{l} (v_1, v_2, 10), (v_1, v_3, 10), (v_2, v_6, 5), (v_3, v_6, t_{3,6}) \\ (v_6, v_2, 6), (v_6, v_3, 6), (v_8, v_2, 1), (v_8, v_3, 1) \end{array} \right\} \\
p_m &= \{0.9, 0.1, 1.0, 1.0, 0.9, 0.1, 0.9, 0.1\}
\end{aligned}$$

and $t_{3,6}$ is calculated as follows:

$$t_{3,6} = t_{3,8} + t_{j_-} - t_{i_-} = 10 + 1 - 6 = 5$$

Now applying Transformation T1, we obtain the reduced probabilistic transition graph as shown in Fig.11.

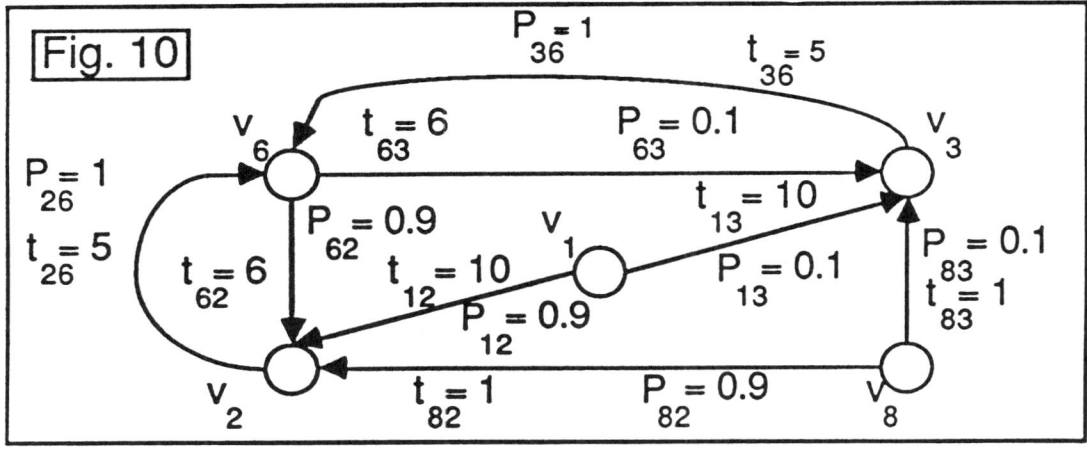

Fig. 10

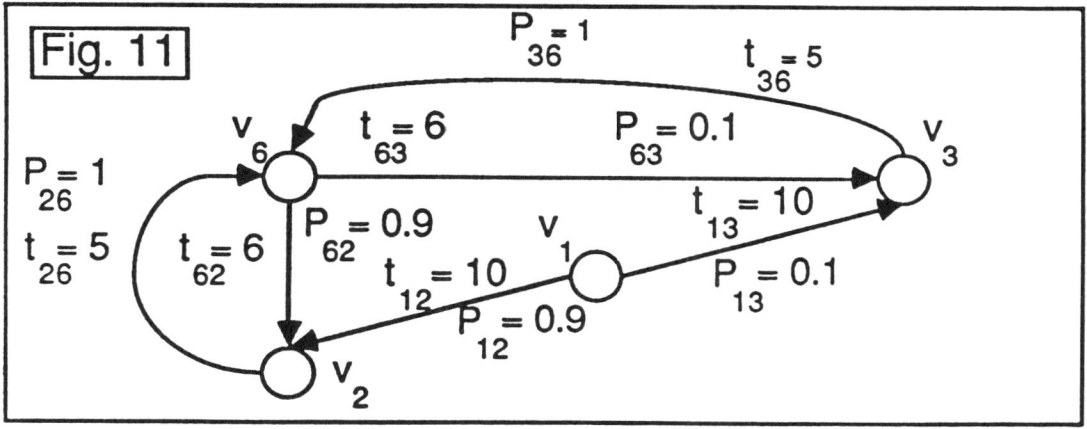

Fig. 11

Definition 9

Let $CVF = \{v_1, v_2, \ldots, v_n : v_i \in V \wedge n > 1\}$. Then, CVF is said to be a *candidate set for vertex folding* if

1. $\#O(v_i) > 1 \quad \forall v_i \in CVF$

2. $O(v_i)$ must be identical $\quad \forall v_i \in CVF$

3. $\forall \bar{k} = 0, 1, \ldots, \#O(v_i) - 1 \quad [\forall v_i \in CVF \quad p_{i,k+\bar{k}} \text{ must be equal}]$

The set of all CVF in a probabilistic transition graph is said to be a *Vertex folding set* and is denoted by VFS. That is, $VFS = \{CVF_i : CVF_i \text{ is a CVF}\}$

Example 2

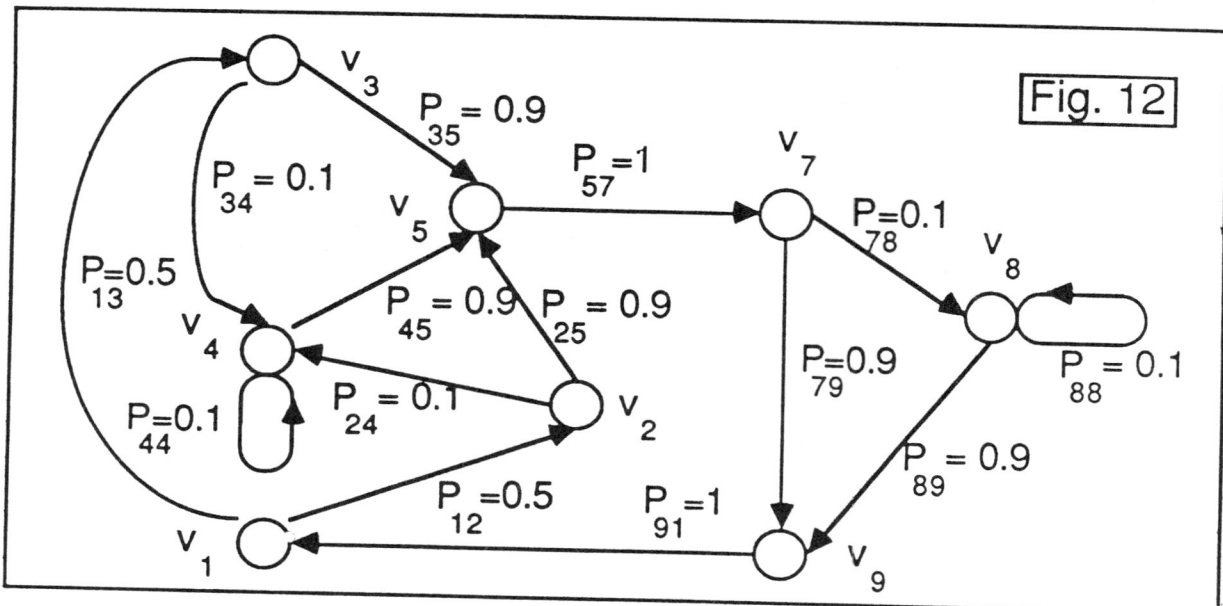

Fig. 12

Referring to Fig.12, we obtain:

$O(v_2) = O(v_3) = O(v_4) = \{v_4, v_5\}$

$p_{2,4} = p_{3,4} = p_{4,4} = 0.1 \quad \wedge \quad p_{2,5} = p_{3,5} = p_{4,5} = 0.9$

Therefore, $CVF_1 = \{v_2, v_3, v_4\}$

$O(v_7) = O(v_8) = \{v_8, v_9\}$

$p_{7,8} = p_{8,8} = 0.1 \quad \wedge \quad p_{7,9} = p_{8,9} = 0.9$

Therefore, $CVF_2 = \{v_7, v_8\}$ and $VFS = \{CVF_1, CVF_2\} = \{\{v_2, v_3, v_4\}, \{v_7, v_8\}\}$
Note: We did not include transition times in Fig.12 since they are not needed for computing CVF.

Definition 10
Vertex folding rule is said to be *enabled* if $VFS \neq \emptyset$.

Definition 11
Let $v_i, v_j \in CVF$. Then, we say that edges (v_i, v_-, t_{i-}) and (v_j, v_-, t_{j-}) for every $v_- \in O(v_i)$ are said to have *equal transition time* if

$$t_{i-} \quad \forall v_- \in O(v_i) \text{ are equal} \quad \wedge \quad t_{j-} \quad \forall v_- \in O(v_j) \text{ are equal} \quad \wedge \quad t_{i-} = t_{j-}$$

and *unequal transition time* if

$$\exists v_- \in O(v_i) : t_{i-} \neq t_{j-}$$

Definition 12
Vertex folding rule is said to be *firable* if it is enabled.

The algorithm which specifies the firing rules for vertex folding is described next.

Rule 8 : Vertex folding
Let vertices v_i and v_j in a graph G be members of the same $CVF \in VFS$. Then, G' as a result of vertex folding (v_j onto v_i) can be obtained as follows:

If $\quad (v_i, v_-, t_{i-}) \wedge (v_j, v_-, t_{j-}) \quad \forall v_- \in O(v_i)$ have equal transition time
    Then Procedure EQUAL
    Else Procedure UNEQUAL
Endif

Procedure EQUAL
    $V' \leftarrow V - v_j$
    Case $(I(v_j) = \emptyset)$ Of
      t: $\quad D' \leftarrow D - (v_j, v_-, t_{j-}) \quad \forall v_- \in O(v_j)$
      f: $\quad$ Case $(v_j \notin I(v_j))$ Of
          t: $\quad D' \leftarrow D - (v_j, v_-, t_{j-}) - (v_+, v_j, t_{+j}) + (v_+, v_i, t_{+j})$
              $\forall v_- \in O(v_j) \wedge \forall v_+ \in I(v_j)$
          f: $\quad D' \leftarrow D - (v_j, v_-, t_{j-}) - (v_+, v_j, t_{+j}) + (v_l, v_i, t_{lj})$
              $\forall v_- \in O(v_j) \wedge \forall v_+ \in I(v_j) \wedge \forall v_l \in I(v_j) \wedge v_l \neq v_j$
        End {inner Case}
    End {outer Case}
End Procedure EQUAL

Procedure UNEQUAL
    Case $(I(v_j) = \emptyset, I(v_i) = \emptyset)$ Of
     (t,t): $G' \leftarrow G$
     (t,f):   Case $(v_i \notin I(v_i))$ Of
          t: T2
          f: T3,T2
       End {Case (t,f)}
    (f,t),(f,f):
        Case $(v_j \notin I(v_j), v_i \notin I(v_i))$ Of
         (t,t): T1
         (t,f),(f,t),(f,f): T3,T1
       End {Case (f,t),(f,f)}
   End{main Case}
End Procedure UNEQUAL
Transformation T3
   If $\exists v_{k+\bar{k}} \in V : v_{k+\bar{k}} \neq v_i \wedge v_{k+\bar{k}} \neq v_j \wedge v_{k+\bar{k}} \in O(v_i)$
     Then T3-A
     Else T3-B,T3-A
   Endif
End Transformation T3

Next, we describe transformations T3-A and T3-B. In transformations T3-A and T3-B, when there is more than one self-loop at v_i and/or v_j, we always select such a pair of edges for which $p_{ii} = p_{ji}$ and/or $p_{ij} = p_{jj}$.

Transformation T3-A

Objective: Removal of all self-loops at v_i and v_j, and constructing junctions instead.

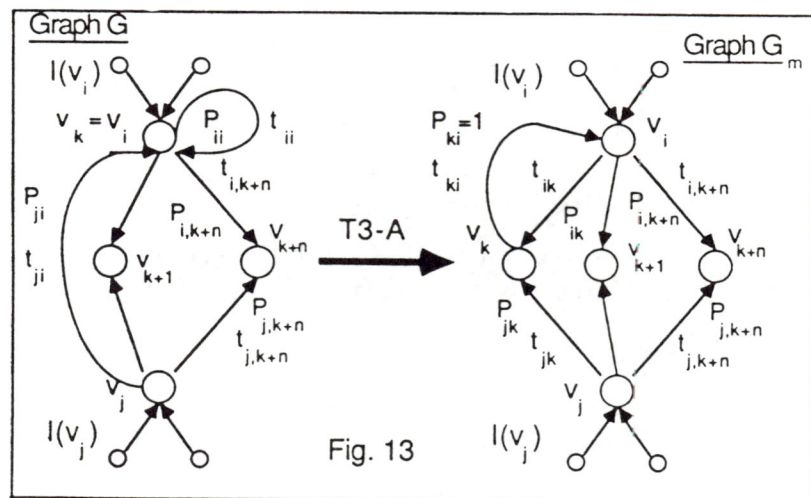

Fig. 13

If $\quad \forall v_{k+\bar{k}} : v_{k+\bar{k}} \neq v_i \wedge v_{k+\bar{k}} \neq v_j \wedge v_{k+\bar{k}} \in O(v_i)$
$\quad\quad [t_{i,k+\bar{k}} \text{ are equal} \wedge t_{j,k+\bar{k}} \text{ are equal}]$

Then $\quad V_m \leftarrow V + v_k$
$\quad\quad D_m \leftarrow D - (v_i, v_i, t_{ii}) - (v_j, v_i, t_{ji}) + (v_i, v_k, t_{ik})$
$\quad\quad\quad + (v_k, v_i, t_{ki}) + (v_j, v_k, t_{jk})$

$$p_m(v_l, v_m, t_{lm}) \leftarrow \begin{cases} p(v_j, v_i, t_{ji}) & \text{if } l = j \wedge m = k \\ p(v_i, v_i, t_{ii}) & \text{if } l = i \wedge m = k \\ 1 & \text{if } l = k \wedge m = i \\ p(v_l, v_m, t_{lm}) & \text{otherwise} \end{cases}$$

$$\forall (v_l, v_m, t_{lm}) \in D_m$$

and t_{ik}, t_{jk} and t_{ki} are given as follows:

$t_{ik} \leftarrow t_{i\_} \quad$ for any $v_\_ \neq v_i \wedge v_\_ \neq v_j \wedge v_\_ \in O(v_i)$
$t_{jk} \leftarrow t_{j\_} \quad$ for any $v_\_ \neq v_i \wedge v_\_ \neq v_j \wedge v_\_ \in O(v_j)$
$t_{ki} \leftarrow (t_{ii} - t_{ik}) \vee (t_{ji} - t_{jk})$

Apply T3-A until all self-loops at v_i and v_j are removed since one application of T3-A removes just one self-loop at v_i or v_j. t_{ki} must be non-negative.

Transformation T3-B:

Objective: Select a self-loop either at v_i or v_j and construct a junction at $v_k \neq v_i \wedge v_k \neq v_j$ by removing the selected self-loop.

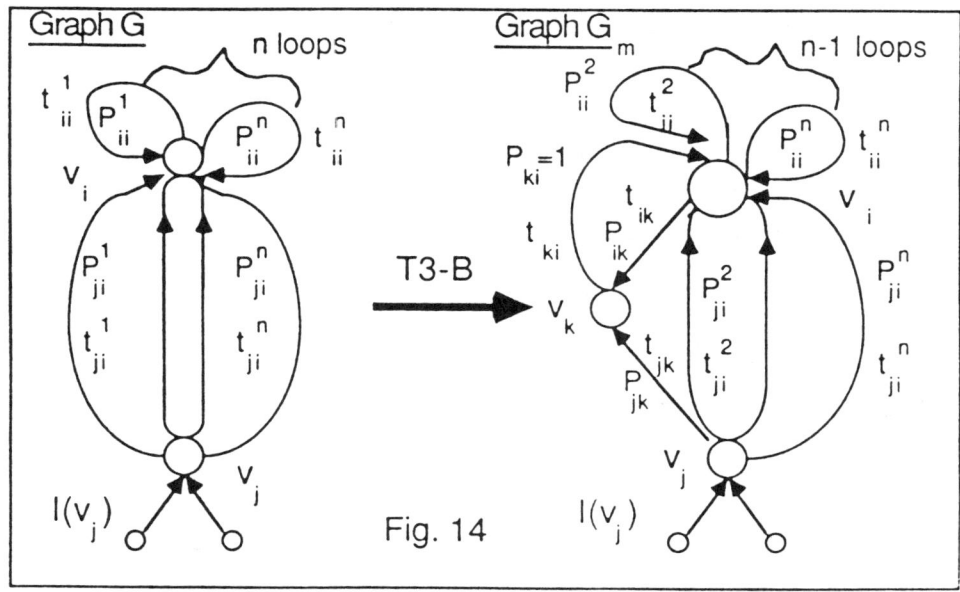

Fig. 14

The graph G_m from G can be obtained as follows:

$$V_m \leftarrow V + v_k$$

$$D_m \leftarrow D - (v_i, v_i, t_{ii}^1) - (v_j, v_i, t_{ji}^1) + (v_i, v_k, t_{ik}) + (v_k, v_i, t_{ki}) + (v_j, v_k, t_{jk})$$

$$p_m(v_l, v_m, t_{lm}) \leftarrow \begin{cases} p(v_j, v_i, t_{ji}^1) & \text{if } l = j \wedge m = k \\ p(v_i, v_i, t_{ii}^1) & \text{if } l = i \wedge m = k \\ 1 & \text{if } l = k \wedge m = i \\ p(v_l, v_m, t_{lm}) & \text{otherwise} \end{cases}$$

$$\forall (v_l, v_m, t_{lm}) \in D_m$$

and t_{ik}, t_{jk} and t_{ki} are given as follows:

If $\quad t_{ji}^1 > t_{ii}^1 \quad$ then $\quad$ choose t_{ik} from $[0, t_{ii}^1]$
$\qquad\qquad\qquad\qquad\qquad t_{jk} \leftarrow t_{ik} + t_{ji}^1 - t_{ii}^1$
$\qquad\qquad\qquad$ else $\quad$ choose t_{jk} from $[0, t_{ji}^1]$
$\qquad\qquad\qquad\qquad\qquad t_{ik} \leftarrow t_{jk} + t_{ii}^1 - t_{ji}^1$

Endif

$$t_{ki} \leftarrow (t_{ii}^1 - t_{ik}) \vee (t_{ji}^1 - t_{jk})$$

3 Application to stop-and-wait protocol

We illustrate here the application of reduction rules(Section 2) to reduce the transition graph(Fig. 15) obtained from timed Petri net analysis of stop-and-wait protocol. Complete description of the timed Petri net model of stop-and-wait protocol and its analysis is given in [MAS 87]. The steps required to obtain the reduced graph (Fig. 23) from the original graph (Fig. 15) are listed below. Each directed edge in Figs. 15-23 is labeled with a tuple (p, t) where p is the probability and t is the transition time. The path representing error-free or successful transfer of messages is shown by bold directed edges.

- Apply vertex reduction rule to vertices—2, 4, 8, 9, 10, 11, 13, 14, 15, 16, 17 and 19 in Fig.15. The result is Fig.16.

- Apply vertex folding rule to vertices—3 and 18 in Fig.16. The result is Fig.17.

- Apply vertex reduction rule to vertex 5 in Fig.17. The result is Fig.18.

- Apply vertex folding rule to vertices—1 and 12 in Fig.18. The result is Fig.19.

- Apply junction removal rule to vertex 7 in Fig.19. The result is Fig.20.
- Apply decision removal to vertex 6 in Fig.20. The result is Fig.21.
- Apply decision removal to vertex 3 in Fig.21. The result is Fig.22.
- Merge all unsuccessful parallel self-loops in Fig.22. The result is Fig.23.

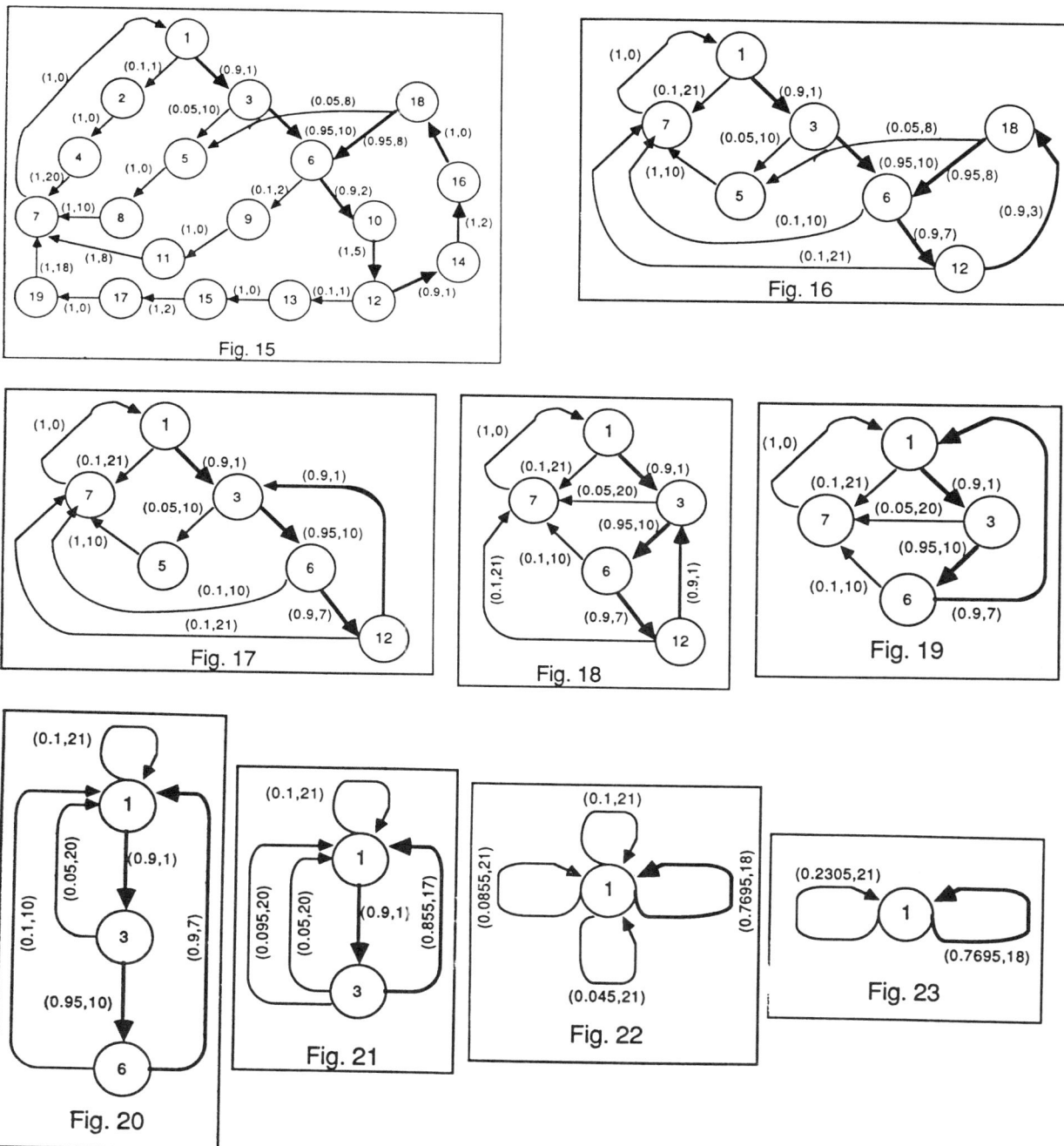

4 Conclusion

The eight rules described above can be used to reduce timed, probabilistic transition graphs to manageable size. The rules may be applied in a variety of orders as required to eliminate certain transitions or vertices and preserve those deemed to be important. From these reduced graphs numerical values of performance parameters such as throughput and delay can be calculated permitting optimum packet size to be obtained. In addition, the algebraic correctness of protocols is easily seen from the same model.

References

[BEI 70] Beizer, B. "Analytical techniques for the statistical evaluation of program running time", Fall Joint Computer Conference, 1970, pp. 519-524.

[GRA 73] Graham, R.H. "Performance prediction", in: Advance Course in Software Engineering, Lecture notes in Economics and Mathematical Systems (Springer-verlag, Berlin, 1973), vol. 81.

[MAS 87] Masapati, G.H. "Performance prediction using Petri Nets", M.Sc. Thesis, Dept. of Computer Science, University of Ottawa, June 1987.

[PET 81] Peterson, J.L. "Petri Net Theory and Modeling of Systems", Englewood Cliffs, NJ: Prentice-Hall, 1981.

[RUD 83] Rudin, H. "From formal protocol specification towards automated performance prediction", Protocol specification, Testing and Validation, III, 1983, pp.257-269.

[ZUB 86a] Zuberek, W.M. "Inhibitor D-Timed Petri nets and performance analysis of communication protocols", INFOR, vol.24, No.3, 1986, pp.231-249.

[ZUB 86b] Zuberek, W.M. "Modified D-timed Petri nets, timeouts, and modeling of communication protocols", in: Proceedings. 6th Int. Conf. on Distributed Computing Systems, 1986, pp.452-457.

EXTENSIONS TO COMMUNICATING SEQUENTIAL PROCESSES TO ALLOW PROTOCOL PERFORMANCE SPECIFICATION

John J. Zic,
Basser Department of Computer Science,
University of Sydney,
NSW 2006 Australia

ABSTRACT

Formalisms based on Hoare's Communicating Sequential Processes (CSP) and Milner's Calculus of Communicating Systems (CCS) for verifying protocols are currently being used by the International Standards Organisation (ISO). However, these models need to be extended if protocol performance specification and verification is to be done, as neither of these models have timing information (other than sequencing) nor a way of specifying controlled loss of information.

This paper presents two extensions to Hoare's CSP that are felt by the author to provide suitable mechanisms for specifying protocol performance. Firstly, the effects of introducing time into CSP are presented, based on the work done by Reed and Roscoe. Secondly, the traces model is modified by associating probabilities with event sequences.

Finally, some example specifications are given using these two extensions.

Symbols Used

$\rightarrow$	prefix operator
P/s	process P after event s
$<\alpha, \beta, ...>$	process trace consisting of events α, β ...
$P \backslash a$	process P with event a hidden
$\mu X.P(X)$	recursive defintion of a process, such that $X = P(X)$
$c\,!\,x$	output the value of x onto channel c
$c\,?\,v$	from channel c input a message and assign it to v
$\|$	general choice operator
$\mid$	deterministic choice operator
$\sqcap$	nondeterministic choice operator
$[\![\pi]\!]$	probabilistic choice operator
$_\lambda Q(\Sigma)$	the left quotient of length λ of a sequence Σ
$\parallel$	parallel composition
;	sequential composition
$\|\|\|$	interleaving
$\mathbb{I}_+$	set of positive integers
$\mathbb{R}_+$	set of positive real numbers
$\mathbb{Pr}$	set of reals in the range [0,1]
$\#\Sigma$	length of a sequence Σ
$\Sigma_1 {}^\wedge \Sigma_2$	Σ_2 concatenated with Σ_1
$\upharpoonright$	set restriction
$\Sigma_1 \leq \Sigma_2$	sequence Σ_1 is a prefix of sequence Σ_2
$fix(X)$	the fixed point of X

Introduction

The use of formalisms such as those of Communicating Sequential Processes (CSP) [1] and the Calculus of Communicating Systems (CCS) [2] in protocol specification and verification is gaining acceptance throughout the protocol engineering community. The International Standards Organisation (ISO) has adopted LOTOS (which is based on CCS) as one of its protocol verification and specification systems. It is also investigating other formalisms, such as Petri and Predicate Nets; the Pascal-like Estelle; and the System and Description Language, SDL. The requirements for a specification system are that it is sufficiently powerful mathematically to model concurrency, communication, nondeterminism and it provide a high degree of abstraction power. An additional requirement may be that the specification is executable. Some work on using the first-order predicate language, Prolog, on specifying the transport layer of the OSI model has been done by Logrippo [3]. Unfortunately, these models (CSP/CCS/LOTOS) are unsuitable for performance criteria specification, which require a mechanism to denote the passage of fixed amounts of time and the ability to specify that event sequences will occur with given probabilities.

This paper presents two extensions to CSP to enable protocol performance specification. Firstly, time is introduced into the CSP model (based on the work done by Reed and Roscoe [4]), and some of its major features are presented. Secondly, stochastic determinism is introduced by the use of a new class of choice operators, probabilistic choice. This class of operators allows the specification of probabilities of event sequences (or traces). A brief exposition of their characteristics with respect to CSP is also presented.

Finally, a few examples of the use of these two extensions are presented.

Specifications

Before commencing on descriptions of the two extensions, what is meant by a specification? Specifications of complex systems are most commonly done by use of ad hoc techniques (including natural language), at least in the initial stages of the system design. As the design progresses, this lax notation is usually refined into one that is more precise and unambiguous. Interpreting these ad hoc specifications usually results in errors of misunderstanding of what is being specified.

In order to remedy this situation, software engineering groups are advocating the use of a more formalised system of specification. These may be done at an axiomatic level, with typed operations in specific domains and ranges; or may take on an operational approach, where the implementational characteristics are specified. Unfortunately, there still exists a major problem – the specification, although verifiably correct, may be specifying the wrong system. "One of the problems in formally specifiying a system is that we don't always specify the one we want" [11].

This paper adopts the following usage:

A *specification* S in a given complete semantic domain D is a mapping from D to $\{T, F\}$. (1)

A specification S is said to be *satisfiable* in a domain D if $\{\exists Q \in D \mid S(Q) = T\}$. This is written as Q **sat** S. (2)

The mapping from the semantic domain to $\{T, F\}$ is, in this paper, the Predicate Calculus. Further details on this subject may be found in many works on specification systems, including the work by Hoare [1], Jones [10], Bergstra, Klop and Olderog [4], or Olderog [9]. These two definitions allow a basis for reasoning about correctness.

A discussion of the Timed CSP model is now presented.

TIMED CSP

In trying to specify protocol performance criteria, recording event sequences of deterministic processes as in the untimed CSP models is insufficient. Specifiable timing information is needed in order to model a network's performance. For example, consider the difficulty in attempting to specify (using untimed CSP) a telephone system's "give up" signal after a number that is being called is not answered within a specific time (usually about a minute). This type of specification is quite common in performance criteria of real-time systems.

The author in [5] proposed some informal extensions to the basic model of CSP to include time-stamped events, process local clocks and a special process which act as single event buffer with specified delays. Independently, Reed and Roscoe [op. cit.] had formalised a similar theory. A summary of their results is presented below.

The following postulates may be used for performance specification of distributed systems such as protocols.

Postulate 1. To describe and verify real-time aspects of a system of distributed processes, a global clock process is required to maintain timing information.

This is achieved by using the global clock to effectively label the untimed CSP events. An event in the Timed CSP model is a pair, (t, e), where t is the time at which event e occurred. Process local clocks can be derived easily from a global clock process if required. The author feels that the difference in the notation of timed events as a pair or as a time-stamp is irrelevant, and has adopted the former throughout this paper.

Postulate 2. After engaging in an event, every process requires a small, finite time before it may be ready to engage in the next event (including any recursive calls to itself). This delay is called the System Delay Constant.

This postulate appeals to the realistic view that a process can engage in only a finite number of events in any finite time (that is determined by the global clock). Each process can be made to run at some finite speed by allowing a delay of some fixed amount between participation of one event (in the process alphabet) and the readiness of the process to engage in the next event.

In order to provide a method of delaying events (which typically happens in a loosely coupled network) a special *WAIT* process is also introduced. It does nothing but provide a delay by a specific amount, and then terminates successfully.

Postulate 3. After engaging in some sequence of events, a process may engage in a large number of internal events, which, in the limit, may lead to divergence. Every process may therefore be described in terms of its timed stability with respect to the degree of internal actions.

The timed stability model is based on specifying processes as ordered pairs, (σ, α) where σ is a sequence of timed events, or a timed trace, and α being the time (called the *process stability time*) at which the process is ready to engage in new events after having engaged in the timed trace σ. This model describes a continuum of process behaviors, ranging from "process is deterministic" to "process is divergent". The parameter α takes on real number values in the range $STAB = [0,\infty]$, whereas the untimed models provide only boolean values for this parameter.

Postulate 4. Every event that is hidden from its environment in a process abstraction (by use of hiding) is assumed to occur as soon as possible.

Reed and Roscoe [op.cit.] summarise this postulate as:

"By hiding, we remove external control. Hence, any time that a process is willing to engage in an internal action, it is permitted to do so".

Some notation and results

The way in which the progress of a process is described in the Timed CSP model is by allowing a distinction between the actual event (which is the untimed CSP model), and the time at which the process is ready to engage in the event. This distinction is needed because of the introduction of the system delay constant.

Let Σ denote the process alphabet in the usual untimed CSP notation. Events superscripted with "r" denote events which the process engaged in as soon as they became available. Let the set of such superscripted events be Σ^r which is given by $\Sigma^r = \Sigma \cup \{e^r \mid e \in \Sigma\}$.

The set of all *timed events* is represented by $T\Sigma = [0, \infty) \times \Sigma^r$. Typically, this is a set of pairs (t, e), where t is the time at which event e occurred.

The set of all *timed traces* is denoted by

$$(T\Sigma)^*_\leq = \{s \in T\Sigma^* \mid \text{if } (t,e) \text{ precedes } (t',e') \text{ then } t \leq t'\}$$

For the set of all timed traces $(T\Sigma)^*_\leq \times STAB$ we can define

$$Traces(S) = \{\forall s \in (T\Sigma)^*_\leq \exists a \in STAB, (s, a) \in S\}$$

The process $\bot$ represents the bottom (the term "bottom" arises from recursive fixed point theory; it is the same as $\mu X.X$ of the continuum of processes. It cannot engage in any events with its environment and is completely divergent.

Let TM_s be the set of subsets of $(T\Sigma)^*_\leq \times STAB$ that satisfy the following conditions:

1. Each process trace has a unique stability value.
2. Once an event is available, it may be engaged normally.
3. Events that occur at the same time can have no order imposed on them.
4. The stability value of a process' trace cannot be less than the time of the last event in the trace.
5. Each process can engage in a finite number of events in any finite time.
6. Once an event is available, it is continuously available until it is engaged.
7. The range of future behaviors of a process after it has reached stability does not change until some other event occurs.

A semantic mapping from the domain of CSP onto TM_s may be found in terms of the following CSP terms:- $\bot$, $STOP$, $SKIP$, $WAIT$, $\rightarrow$, $|$, $\sqcap$, $\|$, $\||$, $;$, $\setminus$, f, f^{-1}, and $\mu X.F(X)$. All operators still obey the laws exhibited by the untimed CSP.

However, even though a large number of the algebraic laws for the operators hold from the untimed model, there are three exceptions which do not because of the introduction of time. These are:

$$P \| STOP = STOP \quad \text{if } P \neq \bot,$$
$$= \bot \quad \text{if } P = \bot;$$

$$(a \rightarrow P)\setminus b = (a \rightarrow P\setminus b) \quad \text{if } a \neq b,$$
$$= P\setminus b \quad \text{if } a = b;$$

and

$$(a \rightarrow P) \|| (b \rightarrow Q) = (a \rightarrow (P \|| (b \rightarrow Q))) \mid (b \rightarrow ((a \rightarrow P) \|| Q)).$$

The first and second only fail because of the passage of time. The third fails because of the improvement inherent in parallel execution over that of sequential execution of processes. Consider the following simple counter-example. Let $P = a \rightarrow WAIT(t_P); P$ and $Q = b \rightarrow WAIT(t_Q); Q$ then LHS of the last equation gives a stability time of $max(t_P, t_Q)$ whereas, the RHS gives stability time of $(t_P + t_Q)$.

Having arrived at this point, what can be said about the proof techniques offered by the Timed CSP model? Can it be inferred, given a specification and an implementation of a process, that the process and all recursive calls of the process satisfy the specification? Referring back to the earlier definitions (1) and (2), the following theorem is postulated.

Theorem: if C^r is a contraction mapping such that $C^r: TM_s \rightarrow TM_s$ and S is a continuous, satisfiable specification, then if $(\exists Q \in TM_s, Q \text{ sat } S \Rightarrow C^r \text{ sat } S)$ then $fix(C^r)$ **sat** S.

It is this theorem, when used in conjunction with postulate 2 that provides the necessary tools for proving that a process satisfies its specification. It should be noted that a similar theorem exists for the untimed CSP model and is given by Hoare [op.cit., p62]:

If $F(X)$ is left guarded, and $STOP$ sat S, and
$(X$ sat $S \Rightarrow F(X)$ sat $S)$ then $\mu X.F(X)$ sat S.

Reed and Roscoe state that the timed stability model provides only partial correctness, giving only an upper bound on the possible traces of a process. Because of the inherent unfair nondeterministic nature of concurrent systems, the model fails to guarantee that all traces will occur, and so may not detect deadlocked states. In the case of protocol specification and verification, it is vital that "proof of correctness" is done on the basis of an untimed model, rather than a timed model. Only once the model has been proven correct for all possible timings, can performance specification and verification can be performed.

However, if a mechanism that ensures fairness is incorporated the timed model may provide a sufficiently powerful model to enable performance verification. This fairness mechanism is introduced into the extended CSP model by stochastic determinism.

STOCHASTIC DETERMINISM

The relationship of stochastic determinism to the deterministic (and nondeterministic) process models in CSP is very similar to that of stochastic sequential machines (SSM) to finite state machines (FSM). Quite an extensive theory has been built up around SSM, as exemplified in the book by Paz [6].

This form of determinism, by associating probabilities with a process' traces, ensures fairness. Other work has been done by Bergstra, Klop and Olderog [7] who have added new semantics to the Failures model of Hoare [1]. However, this is felt by the author not to be suitable for protocol performance specification because protocol engineers typically specify performance in probabilistic terms.

The mechanism by which stochastic determinism is implemented is by associating probabilities with CSP's nondeterministic choice operator. A formalised treatment of some of the characteristics of this family of operators is given by the author in [7]. Work is in progress by the author on the complete formalisation of this extension, and its interaction with the Timed CSP model.

Consider the following nondeterministic loss process, whose behavior is expressed in untimed CSP. *Loss* has one input and one output channel (*left* and *right*, respectively):

$Loss = (left\,?\,x \rightarrow right\,!\,x \rightarrow Loss) \parallel (left\,?\,x \rightarrow Loss)$.

This is of limited value in performance analysis because of its unfair nondeterministic nature. It could input from the left forever without ever outputting a single thing to the right, just as would an extremely noisy wire. A protocol designer typically gives a throughput measure for a given (stochastic) error rate when attempting to specify performance criteria of a protocol. This implies that a method of introducing a controlled, specifiable loss mechanism needs to be introduced into CSP by making nondeterminism fair. Fairness in the proposed model is ensured by assigning certain probabilities to event sequences at any given time in the execution of the network of processes, echoing what is normally expected in designing a system.

Let P and Q be any two processes. Let R be the process that can be represented by the union of the traces of P and Q. Write "$P[\![\pi]\!]Q$" when the probability of finding a trace of Q in the initial subsequence of any given length of R is π, and the probability of finding a trace of P in the same initial subsequence of R is $1 - \pi$.

The initial subsequence of length λ of a trace is sometimes referred to as the *left quotient of length* λ. Its behavior is described by the semantic equation
$\forall \lambda \mid \lambda \in \mathbb{I}_+, {}_\lambda Q: traces \rightarrow traces$.

For example, for the *clock* process given by Hoare [1] the left quotient of length three of the clock's traces is:

$_{3}Q\ (traces(clock))$
$= {}_{3}Q(\{tick\}^*)$
$= \{<>, <tick>, <tick, tick>\}.$

The traces of a process, P, which has an alphabet $\alpha(P) = \{a_1, a_2, \ldots, a_n\}$, can be written as

$traces(P) = \{<>, <b_1>, <b_1, b_2>, \ldots, <b_1, b_2, \ldots, b_i>, \ldots \},$

where each $b_i \in \alpha(P)$.

Note – there is no ordering implied in the selection of each b_i from the process alphabet. For example, b_1 doesn't have to be event a_1. The only criterion is that the mapping is unique.

That is, $traces(P) = \{\sigma_n\}$, $\#traces(P) \to \infty$, with $\sigma_0 = <>$, $\sigma_{n+1} = \sigma_n{}^\wedge <b_n>$ for $0 < n < \infty$ and $b_n \in \alpha(P)$.

Applying the left quotient function of length λ to the traces of P results in the restriction of the set of traces of a process to the first λ elements of this traces set.

Let $S = {}_\lambda Q(traces(P)) = \{\sigma_n\}$, $\#S = \lambda$,
$\sigma_0 = <>$, $\sigma_{n+1} = \sigma_n{}^\wedge <b_n>$ for $0 < n \leq \lambda$ and $b_n \in \alpha(P)$.

The family of probabilistic choice operators written as "$[\![\pi]\!]$" map process traces into real numbers in the range $[0,1]$ (probabilities). Let $X = traces(P[\![\pi]\!]Q)$, then the mapping can be described by a function that behaves as

$\tau: traces \to \mathbb{P}r,$
$\tau(X) \quad = \pi \quad\quad\quad\, \text{for } X = traces(Q),$
$\quad\quad\quad = 1-\pi \quad\quad \text{for } X = traces(P),$
$\tau(traces(P)) + \tau(traces(Q)) = 1.$

This can be extended into an n-ary choice:

Let $X' = traces\big(P_0 [\![\pi_1]\!] \ P_1 \ \ldots \ [\![\pi_n]\!] \ P_n\big),$

Then
$\tau': traces \to \mathbb{P}r,$
$\tau'(X) \quad = \pi_1 \quad\quad \text{for } X' = traces(P_1)$
$\quad\quad\quad\ \ldots$
$\quad\quad\quad = \pi_n \quad\quad \text{for } X' = traces(P_n),$
$\quad\quad\quad = 1 - \sum_{i=1}^{n} \pi_i \text{ for } X' = traces(P_0),$

$\sum_{i=0}^{n} \tau'(X_i) \doteq 1 \quad\quad \text{for } X_i = traces(P_i).$

So, for any two processes P and Q, the operational definition of "$[\![\pi]\!]$" is given by:

$P[\![\pi]\!]Q \cong$
$\forall (\sigma, \lambda) \mid (0 \leq \lambda \leq \infty) \wedge$
$\quad \sigma \in \big(traces(P) \cup traces(Q)\big),$
$\quad\quad pr\big(\sigma \in {}_\lambda Q(traces(P))\big) = 1-\pi,$
$\quad\quad pr\big(\sigma \in {}_\lambda Q(traces(Q))\big) = \pi.$ \hfill (3)

Generalised to a n-ary choice operator this becomes:

$P_0 [\![\pi_1]\!] \ P_1 \ \ldots \ [\![\pi_n]\!] \ P_n \cong$
$\forall (\alpha, \lambda) \mid (0 \leq \lambda \leq \infty) \wedge$
$\quad \sigma \in \big(traces(P_0) \cup \ldots \cup traces(P_n)\big),$
$\quad\quad pr\big(\sigma \in {}_\lambda Q(traces\ (P_1))\big) = \pi_1,$
$\quad\quad \ldots$
$\quad\quad pr\big(\sigma \in {}_\lambda Q(traces\ (P_n))\big) = \pi_n,$
$\quad\quad pr\big(\sigma \in {}_\lambda Q(traces\ (P_0))\big) = 1 - \sum_{i=1}^{n} \pi_i.$ \hfill (3a)

where $pr(u)$ refers to the probability associated with u.

$P[\![\pi]\!]Q$ gives a probability distribution of process behavior over a sequence of events that arise from both processes. It should be noted that this probabilistic choice operates at the same level as nondeterministic choice, in that choices are made on the process side, not necessarily on the first event offered by the processes.

The introduction of stochastic determinism into a process results in events being divided into either unit or non-unit events. If the action of prefixing the process with an event doesn't alter the above probabilities then the event is called a *unit event*:

If P is a process, then z is a *unit event* if

$\exists (z, \lambda) \ \forall \mu \mid \mu \in (traces(P)),$
$pr\big(z \to \mu \in {}_\lambda Q(traces(P))\big) = pr\big(\mu \in {}_\lambda Q(traces(P))\big).$ \hfill (4)

It immediately follows from this definition that for any unit event z, if $P[\![\pi]\!]Q$ then $(z \to P) [\![\pi]\!] (z \to Q) = z \to (P[\![\pi]\!]Q)$. (5)

Markov processes, and certain other classes of sequential processes, have no unit events defined because prefixing alters their execution probabilities.

Some properties of the family of probabilistic choice operators.

In the following examples, P, Q, and R are arbitrary processes (including *STOP*, *SKIP*, *WAIT*, or $\bot$)

$P[\![1]\!]Q = Q \quad P[\![0]\!]Q = P$

Property 1. Identity

$\forall \pi \mid \pi \in \mathbb{P}r, P [\![\pi]\!] P = P.$

Property 2: Association across the family of operators.

$P [\![x]\!] (Q [\![y]\!] R)$
$= \left(P \left[\!\!\left[\frac{x'(1-y')}{(1-x'y')}\right]\!\!\right] Q \right) [\![y'x']\!] R.$

Property 3: Symmetry.

$[\![x]\!]$ is symmetric (by definition (1))
$P [\![x]\!] Q = Q [\![x']\!] P$ if $x' = 1-x$.

Property 4: Distribution through some CSP operators.

Distributive properties of this operator family are much the same as that of the nondeterministic choice across the traces of a process. The traces of $P[\![x]\!]Q$ are just the union of the traces of P and Q. However, these sets now have a probability distribution associated with them.

Property 4.1: Prefixing distributes through $[\![x]\!]$ provided that the event prefixing the process is a unit event. (See earlier section)

Property 4.2: Hiding

If a is a unit event then

$((a \to P) [\![x]\!] (a \to Q)) \backslash a$
$= (a \to (P [\![x]\!] Q)) \backslash a$
$= P [\![x]\!] Q.$

Property 4.3: Recursion

Unlike nondeterministic choice, probabilistic choice does distribute through recursion. Consider the following two processes.

$P = \mu X.((a \to X) [\![x]\!] (b \to X))$
$Q = (\mu X.(a \to X)) [\![x]\!] (\mu X.(b \to X))$

In the case of process P, sequences of a and b are intermixed with each other with probabilities of $(1-x)$ and x, respectively. Process Q also produces similar sequences, since the probabilistic choice function is *forcing* a specific probability on them. Nondeterministic choice, on the other hand, produces different sequences for P and Q, since it is not fair in the selection of the left or right hand sides of the operator in Q. Once one or other side is selected, it may remain there for the duration of the process execution.

Property 4.4: Distribution through parallel and interleave composition operators

Parallel composition of processes using the "||" operator requires that all the subprocesses, and their environment, have alphabets that are not disjoint. Write

$traces(P_1 || P_2 || \ldots || P_n) = traces(P_1) \cap traces(P_2) \ldots \cap traces(P_n)$

since this is the only way that the processes can engage each other.

The class of operators can be shown to be distributive through parallel composition, that is

$(P[\![\pi]\!]Q) || R = ((P||R) [\![\pi]\!] (Q||R))$

under the traces model.

Similarly, it is also distributive through the interleave operator: $(P[\![x]\!]Q)|||R = (P|||R)[\![x]\!] Q |||R)$.

EXAMPLES

In all of the following examples, a process' alphabet (as defined in CSP) is divided into the channel names and the message and events that the process can engage in. That is $\alpha = Channels \times Messages \cup Events$, where *Channels* is the set of all channels attached to a process, *Messages* is the set of all communication events that the process is prepared to engage in, and *Events* is the set of all other events of the process. Let $\varepsilon = Messages \cup Events$. A sequence of messages on a particular channel, c, of a process P, is represented by the (special) trace $Comm_c(P) \in Messages$. Note that $traces(P) \supseteq Comm_c(P)$.

Example 1 Simple one way asynchronous communication

In this simple example, an attempt to specify and implement a one way asynchronous communication system is made. Three processes are used – a transmitter process, *sender*, an unbounded buffer, *buffer* (which can be regarded as the asynchronous communication channel), and a receiver process, *receiver*. These three are run concurrently. The specifications for the overall system are quite lax – message order from the transmitter process output channel to the receiver process input channel must be preserved, and all messages that are sent by the transmitter must be eventually consumed by the receiver. This may be expressed as

$S_0 : \forall (Comm_{out}(sender), Comm_{in}(receiver)) \mid$
$\quad Comm_{in}(receiver) \leq Comm_{out}(sender).$

The transmitter process, *sender*, starts off with some finite set of messages, $S = \langle x \rangle \smallfrown s$, which is reduced in length until this set is empty. The process does nothing when it has no more to send, and cannot refuse[†] to engage in any communication on its output channel:

$Channels(sender) = \{out\},$
$\varepsilon(sender) = A_s,$
$S_s: sender$ **sat** $Comm_{out}(sender) \notin ref \land$
$\quad (\text{if } s \neq \langle \rangle$
$\quad \text{then } (Comm_{out}(sender_{\langle x \rangle \smallfrown s}) =$
$\quad\quad\quad \langle x \rangle \smallfrown Comm_{out}(sender_s))$
$\quad \text{else } Comm_{out}(sender) = \langle \rangle)$

This is implemented in CSP as:

$sender = tx_S$
$tx_{\langle \rangle} = SKIP$
$tx_{\langle x \rangle \smallfrown s} = out \,!\, x \rightarrow tx_s$

The buffer process, which is called *buffer* has two channels, one input and one output. It never stops, and cannot refuse any event offered on either channel. It is intially empty.

$Channels(buffer) = \{in, out\},$
$\varepsilon(buffer) = A_b,$ and
$S_b : buffer$ **sat**
$\quad (Comm_{out}(buffer) \leq Comm_{in}(buffer)) \land$
$\quad (\text{if } Comm_{out}(buffer) = Comm_{in}(buffer)$
$\quad \text{then } Comm_{in}(buffer) \notin ref$
$\quad \text{else } Comm_{out}(buffer) \notin ref)$

A CSP implementation is:
$buffer = P_{\langle \rangle}$
$P_{\langle \rangle} = in \,?\, x \rightarrow P_{\langle x \rangle}$
$P_{\langle x \rangle \smallfrown s} = \quad out \,!\, x \rightarrow P_s$
$\quad\quad\quad \mid in \,?\, y \rightarrow P_{\langle x \rangle \smallfrown s \smallfrown \langle y \rangle}$

The *receiver* starts off empty and is always ready to engage in an input, and it also never terminates.

$Channels(receiver) = \{in\}$
$\varepsilon(receiver) = A_r,$ and
$S_r : receiver$ **sat**
$\quad (Comm_{in}(receiver) \notin ref) \land$
$\quad (\forall a \mid a \in Messages,$
$\quad\quad Comm_{in}(receiver_s) \smallfrown \langle a \rangle$
$\quad\quad = Comm_{in}(receiver_{s \smallfrown \langle a \rangle}))$

[†] The notation for this is based on a process' Refusal Set, *ref*, being an arbitrary set of events that immediately cause the process to deadlock. An arbitrary trace is denoted by *tr*.

CSP implementation:

$receiver = rx_{\langle\rangle}$
$rx_s = in\ ?\ x \rightarrow rx_{s\frown\langle x\rangle}$

Provided that $A_s \supseteq A_b \supseteq A_r$, and that the channels can be shared to allow communication between processes, then the three processes may be connected to each other using parallel composition, *sender* ∥ *buffer* ∥ *receiver*. Let this composition be called *ASYNC*. Does it satisfy specification S_0?

If each of the above processes satisfies its own specification (proof is left as an excercise for the reader), then

$ASYNC$ **sat** $S_s(tr \upharpoonright A_s) \wedge S_b(tr \upharpoonright A_b) \wedge S_r(tr \upharpoonright A_r).$

Hence it is required to prove that

$S_s(tr \upharpoonright A_s) \wedge S_b(tr \upharpoonright A_b) \wedge S_r(tr \upharpoonright A_r) \Rightarrow S_0$

so as to prove that $ASYNC$ **sat** S_0.

Consider now the communications on each of the channels of the compostion. If any communication is going to occur, then the processes need to share channels. Let the channel connecting *sender* to *buffer* be sb, and the channel connecting *buffer* to *receiver*, br. Since $Messages(sender) = Messages(buffer) = Messages(receiver)$ for any communication to occur, it follows that

$Comm_{out}(sender) = Comm_{in}(buffer) = Comm_{sb}(ASYNC) \wedge$
$Comm_{out}(buffer) = Comm_{in}(receiver) = Comm_{br}(AYSNC).$

So it is sufficent to prove that

$S' : Comm_{br}(ASYNC) \leq Comm_{sb}(ASYNC) \Rightarrow S_0$

But $S' \Rightarrow S_b$, which certainly meets S_0. So $ASYNC$ **sat** S_0 provided that the channels can be shared by the processes in the manner specified above.

Example 2 Asynchronous one way communication on a noisy channel.

The process *buffer* given above is deterministic, in that no communication can be refused on either its input or output channels. This is behaving as a reliable buffer, which is bound to output (eventually) whatever was input. Consider the introduction of the process, *Loss*, which behaves as follows. *Loss* inputs a communication, and then non-deterministically either immediately outputs the communcation or loses it. It can never refuse any input communication, and does not provide any storage of communications.

Since the process can now lose communications, the traces of its output and input channels are no longer related to each other by the prefix relation of the buffer. All that can be said about them is that the output channel traces are a subset of input channel traces. So our preliminary specification is:

$Channels(Loss) = \{in, out\},$
$S_{Loss}:\quad Comm_{in}(Loss) \supseteq Comm_{out}(Loss) \wedge$
$\qquad\qquad Comm_{in}(Loss) \notin ref$

It is proposed that the example given earlier satisfies this specification. That is,

$Loss\ = (in\ ?\ x \rightarrow out\ !\ x \rightarrow Loss)\ |\ (in\ ?\ x \rightarrow Loss)$
$\quad\ = in\ ?\ x \rightarrow ((out\ !\ x \rightarrow Loss)\ \sqcap\ Loss)$

by definition of the general choice operator, and distribution law of prefixing.

It is required to show that *Loss* **sat** S_{Loss}.

Informally, the process certainly meets the criterion that the output channel's trace is a subset of the input, since it has no internal generation of new events that appear on the output. It is also left-guarded, and so can never refuse to engage in the input event. Hence the process described satisfies the specification.

The degree of the unreliability of communication can now be specified, and implemented using the stochastic choice operator. Let a new process, $Loss'$, have a probability of 0.1 of losing an event that appears on its input channel. The probability that the message will appear on its output channel is 0.9. Any input once again cannot be refused. A specification of this process is:

$Channels(Loss') = \{in, out\}$,
$S_{Loss'}: Comm_{in}(Loss') \notin ref \land$
$\quad pr(Comm_{out}(Loss') = <>) = 0.1 \land$
$\quad pr(Comm_{out}(Loss') = Comm_{in}(Loss')) = 0.9$

This is satisfied by the following CSP process:

$Loss' = in\,?\,x \to \big((out\,!\,x \to Loss')\,[\![0.1]\!]\,Loss'\big)$ \quad (6)

Proof: By the definition (3),
$\big((out\,!\,x \to Loss')\,[\![0.1]\!]\,Loss'\big)$ is defined to be:

$\forall (\sigma, \lambda) \mid (0 \leq \lambda \leq \infty) \land$
$\sigma \in \big(traces(out\,!\,x \to Loss') \cup traces(Loss')\big),$
$\quad pr(\sigma \in \lambda\mathbf{Q}(traces(out\,!\,x \to Loss'))) = 0.9 \land$
$\quad pr(\sigma \in \lambda\mathbf{Q}(traces(Loss'))) = 0.1$

Since $in\,?\,x$ is a unit event, it may be taken inside the brackets of equation (6), and so

$\forall (\sigma, \lambda) \mid (0 \leq \lambda \leq \infty) \land$
$\sigma \in (traces(in\,?\,x \to out\,!\,x \to Loss') \cup$
$\qquad traces(in\,?\,x \to Loss')),$
$\quad pr(\sigma \in \lambda\mathbf{Q}(traces(in\,?\,x \to out\,!\,x \to Loss'))) = 0.9 \land$
$\quad pr(\sigma \in \lambda\mathbf{Q}(traces(in\,?\,x \to Loss'))) = 0.1$

Since $traces(in\,?\,x \to Loss') \Rightarrow Comm_{out}(Loss') = <>$
and $traces(in\,?\,x \to out\,!\,x \to Loss') \Rightarrow$
$\quad (Comm_{out}(Loss') = Comm_{in}(Loss'))$,
it follows that $Loss'$ **sat** $S_{Loss'}$.

Example 3 Asynchronous one way communication channel with fixed delay

The above example is extended so as to include another process in the chain which will delay all messages by a fixed time of D seconds. This new process will behave as follows.

S_1: The process puts out at least as many messages as it inputs after it has reached a stable state:
$(s, \alpha) \in Q \Rightarrow \Sigma(s) \supseteq \{Messages_{in} \cup Messages_{out}\} \land$
$\#Comm_{out}(delay) \leq \#Comm_{in}(delay)$.

S_2: Once stable, the process will output a message if it has received more messages than it has output:
$(s, \alpha) \in Q \land a < \infty \land \#Comm_{out}(delay) < \#Comm_{in}(delay)$
$\Rightarrow s\!^\frown\!<(\alpha, e)> \in Traces(Q)$, where $e \in Messages(Q)$.

S_3: Once stable, if the process has output the same number of messages as it has input, then the process is ready to accept input:
$(s, \alpha) \in Q \land \alpha < \infty \land \#Comm_{out}(delay) = \#Comm_{in}(delay)$
$\Rightarrow s\!^\frown\!<(\alpha, e)> \in Traces(Q)$, where $e \in Messages(Q)$.

S_4: The process is initially stable, and never delays a message by more that D seconds after becoming stable once again:
$(<>, 0) \in Q \land (s\!^\frown\!<(t, \alpha)>, \alpha) \in Q \Rightarrow \alpha \leq t + D$.

The specification S of this process, $delay$, is the conjunction of all the above conditions: $S_1 \land S_2 \land S_3 \land S_4$

It is hypothesised that the following process will satisfy this specification.

$delay = in\,?\,x \to WAIT\ d\,;\,out\,!\,x \to delay$

Since all recursive functions in the timed CSP model such as $\mu F.F$ have a contraction mapping $fix(C^r)$, (with $C^r(Q) = WAIT\ d\,;\,Q$) by postulate (2), we can rewrite the above in terms of a specific solution.

$C^r = in\,?\,x \to WAIT\ d\,;\,out\,!\,x \to WAIT\ \delta;\,Q.$

Now, for the above solution, $STOP$ **sat** $S_1 \land S_2 \land S_4$, $in\,?\,x \to STOP$ **sat** S_3, and provided that $\delta \leq D - d$, C^r **sat** S_4.

Hence by the above theorem, $delay$ **sat** S since $fix(C^r)$ **sat** S.

Conclusion

By introducing both time and probabilities to CSP's traces model, a useful specification and analysis tool for protocol performance may be realised. The semantics of the combined time and stochastic determinism models is currently being investigated by the author.

Acknowledgements

The author wishes to thank Telecom Australia for providing a research grant for part of this work. Special thanks also to Dr. Bob Kummerfeld, Prof. Jennifer Seberry, Prof. Norman Foo, Bruce Janson, Janet Wiles and Mark Grundy for suggestions and discussions of material in this paper.

Bibliography

[1] Hoare, C.A.R. "Communicating Sequential Processes", Prentice-Hall International series in Computer Science, Prentice-Hall International, UK, 1985

[2] Milner, R. "A Calculus of Communicating Systems", Lecture Notes in Computer Science 92, Springer-Verlag, New York, 1980

[3] Logrippo, L., Simon, D., Ural, H. "Executable Description of the OSI Transport Service in Prolog", Proceedings 4th International Workshop on Protocol Specification, Testing, and Verification, North Holland, 1984

[4] Reed, G.M., and Roscoe, A.W., "A Timed Model for Communicating Sequential Processes", Automata, Languages, and Programming 13th International Colloqium Proceedings, Lecture Notes in Computer Science, Springer-Verlag, Berlin, New York, 1986

[5] Zic, J.J., "A New Communication Protocol Specification and Analysis Technique", Technical Report TR287, July 1986, Basser Department of Computer Science, University of Sydney

[6] Paz, A. "Introduction to Probabilistic Automata", Monographs and texts in Computer Science and Applied Mathematics, Academic Press, New York and London, 1971

[7] Bergstra, J.A., Klop, J.W., Olderog, E.-R. "Failures without Chaos: A New Process Semantics for Fair Abstraction", Report CS-R8625, August 1986, Centrum voor Wiskunde en Informatica (CWI), Amsterdam

[8] Zic, J.J., "Stochastic Determinism as an Extension to Communicating Sequential Processes", Technical Report TR306, May 1987, Basser Department of Computer Science, University of Sydney (Submitted for publication).

[9] Olderog, E.-R., "Specification oriented programming in TCSP", Logics and Models of Concurrent Systems, NATO ASI Series F, volume 13, Edited by Krzysztof R. Apt. Proceedings of the NATO Advanced Study Institute in Logics and Models of Concurrent Systems, La Colle-sur-Loup, France, 8-19 October 1984, Springer-Verlag Berlin New York Tokyo, 1985.

[10] Jones, C.B. "Systematic Software Development using VDM", Prentice-Hall International series in Computer Science, Prentice-Hall International, UK, 1986

[11] Morris, K. comment in an Honours seminar, Basser Department of Computer Science, University of Sydney, May 1983.

The IC* System for Protocol Development

David M. Cohen
Bell Communications Research
435 South Street
Morristown, New Jersey 07960

Timothy M. Guinther
Bell Communications Research
444 Hoes Lane
Piscataway, New Jersey 08854

Abstract

The realization of a new protocol is a long and complicated procedure whose inherent technical difficulty is exacerbated by the scarcity of useful tools. This paper discusses the initial use of a system that is being developed by Bell Communication Research to help in the specification, analysis, and implementation of communications protocols. This paper describes the application of this system to the specification and implementation of an industry standard protocol.

1. Introduction

Despite the considerable research that has been done in protocol methodology [1], [2], [3], [4], there are still very few tools to aid the implementation of a new protocol. The needed tools require that protocols be specified in a formal model that can capture the precise semantics of the protocols. Using a specification language, such as English, that lacks semantic precision, prevents the development of useful tools since any specification may have many equally valid but conflicting interpretations. Tools to produce and study simulations and prototypes are needed since a major difficulty in implementing a protocol is understanding the protocol's reaction to unusual situations and sequences of events.

This paper discusses the use of the IC* model and environment to specify and study communications protocols. The IC* model of computation [5] is a new, precise, parallel model of computation that is being developed by Bell Communication Research. It is the basis of the IC* project which is an effort to create an environment [6] for the design, analysis, and implementation of complex systems such as communications protocols. The IC* environment includes a language to specify protocols, tools to generate simulations and prototypes of a protocol directly from its IC* specification [7], and tools to observe and control a running simulation.

This paper will discuss the current IC* protocol language and the application of the IC* system to the specification and simulation of an industry standard communications protocol, the 3270 Display Systems Protocol (DSP). DSP is the de facto standard protocol for communicating synchronous data from IBM 3270-type devices across an X.25 packet-switched network. The initial specification of DSP is an English-text document proposed in June 1983 by Telenet, Tymnet, and Transcanada Telephone. A formal specification of the DSP protocol was written in the IC* protocol language, and this formal version was automatically translated, by the IC* systems, into a simulation of the protocol which was studied using the IC* tools. An IC* based prototype will be used to provide actual DSP services for an experimental network being developed at Bellcore.

2. Overview of the IC* protocol language

As discussed in the survey article [8], a formal specification language needs to have precise semantics and a notion of state and time. It needs enough precision to capture the full semantics of a protocol specification and yet has to be simple enough to be used in engineering practice. The utility of using precise state-based models to specify protocols has been demonstrated by work at IBM Zurich Research Labs [9], [10], and by systems such as the SPANNER [11] [12], and COSPAN [13] systems used at AT&T Bell Labs.

The IC* protocol language developed at Bellcore is a modular, parallel language that allows for non-deterministic specification and varying levels of abstraction and whose grounding in the IC* model give it precise semantics. Because the language is modular and allows for non-determinism, a specifier can write a partial specification that still has a precise semantic model that can be reasoned and argued about and tested. It thus allows for incremental design with the specifier adding details to resolve non-determinancy as decisions are made or more information becomes available.

The basic elements of the current IC* protocol language are *capsules*, *state variables*, *fragments*, and *connections*. A capsule consists of a declaration of state variables, a list of fragments, and an optional list of connections. State variables may be thought of as variables in a programming language, but unlike variables in a typical programming language, the user specifies how many bits are in each state variable. The user can also define explicit random variables which can be used in the is the point in time when the changes in the state variables caused by the selected effect take place. The interval of time between the trigger and posting time is specified by the *delay* expression. The *delay* expression is a function of the state variables and random variables. The user may use the built in implicit random variable and write **[min, max]** to specify that the delay is uniformly distributed between the values **min** and **max**.

The *effect* expression is a list of equations relating the values of the state variables at the trigger and posting times. The left-hand side of each equation is a set of values of state variables at the posting time and its right-hand side is a composition of functions on the values of the state variables at either the trigger or posting time. These functions are either library functions or they can be user specified and can be programmed in an ordinary sequential programming language. However, these functions must have very precise semantics with no hidden side effects.

The connections give static time invariant relationships between the state variables. The connection may be between state variables in the same capsule or between state variables in different capsules. For example, a connection may specify that state variable **a** of capsule **A** always has the same value as state variable **b** of capsule **B**. This connection would be written: **A.a = B.b**. A specification typically consists of several capsules and a list of connections between the states in the different capsules. Connections give the specifier a very flexible way to combine many smaller capsules into a large specification.

The fragments specify relationships between state variables at the current time and state variables at some future time. The state variables used in different fragments refer to entirely different variables unless the variables are related by defining a connection between them. The connections are used to compose specifications of larger systems from smaller systems.

A *capsule* is a collection of fragments that implicitly share a common name space, i.e., there is an implicit connection that defines an equality relationship between state variables in different fragments in the same capsule that have the same name. Explicit connections among the variables within a capsule are also permitted. The name space is not shared across capsules and explicit connections are required to establish relationships between state variables in different capsules.

Capsules can be written in a template form which may use formal parameters to specify the size or number of different types of objects. For example, a capsule may contain "N" fragments of a certain type each of which may refer to a parameterized state. Connections can also be written in template form using formal parameters. These parameters are assigned values at *instantiation* time. An instance of a system can be constructed by instantiating the capsules, fragments, connections, and states.

Frequently more than one detailed specification meets the given set of high-level requirements and it is useful to have a notion of equivalence. Two specifications are said to be *equivalent* modulo a set of connections if any capsule that is connected to them via these connections can not distinguish between them. Thus unimportant differences between specifications can be factored out in a precise fashion and alternative specifications can be given.

The IC* language can be used to write both functional and performance specifications and to define data as well as procedural abstractions [14].

3. Brief overview of IC* tools for simulation

Because of the problem of state space explosion, simulation is felt by some to be the best way to study a system [15] before prototyping or implementing. The IC* system was designed to encourage simulation and has tools that produce simulations automatically from an IC* description and which allow real-time interaction between the user and the simulation.

One of the major problems in simulating a large system is interpreting the enormous amounts of data a simulation can produce. This information has to be filtered so that the designer can make sense of how a part of the system affects its global behavior. The IC* environment's I* system provides real-time filtered observation of a running simulation. A simulation is observed through symbolic animation using both visual and audio icons. The user can see both text and high resolution animated color graphic displays, such as moving gauges, dials, etc. The user can also hear speech, sound effects, and musical patterns whose changes are controlled by the simulation.

The I* system is used by attaching a set of state variables as inputs to a *filter* and the output of a filter to a *gauge*. There are several types of filters and each type performs some transformation of its input values such as scaling, averaging, or evaluating the maximum of its inputs. The filters and the connections between the filters and the state variables are specified in the IC* language. The system has libraries of visual and sound gauges. The user can select any gauge to see or hear the output of a filter. Several gauges can be connected to the same filter, so the user can determine which gauge best portrays the data. Sound gauges can be very helpful in multiplexing the inputs from many different filters.

An interactive user interface to the IC* environment is provided by the N* system which also manages the library of IC* descriptions. The N* system is used to compose many IC* capsules, including some from its libraries, into an instantiated description and to answer questions about the resulting description. The N* system can then be used to order the S* system to compile and execute a simulation of the instantiated IC* description.

The results of the simulation can be observed either via the I* system or through the history files that are produced during the simulation. Many errors are uncovered during simulation by noticing, via the I* system, that something is going wrong and then backtracking through the history files to pinpoint the source of the problem.

Since even partial descriptions can be simulated, the user can specify, study, and simulate the protocol in an incremental fashion. The initial object of study may be a high-level view of the whole protocol that is gradually made more detailed or it may be a detailed view of some aspect of the protocol that is then combined with descriptions of other parts of the protocol.

4. Specification of the 3270 Display System Protocol

The 3270 Display System Protocol (DSP) is the de facto standard protocol for communicating synchronous data from IBM 3270-type devices across an X.25 packet switched network. As such, it specifies how data and control information are exchanged between packet assembler/disassemblers (PADs) to manage a logical connection across an X.25 network between a 3270-type device at a terminal PAD (TPAD) and a host at a host PAD (HPAD). It defines messages and procedures to establish and disestablish logical connections, transfer data between PADs, and resolve errors in both the IBM and X.25 networks.

The initial specification of DSP is an English-text document proposed in 1983 by Telenet, Tymnet, and Transcanada Telephone. IC* has been used to prototype a more formal specification of the DSP protocol, and based on this formal version, simulate the operation of the protocol. Eventually, the prototype will be used to provide actual DSP services for an experimental network (OSN*IN) being developed at Bellcore.

The initial, English-text specification of DSP is divided into sections corresponding to the phases of a DSP session, call establishment, data transfer, error recovery, and call clearing. The IC* specification developed naturally from this framework and the procedures and message formats used in each of these phases have been specified.

4.1 The Specification of DSP Using IC* — Call Establishment

In the call establishment phase, DSP defined messages are exchanged between the TPAD and the HPAD to establish a logical connection. When a 3270 terminal user instructs the TPAD to place a call, the TPAD will generate and send a DSP defined message to the appropriate HPAD. When the HPAD receives this message, it determines whether the call can be accepted and responds accordingly using DSP defined procedures and messages. Several DSP messages are exchanged between PADs before the connection is available to transfer data.

Using IC*, this phase is specified more precisely as some input, received at a PAD, producing a state transition with associated output. This state table based technique uses the fragment structure to specify the input, state transition and output. The cause portion of a fragment specifies the input and current state required to make the state transition and generate the output specified in the effect portion of the fragment.

All fragments specifying some aspect of call establishment were grouped into a capsule to form the IC* specification of the call establishment phase. Initially, the entire specification consisted of two such capsules, for DSP at the TPAD and HPAD.

The intermediate PSN was unspecified and simulated using a connection between variables in the two capsules. A message is sent when a variable is populated by the source and received when the destination detects the change. Later, when a more detailed interface to the PSN was needed, a capsule to simulate an X.25 PSN was written and the connection redirected to it. To boot the simulation, an additional fragment was added to the TPAD capsule which detected the initial state and simulated a user requesting a connection. Eventually, this fragment was removed when a capsule to simulate a user was written.

4.2 The Specification of DSP Using IC* — Data Transfer

After a connection is established and initialized properly, data transfer between the terminal and host application may take place. When a PAD receives data over a BSC line, it examines and replaces the BSC header and trailer with an appropriate DSP envelope. The DSP data message is then packetized and sent across the PSN to the destination PAD where the reverse process is performed.

The DSP envelope is used by the source PAD to convey information about the data to the destination PAD. DSP specifies how the source PAD derives values for the DSP envelope's fields from the BSC trailer and current state of data transfer. The IC* specification of this phase consists of fragments which check for possible combinations of state and BSC trailer values and form DSP envelopes accordingly.

Variables are used to store the current state and BSC trailer values. The cause portion of a fragment at the source PAD tests these variables for certain values. The associated effect portion updates the current state and forms the DSP envelope appropriate for the state and trailer values matched in the cause.

For example, the following fragment specifies how the first segment of a data block containing transparent text is enveloped using DSP. By convention, variables starting with "in_" are used to hold values obtained from input. Assume a parsing function has populated these variables. Variables starting with "exp_" are used to store current state information.

** cause **

context = TRANSFER
in_trailer = DLE_ETB
exp_first = YES

** effect **

exp_first' = NO
xpr_text' = YES
seq' = modinc(seq, MOD)
out_dsp_msg'=concat("01000000",seq,in_3270_data,ETB)

This fragment reads as, if data is received with a trailer byte of DLE ETB, and a first segment is expected, then change the state to indicate a subsequent, transparent segment is expected, the sequence number used in the next message, and the DSP data message which should be sent. The final effect statement forms the DSP data message by concatenating bits to indicate this message is a first segment(bit $0 = 0$) and contains transparent text(bit $1 = 1$), the sequence number of the message, the 3270 data, and the appropriate DSP trailer byte.

At the destination PAD, the DSP envelope is inspected and validated before being replaced with BSC framing characters. This is the reverse of what is done at the source PAD, but the translation process of inspecting and replacing is essentially the same. The cause portion of a fragment at the destination PAD inspects and validates the DSP envelope by testing its fields and the current state for specific values. The effect portion replaces the DSP envelope with BSC framing characters and makes necessary state changes.

The following fragment specifies how the DSP data message sent in the previous example would be handled at the destination PAD.

** cause **

context = TRANSFER
exp_first = YES
in_subs = NO
in_xpr = YES
in_seq = exp_seq
in_trail = ETB

** effect **

exp_first' = NO
exp_xpr' = YES
out_bsc_data'=conn(DLESTX,in_3270_data,DLEETB)

This fragment can be read as, if a first segment is expected, and the data received is a first segment(bit $0 = 0$, or in_subs = NO), and it is transparent data(bit $1 = 1$, or in_xpr = YES), and the sequence number of the message is the expected one, and the trailer byte of the message is ETB, then change the state to indicate a subsequent, transparent data segment is expected and generate the BSC data segment to be sent to the destination.

The IC* specification of the DSP data transfer phase consists of all the fragments which define how the DSP envelope is formed and used to transfer data. Such fragments naturally partition into two capsules, one to specify how the DSP envelope is formed at the source PAD and another to specify how it is validated and used at the destination PAD. As before, a connection between variables at the source and destination capsules was used to simulate passing messages. A capsule to parse incoming messages into the fields it contains proceeds and filters values to the appropriate capsules. This capsule could be thought of as a specification of the format of DSP messages.

Thus far, the specification of DSP at a PAD consists of four capsules, one to establish a call, others to send and receive data, and a one to parse incoming messages. Connections are used to specify the interactions these capsules have and to enable simulations. To indicate the current state of the call, a context variable is present in and connected among all the capsules at a PAD. To simulate data flows between PADs, a connection between variables at the PADs is used. Finally, the parsing capsule uses connections to filter values obtained from fields of incoming messages to the appropriate capsules.

4.3 The Specification of DSP Using IC* - Error Recovery

DSP defines messages and procedures to recover from errors and failures in both the BSC and X.25 networks. Device failures and undeliverable data occur in the BSC network while out of sequence data and X.25 Reset packets are received from the X.25 network. Since errors can disrupt normal processing of messages, and can occur concurrently, and need to be assigned priorities, the error recovery routines specified by DSP manage and impact almost every aspect of the protocol.

A separate IC* capsule was written to specify DSP error recovery. Most of the complexity involved in writing this capsule came from specifying the interaction of concurrent error recovery routines. To resolve an error, both the type of error, and its priority, with respect to the current state of other error recovery routines, needs to be considered. Hence, these conditions are specified and tested for in the cause portion of a fragment which initiates error recovery. The effect portion of such a fragment proceeds with the error recovery. Depending on the error, this might involve sending a DSP error message, changing the error recovery state, or initiating a process, such as resending data, in another capsule.

For example, the following simplified fragment specifies that if an error occurs receiving data, and no other error routines are active, and an X.25 Reset packet is not received at the same time, then send a DSP Reset message and wait for a response Reset message.

```
** cause **

data_error = TRUE
context = IDLE
network_type <> X25_RESET

** effect **

dsp_reset_msg' = concat
            ("00000000", RESET, last_seq, exp_seq)
context' = WF_RESET
```

Connections between variables in the error recovery and other capsules indicate the interaction error recovery has with other protocol processes. Since errors occur at different places and phases of processing, they are naturally detected in different capsules. Such capsules use connections to report the error to the error recovery capsule. For example, an out of sequence data message is detected only after it has been parsed and analyzed, while an X.25 Reset packet is a detectable error upon receipt. The capsule which specifies how data is received would detect an out of sequence message and notify the error recovery capsule using a connection to a variable such as "data_error" of the previous example.

4.4 Advantages of Using IC*

The DSP prototyping and other protocol specification work using IC* evidence the system's usefulness and advantages. IC* is able to specify the many aspects of a complex communication system consisting of diverse network components and protocols.

The language provides a natural and intuitive means of specifying concurrent and intricate control and data flows, precise interfaces, state transitions with associated actions, and other aspects of a protocol's specification. For example, state transitions with associated actions are specified easily and precisely using the fragment structure. The cause portion of a fragment can specify the input and current state that are required to make the state transition and the effect portion can specify the action to perform. Moreover, the simulation system can "execute" this fragment while simulating the operation of the protocol to verify the fragment's correctness.

The simulation system can be used at each stage in the development of a specification to simulate the actual operation of the protocol directly from its IC* representation. Much of the difficulty involved in specifying and implementing a protocol is understanding the protocol's behavior such as its reaction to complex, asynchronous events and interactions. Simulations have proven very helpful in detecting unexpected situations and undesirable behavior that is due to an incorrect or incomplete specification.

Desirable software engineering techniques such as modularity, incremental development, and varying abstraction levels are provided and encouraged by IC*. For example, capsules provide modularity by grouping related fragments, encourage incremental development by specifying new components or distributing and extending detail among inter-related capsules, and provide varying levels of abstraction from low-level views of a capsule's internals to high-level views which aggregate capsules into logical entities.

5. Summary

This paper discussed the application of the IC* system to the specification, study, and simulation of a standard communications protocol, the 3270-DSP protocol. The similarity between the IC* protocol language and the intuitive state diagrams commonly used by engineers made writing the protocol in the IC* language fairly straightforward. The IC* language provides a natural and intuitive way to specify concurrent and intricate control and data flows, precise interfaces, state transitions with associated actions, and other aspects of a protocol's specification. Since the language has inherent parallelism and even partial specifications may be directly translated into simulations, the IC* language and environment encourage desirable software engineering techniques such as modularity, incremental development, and varying levels of abstraction. Using the IC* language and tools greatly eased the process of studying the protocol.

References

1. "Protocol Specification, Testing, and Verification, II", C. Sunshine, editor, North Holland, 1982.

2. "Protocol Specification, Testing, and Verification, III", H. Rudin and C. H. West, editors, North Holland, 1983.

3. "Protocol Specification, Testing, and Verification, IV", Y. Yemini, R. Strom, and S. Yemini, editors, North Holland, 1985.

4. "Protocol Specification, Testing, and Verification, V", M. Diaz, editor, North Holland, 1986

5. To appear in IEEE Transactions on Software Engineering

6. E. J. Cameron, D. M. Cohen, B. Gopinath, W. M. Keese, and P. Uppaluru, "The IC* Model and Environment", Advance Papers, Vol. II, First International Workshop on CASE, Cambridge, Massachusetts, May 25-29, 1987, pp. 639-651.

7. D. M. Cohen, E. J. Isganitis, "Automatic Generation of a Prototype of a New Protocol From Its Specification", Globcomm Dec 1986.

8. T. Piatkowski, "The State of the Art In Protocol Engineering", ACM Communications Architectures and Protocols, August 5 - 7, 1986, pages 13 - 18.

9. Rudin, H. and West, C. H., "A validation technique for tightly coupled protocols", IEEE Trans. on Computers, C-31, 7, July 1982, 630 - 636.

10. Zafiropulo. P., West, C. H., Rudin, H., Cowan, D. D., and Brand, D., " Towards analyzing and synthesizing protocols", IEEE Trans. Commun., COM-28, (April 1980), 651 - 661.

11. S.Aggarwal, D. Barbara, and K. Z. Meth, "Specifying and Analyzing Protocols with SPANNER", Proc. of IEEE Int'l Conf. on Communications, Toronto, Canada, June 1986.

12. S.Aggarwal, D. Barbara, and K. Z. Meth, "SPANNER: A Tool for the Specification, Analysis, and Evaluation of Protocols", to appear in IEEE Transactions on Software Engineering.

13. J. Katzenelson and R. P. Kurshan, "S/R Language ...," Proc. Fifth Ann. Int'l Phoenix Conf. on Computers and Communications, Computer Society, Los Alamitos, Calif, 1986, pp 286-292.

14. "Abstraction and Specification in Program Development", B. Liskov and J. Guttag, The MIT Press, 1986.

15. C. H. West, "Protocol Validation by Random State Exploration", in the"Protocol Specification, Testing, and Verification, VI" Conference in Montreal, 1986.

PART 8. RESOURCE SHARING IN DISTRIBUTED SYSTEMS

L. Schreier

SRI International, USA

A Yellow-Pages Service for a Local-Area Network

Larry L. Peterson

Department of Computer Science
University of Arizona
Tucson, AZ 85721

ABSTRACT

We introduce a yellow-pages service that maps service names into server addresses. The service is novel in that it associates a set of attributes with each server. Clients specify the attributes the server should possess when requesting a service and the yellow-pages service determines what servers satisfy the request. In addition to describing the implementation of the yellow-pages service within a local-area network, we show how the service can be integrated with the available internet communication protocols to enable clients from throughout the internet to access local servers.

1. INTRODUCTION

This paper describes a yellow-pages service that maps the name of a service into the address of a server willing to provide the service. The service is designed for an *autonomous system* consisting of a collection of autonomous, heterogeneous hosts connected by a local-area network. The autonomy implies that each host decides for itself what services it is willing to provide. The heterogeneity implies that the servers providing a given service are not identical. Also, each host in the system is reachable from throughout an internet, such that clients in remote systems might invoke services available in the local system.

Our design differs from conventional name servers (e.g., [3,7,12]) in two ways. First, associated with each server is a set of *attributes* that describe the characteristics and properties of the server. A client that wishes to engage a service queries the yellow-pages service for the address of a server, specifying the name of the service and any attributes the server should possess. The yellow-pages service returns the address of one or more servers that satisfy the client's requirements.

Second, clients from throughout the internet contact servers available within the autonomous system through an intermediate agent that uses the yellow-pages service to select an appropriate server. Specifically, a *flagship* host in the local system advertises a set of services offered by the system with an internet naming service. Clients connect to the flagship host as though the server is available on that host. A *forwarding mechanism* running on the flagship host then "patches" the client through to an actual server that provides the service. The forwarding mechanism queries the yellow-pages to determine the address of the lightest loaded server the implements the service. Indirection through the forwarding mechanism and the selection of a suitable server are hidden from the remote client.

The paper is organized as follows. Section 2 gives a structural overview of the yellow-pages service, Section 3 gives several detailed examples, and Section 4 describes the forwarding mechanism. The mechanisms described in these three sections have been implemented in a testbed system consisting of a collection of VAXes and Sun Workstations running UNIX[1] and connected by a 10 megabit ethernet. The hosts in the system are reachable from throughout the DARPA Internet using the TCP and UDP protocols [9,13]. Finally, Section 5 reports our experiences and Section 6 offers some conclusions.

2. ARCHITECTURE

A set of servers implement the yellow-pages service. Each server maintains a database of information about the available services and servers. Clients within the system invoke operations on one or more servers using the Sun Remote Procedure Call mechanism [11]. The rest of this section describes the basic objects and operations of the yellow-pages service.

This work supported in part by National Science Foundation Grant DCR-8609396.

© 1988 ACM 0-89791-245-4/88/0001/0235 $1.50

---

[1] UNIX is a trademark of Bell Laboratories.

2.1 Attributes

An attribute is a syntactic object that denotes a property or characteristic of a server. An attribute is defined as

$$attribute \equiv \langle type, operator, value \rangle$$

For example, `queue<3`, `architecture=postscript`, `pixels=300`, and `pages_per_minute>=8` are string representations of attributes that are meaningful in the context of a print service, where 'queue' is the type, '<' is the operator, and '3' is the value of the first attribute. Attributes associated with a given server are recorded in the yellow-pages database. Clients submit a set of attributes when querying the yellow-pages for a server that provides a particular service.

Attributes are classified along two dimensions. Along one dimension, attributes are distinguished based on whether they are *static* or *dynamic*. Static attributes correspond to those properties of a server that are fixed; e.g., the speed of a printer or the architecture of a processor. Although static attributes may change, for example due to upgrades, such changes are infrequent and easily tracked by updates to the yellow-pages database. In contrast, dynamic attributes change continuously; e.g., a processor's load or the number of jobs in a print queue. The important characteristic of a dynamic attribute is that it changes with much greater frequency than the yellow-pages service is asked to make a decision based on the attribute. For practical reasons, therefore, a server's dynamic attributes should be computed only on demand.

Along the other dimension, attributes are distinguished according to whether they are *absolute* or *relative*. Absolute attributes correspond to those properties of a server that can be determined independent of any other servers; e.g., its architecture or its load. Relative attributes, in contrast, are computed over a collection of servers; e.g., the processor with the minimal load or the printer with the maximum output rate.

A client queries a yellow-pages server to learn the address of one or more servers that provide a given service. In addition to giving the name of the service, the client requests that the server chosen to provide the service satisfy a set of attributes. The set of requested attributes is given by:

$$requested\_attr \equiv \langle mandatory, optional \rangle$$

where *mandatory* is a set of attributes identifying those properties the server "must" possess and *optional* is the set of attributes that denote those properties the client would "like" the server to possess. For example, a client requesting a print server for the purpose of printing a postscript file would specify that the server must be able to interpret postscript and it should be the lightest loaded of those servers that qualify.

2.2 Database

Associated with each yellow-pages server is a database of information about the services available in the system. The database contains bindings of each service to a set of servers that provide the service.

$$service \longrightarrow \{server_1, server_2, ...server_n\}$$

A server, in turn, is defined by:

$$server \equiv \langle address, registered\_attr \rangle$$

where *address* is a character string that is meaningful to the client — for example, the address of a print server is simply given by the name of a printing device — and *registered_attr* is a set of static, absolute attributes associated with the server.

The database also binds each type of attribute associated with a given service to a pair of procedures;

$$\langle service, type \rangle \longrightarrow \langle comp\_proc(), eval\_proc() \rangle$$

The first, called a comparison procedure, determines if a registered attribute satisfies some requested attribute. It is defined by a boolean function that takes an operator and the value of two attributes as arguments. Each comparison procedure, therefore, defines the meaning of the operator and value fields for the attribute type. The second, called an evaluation procedure, dynamically generates the specified type of attribute and adds it to the set of attributes registered for a given server. It takes a server as an argument, generates an attribute of the appropriate type, and augments the set of attributes associated with the server to include the dynamic attribute.

The yellow-pages server supports a pair of operations — `register` and `unregister` — that allow clients to change the set of servers bound to a given service. The comparison and evaluation procedures, however, are defined when a yellow-pages server is configured and cannot be changed at runtime.

2.3 Operations

2.3.1 Registering and Unregistering

Clients add servers to the database and remove servers from the database with the operations

    `register(service, address, registered_attr)`

and

    `unregister(service, address)`

respectively. Both operations broadcast the update request to all yellow-pages servers in the system. In practice, the server itself is the client of the yellow-pages service that performs the `register` and `unregister` operations.

Each yellow-pages server timestamps every service in its database based on when the last update was made. A server may verify the freshness of the bindings in its database by querying another yellow-pages server with the

    `(time, server_set) = get_servers(service)`

operation, where `time` is the time of the last change to the service's bindings and `server_set` is the collection of servers currently bound to the service. The invoking server decides which binding to record in its database based on the timestamp. In practice, the `get_servers()` operation is only used to initialize (restart) a yellow-pages server.

2.3.2 Lookup

Clients query the yellow-pages service for the address of one or more servers that provide a given service with the operation

```
address_set = lookup(service, requested_attr,
                    mode)
```

The set of attributes taken as an argument by `lookup()` is partitioned into mandatory and optional subsets. The mode argument specifies whether the client wants to receive addresses for any or all of the servers that satisfy the requested attributes. The `lookup()` operation is invoked relative to a single yellow-pages server. A client learns the address of the available yellow-pages servers with a

```
address_set = find()
```

operation; `find()` is implemented by broadcasting a request over the local-area network.

A yellow-pages server selects an address to return to the client as follows. First, it determines what, if any, servers satisfy all the mandatory attributes. It then considers, in order, the optional attributes, until a single server remains or the list of optional attributes has been exhausted. Before determining whether or not a given requested attribute is a member of the set of attributes registered for a given server, if the requested attribute is either dynamic or relative, then the attribute is computed for the server and added to the server's registered set. Finally, if the mode indicates only one address is to be returned and the selection algorithm determines that a set of servers satisfies the requested attributes, then a single server is selected at random and its address is returned.

The selection algorithm is given by procedure `select()` in Figure 1. The algorithm is expressed using standard set notation and a simple record construct, in which `attribute.type` denotes the type of the attribute. The routines `evaluate_dynamic()` and `evaluate_relative()` augment the attributes registered for the specified set of servers to include dynamic and relative attributes, respectively. `evaluate_dynamic()` calls the evaluation procedure bound to the specified attribute, while `evaluate_relative()` computes a relative attribute over the set of servers when the specified attribute has a value equal to the string `"min"` or `"max"`. The use of comparison procedures is hidden within the set membership and set inclusion operations. That is, to determine if attribute a is in attribute set A, a is compared with each $a' \in A$ using the comparison procedure bound to the type of attribute a.

```
server_set = select(service, server_set, requested_attr)
{
        for each attribute ∈ requested_attr.mandatory
        {
                evaluate_dynamic(attribute, server_set)
                evaluate_relative(attribute, server_set)
        }
        for each server ∈ server_set
                if requested_attr.mandatory ⊄ server.registered_attr
                        server_set = server_set − server
        if |server_set| ≤ 1
                return(server_set)

        for each attribute ∈ requested_attr.optional
        {
                evaluate_dynamic(attribute, server_set)
                evaluate_relative(attribute, server_set)
                for each server ∈ server_set
                        if attribute ∉ server.registered_attr
                        {
                                server_set = server_set − server
                                if |server_set| = 1
                                        return(server_set)
                        }
        }
        return(server_set)
}
```

Figure 1
Selection Algorithm

3. EXAMPLES

The yellow-pages service provides a general mechanism for locating a server that implements a given service. The way in which this mechanism is used differs from service to service. In particular, each service is free to chose a collection of attribute types that are meaningful for the service, along with the corresponding comparison and evaluation procedures. This section gives three examples of how the yellow-pages service has been used in the testbed system.

3.1 Print Service

A print service produces hardcopy output for users. A representative set of servers providing the print service is given in Figure 2. The speed attribute is given by the device's output rate in number of pages per minute; the res attribute is given by the printer's resolution in pixels; and the arch attribute corresponds to the target language of the printer. The database also binds the print service and the dynamic attribute load to the evaluation procedure printer_load(), which takes a server as an argument, calls the system printer status command to determine the number of jobs in the work queue for the printer, and augments the set of registered attributes to include the load attribute.

Consider a client of the print service that wants to print a postscript file. The client might invoke the lookup() operation with the mandatory attribute arch=ps and the optional attribute load=min. Given such a request, the selection algorithm first narrows the registered set of servers down to lw0, lw1, lw2, and lw3 based on the mandatory attribute. It then calls the printer_load() procedure to generate the load attribute for these four servers, augmenting the set of attributes bound to each server to include the load attribute. For example, as a result of applying printer_load() to lw0, its set of attributes might be extended to

{loc=756:7th:cer:GS, speed=8, arch=ps,
 res=300, load=2}

Next, the selection algorithm evaluates the relative attribute load=min. If, for example, lw1 and lw3 are the only printers with a load of 0, then their attribute set would be extended to

{loc=705:7th:greg:GS, speed=8, arch=ps,
 res=300, load=0, load=min}

and

{loc=708:7th:rick:GS, speed=8, arch=ps,
 res=300, load=0, load=min}

respectively. Finally, it selects the servers whose set of registered attributes contain the optional attribute load=min, yielding lw1 and lw3. Assuming the client invoked the lookup() operation with mode=ANY, one of the two servers is picked and its address is returned. Note that although conceptually the set of attributes registered for a given server includes dynamic and relative attributes, the selection algorithm does a lazy evaluation of such attributes; i.e., only for those servers still under consideration by the selection algorithm.

As another example, suppose the client wishes to retrieve the address of the printer based on its location; e.g., "the printer in Rick's office". In this case, the client invokes the lookup() operation with the mandatory attribute loc=rick. Any number of optional attributes are ignored because the mandatory attribute loc=rick selects a single server. The comparison procedure bound to the attribute type loc treats the value as a list of items separated by colons and determines whether or not the requested value is a member of that list.[2]

Finally, if the client invokes the yellow-pages service with an empty set of mandatory and optional attributes and mode=ALL, lookup() returns the address of all registered print servers. In this case, the client is free to select a single server based on whatever criteria it choses.

⟨lw0, {loc=756:7th:cer:GS, speed=8, arch=ps, res=300}⟩
⟨lw1, {loc=705:7th:greg:GS, speed=8, arch=ps, res=300}⟩
⟨lw2, {loc=721:7th:main:GS, speed=8, arch=ps, res=300}⟩
⟨lw3, {loc=708:7th:rick:GS, speed=8, arch=ps, res=300}⟩
⟨ima, {loc=732:7th:dev:GS, speed=24, arch=imagen, res=300}⟩
⟨ip, {loc=732:7th:dev:GS, speed=10, arch=imagen, res=300}⟩
⟨lp, {loc=732:7th:dev:GS, speed=40, res=10}⟩

Figure 2
Set of Registered Printer Servers

---

[2] Because loc is not a dynamic attribute, the evaluation procedure bound to loc in the database is null.

3.2 Processor Service

A processor service consists of a pool of hosts that can be used to execute user jobs. Figure 3 gives an example set of processor servers that might be registered with the yellow-pages service. The `tf` and `comp` attributes identify and text formatters and compilers available on the host, respectively, and the `speed` attribute reports the processor's speed relative to a VAX 780. Also, the dynamic `load` attribute, as computed by the evaluation procedure `processor_load()`, is given by the processor's load average.

Suppose, for example, that a client wants to compile a C program, producing object code for a Sun, as fast as possible. The client might request a processor server with the mandatory attributes `arch=sun` and `comp=cc` and the optional attributes `load<1.5` and `speed=max`.[3] The selection algorithm first narrows the set of available servers to those that correspond to Suns; of those, it next eliminates the processors with a current load greater than or equal to 1.5; and of the remaining servers, it returns the one with the maximum speed. To return all Sun's with a load average under 1.5 — so as to locate a pool of processors to perform multiple compilations in parallel — the `speed=max` attribute might be dropped and `mode` set to ALL.

It is important to understand that the policy adopted by a given system regarding the registration of servers is independent of the yellow-pages service. In this example, the processor servers consist of a pool of "public" processors and a collection of "private" workstations. The public processors are registered with the yellow-pages service when they first become available, while users are free to register and unregister their workstations depending on whether they are willing to allow other jobs to run on them (e.g., the user registers the workstation when logging off and unregisters it when logging on).

3.3 Talk Service

A talk service allows a pair of users to write messages to each other's terminal in real-time [4]. By dynamically assigning the attribute `user` to those hosts (i.e., talk servers) on which a particular user is logged on, the yellow-pages service can be used to locate the host to which a talk connection should be established. For example, to talk to user `rick`, a client simply requests a talk server that satisfies the mandatory attribute `user=rick`. The evaluation procedure `locate_user()` bound to the attribute type `user` determines the host for which the attribute is true. `locate_user()` assigns the `user` attribute only to the host on which the user was most recently active.

4. FORWARDING MECHANISM

This section describes how the yellow-pages service is integrated with the internet transport protocols, thereby allowing clients from throughout the internet to access servers within an autonomous system. Because the testbed is a local-area network in the DARPA Internet, the servers that are accessible to remote clients are necessarily limited to those servers listening at a well-known port on one or more of the system's hosts [10].

A single host in the local system is designated as the *flagship* host; for example, the host named `arizona.edu` is the flagship host for the University of Arizona. The system advertises the flagship as offering a set of services to Internet clients by registering a set of resource records — potentially one for each service — with the domain naming system [5,6]. For example, an MX resource record indicates that the mail service for the system is available at the flagship host [8]. A client consults the domain name server to learn the address of a host at the system that

---

```
⟨megaron,     {speed=6.0, arch=vax, tf=tex:ps:troff, comp=cc:f77:pascal:lisp}⟩
⟨bocklin,     {speed=1.5, arch=vax, tf=tex:ps:troff, comp=cc:f77:pascal:lisp}⟩
⟨arizona,     {speed=1.0, arch=vax, tf=tex:ps:troff, comp=cc:f77:pascal:lisp}⟩
⟨baskerville, {speed=4.0, arch=sun, tf=troff, comp=cc:f77}⟩
⟨univers,     {speed=2.0, arch=sun, tf=troff, comp=cc:f77}⟩
⟨bodoni,      {speed=2.0, arch=sun, tf=troff, comp=cc:f77}⟩
⟨aurgia,      {speed=2.0, arch=sun, tf=troff, comp=cc:f77}⟩
⟨plantin,     {speed=1.5, arch=sun, tf=troff, comp=cc:f77}⟩
⟨caslon,      {speed=1.0, arch=sun, tf=troff, comp=cc:f77}⟩
⟨raffia,      {speed=1.0, arch=sun, tf=troff, comp=cc:f77}⟩
```

Figure 3
Set of Registered Processor Servers

---

[3] The two optional attributes correspond to the client's estimation of the best response time for this particular compilation.

offers a particular service and the address of the flagship host is returned. The client then contacts the server by sending one or more packets addressed to the well-known port on the flagship host. The flagship host, in turn, forwards the packets to a server within the system. Thus, the forwarding mechanism is analogous to the strategy of accessing a server at well-known port: The flagship serves as the "well-known host" for the system.

Consider how the forwarding mechanism is implemented within TCP in more detail. The TCP module running on the flagship host is modified to include the forwarding mechanism. Associated with the forwarding mechanism is a table that binds well-known ports to the addresses of servers. The table contains bindings of the form

$$well\text{-}known\text{-}port \longrightarrow \{addr_1, addr_2, ...addr_m\}$$

where each server address is given by a port, host address pair. When a packet arrives at the TCP module addressed for some port, the forwarding mechanism is consulted to see if forwarding is to take place for that port; i.e., if there is an entry in the table. If the packet is from a new client, the forward server randomly selects one of the available servers and forwards the packet on to it. That is, the forwarding mechanism sets the packet's destination address to the server's address and resends the packet. The pair

$$\langle port_{client}, host_{client}\rangle \longrightarrow \langle port_{server}, host_{server}\rangle$$

is then recorded in the protocol control block normally associated with the connection. Subsequent packets sent on the same connection are forwarded to the same server.

The TCP module running on the server host is aware that forwarding is taking place and sends all reply messages directly to the client. TCP on the server host sets the packet's source address to that of the flagship host, thereby making it appear to the client as though it is still communicating with the flagship host. The client, therefore, is never aware that the forwarding is taking place.

The path followed by all packets exchanged between the TCP module on the client host and the TCP module on the server host is given in Figure 4. The packets traversing each leg of the path have a source and destination address as follows:

(a) SOURCE: $\langle port_{client}, host_{client}\rangle$
DESTINATION: $\langle port_{well-known}, host_{flagship}\rangle$

(b) SOURCE: $\langle port_{client}, host_{client}\rangle$
DESTINATION: $\langle port_{server}, host_{server}\rangle$

(c) SOURCE: $\langle port_{well-known}, host_{flagship}\rangle$
DESTINATION: $\langle port_{client}, host_{client}\rangle$

A load manager executing on the flagship host is responsible for binding each well-known port to a set of servers in the forwarding mechanism's table.[4] The load manager's objective is to distribute remote work over the local servers so as to balance their load. In the case of generally available services, such as the mail service, the manager becomes a client of the yellow-pages service by periodically querying for all processor servers with a load under a certain threshold. The manager then updates the forwarding mechanism's table accordingly. Note that because the forwarding mechanism is embedded in TCP, remote clients are not able to request servers that satisfy a particular set of attributes; only the load manager is a client of the yellow-pages service.

5. EVALUATION

It is clear that providing a yellow-pages service that supports attributes is justified. First, as system resources become more and more heterogeneous, there is an increasing need on the part of users to "discover" the characteristics of a given resource. That is, the yellow-pages service serves as a system-wide *help* mechanism. Second, by being able to evaluate the properties of a collection of servers, the yellow-pages service provides an automatic mechanism for selecting the server that best meets the user's needs. Such a service seems to be well suited for "network interfaces" such as the one described in [2]. Finally, the yellow-pages service provides a natural place to implement the system's policy for sharing the load on servers. That is, requests for services can be dispatched throughout the system according to each server's current load.

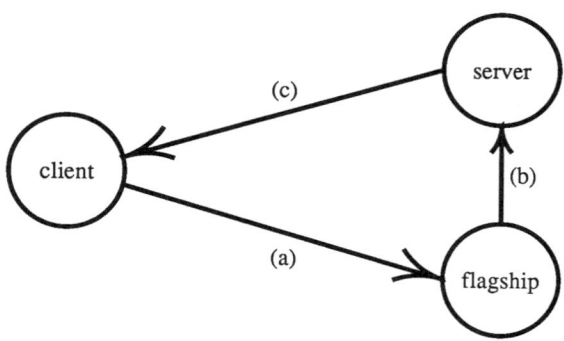

Figure 4
Remote Client; Local Flagship and Server

---

[4] The load manager is not implemented in the prototype. Instead, the forwarding mechanism's table is statically defined to a set of servers for each service.

5.1 Performance

A yellow-pages server with a database containing information about the three services described in Section 3 was tested for a variety of requested attributes. In the case of a simple query that contains no dynamic attributes, an invocation of the `lookup()` operation between a client and server executing on a pair of Sun 3/75 workstations takes 35 msec when the database is resident in memory. A query that contains a dynamic attribute depends on the performance of the evaluation procedure. The procedure `processor_load()` associated with the processor service, for example, is based on the Sun RPC `rstats` program [11]. An invocation of the `lookup()` operation for the processor service with `load` as one of the requested attributes takes 1.4 seconds on average. As a consequence, using the yellow-pages service to locate lightly loaded processors is only worthwhile for large computations; using dynamic attributes is almost always worthwhile for the print and talk services, however.

The forwarding mechanism adds an extra hop to the route traversed by a TCP packet. While this intuitively results in a 50% performance penalty for a virtual circuit between two hosts on the same local-area network, the relative penalty is insignificant when the client is remote. This is because traversing the Internet, not the extra hop across the local-area network, dominates the communication cost. To get a handle on the impact, we conducted several experiments involving connections from a remote client directly to a local host and indirectly to a local host through a forwarding mechanism on the flagship host. The performance penalty incurred by the forwarding mechanism is typically less than 2%.

5.2 Design Issues

Server-Heavy Design

The configuration of the yellow-pages service described in this paper clearly places the burden of selecting a server on the yellow-pages server rather than the client. An alternative would be to have the yellow-pages server simply return a set of values associated with a given name and make the client responsible for interpreting the returned value in whatever what it choses. While our limited experience is not conclusive, we identify three arguments as to why the server-heavy design is reasonable.

First, by engaging the selection algorithm at the server rather than the client, the yellow-pages service effectively moves the "function to the data" rather than the "data to the function". That is, the selection algorithm executes on the same host as the database and a relatively small answer — a server address — is returned. In contrast, all the server information bound to a given service would have to be sent in the reply message to the client. Second, by isolating all invocations of the evaluation procedures on a small collection of server hosts, the server is able to cache dynamic attributes across multiple client calls. Finally, because the yellow-pages server can be asked to return all it knows about a given service — either with the `get_servers()` operation or by applying the `lookup()` operation to an empty set of attributes — the client remains able to retrieve uninterpreted information from the server without paying a performance penalty.

Database Management

The collection of yellow-pages servers adopt a simple strategy for maintaining the consistency of their databases: Updates are unreliably broadcast to all servers and servers can refresh their database by invoking the `get_servers` operation. The approach seems justified because the information in the database changes infrequently, only a single entity is responsible for adding and deleting information about a particular server (i.e., the server itself), and the consequence of out-of-date information is not catastrophic (the client contacts the server at the returned address and is informed that the requested service cannot be performed).

Integration

The yellow-pages service is integrated with the internet transport protocols by the forwarding mechanism and the load manager. Although there is no fundamental reason why a remote client could not directly contact one of a system's yellow-pages servers, it is important to note that the forwarding mechanism allows the service requested by the client to be bound to a server at the latest possible moment — during connection establishment — at an insignificant cost. Intuitively, this is significant in an internet where the "distance" between the remote client and the system is an order of magnitude greater than the "diameter" of the system. That is, the approach seems appropriate for an environment in which it takes longer to establish a connection to a server than it does to change the set of servers that offer the service.

The approach is also appealing because it hides information about the servers behind the autonomous system abstraction. In other words, the host in the system that provides a service is invisible to the client requesting the service in the same way that the process on a host that implements a server is invisible to the client invoking the server. Such information hiding lessons the burden on the internet naming mechanism and therefore scales well as more services and servers are made available throughout the internet.

Forwarding versus Redirection

The forwarding mechanism acts as an intermediary between the client and server. This has the advantage of not requiring any changes to the transport protocol because the client is shielded from the indirection. In contrast, the protocol could be modified such that the flagship host informs the client that it should redirect its packets to the server host. While this might be reasonable in the case of a connection oriented protocol (e.g., TCP), it more cost effective to simply forward the packet on to the server host in the case of a connectionless protocol (e.g., UDP). This view is consistent with the forwarding facility provided by VMTP [1].

6. CONCLUDING REMARKS

We have implemented and experimented with a yellow-pages service for a local-area network and a forwarding mechanism that integrates the service with the available internet protocols. Although the results should be interpreted as preliminary, our experience clearly demonstrates the usefulness and feasibility of an attribute-based yellow-pages service. The most significant remaining problem involves refining and evaluating the architecture of the yellow-pages service. In particular, more attention must be paid to the division of responsibility between the client and yellow-pages server and the distribution of yellow-pages servers over the local-area network. Also, the level of granularity with which the selection algorithm can be customized for each service requires further study. The current architecture only allows the evaluation and comparison procedures to be defined on a service by service basis.

REFERENCES

[1] D. Cheriton, "VMTP: A Transport Protocol for the Next Generation of Communications Systems", *Proc. of SIGCOMM '86* (Aug. 1987) 406-415.

[2] T. Korb and C. Wills, "Command Execution in a Heterogeneous Environment", *Proc. of SIGCOMM '86* (Aug. 1987) 68-74.

[3] K. Lantz, J. Edighoffer, and B. Hitson, "Towards a Universal Directory Service", *Proceedings of 4th Symposium on the Principles of Distributed Computing* (Aug. 1985) 250-260.

[4] M. McKusick, M. Karels, and J. Bloom, *UNIX User's Manual Reference Guide*, 4.3 Berkeley Software Distribution (April, 1986).

[5] P. Mockapetris, "Domain Names — Concepts and Facilities," *Request For Comments 882* (Nov. 1983).

[6] P. Mockapetris, "Domain Names — Implementation and Specification," *Request For Comments 883* (Nov. 1983).

[7] D. Oppen and Y. Dalal, *The Clearinghouse: A Decentralized Agent for Locating Named Objects in a Distributed Environment*, XEROX Office Products Division Report OPD-T8103 (Oct. 1981).

[8] C. Partridge, "Mail Routing and the Domain System," *Request For Comments 974* (Jan. 1986).

[9] J. Postel, "User Datagram Protocol," *Request For Comments 768* (Aug. 1980).

[10] J. Reynolds and J. Postel, "Assigned Numbers," *Request For Comments 1010* (May. 1987).

[11] SUN Microsystems Inc., *Remote Procedure Call Programming Guide* (Feb. 1986).

[12] SUN Microsystems Inc., *Yellow Pages Protocol Specification* (Feb. 1986).

[13] USC—Information Science Institute, "Transmission Control Protocol," *Request For Comments 793* (Sep. 1981).

Abstract for

Resource Management in the Cronus Distributed Operating System

Richard Schantz
Ken Schroder
Paul Neves

BBN Laboratories Incorporated
Cambridge, MA 02238

Cronus [1-7] is an object oriented distributed system which operates in a heterogeneous computer environment of interconnected local area networks. As a distributed system architecture, Cronus faces a number of resource management issues not present in non-distributed architectures. Strategies for effectively controlling the redundancy and reconfigurability inherent in Cronus are needed to take advantage of the distributed system environment. These strategies for resource management are often conveniently separated into policies and mechanisms. A policy is a goal or guideline set by a system administrator or component designer constraining the decisions made by a resource allocator. A mechanism is an internal system structure designed to implement a class of policies.

In the Cronus distributed system model, there are currently two general aspects of resource allocation mechanisms which are particular to the network environment and must be effectively managed. One of these is the binding of a client request to a particular resource manager for those resources which are available redundantly. Redundancy comes in two forms: replicated objects, (e.g., a mutli-copy file) and replicated managers (any manager for a type can create a new instance of that object type). For both forms the selection of an object manager to provide the given service is an important resource management policy decision. The other important aspect of resource management mechanism is the ability to reconfigure parts of the system by dynamically migrating objects. Object migration is a powerful tool for matching system resources to tasks in a manner that attempts to maximize some measure of system performance, reliability, or survivability. Both static reconfiguration (e.g., choosing or amending the placement of object managers and their associated objects), and dynamic reconfiguration (e.g., moving an individual object in direct response to demand for its use possible in the Cronus architecture and design.

The general approach to resource management in Cronus is to individually control the management of the classes of objects which make up the system. This approach extends Cronus resource management concepts beyond system resources to the abstract resources developed by applications. Resource management for an individual abstract resource (type) and for groups of related resource types (services) in Cronus is based on combining a number of carefully planned mechanisms which are part of the system architecture. In addition to resource management by resource type, a client specific policy which considers collections of object types used in a specific context can be constructed.

In Cronus we achieve system wide and easily controllable resource management by requiring the object managers to cooperate in enforcing a resource management policy for their resource type. An object manager can redirect operations to a peer manager on another processor on the basis of current resource status. In the case for creation of a file to an alternate file manager which may have more storage available. Part of the basis for decisions to redirect requests are parameters, settable dynamically by system administrators through monitoring and control functions, which control the resource management strategy. The creation of objects and resource management in general thus becomes a responsibility that is decentralized among object managers on each processor based on a global allocation policy, both in terms of sharing current status and possible redirection of operations between managers.

The Cronus resource management model is based on the integration of the following set of primitive mechanisms:

- the kernel routes requests for a given type to any available manager of that type, using the Locate mechanism
- Cronus managers redirect requests to a more appropriate peer to accomplish resource management objectives
- managers periodically collect current status of their peers, via a standard mechanism (ReportStatus), to be used as a basis for selecting a site for redirecting an operation
- users and applications optionally indicate specific location preferences with requests
- an operator can monitor and regulate the functioning of the resource management policy
- applications can use the basic system mechanisms (e.g. broadcast or multicast, ReportStatus operations) to build special-purpose resource management strategies tailored to their need

---

Cronus development has been supported by the Rome Air Development Center, under contracts F30602-81-C-0132 and F30602-84-C-0171.

There is a hierarchy of desirable locations for implementing resource management policies: object managers, shared libraries, and finally client programs or users themselves. Managers are the most desirable because they are readily identifiable with a limited set of object types which are likely to have similar policy goals. Also, managers are addressable as a group for administrative control to regulate the policy parameters, and for peer manager cooperation to implement the policy. Many decisions are negotiated between managers based upon information periodically obtained via the ReportStatus operation. The Cronus Monitoring and Control System uses the same ReportStatus operation to present the operator with a global view of how well the resource management policy is proceeding.

In this paper we elaborate on these approaches to distributed resource management in Cronus, including appropriate background, detailed system design, and experiences with incorporating these ideas into three different resource managers.

REFERENCES

[1] Richard E. Schantz and Robert H. Thomas, *Cronus, A Distributed Operating System: Functional Definition and System Concept*, BBN Laboratories, Technical Report 5879 (June 1982, Revised January 1985).

[2] Richard E. Schantz and Robert H. Thomas, *Cronus, A Distributed Operating System: System/Subsystem Specification*, BBN Laboratories, Technical Report 5884 (June 1982, Revised February 1986).

[3] R. Schantz, R. Thomas, R. Gurwitz, M. Barrow, G. Bono, M. Dean, K. Lebowitz, K. Schroder, and R. Sands, *Cronus, A Distributed Operating System: Phase 1 Final Report (Interim Technical Report No. 4)*, BBN Laboratories, Technical Report No. 5885 (January 1985).

[4] R. Schantz, K. Schroder, M. Barrow, G. Bono, M. Dean, R. Gurwitz, K. Lam, K. Lebowitz, S. Lipson, P. Neves, and R. Sands, *Cronus, A Distributed Operating System: Cronus DOS Implementation, Final Report (Interim Technical Report No. 6)*, BBN Laboratories, Technical Report No. 5885 (February 1986).

[5] James C. Berets and Richard M. Sands, *Introduction to Cronus: A Distributed Operating System*, BBN Draft Report (January 1987).

[6] R. Schantz, R. Thomas, and G. Bono, *The Architecture of the Cronus Distributed Operating System*, Sixth International Conference on Distributed Computing Systems (May 1986).

[7] R. Gurwitz, M. Dean, and R. Schantz, *Programming Support in the Cronus Distributed Operating System*, Sixth International Conference on Distributed Computing Systems (May 1986).

Strategies for Decentralized Resource Management

Michael Stumm
University of Toronto
Toronto, Canada M5S 1A4

Abstract

Decentralized resource management in distributed systems has become more practical with the availability of communication facilities that support multicasting. In this paper we present several example solutions for managing resources in a decentralized fashion, using multicasting facilities. We review the properties of these solutions in terms of scalability, fault tolerance and efficiency. We conclude that decentralized solutions compare favorably to centralized solutions with respect to all three criteria.

1 Introduction

Decentralized resource management in distributed systems has become more practical with the availability of communication facilities that support multicasting. In this paper we consider three resource management problems and present decentralized solutions that use multicasting facilities. We review their properties with respect to scalability, fault tolerance and efficiency. The problems we consider are: (1) finding objects in a distributed system, (2) monitoring host resources for scheduling purposes, and (3) allocating hosts for specific functions.

This paper is structured as follows. Section 2 reviews the uses, costs and advantages of multicasting for decentralized applications. The decentralized naming facility of the V distributed system [4] is presented and used as an example. Section 3 presents a decentralized facility for scheduling tasks in a distributed system and describes its implementation for the V system. Section 4 focuses on our current research in progress. It shows that some tasks that are part of a parallel computation executing as a task group may have special scheduling requirements. For example, we show that some of these tasks cannot share processors with other processes without significantly degrading the performance of the parallel computation. We then present a decentralized method for allocating hosts to accommodate tasks with these special requirements.

2 Background

Many local area networks support *multicast* transmission, where a packet is delivered to a set of zero or more destination hosts based on a single multicast address. In general, multicast is more efficient than *broadcast*, where a packet is transmitted to *all* hosts, since fewer hosts receive and need to service the packet. It is also more efficient than a sequence of unicast transmissions, both in terms of the number of network packets transmitted and the number of packet events at the transmitting site.

Multicasting has an additional advantage over a sequence of unicast transmissions in that multicast addresses can be used as a binding mechanism by associating function with an address rather than location. For example a multicast address can be used to identify the set of hosts that are running file servers. A client can then contact the file servers (with a single packet) without knowing the identity or number of the individual hosts, but only the appropriate multicast address.

The practicality of multicasting in distributed systems and distributed applications has been well recognized. Efforts are currently underway to provide similar functionality in internetworks [3,9,8]. Distributed operating systems are beginning to provide similar functionality at the process level. For example, the V distributed system [7] provides support for *process groups*, where the processes of a group may span multiple physical hosts [6]. A multicast address is associated with each process group and a process may be a member of multiple groups. A message may be sent to a process group by addressing it with the process group identifier. The message is passed to the processes in the group using the network-level multicasting facilities where appropriate.[1] Two important uses

---

[1]The basic communication model provided by the V kernel is that

of group communication in V are to *query* a process group for information or to *update* a process group with (new) information.

The availability of group communication based on multicasting has made it economically feasible and practical to use fully decentralized solutions for distributed problems, including problems related to resource management. For example, obvious uses of group communication are for querying a set of hosts to find the location of a particular object or to query a set of hosts to determine their load in order to make a scheduling decision.

While decentralized solutions are possible by using broadcasts (as demonstrated by the worm program [19]), the cost of doing so would be prohibitive in large systems if used widely and frequently. Similarly, using unicast communication at the application level often complicates applications to a point where centralized solutions become simpler and more economical.

Nevertheless, the cost of group communication can also be high, if not used prudently. Each multicast transmission will cause an interrupt and require service at every host in the multicast set. Also, each query multicast can cause the reply of many packets, resulting in increased network traffic and an increased number of packet events at the host that transmitted the query. These costs can be reduced in a number of ways:

- cache information to reduce the amount of multicasting necessary.

- generate a reply to a query only if the response contains useful information.

- organize processes in (possibly multiple) groups, such that only minimal sets must be addressed.

As an example, consider the decentralized naming facility of the V system designed and implemented by Cheriton and Mann [4]. This facility is used to locate objects maintained by object managers and identified by clients with high-level names. In this scheme, the global (hierarchical) directory is distributed across all object managers such that each manager stores and maintains that portion of the directory corresponding to the objects and services it implements. When a client wishes to locate an object given its (high-level) name, it multicasts a query to a set of object managers. The manager of the named object will respond to the query with an appropriate reply message.

Clients can significantly reduce the number of queries by caching the information they obtain from the responses to their queries. Whenever a manager responds to a query it identifies the prefix of the object name that identifies the root of the name tree for which it exclusively is the manager. This prefix-manager pair is then cached by the client. Hence, whenever a client wishes to locate an object, it first looks in its cache for an entry that maps the name to an object manager. If such an entry is found, the operation and name can be sent directly to the manager in question using unicast network access. (Otherwise, a query multicast is necessary.) The cache effectively stores the last known location of objects and is maintained on a per task basis. Measurements indicate that with a suitable management of the cache, a hit ratio of 99.7% can be achieved in practice [4].[2]

Client cache entries may become invalid, however, for example when a portion of the name tree moves from one manager to another or when a manager crashes. These invalid entries are detected on use, either through an error indication directly from a manager (when it no longer manages the named object) or an error indication from the communication system (when the manager cannot be reached). In this case, the invalid cache entry is deleted and the named objects manager is again sought by multicasting a query.

The overhead of multicasts are further reduced by associating a process group with each node of the naming hierarchy under which multiple object managers maintain a subtree of the name space. For example every object manager is in the group of managers associated with the root of the naming hierarchy. If a manager, M1, manages the name space of the subtree with the root `/A/B` and manager M2 manages the name space under `/A/C` then both M1 and M2 will be a member of the process group associated with `/A`. Assuming no other manager belongs to this group, then if a client wishes to locate a file "`/A/C/D`" and knows the group identifier associated with `/A`, but not the identity of the manager M2, it will query the group associated with `/A`, affecting only those two hosts on which M1 and M2 are running, rather than all object managers.

Finally, network traffic can be reduced by having only those managers reply to a query that manage the object being sought. Using the above example, manager M1, managing the subtree under `/A/B`, does not reply to a query for `/A/C/D`. A negative response carries no useful information for the client, since it does not know the members of the group or the number of managers in the group. Moreover, having processes generate replies only when the reply is useful to the client reduces the number of packets that are simultaneously sent back to the client. This helps avoid possible systematic errors at those clients that have trouble receiving multiple packets that arrive back to back.

The naming example illustrates a number of additional features typical of many decentralized solutions based on multicasting. Firstly, in this application, multicasts need not be reliable, as long as a small number of repeated transmissions results in *group coverage* [3]. A

---

of *message transactions* that is initiated by a client `Send` operation that transmits a request message to a *server*. The client blocks until a reply message is returned by the server. The V kernel provides for reliability by retransmitting the message when appropriate, signaling an error when communication with the server breaks down.

Sending to a group is similar except that the client is blocked until at least one member of the group has received the message and sent back a reply. Additional replies can be received with `GetReply`. The V kernel also provides for a *real-time* `Send` that does not block because no replies are allowed in this case. The message is then sent as an unreliable (best efforts) datagram.

[2] A number of additional strategies are used to increase the hit rate. For example, each task inherits its name cache from its creator, thus reducing cache misses at task startup time.

multicast is retransmitted if a response is not received within a timeout period equal to the length of the expected response time. A client can safely assume that an object is not reachable if no response is received from the server after several retransmissions.

Secondly, the naming scheme described is fault tolerant in that a node failure will not affect naming. The failure of a client node will have no effect on the naming mechanism for the rest of the system. If a manager fails then only that portion of the name space become unavailable for which the objects are also unavailable. In contrast, with a centralized name server, objects may become inaccessible when the name server fails. Also, a centralized, but replicated server is more expensive to keep if they are to survive individual crashes.

Finally, the naming mechanism described here is scalable to very large systems consisting of thousands of nodes[4], since multicasting is used only infrequently (0.3% of the time) and often directed only to a small subset of all hosts. In a large system, it is probably advisable in any event to use *scoped multicasts*[3], where the transmission of a packet is also controlled by a distance parameter specified by the client. A client searching for an object is typically interested in a replica of the object in proximity and would initially query only nearby managers and, if unsuccessful, gradually increase the scope of its queries.

3 A Decentralized Scheduling Facility

3.1 Introduction

In this section we present the design of a decentralized global scheduling facility. The goal of such a facility is twofold: (1) to aid the user in exploiting remote resources by running programs at remote sites, and (2) to balance the load among the hosts in order to reduce the average response time of tasks. For example, users on workstations based on older technology will observe a response time improved by an order of magnitude if their programs are executed on newer, faster workstations. Similarly, a computationally intensive application will complete significantly faster on an idle host than on a busy one.

The scheduling facility described here was designed to be scalable to a large number of hosts and to be capable of scheduling at a high frequency so that every task that is started could be scheduled. But the design is based on a number of assumptions. First we assume that facilities exist for remote execution and (possibly) migration of tasks. Further, we assume that tasks execute in a network-transparent execution environment, that is, any instance of a program can safely execute on any one of a number of compatible hosts, behaving identically as far as the user is concerned. Many of todays systems provide such functionality [1,10,14,17,18,20].

We also assume that the cost of file access is equal across all hosts. This is generally the case when files are down-loaded from a network file server. (If this is not the case then scheduling should be restricted to tasks with a sufficiently long expected execution time, so that the cost of additional file transfers is negligible relative to the total execution time.) Finally, the original design was based on the assumption that the distributed system is mainly workstation based. This is important with respect to the policies we implemented, since workstation based systems have a large amount of computational power that goes mostly unused. For example, our implementation site had over 70 workstations with an aggregate processing power of more than 150 MIPS, yet the average processor load was only about 20% during the busiest times. Only a fraction of the total number of hosts are used at any given time. We expect this low level of average processor utilization to become more pronounced as faster processors (10-80 MIPS) and multiprocessor workstations come to the market in the next few of years.

3.2 Selecting an Execution Site for a Task

The scheduling facility is based on hosts publishing their state information: Every host constantly monitors its own state and multicasts it to all interested parties whenever it changes significantly. The state information of a host includes attributes that define the configuration (i.e. processor type, devices, coprocessors, etc.) and the expected load of its resources, such as processor and memory. Each interested host maintains a cache containing the state information of other hosts. This cache is updated every time new information is received and is consulted every time a task is scheduled. If the system contains very many hosts, then the information of only the N "best" hosts needs to be cached.

A program is scheduled by first determining what executable files are available for that program. There may be several, each for a different configuration or host type. Also, any special requirements an executable file may have, such as minimal memory requirements, is determined. A set is then constructed, consisting of the M most lightly loaded hosts (as indicated by our cache) that are eligible execution sites, as determined by the requirements of the program or specified by the user. The number of hosts considered, M, will be a function of the load distribution, so as to consider only "lightly loaded" hosts. The load measure maintained for each host is appropriately scaled to reflect its processing power.

If the local host belongs to this set, then it is chosen, biasing the choice towards local execution. Otherwise, hosts are randomly chosen from this set and probed to verify that the cached information is still valid (to within a certain degree of accuracy). If a probe identifies an inaccurate cache entry, then the cache is updated and the set is modified appropriately; otherwise that host is chosen for execution. (Our implementation indicates that the cache will be accurate enough so that a second probe will very rarely become necessary. The number of probes can therefore be limited to a small number.) The randomness in the selection process helps avoid *scheduling clashes* where several hosts simultaneously select the same execution site for their programs.

This scheme uses a policy similar to the *Threshold* policy analyzed by Eager et.al.[11], except that the decision whether to execute a program remotely is made based on approximate global information as opposed to the state of the local system alone. Also, instead of probing hosts completely at random, an attempt to make to guess "intelligently" as to which ones would perform best. Eager et.al. conclude that the Threshold policy which uses only a very small amount of system state information yields performance close to that of a theoretically optimal policy. Our policy had to differ from the Threshold policy to accommodate differences in assumptions concerning the characteristics of the underlying system, especially in terms of workload distribution and heterogeneity.

A key issue is how to measure the load of a host. Two important factors are the load on the processor and the load on the memory system as indicated by the amount of ongoing paging activity (or the amount of free memory on a system without demand-paged virtual memory). Although the processor load is more important with respect to its effects on response time, the effects of the memory load should not be underestimated. Adding a new task can significantly increase the page swapping activity, thereby decreasing the performance of all tasks running on that host. (Another possible load factor, a hosts networking activity, is not considered significant enough, especially since much of it is already captured by the processor load.)

Note that the multicasts used for distributing load information need not be reliable. Stale cache entries are detected and updated on use, i.e. when probing a remote host. Moreover, the facilities function correctly in spite of host failures. Orphaned cache entries (those of crashed hosts) indicating light load are also detected on use: The first host to detect an orphan, multicasts that information to all other hosts. Orphaned entries indicating heavier load are seldomly detected on use. Hence, these entries must periodically be found and disposed of using a separate mechanism for this purpose. (Note that it is not reasonable in larger systems to periodically validate each entry by querying the host in question, as this would cause considerable network traffic if done by each host.[3])

3.3 Implementation

We describe the implementation of this scheduling facility for the V distributed system [7]. The V-system consists of a distributed kernel and a distributed collection of server processes. Each host has a *program-manager* that provides program management for programs executing on that host and an *exec-server* that provides a shell-like service for interpreting command lines and starting programs for the user. The program-manager monitors the host on which it is executing and maintains the cache containing state information of all other hosts in the system. It makes this information available to all other local tasks.

The load of a host is measured by monitoring the CPU utilization, as measured by time allocated to the idle-process (an eternal process with the absolute lowest runnable priority) and is scaled by a factor representing the processing power of the host[4]. Two exponential smoothing functions with different weights are applied to this value. One tracks longer term trends and is smoother while the other tracks shorter term trends. The available memory is monitored in a similar fashion.

The computed long-term values (together with configuration information) are multicast to all other program-managers, if they differ significantly from the values that were last multicast (i.e. by more than 10% of maximum value). Each host that receives the multicast message updates its cache appropriately, as described in the previous subsection. A newly started host can initialize its cache by obtaining a copy from any one of the other hosts.

To schedule a task, the exec-server (or any other program wishing to schedule a task) reads the cache from the program-manager and selects one of the hosts represented therein. A probe is sent to that host by sending a load-request message to its program-manager, asking it to load and start executing the specified program. The basic procedure is the same as outlined in [17]. The load value used to select a host is included in the load-request message. If this value is much lower than the short-term load value, then the request is turned down, and if it is much lower than the long-term value, then besides turning down the request the requester is also asked to correct its cache entry.

Once started, the program is run in its own address space and is provided with a network-transparent execution environment. Except for the time needed for scheduling, the fact that a task may be executing remotely, is transparent to the user[5]. The difference between loading a task locally or remotely is equal to the difference between a local and remote message transaction, since all files are loaded over the network (ca. 1.5 ms vs. 3 ms [7]). Hence, even small tasks can safely be scheduled remotely. Also, a user will not notice any sluggishness when interacting with remotely executing interactive programs, since all inter-process communication is based on message passing that differs only by a factor of two for the local and remote cases (again 1.5 ms vs. 3 ms). In fact, we were surprised to find users on slower workstations notice a significantly improved responsiveness in running interactive tasks, such as editors, remotely on newer, more powerful workstations.

Most file systems, including those used in V, do not have facilities for maintaining information about files, such as execution host type, memory requirements, expected run time, task type, etc. Currently, this information is encoded in the file name (i.e. /usr/bin/cat.m68k

---

[3]500 hosts probing each other once an hour would generate 138 packets a second

[4]CPU utilization is reasonable only because we are dealing with heavily underutilized hosts, for otherwise the utilization would be constant close to 100%. For systems with a higher average load, ready-process queue length averages probably are a better measure[12].

[5]Some programs have location dependent semantics.

or /usr/bin/cat/vax) or maintained in separate tables. This is clearly a deficiency. We are currently evaluating a number of proposed solutions for maintaining information about files.

Additionally, searching through directory structures along a given search path on a file server can lead to a large number of messages. For example, in our first implementation almost 100 messages were generated per executable file lookup. This can be alleviated, however, either by introducing a hashed bit-map indicating which executable files exist in a user's search path, or by caching directory entries locally.

Measurement of our implementation indicate that for a system with 50 hosts, 10 state-information messages are broadcast to all hosts per minute during bury periods. This is with a natural workload with a load average of about 20%. Our simulations indicate that the number of broadcast message would increase to about 15 with a higher load average of 60%. Each host will service each message broadcast at a cost of approximately 1.5 to 2 milliseconds in processing overhead (depending on host type). In order to compute the local load average, the program-manager must query the kernel for the time allocated to the idle process. It does so every 5 seconds at a cost of approximately 1 ms.

The scheduling facility described provides the mechanisms for implementing many kinds of policies. Our implementation supported the policy of scheduling every task that is started in the system, (unless the user directs the exec-server to follow a different policy). Initial measurements indicate that the response time of large programs decreased by about 10% on average with this policy. This measure alone is not very meaningful, as it depends heavily on the type of hosts running at the time, the distribution of the arrival rate at the individual hosts, the distribution of the load, the type of tasks that are executed, etc. Because of the low load averages, most tasks started on the more powerful hosts execute locally. The benefit of remotely executing programs is due mostly to offloading tasks from the older, slower Workstations to the newer faster ones. For example, to *TeX* a 20 page document on an otherwise unloaded *Sun-2* workstation requires approximately 240 seconds, but only 100 seconds on an otherwise unloaded *Sun-3*, 150 seconds on a *Sun-3* that already has a load average of 50% (as measured by CPU utilization) and 200 seconds on a 75% loaded *Sun-3*.

3.4 Comparison to Other Policies

Our scheduling is based on a Publishing policy. A number of other policies are also suitable for decentralized scheduling. For example, a Querying policy can be used to query the current load of hosts and schedule a new task to the most lightly loaded host that responds. This approach is similar to that used by the naming facility, except that that the load measure indicated in response to a query is much more volatile and therefore less suited for caching. A query must therefore be multicast each time a task is scheduled. Other policies do not make use of load information when choosing an execution site for a task. For example, a host is selected randomly with the Random policy and a Cyclical policy attempts to assign tasks to hosts in a round robin fashion.

All of these studies have been well studied using both analytical models and simulations [11,22,21]. Simulations we undertook indicated that (given a workload typical of our system) Publishing and Querying performed comparably under light to medium system loads and that the Querying policy performed slightly better under higher loads and for computationally intensive tasks. Moreover, it was found that the Random and Cyclical policies performed significantly worse.

The major reason for choosing a Publishing based scheme over Querying was scalability. In Publishing based schemes, the number of messages is a function of the number of hosts. The overhead can be tuned to an acceptable level. Our implementation indicated that given the smoothing functions used approximately 20 messages per minute were generated per 100 hosts during busy periods a day, when hosts multicast their state information when the load changes by more than 10%. About four times as many messages were generated when state information is multicasts with load changes of 5%. Our simulations, indicated that the number of messages published would not increase significantly under higher system loads.

Although Querying has the advantage that the most current load information can be obtained, it delays the start of a task until responses are received from a query. Also, in Querying based schemes the number of messages is a function of the number of tasks scheduled. Not all hosts have to be queried each time a task is scheduled — for example, hosts can join a group depending on their load and clients can first query lightly loaded hosts — but the number of messages generated in large systems can easily limit the number tasks that can be scheduled. Figure 1 compares the number of network messages in Publishing to the number of messages in Querying for different scheduling frequencies, assuming only 9 hosts receive and respond to an average query. (Note, however, that all of the messages due to Publishing are multicasts, in contrast to Querying, where only the query is multicast.)

Finally, with Publishing, all packet events are evenly distributed across all hosts, whereas hosts that issue a query incur most of the packet events themselves. Hence, precisely those hosts that want to distribute some of their load will momentarily have an even higher load (due to packet processing) every time they need to schedule.

Our simulations also indicated that centralized policies do not perform better than Publishing or Querying given a workload typical of our system. In centralized schemes the number of messages transmitted is also a function of the number of tasks scheduled (one additional message per task), although non of them are multicasts. With a high rate of scheduling, a centralized scheduling server will potentially become a bottleneck unless it is run on a dedicated server host. This in turn complicates the fault tolerance aspects of such centralized servers.

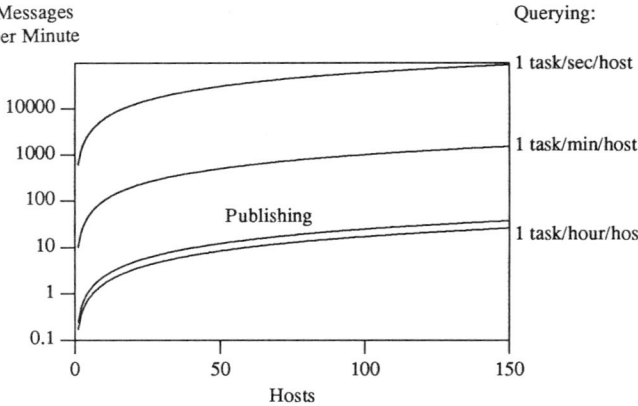

Figure 1: Publishing vs. Querying: number of network packets transmitted.

3.5 Migration

Migration facilities are mainly useful for ejecting all foreign tasks from a host (so that it can be rebooted, for instance). But migration can also be beneficial for load balancing purposes; a task will complete more quickly if it can be migrated to a host with a significant lighter load. This may be necessary, for example, after a scheduling clash, when several hosts simultaneously select the same site for processor-bound tasks.

The scheduling facilities described so far can be extended to handle migration. The global state is periodically reevaluated to decide for each task whether to migrate it to another site. This is associated with more overhead, however, since the local load must be discounted by the proportion due to the process being considered for migration, when comparing the local load to that of a remote host. Hence, the load inflicted by each task must also be measured and monitored.

There are several complications associated with migration. First, there is a danger of instability where tasks migrate from one host to another. This can be solved by requiring the difference in load between the two hosts to be larger than a threshold and by requiring that a task may only migrate if its expected time to completion is large enough. This also has the effect of offsetting the cost of migration by improved performance at the new site.

A second complication is that the measure of the load inflicted by a task must be compatible with the measure of the processor load for the arithmetic to be meaningful. Finally, the decision whether to migrate and to where to migrate cannot always be made by the "system" without additional information from the application. In some instances it is easier to let the application make the migration decisions. For example, some tasks may require efficient access to certain devices and should not be migrated at all or only to a certain subset of the hosts. Others may have residual dependencies (e.g. a compilation that uses local temporary files) that should also be moved. As another example, the purpose of some tasks are to function as watchdogs, that is, to monitor other tasks to detect their failure (and commence recovery procedures). Since tasks often fail because the host on which they are executing fails, a watchdog should never be migrated to the same host on which the task it is monitoring is executing and vice versa.

4 Allocating Resources for Parallel Programs

In this section we consider some scheduling requirements of parallel programs. Programs can be structured for parallel processing in many ways. Some can be structured to execute on a cluster of hosts connected by a local area network [5,13], treating the cluster as a loosely coupled parallel machine. Workstation clusters are particularly suited for executing parallel computations of this type, since a large portion of the workstations are idle at any given time, especially at night. These parallel computations execute as *task groups*, where the tasks execute in parallel (on different hosts).

Depending on the structure of the computation, the tasks that belong to a task group may require special consideration when being scheduled. We present two such requirements and propose modifications to the scheduling facility of the previous section that accommodate these special requirements.

First we consider programs that execute synchronously, that is, the tasks execute in lock step, synchronizing at the end of each iteration. For example, algorithms for dynamic programming or Gaussian elimination can be structured in this way. Tasks belonging to such synchronous computations, which we call *S-tasks*, should not share the processor assigned to them with any other task. Even slight variations in the processing power made available to an S-task can decrease the performance of the entire computation drastically, because all tasks must periodically wait for the slowest task to complete its iteration and a single, slowly running task can prevent the computation from attaining the expected speedup. For example, consider a parallel synchronous computation (with perfect speedup behavior) executing as 5 tasks, where 4 of them have exclusive use of the processor they are executing on, but one of them has only access to 70% of its processor. This computation will complete more quickly if executed using only 4 tasks if they can run alone on the processors to which they are assigned.

To accommodate for S-tasks in scheduling, we reserve a subset of all hosts to execute S-tasks, at most one at a time. We call these hosts *S-hosts*. In a large system with an overabundance of processing power, an attempt is made to always keep a few S-hosts idle, ready for new S-tasks. (In order not to waste these cycles completely, one can still allow short tasks to be executed on S-hosts, when not being used by an S-task.)

Naturally, the number of S-hosts would have to vary dynamically, adapting to the current state of the system. The number of available S-hosts would be a function of the total number of hosts, the relative number of S-hosts in use, the average load on non-S-hosts, etc. The scheduling facility described in the previous section can be slightly modified to include in the state information whether a host is an S-host or not. Then each host can periodically reevaluate the global and local state to determine if it should become or cease being an S-host, depending on the global state as represented by the local cache. In this scheme, the set of all hosts is partitioned into two disjoint subsets, the S-hosts and the non-S-hosts, in a fully decentralized manner, adapting to the changes in the system. A change in the status of the host is considered significant. A host therefore multicasts its state whenever, it changes from one set to another.

We are currently studying how best to implement these adaptive subsets. A number of tradeoffs are involved. On the one hand, one would like to have the subsets adjust to changes in the system relatively quickly. On the other hand, one would like to minimize the number of transitions and in all cases achieve stability. These tradeoffs are complicated by the fact that hosts base their decisions on partially incorrect information (due to the unreliability of multicasts). We would like to better understand the effects of different choices in threshold values and the effects of the unreliability of multicast transmissions. We are also looking into using a more probabilistic decision procedure to decide whether a host should make a transition from one set to another.

Next we consider scheduling requirements of tasks that are part of a parallel computation with less than perfect speedup behavior. As a general rule of thumb, two tasks that are members of different task groups should not execute on the same processor at the same time. This requirement can be explained by observing that the efficiency of a parallel computation cannot increase with the number of processors; the shape of the speedup curve will always be concave. As an example, consider a parallel alpha-beta searching algorithm within a game of checkers [5]. Figure 2 depicts the average speedup obtained on a cluster of Sun-3's running the V kernel [7]. The speedup with 5 processors (ca. 4) will always be greater than or equal to half the speedup with 10 processors (ca. 3). Therefore, if, for example, we wish to run two such computations at the same time, then it is more efficient (the computations will complete more quickly on average) if each computation used 5 separate processors, rather than if each computation time-shared the same 10 processors. The two computations will also complete less quickly on average if 10 processors first run the tasks of the first computation followed by those of the second computation.[6]

This requirement makes it difficult to schedule many

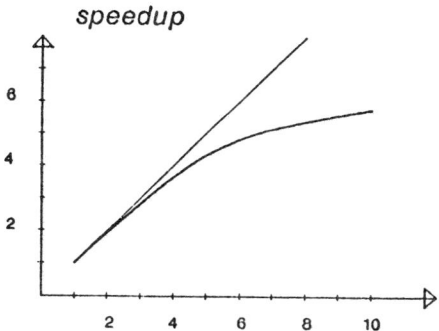

Figure 2: Speedup of Alpha-Beta searching on a workstation cluster.

competing task groups, because either (1) a program is restricted to using a small number of hosts in anticipation that other programs will also run, but limiting the program from exploiting the available processing power, or (2) a program is allowed to "grab" as many hosts as it wishes, potentially blocking out other parallel programs. A third alternative is to require the program to be capable of adjusting the number of hosts it is using dynamically during execution. This alternative is fair, yet allows programs to exploit as much parallelism as is available, but at the cost of potentially having to periodically restructure the workload within the parallel application.

Having self-adjustable parallel programs may not be as difficult as it may sound. Cheriton and Stumm [5] describe a model for structuring parallel computations for a workstation environment that is capable of running while the number of processors available to the computation varies. Some parallel programs, such as simulations described by Jefferson [15], must be capable of dynamically adapting the load on each processor to changing processing requirements. The methodology he uses can be generalized for releasing and adding processors to a parallel computation.

If we wish to implement a policy where each host may execute at most one task belonging to a task group (but may run other "normal" tasks) and where the parallel computations are capable of adjusting the number of tasks they run in parallel, then we propose the following solution. First, tasks belonging to parallel computations register themselves as such with the program-manager on the host on which they are executing. The fact that a host is executing one of these tasks becomes part of the state it maintains and publishes.[7] (It is in the interest

---

[6]Using the same line of reasoning, one can also argue that parallel computations should use the most powerful processors in the system, since a parallel computation will always complete more quickly when using two fast processors than if run on 6 processors one third the power of the fast ones, although this may contradict scheduling policies concerning interactive jobs.

[7]With tasks executing on hosts to use up the processors "slop", it becomes necessary to modify the definition of the load of a host

of the tasks to register themselves.) A parallel program can determine the number of hosts available for executing its tasks from the local cache of state information and decide how many tasks it should run in parallel and schedule them to execute on an appropriate host.

It may happen that an application would like more hosts than are immediately available. For this purpose we assume that each parallel program in execution is being controlled by a master process. Each such master process joins a well known group and is responsible for negotiating with other master modules and for restructuring the computation if required to do so. If an application would like to use more hosts than are currently available, then it sends a query message to the group of parallel program managers, to determine their identity and the number of tasks they are using. He may request some of these computations to release processors, as long as his task group does not become larger than those he is forcing to restructure. A parallel computation must reduce the number of tasks if asked to do so. A computation releases a processor by migrating its task onto a processor that it already possesses before restructuring. The master process of a computation may periodically reevaluate the global state to determine if it should expand the number of processors it is using.

Hence, in this scheme, task groups compete for processors. If each processor attempts to maximize its number of tasks, then each task group will approximately be equal size. It is possible to refine the scheme by having the master modules specify the speedup characteristics during the negotiation process, to allow computations with better speedup to have more processors. It would also be straight forward to modify the scheme to accommodate task group priorities.

5 Conclusions

We presented several example solutions for problems associated with resource management in distributed systems, including (1) naming, (2) global scheduling and (3) allocating hosts for specific functions. Traditionally, these services have been provided for by centralized servers, i.e. name servers and scheduling servers. We argued that decentralized solutions to these problems have become more practical with the availability of multicasting facilities in modern networks. If these multicasting facilities are used prudently, then decentralized solutions benefit from a number of advantages in terms of scalability, performance and reliability, when compared to centralized solutions, as shown in our examples.

While the use of multicasts generally reduces communication costs (when compared to using broadcasts or a sequence of unicasts) in terms of both network traffic and the number of packet events that must be serviced by hosts, the aggregate cost of all multicasts can become very high in a large system if used indiscriminately. We

---

to include that proportion of the processor utilization consumed by "normal" tasks and that proportion consumed by tasks belonging to parallel computations.

presented a number of strategies to reduce these costs and showed that by far the most effective reduction of multicast use can be achieved by introducing a local caching mechanism to store information. In each of our examples, application level strategies could be applied to detect stale cache entries or to reduce their effects. Hence, the approaches taken here are all examples of applying Cheriton's problem-oriented shared memory[2] techniques.

We believe that the strategies chosen are applicable to many other problems in resource management. As another example, consider a distributed shared virtual memory system [16]. If we assume a page ownership protocol for maintaining consistency, then each page in memory will have an associated owner. Ownership of pages will (generally) change over time. Multicast facilities can be used by the client on a page fault to locate the appropriate owner. The number of multicasts can be reduced significantly in practice, if each client caches the last known owner of each page. This solution is essentially identical to the one proposed by Li [16].

Some of the problems we considered appear to fundamentally require decentralized solutions. For example, in dealing with migration and the scheduling of task groups or parallel programs in execution, we found that some of the scheduling and allocation functions had to be performed by the application, as opposed to a "system" module. The information and algorithms needed to decide what actions to take were too complex and application dependent to be abstracted into simple generic models suitable to be handled by the system (and therefore also centralized servers). In order to make these decisions, applications need efficient access to complex state information concerning a large portion of the distributed system. Since this may entail a large amount of information, it will be obtained more efficiently if maintained on a per host basis rather than a centralized server (especially if this information in made available by using local virtual memory mapping techniques rather than copying).

In conclusion, we view the examples described in this paper to be useful facilities for distributed systems. Their properties with respect to scalability, fault tolerance and efficiency also make them suitable for larger internetwork environments as soon as these environments provide for multicasting facilities. In the future, we expect to see solutions, similar to the ones described here, applied to an increasing number of problems.

Acknowledgments

P. Brundrett helped implement and find bugs in the scheduling facility. S. Shi performed the simulations of the scheduling policies. Discussions with members of the Distributed Systems Group at Stanford, S. Curran, O. Krieger, A. Sanwalka, B. Thomson and S. Zhou were also very helpful.

References

[1] R. Agrawal and A.K. Ezzat. Location Independent Remote Execution in NEST. *IEEE Trans. on Soft. Eng.*, SE-13(8), 1987.

[2] D.R. Cheriton. Problem-oriented shared memory: A Decentralized Approach to Distributed System Design. In *Proc. 6th Intl. Conf. on Distributed Computer Systems*, May 1986.

[3] D.R. Cheriton and S.E. Deering. Host Groups: A Multicast Extension to the Internet Protocol. In *Proc. 9th Data Comm. Symp.*, September 1985.

[4] D.R. Cheriton and T.P. Mann. *A Decentralized Naming Facility*. Technical Report STAN-CS-86-1098, Department of Computer Science, Stanford University, February 1986.

[5] D.R. Cheriton and M. Stumm. The Multi-Satellite Star: Structuring Parallel Computations for a Workstation Cluster. *Distributed Computing*, to appear.

[6] D.R. Cheriton and W. Zwaenepoel. Distributed Process Groups in the V Kernel. *ACM Trans. on Computer Systems*, 3(2), 1985.

[7] D.R. Cheriton and W. Zwaenepoel. The distributed V Kernel and its Performance for Diskless Workstations. In *Proc. 9th ACM Symp on Operating System Principles*, 1983. appeared in Operating System Review 17(5).

[8] S. Deering. Host Extensions for IP Multicasting. July 1986. RFC 988.

[9] S.E. Deering and D.R. Cheriton. Host Groups: A Multicast Extension to the Internet Protocol. December 1985. RFC 966.

[10] F. Douglis. *Process Migration in the Sprite Operating System*. Technical Report UCB/CSD 87/343, Computer Science Division (EECS), University of California, Berkeley, California 94720, 1987.

[11] D. Eager, E. Lazowska, and J. Zahorjan. Dynamic Load Sharing in Homogeneous Distributed Systems. *IEEE Trans. Soft. Eng.*, SE-12(5):662–675, 1986.

[12] D. Ferrari and S. Zhou. *An Emperical Investigation of Load Indices for Load Balancing Applications*. Technical Report UCB/CSD 87/353, Computer Science Division (EECS), University of California, Berkeley, California 94720, 1987.

[13] R. Finkel and U. Manber. DIB — A Distributed Implementations of Backtracking. *ACM Transactions on Programming Languages and Systems*, 9(2):235–256, 1987.

[14] R. Hagmann. Process Server: Sharing Processing Power in a Workstation Environment. In *Proc. Principles of Distributed Computing*, 1986.

[15] D.R. Jefferson and H.A. Sowizral. Fast Concurrent Simulation using the Time Warp Mechanism. In *Proc. of te SCS Dist. Sim. Conf.*, 1985.

[16] K. Li. *Shared Virtual Memory on Loosely Coupled Multiprocessors*. PhD thesis, Yale University, Dept. of Computer Science, 1986. Tech. Report YALEU/DCS/RR-492.

[17] M.Theimer, K.A. Lantz, and D.R. Cheriton. Preemptive Remote Execution Facilities for the V-System. In *Proc. 10th ACM Symp. on Operating System Principles*, 1985. appeared in ACM Operating System Review.

[18] M.L. Powel and B.P. Miller. Process Migration in DEMOS/MP. In *Proc. 9th ACM Symp on Operating System Principles*, 1983. appeared in Operating System Review 17(5).

[19] J.F. Shoch and J.A. Hupp. The Worm programs - some early experiences with a distributed computation. *CACM*, 25(3), March 1982.

[20] B. Walker, G. Popek, R. English, C. Kline, and G. Thiel. The LOCUS Distributed Operating System. In *Proc. 9th ACM Symp on Operating System Principles*, 1983. appeared in Operating System Review 17(5).

[21] Y. Wang and R. Morris. Load Balancing in Distributed Systems. *IEEE Trans. Comp.*, C-34(3), 1985.

[22] S. Zhou. *A Trace-Driven Simulation of Dynamic Load Balancing*. Technical Report UCB/CSD 87/305, Computer Science Division (EECS), University of California, Berkeley, California 94720, 1986.

RESOURCE MANAGEMENT IN A DISTRIBUTED INTERNETWORK ENVIRONMENT

Greg Skinner[*]
Joan M. Wrabetz[*]
Louis Schreier[*]

SRI International
Menlo Park, California 94025

ABSTRACT

The resource management system is designed to support location-transparent access to resources and to improve performance in a distributed internetwork environment. In this environment, access to one of several machines that have a given resource is determined by the effective bandwidth and reliability of internetwork communications, the ability to interact with the machines offering the resources, and the load on those machines. Using these criteria, the resource management system enables applications to determine and obtain access to the "best" copy of a resource. Should the resource become unavailable from one machine, the resource management system can dynamically direct the applications to another machine known to offer the same resource. This paper discusses some of the problems that motivated the design, an implementation for a UNIX workstation environment, and future directions for the resource management system.

INTRODUCTION

In a distributed internetwork environment, resources are dispersed among many heterogeneous machines and operating systems. If that environment is to reliable and survivable as well, redundant resources should be provided to increase availability and to guarantee continuous operation. This is true of a tactical environment in which both communications and processing may be unreliable. Thus, resources will not always be accessible. Further, they may migrate to new locations either to improve system performance, or to meet survivability requirements. Despite the dynamics of this environment, resources must be kept available to users requesting them. Therefore, resources must be managed such that access can be guaranteed to be reliable and efficient without regard for their physical location.

In addition to providing access, resource management must also provide the capability to reconfigure resources. Such reconfiguration may be required for several reasons. First, in order to maintain system reliability resources may need to be migrated when hosts are shut down or have failed, or when hosts move to a new location or take on a new function. Second, in order to maintain consistent performance, resources may need to be dynamically migrated during periods of peak usage, during system partitions, or when hosts have failed because fewer resources are available. Under such circumstances, it is useful to provide additional resources at heavily loaded parts of the distributed system. Finally, in addition to creating or migrating resources, information must be kept about their location so that access can be granted and consistency among replicas maintained.

A third function of resource management is to monitor and display status information for the system's operators. Resource monitoring also provides the underlying information for deciding how to allocate resources and reconfigure the system. Moreover, in a large distributed system typical of tactical environments, it is desirable to decentralize this monitoring function, and to provide an architecture that minimizes the cost of propagating the information it collects.

BACKGROUND

The resource manager is being developed at SRI International (SRI) under the auspices of the ADCCP (Army Distributed Command and Control Project). One of the goals of ADCCP is to investigate the design of system architectures that satisfy the requirements for

---
[*]The authors are with SRI International in the Information Sciences and Technology Center, 333 Ravenswood Avenue, Menlo Park, CA 94025. This work is being funded under the ADCCP program by the Communications and Electronics Command under Contract DAAB07-86-DA035-DO No. 13.

Permission to copy without fee all or part of this material is granted provided that the copies are not made or distributed for direct commercial advantage, the ACM copyright notice and the title of the publication and its date appear, and notice is given that copying is by permission of the Association for Computing Machinery. To copy otherwise, or to republish, requires a fee and/or specfic permission.

© 1988 ACM 0-89791-245-4/88/0001/0254 $1.50

survivable Command, Control, Communications, and Intelligence (C³I) applications. To meet this goal, SRI is developing a prototype distributed system to investigate ways for providing access to C² information resources in an unreliable internetwork environment, that is where partitioning is common and resources are often unavailable.

This paper describes the architecture and implementation of a resource management system that provides the functions described above.

ARCHITECTURE

The resource management system is made up of three elements: A *replicated nameserver*, a *distributed resource monitor*, and *resource managers* (See Figure 1). The replicated nameserver provides reliable, dynamic mappings between services and hosts to support both the allocation and reconfiguration of services. Updates to the nameserver are automatically replicated to other copies of the nameserver, thus propagating location information in real-time. This fully automated replication and management of the nameserver is in contrast to current nameserver implementations such as SUN MicroSystems Inc., Yellow Pages [1].

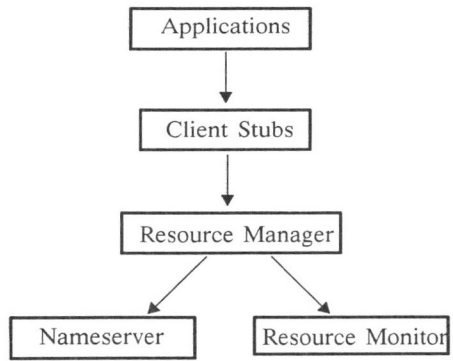

Figure 1. Resource Management System

The distributed resource monitor provides dynamic status information about the hosts, communications, and services used in making allocation and reconfiguration decisions. In many systems resource monitoring is done by having resources (or their servers) broadcast status information [2,3]. Broadcasting in an internetwork, however, will increase communication traffic to potentially unacceptable levels. In addition, broadcast communications are not reliable. Alternatively, status can be collected by polling resources. For example, the Automated Network Manager (ANM), consists of a central polling entity that collects status from resources [2]. Having a central status collection agent does not provide fault tolerance when the distributed system is partitioned and all resources do not have access to the collection agent. Thus, in our distributed system, centralizing the collection agent is inappropriate and decentralized status collection is used by the resource monitor. Because distributed status collectors must have full system status information, they must share information. Because broadcasting is not feasible, these monitoring agents propagate information between themselves using a transactional interaction.

In addition, in order to maximize efficiency in the internetwork, status collection is also designed to be hierarchical. Monitoring agents have limited status collection responsibilities and propagate their status information only among peers. This hierarchical status collection architecture *is* scalable, because the levels of the hierarchy can be extended as necessary with entities propagating information only within their level of the hierarchy and to a single superior agent.

Resource allocation is provided within the distributed system by resource managers. These managers are RPC-based services that can be accessed by any client, and determine for a requesting client the "best" available service from a set of equivalent services. These resource managers are not associated with the resources that they make determinations about, nor do they handle binding directly. They simply provide the client with a server allocation, so that the client can then bind to a service in a location-transparent manner. This is in contrast to other systems in which the resources themselves (or their object managers) manage allocation and binding. For example, in the CRONUS Operating system, resource object managers make allocation and binding decisions, by refusing allocations and forwarding requests to other object managers [4].

In our distributed system, the resource allocation function is separated from the resources themselves for several reasons. First, the cost of locating a resource and potentially being refused allocation by that resource, or being forwarded is very costly in a large unreliable distributed system connectivity. Second, our distributed system is based on a client/server model in which the binding between clients and servers is expected to be transactionally oriented. Servers are strictly passive RPC-based services that respond to calls from a client. In addition, in order to maximize reliability and simplify recovery from failures, services do not maintain state information between invocations. Thus, it would be difficult for these services to make good allocation and binding decisions or to handle the binding operation. Therefore, clients in this system need the help of an intermediary to locate and bind themselves to a server when multiple copies are available. It is this function that is provided by the resource managers. Resource managers are services that clients access via RPCs to request an allocation suggestion for the "best" server of a specified type. Using this information, an application can then access a resource on a processor best able to service the request. If the selected processor is unable to handle subsequent requests, the resource manager dynamically selects another processor from which the resource is available. *

The resource manager makes a decision as to the "best" available service for a requesting client using heuristics that take into account the locations of the available copies of the requested service, the dynamic system status, and the communications status between the client and the potential server. In our distributed system, status-based heuristics are being used for resource allocation and will be used for dynamic reconfiguration.

IMPLEMENTATION

The resource management system is written in the C language and runs as user processes in the 4.2 BSD UNIX operating system. Interprocess communication (IPC) between resource management modules is accomplished with an implementation of Sun RPC that has been extended to support reliable, location-transparent IPC [5,6]. Status information is stored dynamically in memory using routines similar to those of the UNIX *dbm* library.

The resource management system consists of three major modules: a *distributed nameserver* that maintains a list of servers that offer a given resource; a *resource monitor* that collects and distributes status information about the resources in the internetwork; and a *resource manager* that executes a heuristic on that status information to determine the "best" server to use.

Communication in this internetwork distributed system uses the client/server model, where client processes (applications) obtain services from server processes (resources). The rationale behind this model is that communication links and processors are most economically used when the data are processed where they reside, instead of being transferred to the processor where the client process is located. Because the internetwork may be congested, unreliable, or partitioned, large data transfers are less likely to succeed, on the average, than small ones. The communication costs involved in transferring all of the data are considerably greater than those of invoking a process on a server site where the data are located.

Applications usually make an RPC to a service by specifying the name of the host on which the service runs. But given the large number of hosts and the likelihood of internetwork or processor failure in this environment, it is difficult to know which host is the "best" one to use. In addition, it is desirable for the details of the internetwork to remain hidden from applications. For these reasons, the system has been designed so that application requests automatically use the resource management system to access appropriate servers.

To support location-transparency, an application makes a call to a surrogate service called a client-stub. The client stub calls the client side resource manager routine, which checks a cache for the "best" host. If the cache is empty, an RPC is made to the server side resource manager. The server side accesses the replicated nameserver database to obtain a list of server host names. A "best" host is picked from the list based on collected host status information, which is returned to the client side resource manager, stored in its cache and returned to the application. That server host name is then used in a standard RPC to the requested service. This whole process is invisible to the calling application.

The nameserver is implemented as an RPC-based service for a database of mappings between service names and hosts. The nameserver database is replicated throughout the internetwork and is updated dynamically to reflect changes in service locations. The replication mechanism we developed is described in Wrabetz, et al., [6]. This nameserver provides dynamic naming to support both location-transparent allocation and reconfiguration.

The resource monitoring architecture consists of status servers associated with resources (hosts, printers, gateways, services) and resource monitors that collect status from an assigned subset of these servers. Resource monitors are daemons that periodically collect and propagate information in a three stage process. First, each monitor polls the host status servers in its assigned domain by making an RPC to collect host and service information. Second, each monitor polls its peers collecting their status information. Finally, this information is stored in a database. A separate-server process manages this database.

Resource monitors collect the following information from their hosts: the time-of-day, the load average, the round-trip time to the host, whether the host is up or down the amount of time the host has been up, the number of users currently logged in, and service information for all services running on that host. Only the round-trip time and up/down status are collected for gateways and printers. The round-trip time is obtained by measuring the time it takes an ICMP echo request

---
*Note: Each application selects its own "best" copy of the resource.

packet to travel from a resource monitor to each monitored processor and then return with a reply [7]. The remaining information for each host is obtained via an RPC to the host status server. The host status server obtains status information from the operating system and returns it to the monitor. In addition, resource usage information is obtained from the operating system for each service process running on that host.

A graphics-oriented, window-based tool is available to graphically display the status of monitored processors. These monitored processors are shaded white if they are up, and black if down. Selecting one of the processors displayed with the mouse causes the status information for that processor to be displayed. Moreover, if the processor is a resource monitor, the status for it and all of the hosts it monitors is displayed. The display is updated automatically.

The resource manager uses status information from the resource monitor. A set of heuristics is applied to the information to derive the "best" server allocation for a requesting client. The current heuristic is as follows:

$$\text{best server} = \mathcal{F}[\min(\text{loadave}, \text{round-trip time}, \text{\#users}, \text{serviceload}) \,\&\, \max(\text{uptime}) \,\&\, \text{upstatus}]$$

this function is applied for each triple of requesting client, server host, and service. The current function applies a weighting factor and a filter to "uptime" in order to normalize it and to adjust for monotonically increasing values. The heuristic will be varied after experimentation and practice with its use in various configurations.

FUTURE DIRECTIONS

The resource management system can be extended in many ways. Some of these extensions are already under development, while others are being studied. Our main goals in doing so are to provide support for dynamic reconfiguration, to minimize the network traffic needed to distribute information and to provide additional network monitoring. The resource management system can also be used to depict the distributed system and characterize its behavior.

The capability to dynamically reconfigure the system is not yet implemented within the resource management system. Incorporation of reconfiguration requires adding another resource manager function to manage the creation, migration and removal of services. Unlike the current resource manager function of allocation, reconfiguration would operate both in response to user requests, and in automatic response to dynamic system information. Heuristics for determining automatic responses will be part of this management function and will use resource monitor status information as well as tactical information. Similar heuristics have been developed for load balancing [8]. In addition, our current RPC implementation must be changed to provide dynamic registration of services and multiple instantiations of a service at a single location [5]. Dynamic service registration is already supported within the nameserver.

Adding multicast mechanisms to the resource manager is also being examined [9]. With these mechanisms, the resource monitors could multicast requests for status updates on the networks that contain the processors they monitor, and the resource monitors could then update each other by multicasting their status information. Multicast communications will provide great improvements in the efficiency of status collection and propagation because of the parallelism provided to the collecting agent, and the reduction of message traffic. New mechanisms are now under development for 4.3 BSD UNIX to provide new packet types, routing algorithms, and dynamic group membership operations for multicast. We will attempt to incorporate these mechanisms into the resource manager as soon as they become available.

The resource manager currently collects little information about the state of the underlying communication media. Internetwork topology, load, and routing conditions would provide additional information for the resource manager's server-selection process. Such information is not generally available though, because it requires knowing which protocols to use to communicate with other internetwork components, such as packet-switched nodes, gateways, and packet radios, although efforts are underway to automatically monitor these components [2].

SUMMARY

The resource management system is a valuable tool for improving and analyzing the performance of a distributed internetwork system. It provides dynamic location-transparent access for system resources, as well as the monitoring and display of status information about communications, processing and information resources. The resource manager integrates these capabilities to provide "best" service decisions. It provides the distributed system with the capability to make intelligent, dynamic decisions about resources in order to enhance reliability and performance leading to increased survivability.

Future work will lead to a better understanding of the complex interactions of distributed system resources, and to better ways to manage them and improve their performance.

REFERENCES

1. SUN MicroSystems, Inc., "Yellow Pages Protocol Specification", February 1986.

2. Stillman, M., "ANM User's Guide", Bolt, Beranek, and Newman, Inc., December 1986.

3. Agrawal, R. and Ezzat, A., "Execution Location Independent Remote Execution in NEST", Proceedings of the IEEE 1985 Conference on Parallel Processing, August 1985.

4. Shantz, R. et.al., "CRONUS, A Distributed Operating System: Phase 1 Final Report", Bolt, Beranek, and Newman, Inc. Report No. 5885, January, 1985.

5. SUN MicroSystems, Inc., "Remote Procedure Call Protocol Specification", May 1985.

6. Wrabetz, J., Schreier, L., and Davis, M., "An Overview of an Experiment Distributed System", submitted to IEEE Transactions on Software Engineering, 1987.

7. Postel, J., "Internet Control Message Protocol—DARPA Internet Program Protocol Specification", RFC 792, Information Sciences Institute, September 1981.

8. Pasquel, J., "Using Expert Systems to Manage Distributed Computer Systems", Computer Systems Research Group, Dept. of Electrical Engineering and Computer Science, University of California, Berkeley, California January 5, 1987.

9. Deering, S., "Host Extensions for IP Multicasting", RFC 988, Stanford University, July 1986.

PART 9. COMPUTER-SUPPORTED COLLABORATIVE WORK

J.J. Garcia-Luna-Aceves

SRI International, USA

A NETWORK ENVIRONMENT FOR COMPUTER-SUPPORTED COOPERATIVE WORK

James Whitescarver
Prithviraj Mukherji
Murray Turoff
Ronald J. DeBlock Jr.
Robert M. Czech
Bijoy K. Paul

New Jersey Institute of Technology

ABSTRACT

A second generation computer supported cooperative work system called Electronic Information Exchange System (EIES2) is described in this paper. The EIES2 communications environment allows users to network across geographical constraints using asynchronous or synchronous communications. The architecture of the network environment is decentralized, and is implemented using modern standards, and an easy-to-use user interface.

At the heart of EIES2 is a high-level, object oriented pseudo machine which incorporates a distributed, communications-oriented database.

The set of tools provided by the EIES2 communications environment is well suited for implementing group communication systems that have an extensive set of user features built into it. These tools are well suited to support the group communication model described by the AMIGO task force (IFIP 6.5 and ISO TC97/SC18/WG64). The EIES2 application layer protocols, using CCITT/ISO X.410 Remote Operations, support a distributed object oriented database.

1. INTRODUCTION

Computer-based systems are being used with increasing frequency as tools for cooperative work [1]. Since most organizational activities are dependent on communications, the goal of cooperative work is to improve organizational productivity by structuring and facilitating communications [2]. A cooperative work environment supports electronic mail, decision making, computerized conferencing, multi-media document processing, graphics, integration with on-line information services, personal communications management and information management. It must also include facilities for tailoring the communications environment to meet diverse cooperative work application needs ranging from crisis management to long-term planning. Facilities are needed to support group processes such as information exchange, data collection, voting, rank ordering, alternatives analysis and task support. These facilities should be provided in an environment consistent with the organization's needs for planning, operation, monitoring and controlling its activities. Programmability and flexibility are desired to meet future cooperative work application needs.

Collaboration and task force activities often cross organizational and geographical boundaries. Communication outside of the user's local environment are often necessary, and these communications should be transparent to the user. New international standards, the CCITT X.400 series, offer the promise that users of CSCW systems might have the same connectivity enjoyed by users of traditional phone and mail system. The Advanced Group Communication Model For Computer-based Communications Environment (AMIGO Project), is providing a framework for standards for group communications [3]. With the advance of technology, the cooperative work environment must be capable of incorporating new technologies and operating in heterogeneous networks of user machines. New standards are needed to support CSCW applications.

The Electronic Information Exchange System II (EIES2) provides a foundation on which CSCW systems may be built and defines protocols that can allow them to operate interactively with each other.

1.1 COMPUTER-SUPPORTED COOPERATIVE WORK APPLICATION OVERVIEW

1.1.1 ASYNCHRONOUS VERSUS SYNCHRONOUS CSCW
Synchronous computerized human communication tools are virtually instantaneous, like present-day telephone service. Synchronous group communication tools represent a special case, in which the participants are on-line in the same activity at the same time.

Asynchronous tools such as electronic mail, provide store and forward capabilities. The computer's memory is used to eliminate the requirement of time concurrence in communications.

Synchronous tools will continue to be important for small groups, but the potential of computer-supported communications is largely in asynchronous mechanisms. This is because they can allow a virtually unlimited number of participants, and because they can allow each individual to have control over his communications processes. Users can participate at their convenience. The communications network serves them, rather than their becoming slaves to constant interruptions, communications and other activities scheduled for the benefit of others. This offers the potential for improved quality of participation.[4]. The aim of these systems is to reduce information overload [5] and develop a knowledge base of communications to provide individual and group leverage [6].

Simple electronic mail can support individual communications with other individuals or groups. This may be called "one-to-one," or "one-to-many" communications [Stevens]. Computerized conferencing applies to a much broader range of applications by supporting "many-to-many" communications. Computer-mediated communications tools provide additional facilities for group processes. Simple group tasks involve list generation, rank ordering, voting, selecting and organizing. These tasks can be facilitated with software tools. Structured communications futher supports group tasks by providing automated support for the social processes and human roles in the group process.

1.2 APPLICATION AREAS

Information Exchange:

Synergy development - The access to a large number of people from varied disciplines and geographical locations offers the potential to avoid redundancies and develop more creative and complete problem solutions. Inquiry Networking provides timely and easy access to expertise and an accumulated database where answers to similar questions may easily be found.

Electronic Meetings and Group Decision Support:

The quality of meetings can be improved by providing enhanced facilities for presenting, recording, organizing, indexing and retrieving the various pieces of information presented, decisions reached and so on. CSCW systems provide a natural basis for this kind of augmentation. More importantly, specific structures can be implemented to support different situations with varied information exchange characteristics such as Brainstorming[7], Crisis Management [8], Planning group support[4] and legal,technical and policy review meetings. Meetings that would be expensive or impractical due to time or geographical constraints can take place on-line and still produce quality results.

Office Management Systems:

Project Management Support Facilities - task assignment and status reporting activities are suited very well to the functions supported by a cmc facility. Typical office management activities such as calendar management, resource scheduling, personal time management, reminders, document processing, office forms processing, and data collection and analysis are possible within a full-fledged CSCW networked utility.

Education (The Electronic Classroom):

Electronic Classrooms- using tailorable features within CSCW networks is an effective alternative to face-to-face instruction[9]. This process is also applicable to dissemination of instructional methods and procedures.

1.3 EIES2 OVERVIEW

The Electronic Information Exchange System II (EIES2) provides an integrated collection of tools for defining and operating computer-supported cooperative work (CSCW) systems. Facilities are provided to tailor group communication facilities and user interfaces in a network environment. Standard application layer protocols for remote operations are used to support a distributed database of communication objects in an arbitrary network of application entities (AEs).

A high-level tool, the Communications Language Processor (CLP), is provided to define the protocol data units (PDUs) for existing, and future standards. The CLP uses standard abstract syntax notation (ASN.1/X.409) as defined by the ISO and CCITT. This standard has been applied to define virtually all the new application layer standards.

EIES2 employs the X.410 application layer protocols for remote operations. The X.410 remote operations protocol is also achieving a high degree of acceptance as a new application layer standard. The EIES2 protocols provide an extremely general base, employing the existing standards as much as is practical, upon which future CSCW standards may be built.

EIES2 provides its own distributed SmallTalk environment for CSCW application development. This maps well to the network environment of CSCW, and provides for a high degree of security. The object model is extremely well suited to CSCW development.

2. EIES2 FEATURES

2.1 DISTRIBUTED AND DECENTRALIZED FUNCTIONALITY

Typically the CSCW environment must support a potentially large number of users using several different computer facilities. Many modern organizations off-load from their central mainframe computers to department mini-computers, work group systems, and personal computers. The EIES2 cooperative work facilities operate in these environments and are transparent to the user.

EIES2 supports both horizontal distributed processing, and vertical decentralization of processing. Horizontal distribution is achieved through support of ° remote operations on remote data objects. Vertical decentralization is implemented through a layered interface between the user and the application. The EIES2 network environment makes the network architecture transparent to the user and the application developer.

2.2 ENVIRONMENT INDEPENDENCE

Although EIES2 has been developed for the UNIX* environment, it is designed to

---

* Trademark of AT&T

maximize its independence from its operating system and hardware base, thus facilitating mobility. Figure 1 illustrates the distributed multi-vendor operation of EIES2.

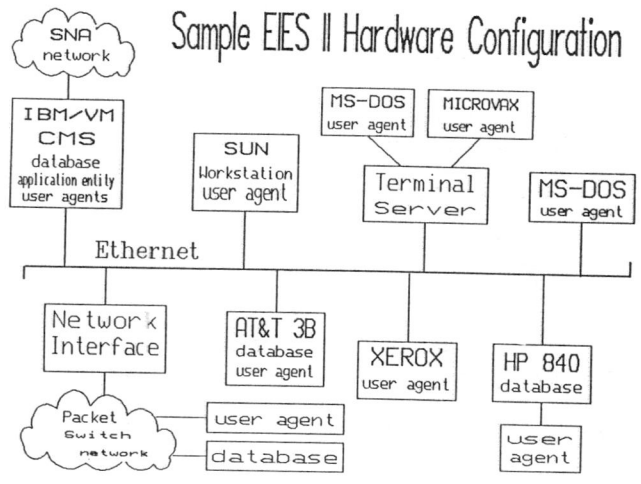

Figure 1

The C programming language is used for the development of the primitive functions. The programs are tested in several environments with different compilers to help ensure portability. A layered implementation isolates potential system dependencies to the lowest layer and minimizes the effort required to support new environments. Standard library functions and virtual device interfaces are used to decouple the database and its interface from the operational environment. An environment-independent data representation (X.409) is used for all data stored in the database and communicated between application entities. A high-level, communication-oriented, pseudo-machine guarantees that the CSCW applications themselves will be environment independent.

2.3 USER FUNCTIONALITY

Computer-Mediated Communications systems being developed at NJIT (EIES II and TEIES) reflect the hypothesis that the next generation of these systems need to be designed for everyday use. It is assumed that messaging and computer-based conferencing will serve as the principal communications medium in an organization.

Another important hypothesis underlying our design work is that the process of using a computer-based system to communicate with individuals and groups provides an ideal "cognitive model" for allowing people to communicate with other computer services. Such services would include the normal components of Management Information Systems and Decision Support Systems. Therefore, a proper design would allow for the integration of computer services of all sorts directly as part of the interface providing for human communications.

Since it takes time and effort to learn a new communications medium, an individual must be offered more than he is used to if he is eventually going to prefer it to other means of communication. The key observation that indicates what is this "more" is related to the fact that the vast majority of communication tasks in organizations are never independent of one another. Most real tasks require a long sequence of sub-tasks. A single phone call, search of a file drawer, a memo, an office visit, etc. are all part of a sequence of events related to a single task. Very often the completion of a sub-task is a communication to gather or request information from others and the major task cannot be carried forward until that feedback occurs.

Given this realization, it becomes crucial that a Computer-Mediated Communications system must be able to provide the association and data base capabilities to allow users to integrate, organize and retrieve communication objects in a manner that addresses their major task objectives. To meet this need, TEIES and EIES II incorporate a number of open ended concepts that allow individual communication objects to be tailored and structured around specific applications and task objectives.

We will describe here a few of these features and discuss their relationship to serving the user in their everyday organizational role.

- A. Groups: A group is a collection of members which can own all sorts of files and communication objects that a member can. As a result groups can share common indexes that are used to reference and filter individual communications. This means that a work group can contribute and share communications anywhere on the system by contributing to the shared index.

- B. Lists: Supporting the interface is an easy-to-use approach for providing the users ways of forming, organizing, and handling lists of communcation items items and all AUTHORED items are standard user lists, each of which can be retrieved as a whole. However, these and other lists can be selectively tailored by "keys" that the individual or group can create, assign and share. The functions for manipulating a list apply to any type of list found in the system. Once a user has mastered those functions, he can deal with any of the types of communication objects he might encounter.

- C. Notifications: Notifications are a short (one or two line) notices of any sort of communication transactions that a user should be aware of. For example, if a person edits a message or comment that the user has already seen, then the user receives a notification that the edit has occurred. This notification is also a "handle" to retrieve the object it refers to. By pointing to the notification and indicating the command GET, the original item will be brought to the screen.

  There are approximately thirty types of possible notifications that have been defined for the initial design. Many of these can be conditional; the user decides whether he wants to receive them or not.

- D. Activities: A large number of possible activities may be attached to a conference comment or message. A simple example is a DOCUMENT activity. In this case the content of the item provides an abstract and table of contents for the DOCUMENT. Anyone who receives the comment or message may choose to perform a DO action on that comment which, in this case, would allow that receiver to display whatever portions of the document they wanted to see, based upon the table of contents.

  Other examples of activities are programs written in any available programming language, a form to fill out, a survey or voting activity, a pre-formatted request to a data base somewhere on the system, et cetera.

- E. Directory: The directory is a file of all members, groups and conferences that exist on the system. The directory includes a set of indexes including "interests of members", "topics of concern" in groups and conferences, and the "skills & talents" of members. The directory also allows those with appropriate privileges to review the assignments or memberships held by various members.

- F. Conference Structure: Conferences will have a wide variety of tailorable parameters, allowing them to be structured for particular communication objectives.

The most crucial CSCW structuring feature is the incorporation of a large variety of human roles which are supported by the software. The "indexer role", for example, has the power to modify any of the keys and to rework the comment index. The conference "organizer" can oversee what activities are allowed and when.

The conference "owner" decides who allocates these roles within the conference membership and to what extent some of the power of these roles is made available to the general membership.

Various collections of structure parameters and roles have been collected into seven basic conference types designed to serve different communication objectives. These are:

A. Discussions: The simplest conference type, discussions allows a straightforward two- level (root comments and replies) structure.

B. Project Management: This conference structure incorporates activities specifically designed to track individual tasks and the assignments to those tasks.

C. Seminars: A set of activities specifically designed to allow an instructor to create a "Virtual Classroom", replacing the traditional classroom in a remote learning situation. The instructor is able, for example, to give and track assignments. A unique example is a series of discussion QUESTIONS which constitute a reply situation such that no member of the conference can see the replies already made to a comment until he himself has replied.

D. Information Exchange: Oriented to support the exchange of unpredictatable information when the group of people is large.

E. Data Collection: This structure allows a group to collaboratively develop a shared data base or to collectively validate the inputs for a data base. It may also include analysis activities to operate on the data provided by conference members. An example is the gathering of budget data from diverse projects into a single organized budget for planning or analysis purposes.

F. Composition: Structure for the collaborative composition of a document. A set of root comments form the outline of the document; the document owner can individually tailor who is allowed to write or edit selected portions of the outline. Associated tracking, via notifications, indicates document modifications.

G. Simulation games: A special structure being developed to allow the set-up of event-oriented role-playing games; it allows the owner to fill in the material governing the particular role-playing game.

The above conference structures are actually tailored choices selected from among the many fundamental tailorable parameters available on the system. Since the system is open-ended, other types can easily be tailored to fit particular applications. The ones we have illustrated above evolved through the history of Computer Conferencing and reflect facilities that have proved to be desirable in specific situations [10] [11] [12] [13] [14]

In summary, we feel very strongly that the use of these systems on an everyday basis is dependent upon the degree to which features are flexible, and tailorable to individual applications within an organizational context. System usage also depends on the degree of integration of the communication processes achieved with all the services and facilities that a modern computer can provide the individual in a personal, group or organizational setting.

2.4 <u>EVOLUTIONARY FLEXIBILITY</u>

The long-term utility of the EIES2 CSCW environment depends on its ability to grow and evolve. It must provide a tool-building environment which can be maintained easily.

To meet this objective, basic EIES2 functions are developed as layered modular systems. Each system is independent of every other system, the programming interface remaining consistent. The functionality of each layer is a relatively simple extension of the layer beneath it.

At the highest levels a fully-protected environment of encapsulated object classes and operations enforces strict control over access to data objects. This can guarantee that added facilities will not corrupt the database and that access permissions are not violated.

Abstraction allows algorithms to be independent of the objects on which they operate; thus, tools may provide support far beyond the context for which they were originally designed. The price of abstraction, however, is processor overhead. To reduce this overhead in the future, provisions are being made so that tools built upon tools may be compiled.

This compilation process involves the evaluation of constant subexpressions, and the reduction of abstraction for specific applications of tools.

3. SYSTEM ARCHITECTURE

The EIES2 Database Interface supports communication processes, the structured items they utilize, and the user interface. An integrated interface provides tools for the systems programmer, the application designer and the user, connecting them to a network of cooperative work facilities.

Communication processes are grouped into application entities (AE's). Each AE supports a set of operations. Initially a database application entity (DBAE) and a user agent application entity (UAAE) are supported (figure 2).

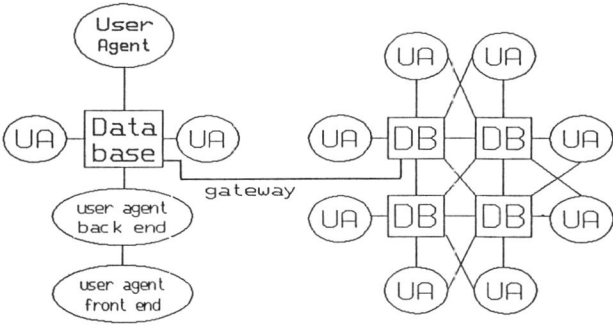

Figure 2

In the cooperative work environment additional AE's are required, including message transfer agents, directory service agents, group communication agents, and archive management agents. Communication between AE's takes the form of remote operations as defined in CCITT X.410.

Application processes are interpreted by the Communication Processor (CP). The CP is a general purpose pseudo-machine; its architecture and high level functions are targeted for the support of cooperative work environments. The CP is logically connected to the communications database, the operating environment, the network interface, and the user interface.

The communications database provides a structured virtual memory for the CP. The network interface provides communication between AE's locally or globally.

The EIES2 Communication Language Processor 2 (CLP) supports an abstract syntax notation for type and value definitions. CLP is used to define the initial EIES2 system and will also serve in defining extended applications.

3.1 CONCEPTUAL MODEL

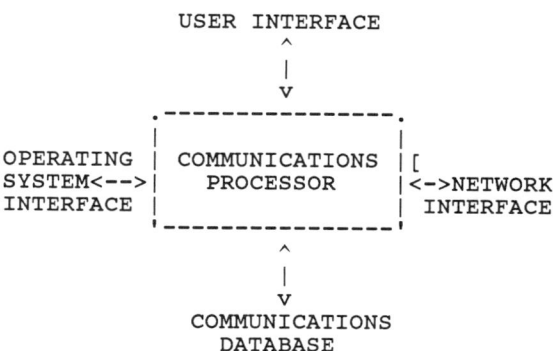

3.2 COMMUNICATIONS PROCESSOR (CP)

The Communications Processor is an object-oriented, stack-based bytecode pseudo-machine. The CP is modeled after SmallTalk-80*, developed at XEROX PARC. It is an extended version of the SmallTalk bytecode interpreter defined in [15] (also known as "The Blue Book").

3.2.1 CREATING CLASS DEFINITONS
Two high level functions are used to create class definitions and to add them to the database. They are the SmallTalkASeMbler (stasm) function and the create function. Stasm is an assembler style language which is either generated by EIES2 SmallTalk or which is used to create class definitions directly. Create is a program used to add new class definitions (as created by stasm) to the database. It also can be used to replace existing class definitions. A class definition encapsulates the functionality of objects of a particular type by defining the set of methods that may be invoked on that class of objects.

3.2.2 MESSAGE SEND

When a method is called, we are actually sending a message to an object. If a remote object is the receiver, a send operation protocol data unit is generated, containing a process identifier, the receiver reference, the message selector, and the arguments. The remote operation server then dispatches the OPDU to the remote application entity, and the process is suspended until a result is returned.

---

* Smalltalk-80 is a trademark of XEROX Corp.

The CP finds the receiver on the stack and determines its class. A new method context is then created and pushed on the stack. The class definition is found in the class index, and the method index for the class is scanned for the method name. If the method is found, the bytecodes are read in and execution begins. If the method is not found, the superclass of the object is determined from the class definition, and the search begins again with the superclass. This continues until the method is found or the search reaches the top of the class hierarchy.

3.2.3 X.409/ANS.1 DATA FORMAT

The CP processes data which is stored in X.409 type, length, contents (TLC) format compatible with the X.409/ASN.1 standard.

```
.------------------------------------.
| TYPE | LENGTH | CONTENTS           |
'------------------------------------'
```

The length and type are themselves of variable length; in fact, an indefinite length format is provided, allowing a virtually unlimited number of data lengths and types. Most data objects require only one octet (byte or character) for the length and type. This overhead is small compared to the advantages of storing strongly typed variable length data with one simple mechanism.

The type includes three fields: class, format, and ID. The X.409 class indicates whether the type is:
  Universal   - as defined by the CCITT and ISO,
  Application-wide   - for example X.400 or T.73 standards,
  Context-specific   - the same type number can be reused in different structures,
  Private-use   - global types for use by EIES2.

The X.409 class should not be confused with the EIES2 object classes mentioned in the previous section. The format field specifies whether the contents are a primitive data element or a constructor. A constructor type indicates that the contents field is itself composed of one or more data objects in X.409 TLC (type, length, content) format. Constructor types are used to define data structures and to break very long simple data objects into easily managed pieces. The ID specifies which type, within the X.409 class, is being indicated.

3.3 EIES2 NETWORK INTERFACE

Figure 3 depicts the EIES2 Network Interface. The Network Interface connects EIES2 compatible Application Entities (AE's) allowing distributed and decentralized processing. AE's may run on the same CP, and CP's may run as separate processes on the same machine or on separate machines, either tightly or loosely coupled. The type of connection is transparent to the application.

EIES II Network Interface

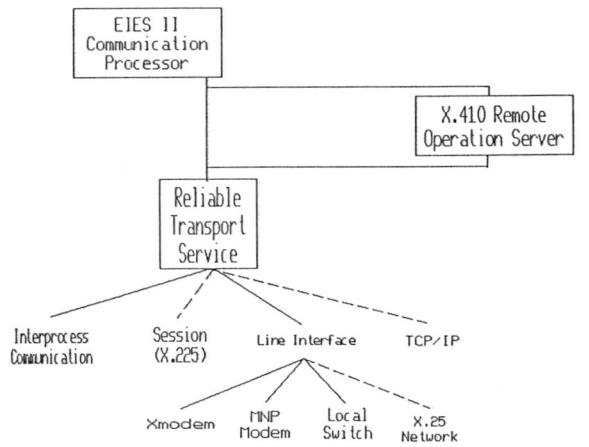

Figure 3

The communication between one or more AE's is handled by two systems, the Remote Operations Server (ROS) and the Reliable Transfer Server (RTS). These facilities are extremely important to the EIES2 distributed system architecture, since one process executed by an AE may invoke several remote messages, each of which would be executed by other remote AE's thus "distributing" the original task.

3.3.1 REMOTE OPERATION SERVER

The ROS allows one AE to establish an association with another AE. Each member of a pair of AE's may request operations from, or perform operations for, the other AE. Mechanisms are also provided for returning results of any remote operation or error messages or for rejecting notifications. The remote operations invoked by the Communications Processor of the AE are defined in CCITT X.409 recommendation. The actual invocations are in the form defined in the CCITT X.410 recommendation. The invoking operation of an AE involves the exchange of Operation Protocol Data Units (OPDU's). The OPDU's are transferred by the RTS and are specified using the X.409 notation.

The remote operations can be divided into five different categories, Invoke, Spawn, Fetch, Copy and Delete. The Invoke operation is mainly used for interactive applications, because the sender is looking for a result of the operation. For this reason, all invoke operations are performed in parallel. The argument for this operation includes an object identifier, a message selector and method arguments. The Spawn operation is invoked when no return is expected. Thus Spawn operations are used for batch applications and all spawned operations are performed serially on a first-come, first-served basis. The Spawn argument is same as the Invoke argument. The Fetch operation is used to obtain a temporary copy of an object. The Copy operation provides a permanent copy of an object. The Delete operation is used to delete a remote copy of an object. Both Fetch and Copy operations are subject to object access rules.

The OPDU's are of four different types: Invoke, ReturnResult, ReturnError and Reject. All four OPDU's have the invokeID element in common. The invokeID is assigned by the AE to indicate which CP process has requested service. This insures that a message unit will not be lost in a network, because its originator can always be identified by its invokeID field. The EIES2 implementation of the OPDU also adds a RemoteReference element. The RemoteReference element contains an AE identifier and an object identifier, providing an identification mechanism for remote objects.

The Invoke OPDU requests that an operation be performed by a remote OPDU. An AE need not wait for the results of an Invoke before issuing another, hence the need for the invokeID. The remote operation to be performed is indicated in the operation element. The argument element consists of a message selector and method arguments, and indicates the object and the Smalltalk method to be performed. If the operation expects a result, the ReturnResult OPDU reports successful completion of operation. The ReturnError OPDU reports unsuccessful completion of an operation, and the Reject OPDU reports the receipt of a malformed OPDU.

3.3.2 RELIABLE TRANSPORT SERVER

The RTS has two major components: the RTS-user and the RTS-provider. The RTS-user handles requests for services from the AE. It builds the appropriate PDU's and "hands" them to the RTS-provider. The RTS-user also maintains a list of addresses of remote AE's and the association number (used in the transfer of PDU's). The RTS-provider actually performs the transfer of PDU's. It translates PDU's from the RTS-user into the appropriate types for the remote AE. The RTS-provider also maintains a table based on association number containing information about each association. The table includes the network address of the remote AE as well as information as to the type of interface and devices used. The RTS-provider uses operating system facilities for interfacing a pair of AE's.

The RTS-user is extendable and can accommodate any type of network interface provided by the local operating system. Examples include: interprocess communication; line interfaces (synchronous and asynchronous) which provide access to modems, data switches and X.25 networks; and high bandwidth networks such as Ethernet.

3.4 EIES II DATA MANAGEMENT SYSTEM

The EIES II Data Management System (DMS) provides a structured virtual object memory for the SmallTalk bytecode interpreter used in the Communications Processor (CP). Provisions are made for operations performed on entire objects or on the internal structure of an object. Operations may be performed on objects in memory, on linear disk segments or on disk indexes. Data is stored and defined using the X.409/ASN.1 international standards. Object size is limited only by storage capacity.

The CP operates on both local and remote objects. If a remote object is to be used, the Remote Operations Server (ROS) is invoked.

3.4.1 OBJECT LEVEL

The top layer of the DMS (see figure 4) is the Object Level. It provides facilities for access and storage of SmallTalk objects using an object cache. The major operations on this level are GET and WRITE. The object cache minimizes disk access, for it is a large block of memory which is set aside to store objects.

When the CP accesses a local object, it invokes the GET operation. If the object is not found in the object cache, it is retrieved from the virtual disk using lower level DMS facilities. If the CP has performed any update operations on the object, it will then use the WRITE operation to store the object on the disk.

3.4.2 POINTER LEVEL

The Pointer Level provides access to X.409 data structures for use by the CP, Object Level and ROS. The Pointer Level also provides an association between the object and its corresponding type definition as determined by its context. Its abstract addressing mechanism allows data to reside in memory segments or indexes, while providing an orthogonal set of operations.

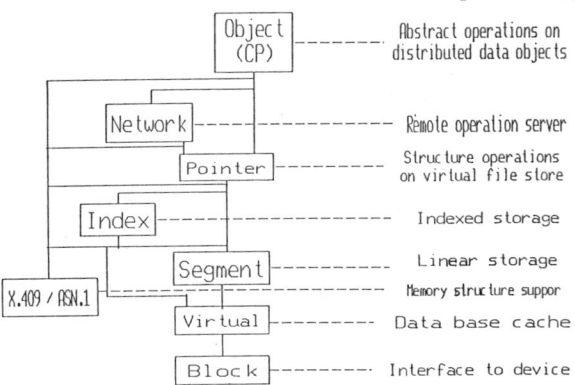

Figure 4

It supports user-transparent data reference mechanisms to support a full network data model.

The X.409 data type definitions compiled by the Communications Language Processor (CLP) are used to build tables used by the Pointer Level to verify all operations. This structure assures that only valid data structures are created and used. A table of primitive types and operations allows type-independent operations to properly handle any type of object.

The user is only required to indicate the location of the object on initial access. When an object is to be created, the user must specify whether it will reside in memory, on a segment, or on an index. Afterwards, a structure known as a control block is used to access the object.

The pointer level provides operations for stream and hierarchical read, stream and hierarchical write, update, find and reference. References are handled transparently if they are not explicitly part of the type definition.

3.4.3 SEGMENT LEVEL The Segment Level supports variable-sized linear data segments on disk. Segments consist of collections of blocks on a disk file, and are used to access data in a linear fashion. The Segment level maintains segment pointers to allow access to currently active segments, and provides a permanent table of segments on an index for each volume.

The segment operations permit the creation and deletion of segments, the reading and writing of data, and the locating of any point on the segment. Data may be inserted or deleted at any point.

3.4.4 INDEX LEVEL The Index Level maintains indexes on disk storage. It uses a B-tree structure to provide rapid access of records. The Index Level allows variable length keys and data.

3.4.5 VIRTUAL DISK LEVEL The Virtual Disk Level manages the images of disk blocks in memory. It supports the Segment and Index levels by providing rapid access to disk blocks already in memory. Overhead is reduced since recently used blocks do not have to be read from the disk. Many updates can be performed on the image before it is written back to the disk.

3.4.6 DISK BLOCK LEVEL The Block Level provides access to the disk through C library functions. The device is accessed only at this layer so that system dependence is minimized. Raw devices may be used to eliminate the overhead of the local file system.

3.4.7 X.409 SUPPORT The X.409 support facilities provide the C programmer with a set of convenient and consistent operations allowing access to X.409 data structures. These operations allow the programmer to create and access data in these structures. By utilizing temporary memory management, prior knowledge of the size of a structure being created is not required. Additional facilities permit easy conversion between X.409 data formats and C data structures (including printable strings).

3.5 OPERATING ENVIRONMENT INTERFACE

The operating environment interface provides an interface to the local system. It provides access to local files and devices, including the system clock, interprocess communications, semaphores, and operating system commands.

The initial environments supported are UNIX* System V. Support for IBM VM/CMS, and Microsoft MS-DOS are planned.

The operating environment interface is implemented using C library routines. The resulting EIES2 virtual operating environment interface isolates system dependencies from all other system components.

---

* Trademark of AT&T

3.6 USER INTERFACE FACILITIES

The user interface connects the user to one or more Application Processes (AP's) or AE's. It provides facilities to enter, select, display and update EIES2 data structures. The user interface also provides facilities to control interactions characterized by multiple applications. It provides access to all functions of the communication processor by using the SmallTalk language.

The terminal is modeled as a multimedia device supporting many virtual interfaces. High-level interface functions allow the support of terminals with radically different physical characteristics. The structure of the terminal interface is shown in figure 5.

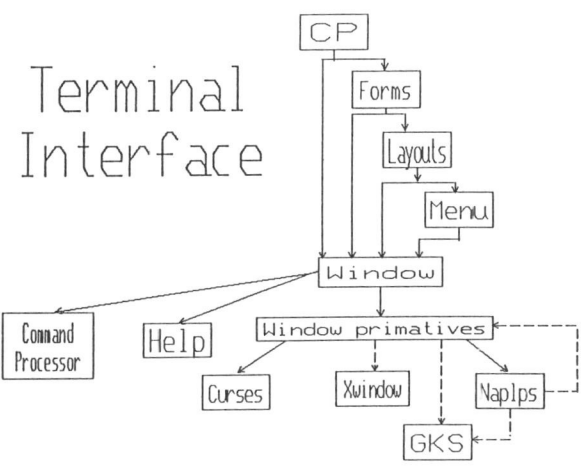

Figure 5

3.6.1 VIRTUAL DEVICE MODELS
The window function interface and menu function interface are defined by the AT&T UNIX PC high-level Terminal Access Method (TAM) specifications. The text facility provides the standard Simple Formatted Document (SFD) formatting, full screen operations, and pointer-structured text operations. A simplified, EIES1-like, line-oriented editor will also be available. Local text editors on the host system may be used where practicable. The user interface to these functions depends on the virtual device model being used and the particular terminal characteristics.

3.6.1.1 DUMB TERMINAL INTERFACE
The dumb terminal interface provides a line-oriented interaction. Menu and form layouts are processed in order from top to bottom. Information is displayed line by line until an input field is encountered. If the user chooses the normal help level, the information line is printed, the input is accepted, and display continues on the next line. For fields already containing information, the old value is printed first and then the new value is requested. Controls allow the user to move up and down on a field by field bases.

3.6.1.2 HALF DUPLEX SCREEN INTERFACE
The half duplex screen interface supports asynchronous, cursor-addressable CRT terminals. It is intended to support terminals over packet networks or wherever a software character echo would be impractical. In this interface, the formatting of the screen and the typing of information will not take place simultaneously.

3.6.1.3 FULL DUPLEX SCREEN INTERFACE
The full duplex screen interface provides optimal flexibility. The user may type at any time independent of screen updates. Intermediate screen updates are skipped when the user types ahead of the reformatting operations, for example, if line speed is slow, or if processor load is great. This provides uniformly good performance without compromising interface functionality.

3.6.1.4 FULL-SCREEN BLOCK MODE INTERFACE
The block mode, full-screen interface will support full-screen 3270 type terminals and certain block mode asynchronous terminals. The features of this interface are limited by the terminal functions.

3.6.2 THE FORMS PROCESSOR (FP)
The ability to communicate with forms rather than simple text is extremely useful in the CSCW environment. A Form represents an implementation of structured messages as described by Malone [16]. In the AMIGO Model the EIES2 Form structure represents a Message Type in the context of Activities defined for group communications [3]. A Form can also be "attached" to a message or to a conference comment. When the user views the incoming message or the comment, he also will be prompted by the system to fill out the Form. When the user completes the form, the information carried by the form will be returned to the sender or other activity agent.

3.6.2.1 LAYOUT PROCESSOR
The EIES2 layout serves as a template for structured Input and Output. It provides support for the Form System and the User Interface in several areas: for input, display, and update of strongly typed information in a specific screen format (when that format can be supported by the terminal).
Screen formats may be generated in two ways, by using the Communication Language Processor (CLP), or by composing a template interactively. The CLP compiles a set of value definitions written in X.409,

and produces a layout object which is the actual template structure, specifying fields, data and respective screen locations. The template composed interactively is based on a previously compiled set of definitions which are general enough to support any user-defined format. The Forms Processor relies heavily on the interactive template generation.

3.6.3 MENUS The Menu facility provides for horizontal or vertical pop-up menus. Items may be selected by number, letter, and by cursor control.

3.6.4 WINDOWS The window sub-system provides device independent support for terminal input and output. The Window subsystem also provides multiple pop-up windows and maintains an answer- ahead buffer. Controls indicating exception situations during terminal I/O operations are maintained and can be accessed by any upper level subsystems. These controls interface with the help processor, the command processor, and the CP to support consistent input processing.

The layout and menu processors utilize the Window subsystem for displaying its template and the information in it.

3.7 COMMUNICATION LANGUAGE PROCESSOR (CLP)

CLP accepts data structure definitions in X.409 abstract syntax notation. These are converted to X.409 internal representation in a two-pass process. The first pass consists of a lexical and syntax analysis and creates a symbol table for use in the later pass. Pass two creates the X.409 internal structures for the defined types and values, passing them to EIES2 segments. The internal structures are laid out; each X.409 module goes on a separate segment. Type definitions generate a DefType data structure that includes all the information relevant to the type. Value definitions generate the X.409 internal format associated with that type.

During the second pass, an M4 macro table is created. The macro definitions allow the C Language programmer to use the type and value names defined in X.409. The macros provide effective access to the type tables for the programmer and improve the readability of EIES2 support programs written in C. The CP type tables are created with another set of routines closely related to the CLP.

3.8 EIES2 DISTRIBUTED SMALLTALK

The information flow in the EIES2 environment is illustrated in figure 6.

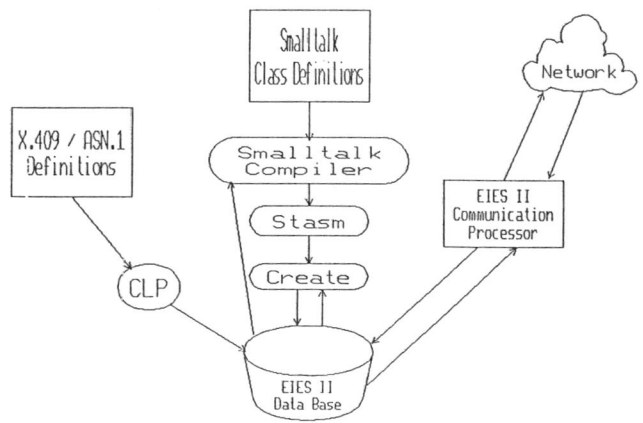

Figure 6

The communication processor is data-driven, based on the database object and method definitions. The processing done by a particular CP is determined solely by the messages received by the objects local to that CP. Network load can be balanced simply by migrating objects between CPs. Figure 7 shows an example of vertical decentralization with three AEs and their hosts, objects, and methods. It is the associated objects that determine the function of the particular AE.

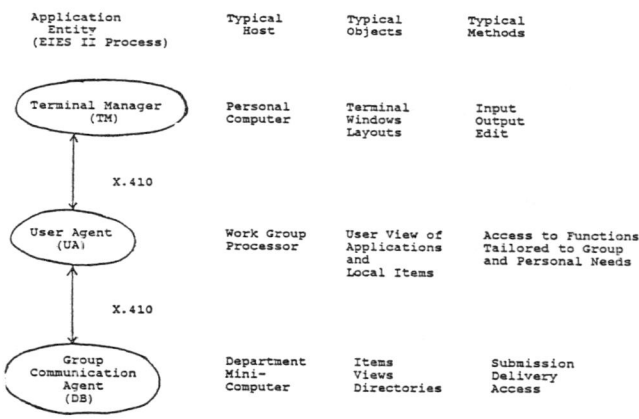

Figure 7

EIES2 provides its own distributed SmallTalk* environment for CSCW application development. SmallTalk provides a message-based architecture that is extremely well-suited to the CSCW environment. In the EIES2 object model of SmallTalk, objects receive messages and perform methods based on the class of the receiver. This conforms well to the network environment of CSCW, and additionally provides a high degree of security. In addition, SmallTalk has excellent meta-language properties. Object classes and methods define the statements that are valid for the objects. As higher-level capabilities are defined, so are higher level statements. This effectively elevates the language from the level the machine to the level of the application.

Figure 8 exhibits a scenario where each object referenced in a smalltalk statement is resident on a different AE and the message send operation involved in its evaluation. Neither the user nor the

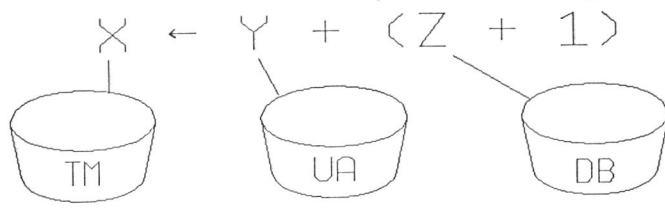

Figure 8

application developer need be aware of where the object is located on the network.

3.9 CURRENT EIES2 STATUS

The current EIES2 development environment has a wide variety of tools which is the foundation upon which advanced features and enhancements are being developed. The existing model includes an easy-to-use learner interface that supports: mail; conferencing; notifications; directory; keyword searching; options to LIST, SCAN, and VIEW TEXT; context-sensitive help; and an answer-ahead feature to provide short cuts.

Advanced features currently being implemented include: the ability to design forms; the ability to transfer binary files; a microcomputer user interface; personal keywords to enable the user to define the way information is organized; support for multi-authored documents; audit trails to provide sequential record of user's menu choices; and tickets to provide selective access to information.

The principal funder of this project, the New Jersey Office of Telecommunications and Information Systems of the State of New Jersey, is beta testing the Phase I version of EIES2. Additional support for this project was obtained from Computer Sciences Corporation, and AT&T Information Systems. Partnerships are being sought to apply the technology further, in the development of distributed CSCW applications, the development of application layer standards support, and in interfacing the EIES2 application functions with lower layer services in various network environments (Figure 9).

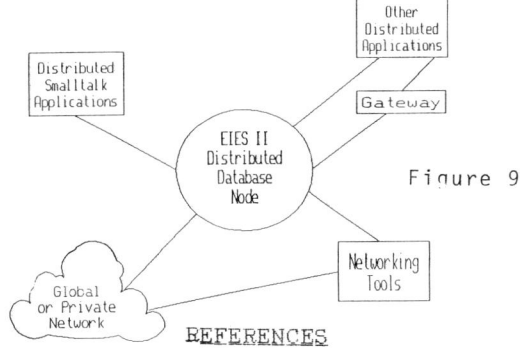

Figure 9

REFERENCES

1. K. Kraemer, and J. King, "Computer-Based Systems for Cooperative Work and Group Decision Making: Status and Use and Problems in Development", Proceedings CSCW'86 Conference on Computer Supported Cooperative Work, 1986.

2. Thore Danielsen, T Folkow, P Richardsen, "Relation and Inheritance in Group Communication", Proceedings IFIP 6.5 International Working Conference on Message Handling Systems, April 1987.

3. T. Danielsen, A. Patel, P. Pays, K. Smaaland, R. Speth The AMIGO Project, Advanced Group Communication Model For Computer-based Communications Environment Proceedings of Conference on Computer-Supported Cooperative Work, 1986

4. Hiltz, Roxanne & Murray Turoff, The Network Nation: Human Communication via Computer, Addison Wesely, 1978

---

* Trademark of Xerox Corp.

5. Hitlz, Roxanne & Murray Turoff, Structuring Computer-Mediated Communications to avoid Information Overload, Communications of the ACM, July, 1985.

6. T. Malone, K Grant, F Tubak, S Brobst, and M. Cohen, "Intelligent Information-Sharing Systems", Communications of the ACM (CACM), May 1987.

7. M. Stefik, D.G. Bobrow, S.Lanning, D Tarter, "WYSIWIS Revisited: Early experiences with Multi-user Interfaces", Proceedings CSCW'86 Conference on Computer Supported Cooperative Work, 1986.

8. M. Stefik, G. Foster, D. Borrow, K. Kahn, S. Lanning, and L. Suchman, "Beyond the Chalkboard: computer Support for Collaboration and Problem solving in meetings", Communications of the ACM (CACM), January 1987.

9. S. R. Hiltz The "Virtual Classroom": Using Computer-Mediated Communication for University Teaching Journal of Communication, Spring 1986

10. Bahgat, Ahmed; A Decision support System for Zero-Base Capital Budgeting, Ph.D. in Management Thesis, Rutgers Graduate School of Management, Newark, N.J. 07102, October 1986

11. Hiltz, Roxanne, On Line Communities: A case study of the office of the future, Ablex Press 1984

12. Hiltz, Roxanne & Murray Turoff, The Network Nation: Human Communication via Computer, Addison Wesely, 1978

13. Turoff, Murray & Roxanne Hiltz, Computer Support for Group versus Individual Decisions, IEEE Transactions on Communications, Con-30, Number 1, January, 1982

14. Turoff, Murray, Information & Value: The internal information marketplace, Journal of Technological Forecasting and social Change, Volume 27, Number 4, July, 1985.

15. Adele Goldberg and David Robson, SmallTalk-80 The Language and its Implementation, Addison-Wesley, 1983

16. Thomas W. Malone, Kenneth R. Grant, Kum-Yew Lai, Ramana Rao, David Rosenblitt Semi-Structured Messages are Surprisingly Useful for Computer-Supported Coordination Proceedings of

Integrating X.400 Message Handling into the IBM VM/SP Environment

Kristian Fischer and Wilhelm F. Racke
IBM - European Networking Center
Tiergartenstr. 15
D-6900 Heidelberg
West Germany

Abstract

A prototype X.400 message handling system for IBM's VM/SP operating system is discussed. The system is designed to provide smooth integration of X.400 services into the predominantly used means of interpersonal communication in the VM/SP environment (RSCS). The system provides native X.400 services to its users and therefore is not a gateway between RSCS and X.400 protocols.

Introduction

Computer networks (1) have been used for interpersonal messaging for almost 20 years. Major examples for such networks are the ARPANET, the CSNET, and BITNET. In the early 1980es the International Telephone and Telegraph Consultative Committee (CCITT), the international technical board of the national public telephone and telegraph companies (PTTs), published the X.400 series of recommendations for message handling systems (2). The recommendations are based on the OSI reference model for open systems interconnection (3). In the terminology of this model the recommendations define protocols for the upper layer of this model, the application layer. To provide an underlying transport system they refer to the OSI standards for the lower layers.

This series of recommendations is of particular importance for several reasons:

- The PTTs intend to provide public electronic messaging service based on the recommendations. This could integrate a much larger community of people into one network than is possible with current computer networks.

- The research community, who is currently the predominant user of electronic messaging in the major countries of Europe, has decided to employ X.400 protocols. For example the German Research Network (DFN (4) and the Italian Research Network (OSIRIDE (1)) have decided to use these protocols. The European Academic Research Network (EARN), currently using RSCS protocol, will migrate to X.400 protocols.

- The X.400 recommendations are one of the first application layer standards of the OSI reference model. As such they are influencing the development of other application layer standards and promoting the use of implementations of the standards for the lower layers of the reference model.

The X.400 system that is discussed in this paper(5), has been developed in a joint project by IBM's European Networking Center, the Gesellschaft fuer Mathematik und Datenverarbeitung (GMD) - a German government sponsored research agency - and the Queen's University in Kingston, Canada. The system was developed with the intent of understanding the X.400 standards and learning how the X.400 services can be integrated into an existing communication system as it is provided by the VM/SP operating system. The system will be provided to the Deutsche Forschungsnetz Verein (DFN) in order to help integrate IBM systems into the research network that is organized by DFN, and as part of an EARN experiment to investigate migrating the interpersonal messaging part of EARN from RSCS to X.400 protocols.

The paper is divided into four parts. In the first part the main characteristics of the CCITT X.400 recommendations for message handling systems are explained. This system model is contrasted with the interpersonal communication in VM/SP based computer networks. In the second part the main concepts which are the basis for the system design are discussed. In the third part the architecture of the system is presented and the fourth part deals with experiences in the use of the system in terms of interoperability with other X.400 systems. Furthermore an outline is given of the future work which could be done based on the system.

Electronic Messaging: The X.400 model and the VM/SP Facilities

The X.400 recommendations are based on a model of a message handling environment. It describes the interaction of a set of processes that is required to provide message handling service to a user community which is distributed over a computer network. The description is independent of the physical structure of the computer network.

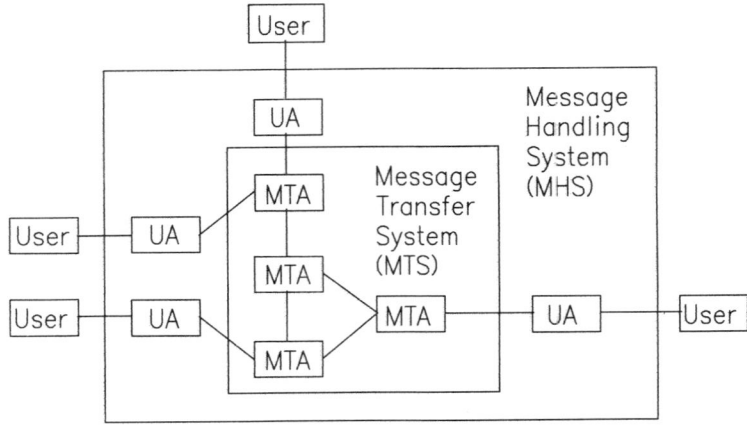

Figure 1. Message Handling System Model

The system model is described in figure 1. The users are considered to be originators and recipients of messages and are served by processes called User Agents (UAs). They allow a user to compose a message, to input necessary address information and to send a message. At the reception of a message such processes are responsible for functions such as the readable representation of messages at the screen or the storing of messages in a document store.

For sending and receiving of messages the user agents make use of the services that the Message Transfer System provides for them. This system is a store and forward system and consists of a set of interconnected Message Transfer Agents (MTAs). Each UA is connected to one and only one MTA, but an MTA may cooperate with none or more UAs. The task of an MTA is the distribution, routing and reliable transfer of messages. In order to find an analogy in social systems, one might compare the message transfer system with the task of the mail service as far as the distribution of letters is concerned, and one might compare an UA with the task a secretary performs for someone as far as the organization of mail is concerned.

X.400 is aimed to describe a worldwide message handling system. The magnitude to which such a system can grow up makes it necessary to organize the set of MTAs in a hierarchical structure. On the top level this structure consists of a set of countries and below that of a set of Administration Management Domains (ADMDs), which are the national PTTs, and a set of Private Management Domains (PRMDs), which typically are larger organizations such as companies or universities.

Each user in the message handling environment is addressed by her or his Originator/Recipient-name (O/R-name). This name is hierarchically structured and the components it may consist of include

- Countryname,
- ADMD-name,
- PRMD-name,
- Organization name and
- Personal name with the components surname, given name, initials and generations qualifier.

The first three components mirror the hierarchical organization within the message transfer system. Because the routing of messages is based on the hierarchical structure of an OR-name this has the advantage that the MTA normally needs only one entry in its routing directory for all the users in each different country or - for her/his country - for all the users in each different ADMD or PRMD. Within an domain the set of MTAs needs not to be organized according to the structure of the lower level OR-name components that are used within that domain.

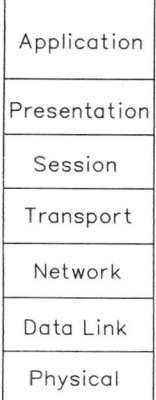

Figure 2. Reference model and X.400 standards

When one wants to connect a computing system to the X.400 message handling system, an implementation of the UA, the MTA, and of the standards for the lower levels of the OSI reference model are needed. The standards involved are shown in their relation to the OSI Reference Model in figure 2. In the standards for each level there is described

- the protocol, that has to be implemented for communication with a peer implementation, and
- the services (in terms of a set of service primitives) that have to be provided for the implementations of the layers on top.

An X.400 implementation involves, besides the implementation of UA and MTA, primarily the implementation of the layer 4 and 5 standards because

- a public X.25 (6) service is available in Europe, and
- the X.400 recommendations reference no service primitives of the presentation layer because there was no presentation standard available when the recommendations were published. Instead the presentation of protocol data units is defined in X.400 itself. Future versions of the recommendations will refer to the presentation standard.

The standards for the transport layer and for the session layer (7) are not discussed in this context.

In terms of the layered view of communication systems the X.400 recommendation further divides the application layer in two sublayers, namely

- the Message Transfer Sublayer, which contains the functions of the message transfer system, and
- the User Agent Sublayer, which contains the functions provided by the user agents.

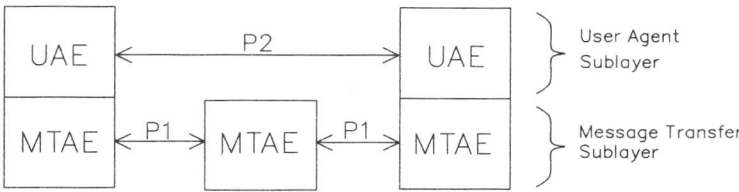

Figure 3. Sublayers and Protocols in X.400

The protocols of these two sublayers, that are involved in the transmission of a message between two user agent entities (instances of implementations are denoted as entities) are shown in figure 3. In the scenario shown a message can be routed from the originator's MTA entity to a relaying MTAE and then to the recipient's MTAE. The UAEs employ the P2 protocol for their communication. Some features this protocol includes are

- specifying multiple primary, copy, and blind copy recipients,
- specifying a message identifier,
- specifying cross-references to other messages via message identifiers, and
- specifying a subject.

The MTAEs employ the P1 protocol to provide a message transmission service to the user agents. An interesting property of this protocol is that messages with multiple recipients routed over the same path are transmitted as a single copy. The services the message transfer sublayer provides for the user agents include:

- request for delivery report of a message on a per recipient base,
- selection of the priority of a message,
- provision of delivery and submission time of the message.

According to the X.400 recommendation the MTA is divided into three parts

- The Reliable Transfer Server uses the services of the session layer to implement the reliable transfer of a message to a peer MTA.
- The Association Manager makes the RTS build up and bring down associations to peer MTAs.
- The Message Dispatcher performs the P1 protocol once a association is build up to a peer MTA.

The model behind the interpersonal communication in the VM/SP operating system can best be described as a physical model: each user is considered to be sitting at her/his own machine (a virtual machine). This machine has attached to it a so-called reader, which can be considered as a device which can receive data items from other "user machines". Such input data items are denoted as spoolfiles.

The transmission of the spoolfiles is a service of the VM/SP operating system if the user machines run on the same host. Otherwise they can be transmitted by the RSCS protocols (8) over leased lines. An RSCS network as a whole operates as a store and forward network in a similar fashion like the X.400 message transfer system.

Associated with each spoolfile is some header information which includes

- the originator and the recipient of the message,
- a timestamp, and
- an indication whether or not the delivery of the message is to be reported.

The address of a user consists of its userid and its nodeid, which is an identifier for the host in the RSCS network. In the case of local message transmission the userid suffices for addressing. For sending and receiving of messages the user is supported by the operating system that is run on her/his virtual machine. The most common choice for that is CMS, which provides the NOTE-command for sending notes. This command can be seen as implementation of what are user agent functions in the X.400 model. It basically provides the user with the facility to compose a note, address the note to multiple primary and copy recipients, and to add things like subject and references to the note. The addresses of the recipients are retrieved from a nicknames file, which allows the user to reference the address information for a partner by a nickname. In addition, some commands that operate on the reader of the user's virtual machine provide services like viewing the list of reader files or browsing through the files.

Important in the context of mail processing in the VM/SP environment is the Professional Office System (PROFS (9)) that provides additional services like storing of messages in a document store and retrieving of messages through selected queries. This system also operates on the reader of the user machine and can access the user's nicknames file.

Design Concepts

When designing a X.400 message handling facility for a operating system like VM/SP one has to find ones way between two extreme design concepts

- the design of a gateway between the local protocols for interpersonal communication and the X.400 protocols on one side, and
- the design of a standalone X.400 Message Handling System on the other side.

The problem with the first concept is that it allows only the provision of those X.400 services for the user which can reasonably be mapped onto services of the local communication system. As for X.400 message handling in particular a major part of the capabilities of the O/R-name based addressing gets lost when these addresses have to be obtained by translation from the addresses in the VM environment (node/userid).

The problem with the second concept is that it confronts a user with two different interfaces depending on whether she/he wants to communicate with partners in the local system or in the X.400 system.

The concept for the design of the prototype X.400 system is a compromise between these extremes. The system does not generate the parameters of the X.400 services automatically from the information available in the RSCS protocol, but the user can put in the values for the service parameters. In particular a O/R-name for the user can be chosen according to her/his position in an organization as it is intended by the X.400 recommendation. In a gateway solution it would have to be derived from the the user's node/userid.

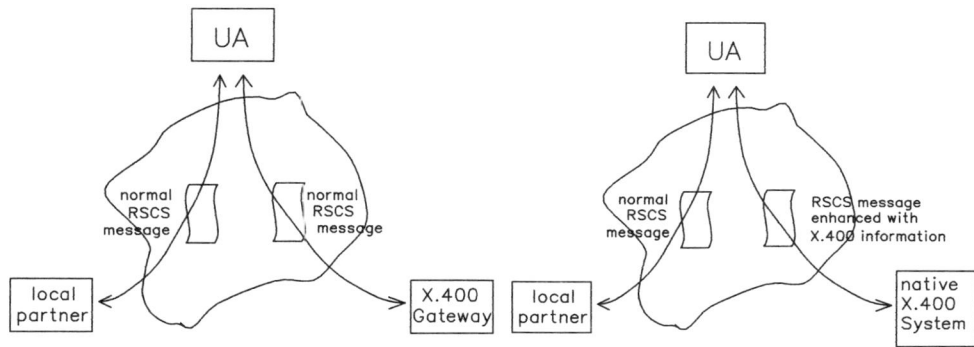

Figure 4. Difference between a native X.400 system and a gateway

The difference between our design concept and a gateway concept is shown in figure 4. In a gateway concept a message containing the same kind of information is sent from the user agent to the local users and to the X.400 gateway. The gateway has to build a X.400 message from the information available in this message.

In our concept, the message for the X.400 partners is composed by the same user agent as the one for the local partners, but it contains additional information as required for the composition of a X.400 message. The user interface gets the X.400 parameters as far as possible from the normal message composition screens and asks for input of X.400 specific information only if the user requests it. However, in order to keep the interface simple only a selection of the quite large set of service primitives is offered.

The functions of the user agent can be considered to belong to two groups. The first group contains functions such as editors or mail stores which are normally available in office systems or operating systems. The PROFS office system has been chosen as basis for the implementation of the functions of this first group, because it provides a rather complete set of user agent functions for composing and storing messages. The second group contains functions which are X.400 specific. Examples in this group are functions for handling the P2 protocol, communicating with the MTA, and decoding/encoding of messages. The functions of this part are to be implemented as part of the X.400 system. It has been a major aim of the design to provide a clean and easy to use interface between these parts of the user agent, that implement the two groups of functions. It is intended to provide easy access to the X.400 services not only for PROFS but for any office- or message handling system. In fact there is also a extension to the CMS NOTE-command which provides access to the X.400 system via this interface. The interface is indicated in figure 5 a as a bold line within the user agent.

The second interface our system provides is the MTA service interface. It is indicated in figure 5 a as the one bold line on top of the MTA. This interface allows one to put a different user agent on top of the MTA to provide different parts of the MTA services to the user. Furthermore the P1 protocol as implemented by the MTA can not only be used for interpersonal messaging with the P2 protocol, but as a general service for the asynchronous distribution of messages. The MTA service interface allows any application process to use this service.

In many organizations a typical configuration consists of not one host at a site but a set of hosts connected by a local network such as a RSCS network. In such an environment one normally wants to provide access to X.400 services to users at different hosts, but one might want to run only one MTA. The advantages of running one MTA instead of multiple MTAs in a local network include

- Only one directory is required, which can more easily be updated than multiple directories.
- Only one access to the public X.25 network is needed.

Figure 5 b shows such an environment. The MTA in the prototype X.400 system is designed to be able to serve users sitting at different systems in a local RSCS network. For this the MTA directory must map the OR-names of the users of the MTA onto the corresponding addresses in the local network.

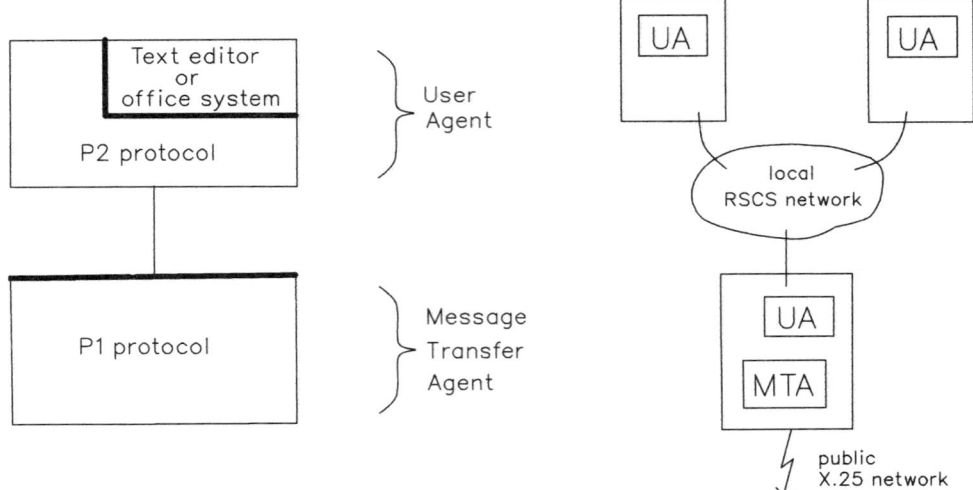

Figure 5. A) Interfaces b) MTA serving remote users

In summary, the design concepts for the prototype X.400 system were:

- Smooth integration of the X.400 message handling services into the message handling services of the VM/SP environment.
- The system is designed to be open to user-provided user-agent functions.
- The system itself is designed to have its components distributed in an RSCS network in order to serve users at different systems.

Architecture of the System

The logical structure of of an X.400 message handling system as it is given in the X.400 series of recommendations has been introduced in the first section. It served as the the basis for defining the structure of the implementation as a set of communicating processes.

As a straight forward way for the implementation of processes in the VM/SP environment, it was decided to implement each process as a virtual machine which runs the single tasking CMS operating system. For the communication between Virtual Machines there are mainly two operating system services available:

- The transmission of spoolfiles is a means for asynchronous exchange of messages.
- The Inter User Communication Vehicle (IUCV) is a means for the synchronous exchange of fixed length buffers.

The functions that are implemented in the different virtual machines of the prototype and the means of communication between the machines is shown in figure 6. The differences between this structure and the logical structure is partly a consequence of the design concepts as discussed in chapter 2 and partly a consequence of design decisions in favor of the ease of implementation and and the simplicity of interfaces.

Firstly it can be seen from the figure that there is not a implementation of the presentation layer as a separate virtual machine. Instead it was decided to implement the presentation function (encoding of protocol data units according to recommendation X. 409) as a service that is directly accessed by the UA, the MTA, and the RTS. This way the data is passed from CUA to Mta and from MTA to RTS in its final encoding as far as possible.

Secondly the MTA which is defined to consist of Message Dispatcher, Association Manager and Reliable Transfer Server has been split into two parts. The reason for this decision is the difference in the kind of function that has to be performed by the RTS and association manager on one side and message dispatcher on the other side. The Message Dispatcher does not have to keep any knowledge about the association with peer MTAs and can therefore be implemented as a protocol automaton with very few states. However the functions it has to perform for encoding/decoding, relaying and routing are rather complex. On the other hand the

Association Manager and the RTS as the direct user of the session services have to keep information about the associations with peer MTAs and therefore have protocol automata with a larger set of states whilst the functions performed in the single states or state transitions are rather simple. The implementation of the two groups of functions in two different virtual machines

- allows the employment of different construction methodologies according to their different characteristics, and
- it yields a simple interface between the two virtual machines.

Furthermore the RTS and the session implementation are put into one virtual machine because the session service primitives require quite frequent interaction with their user. This can be implemented more efficiently with intra virtual machine communication rather than with inter virtual machine communication.

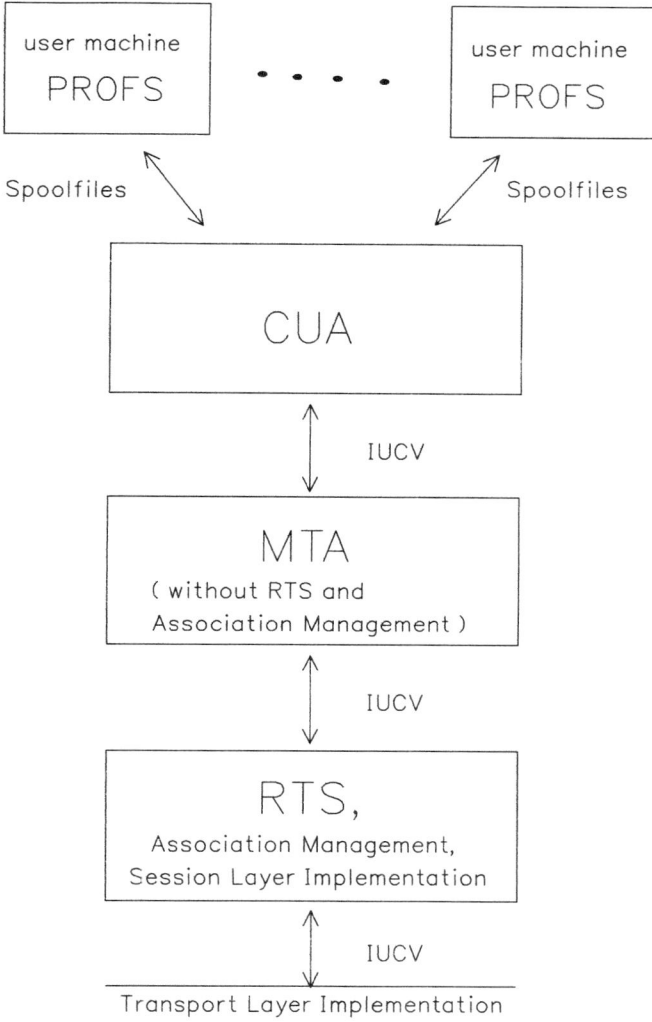

Figure 6. Virtual machines of the X.400 system

The most unusual part of the architecture of the system is the division of the user agent into two parts. The first part of the UA runs in the virtual machine of the user and is a slight extension of the PROFS system. The second part is the Common User Agent (CUA) which is a service machine common to all the users. It implements the P2 protocol, the encoding/decoding of the messages and the use of the MTA services via an IUCV interface.

For the extension of PROFS the office system itself did not need to be extended but a published interface of the system (user exits) could be employed to bring in code that

- allows a user to use X.400 specific services like e.g. request for delivery report or selection of the priority of a message,

- retrieves the originator's and the recipient's OR-names from the CMS names file, where they can be put in with tags defined specifically for this system, and
- puts the message itself and the additional X.400 information in a file which is sent to the CUA.

This allows a PROFS user to compose a message which has both X.400 and RSCS recipients. For all the X.400 recipients of a message only one file is sent to the CUA. This exploits the ability of the X.400 system to transmit messages with multiple recipients at one site as a single message.

The user machine does not need to be run on the same computing system as the CUA but can also be run on an remote system if a RSCS connection exists between the systems. The spoolfile interface between user machine and common user agent makes it easy to connect different office systems or message handling facilities to X.400 services.

The spoolfiles which are sent from the PROFS system to the CUA as well as the ones sent from the CUA to the user machine running PROFS are normal human readable messages with a header containing the X.400 specific information. The structure of this header is described by a LALR(1)-syntax. No X.400 specific code is needed in the user machine for the receiving of messages. They are handled as normal PROFS or CMS spoolfiles and the format of the message header is therefore designed to be easy to survey. In order to accomplish this, it was decided not to represent all the X.400 services in it, but only a subset of them.

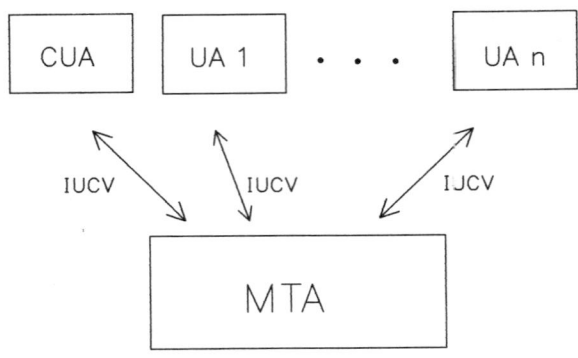

Figure 7. Openness of MTA towards different UA designs

For some potential applications the selection of services of the spoolfile interface might not suffice. Therefore the MTA service interface can in addition to the CUA be accessed by different implementations of the UA functions as indicated in figure 7. The services offered at this interface include

- Logon: A User Agent is allowed to logon to the MTA if it is registered in a MTA configuration file.
- Logoff: A User Agent which is logged on to the MTA may logoff. Messages coming into the MTA for users which are to be reached via a logged-off UA are stored and delivered upon the next logon.
- Submit Request: A message may be submitted to the MTA by any originator who is registered in the MTA's directory. Associated with the submit request is some data which allows the MTA to build the P1 envelope for the message and the message itself. The envelope information is represented in a Pascal data structure and the message itself is expected to be encoded, as required for transmission.
- Submit Confirmation: after a submitted message has been received by the MTA and stored on disk, the MTA takes over responsibility for the message and sends a submit confirmation to the UA.
- Deliver Indication: Associated with the delivery of a message to the UA is some information which is taken from the P1 envelope and the message itself. In addition the local addressing information (node/userid) is passed to the UA in order to support the concept of the distributed common user agent. The information for local addressing is retrieved from the MTA directory. The envelope information and this local address is represented in a pascal datastructure and the message itself is encoded as it has been received by the MTA.
- Notify Indication: The notify indication is used to report the delivery or non delivery of a message to its originator. This service primitive is used by the MTA when it receives a delivery report from a peer MTA, that serves the recipients of a message. The data that is associated with the notify indication is passed as a pascal datastructure to the UA.

The MTA passes/receives with these service primitives the full set of parameters as it is described in the X.411 recommendation. The representation of these parameters is concisely defined as set of Pascal type definitions and the way the MTA expects/sends the data is defined to be a sequence of IUCV buffer transmissions. Therefore this interface provides access to the complete parameter data of the main MTA service primitives.

The main function of the MTA is the relaying of messages: Upon receipt of a message either from an UA or from some peer MTA it

- retrieves for each recipient from its directory either its local address (if it is a local recipient), or the identifier of a peer MTA which is assumed to be able to forward the message (if it is a remote recipient), or an indication that no route can be found for that recipient,
- puts an entry in the queue of the appropriate UA for each local recipient,
- hands over to the RTS one copy of the message for each peer MTA, that serves at least one recipient, and
- creates a delivery report in case that a copy of the message was enqueued for at least one local user (if requested in the message) and creates a nondelivery report in case that no route could be found for at least one recipient.

When the RTS takes over responsibility from the MTA for the reliable transfer of a message to some peer MTA, it receives together with the message an identifier of the peer MTA. It uses this identifier to retrieve from its directory

- the name and the password, that are used to identify the MTA towards this peer, and
- the name and the password, that are expected from the peer to identify itself.

Before the RTS can attempt to obtain a session with its peer MTA, it has to pass the peer MTA name down to the transport layer where it is finally mapped to the X.25 address, transport protocol identifier, and transport service access point of the peer. The above mentioned first name/password pair is then passed with the connect request to the peer. In the case of an acceptance of the connection the name/password pair that it passes back is verified against the above mentioned second name/password pair. After the establishment of a connection the RTS provides for reliable transfer of the message even when the session connection happens to be temporarily unavailable. However the reliability can be reached only as far as the operating system provides reliability for disk store.

To summarize this section, the major conceptual design decisions in the prototype are:

- The Presentation Layer of the OSI Reference Model has been identified as a set of functions which are implemented as a service equally accessible by MTA and UA.
- In both sublayers of the X.400 system, the UA-layer and the MTA-layer, the system has a substructure which is a consequence of our design concepts:
  - In the MTA-layer the association management and reliable transfer service are joined as one process. The message dispatcher is put into a second process.
  - The UA-layer is split into two parts. One part implements the user-supporting functions like editing and retrieval of messages. This part runs under the control of the user. The other part implements the UA functions which are not related to the user interface. It runs as one commonly used service process, the CUA.

Experiences with the System and future Work

An earlier version of the prototype has been demonstrated in a multivendor demonstration at the CeBit Fair 1986 in Hannover, Germany. The main technical effect of this demonstration was the agreement on a subset of the X.400 services, that yielded a powerful message handling system on one side and a allows the construction of rather simple prototypes on the other side. The definition of such a subset, called profile, is necessary because of the large amount of X.400 services that are not essential for the basic operation of a a message handling system and because of the absence of length restrictions for the service parameters in the X.400 recommendation.

The next step in the development of a public message handling system out of the X.400 recommendations is the demonstration at the TELECOM'87 exhibition in Geneva, Switzerland. In this exhibition the discussed prototype will be operated in a joint demonstration of 20 organizations. Among these organizations are several PTTs from European countries, the US, and Japan. They operate a set of interconnected MTAs - representing one administration management domain each - which provide the backbone message transfer system for a set of private management domains. They consist of MTAs and are operated by the different vendors. The technical contribution of the establishment of this scenario is, that for the first time a network of reasonable size is operated in an configuration as it is intended by the X.400 recommendations: i.e. PRMDs use the message relaying service of ADMDs to exchange messages.

Based on the implementation of X.400 messaging we see several topics for future work. Two of them are discussed here. First, the organization of naming in large messaging systems is a problem to be attacked by the ADMDs and PRMDs. In any case it will be necessary to provide some sort of directory service. A minimum requirement of such a service is that it is possible to determine the O/R-name of a person. Work in this arena is under way in the standards committees (10), but prototype implementation will raise certainly many questions in topics like implementation of large distributed databases, or privacy of information.

The second topic is the extension of interpersonal messaging for the exchange of (possibly large) structured multimedia documents. The basic standard for a common representation of e.g. integrated text/graphic documents is already a draft international standard (11) and work for the integration of e.g. interactive operational structures is under way (12). For the exchange of such documents the X.400 message transfer system will probably be only one of several possible means of transportation. Other more interactive protocols might be required to avoid the unnecessary transport of voluminous information for media like sound or video.

Acknowledgements

The authors would like to thank our partners at the GMD in Darmstadt, the Queens University in Kingston and the members of the Office Communication Research department of the ENC in Heidelberg. Each of them has contributed to the development and implementation of of various versions of the prototype.

References

1. J.S.Quateman, J.C.Hoskins: Notable Computer Networks, CACM, Vol.29, No. 10 (October 1986)

2. CCITT Eighth Plenary Assemble: Recommendations X.400 - X.430: Data Communication Networks Message Handling Systems, CCITT Red Book Volume VIII.7, Malaga-Torremolinos (October 1984)

3. J.D.Day, H.Zimmermann: The OSI Reference Model, Proceedings of the IEEE Vol. 71, No. 12, pp. 1331-1333 (December 1983)

4. DFN Zentale Projektleitung (ed.): Das Message Handling System im DFN (in German), Deutscher Forschungsnetz Verein, Berlin (March 1983)

5. Th. Schuett, J.B. Staton, W. Racke: Message Handling Systems based on the CCITT X.400 Recommendations, to appear in IBM Systems Journal Vol. 26. No. 2 (1987)

6. CCITT Eighth Plenary Assemble: Recommendations X.20 - X.32: Data Communication Networks Interfaces, CCITT Red Book Volume VIII.3, Malaga-Torremolinos (October 1984)

7. CCITT Eighth Plenary Assemble: Recommendations X.200 - X.250: Data Communication Networks Open System Interconnection (OSI) System Description Techniques, CCITT Red Book Volume VIII.5, Malaga-Torremolinos (October 1984)

8. IBM Corporation: Remote Spooling Communication Subsystem Networking: Program Reference and Operations Manual, Order Number SH24-5005-2

9. P.C.Gardener Jr.: A System for the Automated Office Environment, IBM Systems Journal 20, No. 3, pp. 321-344 (1981)

10. CCITT: X.ds Series of Recommendations for directory Systems Version 4, Melbourne, April 1986

11. International Organization for Standardization (ISO): Information Processing - Text and Office Systems - Office Document Architecture (ODA) and Interchange Format - Part 1 - 6

12. CCITT: Document Transfer, Access and Manipulation (DTAM) Draft of the T.400 Series of Recommendations (December 1986)

Laboratory for Emulation and Study of Integrated and Coordinated Media Communication

L. F. Ludwig
D. F. Dunn

Bell Communications Research
Red Bank, NJ

ABSTRACT

In future telecommunications networks, understanding the issues of user-network control, Customer Premise Equipment (CPE) technologies, services and user applications is as important as the classical network problems of channel structure, switching, and transmission. This paper discusses a Bell Communications Research facility, the Integrated Media Architecture Laboratory (IMAL), designed to flexibly emulate a wide range of current and future network and CPE environments with a focus on multiple media communications. IMAL combines off-the-shelf technologies to create an easily clonable emulation environment for studying, planning, demonstrating, and checking the feasibility of integrated media communications.

The IMAL project has assembled workstations which feature speech-synthesis/sampled-audio/telephony capabilities, local 1 MIP computation capacity, and a high-resolution color display integrating text/graphics/image/video under an expanded X Window display management system. (X Windows is an emerging windowing standard to provide high performance device-independent graphics.) The workstations may be augmented as needed by local image digitizers, video cameras, and color image printers producing paper and viewgraph hardcopies. Also, the workstations are interconnected with switches permitting access to one another as well as shared databases, temporary storage, intelligence, and information processing/conversion resources. Communications services are implemented under a distributed, real-time service primitive control scheme. This multiple-media service primitives scheme employs a threaded/dataflow-type architecture to support user-defined, network-defined, and vendor-defined services while including a wealth of flexible features for the study of network architecture, protocol, network management, and billing functions.

1. INTRODUCTION

This paper describes the Integrated Media Architecture Laboratory (IMAL) which began in October of 1986. The laboratory is currently under an expanded development effort based on the original vision. The paper will discuss the motivation, applications, and architecture of IMAL.

1.1 Themes of the IMAL Project

IMAL is intended to facilitate the study and demonstration of a wide range of network capabilities in architecture, signaling, services, and protocol areas. IMAL does this by creating a flexible emulation *environment* in a setting characterized by two main themes:

- Integrated and coordinated media communications employing voice, audio, data, text, image, animated/still graphics, live/still video, and real-time control;

- Service construction from other services and fragments of services called *service primitives*.

The philosophy of the laboratory is held as a critical design feature. This philosophy consists of three themes:

- Attention to the low-cost reproducibility of the laboratory to allow for an easily cloned technology transfer package, educational vehicle, "concept theater", and basic research tool;

- Focus on emulation of both CPE and network features;

- Avoidance of the endorsement of specific coding, interface, signaling, transmission, and switching approaches. Those approaches are viewed as implementational artifacts that do not effect the basic intent of the laboratory yet can be freely emulated by the laboratory.

In addition to the value provided by having multiple copies of something such as IMAL in a wide variety of environments, clone IMAL sites could also be linked together to study long-distance ergonomics of integrated media communications.

1.2 Structure of the IMAL Environment

Figure 1 shows the basic structure of the IMAL environment. This structure is intended to facilitate flexible *emulation* of a wide range of network and CPE configurations.

- All CPE functionality is emulated using a small family of workstation configurations. The highest levels of CPE functionality are emulated using a special custom-designed workstation that includes a spectrum of integrated visual, audio, data, control, computation, and presentation features in a standardized window (modified X-windows) and operating system (modified UNIX™) environment. An emulation of a given application may very well use only a small subset of the capabilities made possible with that workstation configuration.

- All switching and transmission capabilities are emulated by a computer controlled *interconnection network*. This interconnection network supports video, telephony, high-

---

UNIX is a trademark of AT&T.

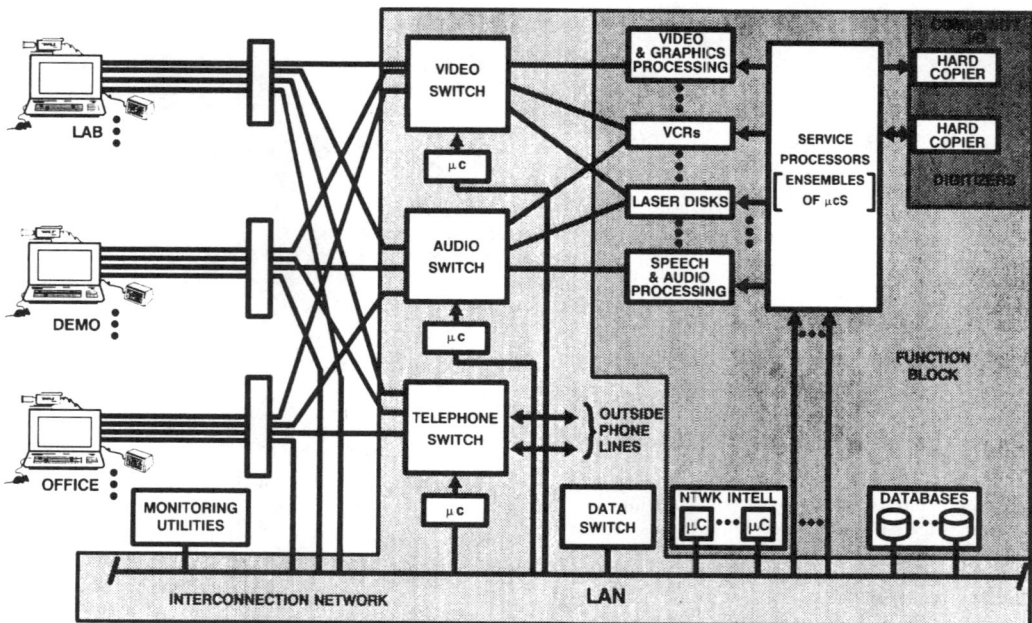

Current IMAL Configuration
Figure 1

fidelity audio, data, and signaling channels. It also features a distributed processor implementation, intelligence for service coordination, and service-description databases set up in a service primitives structure. As affordable, multiple resources (switches, intelligence, databases) can be used to study routing, server, and failure-recovery issues.

- All service features beyond the scope of simple switching and transmission (storage, media conversion, processing, entertainment material, public databases, etc.) are emulated by a collection of equipment termed the *transcendental function block*.

- All community-shared input and output capabilities (paper hardcopy, transparency hardcopy, digitization of hardcopy, etc.) are emulated by a collection of equipment termed the *community I/O block*.

- Monitoring of state and performance are provided by a number of *monitoring utilities*. Current plans include such monitors for the interconnection network and the highest level workstation configurations. The monitor for the interconnection network measures traffic for display and statistical analysis in addition to displaying state information about channels, switches, service invocations, service executions, call progress, billing, information flows, and failure modes. The workstation monitor measures both traffic and internal behavior for display and statistical analysis. The internal behavior information includes attributes such as disk accesses, packet collisions, and CPU loading which can be valuable in emulating performance-limited CPE.

1.3 The IMAL goal

The focus of IMAL is to study the control aspects of networking sophisticated user applications and cross-media control. Figure 2 illustrates IMAL as the intersection of twelve major areas of current interest in modern communications. Thus a single IMAL facility can be useful to a large number of otherwise separate study efforts. As a result, it provides a new way for these otherwise separate study areas to coherently work together in a shared environment, seeing impacts on each other and working together towards synergies and group evolutionary awareness.

2. MOTIVATING MULTIPLE MEDIA AND COORDINATED MEDIA SERVICES

In this section, a wide spectrum of potential applications for integrated media communications which feature a reasonable amount of integrated control are considered. As the reader's own imagination will testify, the examples given here by no means form an exhaustive list. All of the examples

- Use approximately the same shared CPE and network substrates;

- Can be implemented today on a reasonable scale given adequate communications support;

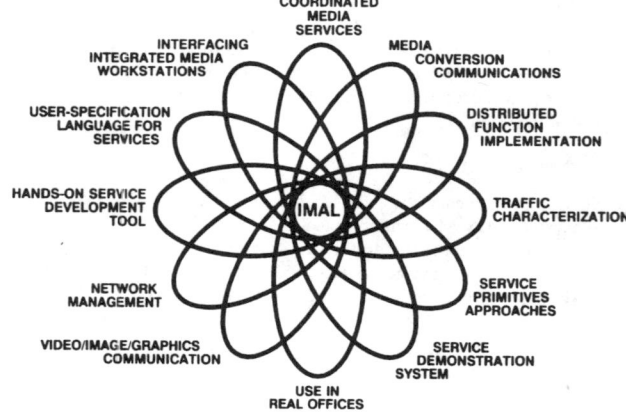

IMAL Goal: Provide An Environment To Support Multiple Studies
Figure 2

- Are easily implemented in a number of different ways within IMAL, permitting comparison.

What is surprising about these futuristic-sounding communications services is that they are realizable today with off-the-shelf products and some software modifications.

2.1 Integrated Media Database Services

Most databases implemented or envisioned today provide access to information of only one type of medium. This medium is typically text with almost all exceptions being audio (voice or music) or single format still image (bit mapped graphics, raster graphics, vector graphics, or still-frame video). An emerging exception to this is in the area of *electronic document archives* where documents are stored as a coordinated combination of text, bit-mapped graphics, and vector graphics [1]. Archived documents are either created in this format or reconstructed in this format by person or machine. Documents are stored in data structures[2] which provide separated parts for text, bit-mapped graphics, vector graphics, and attribute lists (which indicate how these pieces interleave).

Databases for electronic document archiving serve as examples of *integrated media databases* (IMDB) which store information in a variety of media. They also serve as examples of *coordinated* integrated media databases (CIMDB) since there is tight coordination in the display of various media. There are many potential applications for more general forms of IMDBs and CIMDBs:

- Information annotation;
- General information retrieval;
- Training;
- What-is-.../this-is-... functions;

These applications are briefly discussed below.

Information annotation includes concepts such as speech-annotated-text, speech-annotated-image and text-annotated-image. Such annotations are useful in providing supplementary information about a target piece of information; in particular the use of multiple media can be quite effective since different media are often best suited for different types or perspectives of information. Since the presentation of the information is tightly coupled between the media, information annotation employed the CIMDB concept.

In *general information retrieval* a user browses for information through a database; however, the information may be represented in whatever media is convenient. For example, IMAL demonstrations could include an inquiry on baboons which begins by browsing for text articles on the animals. Next, references to obscure regions of the world where the baboons are located leads the user to access a graphical map database which points out named locations on map images with a red overlay arrow. Questions about a particular animal eventually lead to the display of raster images showing photographs of the animal, and inquiries about social behavior lead to the display of short video segments illustrating specific types of group behavior. Note here that each database inquiry results in the display in a single media; this is the IMDB mode. It is also possible for each database inquiry response to involve the display in several media at once in a coordinated fashion; for example, text, image, and video at the same time. These responses require CIMDBs.

Automated training has appeared as an extremely cost effective solution in many industries requiring specialized training with high personnel turnover. Here a training database may consist of text, image, and video segments. One example involves the training of transportation mechanics. Video is used to illustrate assembly/disassembly of engines, fuselages, etc, with potential for coordinated graphical overlay to point out specific items. Image and text are then used to create manual pages with interactive capabilities.

What-is-.../this-is-... functions combine image/video with overlay graphics and mouse-controlled pointers. The what-is-... function allows a user to move a mouse-controlled pointer over a particular component or region illustrated in a image and query the database for its name or additional information. The this-is-... function allows a user to type in the name of a component or region and have it outlined with a graphics overlay from within an image showing it and other related items.

2.2 Adding Communications to Existing Stand-Alone Mixed Medium Applications

Although some vendors are creating LAN oriented applications software, there are a number of stand-alone CPE applications that currently employ no or at most very little communications yet involve mixed media presentation. These include CAD/CAE, desktop publishing, and computer aided graphic artwork. In this section, communications possibilities for these applications are considered.

Computer Aided Design (CAD) and *Computer Aided Engineering* (CAE) employ computers for design rendering, simulation, and display. These systems have appeared in every aspect of engineering design in all disciplines of engineering. *Desktop publishing* permits users with very limited training to create sophisticated page layouts with multiple font text and a variety of graphics image sources. This is accomplished by combining simple-to-use mouse-controlled menus in conjunction with instantaneous display of created or modified input. Such instantaneous display is termed WYSIWYG in the industry (pronounced *"whizy-wig"* as a mnemonic for What-You-See-Is-What-You-Get). Most of the desktop publishing packages include fairly complete features for the creation of graphic art work for use as figures or transparencies. In addition, stand-alone graphics artwork systems, for example Genographics, can produce very high quality artwork.

As suggested by Figure 3, the evolution of communications CPE and stand-alone CPE to multiple media formats suggests natural convergence to a single workstation which could be used for both applications. Therefore, it is natural to consider possibilities for building more sophisticated communications capabilities into traditional stand-alone CPE applications.

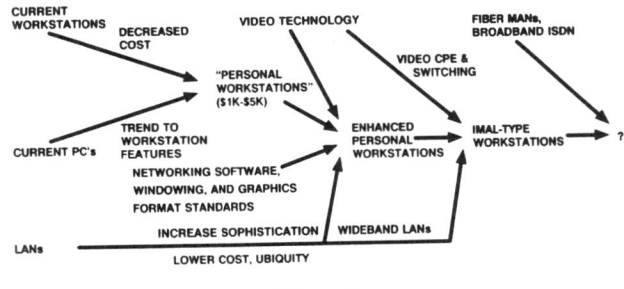

Merging Evolution Of Communications CPE And Stand-Alone
Figure 3

Possibilities include:
- Conferencing;
- Annotation and Markup;
- Integration of the output of incompatible systems;
- Integration with extensive engineering, icon, and graphics databases;
- Integration with standard call and mail utilities;

In the examples the term "display" can mean presentation of either visual (text, graphics, image, video) or audio (sounds, speech synthesis, music, voice) stimulus.

Conferencing permits two or more people physically separated to use a given application interactively in real time. In some cases the application may be specially designed for multiple users, but the more useful situations are ones where the application was designed for usage by a single user. In this case, conferencing telecommunications features can add tremendous value to existing applications. Typical functions required for conferencing are simultaneous display of application display features, group usage of mouse and keyboard input, shared file access, shared resource access, and overlay person-to-person communications features such as voice, pointers on the screen, or video communications.

Annotation and Markup allows notes and visual markups to be overlayed or displayed in conjunction with the output, display, or usage of an otherwise unrelated application. This is useful in both call-type or mail-type services. Examples include penciled overlays on text or images and verbal or text annotations.

Integration of the output of incompatible systems permits a workstation, network resource, or service vendor resource to merge the outputs of unrelated systems. In desktop publishing one may use one resource for drawing graphs, another for artwork, a variety of databases for other text and visual information to provide raw input; from there the user may use a variety of page layout programs to handle different problems and finally produce a single unified output. Similarly in CAD/CAE, it may be very useful to pass textual, numerical, and visual information between a variety of applications optimized for dissimilar functions.

Integration with extensive engineering, icon, and graphics databases is an important special case of the above with some added features. There are two goals here. One is to permit arbitrary applications to have information "dropped into them" from databases in convenient ways. The second is to tie several databases together so that a single inquiry can be served by several databases at once.

Integration with standard call and mail utilities allows an existing or new call to be linked into an already active application or set of applications. This is useful in consulting others about details identified in the work process; first one works alone, then one decides to discuss partial results with someone, then one is electronically able to have another user involved as if they were there in the same room, etc. Most if not all of these features can be supported within the context of a slightly extended window manager.

2.3 Call-like Communications

Most of the above examples are examples of either a workstation-workstation call or a workstation-machine call. Also, either user should have the freedom to add or remove media and channels from a call at any time, subject to any billing or permission constraints requested by users involved. In workstation-workstation calls either user could potentially add or remove media and channels from a call at any time from either side of the connection. Billing for a feature added during a call could be directed to the party invoking the feature, the party invoking the call, or a third party.

It is natural to expect future CPE to support more than one simultaneous active call. This is a basic feature of ISDN; in addition, window-based workstations naturally permit the display of information from multiple independent sources at the same time. For example, a user may be engaged in one call and then decides to place a second call to another party (for additional information, expertise, second opinion, etc.). In many cases, it will be necessary for the user CPE to direct its output to the appropriate call channels. It will also be useful to permit the "merging" of independent active calls. In the preceding example, the user may decide after going back and forth between two active calls with two separate users that a conferencing of the active calls may be desirable. Again, this can involve a variety of media: for example, the first call might be a CAD session where two designers work together on a design drawing; at first one user attempts to consult a text or image database for reference information, and later decides the other user should participate in this database consultation as well. Moreover, from the users' view it is perfectly natural to wish to merge the active calls without disconnecting and re-initiating any of them.

2.4 Deferred Communications

Deferred communications replaces a single call to the ultimate destination with a call to a storage system. This storage system can later be consulted by the ultimate destination at that party's convenience. Note, that deferred communications can be viewed as a pair of workstation-machine calls; one for creation and one for review. Historical examples of deferred communications include paper memo notes, postal letters, computer-mail, telephone answering machines, and emerging voice-mail services. In addition to providing a reliable method of exchanging information between hard-to-reach users, deferred communications can also be used to counteract differences in time-zones, move information to be incorporated into some other application, and facilitate "copy-to" actions.

Deferred communications could be supported for multiple media. In addition, the media can be coordinated, i.e., graphics can be overlayed over video/image/text at key times within the message's duration, etc. In this sense, it follows that deferred communications merely amounts to coupling an IMDB or CIMDB (see Section 2.1) with an editing utility used for creation of the message.

Interesting extensions occur when deferred communications are tied in with media conversion utilities. For example, by incorporating speaker-trained speech recognition systems and speech synthesizers, a simple text-based computer-mail system can be used with any combination of voice or text input or output, permitting telephone or terminal creation and review as convenient. As a bonus, such a system also serves as a voice-dictation system.

2.5 Role of Service Primitives

In all of the previous examples, it is startling to notice how astronomical the potential combinations of "reasonable" user expectations for telecommunications might be. It is this that motivates the use of service primitive systems as a basic tool within IMAL. The current IMAL service primitives system [3] is flexible enough to permit emulated comparisons of a wide variety of possible network service primitive implementations.

Figure 4 illustrates the potential service combinatorics. Each of the user, network, and service vendor domains is working toward support of the telecommunications features shown. It is impossible to address the sophistications and combinations using the existing methodology of monolithic software generics and hardware upgrades oriented around adding only one feature service at a time. In addition, it is likely that many services may become linked or incorporated into others. For example, users may subscribe to automated calendar management services or have one in their own network-accessible systems. A service vendor could link these with a network-provided call forwarding service to form a meeting scheduling service; subscribers could name meeting participants and constraints and the automated service would forward potential dates and places to participants, optimize, and finally distribute word of the meeting time and place as well as supporting documentation using call and mail utilities.

A reasonable set of goals for network-level service primitive systems include:

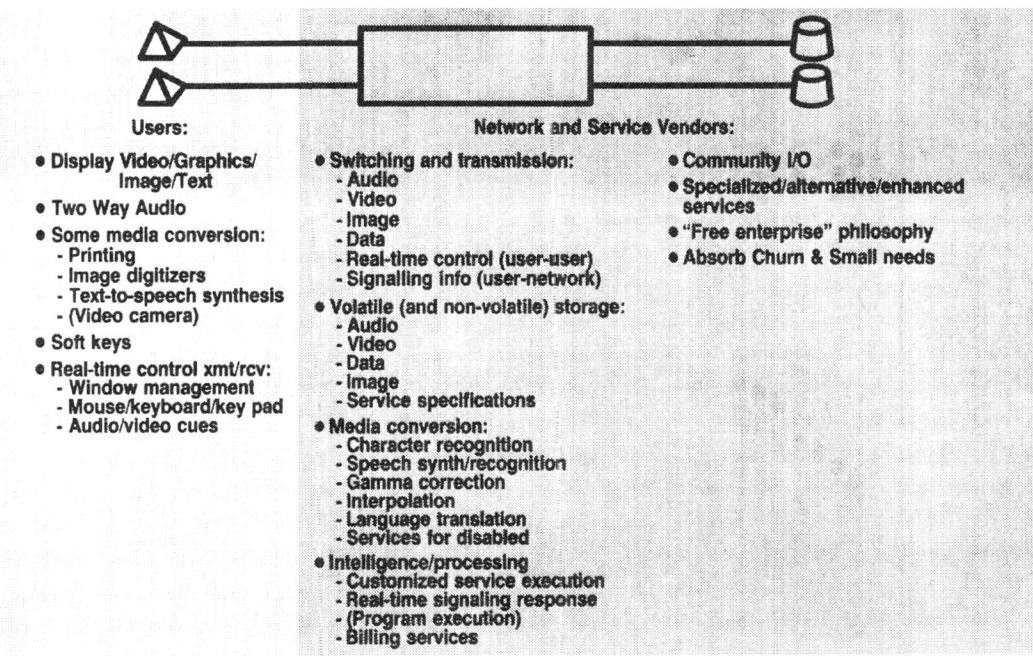

Potential Service Complexities
Figure 4

1. Span of the possible service combinatorics made possible by technology;
2. Linking of existing services;
3. Management and linking of simultaneous calls.

The IMAL environment can employ a variety of techniques for implementing these capabilities. Current plans are to use the threaded/flow approach described in [3], although, ISDN-based service subscription systems and other methodologies could be implemented for exact or simulated emulation.

3. THE IMAL ARCHITECTURE

The IMAL Architecture was outlined in Section 1.2. Here each item identified in that Section is discussed in more detail from the implementation point of views.

3.1 Workstations

The planned IMAL workstations are of three types:

1. "High-End" workstations (widest set of features and sophistication);
2. "Low-End" workstations (a PC with graphics/video display features and a telephone);
3. "Primitive" workstations (a PC supplemented with a video monitor and a telephone).

At this writing, only the High-End workstation is implemented. This workstation is intended to act as a placeholder for arbitrary future CPE by incorporating a collection of most foreseeable CPE terminal capabilities. As part of future work, the Low-End and Primitive workstations will be implemented to study functions in a more limited computational/display environment.

The features of the High-End workstation are inspired from the observations reported in [4]. An overview of the High-End workstation we have created is illustrated in Figure 5. It provides:

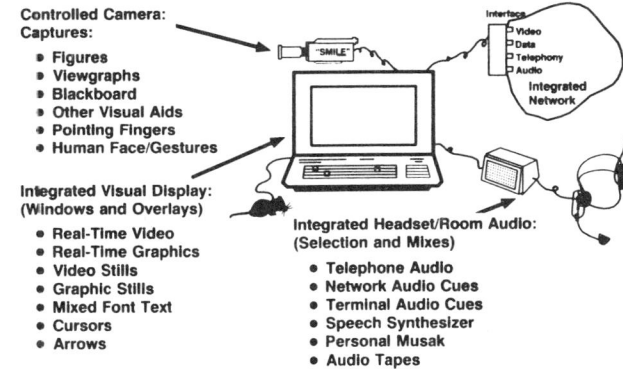

High-End Workstation
Figure 5

1. A 1 MIP computer supporting a multi-tasking operating system for control of all workstation features as well as local execution of user applications.

2. A high-resolution color graphics screen under the control of a window management system capable of integrating mouse-cursors, pointers, data-terminal emulators, mixed-font text, bit-map or raster image, still or animated graphics, and still or animated video within a multiple window environment. Each window acts as a virtual screen supporting separate or related applications as needed. A mouse cursor is used to direct keyboard and mouse-button inputs to one specific active process on a workstation. Pointers, whose position on the screen may or may not be controlled by a mouse, are used to call attention to specific points on the screen. Unlike mouse-cursors, pointers do not direct keyboard or mouse-button input.

3. A high-fidelity audio system integrating telephony, speech synthesis output, generalized audio stimulus, network-provided audio material, and a local cassette tape output into a miked headset and speaker-phone arrangement. Signals can be mixed and switched on/off as needed and directed in different formats to headset/speaker and to outgoing audio channels. Generalized audio stimulus, which generalizes sounds similar to call-progress signals and data-terminal beeps, are stored and created by a local audio sampler. Such audio samplers are effectively computer-controlled audio RAMs which can download, playback, record, and modify recorded sounds.

4. Hardcopy I/O systems including a pan-tilt video camera arrangement, image/text printers, and hardcopy digitizers may be expanded to include provisions for creating data tapes/floppies and audio tapes at the workstation.

In particular the workstation should be constructed with as much off-the-shelf and standardized elements as possible. At this writing, the best if not only choice for the software substrate is some version of UNIX [5] supplemented by the X-window window management system [6].

Figure 6 shows the IMAL realization of the High-End workstation. The current implementation uses a 1MIP computer module running UNIX. The display is a 1024x1280 pixel color graphics monitor. The text/graphics/video integration is accomplished with a graphics controller fitted with special on-board microcode, PLA modifications, and UNIX kernel modifications to support X-windows and a special device driver. (This special driver requires shared memory between user and kernel with absolute addressing to permit high-performance DMA and control. The software and microcode work required to accomplish this included vast efforts by R. Goodwin and M. Levine of the MIT ATHENA Project in addition to our own work. IMAL is currently beginning work to incorporate the portable version of the SUN NeWS™ POSTSCRIPT windowing [7] and image rendering standards [7] as well. It is noted that both X-windows and NeWS are cooperatively working on a merger of the two windowing systems.)

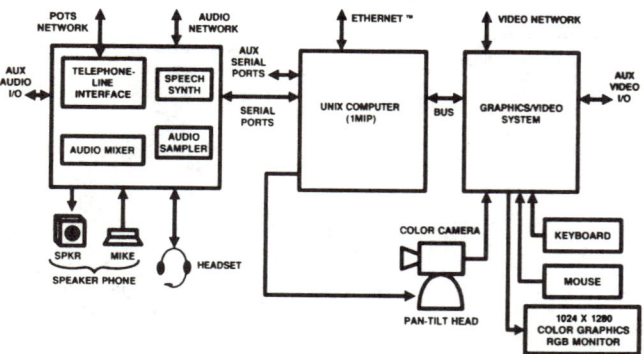

IMAL Workstation Realization
Figure 6

Figure 7 shows a software model of the workstation. There are three subsystems:

1. The graphics/video environment;
2. The UNIX environment;
3. The audio/pan-tilt/peripheral control environment.

___
NeWs is a trademark of SUN Microsystems.

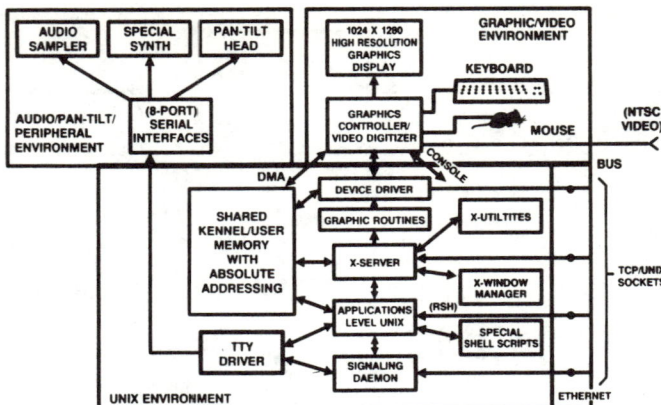

Figure 7

The keyboard and three-button rolling-ball mouse used by the workstation are hosted by the two serial ports provided on the graphics controller. The graphics controller also hosts the 1024x1280 RGB high resolution graphics monitor screen. An NTSC video signal is also provided directly to on-board digitizing and encoding hardware in the graphics controller. The resulting graphics/video system has three interfaces to the UNIX environment:

1. Control-message interface to the interrupt-driven device driver;
2. Direct Memory Access (DMA) interface to the special absolute-addressed shared user/kernel memory space for file and image transfer;
3. Console interface for UNIX booting, executive, and administrative functions.

The special absolute-addressed shared memory and the interrupt-driver device driver are both located in the UNIX environment. Each of these special features requires extensive modification of the UNIX kernel but are needed to obtain high performance in keeping with the powerful graphics capabilities. Overall, the UNIX environment consists of the following elements:

1. Interrupt-driven device driver for the graphics system;
2. Absolute-addressed shared user/kernel memory system;
3. C-language interface to the device driver;
4. X-window system:
   - Modified X-server;
   - Modified X-window manager;
   - Common plus new X-utilities and X-applications;
5. UNIX applications programs;
6. Special-function UNIX shell-scripts;
7. Signaling daemon;
8. Ethernet system:
   - Signaling daemon interface;
   - UNIX applications "rsh" interface (for remote shells);
   - Direct X-server interface;
   - Direct device driver interface;
   - Interrupt-driven serial-port device driver for the audio/pan-tilt/peripheral control environment.

Note the variety of interfaces and utilities provided in this part of the workstation design. These functions provide a wide range of CPE emulation capabilities to be easily invoked and manipulated by C-language programs.

Figure 8 shows the audio subsystem of the workstation which centers around a stereo-output audio mixer with separately mixed "effects" channels. The mixer accepts

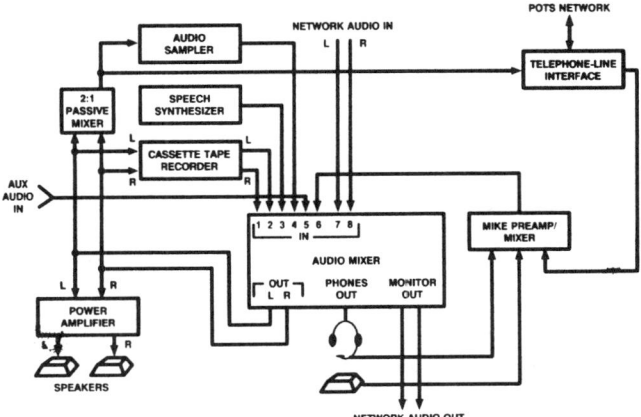

Figure 8

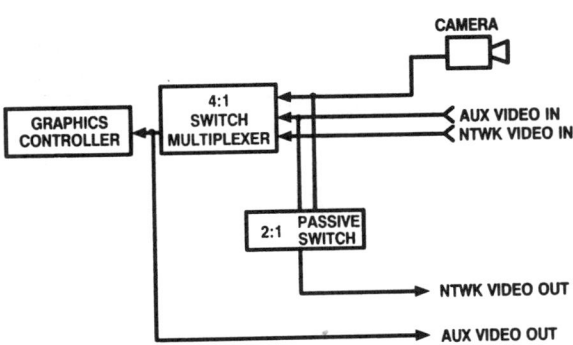

Video Subsystem
Figure 9

stereo inputs from the network and cassette tape recorder as well as monoaural inputs from the speech synthesizer, audio sampler, microphone preamp, and a free "auxiliary input" which could be used with outside audio sources such as VCR audio or an electric guitar. The mixer's main audio output is internally routed to a headphone amplifier driving a headset (for private audio listening) and externally applied to a power amplifier and speakers for room-scale audio. A directional microphone/preamp system is used to implement "hands-free" speakerphone functions. This preamp includes a mixer which is also fed the signal from a headset microphone and the earpiece signal from a telephone-line interface system. The telephone-line interface is created from a telephone-headset system and a standard POTS phone. Audio storage and playback functions are provided by a cassette tape recorder and audio sampler; each can record the same audio signals applied to the headphones and speakers. A small passive mixer is used to mix the stereo audio signals from the mixer into a monoaural signal fed to the single high-impedance audio inputs of the audio sampler and telephone-line interface. The mixer also provides separately mixed "effects" channels which are used to produce outgoing stereo audio to the network.

Figure 9 shows the video subsystem of the workstation. The four main elements are the graphics controller, a high-quality color video camera with NTSC output, a quad switching/multiplex module, and a passive (i.e., contact-closure) video switch unit (optional as will be discussed). The switching module permits the workstation video window to display live video signals provided by the network, the workstation camera, or an auxiliary video source at the workstation such as a VCR or video laserdisk. The module also provides a monochrome multiplex of all of the video sources, one allocated to a particular quadrant of its output when displayed. The workstation also provides two NTSC video outputs: one to the network and one to an auxiliary output such as a VCR a user may connect to the workstation. The auxiliary output is a copy of the signal sent to the workstation video window. The network output can be selected from the workstation's camera or auxiliary video input as shown in Figure 9. As a remark,

it is noted that most of our current workstations are not even provided with auxiliary audio and video inputs and outputs since the IMAL network has such rich service resources; a stand-alone workstation product, however, could easily be expected to incorporate auxiliary inputs and outputs to permit interworking with other CPE equipment.

3.2 Formats of Transmission and Switching Channels

In the IMAL control scheme transmission and switching channels are regarded and are administered as "resources". In this Section the channel formats, transmission methods, and switching methods are discussed. The transmission and switching channels are administered as resources by switch manager routines running as background processes on a switch-control computer. This switch computer will employ a high-performance background daemon process fitted with sockets to allow communication with other active processes on computers in IMAL. The background daemon serves as an interface between network signaling channels and switch management programs. The switch management programs are examples of "resource managers" in the IMAL control scheme; they accept switching requests through signaling daemons, make allocation decisions, and pass on appropriate commands directly to switch control programs. The switch control programs are either software switch fabrics themselves (as in the data switch discussed below) or consist of serial port device drivers designed to control the external video, audio, and telephone switching hardware discussed below.

All computers used in IMAL include 10Mbps Ethernet ports which are used for both signaling and data communications. Data and signaling channels are statistically multiplexed inside each computer via TCP and Berkeley UNIX sockets. Consequently, the transmission of all data and signaling channels in IMAL is implemented via a single Ethernet system.

Switching for signaling channels is done directly on the Ethernet by simply specifying the address of the final destination. Switching for data channels could also be done in this way or a separate background process on a switch computer could act as a centralized data channel switch. This high-performance daemon process links sockets with cross-connections so as to implement a software switching fabric. The resulting logical architecture for the data channels is the star shown in Figure 10.

All video switch and transmission channels are NTSC carried over video coax. All high-fidelity audio switch and transmission channels are in stereo configuration, each of the two channels is implemented as 600-ohm balanced line. Video and stereo high-

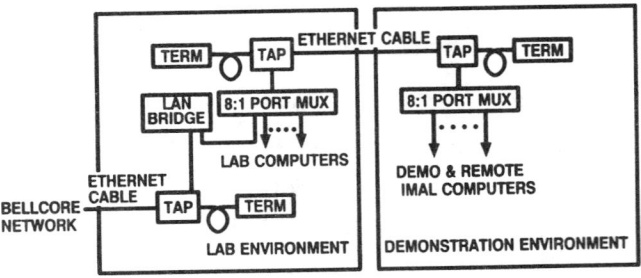

LAN System For Signaling And Data Communications
Figure 10

fidelity audio channels are switched by a production switch. The switch is controlled by a serial port and permits each of the three 16x16 crossbars to be independently switched. The serial port is hosted by the switch computer, described above, which supports a background daemon that serves as an interface between the switch's serial control port and network signaling channels.

Telephony switching and signaling gateway functions will be soon implemented on a rack mounted computer controlled PBX to permit interactions with call processing. The switch is controlled by a serial port hosted by the switch computer described above. The switch computer supports a background daemon that serves as an interface between the switch's serial control port and network signaling channels.

3.3 Other Shared Resources

In addition to transmission and switching resources, IMAL also provides a number of other shared raw resources from which services may be constructed. They currently (or will shortly) include:

- Computer-controlled VCRs with timecode for controlled playback, search, editing, and synchronization of computer events;
- A computer-controlled writable video laserdisk supplemented with additional read-only video laserdisks (stores both video stillframes and live audio/video segments under timecode control);
- Writeable data laserdisks (data-format image archive);
- Speech synthesis and speaker-trained speech recognition equipment;
- Speech/Audio processing system;
- Four-way conferencing bridge;
- Audio cassette tape and compact disk players;
- FM radio and commercial broadcast television receivers;
- Video and graphics processing hardware for image processing and enhanced graphics functions;
- Database archives for on-line text reference and downloadable programs;
- Computers for execution of programs downloaded from databases or users.

These raw resources are managed by resource management programs and are used to build services via the service primitives control scheme mentioned below [3]. Almost if not every service cited in this document, from mixed media interactive tutorials to integrated audio/text/graphics/video/graphics-overlay mail and calls, can be constructed in this manner (in addition to many other services).

3.4 Service Primitives

The key to managing the immense possibilities both within IMAL and within future telecommunications networks is a flexible, powerful, and simply used service primitives system. Full detail of the service primitives system employed in IMAL [3] is beyond the scope of this Section and hence will only be outlined here. It is capable of the functionality described in Section 2.6 with very fine granularity.

The IMAL service primitives method uses an architecture for the direct implementation of dataflow descriptions of services. An example of such a description is shown in Figure 11. Each

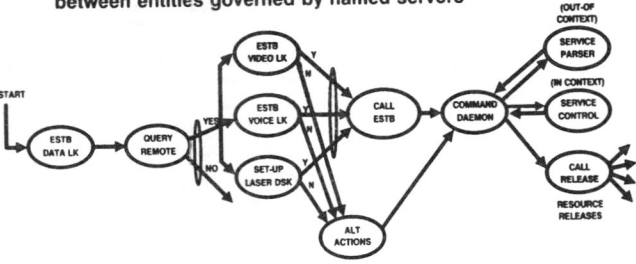

Service Descriptions
Figure 11

named process can be a raw resource function (such as those discussed in Sections 3.1 and 3.2), a service element (i.e., raw resource functions with controlling programs), or a full stand-alone service. Thus the IMAL method is one for supporting the *implementation* of general service primitives architectures; in fact, it is a *programmable services primitives engine* on a network scale. It should be noted that explicit attention has been given to architectural, operations, maintenance, administrative, fault-tolerance, failure recovery, billing, and monitoring design issues that are relevant to large-scale network implementations. The IMAL method thus provides a substrate for implementing a variety of approaches to the same design statement or goal. As a result, it permits
study of a wide range of single issue, synergistic, and evolution concerns.

The IMAL method uses a software substrate which equates hard and virtual resources with algorithms. A system for fetching service descriptions from databases and constructing dataflows between named entities provides the basic foundation for the method. A named entity is either a resource (controlled by a resource manager) or another algorithm which may itself control other algorithms and resources. A given entity may exist and execute its tasks anywhere in the network and can itself be of a distributed nature. Branching, concurrency, pipelining, and arbitrary degrees of decentralization are naturally supported. It is straightforward to pipeline the setup and execution phases of the dataflow so that parts of the dataflow which are already set up may execute as remaining parts are themselves being set up; this permits conditional setup of a dataflow as a function of events encountered in earlier parts of its execution. Since an existing stand-alone service can be linked to (i.e., peer connections) or included in (i.e., hierarchical connections) another service, the system acts very much like a threaded interpretive language. It is also straightforward to replace service description fetches from databases with user downloads, permitting user definition of services from service primitives.

desired class. Three monitors are provided:

1. A *channel monitor* showing explicit channel connections between users, switches, and resources. The monitor shows all changes as they happen, giving an instantaneous view of actively allocated communications channels. Circuit switched connections are shown as lines through switch fabrics; these lines exist for the full duration of the connection and then are removed. Packets are shown in a similar manner except 100-500 msec flashes are used for each packet so they can be seen by the human eye.

2. A *service setup monitor* shows user signaling, SEC creation, service description fetches, resource allocation, and contingency actions. This monitor is very elaborate and displays a large amount of information. Color coding is used extensively to distinguish distinct calls, parent servers, and control message types.

3. A *service execution monitor* shows the execution of dataflows that begin once they have been set up. During call set-up phases, resources are displayed on the screen as they are allocated. During the subsequent execution of the dataflow, each new action is drawn as an arc from source entity to destination entity in a flash of bright color. After the flash the arc remains in darkened color for later review.

4. SIMULATING LARGE-SCALE NETWORKS

Some rough plans have been made for the eventual analytical modeling of large-scale implementations of IMAL which could be used to create real-time simulations. Given that this is possible, IMAL could be "embedded" in a real-time simulation in such a way that it behaves as an infinitesimal slice of a large-scale network of the same type. The performance of resource management, network management, control architecture, billing, fault recovery, and other schemes could be tested in a hands-on environment against simulated traffic and failure mode conditions.

5. CURRENT STATUS

At this writing most of the hardware configurations have been installed and debugged. Also, workstation software is largely complete, monitoring software is about half finished, and the final implementation of the first IMAL service primitives system implementation is just starting. Imal has been giving demonstrations to various audiences since 2 weeks after its inception in October 1986. Prior to the current implementation a number of scattered feasibility test subsystems were implemented for preliminary study of the service primitives approach. The studies helped form the foundation for the current coding which, aside from extensive tricks to obtain high performance, is relatively straightforward to implement thanks to a strong design phase. Serious work on complete resource managers compatible with the new service primitives system Rather than naming specific primitives explicitly as is done in traditional service primitives approaches, the IMAL method only needs to explicitly define and implement the following elements:

1. Service description database system;
2. Service Execution Coordinators (SECs) and their servers;
3. Resource managers;
4. Control messages and their precise formats;
5. Overall systems management utilities;
6. Monitoring and reporting utilities.

Using this approach, creation of explicit service primitives and services themselves can be done with very short "programming-language" type files which are much easier to create and change. In addition to being a very useful research tool, this approach has value in actual deployment since it naturally permits easy introduction and evolution of service primitives. Much more detail on the IMAL threaded/flow service primitives method may be found in [3].

3.5 Network Monitors

IMAL provides a network monitors that can be enabled or disabled as needed for examining calls and transactions of a will be starting soon. Services are currently implemented with patched and stand-alone approaches; these services will be incrementally migrated to the new service primitives system as functions become available. Porting of CAD, desktop publishing, and other applications programs has been started but is largely limited to date.

6. REFERENCES

[1] Scan-Tek corporate presentation at ELECTRONIC IMAGING WEST, *Digital Scanners and Automatic Digitizers for Engineering Applications*, Session II, Anaheim, California, February 16-19, 1987.

[2] Formtek corporate presentation at ELECTRONIC IMAGING WEST, *Digital Scanners and Automatic Digitizers for Engineering Applications*, Session II, Anaheim, California, February 16-19, 1987. O.LI L. Ludwig, "A Threaded/Flow Approach to Reconfigurable Distributed Systems and Service Primitives Architectures", Sigcom 87.

[3] J. Bairstow, "Personal Workstations Redefine Desktop Computing", *High Technology*, Volume 7, Number 3, March 1987, pp.18-23.

[4] *UNIX User's Manual*, USENIX Association, March 1986 edition.

[5] R. W. Scheifler, J. Gettys, "The X window System", MIT ATHENA Project publication, October 1986 revision, Cambridge Massachusettes.

[6] CONRAC Division, CONRAC Corporation, *Raster Graphics Handbook*, 2nd edition, New York: Van Nostrand Reinhold Company Inc., 1985.

Telescience and Advanced Technologies

B. M. Leiner

Research Institute for Advanced Computer Science, USA

August 7, 1987

Abstract

Space Station and its associated laboratories, coupled with the availability of new computing and communications technologies, have the potential of significantly enhancing scientific research. Telescience involves the interaction of scientific researchers and equipment on earth with on-board personnel and equipment as well as with other researchers, remote ground-based resources, mission control personnel, and space station developers. To assure that this potential is met, scientists and managers associated with the Space Station project must gain significant experience with the use of these technologies for scientific research, and this experience must be fed into the development process for Space Station.

In this talk, a pilot program is described that is attempting to address this problem. University researchers are conducting rapid prototyping testbeds employing new telescience technologies and ideas. These testbeds are specific research experiments within the scientific discipline areas that will use Space Station laboratories. The experiments are being carried out in a coordinated manner to allow the critical questions to be answered by groups of scientists working with technologists in a rapid prototyping testbed environment.

The rapid prototyping testbeds are not like a typical testbed. Rather than being used to evaluate and integrate systems on the way to deployment, the rapid prototyping testbeds constitute a Technology Evaluation Environment (TEE), allowing users to interact with advanced technologies in the conduct of scientific research in order to develop the required base of experience to permit development and evaluation of requirements and specifications.

PART 10. DISTRIBUTED SYSTEMS

L. Schreier

SRI International, USA

MODELS OF A VERY LARGE DISTRIBUTED DATABASE

Mark Blakey

Research Laboratories
Telecom Australia

and

Department of Computer Science
Monash University

ABSTRACT

The problems inherent in managing a database distributed over a very large number of sites are considered. The applications of such databases to the provision of telecommunications and other public services are discussed. It is shown that the distribution and maintenance of the directory information describing object locations poses some fundamental problems. A new partially informed class of distributed databases is described which distributes the directory information on a "needs-to-know" basis. The class is described by models of the network topology, and by the knowledge available to each site. These proposals are sufficiently general to support the partitioning of data relations into distribution fragments, and for those fragments to be replicated at multiple sites.

1. INTRODUCTION

Recent developments in computers and communication technologies are enabling a rich variety of advanced information-based and transaction processing services to be offered over public networks. Typical applications include electronic funds transfer, airline reservation systems and real estate listings. Sophisticated telecommunication services, such as on-line directory services, are also emerging. All of these applications rely on an underlying Distributed Database (DDB) technology. Most present day services make relatively modest demands of the DDB given that information is distributed across a small number of sites (typically 20 or less) so that the information processing demands are readily supported by existing commercial DDB systems (see [3,4] for example). It is, however, likely that applications will evolve requiring much higher degrees of distribution. New telephony services such as automatic call redirection could, for example, be established by incorporating a DDB site into each telephone exchange. Manufacturing and operational efficiencies may also be significantly improved by enabling direct communications between an enterprise's databases (e.g. warehouse contents which may themselves be distributed) and those of its clients and suppliers. Applications such as these require DDBs distributed over a very large number of sites (possibly hundreds) so that new techniques must be found to assist in their management.

Some of these applications will naturally require that data objects be partitioned into fragments [5], suitable for storage allocation at specific sites, and that some fragments be replicated at multiple sites. These requirements, together with the size and dynamic nature of the network, pose some fundamental problems in the design of the system's internal data directory that associates fragments with storage sites. These problems are further compounded by the common requirement that the partitioning and distribution of objects be transparent to system users and application programs. Centralizing the directory to a special nominated site is undesirable because (1) failure of that site effectively prohibits any distributed transaction processing, and (2) an additional overhead of a directory interrogation is imposed on each transaction. The alternative arrangement of fully replicating the directory at every site is also undesirable as (1) an unreasonable storage burden is imposed on every site, and (2) an exorbitant amount of network traffic will result whenever data is relocated (i.e. every directory copy would have to be updated).

These problems may be solved by partitioning and distributing the directory information on a "needs-to-know" basis. Each site has a restricted view of the rest

---

This work is a synopsis of a doctoral project being undertaken by the author at Monash University, Australia. A more detailed account of this material is given in [1,2].

Permission to copy without fee all or part of this material is granted provided that the copies are not made or distributed for direct commercial advantage, the ACM copyright notice and the title of the publication and its date appear, and notice is given that copying is by permission of the Association for Computing Machinery. To copy otherwise, or to republish, requires a fee and/or specfic permission.

© 1988 ACM 0-89791-245-4/88/0001/0294 $1.50

of the network and of the data objects stored by the visible sites. These proposals define a new class of *Partially Informed Distributed Databases (PIDDB)*. In effect, this proposal partitions the directory information so that sites may need to communicate with other sites in the network to discover the identities and location of those fragments that are not described by the local knowledge. Despite the partial knowledge held at each site, these systems will allow any distributed data object to be located from any site.

The following sections present an overview of the PIDDB class. A more complete description, involving non-trivial formalisms and algorithms, may be found in [1,2]. Models are presented in Section 2 that describe the logical network topology, and the knowledge available to any site. An extension of these models that supports *distributed objects* is outlined in Section 3. The objectives and overview of a distributed algorithm for dynamically determining data locations is presented in Section 4. The relationship of this algorithm to PIDDB query processing is also discussed.

2. NETWORK TOPOLOGY

A logical model of the network topology is proposed below that specifies what kind of information sites possess about the rest of the network and how this information is organized. This model anticipates the development of an efficient and distributed algorithm for dynamically determining data locations. The topology defines the *meta-database* known to each site. It is implicit in the definition of the PIDDB class that no site would know the entire meta-database. The portion known to a site constitutes its *local knowledge view (LKV)*. The proposed topology does not require that sites store any data fragments in order to be able to initiate or execute queries (although their meta knowledge is subject to a series of constraints on the LKV).

The topology partitions the network into sets of neighbours called *N-Sets*. All N-Sets contain at least one site and all sites are assigned to at least one N-Set. Sites in a common N-Set know of each others existence and may possess extensive descriptions of the data fragments possessed by each neighbour, although these descriptions may be incomplete or even null (subject to the constraints on the LKV). At least one site in each N-Set would be nominated as an *entry point*. These sites are distinguished by being known (i.e. name and network address) by sites in other N-Sets. All incoming data location or update requests from outside an N-set would be directed into an entry point site. These sites locally distribute the requests within the N-Set as appropriate. Sites assigned to multiple N-Sets define the overlapping *articulation points* between those sets. Articulation points would typically arise where a site makes frequent access to differing N-Sets so that membership of those sets becomes attractive. Groups of N-sets overlapping in this way define a *neighbourhood*. Articulation points would commonly be entry points to improve the efficiency of the data location procedure.

A network would typically be partitioned into a number of disjoint neighbourhoods. These neighbourhoods must however be connected in some fashion so that the location or existence of remote data can be determined. *Hyper-Sets (H-Sets)* of N-Sets are introduced to provide this connection. H-Sets define the *mappings* of fragment names onto the N-sets possessing replications of those fragments. H-Sets may contain any arbitrary collection of N-Sets and neighbourhoods, however neighbourhoods may not span H-Set boundaries. H-Sets may be nested, but other forms of overlap are not permitted. Nesting would typically be useful in large networks where groups of sites were administered by differing agencies; each H-Set would correspond to an autonomous management domain. Such complex networks require a global H-Set (H_g) that encloses the entire network to ensure that disjoint partitions of knowledge do not occur. Since H_g provides connectivity between disjoint sub-networks, its definition must be known within every H-Set.

The N-Set/H-Set model is suitable for modeling the network topologies commonly encountered in practice (e.g. star, ring, hierarchical). In many cases either N- or H-Sets can be used to model a part of the network. The specific design depends on factors such as the anticipated frequency of access between sets of sites, and on the desired degree of autonomy for such sets. As an example, consider the network of nine sites organized into the logical hierarchy of Figure 1. Many PIDDB representations of this network are possible. One topology, in which all sites are grouped into a single global H-Set H_g is shown in Figure 2a. Sites and N-Sets are represented as solid circles and enclosing ellipses respectively. The articulation points at sites 2, 3 and 5 link the entire network into a single neighbourhood. The N-Set boundaries group together those sites expected to frequently access one another.

The constraints on the LKV require that at least one site in each N-Set possesses a description of the immediately enclosing H-Set. This ensures that all sites can locate each of the other sites in that H-Set. Extending the sample topology to very large networks is, however, problematic. Single H-Set topologies reduce N-Set autonomy as data or topological updates must be acknowledged by large numbers of sites. It is also likely that communications between sites in certain pairs of N-Sets would occur infrequently. These considerations provide the motivation for partitioning the network into *multiple* H-Sets. Such an arrangement minimizes the propagation domain of an update and reduces the amount of information that sites must possess about other portions (i.e. H-Sets) of the

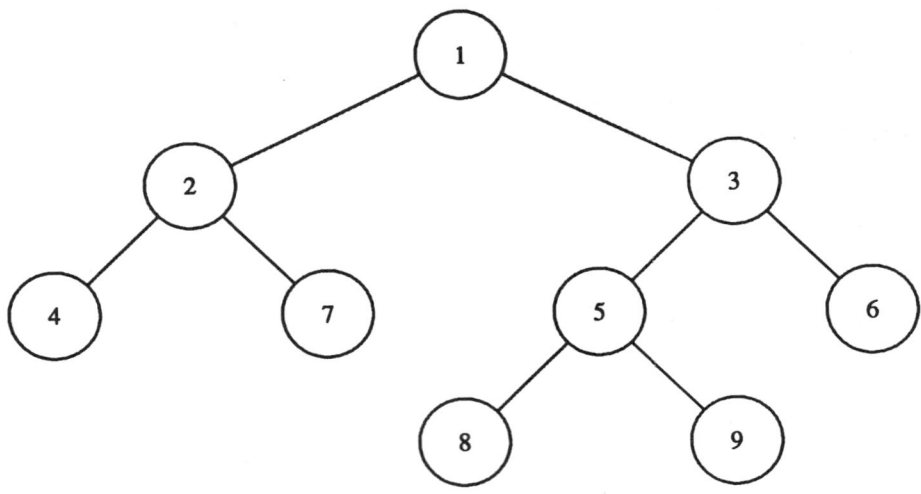

Figure 1: Example of an Hierarchical Network

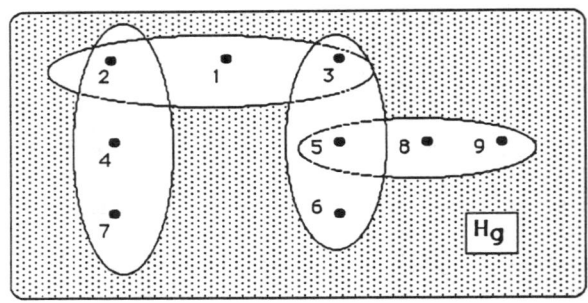

a) Single H-Set Representation

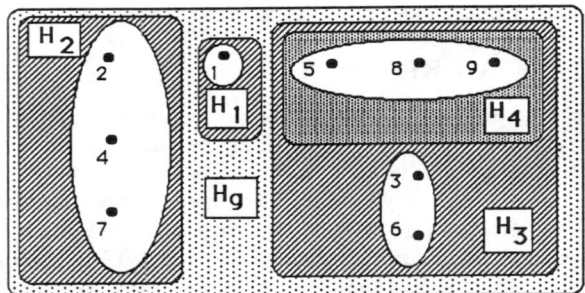

b) Multiple H-Set Representation

Figure 2: Representations of the Hierarchical Network of Figure 1

network. As an example, a multiple H-Set representation of the network of Figure 1 is given in Figure 2b. This topology partitions the network into 5 H-Sets, shown here as shaded regions. H-Sets at the same level of nesting (with respect to H_g) are shaded similarly.

2.1 Gateway N-Sets and the Knowledge Kernel

Each H-Set includes a distinguished gateway N-Set N_g through which all communications with other management domains (i.e. remote H-Sets) are directed. Gateways local to the immediately enclosing H-set (H_l) are denoted N_{gl}; gateways to a remote H-set (H_r) are denoted N_{gr}:

$$N_{gl} \in H_l$$
$$N_{gr} \in H_r$$

The three principal reasons for introducing gateways are: (1) the volume of traffic between H-Sets may be significantly reduced, (2) secure communications may be established between domains (i.e. authentication protocols can be employed between gateway N-Sets), and (3) the characteristics (e.g. speed, storage, communication channels etc.) of the gateway sites can be chosen to avoid communications bottlenecks.

All sites within N_g possess a *knowledge kernel*. This contains information about:

- the local (immediately enclosing) H-Set H_l,
- the set of remote H-Sets knowing H_l,
- the global H-Set H_g,

2.2 Enclosure Hierarchy Trees

The relationships and relative nestings between H-Sets may be described by an *Enclosure Hierarchy Tree (EHT)*. Each node of an EHT represents a specific H-Set and indicates that it contains or *owns* each of the descendant subtrees. N-Sets are not explicitly represented in EHTs. The EHT including H_g spans the entire network and is called the *Global Enclosure Hierarchy Tree (GEHT)*. The GEHT for the sample topology of Figure 2b is shown in Figure 3.

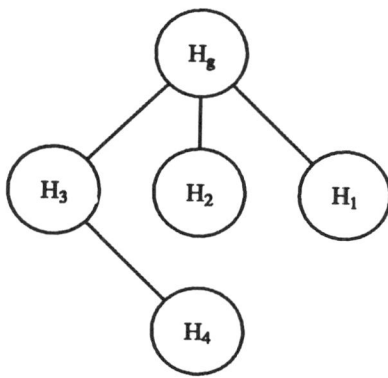

Figure 3: Sample GEHT (Network of Figure 2b)

It is unlikely that any site would know the GEHT. Instead each site possesses a *Local Enclosure Hierarchy Tree (LEHT)* describing only that portion of the topology known locally (i.e. the LEHT defines the LKV). The nodes of an LEHT represent knowledge *about* H-Sets and define *where* this knowledge resides. The relative positions of nodes within an LEHT are consistent with the relative H-Set nestings defined by the GEHT. Individual sites could not otherwise deduce the relationships between the known H-Sets. This information is typically used when determining which remote H-Sets may be able to assist in the refinement of a query. It is also required when changes to the network topology alter the GEHT. Sites informed of the update could not otherwise infer the scope of the change. Eight types of LEHT nodes have been identified representing four different classes of knowledge.

2.3 Network Topology Schemas

The PIDDB topology proposed above is not yet complete enough for the development of operational procedures such as the data location algorithm. An overview of the *conceptual schemas* defining what information is associated with N-Sets and H-Sets, is given below. The schemas are expressed as sets of n-ary tuples of data elements; the ordering of tuples within sets and of elements within tuples is not significant. Underscored elements in the schema definitions indicate that the *name* rather than the *value* of the object is referenced. Some of the parameters included in the schema definitions will not always be available (e.g. status of another site). These parameters are enclosed in square braces ([]) to indicate that their inclusion is *dependent* on their availability.

2.3.1 Notation

Before presenting the detailed schemas, some notation and knowledge operators are required. In addition to the usual structural and value instance information, an object in a PIDDB is not fully described without knowledge of its location. The boolean operator ϕ is useful for expressing or testing this knowledge:

ϕ^n OBJ is *true* if object OBJ is possessed by site S_n.

Another operator, Φ, is a macro that defines the set of sites possessing OBJ.

$$\Phi(OBJ) = \{S_n : \phi^n OBJ\}$$

The relational data model [6,7] is assumed throughout this paper: fragment α of relation x is denoted R_x^α. Two further definitions are required:

$F(R_x)$ The *fragmentation schema* defining the partitioning of relation R_x into the set of fragments $\{R_x^\alpha\}$,

$A(R_x^\alpha)$ The *fragment allocation schema* defining the assignment of fragment R_x^α to its set of storage sites $\Phi(R_x^\alpha)$. This schema also includes the cardinality $|R_x^\alpha|$.

Queries may or may not be defined with respect to these schemas. Queries that are not refined with respect to either schema are *completely unrefined*. Those defined with respect to the fragmentation schema are *partially refined*. Queries that are also defined with respect to the allocation schema are *fully refined*.

The allocation schema does not constitute a fragment directory in the sense described in §1. Rather, this schema *together* with the topological (i.e. N-Set and H-Set schemas) and knowledge models (i.e. LEHT) constitute the distributed directory.

2.3.2 N-Set Schema

Sites possess extensive knowledge about their *neighbours*, limited knowledge about certain other N-Sets, and no knowledge about any other site. Each site S_n in N-Set N_i would typically be described by its communication parameters C_n, usage costs U_n, current status D_n, the set of fragmentation and allocation schemas held by S_n (F_n and A_n respectively), and boolean indicators P_n and E_n that are *true* if S_n is an articulation point and/or an N-Set entry point respectively. Another boolean N_g associated with each N-Set is *true* if N_i is a gateway N-Set. These parameters constitute the schema:

$$N_i = <\underline{N_i}, N_g, N_s>$$

where $\underline{N_i}$ identifies the N-Set and N_s describes the set of sites participating in N_i:

$$N_s = \{<\underline{S_n}, P_n, E_n, [F_n], [A_n], [C_n], [U_n], [D_n]>\}$$

where $\underline{S}_n$ identifies[1] a specific site. F_n and A_n simplify the data location process within an N-Set as all sites know what data their neighbours possess. It is not therefore necessary to explore the local N-Sets during query processing when these elements are available. The policy adopted for inclusion and maintenance of these elements is local to each N-Set and may vary between N-Sets.

2.3.3 H-Set Schema

The fundamental purpose of the H-Set schema is to express the *mappings* of data fragments onto their containing N-Sets. The H-Set schema therefore contains mapping tuples expressing facts such as fragment R_x^α resides in N-Set N_k:

$$<\underline{R}_x^\alpha, \underline{N}_k>$$

The H-Set schema also includes parameters to ensure that the network is both navigatable and maintainable. For example, sites require knowledge of the identities of at least one ancestor[2] H-Set, and each of the descendant H-Sets. The names of these H-Sets are represented by the sets $\underline{H}_a$ and $\underline{H}_d$ respectively. Two further parameters complete the H-Set schema. C_i is a boolean that is *true* if H_i is the local H-Set H_l. N_h identifies the set of N-Sets participating in H_i and is required to distribute updates of the H-Set schema or extension. The complete H-set schema is expressed by the tuple:

$$H_i = <\underline{H}_i, F_i, C_i, \underline{H}_a, \underline{H}_d, N_h>$$

where $\underline{H}_i$ identifies the H-Set, and F_i is the set of tuples associating fragments with their storage N-Sets in H_i.

3. DISTRIBUTED OBJECTS

Large database systems often serve as repositories of information relevant to a number of applications. It is unlikely that all users of such systems would be interested in all of the available data. The *view* concept [7,8] simplifies the apparent structure and contents of the database to include only those portions relevant to an application or a users interest. A view is a description of a *virtual object* that identifies the components of the fundamental *base objects* (e.g. relations) included in the view, and defines how these components are combined to instantiate a virtual object.

Distributed systems introduce additional complexity into the view management problem as view components may be both logically and physically distributed across a computer network. An application of the view concept arises in the PIDDB context as a mechanism for modelling *distributed virtual objects*. A distributed object is an instantiation of a virtual object whose components reside at differing locations. This concept permits agencies to cooperate to "provide" *services* to the rest of the network. A telecommunications administration may, for example, wish to define virtual objects combining parts of, say, its telephony and electronic mail directories. Users may then directly interrogate the integrated directory without knowledge of its structure or distribution. The base objects of such integrated services may be owned by *different* administrations. This class of view is commercially significant as it permits information providers to "repackage" their individual information pools into a number of distinct service offerings that would typically be used and tariffed quite differently.

The network is partitioned into two types of domains with respect to each distributed object:

1. *Service Provider Domains (PDs)* which own some component(s) of the object, and

2. *Subscriber Domains (SDs)* which know of or possess an instantiation of the distributed object.

Distributed objects are indistinguishable from other base objects within the SDs and may be represented via LEHTs in the usual way.

The view defining a distributed object may be arbitrarily complex and may contain other views as subcomponents. The structure of these views is defined by a *dependency* or *view graph*. View graphs are both directed and acyclic. The direction of the edges indicates the nature of the dependencies (i.e. arrow heads point towards the more basic objects). Cycles in this graph would represent *recursive* view definitions that could not be instantiated. An example of a view graph for a distributed object is given in Figure 4. R_a, R_b and R_c are base relations which may reside at differing sites. R_{abc} is a view on these relations (e.g. a natural join following projection or selection over each component). R_{abcd} is another view defined in terms of R_{abc} and R_c. Two nodes in this graph are dependent on R_c illustrating why a tree description would be inadequate.

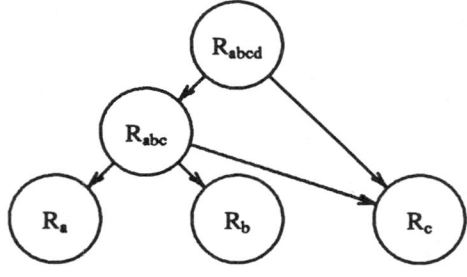

Figure 4: Sample View Graph

---

1. It is implicit that the site name $\underline{S}_n$ is sufficient to uniquely identify a specific network address.
2. An *ancestor* H-Set encloses H_i. Similarly, a *descendant* H-Set is nested within H_i.

The PDs are responsible for ensuring that each of the SDs receive updates whenever (1) a change in a base object causes a resultant change in a distributed object, or (2) the view definition is altered resulting in changes to the distributed object.

4. PIDDB QUERY PROCESSING

The special nature and requirements of PIDDB query processing are identified below by developing the ramifications of the conceptual framework proposed above. The distribution of responsibility for evaluating and combining portions of the input query, and the requirements of the data location algorithm to support it are presented.

4.1 H-Set Decomposition

The PIDDB framework imposes the constraint that all communications between H-Sets must be via their gateway N-Sets, and that these N-Sets are the only ones known to other H-Sets. It is also implicit that sites can access fragments in remote H-Sets *without* knowing their specific storage locations. It is therefore a natural extension of these principles to *partition* queries involving multiple H-Sets into sub-queries that can be independently evaluated within each H-Set. The gateway sites are then responsible for locating and accessing fragments within their local H-Set on behalf of sites in other H-Sets. Query evaluation therefore requires a *master schedule* concerned with finding an optimal strategy for transporting and combining the partial results produced by each participating H-Set. The initial partitioning of the query is called *H-Set decomposition*. One ramification of this decomposition is that the data location algorithm need not refine the locations of remotely owned relations beyond identifying the relevant gateway N-Sets N_{gr}. This also suggests that data location is an independent phase of query processing that terminates within each H-Set before evaluation of the local sub-query commences. While this Section is predominantly concerned with the data location algorithm, it is necessary to consider its relationship to the larger query processing problem. An operational basis for managing the generation, evaluation and combination of the partial queries is proposed below. The initiating site S_{init} coordinates the overall activity in this scenario and is responsible for:

1. performing the initial H-Set query decomposition,
2. distributing the partial queries to the gateway N-Sets of the identified H-Sets,
3. determining the locations of each of the data objects required for the local sub-query executable within H_l,
4. evaluating the local sub-query,
5. planning and executing a master schedule for distributing and combining the partial results produced within each H-Set. (This step could be delegated to N_{gl} to minimize interactions within H_l.)

An example of H-Set decomposition in PIDDB query processing is demonstrated in Figure 5. Messages associated with data location and master schedule

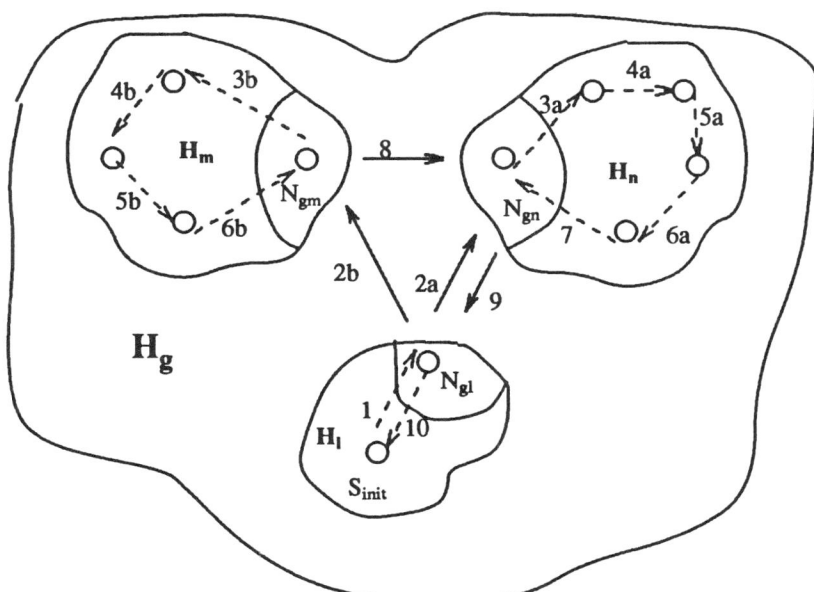

Figure 5: H-Set Query Decomposition

coordination are not shown. Only gateway N-Sets are identified; other N-Set boundaries within each H-Set are ignored for simplicity. Dashed arcs represent the optimal query evaluation sequences within each H-Set. Solid arcs represent the master schedule and illustrate the distribution and combination of the partial queries and results respectively. The numbers on the arcs indicate the chronological order of the messages. Messages distinguished by lower case letters are issued simultaneously.

The partial queries would typically be distributed simultaneously (messages 2 in the Figure). Each H-Set assisting H_l invokes the data location algorithm within its local gateway N-Set to plan and then execute an optimal schedule for evaluating the local sub-query. This is represented by messages 3a to 7 and 3b to 6b in the example. The partial results are then combined according to the master schedule planned within H_l. This would typically require exchanging additional messages with H_l to report the cardinalities of the partial results. (The master sequence cannot be completely planned until this information becomes available. The coordination messages reporting cardinalities and returning instructions are omitted from the Figure for clarity.) In the example scenario, it is assumed that the partial result produced in H_m is smaller than that produced within H_n, and that the final result is significantly smaller than either partial result. The optimal strategy is therefore to send the result produced in H_m to H_n (message 8), and then to return the final result to H_l (message 9). Message 10 relays the final result to S_{init}.

4.2 Objectives of Data Location

The PIDDB query processing paradigm proposed above provides a basis for defining the objectives of the data location algorithm:

1. to identify the set of relevant fragments possessed within H_l (i.e. fragments that are implicitly referenced by the user's global query),
2. to determine the specific storage sites and cardinalities of each relevant fragment in H_l,
3. to determine which remote H-Sets contain sites owning relevant relations[3] that are not available within H_l.

Many heuristic techniques for finding an acceptably efficient[4] query evaluation strategy are described in the literature and are suitable for evaluating the partial queries within each H-Set. Early examples, based on semi-join techniques [5,9], include the SDD-1 query processor [10] and the techniques developed by Hevner et. al. [11,12]. More recent developments were described by Chiu and Ho [13], Chu and Hurley [14] and by Lafortune and Wong [15]. The fragment cardinalities obtained during data location are required by these techniques to plan an efficient schedule for transferring partial results between sites within an H-Set. This schedule cannot be planned until all of the required locations and cardinalities have been determined. Data location is therefore an independent and preliminary phase of query processing that completes within each H-Set before evaluation of the local sub-query commences.

4.3 Phases of Data Location

The global query, denoted gq, explicitly references a set of relations. Two refined representations of gq, namely fq and aq, are proposed. The canonical fragmentation query fq is derived by analysing the relevant fragmentation schemas to replace each relation in gq by an appropriate set of data fragments. The canonical allocation query aq is derived by augmenting fq with additional information that defines the cardinality and location of each relevant fragment. The data location problem can be phrased in this context as the task of refining gq to fq and then refining fq to aq.

The fragmentation schemas required to produce fq may not all be locally available at S_{init}. It is therefore necessary to locate the required fragmentation schemas before the locations of specific fragments can be determined. There are therefore two logically distinct and serial phases of data location:

- a preliminary *knowledge acquisition phase* (*K*-Phase) during which the locations of the required fragmentation schemas are determined, and
- a *sites identification phase* (*S*-Phase) during which the identities, locations and cardinalities of the relevant fragments are determined.

The *K*-Phase determines where the required fragmentation schemas are possessed. It is implicitly assumed by invoking the *S*-Phase at these sites that they can identify and locate the required fragments. The proposed data location algorithm relies on the observation that sites capable of identifying any fragments implied by gq must also be capable of determining the locations and cardinalities of those fragments. Theorem 1 states this observation more formally. The knowledge and topological models proposed in [1] are used to prove this theorem in [2].

---

3. The set of relevant *fragments* implied by these *relations* are determined by the instances of the data location algorithm in the remote H-Sets.
4. It is typically necessary to employ *acceptably efficient* schedules as discovery of an *optimal* solution is often intractable.

Theorem 1: Refinement Capabilities

Suppose that, as a result of the *K*-Phase, S_{init} determines that S_n possesses each of the fragmentation schemas necessary to refine a subset gq' of gq to fq'. Then if S_n is capable of refining gq' to fq' it must also be capable of refining fq' to aq'.

4.4 Query Taxonomy

A number of distinct query versions are appropriate as data location proceeds. A total of 16 query versions in four classes have been identified. This taxonomy provides a precise basis for the development of the *K*-Phase and *S*-Phase data location algorithms. The *input* class contains a single member that is the user's input query. The next two classes cater for the requirements of the data location algorithm: the *knowledge* and *sites* queries cater for the *K*-Phase and *S*-Phase respectively. The final *evaluation* class is concerned with H-Set decomposition for query evaluation. An overview of the various query versions is given in Table 1. All of these queries are generated at S_{init}, except fq_j^s and aq_j^s which are generated at the sites refining gq_j^s during the *S*-Phase of data location.

The relationships between these queries are illustrated as a directed graph in Figure 6 where each node represents a specific query. The edges identify the specific dependencies: the query at the head of an edge is derived from and generated after the query at the tail. gq_{init}^s is, for example, a subset of gq^{sl} which in turn is generated using the information contained in gq and gq^k.

The fundamental objective of data location can be restated in terms of this taxonomy as the task of transforming the input query gq to the local allocation schema sub-query aq^l and the remote global schema sub-queries gq^r that are sufficiently detailed to enable planning an optimal execution strategy.

4.5 Overview of Data Location

Theorem 1 provides an operational basis for the data location algorithm. A series of 14 conceptual

\multicolumn{3}{c}{**TABLE 1: PIDDB Query Taxonomy**}		
Class	**Query**	**Content**
Input	gq	The user's input query defined on the global schema.
Knowledge	gq^k	*K*-Phase input version of gq identifying each relevant relation
	gq^{sl}	*K*-Phase output/*S*-Phase input identifying relations with N-Sets in the local H-Set H_l.
	gq^{sr}	*K*-Phase output identifying relations with remote H-Sets H_r.
Sites	gq_{init}^s	The portion of gq^{sl} refinable by S_{init} (i.e. each of the relevant fragmentation schemas implied by gq_{init}^s has been determined by the *K*-Phase to be possessed by S_{init}).
	gq_j^s	The portion of gq^{sl} refinable by N-Set $N_j \in H_l$ (i.e. each of the relevant fragmentation schemas implied by gq_j^s has been determined by the *K*-Phase to be possessed within N_j).
	fq_{init}^s	The partially refined version of gq_{init}^s.
	fq_j^s	The partially refined version of gq_j^s.
	aq_{init}^s	The fully refined version of fq_{init}^s.
	aq_j^s	The fully refined version of fq_j^s.
	aq^s	The aggregate of the aq_j^s and aq_{init}^s generated within H_l.
Evaluation	gq^l	The portion of gq such that each of the fragments implied by the relations referenced in gq^l is possessed by some site in H_l.
	gq^r	The portion of gq such that each of the fragments implied by the relations referenced in gq^r is possessed by a site within some remote H-Set H_r.
	gq_y^r	The portion of gq^r refinable within remote H-Set H_y.
	fq^l	Partially refined version of gq^l.
	aq^l	Fully refined version of fq^l.

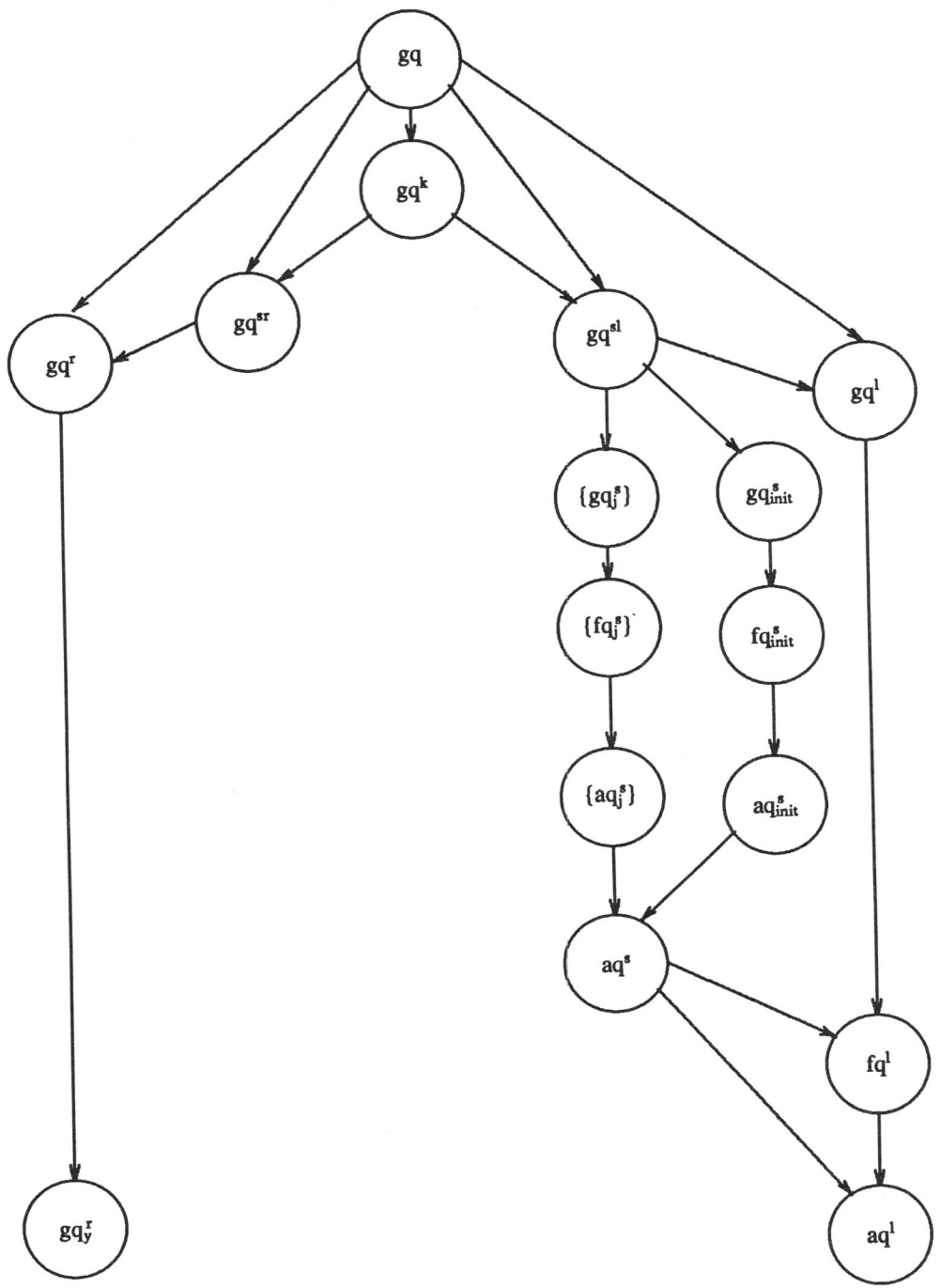

Figure 6: Dependencies Between PIDDB Queries

algorithms that collectively constitute the data location algorithm are presented in [2]. A simplified overview (incorporating both the *K*-Phase and *S*-Phase) is given below.

4.5.1 Simplified Algorithm

The algorithm demonstrates the application of part of the proposed query taxonomy and is concerned with identifying the local sub-query gq^{sl} and with locating the fragments implied by it:

1. for each R_x named in gq^k such that $\neg \phi^{init} F(R_x)$, S_{init} uses its local knowledge view to determine a set of candidate N-Sets possessing the relevant fragmentation schemas:

$$\{N_j \in H_l: \exists\, S_n \in N_j: \phi^n F(R_x)\} \quad (4.5a)$$

   Hence refine gq^k to gq^{sl}.

2. decompose gq^{sl} into a set of partial queries such that each partial query can be fully refined within one of the identified N_j:

$$\{gq_j^s \subseteq gq^{sl}: \bigcup_j gq_j^s = gq^{sl}\} \quad (4.5b)$$

   on the basis that for every R_x named in gq_j^s

$$\exists\, S_n \in N_j: \phi^n F(R_x) \quad (4.5c)$$

3. distribute the partial queries gq_j^s to their respective N-Sets.

4. await the partial responses aq_j^s and assemble the final result aq^s.

Step 1 identifies that portion of the global query refinable within H_l. Step 2 defines an *N-Set query decomposition* that identifies the portion of gq^{sl} refinable by each N_j. The criteria for N-Set selection in given in expression 4.5a. The constraint defined in expression 4.5b ensures that each relation in gq^{sl} is represented in some partial query; the constraint of expression 4.5c reflects the N-Set selection criteria of expression 4.5a.

This algorithm assumes that S_{init} has a sufficient local knowledge view to complete the N-Set decomposition of step 2. This is <u>not</u> necessarily true in general: it is the task of the preliminary *K-Phase* identified above to collect sufficient knowledge before attempting N-Set decomposition.

Sites in the selected N-Sets $\{N_j\}$ fully refine the decomposed query gq_j^s by applying Theorem 1. An overview of their algorithm is (note that "local" and H_l are with respect to the site in N_j, not the originating site):

1. use the locally held fragmentation schemas to refine gq_j^s to fq_j^s.

2. refine fq_j^s to aq_j^s by determining the locations and cardinalities of each R_x^α named in fq_j^s such that,

   a. if $\phi^l A(R_x^\alpha)$ then, by definition, $\Phi(R_x^\alpha)$ and $|R_x^\alpha|$ are available; fq_j^s may be refined to aq_j^s with respect to R_x^α.

   b. if $\neg \phi^l A(R_x^\alpha)$ then request $A(R_x^\alpha)$ from another site in H_l (using a description of H_l to identify the assisting site); fq_j^s may now be refined to aq_j^s with respect to R_x^α.

3. return the partial result aq_j^s to S_{init}.

An example of the manner in which the complete data location algorithm would explore the PIDDB topology is given in Figure 7. N_i and N_j represent two typical N-Sets local to S_{init}. If data location cannot be completed within these N-Sets than the neighbourhoods within H_l are searched. NH_l and NH_a represent the local and some other neighbourhood respectively within H_l. If these are also found to be inadequate then a wider domain search involving other H-Sets is invoked. H_m

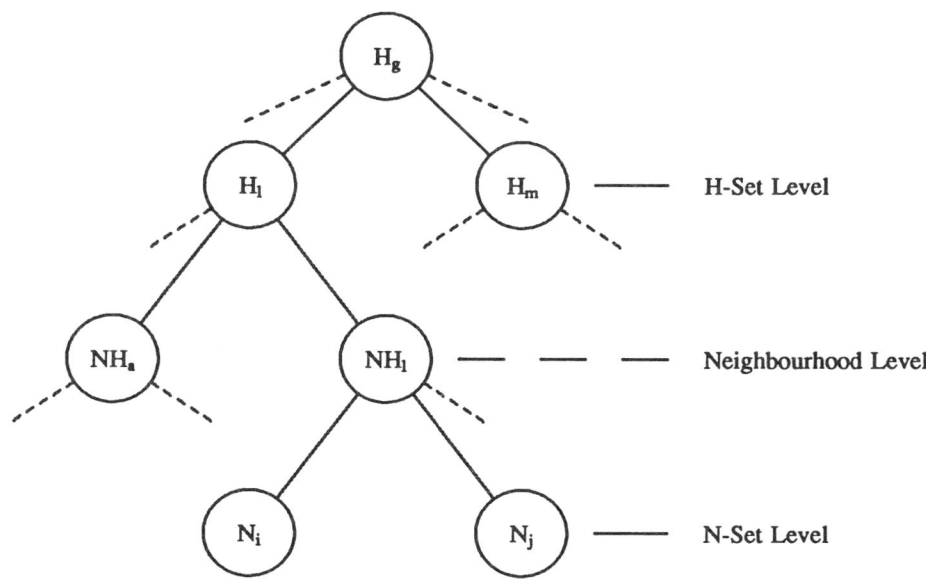

Figure 7: Overview - Levels of Data Location Search

represents another typical H-Set that may be investigated. Finally, if the available or acquired knowledge proves inadequate then the global H-Set H_g enables a systematic and exhaustive search of the entire topology to be undertaken.

4.6 Overview of S-Phase Algorithms

A simplified overview of the S-Phase algorithms is presented below. This overview develops steps 2 to 4 of the simplified data location algorithm for S_{init}:

1. initially decompose gq^{sl} into two components:
    a. $gq^s_{init} \subseteq gq^{sl}$ such that for every R_x named in gq^s_{init}, $\phi^{init} F(R_x)$
    b. gq' such that $gq' = gq^{sl} - gq^s_{init}$
2. locally refine gq^s_{init} to aq^s_{init}
3. perform N-Set decomposition on gq' to produce $\{gq^s_j\}$ and distribute sub-queries to the corresponding N_j
4. await aq^s_j responses, combine with aq^s_{init} and assemble aq^s. Delete the corresponding gq^s_j from $\{gq^s_j\}$ as each response is received
5. terminate when $\{gq^s_j\} = \emptyset$

Step 1a identifies those portions of gq^{sl} refinable by S_{init}. Step 1b finds the residue refinable by other N_j. This residue is (N-Set) decomposed in step 3 into the portions relevant to specific N-Sets. While many partitions may be possible, it is implicit that the *optimal* partitioning would be found. This minimizes the number of N-Sets involved by selecting those containing several relevant fragments in preference to those containing only a single fragment.

5. CONCLUSION

A model for managing very large distributed databases has been presented. This model involves restricting the meta knowledge available to any site and defines a new class of Partially Informed Distributed Databases (PIDDB). This class is fully transparent with respect to data fragmentation, location and replication. It is inherently suitable for very large systems and preserves the autonomy of sub-domains. No assumptions are made regarding the initial or current allocation of data fragments to sites so that replications may readily be created or deleted within their owning domains.

A mechanism has been described that permits information providers to cooperate to define *distributed virtual objects* using components of their individually owned objects. These objects are instantiated and distributed as snapshots.

The relationship of data location to PIDDB query processing has been developed and a mechanism for coordinating query evaluation has been proposed. It was shown that differing versions of the initial global query exist as data location proceeds. A descriptive query taxonomy was introduced to provide a concrete basis for the development of the data location algorithm. A total of 16 different query versions have been identified.

Data location has been found to consist of two distinct and serial phases: a knowledge acquisition phase (K-Phase) and a sites determination phase (S-Phase). The K-Phase is concerned with determining which domains (local N-Sets or remote H-Sets) contain sites possessing the fragmentation schemas relevant to the global query. The S-Phase is concerned with applying the knowledge acquired during the K-Phase to identifying, locating and determining the cardinalities of the relevant fragments. Conceptual algorithms have been presented that define the basis of the procedures required to develop a prototype system.

6. ACKNOWLEDGEMENT

The support of Telecom Australia to undertake this work is appreciated. The permission of the Director Research, Telecom Australia to publish this paper is acknowledged. Thanks are also due to Dr Ken J. McDonell, Department of Computer Science, Monash University, for his numerous constructive suggestions during the preparation of this paper.

7. REFERENCES

1. M. Blakey, Partially Informed Distributed Databases: Conceptual Framework And Knowledge Model, Tech. Rep. 80, Dept. of Comp. Science, Monash Univ., Melbourne, Australia, Dec., 1986.

2. M. Blakey, Partially Informed Distributed Databases: Data Location Algorithm, Tech. Rep. 87/85, Dept. of Comp. Science, Monash Univ., Melbourne, Australia, May, 1987.

3. C. Mohan, B. Lindsay and R. Obermarck, Transaction Management in the R* Distributed Data Base Management System, Report RJ 5037, IBM Thomas J. Watson Research Center, Yorktown Heights, New York, Feb., 1986.

4. J. B. Rothnie, Jr., P. A. Bernstein, S. Fox, N. Goodman, M. Hammer, T. A. Landers, C. Reeve, D. W. Shipman and E. Wong, Introduction to a System for Distributed Databases (SDD-1), *ACM Trans. on Database Sys. 5* , 1, (1980), 1-17.

5. S. Ceri and G. Pelagatti, *Distributed Databases: Principles and Systems*, McGraw-Hill, New York, 1985.

6. E. F. Codd, A Relational Model of Data for Large Shared Data Banks, *Comm. ACM 13* , 6, (1970), 377-387.

7. C. J. Date, *An Introduction to Database Systems, Volume 1, 4th Edition*, Addison-Wesley, Reading, Massachusetts, 1986.

8. J. D. Ullman, *Principles of Database Systems*, Comp. Science Press, Rockville, Maryland, 1982.

9. P. A. Bernstein and D. M. Chiu, Using Semi-joins to Solve Relational Queries, *J. ACM 28*, 1, (Jan. 1981), 25-40.

10. P. A. Bernstein, N. Goodman, E. Wong, C. L. Reeve and J. B. J. Rothnie, Query Processing in a System for Distributed Databases (SDD-1), *ACM Trans. on Database Sys. 6*, 4, (1981), 602-625.

11. A. Hevner and S. B. Yao, Query Processing in Distributed Database Systems, *IEEE Trans. on Software Eng. SE-5*, 3, (May 1979), 177-187.

12. P. M. G. Apers, A. R. Hevner and S. B. Yao, Optimization Algorithm for Distributed Queries, *IEEE Trans. on Software Eng. SE-9*, 6, (Jan. 1983), 57-68, IEEE.

13. D. M. Chiu and Y. C. Ho, A Methodology for Interpreting Tree Queries Into Optimal Semi-join Expressions, *Proc. ACM SIGMOD International Conf. on Management of Data*, Ann Arbor, Michigan, ACM, New York, Apr., 1980, 169-178.

14. W. Chu and P. Hurley, Optimal Query Processing for Distributed Database Systems, *IEEE Trans. on Computers C-31*, 9, (Sep. 1982), 835-850.

15. S. Lafortune and E. Wong, A State Transition Model for Distributed Query Processing, *ACM Trans. on Database Sys. 11*, 3, (Sep. 1986), 294-322.

A Threaded/Flow Approach to Reconfigurable Distributed Systems and Service Primitives Architectures

Lester F. Ludwig

Bell Communications Research
Red Bank, New Jersey

ABSTRACT

This paper discusses a methodology for managing the assembly, control, and disassembly of large numbers of independent small-scale configurations within large-scale reconfigurable distributed systems. The approach is targeted at service primitives architectures for enhanced telecommunications networks, but can apply to more general settings such as multi-tasking supercomputers and network operations systems.* Study of the methods presented here was a key motivation in founding the Bell Communications Research *Integrated Media Architecture Laboratory (IMAL)* [1].

The Threaded/Flow approach uses data-flow constructs to assemble higher level functions from other distributed functions and resources with arbitrary degrees of decentralization. Equivalence between *algorithms* and *hard and virtual resources* is accomplished via threaded-interpretive constructs. Function autonomy, concurrency, conditional branching, pipelining, and setup/execution interaction are implicitly supported. Some elementary performance comparisons are argued.

This work is motivated by telecommunications applications involving coordinated multiple-media in open architectures supporting large numbers of users and outside service vendors. In such networks it is desired that services may be flexibly constructed by the network, service vendors, or by users themselves from any meaningful combination of elementary primitives and previously defined services. Reliability, billing, call progress, real-time user control, and network management functions must be explicitly supported. These needs are handled with apparent high performance by the approach.

1. INTRODUCTION

This paper discusses a methodology for managing the assembly, control, and disassembly of large numbers of independent small-scale configurations within large-scale reconfigurable distributed systems. The methods are targeted at service primitives architectures for enhanced telecommunications networks discussed at the end of the paper. However, the approach also applies to more general settings such as multi-tasking supercomputers and network operations systems as well as very general settings involving a functionally-distributed system which is reconfigurable.

The approach employs a functional substrate which equates hard resources, virtual resources, and algorithms. This permits an existing service (typically an algorithm) to be freely combined with resources of different types in a unified way; in fact, services and resources are managed and allocated in the same basic manner. A system for fetching service descriptions from databases and constructing data-flows between named entities provides the basic foundation for the method. A named entity is either a resource (controlled by a resource manager) or another algorithm which may itself control other algorithms and resources. A given entity may exist and execute its tasks anywhere in the network and can itself be of a distributed nature. Branching, concurrency, pipelining, and arbitrary degrees of decentralization are naturally supported. It is straightforward to pipeline the setup and execution phases of the data-flow so that parts of the data-flow which are already set up may execute as remaining parts are themselves being set up; this permits conditional setup of a data-flow as a function of events encountered in earlier parts of its execution. Since an existing stand-alone service can be linked to (i.e., peer connections) or included in (i.e., hierarchical connections) another service, the system acts very much like a threaded interpretive language. It is also straightforward to replace service description fetches from databases with user downloads, permitting user definition of services from service primitives. Filters to preserve integrity of the network will require straightforward design but are not explicitly considered here to limit the discussion.

The approach presented here was developed for use in ISDN prior to the CCITT standards that established ISDN as it is recognized today. It differs somewhat in style from conventional trends in distributed processing since the key application concerns control in the context of extremely large-scale telecommunications (campus-wide, city-wide, or nation-wide) networks. The emphasis is on executions of well-defined control procedures rather than execution of arbitrary user programs.

1.1 Need For Service Primitives In Advanced Telecommunications Networks

The main reasons for resorting to a service primitives approach in a telecommunications network are the potential combinatoric complexity of service details, evolution of services in un foreseen directions, and a need for simple ways of linking existing services and and other functional elements to create new expanded services.

---

* *Most of this work was performed in 1982 and refined from 1983 - 1986 while the author was at U. C. Berkeley.*

Permission to copy without fee all or part of this material is granted provided that the copies are not made or distributed for direct commercial advantage, the ACM copyright notice and the title of the publication and its date appear, and notice is given that copying is by permission of the Association for Computing Machinery. To copy otherwise, or to republish, requires a fee and/or specific permission.

© 1988 ACM 0-89791-245-4/88/0001/0306 $1.50

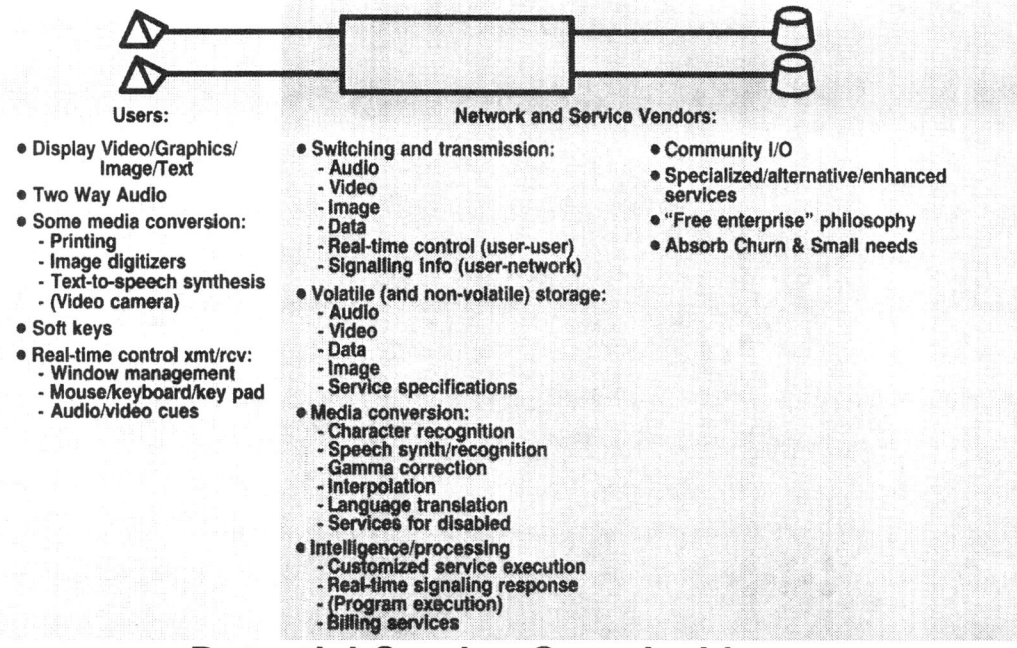

Potential Service Complexities
Figure 1

Figure 1 illustrates the potential service combinatorics. Each of the user, network, and service vendor domains is predicting and working toward support of a number of telecommunications features as shown. It is startling to notice how astronomical the potential combinations of "reasonable" user expectations for telecommunications might be. It is impossible to address these sophistications and combinations using the existing methodology of monolithic software generics and hardware upgrades oriented around one additional single-feature service at a time. In addition, it is natural to expect services to become linked or incorporated into others. For example, users may subscribe to automated calendar management services or have one in their own network-accessible systems. A service vendor could link these with a network-provided call forwarding service to form a meeting scheduling service; subscribers could name meeting participants and constraints and the automated service would forward potential dates and places to participants, optimize, and finally distribute word of the meeting time and place as well as supporting documentation using call and mail utilities. Later, another service vendor may link this meeting scheduling service with a travel booking service to automatically arrange transportation. From the user viewpoint, it is natural to expect that such capabilities should be made available from an advanced communications and applications environment.

The highly succinct explanations above illustrate that the key to managing the immense possibilities within future telecommunications networks is a flexible, powerful, and simple-to-use service primitives system. A reasonable set of goals for such a service primitive system include:

1. Span the possible service combinatorics made possible by technology, including the management and linking of simultaneous calls;
2. Support simple ways of linking existing services and other functional elements;
3. Provide monitoring, billing, and reliable failure recovery functions;
4. Provide ways for the network, its users, or outside service vendors to create their own services in an open architecture.

The service primitives solution suggested in this paper uses an architecture for the direct implementation of data-flow descriptions of services. An example of such a description is shown in Figure 2. Each named process can be an elementary resource function a service element (i.e., raw resource functions with controlling programs), or a full stand-alone service. Because of this, what is viewed as a fundamental "service primitive" can be quite arbitrary: they could be any subset of the possible collections of raw resource functions, explicitly constructed primitive service elements, or existing stand-alone services. This allows a network or service architect to

- A data flow description of transactions and interconnections between entities governed by named servers

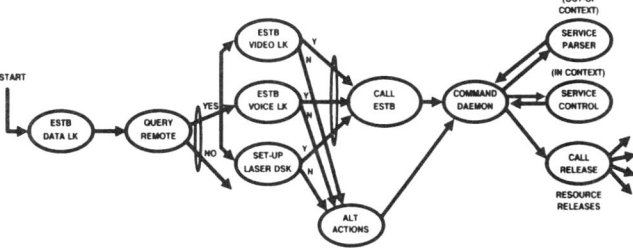

- Each entity is either a "process" or a "resource"
- Each process may have subprocess (specified at lower levels)

Service Descriptions
Figure 2

experiment with custom designed collections of service primitives which may be freely modified. Because of this, the suggested approach is actually a generalized service primitives architecture; in fact, it is a *programmable services primitives engine* on a network scale with explicit attention given to architectural, operations, maintenance, administrative, fault-tolerance, failure recovery, billing, and monitoring design issues that are relevant to large-scale network implementations.

Rather than naming specific primitives explicitly as has been suggested in other service primitives methods, this approach only needs to explicitly define and implement the following elements:

1. Service description database system;
2. Service Execution Coordinators (SECs) and their servers;
3. Resource managers;
4. Control messages and their precise formats;
5. Overall systems management utilities;
6. Monitoring and reporting utilities.

With this substrate, creation of explicit service primitives and services themselves can be done with very short "program-like" files which are easy to create and change. This approach naturally permits easy introduction and evolution of service primitives. It also lends itself well to laboratory experimentation.

1.2 Strategy of the Paper

Figure 3 illustrates the evolution of the ideas as developed in this paper. The development is structured as follows:

1. Drawing from threaded-interpretive language ideas [2], a generic method for constructing functions from resources and previously created functions is developed. The method employs two parts: (1) descriptions of particular configurations within the reconfigurable system and (2) the passing of parameters, files, or software to specific functional elements in the configuration. *This method permits functions to be associated in a well-defined manner with linguistic descriptions, but does not provide a means of handling the actual assembly or disassembly of the functions it concerns.*

2. Threaded-interpretive language ideas are then used a second time; here they are coupled with data-flow concepts [3,4,5,6] to create a specific means of handling data-flow type subroutines. The result is used, subject to the structure of configuration description method just discussed, to create a means for the assembly and disassembly of the configurations.

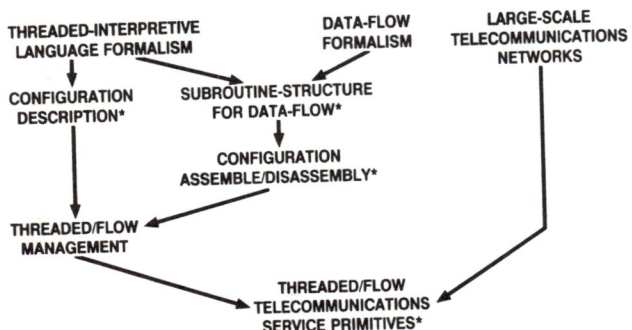

Development Of The Control Synthesis. The Author Views Items Denoted (*) As New Work In The Area
Figure 3

3. The two items listed above are united to create an overall method for managing the assembly, control, and disassembly of large numbers of independent small-scale configurations within large-scale reconfigurable distributed systems. The approach permits arbitrary degrees of decentralization. It also permits configurations to be partially assembled, used as such, and then continue assembly/disassembly steps as a function of the outcomes of this usage (i.e., assembly, usage, and disassembly may be freely pipelined). *The development to this point is general, applying to settings such as multi-tasking supercomputers, enhanced telecommunications networks, and network operations systems.* The approach to this point is entitled a "Threaded/Flow" approach for lack of more creative thoughts.

4. The abstract Threaded flow approach is combined with perspectives concerning large-scale telecommunications networks to form a service primitives method for enhanced telecommunications networks. Discussion of full detail is somewhat suppressed here in view of the audience and potential legal and proprietary issues currently under consideration.

Most of the paper focuses on the abstract Threaded/Flow approach. The items listed above are supplemented with remarks on performance, server design, and analytical study. With the exception of the analytically-oriented Sections 6 and 8, the level of this paper is comparable to that of technical introductions to the OSI reference model.

In this paper a number of special terms are defined and used in subsequent discussion. These terms are printed in **bold type** where they are first mentioned and defined.

2. CONFIGURATIONS WITHIN A LARGE-SCALE DISTRIBUTED SYSTEM

Figure 4 illustrates the basic setting, i.e., a large-scale reconfigurable system with distributed **functional elements.** The functional elements are treated as shared resources which are allocated by one or more **servers.** Each server may administer multiple functional elements. The functional elements may be either hard or virtual resources. Servers allocate these resources, in accordance with currently active network management policies, to a specific task on the basis of **resource requests.** In particular, each specific task will require one or more resources which must be arranged and interconnected with information flows. A specific arrangement and interconnection is termed a **configuration.** The large-scale reconfigurable system exists so that configurations can be assembled on request from the pool of available functional elements, applied to serve a specific task, and then dismantled to free resources for subsequent tasks. In particular it is assumed the large scale system can support a large number of such configurations simultaneously and that most of these configurations will be created, operated, and dismantled independently from one another. Figure 4a shows the overall collection of resources and servers, while Figures 4b and 4c illustrate two possible sets of active configurations. The collection of active configurations present at a given instant may be viewed as the **configuration state** of the large-scale reconfigurable system. Hence, Figures 4b and 4c illustrate two possible configuration-states.

2.1 Uniqueness & Operations On Configuration-States

To clarify terminology, it is required that a given resource may only be employed in at most one configurations. Two or more configurations can be **merged** to form a new configuration at which time the original configurations involved are no longer separately recognized as a feature of the configuration-state; i.e., a merger results in a change of configuration-state. Two or

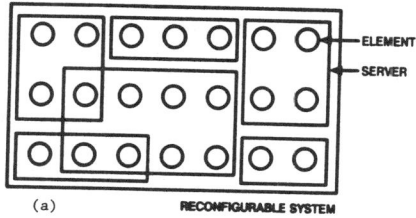

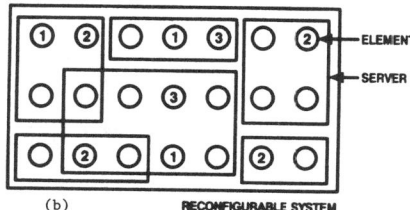

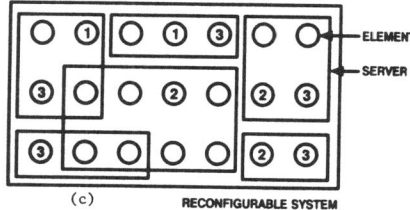

Independent Configurations Within A Reconfigurable System: (a) Setting, (b) A Configuration State, (c) Another Configuration State
Figure 4

more configurations may also be linked together at higher levels but such an arrangement will not be viewed as affecting the configuration-state.

2.2 Configuration Servers

In general, the large-scale reconfigurable system will be able to realize a large number of possible configurations. Also in general, and in most cases by design, the large scale system will be able to support multiple independent copies of the same configuration. Thus, if the admissible configurations are $C_1, C_2, \ldots C_K$, there can be n_1 copies of configuration C_1, n_2 copies of C_2, ..., and n_k copies of C_k all active at a given instant, subject to resource limitations:

$$(n_1, n_2, \cdots, n_k) \in L$$

where L is some set of admissible configuration states (mathematically, L is a subset of the collection of non-negative integer-valued k-tuples Z_+^k).

The outside world presents the large-scale reconfigurable system with requests for configurations. Assumed here is that these requests are largely independent of one another and that each configuration is limited to employing only a small fraction of the resources available in the system. These assumptions validate the need for **configuration servers**, i.e., entities which accept or reject configuration requests based on the current configuration state. An accepted request is passed to resource servers in the form of resource requests (which are translated into actual resource allocations by the resource servers). This is illustrated in Figure 5. It is noted that the configuration server may not have full information of the configuration state; more than likely it will work from simplified information provided by the resource servers.

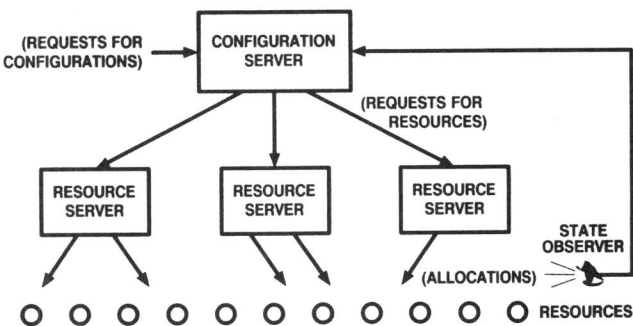

Configuration Server Setting
Figure 5

2.3 Hierarchical Features

The purpose of configurations is to implement higher level functions. That is, each configuration performs a function itself, comparable to the functions provided by the functional elements themselves, but with more sophistication. For convenience call the functions provided by configurations **configuration functions**. At this point two key observations are relevant:

1. Since both configurations and functional elements implement functions, configuration functions and functional elements may be viewed as being equivalent except for the level of sophistication;

2. Just as functional elements may be brought together to form configurations, it is also possible to construct configurations out of configurations themselves.

These two observations may be combined to yield third and fourth observations:

3. The collection of configuration functions together with functional elements can be used as an extended collection of elements, from which higher level configurations may be created.

4. This process can be iterated as follows:

    - Define functional elements as "level.0" configuration functions
    - For K = 1, 2, 3.. - define **"level.K" configurations** as configurations created from the pool of resources consisting of "level.K-1", "level.K-2", ... "level.0" configuration functions which include at least one "level.K-1" configuration function.

In this way, just as in structured programming, Lego-blocks,* or an Erector-Set,* raw functions at any level of sophistication can be drawn upon in a unified way to construct more sophisticated configurations.

The nature of the fourth observation is not unlike that of a threaded interpretive language. The resulting possible constructions are illustrated in Figure 6. For the moment a "level.K" configuration can be thought of as being administered by **"level.K" configuration servers**, an artificial concept to be used temporarily.

It is explicitly noted that the layering discussed here results from a general hierarchical construction *and has nothing to do with the seven-layer OSI reference model.*

---

* American children's toys featuring elements which can be assembled in easily nested modules.

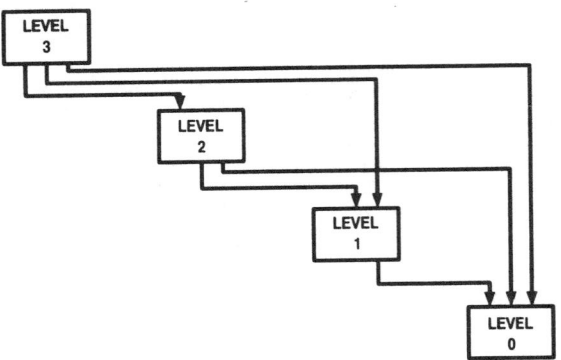

Hierarchy With Triangular Connectivity
Figure 6

2.4 Naming Complexities

For each value of K=0,1,2, ··· let there be N_K different "level.K" configuration functions. Then a fully capable "level.K" configuration server must be internally aware of each of the

$$\sum_{i=0}^{K-1} N_i$$

different configuration functions available to it, yet deal with requests for only N_K types of configuration functions. This suggests an implementation strategy for controlling complexity as illustrated in Figure 7. A simple database recognizes function names and routes requests to configuration servers of an appropriate level. These configuration servers need only worry about a few (i.e., N_K at level K) configuration descriptions. This conceptual structure may be used either directly or indirectly in implementing user interfaces and/or look-ahead pipelining during configuration set-up (to be discussed later).

Definition Management
Figure 7

3. CONFIGURATION ASSEMBLY

Configuration functions are an important advantage offered by a reconfigurable system. However, these functions are only available after a configuration has been assembled. Further, unless configurations are disassembled after their use by the requester, resources will be wasted and assembly of configurations will soon be impossible. Thus, the control required for the assembly and disassembly of configurations is of key importance for realization of this concept. In addition, it is naive to believe that large-scale reconfigurable systems could be well centralized, especially if subject to any reasonable amount of evolution or change. Although this paper targets large-scale reconfigurable systems that are decentralized, it is natural to suspect that almost all practical large-scale reconfigurable systems will have to be at least somewhat decentralized. It is here that data-flow like constructs are very useful. As it turns out, the resulting features made possible by decentralized assembly control have some interesting potential performance advantages in many situations which can be well characterized. As a result, potential exists for well-defined design principles concerning degrees of decentralization appropriate for a given situation.

Consider a request for a "level.K" configuration function by a user of the large-scale reconfigurable system. Depending on implementation, the user may or may not specify the precise level of the function. Further, the level may or may not be useful in administering assembly of the requested configuration.

It is assumed that full information describing how each configuration is to be assembled is represented as software files to permit easy evolution and change. The full information describing how each configuration is to be assembled is called a **configuration assembly description** and is assumed to be stored in databases that are made available to configuration servers. Other arrangements are possible, including one where users are free to provide this full description themselves.

The goal is to create a mechanism which simplifies configuration description software as much as possible yet operates with high performance in an environment where configuration functions (at least a "level.0") are distributed. The suggested approach is to use a data-flow like substrate between configuration servers at all levels. This data-flow substrate provides a message-passing system that is:

1. Oriented towards the execution of tasks and processes;
2. Supports branching, conditionals, and concurrency;
3. Operates transparently and naturally in either centralized or decentralized environments.

In particular, the degree of decentralization is determined precisely by the configuration assembly description.

3.1 The Data-flow Formalism

The mechanism used for configuration assembly is more precisely a type of "control flow" (see, for example, [3]) since it is intended for control rather than computation. The structure of the configuration assembly mechanism is almost identical to the traditional data-flow formalism which is well documented (see, for example [3,4,5,6]).

The basic features of the data-flow formalism are illustrated in Figure 8. In the Figure, processes are represented by labeled

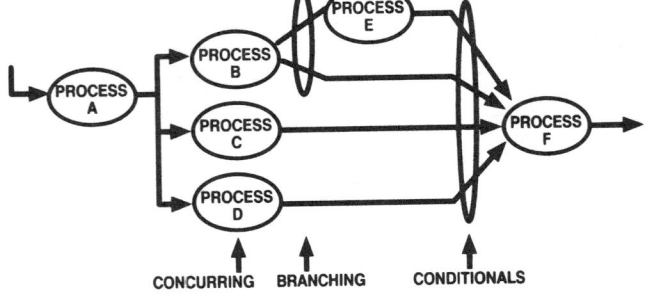

The Data-Flow Formalism
Figure 8

ovals. These ovals are interconnected by message-passing paths which are represented by arrows. These paths carry completion tokens which are used to signify that the previous process has been completed. These tokens also may carry information created by the previous processes if appropriate. A given process collects these tokens until a logical condition involving them (and related time-out events) is satisfied and then begins its own execution. At the completion of its execution (or part-way through, as appropriate), tokens are generated and sent to subsequent processes in the data-flow. These tokens may be created and sent to locations as a function of the outcome of the process. Each process executes independently and may exist in any processor within a distributed processing environment.

As a result of the features identified in the previous paragraph, a data-flow naturally permits conditionals, branching, distributed execution, and concurrency. In addition, data-flows can be executed with arbitrary degrees of decentralization as suggested by Figure 9. Figure 9a shows an abstract data-flow involving five processes {A,B,C,D,E}, an outcome-dependent branching at process A, multi-step completion token generation at process B, concurrency of processes C and D, and a logical relation governing the execution of process E. Figures 9b-d show three different implementations with increasing degrees of decentralization. Figure 9b shows no decentralization; all processes are executed by a single multi-tasking processor. *In this case the data-flow scheduling and token-routing is totally contained within the single multi-tasking processor.* Figure 9c shows an environment involving five processors; one processor is used as a centralized controller/scheduler, a second processor executes processes A and E, and the remaining three processors each execute processes B, C, and D. In this case, single start and completion tokens are exchanged between the centralized controller/scheduler and the other process-executing processors as illustrated. *In this case the data-flow scheduling is handled by the centralized controller/scheduler but the actual processes are executed in a distributed environment.* Figure 9d shows another environment involving five processors; in this case each processor uniquely executes one of the five processes {A,B,C,D,E}. There is no centralized control or scheduling. *In this case, the entire data-flow is implemented in a fully decentralized nature.*

The above example is illustrative of the fact that the same rather involved data-flow can be directly supported by a wide variety of environments involving many different types and degrees of decentralization. In addition to this and other useful properties cited above, data-flows also enjoy considerable endorsement outside of the computer literate community, in particular data-flows are useful for specifying corporate, administrative, and financial procedures [6]. As a result, data-flow flavored schemes offer potentials for simplifying configuration specification and user interfaces.

3.2 Performance-Based Design Considerations

Assuming some decentralization is required in the large-scale reconfigurable systems, interesting observations can be made concerning the role of centralized coordination of a data-flow execution in comparison to decentralized execution.

3.2.1 Execution

Consider the simple data-flow shown in Figure 10a. This abstract data-flow contains N processes which execute in sequence. Figure 10b shows a centralized coordination of the execution of this data-flow. Including "start" and "finish" tokens, a total of $2(N+1)$ messages are required. Note that since the coordination is centralized, any failures of a process execution can be identified and hence recovered from during the execution; also, completion of each process is observed and hence available for monitoring,

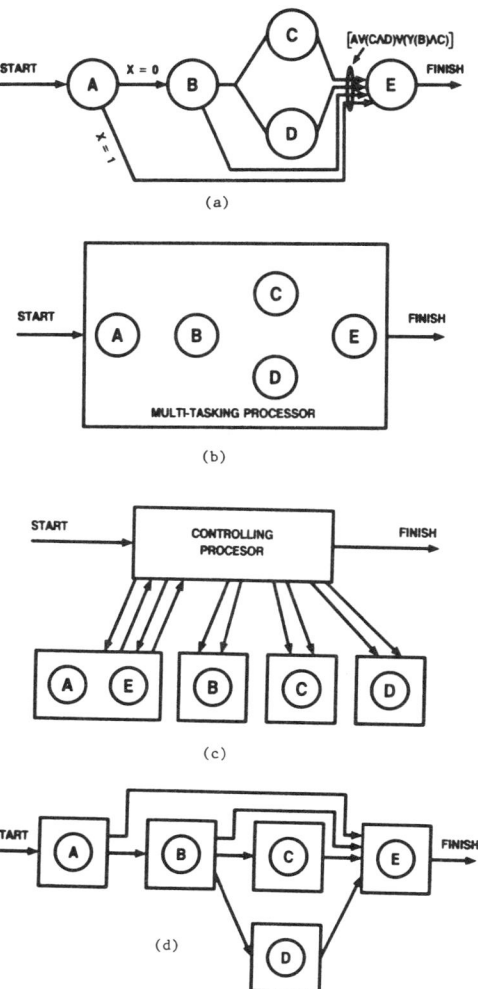

A Data-Flow (a) And Three Implementations With Increasing Degrees Of Decentralization
Figure 9

administration, and accounting (billing) purposes. In particular, completion of the Kth process occurs after $2K$ messages and is observed after the exchange of $2K+1$ messages. Compare this to the decentralized execution shown in Figure 10c. Full execution requires only $N+1$ messages, half as many as before. Without outside observations (such as shown in the dotted lines) failure recovery and monitoring in an equivalent fashion is not possible, so these messages are now considered. Again $N+1$ messages are required, so the total number of messages needed is $2(N+1)$ as in the centralized case. However, the completion of the Kth process occurs after K messages and is observed after $K+1$ messages, half of that for the centralized case. These and some other remarks to be discussed are summarized in the Table below.

In a decentralized system, message count represents one important degree of complexity. Each message must be created, successfully transmitted/routed/received, analyzed and noted upon. The diversity of the types of messages expands the complexity of the system's elements, and the number of messages

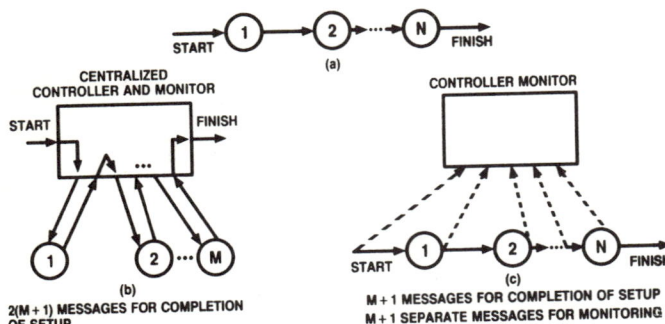

Comparing Execution Complexities (After Allocations Have Been Made): (a) Abstract Data-Flow, (b) Centralized Control/Monitoring, (c) Decentralized Execution With Centralized Monitoring
Figure 10

scales the loading requirements of the message exchange systems (i.e., the data-communications network linking the system elements.) In most systems each message exchange is likely to introduce delay and potential points of failure, comparing the columns of the table, it is observed that the decentralized approach in many ways makes much more intelligent use of the 2N+2 messages required. The key here is that only half of the messages are required for execution of the data-flow. As a result, the data-flow executes faster* and has fewer points of failure. Since the other half of the messages are used for monitoring, another property is also observed: there is a well-defined distinction between execution-oriented messages and monitoring-oriented messages. As a result, execution-oriented messages can be handled in a separately engineered environment emphasizing speed and reliability. The degree of reliability attained in the execution-oriented environment determines requirements on the monitoring-oriented environment. Since the monitoring information is used for billing, statistical records, and failure-recovery, it is reasonable to design the monitoring-oriented environment for slower speed and lesser reliability. It is also noted that since the monitoring and execution messages are generated in parallel (rather than in sequential interleave), the decentralized approach handles *all* aspects of configuration assembly with half the message exchange time (at the expense of an efficiently doubled message rate). A find observation concerns the fact that the centralized controller used in centralized coordination is required to take N actions even if no failure occurs, while nothing comparable is required is the decentralized case.

The preceding analysis may be extended to more complex (i.e., non-serial) data-flows. To do this requires focus on events *local* to the execution of a single given process as shown in Figure 11. Figure 11a shows a given process receiving m tokens from and transmitting n tokens to other processes in the data-flow. It is assumed that the process shown executes **monolithically**, i.e., begins its execution when received tokens satisfy a logical relation, executes without externally-visible steps, and all n transmitted tokens are then sent. (It is noted that, for the sake of analysis, any non-monolithically executing process may be itself decomposed into a new data-flow consisting of only monolithically executing process.) As shown in Figures 11b and 11c, which respectively illustrate the message flow in the centralized and decentralized approaches, only the received tokens need be considered. (This is because a transmitted token for one process also serves as a received token for exactly one other process.) As shown in Figure 11b, the centralized controller requires as many as m messages to be received for evaluating the logical relation permitting execution; when this relation is satisfied a message is sent to the process signaling that it is to now execute. Execution is confirmed with an additional message. Assume that each of the m+1 messages leading up to the execution of the process encounters a non-zero delay time between the completion of the action generating it and the message's reception; let "T_{max}" be the longest of these times "T_{submax}" be the second longest, and "T_{min}" be the shortest. Then the delay "t" between the time the process in the Figure could execute ideally and in reality must satisfy (assuming no race conditions):

$$(T_{max} + T_{min}) \leq t \leq (T_{max} + T_{submax})$$

Also, note that two messages are required between the action last required for process execution and actual execution.

Compare now the decentralized approach as illustrated in Figure 11c. Here, each of the m received tokens were co-transmitted with monitoring messages as illustrated. Upon execution, the process sends a single monitoring message to the centralized monitor along with the n transmitted tokens sent to subsequent processes in the data-flow. As a result, (assuming no race conditions):

$$T_{min} \leq t \leq T_{max}$$

and only one message is required between the action last required for process execution and actual execution. If all message delays are assumed approximately equal, i.e.,

$$T_{min} \approx T_{max}$$

then one sees the decentralized approach emerging with an execution encountering half as much message delay, just as in the serial case.

Comparison of Coordination Methods for Serial Data-flows		
Attribute	Centralized	Decentralized with Centralized Monitoring
Total number of messages for complete execution	2N+1	N+1
Total Number of messages for complete monitoring	2N+2	N+1
Number of messages required to executed K^{th} process	2K+1	K
Number of messages required to observe K^{th} execution	2K+2	K+1
Number of actions required by central point during non-failures	N	0

---

* *Another way to look at this is that for a given user-perceived configuration assembly time, the message network only need operate half as quickly.*

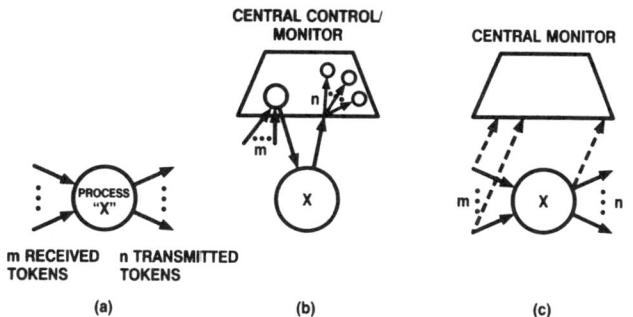

**General Data-Flows
(a) Data-Flow Element, (b) Centralized Execution
(c) Decentralized Execution With Centralized Monitoring
Figure 11**

3.2.2 Allocations Figure 12 illustrates the differences between the centralized and decentralized approach. As shown each case requires the centralized entity to be presented with the full algorithm script. In the decentralized case, each resource must also be given information about its precise role in the script, hence elongating the allocation messages in size but not increasing the number of messages. Although this elongation is not required in the centralized case, it is the only penalty paid at allocation for decentralization with monitoring.

3.2.3 Comparisons Summarized Decentralization with monitoring elongates allocation messages and increases the instantaneous rate of messages during execution. It does not change the total number of messages involved in execution and monitoring nor does it affect the average message generation rate. However, decentralization does speed up execution, reduce message-related points of failure, and increase the rate at which execute-time failures are detected, typically if not almost always by a factor of 2. In addition, it permits separate engineering of monitoring and execution messages (allowing retribution for increasing the instantaneous message generation rate mentioned above) and prevents additional actions by a centralized entity in non-failure modes.

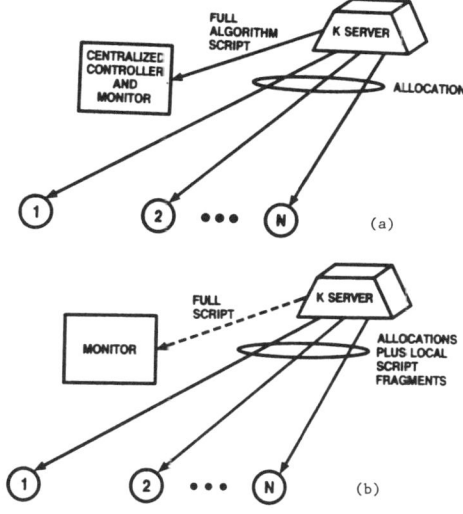

**Comparing Complexity Of Level K Allocations
(a) Centralized, (b) Decentralized
Number Msgs Same; Msgs Slightly Longer Under (b)
Figure 12**

4. RESOURCE AVAILABILITY AND CONFIGURATION DISASSEMBLY

It is important to free resources and other types of server allocations when a user has finished with a configuration assembled in their behalf. This is somewhat obvious for otherwise new configuration requests would eventually find no resources available. As it turns out, there are a number of detailed issues closely related to the freeing and general availability of resources. Here some performance and implementation considerations of resource availability and configuration disassembly are discussed.

Note that a given resource, once allocated, cannot be used by another user until somehow made free. A resource is allocated during a configuration assembly and remains unavailable to other users until some time after its use is completed. Thus for a given configuration request, the time a resource is unavailable to other users may be split into three components:

$$T_{unavailable} = T_{assembly.idle} + T_{usage} + T_{disassembly.idle}$$

The time spent in use (T_{usage}) is connected to revenue and cost; it is for these intervals that the resource is provided in the first place. The times spent idle during assembly ($T_{assembly.idle}$) and disassembly ($T_{disassembly.idle}$) phases, however, represent periods when the resource is wasted. The efficiency of the resource allocation system for the duration of a given configuration can thus be characterized as:

$$\text{Efficiency} = \frac{T_{usage}}{T_{assembly.idle} + T_{usage} + T_{disassembly.idle}}$$

The closer this expression is made to 1, the more potential for actual usage can be obtained. To obtain high efficiencies, one requires:

$$T_{usage} \gg T_{assembly.idle} + T_{disassembly.idle}$$

This is particularly important in systems where a great deal of resource sharing is to be expected. Most instances of large-scale reconfigurable systems would fall into this category for sheer reasons of minimizing cost and component-count complexities.

As discussed earlier, it is desirable to allocate resources quickly during configuration assembly for user performance requirements; users typically wish to have configurations made available quickly after a request is made. This force already motivates minimizing $T_{assembly.idle}$. However, one can see now that it is also desirable to minimize the time required to free up resources at the end of their use (i.e., $T_{disassembly.idle}$).

The most straightforward method of freeing resources is to do so on the receipt of a signal from the user that the configuration is no longer needed. In this case each "level.K" configuration function server is notified by some means to free the allocated resource. This, however, can be done in at least two ways:

1. Notification from higher level servers that the configuration is to be disassembled (this is the same way assembly is done);

2. Broadcast notification to each server involved in the configuration from some central point aware of the completion (this requires "look-ahead" operations to provide the centralized point with all the server addresses in advance).

Resources may also be freed using a number of typically context-oriented techniques. In many cases, time-out conditions can be used to supplement user completion messages. In other cases, resources can be implicitly released because of the nature of the allocation discipline requested (for example, a call-forwarding address query, the dump of a file, video frame, or audio segment, etc.). In other cases, resources may be explicitly freed by the user; this may be done by sending a message terminating specific subsets of an otherwise currently active configuration (turning off the video of an audio/video call, etc.).

All of the options for resource release may be used in the Threaded/Flow approach. The degree of performance required for resource release is a function of the designed server load, cost of the resources, cost of the release mechanism options, etc.

5. PIPELINING CONFIGURATION USAGE, ASSEMBLY, AND DISASSEMBLY

In many cases it is useful to interleave the assembly, usage, and disassembly phases of a configuration. In some cases this would be done strictly for performance reasons, offering the user a speedier setup and freeing resources as quickly as possible. Another reason would be to provide partial grants of a configuration request while waiting for other resources to become available; the user could be offered key subsets of the configuration (say, audio and graphics features) while waiting to obtain the next available resources for the rest of the configuration (say, video features). Another case would be to provide conditional feature implementation (for example, a user may or may not wish to tie in a graphics editor depending upon the type of image found during a database query whose output is directed to a desktop publishing feature). The latter case is especially useful in functions with very extensive user options and interactive qualities.

Figure 13 shows a way of graphically characterizing such pipelining as multi-dimensional curves. The Figure shows diagrams whose axes are

"x": the number of resource allocations made,
"y": the number of resource-level data-flow steps executed at "level.0",
"z": the number of resource releases made.

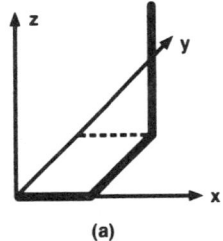 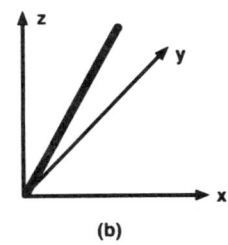

**Non-pipelined (a) and highly pipelined (b) executions
Figure 13**

Assume also that there is only one resource-level data-flow step made for each allocated resource. If each axis is normalized so that the curve is confined to values between 0 and 1, a number of properties, listed below, can be expected. (Variations on the assumptions result in other similar properties.)

1. The curve is non-decreasing in each coordinate (true without normalization);
2. If there are no recursions, the curves must lie within the wedge described by:

$$0 \leq y \leq x$$
$$0 \leq z \leq x$$

3. The shape of the curve determines the degree and style of pipelining. A condition of "no pipelining" is represented by the curve

$$\{0 \leq x \leq 1,\ y=0,\ z=0\} \cup \{x=1,\ 0 \leq y \leq 1,\ z=0\} \cup \{x=1,\ y=1,\ 0 \leq z \leq$$

(see Figure 13a) while "full pipelining" is asymptotically represented by the curve $x=y=z$ (see Figure 13b). Geometric proximity to these limiting curves gives a graphic intuition for the degree and style of pipelining.

The topic of pipelining also includes two other concepts:

1. "Throw-away" parts of a configuration that are unlikely to be used may be preconfigured anyway in case they are needed quickly. This could be done after the principal part of the configuration is assembled but at some time prior to when the user could first possibly require the rarely used feature.

2. Commonly requested configurations may be pre-assembled to some degree. This is useful when used in an adaptive way, basing the number and types of pre-assembled configurations (as well as perhaps the degree of pre-assembly) on automated statistical observations. (This is comparable to a fast-food restaurant, upon noticing a rush on particular types of hamburgers, precooking a few in anticipation of impending requests.) This type of pipelining is an interesting case since in a way this is pipelining the assembly process with the actual *request* process.

6. SERVER DESIGN AND HIERARCHICAL QUEUEING MODELS

The design of servers and network management systems in the Threaded/Flow approach can at first cut be handled with simple design intuition. This is as done in the design of most computer systems since sophisticated analytic and even simulation techniques often contribute little in practice. However, there is in this case excellent opportunity for the development of some new analytical tools capturing features of the Threaded/Flow approach. In this Section, some design considerations and one promising analytical technique currently under development will be discussed.

In general servers may have to manage resources across a variety of demands. Some requests will be for only brief one-time usage, others for bursty long-term usage, others for long intervals at full utilization. In some cases delay in the allocation will be tolerable, and in other cases it will not. Also, servers will have to administer resources subject to network management conditions. For example, under heavy loading priority may be paid to requests associated with configurations that are almost complete rather than new requests in order to maximize revenue. Expensive resources may be allocated only after guarantees that enough other resources are available to complete the configuration assembly. As a result of these observations, it is seen that the design of servers in the Threaded/Flow system is very interesting and worthy of some theoretical study and dependable design techniques.

The modeling of servers and network management systems in the Threaded/Flow system is nicely handed by *hierarchical queueing models*. The first model of this type was a two-level model proposed by Schoute to study the creation of tasks resulting from the acceptance of a call-request in a telephone switch controller [7]. Figure 14 shows a more general hierarchical queueing model involving more layers developed by the author [8]. In this model there are separate queues associated with each server within each level. "Customers" may arrive at any level, but customers at a given level can, while being served by their server, *generate customers for queues at lower levels*. This nicely models many circumstances, such as the scheduling of processes in a batch computer system, allocation of resources within a corporation, or the Threaded/Flow approach presented in this paper. In less obvious ways, the hierarchical queueing model also is useful in modeling resource allocation systems where allocations involve hard or virtual allocations over a range of time-constants. For example, in [8] the allocation of transmission or switch fabric channels to circuit-switched, burst-switched, virtual-circuit, and datagram oriented clients is represented as a two-layer model (a "fast" burst-duration/packet-duration layer plus a "slow" call-duration/connection-duration layer). This is also of great potential use to modeling and designing more general resource servers involved in Threaded/Flow implementations. In [8] the topic is considered in more detail from modeling, analysis, and control design viewpoints. Analytical results appear promising since under standard types of independence assumptions both decomposability [9] and geometric matrix [10] techniques can be applied.

7. APPLICATIONS TO TELECOMMUNICATIONS SERVICE PRIMITIVE SYSTEMS

This discussion is limited in detail due to legal and proprietary issues yet to be resolved. The ideas are fairly straightforward, however. From the service definition viewpoint, this application is based on the following identifications:

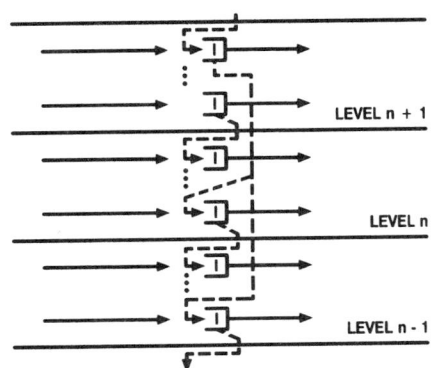

**General Hierarchical Queuing Model
(A Specific Example Is Shown)
Figure 14**

Identification of Threaded/Flow Entities with Service Primitive Entities		
Entity	Service Primitive Concept	Threaded/Flow Concept
simplest resources	resources	"level.0" configuration function (i.e., functional elements)
explicit building blocks	service elements	"level.K" configuration function
functions or services	level.K service	"level.K+1" configuration function ($K \geq 1$)

What has been done here is that the very first level of configuration functions are reserved to create explicit service building blocks called **service elements**. This is done because for most purposes raw resource functions will be too limited to use directly in simple service specifications. In particular, a large-scale network may require finer granularity for its own internal management, operations, and failure-recovery needs than is reasonable to present to users at a user interface. (For example, a resource might be a circuit-switched channel or video laserdisk which, respectively, require routing and linking with specific editors or display controllers before they are of any real use. However, what is viewed as a resource or service element is *completely arbitrary*; these examples could just as easily incorporate routing and editors or display control and be viewed as simple resources.)

Other aspects and augmentations include service description languages, service definitions, service description database management, assembly/usage/disassembly languages and interfaces, open architecture issues, call progress, real-time control, billing, failure-recovery, operations, provisioning, service subscription administration, and network management. A few of these are briefly discussed.

7.1 Administration

The operations, billing, call progress, and real-time control functions are implemented by adding specific functions and messages to the various servers. In particular, the highest-level server is used as the centralized point of contact between these functions, users, and the processing of user requests. Communications between servers follows the same hierarchy used in configuration definition. This permits each server to be only locally responsible for affairs it directly delegates.

7.2 Definitions of Services

Services are defined by specifying configurations and passing specific parameters, files, or software to resources. Configurations are specified by software descriptions. These descriptions consists of specific resource request messages and the specific servers to which the requests are to be directed. All information needed to construct a fully decentralized data-flow can be organized in this manner. Because of the Threaded/Flow construct, an entity named in a description can be a resource, an elementary service element, or a full stand-alone service. A given server, however, does not distinguish between these since it only is concerned with affairs within its level and message exchanges with levels immediately below and above. Note each server is responsible for failure detection and recovery for all the servers and resources it explicitly deals with.

A network defined service is one whose description is provided by a network administered database. A service vendor defined service is one whose description is provided by a service vendor database. A user defined service is one whose description is provided in some manner by the user. User-defined services may be limited to single-layer descriptions of robust services and service elements with significant filtering and security functions; otherwise the integrity of the entire network can be easily compromised.

7.3 Roles for Service Vendors

Service vendors can provide resources, service descriptions, or combinations of both. The interface to a service vendor is expected to be identical to that of a user with the probable exception of support for higher channel capacities.

8. SUGGESTIONS FOR RELATED ANALYTICAL WORK

There is the potential for some interesting formal language work characterizing the intrinsic structure of the Threaded/Flow approach. In addition, category representations [11] using functors are particularly attractive for specifying the synthesis, decomposition, and equivalence of configurations. (It is noted that category theory has seen value of a completely different manner in other work with languages and algorithms; see, for example, [12].) Besides these algebraic studies, there is considerable work that could be done with the notion of hierarchical queueing systems and their control, both from the pure layering and mixed time-constant viewpoints. In addition, there are probably other types of resource allocation and network management models that could be used to study and design the servers used in the Threaded/Flow approach.

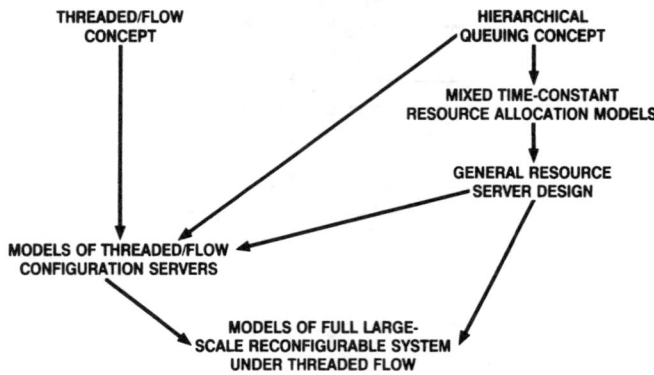

Role Of Hierarchical Queuing Models
Figure 15

9. ACKNOWLEDGEMENTS

The author would like to thank Warren Gifford (Bell Communications Research) and Professor Pravin Varaiya (U. C. Berkeley EECS Department) for their support and encouragement of these ideas over the years. The author is also grateful to Bell Communications Research for supporting the development of the *Integrated Media Architecture Laboratory* (IMAL) [1] where the need for these ideas has provided a wonderful theater for study. In particular, the author wishes to acknowledge the programming design and coding efforts of Chris Bidaut (AGS) and earlier exploratory efforts by Doug Riecken (Bell Communications Research) involved in creating the first working prototype of the Threaded/Flow approach within IMAL. This work has also been nicely complemented by the efforts of summer student Damon Altos (Rutgers University) in creating an extremely sophisticated graphics-oriented monitoring display system for the Threaded/Flow prototype. Finally, but with great thanks, the author acknowledges the valuable editorial review of Laura Pate and Robert Klessig (both of Bell Communications Research).

10. REFERENCES

[1] L. F. Ludwig, D. F. Dunn, "Laboratory for the Emulation and Study of Integrated and Coordinated Media Communication," this SIGCOM conference.

[2] R. G. Loeliger *Threaded-Interpretive Languages* Byte Books, Peterborough, NH, 1981.

[3] M. Broy, ed., *Control Flow and Data Flow*, Springer, New York, 1984.

[4] J. A. Sharp, *Data Flow Computing*, Halsted Press, New York, 1985.

[5] C. R. Vick, C. V. Ramamoorthy, eds., *Handbook of Software Engineering*, Van Nostrand, New York, 1984.

[6] T. Demarco, *Structured Analysis and System Specification*, Prentice Hall, Englewood Cliffs, NJ, 1979.

[7] Schoute, "The Hierarchical Queue: A Model for Definition and Estimation of Processor Loading," *Phillips Technical Report*, SR220-82-3743, October 22, 1982.

[8] L. F. Ludwig, "Hierarchical Queues and the Control of Layered and Mixed Time-Constant Resource Allocations", *to appear*.

[9] Courtis, *Decomposability*, Academic Press, New York, 1977.

[10] M. F. Neuts, *Geometric Matrix Solutions in Stochastic Models*, John Hopkins, Baltimore, 1981.

[11] S. MacLane, *Categories for the Working Mathematician*, Springer, New York, 1971.

[12] P-L Curien, *Categorical Combinators, Sequential Algorithms, and Functional Programming*, Wiley, New York, 1986.

Distributed Shared Memory in a Loosely Coupled Distributed System[†]

Brett D. Fleisch
University of California, Los Angeles

Abstract

This work outlines the development and performance validation of an architecture for distributed shared memory in a loosely coupled distributed computing environment. This distributed shared memory may be used for communication and data exchange between communicants on different computing sites; the mechanism will operate transparently and in a *distributed* manner. This paper describes the architecture of this mechanism and metrics which will be used to measure its performance. We also discuss a number of issues related to the overall design and what research contribution such an implementation can provide to the computer science field.

1.1 Introduction

The past decade has brought about a dramatic change in computing practices. Communication, processing, and storage costs have decreased significantly; the economics of centralized single processor computing environments has given way to distributed network environments where many processors interact to perform roughly equivalent tasks at much cheaper cost. Today it is commonplace to have networks of computers with diverse interaction styles. Such interaction or communication has been called *interprocess communication* (IPC) in the literature.

IPC has formed the basis for many centralized and distributed computing systems. This work will focus on a new communication architecture based on shared memory communication. Our specific goal is to investigate the feasibility of distributed shared memory (dsm) in an operating system kernel. Li[LI86] demonstrated the feasibility of such a system outside of the kernel with a number of numeric applications, but it remains a relatively open question as to how well dsm performs for a variety of non-numeric applications and what the effects of dsm are on other kernel services.

The work will also examine the performance of a number of typical shared memory programs in the dsm system. Specifically we propose to examine symbolic computation performance which emphasizes the rearrangement of data and where the sequence of operations is often highly data dependent and less amenable to compile time analysis than numeric computation.

Lastly, we wish to gain experience with dsm and cross processor address and data sharing. Actual experiences will be most useful for gauging the utility of the mechanism.

1.2 Organization

A roadmap to this document is as follows. In Section 2 we examine past work on centralized and distributed shared memory specifically looking at Kai Li's work and Mach. Section 3 examines the impact of changing technology on communication mechanisms. Section 4 outlines the dsm implementation. In this section we look at the motivations for distributed shared memory, overview our design, describe the configuration issues for dsm, locality, consistency, problem-oriented shared memories, scaling, network errors, synchronization primitives, and details of our prototype. Section 5 looks at performance of distributed shared memory and Section 6 looks at the significance of this work. Appendix I provides the standard System V interface to shared memory.

[†] This research was supported by the Advanced Research Project Agency under contract DSS-MDA-903-82-C-0189.

Permission to copy without fee all or part of this material is granted provided that the copies are not made or distributed for direct commercial advantage, the ACM copyright notice and the title of the publication and its date appear, and notice is given that copying is by permission of the Association for Computing Machinery. To copy otherwise, or to republish, requires a fee and/or specfic permission.

© 1988 ACM 0-89791-245-4/88/0001/0317 $1.50

2.0 Past Work on Centralized and Distributed Shared Memory Architectures

Shared memory multiprocessors have been explored since the early 1970s. Designed around a processor-memory-switch organization, the function of the common shared memory is to provide storage for each of the processors and, in some cases, a communications repository for messages. Shared memory typically is supported by machine instructions for remote memory operations. It may consist of one large address space or *n* address spaces mapped into a large physical address space. Systems which have used shared memory, some of which are multiprocessors, include Hydra[WULF74, WULF75], the Plessey system 250[ENGL74], CM*[JONE77, SWAN77a,b] and the BBN Butterfly[BBN85]. In a distributed setting Spector[SPEC82] used network packets to implement high-speed remote memory operations from Xerox Altos[THAC81] and Linda[CARR86, GELE83] provides shared memory that appears tightly coupled, but is physically distributed.

Many of these systems access shared memory through a hardware switch. This switch may allow the memory to be accessible from all the processors, it may allow memory to be accessible to each processor with overlap for shared access, or it may allow subsets of processors to share disjoint portions of memory. These configurations determine whether access time to shared memory is uniform or hierarchical, that is whether access time varies as a function of the physical structure of the memory.

In a tightly coupled system, proper partitioning of memory regions, organization of processors, and configuration of the communications switch are very important to reduce memory contention and to improve channel bandwidth. Performance is also greatly affected by the choice of synchronization primitives and their relative efficiency. The use of a *cache,* associated with each processor, can greatly improve performance by reducing costly shared memory access. A cache typically contains data recently accessed from shared memory; cache capacity is usually limited because it is manufactured from higher cost memory than main memory.

Since each processor typically has its own cache, it is possible that the memory contents and cached data at one or more sites becomes out-of-date. Typically, caches must be kept consistent between processors as the contents of memory is updated. Known as *multi-cache consistency,* the solutions to this problem are varied[SMIT82].

Shared memory seems like an attractive paradigm. Data never need be transferred between recipients, since sharing is used. The problems involved with passing large data structures in message-passing systems are easily solved with shared memory. However, there are a number of inherent problems. First, in many shared memory systems, machines have to be close together for access time to be acceptable. Second, synchronization of shared memory access can complicate the semantics of access and its performance; other paradigms, message passing as one example, have synchronization implicit. Third, shared memory can introduce a single point of failure in a computer system. Fourth, shared memories typically have two instructions used to place and remove items from the memory known as *fetch* and *store* which can cause problems in a distributed environment. The *fetch* instruction obtains the latest value stored at a given memory address or returns an undefined value if no item has been stored. The *store* instruction replaces a value at a given address. In a distributed environment a given *store* operation may not update all the memories at all sites consistently before some site *fetches* from the same address. In this case, the fetch may return old ("stale") data, a significant problem similar to the one that occurs with caches.

2.1 Kai Li

Kai Li[LI86] experimented with a shared virtual memory system on a loosely-coupled multiprocessor, the Apollo Domain system[LEAC83]. Shared data is paged between processors, some of which have copies of the virtual address space pages. The model assumes ownership of pages can vary from processor to processor either statically or dynamically. Work in this paper concentrates on consistency problems and theoretical performance based on experimentation with centralized and distributed managers to locate the ownership of a page. The last writer to a page becomes the new owner of the page in his work. Unless the local processor owns the page, someone has to be asked, before a write can occur.

Li's work had no hard performance figures because the implementation was done outside of the kernel. He implemented less than 4700 lines of application-level code to implement this mechanism. While results suggest the viability of distributed shared memory on loosely-coupled systems, a serious distributed implementation would have to be built in the kernel of the underlying operating system. Further Li's work provided measurements of numeric applications only; no non-numeric computations were measured.

The model we propose here is considerably different from Li's. Li assumes that distributed shared memory design should be similar to a virtual memory paging system. In particular, page ownership is distributed across sites on a per/page basis. In our model, pages should be grouped into a logical segments with one processor being the owner or primary site for that entire segment's pages. As in Kai Li's work, if the writer is the owner, no penalty is paid to inquire if a write is permitted. Further, there is less administrative overhead in managing this courser granularity, i.e. segments. This will be discussed further in Section 4.

2.2 Mach

The Mach system[RASHID86] permits both copy-on-write and read/write sharing of memory regions between tasks. Copy-on-write sharing between unrelated tasks comes about from message passing. An entire address space may be sent in a single message with no physical data copy made. Read/write shared memory within a task tree is handled by inheritance whereas read/write shared memory between unrelated tasks is implemented using *external pagers* i.e. tasks which allocate and manage secondary storage objects. These external pagers allow data to be mapped into the address space of a given task at one or more locations. The Mach kernel provides consistent shared memory access to all mappings of the same memory object on the same uniprocessor or multiprocessor.

The interaction with external pagers is conducted through Mach *ports*. Because of this it is possible to map the same memory object into tasks on different hosts throughout the system. Each kernel keeps its own cached data consistent while the various pagers coordinate further consistency control.

Mach also makes available a mapped file facility under the UNIX emulation it provides. A single new Unix domain system call called *map_fd* is used (along with an open Unix file descriptor) to make a virtual copy of the file mapped into the address space of the calling Unix process. Mach uses mapped files to implement program loading and also as a replacement for buffer management in the standard I/O library.

External pagers provide a facility for distributed shared memory in a similar way as Kai Li's mechanisms provide. However, because this facility is implemented outside of the kernel its performance will probably not be as effective as a similar service provided in the kernel. The effect of the interaction between external paging and network server use (servers not in the kernel) should make remote performance even less attractive in this implementation.

3.0 Impact of Changing Technology

One of the most significant developments in communication technology over the past 15 years, is fiber optics. Today fiber optics is a viable alternative to copper wire and coaxial cable in many type of computer networks[BALB84]. Thousands of commercial organizations, including firms doing business in banking, finance, electrical power, insurance, oil, and securities use fiber optics to meet a variety of communication needs. One of the most significant benefits provided by fiber optics is the very high bandwidths that can be accommodated by fiber. Bandwidths should range from 100 MBits/sec to 8 Gigabits. Fiber optics also enhances security through lack of radiation and resistance to tapping. Optics also permits relative ease of installation with light-weight cable.

Changing technology greatly affects the design of future communications mechanisms: differences in computing environments, new communications characteristics, and experiences from related work, suggest basic assumptions that have held in the past may no longer hold in the future. For example, fiber optics nets have significantly different processor-network bandwidth ratios than older technology. For example, typical LAN bit rates are 3-10 MBits/second, whereas in the future one can expect fiber optics to have bandwidths ranging from 100MBits/sec to 8 Gigabits/second. The corresponding figures for (Vax-architecture) reflect similar speedups because of the emergence of optical busses. Disk transfer rates will also increase, but probably less dramatically than for busses and networks. These increased rates suggest dsm will become more attractive in the future because large memory UNIX systems will continue to be limited more by their I/O capacity than by memory. A shared memory facility could reduce the number of I/O operations and therefore improve system performance. Our work will examine dsm with keen attention to fiber optics and changing technological trends.

4.0 Distributed Shared Memory

In Section 2 we introduced shared memory architectures. Here we we describe the architecture of a newly proposed distributed shared memory and motivate its development and use. We then discuss how the client uses dsm. Next we describe how the performance success of the implementation is closely coupled with locality of reference and selection of an appropriate segment distribution granularity. The issue of using problem-oriented memories to solve performance problems is presented. Then we propose a way to examine how well shared memory scales. We next discuss network error conditions and their effects on dsm. We present issues related to synchronization primitives and dsm. Lastly, we describe implementation details of our prototype.

4.1 Motivations for Distributed Shared Memory

In the past, a significant limitation of message passing was that to transfer a large amount of data between processes required a significant number of message exchanges[RASH86]. Often, data had to be broken up into discrete packets typically of 1K or 4K and transferred sequentially. This effects the efficiency of the message system and on the complexity of interactions. Accent[RASH81] and Mach[ACCE86] addressed the issue of accommodating bulk transfers in message passing systems. It relied, however, on a scarcely available hardware provision: copy-on-write support. With copy-on-write, no copy of the data is made when data is transferred if both communicants only read the data transmitted. Instead, shared memory is used (actually sharing through the maps) rather than paying the overhead of having the data copied. However, if one of the two communicants subsequently writes the data, a (copy-on-write) fault occurs and a copy is made. Since typically the data is not written to, this scheme appears to improve performance substantially.

The use of sharing for high performance message passing suggests exploration of a more direct sharing model in a distributed network environment. Our new model is a separate and distinct shared memory facility. It may be used for sharing and data exchange between sites in a transparent *distributed* manner in the Locus system[POPE81]. It differs from copy-on-write schemes which preserve "copy" semantics since direct sharing is used. It is similar to the external pager concept discussed earlier (Section 2.2) but is proposed for inside the OS kernel.

Shared memory can be used for:

- fine grain multiprocessing
- fast IPC
- database management and support
- replacement of file access operations

In the first case, several multiprocessor manufacturers (Sequent and Encore) are using a form of shared memory in their versions of UNIX. Fine grain multiprocessing is accomplished by creating processes for available processors and mapping in a shared memory object and synchronizing access through it. In the second case, shared memory has been used to communicate, exchange, and manipulate large data structures. An example of this approach would be in multiphase programs such as the C language preprocessor and compiler. Such programs use files or pipes to accomplish this currently. In the third case, designers of DBMS systems would benefit by being able to share data between potential database client programs and transaction managers or data managers. Systems of this kind need both sharing between processes and sharing of data pages. In the last case, one can reduce the overhead of file management for UNIX-like systems by replacing file I/O with shared memory operations. As the relationship between the costs of memory and secondary storage have changed since UNIX inception, large memory UNIX systems are limited more by I/O capacity than by memory. A shared memory facility could reduce the number of I/O operations and therefore improve UNIX performance.

It has been argued that a distributed shared memory model can be a powerful basis for a decentralized computer service. In particular, Cheriton[CHER85] imagines a common name space tied together with a global shared directory system. Such a system would have global directories residing in the shared memory. As another example of the power of such a service, the machines could agree on the time of day by storing the time in this shared memory. At the extreme, assuming the shared memory was large enough, the system could put everything in this shared memory and operate just like a shared memory multiprocessor. Further, much power is derived because it is easy to program applications in a shared memory model. The management of shared program state is familiar to programmers and transparently managed by the underlying operating system. Lastly, shared memory allows bulk data transfers(sharing) and the passing of complicated data structures to be very efficient.

The implementation we describe in the next section uses software support rather than building the shared memory, in hardware. By implementing shared memory using the software segments mentioned earlier, a wide range of experimental parameters can be varied. Experimental parameters include number of processors, amount of multi-segment consistency, amount of memory, and variety in applications. We would like to be able to experiment with fiber optics for this work, as well. This work would differ from that of the Harris Aerospace fiber optic shared memory[FOLM85] in that memory is distributed rather than centralized. It differs from the Apollo Domain work[LEAC83] in that our segments have stronger concurrency control and our segments are logically replicated rather than demand paged from a primary site.

4.2 Distributed Shared Memory Overview

Because of decreasing memory costs, it is feasible for contemporary distributed architectures to have shared memories that are larger and logically distributed. In comparison to hardware caches, which contain only a portion of a memory image, modern memory technology allows each site to cache the entire shared memory. Figure 1 shows the organization of our proposed distributed shared memory system. Depicted are a number of sites connected by a communication medium. Also shown is one shared memory *image* (or *segment*). The image is seen by all sites which have it "attached". When a site attaches the image all machine instructions are directed to a *local segment* which is a logical copy of the shared memory image. Each site with the shared memory image attached has a local segment which reflects the contents the entire image's data.

The System V system interface to shared memory (see Appendix I) will be used for the dsm system. This model organizes shared memory as a collection of variable size segments. It provides distinct advantages over non-segmented virtual memory systems because it allows the potential of better protection of user segments and allows user to group data into a logical organization whose locality of access could potentially be better than non-segmented organizations. The System V model is a useful one because a number of single site applications have been written and when coupled with our implementation should transparently operate without modification in a multisite configuration. It goes without saying, however, that additional mechanisms will have to augment the standard single-site interface (in a transparent way) to make multi-site configuration specifications and to add multi-site user advice.

4.3 Configuration and Number of Processors

Clients use dsm by attaching a shared memory image to an address using the command *attach*. To locate the appropriate shared memory image to attach, a *key* is associated with each image and a name lookup service[FLEI86] is used by the client to locate the primary storage site for the image. Later, when done, the client issues the *detach* command.

For clients to transparently share addresses of an image, a realization of an image (called a "segment") is attached to the client's address space locally. Clients should attach the segment to the same starting address in all address spaces if the addresses are to be passed among clients. If this is not done, the only other way to share addresses is to use self-relative addressing for all addresses used within the segment.

The total number of processors sharing an image is determined by the attach calls. If all *attach* commands are issued by one site the sharing is equivalent to centralized sharing. If more than one site issues *attach* commands for the same segment, shared memory becomes distributed among client sites.

4.4 Locality

A successful dsm should exploit the *principle of locality* [DENN72] for the various applications which run on it. Smith[SMIT82] points out that the property of locality has two aspects, *temporal* and *spatial* [SMIT82]. Over short periods of time a program references memory nonuniformly, but over a large period of time, portions of the address space which are favored remain largely the same. This property is called *temporal locality* or locality by time. This behavior has been observed in program loops, as one example. *Spatial locality* means that portions of the address space in use consist of a fairly small number of individually contiguous portions of the address space. Locality in space, means that the loci of reference in the future are likely to be near the current loci of reference. This type of behavior can be expected when accessing data items such as variables, arrays, or program instructions.

Because programs exhibit "conventional" locality does not mean they will perform well in the context of dsm. For example, if a program has a high degree of spatial locality, different sites may alternately write locations in the same physical proximity and thus a high degree of network traffic may be required to keep the page consistent. The performance of dsm programs that exhibit a high degree of temporal locality may be worse than in a single site system because of the number of sites making memory references. Worse yet, in both cases this poor performance could cause a cross site thrashing phenomena. Thus, our goal is to examine conventional locality for dsm with the goal of improving performance.

4.5 Consistency

Performance of a dsm system is closely coupled to how well segment consistency is performed. To keep large segments consistent involves choosing a *granularity* for data items to be replicated at and a *replication policy* to implement this choice.

One possible configuration for the grain of replication is the entire segment. In this scheme, one site will store the primary copy of the segment. Any time an item is changed in the segment, the entire segment must be copied between all sites that have copies of the segment. Intuitively, the configuration seems unreasonable because an enormous amount of unchanged data will be propagated between sites. Nonetheless, deferring the propagation of changes with a large unit of granularity can pay off. Depending on the frequency of updates to the segment, the frequency of complete segment copy, and the requirements for immediacy of seeing updates, the scheme could have merit. Consider a time-driven distribution approach to updates. In such an approach, at some fixed interval (say 30 seconds) the changed segment is distributed to all sites that have a copy of the segment. An advantage with this is there is no overhead in keeping track of which subunits of the segment are propagated, since the entire segment is copied to all sites requiring a copy. A significant disadvantage is that updates are not seen for a fixed interval and based on this, recency of data is not guaranteed. Even by waiting the full fixed interval amount of time, recency of data cannot be guaranteed. Furthermore, such a large granularity increases the chance of segment writing contention.

Another possible configuration is that the grain of replication be much smaller, say a *page*. Any changes to a segment's pages are passed to other logical copies for update. The frequency and immediacy of distribution of these updates could be selected to match the end-users application or be strictly mostrecent". The page is a good unit of granularity because programs typically have a high degree of locality in data access. Our prototype implementation will use this unit of granularity.

A variation, using the page as the unit of replication, is that the primary site be different for each page of the segment. Each page of the segment could have its primary storage site, be different from (or the same as) the other pages of that segment. Although the administrative and policy overhead is greater for this level of distribution granularity, there may be benefits. This configuration was experimented with (outside of the kernel) by Li[LI86]. For example, depending on the amount of locality in the application program, pages surrounding the one being updated could be stored at different primary sites. This would provide the benefit of load balancing accesses to surrounding pages using different processors. However, determining the primary site for a particular page is burdensome and may end up being a bottleneck. Also, there are few studies which suggest that locality of access would make this a significantly better policy than associating all the pages of the segment to one primary site. Is the administrative overhead of determining the primary site more than the benefit derived from the load balancing? And if not, does locality of access warrant the policy at all? Much more research needs to be done to answer these fundamental questions. Our prototype will have all a segment's pages use the same primary site. We may change this policy at a later time.

A last possible scheme is a *circulating token* scheme where there is no primary site. Rather, a *token* is passed around the logical ring whose value is the contents of all pages that have been updated. Sites interested in an update obtain the token's value as it circulates. This scheme fits in well with our desire to implement mechanisms that are suitable for fiber optic networks. In one possible implementation, each shared memory image has a token associated with it.

This token (logically) constantly circulates around the network. To access or update one's local segment one must defer until the token has circulated to the local site. To optimize performance, when no updates and reads are being performed the token would not circulate around the ring aimlessly. A known site would have the token when it is not circulating. Unfortunately, the consequences of this optimization are that a token manager site, similar in some ways to a primary site, would have to be used to request the token from. Another optimization to this scheme may be to have separate read and write tokens.

4.6 Problem-Oriented Shared Memories

It has been argued by Cheriton [CHER85] that multi-segment consistency can be relaxed for certain applications that do not require recent data be returned by fetch operations. Specifically, Cheriton argues shared memory semantics should be tuned to a particular application since no reasonable application independent techniques for a shared memory model have been devised. This approach, known as *problem-oriented* shared memory, looks like a very promising approach to building prototypes for certain shared memory applications.

In this work we wish to examine the issue of whether a general shared memory can be built with acceptable performance. We know general shared memory paradigms can be built whose performance is not very good; *a solution whose performance is not acceptable is not a solution*. Clearly, we can always fall back on problem-oriented approaches, some of which relax the consistency constraints we place on our more general distributed shared memory model. It remains an open question as to whether it will be *necessary* to fall back on problem-oriented approaches to meet the needs of certain applications. The best way to examine this issue is to prototype a shared-memory implementation and measure its performance. It is only by actual experience that one can gain insight to answer these questions.

4.7 Scaling

For programming large scale communication systems, we believe dsm will provide a significant benefit over less transparent paradigms. Dsm relieves the programmer from explicitly managing the underlying communication paths and allows the system to do more of the bookkeeping needed for communication management in large scale systems. For example, in message-passing systems, servers that maintain multiple client connections save state records for each client. This record stores necessary information that need not be saved at an application visible level in a corresponding dsm scheme. This relieves the programmer from managing explicit details and therefore we believe this makes scaling a dsm system an easier task for the applications programmer. Such a system should scale in an application-level transparent manner.

A fundamental resource utilization question arises for scaling dsm: as a system scales upwards, how much memory can be shared by users until memory contention becomes a severe problem? To examine this issue, we must consider how much locality there is in applications that choose to use shared memory. Our plan is to set up an experimental configuration with dsm to examine this. This configuration will minimize IPC between processors, use segments as complete caches, and implement low overhead intersegment consistency policies. A variety of applications will be executed in this experimental configuration and we will vary the number of processors in the study and applications.

4.8 Network Error Conditions

A variety of network error conditions can affect dsm. Although some of these errors can be handled easily, more severe errors such as a network partition present a serious problem. In a network partition some isolated processors may have "local" copies of the segment. In this case, segment consistency could only be achieved within a connected partition. If writes were permitted during the network partition, this may leave local copies of the segment within different partitions inconsistent when the system merges. Achieving a consistent "version" of the shared memory segment would be almost impossible. The rapidity of update and the different locations updated could leave a history of changes that would be nearly impossible to reconcile. Although some work has been done in the area of achieving a consistent version of a data object after a network partition[GUY87], there seems no work applicable to a shared memory system. For now we plan to avoid the problem by aborting the shared memory users or by allowing writes in only one of the disjoint partitions.

4.9 Synchronization Primitives

The performance of dsm cannot be assessed without examining the impact of synchronization primitives on the implementation's performance. In a traditional message-passing scheme synchronization is implicit in the message-passing itself: a sending client must have sent a message before a receiving client can receive the message. This implicit synchronization is not present in dsm. Explicit synchronization must be provided by the applications programmer.

The impact of synchronization will be a critical issue in the overall performance of dsm. Of these mechanisms, many are structured in such a way as to avoid operating system call overhead. For example, the *test and set* instruction is an example of a primitive provided by the hardware for synchronization. It requires no OS intervention and provides an indivisible setting of a memory location after a "testing" instruction. In the face of dsm, however, there may be several different sites that will require their copies be set as a consequence of the "set" portion of the *test and set* instruction. To accomplish this in a dsm environment, two alternative methods could be used. In the first, a new instruction could be provided so that the OS will intercept and update all "copies" of the segment image. However, in making the OS intercept this call, a portion of the benefit of having a low overhead synchronization mechanism that requires no OS intervention has been lost. In the second scheme, the setting of the memory location could trigger the propogation of the entire page to the sites where copies exist. This mechanism would preserve the low-overhead of the *test and set* instruction, but present serious performance problems when used in an intense fashion on dsm. It could cause a cross network page-thrashing phenomena if local updates become too intense. In an ideal environment the hardware could be modified to wait for all the network updates to complete before the *test and set* returns from its "set".

4.10 The Prototype Implementation

Our dsm prototype will be implemented on Digital Equipment Corporation VAXs connected by a 10 MB Ethernet. We will begin work with a version of the Locus operating system which includes System V shared memory for single site systems. We have also implemented a distributed name service facility which allows objects (segments) to be located anywhere on the net in a reliable manner. This naming component served as the basis for distributed services for System V IPC's distributed message passing and distributed semaphores [FLEI86]. Continuing to use this component for segments in a dsm scheme is a natural extension of this previous work.

Although taking the Mach kernel (recently obtained) and modifying it to include these facilities is always possible, the issues this work proposes to address include the concept of transparency and performance. We feel these are best examined by taking existing applications and running them unchanged under a new distributed implementation. Since we are emulating existing System V IPC system calls to do this, we should be able to obtain direct comparisons between applications running non-distributed and distributed. In the Mach kernel, it will be much more difficult to assess the performance implications of distributed shared memory because when memory is shared locally mechanisms internal to the OS kernel are used. When memory is shared across sites in Mach, external mechanisms come into play.

Our prototype implementation will make use of the memory management hardware, and in particular, the page table entries (PTEs) of the VAX. The VAX-11 hardware does not have a reference bit, so what is generally done is the kernel turns off the hardware *valid* bit for pages and follows this scenario: if a process references the page, it incurs a page fault because the hardware *valid* bit is off, and the page fault interrupt handler examines the page. Because the *software-valid* bit is set, the kernel knows that the page is really valid and in memory; it sets the *reference* bit and turns the hardware valid bit on. It will know that the page had been referenced. Subsequent references to the page will *not* incur a page fault because the hardware *valid* bit is on. When the page stealer examines the page, it turns off the hardware *valid* bit again, causing processes to fault when referencing the page, repeating the cycle. Our implementation will adjust this cycle to include a software *shared-memory valid* bit which will be used to determine if the page fault is a cross-net page fault and additional software mechanisms to indicate the site at which to fault the page in or out from. We will also be required to modify the *modify* bit cycle to write back changes to the home site of the page of the segment rather than directly to disk. Our prototype will use a primary site scheme where all pages of a given segment have the same primary site.

A variety of issues arise in reestablishing the necessary environment for dsm if a dsm client issues network tasking commands. The *fork* and *exec* system calls will have to be modified for processes that have dsm attached so that both work properly with cross-site commands. Although the case of *exec* is trivial, the case of *fork* could be a problem because a cross site fork could place a process on a host where a different shared memory segment was already occupying needed memory locations. This conflict could occur in the case of *migrate* as well. Network tasking may require that all attached segments be detached upon moving from site to site and that the client manually reattach segments that have been detached. Alternately, the kernel may be able to handle most of these cases and detach shared segments only in special circumstances, such as a conflict in shared memory locations. How transparent network tasking can be made to operate in the context of dsm, remains an issue that requires further investigation.

5.0 Performance of Distributed Shared Memory

Measuring the performance of computer systems is a difficult task. Two methods are typically used: hardware monitors or software monitors. Hardware monitors usually make extremely gross measurements of aggregate properties; the utility of hardware monitors at the software level is marginal. Software monitors can measure as finely as desired, but in doing so disturb the system being measured. Since they may be very expensive to run, they may perturb measurements considerably. Because of these problems, monitoring and measuring must be done very carefully. Nevertheless, measuring the performance of the distributed shared memory implementation is essential in judging the design and implementation. After being implemented, many seemingly good ideas have gone down the road to oblivion because of poor performance; one of the most significant failures related to IPC was Intel's 432 machine[COX81, HANS82].

This work will examine the performance of dsm by executing a number of non-numeric applications that run on System V architectures. One such program is PC-Interface. Others are also under consideration. We plan to move the code to the Locus environment and compare the performance of the distributed configurations with single-site System V IPC. After being normalized for network overheads a comparison between these configurations should prove enlightening.

It is crucial that the implementation of shared memory be a good implementation to have reasonable measurements. To address this issue, we plan to develop some formalization of the communication model we are measuring. This model may not be a formal model, but it will be precise enough to capture necessary characteristics of the communication. We plan to analyze questions about these general communication paradigms using measured experimental results coupled with this model. Zwaenepoel did something similar in his dissertation[ZWAE85]. He developed a queuing model for a workstation-server model of computation and used empirical performance results as the basis for a "baseline" model of computation. This queuing model could be abstracted away from his specific hardware environment. Similarly, the intent of our model is to isolate the implementation artifacts and to provide a mechanism to generalize the results. Future work will look at this in more detail.

6.0 Significance of the Work

Changing technological trends have made distributed shared memory viable. We propose to develop, implement, and measure this IPC mechanism to see how well it performs in practice. The engineering of a distributed shared memory system inside an operating system kernel along with its performance validation has not been done before. The closest work by Li[LI86] was not a kernel-based implementation; kernel performance remains an open question.

We will examine a number of issues related to shared memory in network environments. Of particular importance will be our examination of configurations for dsm, scaling issues, consistency, problem-oriented shared memory, and network error handling. Coupled with this, we look at these IPC mechanisms in the context of fiber optic networks, which changes our past assumptions about latency and throughput for communication. Examining these issues will add to our understanding of contemporary IPC. To our knowledge, there has been little work assessing the impact of fiber optics and shared interprocess communication.

The work here will describe a set of software primitives and identify architectural features that can be used to support the conversion of applications from (non-distributed) shared memory to distributed shared memory. The software primitives are needed because our implementation of distributed shared memory will be based on software segments rather than transparent paging. Our scheme may be able to use some hints or user advice to configure segment placement, distribution, and for optimizations. Hardware features that can assist the implementation will also be identified.

7.0 Conclusions

This paper has outlined the objectives and significance of a distributed shared memory system. We have overviewed issues related to this system and outlined a prototype implementation which is being implemented by the author at UCLA.

8.0 References

[ACCE86] Accetta, M., Baron R., Bolosky W., Golub, D., Rashid, R. F., Tevanian, A., and Young, M., "Mach: A New Kernel Foundation for UNIX Development," Computer Science Department Technical Report, Carnegie-Mellon University, Pittsburgh, PA, May 1986.

[BALB84] Balbus, P. G., Healey, J. L., Out of the Labs and Into the Streets, *Datamation*, September 1984, pp. 96-106.

[BBN85] BBN Laboratories Inc, Butterfly Parallel Processor Overview, Cambridge, MA, June 1985.

[CARR86] Carriero, N., Gelernter, D., The S/Net's Linda Kernel, *ACM Transactions on Computer Systems*, v. 4, n. 2, May 1986, pp. 110-129.

[CHER85] Cheriton, D. R., Preliminary Thoughts on Problem-Oriented Shared Memory: A Decentralized Approach to Distributed Systems, *Operating Systems Review*, v. 19, n. 4, October 1985, pp. 26-33.

[COX81] Cox, G., Corwin, W., Lai, K., Pollack, F., A Unified Model and Implementation for Interprocess Communication in a Multiprocessor Environment, *Proceedings of the Eighth ACM Symposium on Operating System Principles*, Pacific Grove, CA, December 14-16, 1981, pp. 125-127 (extended abstract).

[DENN72] Denning, P. J., On Modeling Program Behavior, *Proceedings Spring Joint Computer Conference*, Vol, 40, AFIPS Press, Arlington, Va., 1972, pp. 937-944.

[ENGL74] England, D. M., Capability Concept Mechanism and Structure in System 250, *Proceedings of the International Workshop on Protection in Operating Systems*, IRIA, Rocquencourt, France, August 1974.

[FLEI86] Fleisch, B. D., Distributed System V IPC in Locus: A Design and Implementation Retrospective, *Proceedings of SIGCOMM '86 Symposium on Communications Architectures and Protocols*, Stowe, Vermont, August, 1986, pp. 386-396. Also appears in UCLA Computer Science Department Quarterly, 14, 2, Spring 1986, pp. 131-144.

[FOLM85] Folmar, R. Distributed Memory Network: An 8 Gigabit Fiber Optic Tightly Coupled System, *Proceedings of the National Aerospace Electronics Conference*, Dayton Convention Center, May 20-24, 1985, v. 1, pp. 91-94.

[GELE83] Gelernter, D., Generative Communication in Linda, Computer Science Department, Technical Report, Yale University, New Haven, CT, November 1983.

[GUY87] Guy, Richard G., A Replicated Filesystem Design for a Distributed UNIX System, Master's Thesis, University of California, Los Angeles, 1987.

[HANS82] Hansen, P. M., Linton, M. A., Mayo, R. N., Murphy, M., Patterson, D. A., A Performance Evaluation of The Intel iAPX 432, *Computer Architecture News*, v. 10, n. 4, June 1982, pp. 17-26.

[JONE77] Jones, A. K., Chansler, R. J., Durham, I., Feiler, P., Schwans, K., Software Management of CM* - a Distributed Multiprocessor, *Proceedings National Computer Conference*, 1977, pp. 657-663.

[LEAC83] Leach, P. J., Levine, P. H., Douros, B. P., Hamilton, J. A., Nelson, D. L., Stumph, B. L., The Architecture of an Integrated Local Network, *IEEE Journal on Selected Areas in Communications*, Vol SAC-1, No., 5, November, 1983, pp. 842-857.

[LI86] Li, K., Memory Coherence in Shared Virtual Memory Systems, *5th ACM SIGACT-SIGOPS Symposium on Principles of Distributed Computing*, Calgary, Canada, 1986.

[POPE81] Popek, G. J., Walker, B. J., et. al., LOCUS: A Network Transparent, High Reliability Distributed System, *Proceedings of the Eighth Symposium on Operating System Principles*, Pacific Grove, CA, December, 1981, pp. 169-177.

[RASH81] Rashid, R. F., Robertson, G. R., Accent: A Communication Oriented Network Operating System Kernel, *Proceedings of the Eighth Symposium on Operating System Principles*, Pacific Grove, CA, December, 1981, pp. 64-75.

[RASH86] Rashid, R. F, From RIG to Accent to Mach: The Evolution of A Network Operating System, *Proceedings of the 1986 Fall Joint Computer Conference*, Dallas, Texas, November 2-6, 1986, pp. 1128-1137.

[SMIT82] Smith, A.J., Cache Memories, *ACM Computing Surveys*, Vol. 14, Number 3, September 1982.

[SPEC82] Spector, A. J., Performing Remote Operations Efficiently on a Local Computer Network, *Communications of the ACM*, v. 25, n. 4, pp. 246-260.

[SWAN77a] Swan, R. J., Bechtolsheim, A., Lai, K. W., Ousterhout, J. K., The Implementation of the CM* Multi-Microprocessor, *Proceedings National Computer Conference*, 1977, pp. 645-655.

[SWAN77b] Swan, R. J., Fuller, S. H., Siewiorek, D. P., CM* - A Modular Multi-Microprocessor, *Proceedings National Computer Conference*, 1977, pp. 637-644.

[THAC81] Thacker, C. P., McCreight, E. M., Lampson, B. W., Sproull, R. F., Boggs, D. R., Alto: A Personal Computer, In Siewiorek, O., Bell, G., and Newell, A. *Computer Structures: Readings and Examples*, Second Edition, McGraw Hill, New York, 1981. Also appears as Xerox Palo Alto Research Center, Report CSL-79-11, Palo Alto, CA, August 1979.

[WULF74] Wulf, W., Cohen, E., Corwin, W., Jones, A., Levin, R., Pierson, C., Pollak, F., HYDRA: The Kernel of a Multiprocessor Operating System, *Communications of the ACM*, v. 17, n. 6, June 1974, pp. 337-345.

[WULF75] Wulf, W., Levin, R., Pierson, C., Overview of the Hydra Operating System Development, *Proceedings Fifth ACM Symposium on Operating System Principles*, 1975, pp. 122-131.

[ZWAE85] Zwaenepoel, W., Message Passing on a Local Network, Ph.D. Thesis, Stanford University, Department of Computer Science, Technical Report STAN-CS-85-1083, 1985.

Appendix I: System V Shared Memory Interface

shmat(shmid, address, flag): attach shared memory segment

shmctl(shmid, command): allows stat, change permissions, shmid removal

shmdt(address): detach shared memory segment

shmget(key, size, flag): locate a segment

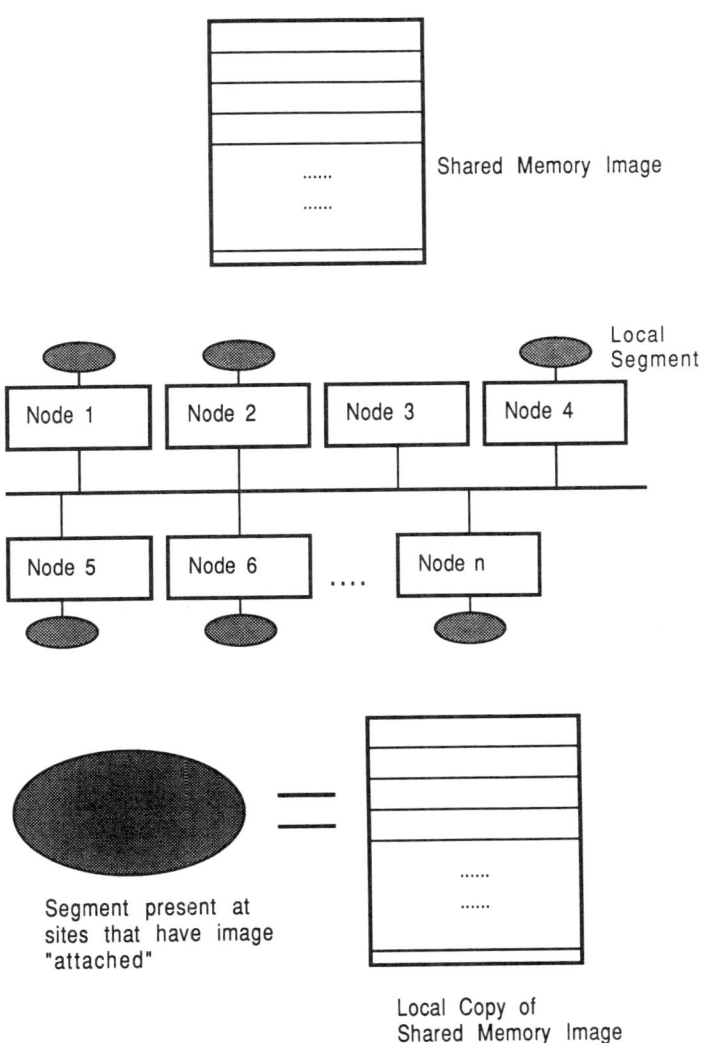

Figure 1

Resource Management Scheme in Distributed Environment

Osamu Nakamura[1] *Nobuo Saito*[2]

Department of Mathematical
Faculty of Science and Technology,
Keio University
3-14-1 Hiyoshi Kohoku, Yokohama, 223 JAPAN

Abstract

The user interface for distributed computing environment needs several kinds of transparency for resources which are distributed on many sites connected to the network. Access transparency and location transparency are general concept for distributed resources.

In distributed environment, there are many resources of the same functions in various sites. For example, cashed resources which are complete duplicated resources exist on many sites in order to realize high performance.

In this paper, the resource management scheme in the distributed environment is described. The sophisticated semantics transparency which is a general scheme for manipulating duplicated resources in distributed environment is provided. The specification language for the environment which provides semantics transparency is also discussed.

1 Introduction

It is very important to consider the semantics of the resources in the distributed environment. Distributed environment should realize the access transparency and location transparency. This transparency in distributed environment is easily done through centralized management, but it does not realize the efficiency of the distributed environment. The advantage of the distributed environment is the replication of the resources in any site.

We introduce the semantics transparency. Semantics transparency is that a user can access resource by semantic name rather than by physical name for the resource. Semantic resource name is in a sense similar to class name of abstract data type. For example, in distributed environment, there are many resources for the same work distributed in several sites.

Another feature of distributed environment is that there are a lot of computing environments in the system. And resources without their environments do not have meaning. For example, in the heterogeneous environment, an object file cannot be executed on a site which has different machine type or different operating system from the specified one. So, it is very important to consider the relationships among the resources in distributed environment.

The resource management scheme in distributed environment which supports the semantics transparency is described in this paper. The resource management scheme which is provided by hierarchical model based on the hierarchy of resource abstraction space is described in section two. In section three, the language for resource management is discussed. An abstract data type is suitable for specifying the distributed environment.

2 Resource Management System

Our resource management scheme in distributed environment is constructed by using a hierarchical model based on resource abstraction space. The details of the resource abstraction spaces are described first, and the category manager which provides the category space and the quantity manager which supports the quantity space are also described in this section.

2.1 Resource Abstraction Space

A hierarchy of resource abstraction space is divided into four layer as shown below:

1. **Local Resource Space**
   a set of resources provided by local operating systems in distributed environment. These are identified by local names and types;

---

[1] Osamu Nakamura is currently a Ph.D candidate at Keio University: osamu%keio.junet@japan.cs.net, and he is also employed by: Software Research Center of Ricoh Company Ltd.
[2] ns%keio.junet@japan.cs.net

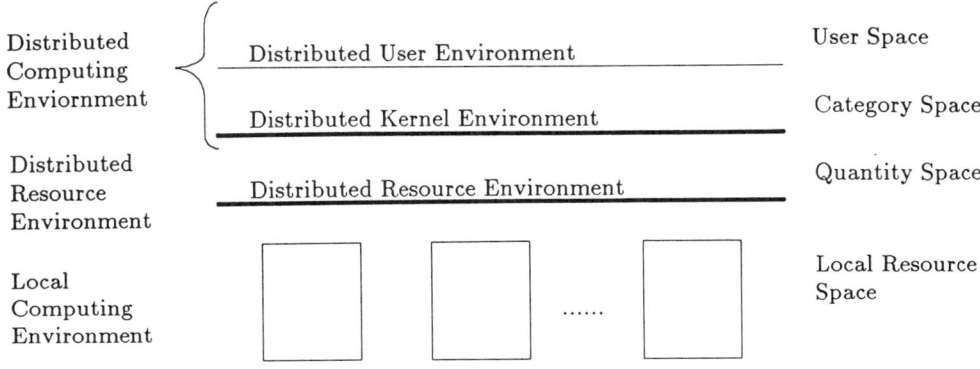

Figure 1: Resource Abstraction Space

2. **Quantity Space**
a set of resources identified by global names and types. Quantity corresponds to an instance of basic abstract data type with a unique name;

3. **Category Space**
a set of abstract resources consisting of component resources and their execution environments. Category corresponds to constructed abstract data type or instances of such abstract data type;

4. **User Space**
a set of user resources for executing application software based on categories.

This structure is shown in Figure 1.

2.1.1 Local Resource Space

Each of the local operating systems in distributed processing environment provides a set of resources for global usage. They are managed by their own operating system, and concrete computation is done by using these resources. The relationship between a resource and its operating system is important because a resource without its execution environment is meaningless in heterogeneous distributed environment.

2.1.2 Quantity Space

All the resources provided by local operating systems are managed together as a set of quantities. A *quantity* is a unified global object with its unique global identifier(a quantity name) and with its basic type. Heterogeneity of local resources are removed and all the quantities are handled in a unified way.

Each of the quantities is mapped to one of the local resources, and its access path is explicitly defined and established.

2.1.3 Category Space

In a user program, it is possible to smoothly carry out its computation by using several quantities, if a user can specify his resource usage requirement. It is, however, not so easy to specify his requirement directly through the global quantity names because he should know all the system resource distributions and management and because there are a lot of the same types of resources doing the same functions in the system. Therefore, it is necessary to provide with users some kind of facilities to help him in specifying resource requirements in his computations.

In order to achieve this goal, we propose a notion of *category* which corresponds to abstract data. The resources are organized as abstract data from the view point of their semantics in a computation. For example, a tool is a resource and it depends on several other resources in distributed environment. Then, this tool is defined as an abstract object which with their supporting resources executes a high level function or facility. A user can easily use this kind of abstract object because he can construct his computation based on high level functions and facilities.

A category consists of a set of resources, and these resources are organized as a hierarchy expressed by a tree. Each of the nodes in a tree is a resource, and it consists of several son resources supporting the functions given by a parent node resource. Or it may directly be mapped to one quantity. A node may be linked to another category already defined in the category space.

A category may include several subcategories in it, and it takes a nested structure. These subcategories can be linked from a node resource, and so we don't distinguish these inner categories from outer ones.

2.1.4 User Space

In a user application program, it is necessary to flexibly specify the resource usage requirement in his computation. A user needs some kind of programming language in order to describe the requirement.

In user program space, the resources are expressed by resource variables. A resource variable represents an instance of a category (or abstract data). This instance is considered to belong to user program space without allowing other users to access to it. In the instantiation, it is possible to give some access restrictions for the usage of categories so that a highly secured distributed environment can be realized.

2.2 Resource Manager

The overview of the resource management system is shown in Figure 2. This system contains the specification language(resource manipulation language), category manager and quantity manager.

Category manager manages all of the categories and instance of categories which represent distributed computing environment. This means that category manager maintains category specification and also manipulates execution of categories. And quantity manager manages all of the resources distributed in the network. Specification language provides the interface between users and this system. The details of the specification language is provided in the next section.

2.2.1 Quantity Manager

Quantity manager manages the resource as quantity. Facilities of the quantity manager are as follows:

1. providing quantities with unique names, types and attributes,

2. managing the location of quantities in distributed environment,

3. transaction processing for the category manager, especially in the resource instantiation.

The quantity manager provides quantities with quantity names which are unique in the network. Location, text or object code, CPU type, input and output types and so on are also maintained as attributes. The quantity manager answers to the query from the category manager about attributes of quantity. This transaction processing mechanism does the same function as the *name server* such as YP(Yellow Page)[1] provided by Sun MicroSystems or Clearinghouse[3] by Xerox does.

Since quantities are managed with types, quantity manager also knows how to access the quantities. For example, resources which are maintained by local operating system as text files, can be accessed by read/write operations, and resources maintained as command can be executed in each operating system.

2.2.2 Category Manager

Category is considered as a module of computing resources in distributed environment and provides the functions of this module. Category can contain subcategories in nested manner, too. It represents an abstracted resource which can handle certain functions in distributed computing. It represents the relationships among component resources, and defines functions provided by this category. It looks like an object in object oriented paradigm. The descendant resources and subcategories support the functions provided by parent resource or category.

An instantiation of category is done in the evaluation of the category. The category manager starts to look for a category which can process the corresponding transactions. First, resources which are included in this category are instantiated. Then subcategories are processed in the same manner recursively. Instantiation of resources is done through the help by the quantity manager described above. Since there are many resources for the same work in distributed environment, it is possible that there are many instances of resources of this category. It is also possible that there are many instances of resources of subcategories. Selection of instances is done by the category manager based on relationships among the resources that are described in category definition.

3 Requirement for Specification Language of Resource Management

In this section, the requirement for a specification language for resource management is discussed. This language is used to define categories in distributed environment. It is designed based on the abstract data type where a resource is defined with its operations together. This language plays a role of kind of shell language in distributed environment.

Modula-2 is used as a base of this language. Its module may correspond to an abstract data type, and a user can use the resources in distributed environment through the instances of abstract data types.

Here are requirements for the facilities prepared in such a language:

- dynamic resource allocation facility,
- resource typing, type hierarchy and type inheritance,
- execution environment through the compilation and interpretation,
- clear definition of statement semantics,
- access control for computer resources.

The followings are the detailed discussion of the above problems.

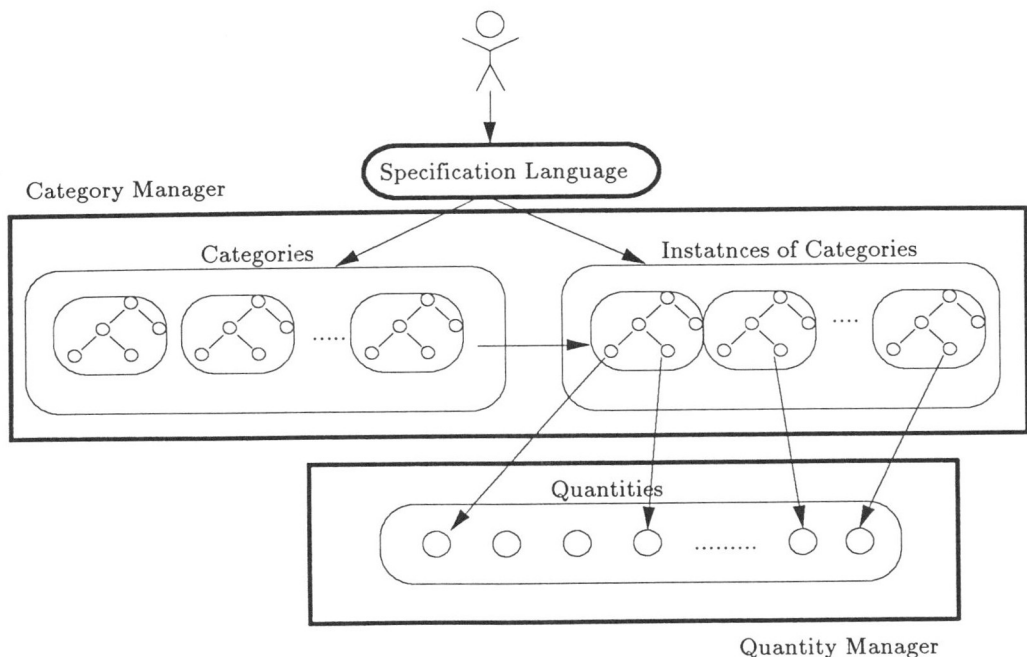

Figure 2: Overview of Resource Management System

3.1 Resource Instantiation and Allocation

It is necessary for the system specification language to have the mechanisms for defining the existing computer resources. For example, it is considered how to access to the hardware resource. A user sometimes wants to specify the instance of the hardware resource, while in another case he wants to specify only the type of resource. For example, when using operating system, he may want to specify a particular site of the system. He is also allowed to specify the operating system class like 4.3BSD and so on.

It is important to realize the instantiation of the resource class. In the instantiation, it is necessary to search existing resources to find appropriate ones which satisfy the type specifications of instances. In the type specification, there may be a hierarchy of types and it is necessary to instantiate all the descendant resource types.

3.2 Type of Resource

It is useful to give a type as one of the attributes for each of the resources in distributed processing environment. Type information can be used to check the semantic correctness of the resource request and resource allocation. There are several basic types for the resources, and of course there are several composite types, too. In fact, the types for categories, abstract data types for resources are all composite types. Composite type usually means a hierarchy of types, and there may be several hierarchical levels for one resource type.

3.2.1 Type Checking

Type checking should be done when the semantic correctness is required to be checked. For example, the laser printer controller Imagen needs to get the Impress code, a special intermediate code for Imagen printing system. It cannot handle the PostScript files. Therefore, it is possible to check the correctness of the input file through the use of its type.

Strong type checking might be hazardous, and it is necessary to introduce a kind of high level type mechanism. Polymorphic type mechanism proposed by R. Milner[2] can be applied to this kind of type system.

Type checking effectively works especially in the distributed processing environment because prechecking of the correctness of the the resources is useful for distributed resources in various remote sites.

3.2.2 Type Inheritance

Resources are constructed as a hierarchy of component resources, and they are defined as abstract data types. Then, there are hierarchical structures among abstract data types, and the type inheritance is a key mechanism in using the hierarchical data type.

Abstract data type has several characteristics, and a derived type can use these characteristics of base types automatically. It is implemented as scope rules of the specification language.

3.3 Statement Semantics

Statements are given in procedure body, and they specify the operations for resources. Usually the operation is an assignment statement, where a variable in the left-hand side represents a resource. Assignment to a variable means to replace the content of the corresponding resource with a value of the right-hand side expression. Usually the right-hand side expression represents a function call which calculates a resource of a specified type.

It is also necessary to initialize the status of the resource. Therefore, the statement of the specification language should do this.

3.4 Scope of Resource Variables

In Modula-2 like language, the import/export mechanism is used to transfer the accesses path. It makes the symbols in one module accessible from another module, and this will introduce the flexible usage of the modules or resources.

Import/export of the resource variables means to control the access to the resource instances, while import/export of the resource types means to transfer the characteristics of the resources.

This scope control mechanisms plays an important role in the type hierarchy, and type inheritance can be implemented through the use of this scope control.

4 Specification Language Proposed

A resource is managed based on the type concept. Ordinary resource management system manages resources only through their names. But in our system, resources are instances of types, and type identifiers are also important. Managing resources with types realizes the followings:

- Semantics check can be done,
- it is possible to select appropriate resources and processes,
- it can realize the semantic transparency.

Specification language is based on Modula-2. Our extensions for Modula-2 are as follows:

1. *Module hierarchy* can be specified in the definition module.
2. *Resource binding* can be specified at the initialization part of the implementation module.
3. *Overloading* mechanism is provided based on type.
4. *Separate compilation* is provided for realizing description ability.

In this section, we provide a specification example for the document processing system TeX using extended Modula-2.

Document processing system TeX has three processors which are AmS-TeX, plainTeX and LaTeX, and it uses two resources, fonts and macros. Fonts and macros are dependent on each of the processors.

Top module of TeX-system is specified as shown below:

```
(*
 * Sample Category Module
 * Document Processor TeX-System
 *)
DEFINITION MODULE TeX-System;
   FROM Document-System IMPORT Dvi_Code,
       Impress_Code, PostScript;
   FROM Document-System IMPORT LaTeX_SRC,
       AmSTeX_SRC, plainTeX_SRC;
   (* Used modules and resources *)
   USE
   MODULE
       TeX-Processor, Utilities;
   (* Procedure Entry for this Category *)
   ENTRY
   PROCEDURE TeX(src: LaTeX_SRC): Dvi_Code;
   PROCEDURE TeX(src: LaTeX_SRC): Impress_Code;
   PROCEDURE TeX(src: LaTeX_SRC): PostScript;
   PROCEDURE TeX(src: AmSTeX_SRC): Dvi_Code;
   PROCEDURE TeX(src: AmSTeX_SRC): Impress_Code;
   PROCEDURE TeX(src: AmSTeX_SRC): PostScript;
   PROCEDURE TeX(src: plainTeX_SRC): Dvi_Code;
   PROCEDURE TeX(src: plainTeX_SRC): Impress_Code;
   PROCEDURE TeX(src: plainTeX_SRC): PostScript;
END TeX-System.

IMPLEMENTATION MODULE TeX-System;
   FROM Document-System IMPORT Dvi_Code,
       Impress_Code, PostScript;
   FROM Document-System IMPORT LaTeX_SRC,
       AmSTeX_SRC, plainTeX_SRC;
   FROM Utilities IMPORT DviToPs, DviToImp;
   FROM TeX_Processor IMPORT LaTeX, AmSTeX,
       plainTeX;

   PROCEDURE TeX(src: LaTeX_SRC): Dvi_Code;
   BEGIN
       RETURN LaTeX(src);
   END TeX;

   PROCEDURE TeX(src: LaTeX_SRC): Impress_Code;
   VAR
       dvitmp: Dvi_Code;
       imptmp: Impress_Code;
   BEGIN
       dvitmp := LaTeX(src);
       imptmp := DviToImp(dvitmp);
       RETURN imptmp;
   END TeX;

   PROCEDURE TeX(src: LaTeX_SRC): PostScript;
   VAR
       dvitmp: Dvi_Code;
       pstmp: PostScript;
```

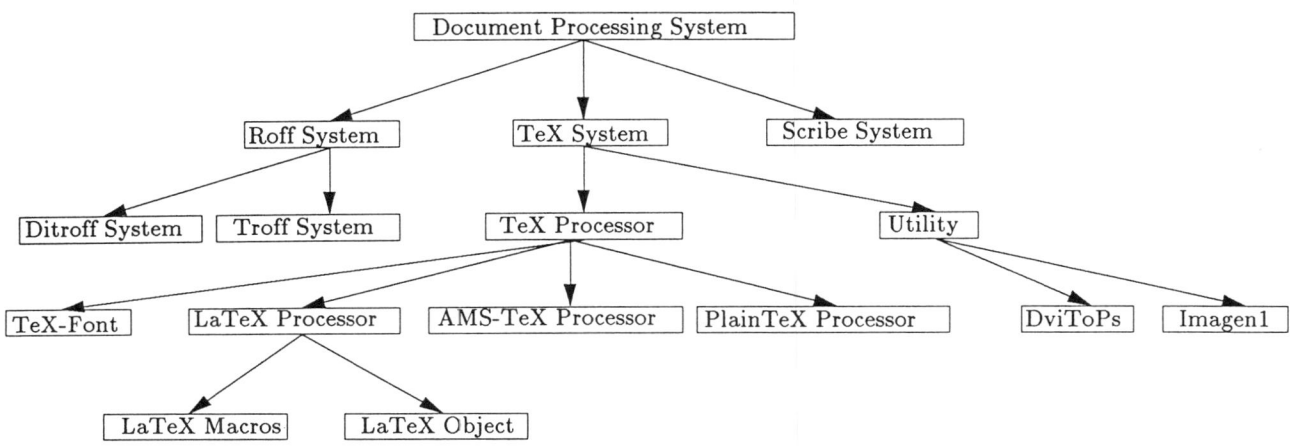

Figure 3: Structure of Document Processing Category

```
BEGIN
    dvitmp := LaTeX(src);
    pstmp := DviToPs(dvitmp);
    RETURN pstmp;
END TeX;

    (* Procedure for AmSTeX text *)
        .
        .
        .
    (* Procedure for plainTeX text *)
        .
        .
        .
BEGIN
 (* Initialization part of the resource variables
*)
END TeX-System.
```

USE entry is used for specifying the subcategories of this category. In this example, *TeX-Processor* and *Utility* are subcategories. **ENTRY** specifies entry points of this abstract data type.

The entry procedure TeX is overloaded, and the correct procedure is selected based on the types of the input and output files. Each of the TeX procedures is implemented by calling the appropriate one imported from the TeX processors and when necessary by calling the appropriate utility functions to convert the dvi-code into a specified target code.

Subcategory TeX-Processor and its subcategory *LaTeX-Processor* is also specified as an abstract data type as shown below:

```
(*
 *TeX-Processor Specification
 *)
DEFINITION MODULE TeX-Processor;
    USE (* Used resources *)
    MODULE TeX-Font,
        LaTeX-Processor,
        AmS-TeX-Processor,
        plain-TeX-Processor;
END TeX-Processor.


(*
 * LaTeX-Processor Specification
 *)
DEFINITION MODULE LaTeX-Processor;
FROM Document-System IMPORT LaTeX-SRC;
    USE
    (* Used resources *)
    MODULE LaTeX-Macros, LaTeX-object;
    ENTRY
    (* Procedure Entry for this category *)
    PROCEDURE LaTeX(src: LaTeX_SRC): Dvi_Code;
END TeX-Processors.

IMPLEMENTATION MODULE LaTeX-Processor;
    FROM LaTeX-Macros IMPORT macros;
    FROM LaTeX-object IMPORT latex;
    PROCEDURE LaTeX(src: LaTeX_SRC): Dvi_Code;
    BEGIN
        RETURN Eval(latex(macros, TeX-Font, src));
    END LaTeX-Processor;
BEGIN
    (* Relationship Condition *)
    LaTeX-object.os = LaTeX-Macros.os;
    LaTeX-object.os = TeX-Font.os;
    LaTeX-object.machine = TeX-Font.machine;
END LaTeX-Processor.
```

LaTeX-Processor uses resources, *LaTeX-object*, *LaTeX-Macros* and *TeX-Font*. These resources are instantiated to satisfy relationship conditions described at the initialization part of the program. All of the resources are managed with some attributes by quantity manager. Instantiation of resources is processed with these attributes. In this example, *os* and *machine* are attributes of the resources.

5 Conclusion

In this paper, the authors proposed resource management scheme which realizes semantics transparency for distributed environment. Semantics transparency enhances the efficiency of resource management in distributed environment.

The semantics transparency is based on the resource types, and specification language for resource definitions is also proposed with an example.

Acknowledgement

We want to thank Tomomitsu Sato, Akira Yamaguchi and Thoru Usami who are the members of distributed processing group of Satio Laboratory. They have been working on this project with us. We also appreciate the help of the other members of Saito Laboratory.

The Ricoh Corporation has provided us with the support for this research work. Special thanks go to Dr. Hideko Kunii of the Ricoh Corporation, who has contributed in realizing good research environment.

References

[1] LYON, B. *Sun Remote Procedure Call Specification*. Tech. Rep., Sun MicroSystems, Inc., 1984.

[2] MILNER, R. A theory of type polymorphism in programming. *Journal of Computer and System Science 17* (1987), 348–375.

[3] OPPEN, D. C., AND DALAL, Y. K. The clearinghouse: a decentralized agent for locating named objects in a distributed environment. *ACM Transaction on Office Information Systems 1*, 3 (July 1983).

PART 11. COMMUNICATION PROTOCOLS

J. Mathis

Apple, USA

Receiver-Initiated Busy-Tone Multiple Access in Packet Radio Networks [1]

Cheng-shong Wu and Victor O.K. Li

Department of Electrical Engineering
University of Southern California
Los Angeles, CA 90089-0272

ABSTRACT

The ALOHA and Carrier Sense Multiple Access (CSMA) protocols have been proposed for packet radio networks (PRN). However, CSMA/CD which gives superior performance and has been successful applied in local area networks cannot be readily applied in PRN since the locally generated signals will overwhelm a remote transmission, rendering it impossible to tell whether a collision has occurred or not. In addition, CSMA and CSMA/CD suffer from the "hidden node" problem in a multihop PRN. In this paper, we develop the Receiver-Initiated Busy-Tone Multiple Access Protocol to resolve these difficulties. Both fully connected and multihop networks are studied. The busy tone serves as an acknowledgement and prevents conflicting transmissions from other nodes, including "hidden nodes".

[1] This research is supported in part by the U.S. Army Research Office under contract DAAG 29-85-K-0116.

I. Introduction

The ALOHA and Carrier Sense Multiple Access (CSMA) protocols have been proposed for Packet Radio Networks (PRN) [1],[2],[4],[5]. However, CSMA/CD [3], which gives superior performance and has been successful applied in local area networks, cannot be readily applied in PRN since the locally generated signals will overwhelm a remote transmission, rendering it impossible to tell whether a collision has occurred or not. In addition, CSMA and CSMA/CD [6],[7] suffer from the "hidden node" problem in a multihop PRN.

In this paper, we develop the Receiver-Initiated Busy-Tone Multiple Access Protocol to resolve these difficulties. In particular, the total bandwidth is divided into two channels, one for the transmission of data and the other for the busy tone. Each packet includes a preamble portion and a data portion. Suppose a source node (sender) wishes to send a packet to a destination node (receiver), it sends a preamble which contains the identification of the destination node on the data channel. If this preamble is successfully received by the receiver, the receiver will send a busy-tone to acknowledge the sender and acquire the data channel for the transmission of the data portion of the packet from the sender. A node can transmit a preamble of a packet only when the tone channel is idle and can transmit the data portion only when the corresponding preamble is acknowledged by the receiver. The busy tone serves two functions. One is as an acknowledgement and the other is to prevent the transmission of other nodes, including "hidden nodes" which may cause collisions.

In the next section, we will describe the protocol in more detail. Markov models are developed to analyze the delay and system capacity of this proposed protocol for both single-hop and multihop systems. The analysis of multihop networks is much more difficult due to the dependencies between nodes. In [8], Boorstyn, et al. studied the CSMA network under the assumption of perfect capture. In [9] Tobagi and Brazio applied the model of [8] to conservative BTMA (that is, all nodes sensing a transmission transmit the busy tone, regardlessly of whether it is the destination node or not), and CSMA with nonperfect capture. All of them considered unslotted systems and assumed preambles with zero length.

II Protocol description

The messages in our system are packetized. Each packet includes a preamble portion and a data portion. The preamble portion contains the indetification of the destination of the packet and the data portion contains the data to be transmitted. The total bandwidth is divided into two channels. The data channel is used for the transmission of data and the tone channel, for the busy tone. Both channels are slotted, with each slot equal to the length of the preamble. We say a slot is busy if there is busy-tone signal in the tone channel; otherwise, the slot is idle. A node can transmit packets only at an idle slot, except when it has already acquired the data channel.

First, we describe the basic protocol. In this protocol, nodes do not provide backlog buffers to store packets. Suppose a source node (sender) wishes to send a packet to a destination node (receiver). First, it senses the busy-tone channel. If the channel is busy, the packet will be rescheduled (that is, it waits a random time and tries again). If the channel is idle, it keeps monitoring the busy-tone channel and sends a preamble which contains the identification of the destination node on the data channel. If this preamble is successfully received by the receiver, the receiver will send a busy-tone and the sender will hear it. After hearing the busy tone from the receiver, the sender begins to transmit the data. As long as the receiver is receiving data from the sender, it continues sending the busy tone. If this preamble is unsuccessful, the sender will not hear the busy tone and it will try again. Figure 1 is an example of channel behavior.

Since the basic protocol, just like the ALOHA protocol, will be unstable at heavy traffic, we introduce the controlled protocol to overcome this problem. A packet which has suffered a collision or is generated during a busy slot is backlogged. The protocol is similar to the basic protocol, except that every node has a backlog buffer to store one backlogged packet. We say a node is in backlogged mode if its buffer is occupied, otherwise the node is in unbacklogged mode. A packet arriving at a node in backlogged mode will be blocked and will be regenerated after a random time. Suppose a packet arrives at a node in unbacklogged mode in a slot. If the slot is an idle slot, with probability p the preamble of the packet will be transmitted at this slot and with probability 1-p the packet will not be transmitted. If the slot is a busy slot, the packet will be put in backlog buffer to wait for the next idle slot. A backlogged node will transmit a backlogged packet with probability q and all backlogged packets will stay at the backlog buffer until it succeeds.

Both of these two protocols can be used in a multihop system directly without any modification. In the next section, we first analyze the single-hop system and then the multihop system.

III. Performance Analysis

1. Single-hop system

Our performance model is based on the following assumptions:

1   The system is fully connected and has N nodes.
2   The arrival of packets, including newly generated packets and rescheduled packets, constitutes a Bernoulli process with probability λ per slot at each node.
3   The length (measured in slots) of the data portion of a packet is geometrically distributed with parameter g.

First, we analyze the basic protocol.

In this protocol, if a packet arrives at a busy slot or the preamble portion of the arriving packet is not successfully received by the destination, we reschedule the packet.

Let P_s be the probability of a successful preamble transmission in an idle slot. Then,

$$P_s = prob\ \{\ exactly\ one\ arrival\ in\ the\ system\ in\ a\ slot\ \}$$
$$= \binom{N}{1}\lambda(1-\lambda)^{N-1}$$

Define random variable X to be the number of elapsed slots up to and including the first successful preamble transmission. We have

$$prob\ \{\ X = x\ \} = P_s(1-P_s)^{x-1}\ ,\ x=1,2,3,...,\infty$$

and

$$E(X) = \frac{1}{P_s}$$

Any successful preamble will be followed by the transmission of the data portion. Thus, we can obtain the throughput η by

$$\eta = \frac{1+E(length\ of\ data\ portion)}{E(X)+E(length\ of\ data\ portion)}$$
$$= \frac{P_s g + P_s}{P_s + g}$$

The 1 in the numerator is for the preamble portion which is counted as useful throughput since the identification of the destination is essential.

Next, we analyse the controlled protocol.

In this protocol, if a packet arrives at a busy slot or at an idle slot and the transmission of the preamble is not successful, we will put the packet into the backlog buffer if it is available.

Define the system state at the beginning of a slot by a vector s. s=(b,t) where b denotes the number of nodes in the backlogged mode at the beginning of a slot, and t=1 if the slot is busy, t=0 if the slot is idle. Let π_s be the steady state probability of the system at state s at the beginning of a slot and $A_{s,s'}$ be the transition probability from state s to state s' in one slot time. Then the system state equation is

$$\pi_{s'} = \sum_s \pi_s A_{s,s'}$$

Using this equation, the fact that $\sum_s \pi_s = 1$, and $A_{s,s'}$ calculated in Appendix 1, we can get the state probabilities and calculate the throughput by

$$\eta = \sum_{b=0}^{N} \pi_{(b,1)} + \sum_{b=0}^{N}\sum_{b'=0}^{N} \pi_{(b,0)} A_{(b,0)(b',1)}$$

The second part of this equation is necessary because we treat the preamble as part of the useful throughput.

Of course, we can obtain other useful results such as the expected number of backlogged nodes

$$E(b) = \sum_{b=0}^{N} b\,(\pi_{(b,1)}+\pi_{(b,0)})$$

or use Little's formula get the expected waiting time of a packet in the backlog buffer as $\frac{E(b)}{\eta}$.

2. Multihop system

The topology of a PRN may be described by a graph G=(N,L), where N is the set of nodes, and L is the set of links. If node i can transmit a message directly to node j, the ordered pair (i,j) is an element of L. Note that (i,j) must belong to L if (j,i) does. When node i transmits a preamble to node j successfully, node j will transmit a busy-tone to acknowledge node j, which will begin the transmission of the data portion, and to inhibit other neighbors from transmitting. We say link (i,j) is active at a slot if node i transmits the data portion of a packet to node j. Let $NB((i,j)) = \{k\,|\,(k,j) \in L\}$ be the neighbors of the receiving node of link (i,j). Define a collision-free set as a set of links that can carry packets simultaneously with no collisions at receiving ends of the links. Let C denote the set of all possible collision-free sets. With this definition, we have the following property:

Property Set of active links A at any slot forms a collision free set, that is $A \in C$.

Proof Assume link $(i,j) \in A$ is an active link at a slot. Any node k, $k \in NB((i,j))$ will hear the busy tone from node j. Our protocol dictates that no neighbors of j, except i who has acquired the data channel, can transmit. Thus link (i,j) is collision free.

This property ensures that our protocol works in multihop networks as well as in fully connected network. Furthermore, collisions may only occur during the transmission of the preamble and several links may be active at the same time. This means we can take advantage of spatial reuse of bandwidth in PRN.

The analysis of the performance is much more complex for a multihop system. To simplify the analysis, we will only study the basic protocol. The analysis is based on the following assumptions:

1. The connectivity of the network is described by a graph G=(N,L).

2. The arrival of packets, including newly generated and rescheduled packets, constitutes a Bernoulli process with probability λ_i per slot at node i. Each packet generated at node i will be destined to node j with probability $p_{i,j}$, where j is a neighbor of node i, and $\sum_j p_{i,j}=1$, for all i.

3. The length of the data portion of a packet from node i to node j is geometrically distributed with parameter $g_{i,j}$.

The set of active links in a slot charaterizes the system behavior at that time. Thus, we the system state $S(t)$ to be the set of active links at slot t. The links with successful preambles in this slot will be added to the set of active links at the next slot and the links completing their transmission at the end of this slot will be subtracted from the set of active links. Then,

$$S(t+1) = S(t) \cup B(t) - F(t)$$

where $F(t)= \{(i,j) | (i,j) \in S(t)$, and completes transmission at slot t},

$B(t)=\{(i,j) |$ transmission of preamble (i,j) succeeds at slot t }.
Please note that $S(t) \cup B(t) \in C$ and $S(t) \cap B(t) = \phi$. We call $B(t)$ a beginning active set.

Since $F(t)$ and $B(t)$ are independent conditioned on $S(t)$ and $S(t+1)$ is as defined above, we find the transition probability, $prob(S(t+1)| S(t))$, is given by

$$prob(S(t+1)| S(t)) = prob(B(t)| S(t)) \times prob(F(t)| S(t))$$

and

$$prob(F(t)| S(t)) = \prod_{(i,j) \in F(t)} g_{i,j} \prod_{(k,l) \in S(t)-F(t)} (1-g_{k,l})$$

The derivation of $prob(B(t)|S(t))$ can be found in Appendix 2.

Now we can solve the system state equations and get the steady state probabilities, π_S. Finally, we define the throughput η to be the average number of active links in the system. Then,

$$\eta = \sum_{S \in C} |S| \pi_S$$

IV Numerical Examples

Figure 2 shows the throughput versus offered traffic for a fully connected system with 20 nodes. First, we note the instability (that is, increasing the arrival rate decreases the throughput) of the basic protocol. This is similar to the instability exhibited by the ALOHA protocol. In the controlled protocol, we use the backlog buffer to "control" the channel input rate.

The maximum throughput of the basic protocol η_{max} occurs at $\lambda = \frac{1}{N}$ which is 0.05 in our example with N=20. This η_{max} is also the maximum achievable throughput of the controlled protocol. We may call η_{max} the system capacity. In our example, the throughput of the controlled protocol is higher than that of the basic protocol because the former provides buffers to decrease the rescheduling rate of arriving packets.

Figure 2 also compares two controlled protocols with different p's. p=1 gives a better throughput at light traffic than p=0.05. The reason may be found in figure 3. The expected number of backlogged nodes for p=1 is less than that for p=0.05. With less backlogged nodes, the probability an arrival is blocked becomes less and the throughput will be higher.

In figure 4, we show two example network topologies with five nodes each. One is fully-connected and the other is partially-connected. Figure 5 shows the throughput versus offered traffic for the two example networks in figure 4. As expected, the partially-connected network gives higher throughput because of spatial reuse.

Conclusion

In this paper, we have described the Receiver-Initiated Busy-Tone Multiple Access Protocol. A Markov model is developed to analyze it. We find that this protocol enjoys good throughput characteristics.

Appendix

1. The calculation of transition probabilities $A_{s,s'}$

$A_{(i,0)(i+k,0)} = prob$ { k of the N-i unbacklogged nodes have arrivals, no packet transmitted successfully | system in state (i,0) at the beginning of the slot }

$$= bin(N-i,k,\lambda)(1-bin(k,1,p)(1-q)^i - bin(i,1,q)(1-p)^k)$$
$$, i=0,1,...,N; k=0,...,N-i$$

where $bin(n,k,\rho) = \binom{n}{k}\rho^k(1-\rho)^{n-k}$ is the probability mass function of the binomial distribution.

$A_{(i,0)(i+k-1,1)} = prob$ { k of the N-i unbacklogged nodes have arrivals, one preamble transmitted successfully | system in state (i,0) at the beginning of the slot }

$$= bin(N-i,k,\lambda)(bin(k,1,p)(1-q)^i + bin(i,1,q)(1-p)^k)$$
$$, i=0,1,...,N; k=0,...,N-i$$

$A_{(i,1)(i+k,0)} = prob$ { k of the N-i unbacklogged nodes have arrivals, current transmission of the data portion will finish in this slot | system in state (i,0) at the beginning of the slot }

$$= bin(N-i,k,\lambda)g \quad , i=0,1,...,N; k=0,...,N-i$$

$A_{(i,0)(i+k,0)} = prob$ { k of the N-i unbacklogged nodes have arrivals, current transmission of the data portion will continue in the next slot | system in state (i,0) at the beginning of the slot }

$$= bin(N-i,k,\lambda)(1-g) \quad , i=0,1,...,N; k=0,...,N-i$$

2. Finding $prob(B|S)$

We use the principle of Inclusion and Exclusion [10] to find $prob(B|S)$.

Define $\bar{B} = \{ B' | B' \supseteq B, B' \cup S \in C, B' \cap S = \phi \}$ to be the collection of all beginning active sets containing B. Then the probability that at least the set B is successful is given by

$$prob(\bar{B}|S) = \prod_{(i,j) \in B} \lambda_i p_{i,j} \prod_{k \in LL}(1-p_k)$$

where $LL = \{UN(S) \cap \bigcup_{(l,m) \in B} NB^*(l,m)\}$

$NB^*((i,j)) = NB((i,j)) \cup \{j\}$

$UN(S) = N - \bigcup_{(i,j) \in S} NB^*((i,j))$.

Note that $UN(S)$ is the set of nodes not blocked by the activation of S, and $\bigcup_{(l,m) \in B} NB^*(l,m)$ is the set of nodes whose transmission will interfere with B. Therefore, LL is the set of nodes which may potentially interfere with B, and we require these nodes to be silent.

We can get $prob(B|S)$ recursively as follows:

$$prob(B|S) = prob(\bar{B}|S) - \sum_{B' \in \bar{B}-\{B\}} prob(B'|S)$$

References

[1] N. Abramson, "The Aloha System - Another Alternative for Computer Communication." AFIPS Conf. Proc., Fall Joint Computer Conference, pp. 281-285. 1970.

[2] L. Kleinrock and F.A. Tobagi, "Packet Switching in radio Channels: Part I - Carrier Sense Multiple-Access Modes and their Throughput-delay Characteristics." IEEE Trans. on Commun. COM-23:1400-1416, Dec., 1975.

[3] F. Tobagi and V.B. Hunt, "Performance Analysis of Carrier Sense Multiple Access will Collision Detection" Comput. Networks 4:245-259, 1980.

[4] Tobagi, F.A. " Analysis of a Two-Hop Centralized packet Radio Network - part I : Slotted ALOHA." IEEE Trans. on Commun. COM-28:196-207, Feb., 1980.

[5] Tobagi, F.A., "Analysis of a Two-Hop Centralized packet Radio Network - part II : Carrier Sense Multiple Access" IEEE Trans. on Commun. COM-28:208-216, Feb., 1980.

[6] Tobagi, F.A. and Kleinrock, L., "Packet Switching in Radio Channels: Part II - The Hidden Terminal Problem in Carrier Sense Multiple Access and Busy Tone Solution" IEEE Trans. on Commun. COM-23:1417-1433, Dec., 1975.

[7] Boorstyn, R. R., Kershenbaum, A. "Throughput Analysis of Multihop Packet Radio Networks." Proc. IEEE Icc, pp 13.6.1-13.6.6 Jun., 1980.

[8] Boorstyn, R. R., Kershenbaum, A., Maglaris, B., Sahin, V. "Throughput Analysis in Multihop CSMA Packet Networks." IEEE Trans. Commun. COM-35:267-274, Mar., 1987.

[9] Tobagi, F. A., Brazio, J. M. "Throughput analysis of multihop packet radio networks under various channel access schemes." Proc. INFOCOM'83, San Diego, Ca, pp. 382-389, Apr., 1983.

[10] Polya, G., Tarjan, R., Woods, D. "Notes on introductory combinatorics." Birkhauser Boston, Inc., 1983

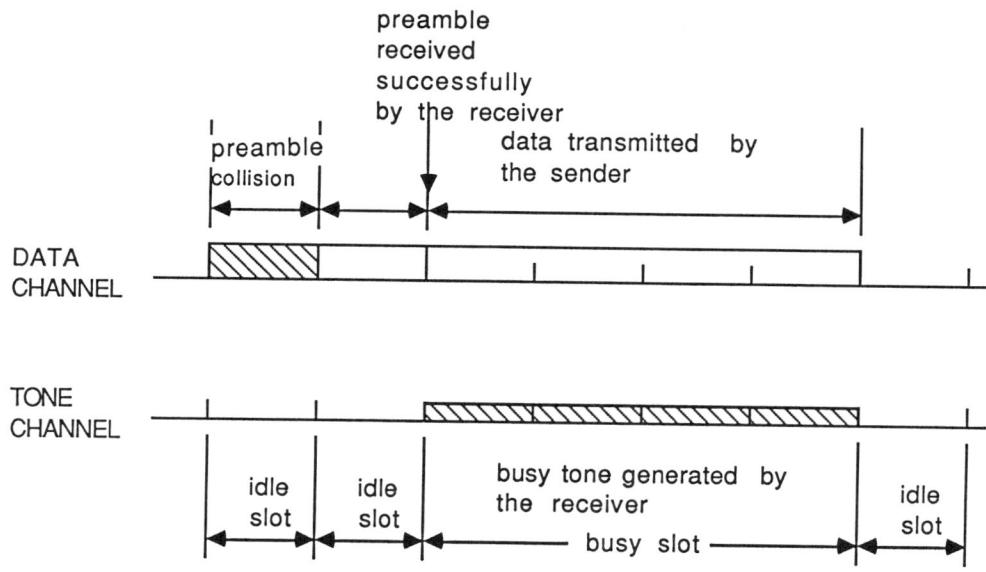

Figure 1. Example of channel behavior

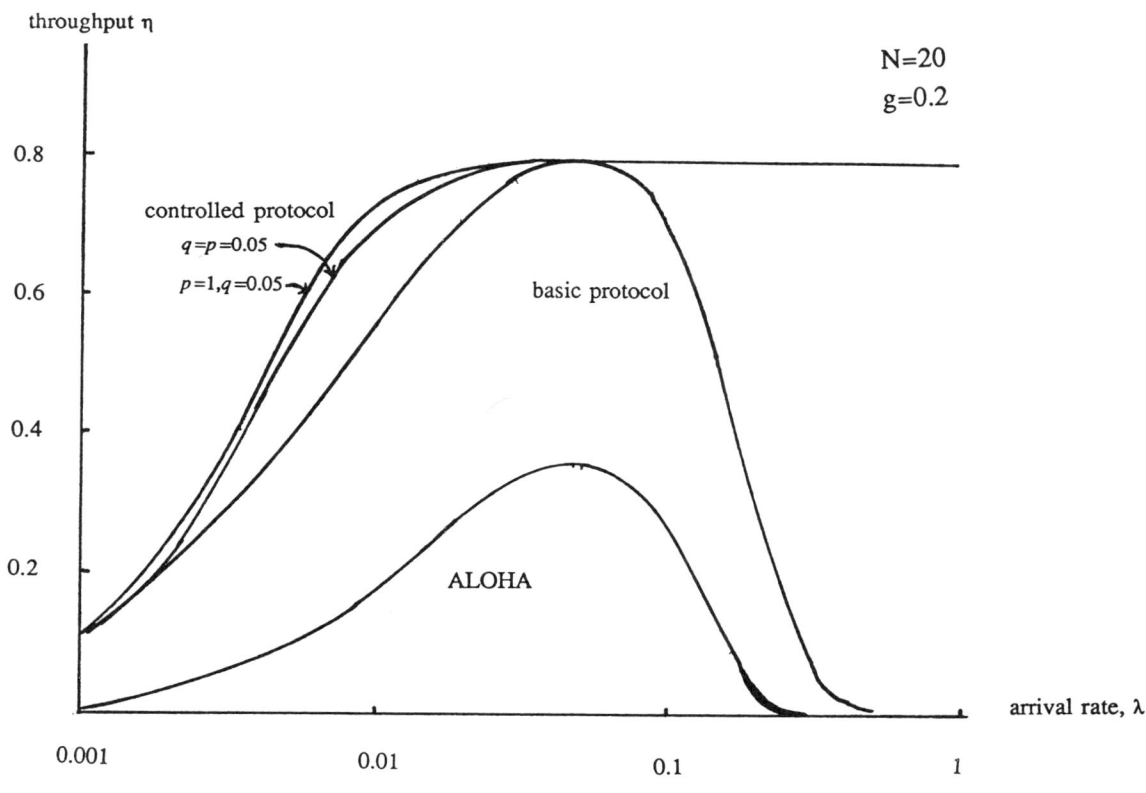

Figure 2. Throughput versus packet arrival rate for a fully-connected network

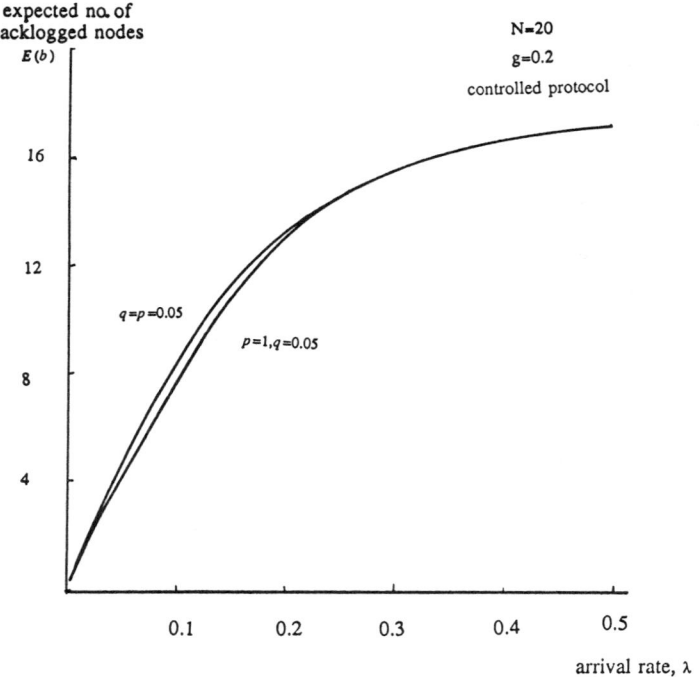

Figure 3. Expected number of backlogged nodes versus packet arrival rate for fully-connected network

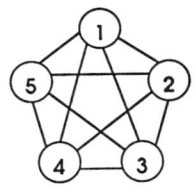

(a) Fully-connected

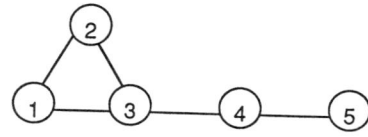

(b) Partially-connected

Figure 4. Example network topologies

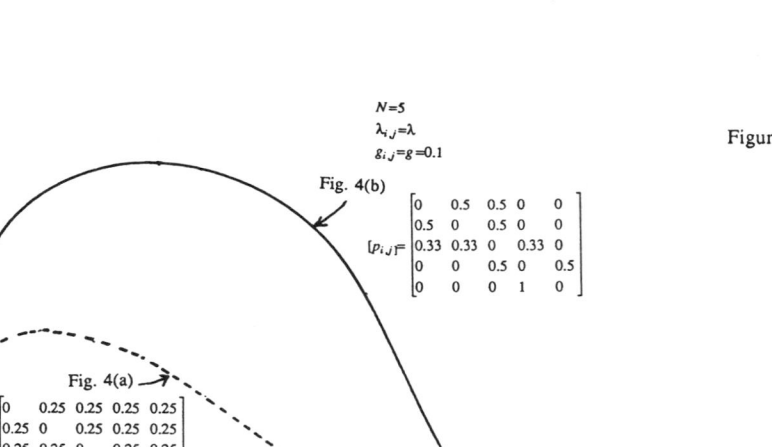

Figure 5. Throughput versus input rate for network examples

A Reliable and Efficient Multicast Protocol for Broadband Broadcast Networks

A. Erramilli
Bell Communications Research, Inc.
331 Newman Springs Road
Red Bank, NJ 07701-7020

R. P. Singh
Bell Communications Research, Inc.
435 South Street
Morristown, NJ 07960-1961

Abstract

A reliable and efficient data transfer protocol is proposed for multicast applications in broadband broadcast networks. The protocol is based on negative acknowledgements, with several enhancements so that it matches most of the functionality of a positive acknowledgement based protocol. The protocol makes the best use of resources in the broadband network environment by conserving processing and trading off transmission and storage resources. The performance of this protocol is compared with the positive acknowledgement based protocol on the basis of maximum throughput as a function of group size for lecture and conference applications.

I. Introduction

Multicast (multipoint-to-multipoint) communication is a natural extension of unicast (point-to-point) communication in which a selected set of users simultaneously communicate among themselves. The primary motivation for multicast communication stems from the wide range of applications that require it, both in a local area network (LAN) and in a broadband packet network. Some important applications include distributed processing, distributed database, office automation, multiuser games, teleconferencing, LAN interconnection etc. The need for a multicast communication is inherent in distributed processing and distributed database applications. It facilitates search of an object among a set of participating processes in parallel, and provides proper coordination of events by simultaneous communication among them. A multicast communication for LAN interconnection allows users to efficiently utilize the large network software base, such as distributed operation systems and databases, developed for different LANs. It allows rapid distribution of ballots in a voting system as well as in a multiuser game. In factory automation, real time distributed data gathering and control of production lines can be more efficiently performed via a multicast communication.

While a LAN, such as an Ethernet bus or a token ring, provides a natural broadcast medium, a broadband packet network is predominantly a unicast network. Multicasting in both situations require a multicast logical address and some mechanism, whereby, in the former, packets are received by a restricted set of users on the network (e.g., address filtering [1]), and, in the latter, packets are copied and are sent to users in the multicast group on a point-to-point basis. Multicasting is obviously easier in a LAN than in a large size public network. Although, multicasting in a store-and-forward type of large public network has been studied before [2], it is only recently, after some useful results on the design of self-routing copy networks have been reported [3], that multicasting in a high speed, high capacity broadband packet network is becoming viable.

Reliability of information transfer is an important issue in a telecommunication network, particularly for data application. Not all data transfer applications require absolute reliability. For example, in some graphics applications small amount of data error will not affect the usefulness of the result. However, some other applications, notably database update and search, require a high degree of reliability. The problem of reliable multicast protocols has been dealt with by many researchers in the literature in various contexts. Decitre et al [4] consider an error detection scheme for multicast communication on a CSMA/CD network, in which the mutual exclusion nature of the contention algorithm is used to generate an absolute ordering of packet traffic from all the senders across all the receivers. Chang and Maxemchuk [5] use a system of primary and secondary receivers to obtain a reliable and efficient data transfer protocol which provides a globally consistent delivery ordering. References [6-8] are other examples of work on this subject. Most of the papers exploit the specific broadcast capability of a LAN to provide reliability efficiently, and it is not clear how these protocols can be implemented in a broadband network. While the focus of earlier work has been mostly on LANs, in this paper we propose a multicast data transfer protocol which can also provide reliable, connection-oriented packet communication among multiple users in a broadband broadcast network.

Broadband networks use fiber optic transmission, and thus are characterized by plentiful bandwidth and relatively low packet error rates, say, of the order of one in 10^{-6}. Further, buffers are relatively inexpensive so that errors due to buffer overflow can be made highly improbable. In broadband networks, therefore, the delay-throughput performance is essentially limited by the amount of processing needed to transport information across the network. As such, any protocol designed for this environment must conserve processing by trading off transmission and storage resources, and by keeping functionality to the necessary minimum. This point of view is a significant departure from classical protocol design which attempts to conserve transmission bandwidth and storage resources. Moreover, the error rates in broadband networks are so low that many of the protocol mechanisms used in more hostile environments can be simplified. Section II discusses the set of assumptions upon which the robust multicast protocol proposed here is based.

In point-to-point communications, robustness is typically achieved by error detection through positive acknowledgements (ACK) from the receiver to the source, i.e., whenever the source sends a data packet, the receiver acknowledges its receipt by sending an acknowledgement to the source. In the multicast case, a direct extension of the ACK scheme implies that for a given data packet there can be as many acknowledgements as the number of receivers. So the efficiency gained by the use of the broadcast capability of the network is negated by the increase in processing required at the source to process each acknowledgement packet. Further, the net throughput is a sensitive function of the number of users in the multicast group. Thus, an ACK scheme is generally unsuitable for multicast communications, and even more so for broadband broadcast networks.

An alternative to this is a negative acknowledgement (NAK) scheme with a sequential numbering of data packets at the source. Here the receiver does not acknowledge receipt of packets under normal operation. It detects errors (i.e., damaged or lost packets) by gaps in the sequence number in the packet stream, and it sends a NAK about the nonreceipt of the packet to the source. In this paper we present a simple and robust NAK-based multicast protocol, and compare its performance with an ACK-based scheme.

There are some inherent advantages in an ACK scheme (and correspondingly, deficiencies in a pure NAK scheme) such as built-in flow control, bounded error recovery times, packet buffer management, etc. These advantages are due to the feedback of information in the form of acknowledgements among the users in the multicast group. Our objective is to enhance the pure NAK protocol so that it matches most of the functionality of the ACK scheme, while having a throughput that stays relatively insensitive to the size of the multicast group. The highlights of our enhanced NAK protocol are: the use of timers and status packets to bound the time taken to recover from packet loss; an implicit back window scheme, useful for buffer management; a provision to detect receiver failures; and a simple congestion control strategy. The added functionality compensates for the lack of feedback, and provides an efficient open loop control of information flow among the users. We describe this protocol in detail in Section III.

In Section IV, the performance of the ACK and NAK schemes is studied using analytical models. We compare the performance of the enhanced NAK protocol with the ACK scheme by examining maximum throughput of the multicast group as a function of its size for both balanced (conference mode) and one-sided (lecture mode) traffic.

Finally, Section V provides some concluding remarks, where the results of the previous sections are used to characterize the environment and applications for which the NAK protocol will be appropriate.

II. Assumptions

The design of a protocol for data transmission directly depends upon the network architecture and environment it has to operate in. The complexity of the protocol is based on the assumptions about the maximum available bandwidth in the network, transmission error rates, cost of various elements of the network, namely, bandwidth, storage (buffer) and processing, the nature of data service, whether the network provides special mechanisms for transfer of information between users, e.g., CSMA/CD on Ethernet or ring, whether it is meant for unicast, multicast or broadcast communication etc. A good protocol meant for unicast narrowband or wideband communication may perform poorly in terms of resource utilization if used in multicast or broadcast broadband communication.

The multicast protocol we propose here is based on the following assumptions:

1. We assume that a multicast group has already been established using some call setup protocol. What we describe below is a data transfer protocol using which the users communicate among themselves reliably.

2. The underlying network is a broadband, broadcast network, characterized by low error rates, low end-to-end delays, inexpensive transmission and storage. The performance bottleneck is primarily due to processing. Thus the protocol presented here has just enough functionality that it provides a reliable data transfer with minimum of processing.

3. There are no intrinsic speed mismatches between the users of the multicast group, which is to say that flow control is not a fundamental objective in this protocol.

4. It is necessary to correctly sequence packets from one user, but an absolute ordering of packets across all the users is not needed.

There are $M+1$ users in a multicast group. Every user of the group has two ports - a receiving port and a transmitting port - through which it receives and sends data, respectively, to every other users under one server or cpu control. There are two modes of communication - lecture mode and conference mode. In the lecture mode, one user of the group generates all the data traffic, and is referred to as the sender. The remainder of the M users receive data packets multicast to them by the sender, and occasionally request retransmission when a data packet is lost. They do not normally communicate among themselves. In the conference mode, all $M+1$ users transmit as well as receive packets. This distinction is not very strict, in the sense that these modes can be interchanged even during a call or session, depending on the traffic flow. The data transfer protocol described below is flexible enough to accommodate this.

III. Data Transfer Protocol

There are fundamentally two ways by which packet error detection can be implemented, depending on whether the onus of detecting packet loss is on the sender or the receiver. If the sender has to detect packet losses, it must receive positive acknowledgements within a certain period of time from all the receivers for each data packet it transmits, which is an inherently inefficient scheme for multicast communication. If, on the other hand, the onus is put on the receiver, it detects the missing packets by monitoring the sequence number of the data packets it receives. Although the latter scheme is more efficient, it does not offer all the advantages which the former scheme provides. For example, the ACK scheme implements an inherent flow control mechanism because the sender can choose to send a new packet only after it has received acknowledgements from every receiver. Further, if it does not receive acknowledgement from any receiver within a specified period of time it retransmits the data packet. It does this up to a given maximum number of time and if the receivers still do not respond, then it is assumed that the connection is no more viable. Additionally, the sender can clear its buffers of the acknowledged data packets. These functions of course come at the cost of efficiency.

We describe below an efficient multicast protocol which is an enhanced version of the pure negative acknowledgement scheme. The pure negative acknowledgement scheme suffers from several drawbacks, all due to a lack of feedback from the receivers under normal operation. For instance, the receivers may have to await an unbounded time to detect the loss of the last packet in a burst. The pure NAK scheme also does not provide a way to detect receiver failure, or flow control to deal with speed mismatches between the receivers and the sender. We have added more functionality to the pure NAK scheme to nearly match the capabilities of the ACK scheme, without significantly sacrificing the efficiency.

1. A source multicasts data packets with sequence number n, $n+1$, $n+2$ ... $mod N$ to M receivers. Every user of the multicast group maintains a separate list of data packets it receives from the other users. In an $M+1$ user group each user receives M separate streams of packets. It is assumed that sequencing across the sources is not important, but it is necessary to do so across the data packets from each source. Specific applications will determine as to how many sources can transmit at the same time. For example, in a multicast graphics application this number will depend on the number of simultaneous windows available on the screen at the receivers.

2. The receivers monitor the packet stream from each source separately. A gap in the sequence number implies a missing packet, and the receiver(s) sends a directed NAK to the source. The NAK bears the sequence number of the next packet expected by the receiver. For example, if a receiver sees the sequence number n, $n+2$ it sends a NAK with sequence $n+1$. The source retransmits the NAKed packet. The receiver continues sending a NAK with the sequence number $n+1$ each time it receives an out of sequence packet from the source, e.g., $n+3$, $n+4$ etc.

3. *The last packet in a burst:* If the last packet in a burst is lost, the receiver(s) should not have to wait for the next burst to recover. So every time a packet is sent, the source starts/resets a timer. If the timer expires, the implication is that no NAK packet has been sent for T_1 ms, and the source will send a "status packet" bearing the sequence number of the next packet it will send. The source can do this for a maximum of K times, giving the receivers K opportunities to recover from the loss of the last packet in a burst. T_1 and K are design parameters which are related to the probability of packet loss, the expected burstiness of the data traffic and the network delays. We discuss this dependence in the next section.

    In the conference mode, every user sends data as well as status packets, whereas only the source sends these packets to the receivers in the lecture mode; the receivers do not send anything other than the NAK packets, and status packets.

4. *Buffer Management:* One advantage of an ACK scheme is that the source is assured that the data packet has been received by all the receivers, and it can flush the packets from its buffers. Such an indication is not normally available with the NAK scheme. One can define a "back window" B such that the source holds in its buffer the last B packets it has sent. The receivers once again have B opportunities to recover from the loss of a packet. Packets outside this window can be flushed. Note that the NAK protocol trades increased storage for reduced processing, which generally agrees with the trend in the cost of these two elements. B is a design parameter which is a function of the probability of packet loss and expected network delays. This is discussed in the next section.

5. *Receiver failure:* In an ACK scheme, receiver failure is detected when the source times out the maximum number of times. With what has been described so far, the source can continue operating without being aware of the receiver failure. Sanity is monitored by assuring some activity on the part of all users, for example, by letting each user send status packets every T_1 ms indefinitely during idle periods. T_1 bounds the time to recover from packet losses, and cannot be very long; this results in excessive status packet traffic, particularly for large M. A better alternative is for the users to send the status packet K times at T_1 ms intervals at the end of a burst, and then continue sending the status packet as a sanity check at much more infrequent intervals, say, T_2 ms ($T_2 \gg T_1$). The status packets sent at T_2 ms will be referred to as "sanity" packets. In the lecture mode, the sender will be transmitting a combination of data, status and sanity packets, depending on the traffic, while the receivers will only be sending status or sanity packets. In the conference mode, all the users will be sending a mixture of data, status and sanity packets. In this way, all the users can monitor each others' health on the basis of their activity.

6. *Flow control:* The NAK scheme does not provide flow control under normal operation. This is not important if there is no inherent speed mismatch between the receivers and the source, and there are a sufficient number of receiver buffers. However, if the buffer space at some receiver is becoming low, it can send a "timed-choke" packet to every user of the group, indicating that it cannot receive new packets for some time, say, T_3 ms. It can periodically do so until it is ready to communicate.

IV. Performance Analysis

The values of the protocol parameters T_1, K, B, T_2, and T_3, are negotiated among the users during the call setup. These depend on the various network parameters, e.g., probability of packet loss (assumed 10^{-6}), burstiness of the data traffic, and expected network delays. T_1 is typically of the order of several times the maximum round trip network delay which is quite small (typically round trip delay, which is the sum of the transmission, terrestrial propagation and packet processing delays, is less than 80 ms), and is smaller than the inter burst time (typically 500 ms [10]). The round trip delay amounts to the time elapsed between the sending of a data packet and the reception of a NAK packet. T_1 bounds the time taken to recover from errors and for this reason can be equal to the error recovery time value in the ACK protocol. The choice of K depends on the error rate, and if K is chosen to be 4, then there are 4 opportunities for the receivers to detect the loss of a packet. This results in an insignificant total probability of packet loss of 10^{-24}.

Similarly, the size of the back window B for buffer management should be such that a receiver has enough opportunities to send NAKs and the sender to receive them, given a probability of packet loss. A large network delay and a higher probability of packet loss implies a large B and the vice versa. The value of T_2 is usually quite large, say, of the order of a few seconds. The value of T_3 depends on the momentary buffer congestion at a user and the time taken to recover from it. The performance of the protocol is a sensitive function of the parameter values. For example, a smaller T_2 means a lower throughput, since then there will be more overhead packets.

Next we compute the maximum throughput, denoted by λ_{ack} and λ_{nak}, in packets/sec of the data traffic for the ACK and NAK schemes, respectively, in the lecture as well as conference modes as a function of the size of the multicast group. Since we have assumed that processing is the bottleneck, we compute λ_{ack} and λ_{nak} based on the total time it takes to process each data packet for reliable delivery. It is assumed that NAK packets have a very negligible effect on throughput. This will be true if the error rates are low, and the number of NAK packets generated per lost packet is not large. This, in turn, is the case if the round trip delay is small.

Lecture Mode:

In the positive acknowledgement scheme, it is obvious that the sender is the bottleneck. The total throughput is limited by the throughput of the sender which handles the most traffic; it transmits data packets and processes M acknowledgements from all the receivers. Each receiver, on the other hand, receives data packets and sends one acknowledgement per data packet to the sender. Thus, the sender processes M more packets than the receivers, and the processing load at the receivers can be ignored. While in the NAK scheme proposed here, the sender sends data, status and sanity packets, and receives sanity packets from each receiver every T_2 ms. The receivers in the normal course process all the packets received from the sender, and multicast sanity packets at T_2 ms intervals. Assuming that the sending and reception of a packet requires the same amount of processing, all users, unlike in the ACK scheme, see the same amount of traffic. Thus, the throughput is equal to that of any user of the group.

ACK scheme: A positive acknowledgement multicast protocol is a generalization of the stop and wait protocol [9] for unicast communication [6,7]. Here for every data packet, the sender processes M acknowledgements (there are a total of $M+1$ users in the group, including the sender). The sender is modeled as a single server, and the processing load on the sender per data packet $= T_d + MT_a$, where T_d and T_a are the average per packet processing times in ms for the data packets and acknowledgement packets, respectively. Hence, for maximum throughput,

$$\lambda_{ack}(T_d + MT_a) = 1$$

which gives,

$$\lambda_{ack} = \frac{1}{T_d + MT_a} \qquad (1)$$

NAK scheme: In this scheme, the sender sends data packets during the data bursts, sends status packets every T_1 ms for K times, and sanity packets every T_2 ms after that during the silence period. In addition, it receives sanity packets from each receiver every T_2 ms. The receivers process all packets from the sender, occasionally send NAK packets, and every T_2 ms send sanity packets. All users see the same amount of traffic since all packets, data, status and sanity, are multicast. The processing load due to the data traffic at any user is $\lambda_{nak} T_d$ (assuming that T_d is the same in both cases.). To compute the processing load due to status and sanity packets generated at the sender, we assume that the data traffic is Poisson with the average rate λ_{nak} packets per second, and then compute the average rate of status and sanity (overhead) packets. This, when multiplied by T_s, average processing time for these overhead packets, gives the overhead load. The processing load due to the sanity packets from the receivers is simply $\frac{MT_s}{T_2}$.

Now, status and sanity packets are sent whenever data packets are not, and sanity packets are sent every T_2 ms after K status packets have been sent, one every T_1 ms. Given that the data traffic is Poisson with the average data rate of λ_{nak} packets/sec, average rate of overhead packets, denoted by λ_{ss}, is given by

$$\lambda_{ss} = \lambda_{nak}(e^{-\lambda_{nak}T_1} + \ldots + e^{-K\lambda_{nak}T_1} + e^{-\lambda_{nak}(KT_1 + T_2)} + e^{-\lambda_{nak}(KT_1 + 2T_2)} + \ldots)$$

which after summation becomes

$$\lambda_{ss} = \lambda_{nak} \left(\frac{e^{-\lambda_{nak}T_1} - e^{-(K+1)\lambda_{nak}T_1}}{1 - e^{-\lambda_{nak}T_1}} + \frac{e^{-\lambda_{nak}(KT_1 + T_2)}}{1 - e^{-\lambda_{nak}T_2}} \right) \qquad (2)$$

The expression for λ_{ss}, as determined above, is exact, and represents the overhead traffic originating at the sender. With this λ_{ss} term, the maximum throughput in the NAK scheme is determined by the following expression

$$\lambda_{nak} T_d + \lambda_{ss} T_s + \frac{MT_s}{T_2} = 1 \qquad (3)$$

Eqn. (3) is an exact expression for the maximum throughput. We can simplify the expression for λ_{ss} based on the nature of data traffic. If the data traffic is light, then most of the traffic is overhead (corresponding to $\lambda_{nak} T_2 < 1$), which is accounted for in (2). But if the data traffic is moderate, the sender will almost never have to send sanity packets (in eqn. (2) it means that $K\lambda_{nak} T_1 < 1$), and λ_{ss} can be simplified to

$$\lambda_{ss} = \lambda_{nak} \left(\frac{e^{-\lambda_{nak}T_1}}{1 - e^{-\lambda_{nak}T_1}} \right) \qquad (4)$$

Therefore, for maximum throughput in the NAK scheme with medium traffic, the following should hold

$$\lambda_{nak} T_d + \frac{\lambda_{nak} e^{-\lambda_{nak}T_1}}{1 - e^{-\lambda_{nak}T_1}} T_s + \frac{MT_s}{T_2} = 1 \qquad (5)$$

This is a transcendental equation which has been solved numerically for λ_{nak} using the Newton-Raphson method. The expressions for λ_{ack} from (1) and λ_{nak} from (5) are related to the size of the multicast group $M+1$. Fig. 1 shows the plots of eqns. (1) and (5), with $T_1=500$ ms, $T_d=8$ ms, $T_a=T_s=6$ ms, $T_2=5$ sec and $K=4$.

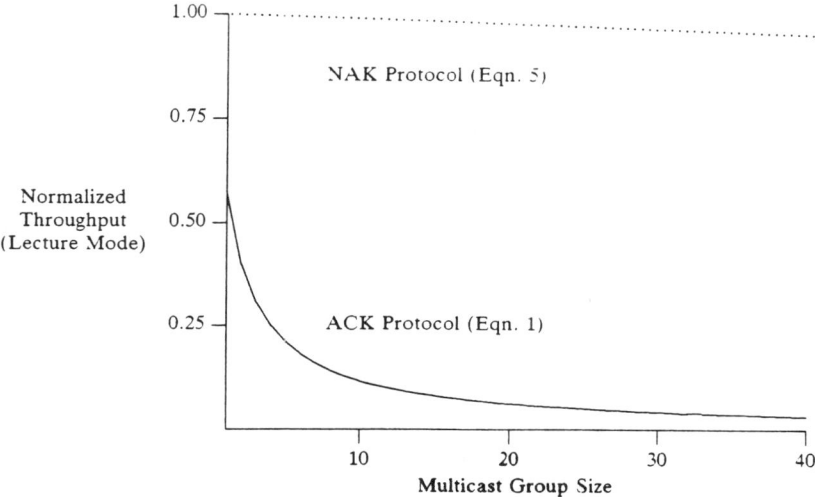

Figure 1. Normalized Throughput versus Multicast Group Size in Lecture Mode

The difference in the values of λ_{nak} obtained from (3), (5) and (7) is very small, and hence the plot of (5) is quite representative of this scheme.

When the data traffic is heavy, further simplification can be obtained. This amounts to saying that the sender is almost always sending the data packets (i.e., $\lambda_{nak}T_1 > 1$), and thus there is no need to send status or sanity packets. Therefore, in eqn. (5) λ_{ss} term drops out and (5) becomes

$$\lambda_{nak} T_d + \frac{MT_s}{T_2} = 1 \qquad (6)$$

which gives

$$\lambda_{nak} = \frac{1}{T_d} \left(1 - \frac{MT_s}{T_2} \right) \qquad (7)$$

The design parameter is T_2 which determines the relative advantage of the NAK scheme under heavy traffic over the ACK scheme. The NAK protocol has more throughput, i.e., $\lambda_{nak} > \lambda_{ack}$ (compare eqns. (1) and (7)) if

$$\frac{1}{T_d}(1-\frac{MT_s}{T_2}) > \frac{1}{T_d+MT_a}$$

that is, if

$$T_2 > \frac{T_s T_d}{T_a}+MT_s \tag{8}$$

Typical values of T_2 (around 5 secs) indicate that (6) holds favorably for a reasonable multicast group size, say, up to $M=40$.

Conference Mode:

In this mode, everyone sends and receives packets from everyone else in the multicast group. So the traffic, both data as well as overhead (acknowledgements, status and sanity packets), is evenly distributed and the total throughput is simply the sum of all the traffic seen by the individual user. In the following analysis, we assume a symmetric environment, and let λ be the traffic generated by one user of the multicast group. Then the total throughput is simply $(M+1)\lambda$ in both schemes.

ACK scheme: The processing load per sent data packet on the server = T_d+MT_a, where T_d and T_a are as defined above; T_d for processing the data packet and MT_a for processing M acknowledgements it receives for the data packet it sends. The processing load at the server due to each received data packet = T_d+T_a; T_d for the received data packet from some other user and T_a for sending the acknowledgement for it. Therefore, the total processing load for each user is determined by

$$\lambda(T_d+MT_a)+M\lambda(T_d+T_a) = 1$$

The total throughput ($\lambda_{ack} = (M+1)\lambda$), then, is given by

$$\lambda_{ack} = \frac{1}{T_d+\frac{2M}{M+1}T_a} \tag{9}$$

The expression (9) becomes independent for large M. To understand this, it should be noted that with this protocol, transmission of a data packet is a significantly more expensive operation than its reception. In a symmetric conference mode among a large number of users ($M \gg 1$), the traffic transmitted by any one user is a small fraction of the total throughput.

NAK scheme: In this scheme, each user sees a combination of data, status, and sanity packets. In a symmetric environment, the total throughput for $M+1$ users is $\lambda_{nak} = (M+1)\lambda$. The processing load at each user is $\lambda T_d+\lambda_{ss}T_s$, where λ_{ss} is as before, but defined with respect to λ. Since the traffic is equally distributed among all users, the processing load at any one user should satisfy the following

$$(M+1)\lambda T_d+(M+1)\lambda_{ss}T_s = 1$$

The total processing load for $M+1$ users, then, can be determined from the following

$$\lambda_{nak}T_d+(M+1)\lambda_{ss}T_s = 1 \tag{10}$$

with

$$(M+1)\lambda_{ss}=\lambda_{nak}(\frac{e^{-\frac{\lambda_{nak}}{M+1}T_1}-e^{-(K+1)\frac{\lambda_{nak}}{M+1}T_1}}{1-e^{-\frac{\lambda_{nak}}{M+1}T_1}}+\frac{e^{-\frac{\lambda_{nak}}{M+1}(KT_1+T_2)}}{1-e^{-\frac{\lambda_{nak}}{M+1}T_2}})$$

The above term for $(M+1)\lambda_{ss}$ holds under the most general conditions, i.e., even when the data traffic is light. Further simplifications can be obtained as before for the medium and heavy traffic. For these two traffic conditions, respectively, the following should be true

$$\lambda_{nak}T_d + \frac{\lambda_{nak}e^{-\frac{\lambda_{nak}}{M+1}T_1}}{1-e^{-\frac{\lambda_{nak}}{M+1}T_1}}T_s = 1 \qquad (11)$$

and

$$\lambda_{nak}T_d = 1 \qquad (12)$$

The parameters T_1 and T_2 can be so chosen that for the group size of interest ($1 \leq M \leq 40$) and at a traffic level of λ_{nak} packets/sec, the overhead traffic is negligible. This corresponds to (12), where the throughput is maximized. Fig. 2 provides the plots of eqns. (9) and (11) which show the normalized ACK and NAK throughputs as a function of the multicast group size, with the same values of parameters as in Fig. 1.

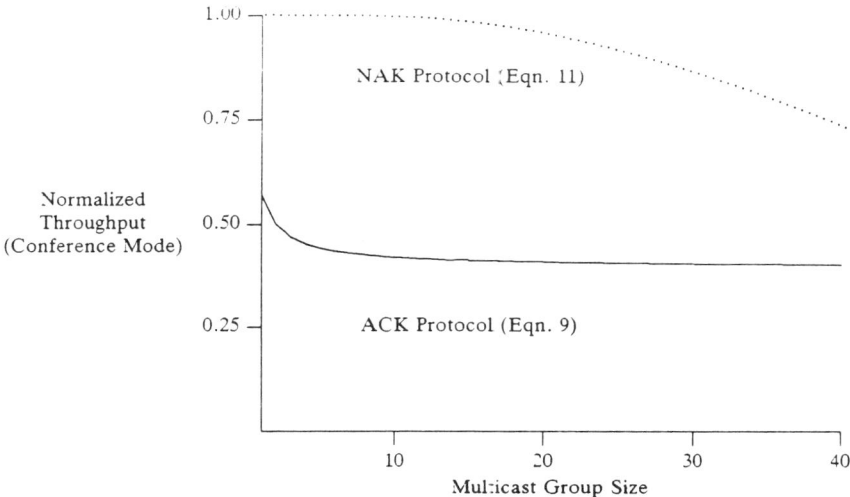

Figure 2. Normalized Throughput versus Multicast Group Size in Conference Mode

The difference in the values of λ_{nak} obtained from (10) and (11) is quite small, both of which differ from (12) which gives the maximum throughput.

V. Concluding Remarks

We characterize the environments for which the enhanced NAK protocol is best suited. As already discussed, the effect of NAK packets on throughput is negligible when the error rates are low, and the round trip delays are small. The NAK protocol will perform better than the ACK protocol as long as the overhead due to status and sanity packets is less than the overhead due to acknowledgements. The parameters T_1 and T_2, relative to the expected traffic, determine the overhead traffic, and should be carefully chosen. The analysis shows that for reasonable values of T_1 and T_2, the NAK protocol is well suited for both lecture and conference modes.

The design parameters T_1 and T_2 are negotiated among users during the call setup. We will describe a multicast call setup protocol which consists of negotiation of the above data transfer parameters among the users in a future paper. The performance of the ACK scheme can be improved by using group acknowledgements. We are continuing our efforts to develop the above results for a group ACK scheme and perform a delay-throughput analysis for performance comparison. We also propose to develop a formal description of the protocol using a formal language, and verify it for correctness.

References

1. D. R. Boggs, "Internet Broadcasting," Technical Report No. CSL-83-3, Xerox PARC, Oct. 1983.

2. D. Wall, "Mechanisms for Broadcast and Selective Broadcast," Ph. D. Thesis, Technical Report No. 190, Computer Science Department, Stanford University, CA, June 1980.

3. T. T. Lee, "Non-Blocking Copy Networks for Multicast Packet Switching," Bellcore Internal Memorandum, 1987.

4. P. Decitre et al, "An Efficient Error Detection Mechanism for a Multicast Transport Service on the Danube Network," in Proc. IFIP workshop on Local Computer Networks, 1982, pp 335-347.

5. J. Chang and N. Maxemchuk, "Reliable Broadcast Protocols," ACM Transactions on Computer Systems, Vol. 2, No. 3, August 1984, pp 251-273.

6. G. Gopal and J. Wong, "Two Protocols for Reliable Broadcast: A Performance Study," in Proc. IEEE GLOBECOM, 1984, pp 11.1.1-11.1.6.

7. J. Wong and G. Gopal, "Reliable Broadcast on Local Area Network," in Proc. IEEE ICC, 1985, pp 43.4.1-43.4.5.

8. S. Ramakrishnan and B. Jain, "A Negative Acknowledgement with Periodic Polling Protocol for Multicasts over LANs," in Proc. IEEE INFOCOM, 1987, pp 502-511.

9. A. S. Tanenbaum, *Computer Networks*, Prentice-Hall, Inc., USA, 1981.

10. R. Jain and S. Routhier, "Packet Trains - Measurements and a New Model for Computer Network Traffic," IEEE-JSAC, Vol. SAC-4, No. 6, Sept. 1983, pp 986-995.

NETBLT: A High Throughput Transport Protocol

David D. Clark
Mark L. Lambert
Lixia Zhang

Laboratory for Computer Science
Massachusetts Institute of Technology
Cambridge, MA 02139

1. Introduction

Bulk data transmission is now finding more and more application in various fields. The major performance concern of a bulk data transfer protocol is high throughput. Theoretically, a packet switched network allows any single user an unlimited share of the network resources. In the absence of other traffic, therefore, a user should be able to transmit data at the raw bandwidth of a network channel. In reality, achievable end-to-end throughputs over high bandwidth channels are often an order of magnitude lower than the provided bandwidth. Experience shows that the throughput is often limited by the transport protocol and its flow control mechanism. It is especially difficult to achieve high throughput, reliable data transmissions across long delay, unreliable network paths.

In this paper we introduce a new transport protocol, NETBLT [2], which was designed for high throughput, bulk data transmission applications. We first analyze the impact of network unreliability and delay on the end-to-end transport protocol; we then summarize previous experience; next we show the design and implementation of NETBLT, followed by our initial experience. Generally speaking, errors and variable delays are two barriers to high performance for all transport protocols. The NETBLT design and experience explores general principles for overcoming these barriers.

2. Impact of Network Unreliability and Delay

2.1. Network Unreliability

If a network were perfectly reliable, an end-to-end transport protocol would have little to do: it would only need to mark the start of a transmission, and then dump all data through the channel.

This research was supported by the Defense Advanced Research Projects Agency of the Department of Defense and was monitored by the Office of Naval Research under Contract Nos. N00014-75-C-0661 and N00014-83-K-0125.

Permission to copy without fee all or part of this material is granted provided that the copies are not made or distributed for direct commercial advantage, the ACM copyright notice and the title of the publication and its date appear, and notice is given that copying is by permission of the Association for Computing Machinery. To copy otherwise, or to republish, requires a fee and/or specfic permission.

© 1988 ACM 0-89791-245-4/88/0001/0353 $1.50

Unfortunately, no real network offers such perfect reliability. The network unreliability manifests itself as packet losses, duplicates, and out-of-order deliveries.

A reliable transport protocol must then detect and recover from all transmission errors. It does so by numbering the data units, and keeping transmission state information at the two communicating ends. The state information keeps track of the status of data under transmission. It also permits recovery from errors whenever they are detected. It is this transmission state that regulates the data flow.

The state at the two ends is constantly synchronized by the arrival of new data and control information (e.g. acknowledgments). The receiving end can easily check and correct duplicate or out-of-order packets. If data or control packets are lost, the most common recovery technique is for the transmitting end to wait for the retransmission timeout and then retry, until a successful retransmission resynchronizes the end state. As will be shown in the next section, however, the detection of lost packets by timers takes a relatively long time, and may easily cause false alarms which in turn trigger superfluous retransmissions.

2.2. Transmission Delay

If there were no communication delays between the transmitter and the receiver, the transmission state at the two ends could be perfectly synchronized, i.e. each end could have a consistent view of the status of every data packet all the time. The transmitter could then retransmit any packet in error immediately after it is detected by the receiver. In this case the throughput would be limited only by the channel bandwidth between the two ends.

In reality, the network round trip delay (RTD) is usually non-negligible and varies randomly. The presence of the RTD causes the control state at the two ends to be out of synchronization: each will have a different view of the status of the data under transmission from time to time, and will not know the other's state changes until some time period later. For instance, after the transmitter sends a packet P, it will not know whether P was successfully received until at least an RTD period; in the meantime, it must keep sending subsequent packets to achieve a high throughput. A transport protocol must tolerate a certain *state out of synchronization* (SOS) between the two ends; the SOS bounds the quantity of data the transmitter is allowed to send before it must stop to resynchronize the state with the receiver.

All transport protocols set a limit on the SOS region in order to bound the state information that must be maintained and the system resources that must be allocated for incoming data. Whenever the transmitter reaches the SOS boundary, the transmission stops and waits for the state resynchronization between the two ends. For instance, a TCP transmitter stops at the window boundary and waits for a new acknowledgment before it can continue. This wait for synchronization can often cause loss of performance.

A small SOS region means a simpler protocol design and implementation. The Trivial File Transfer Protocol (TFTP) [3], for example, takes a lock-step approach and synchronizes the state at every packet transmission[1]. Since the end state synchronization always takes at least an RTD, TFTP can send only one data packet each RTD, and thus performs very poorly over long delay links.

In order to keep transmitting while waiting for the end state to be synchronized, the SOS region must be set larger for longer RTD paths, so that there are always data ready to go. How big an SOS region will be sufficient? Theoretically, there does not exist an upper bound that is absolutely sufficient, because if N errors occur, the ends might need a time period of (N * RTD) to recover, where N ranges from 1 to infinity. In practice, we must assume a bound on the number of errors beyond which performance will suffer.

In summary, it is the requirement for reliable data transmission that make the transport protocol maintain a transmission state at the two ends. Communication delays cause each end's state to be out of synchronization with the other's. Finally, this SOS region must be sufficiently large to achieve a high throughput over long RTD paths.

3. Previous Experience

Previous experience with the performance of transport protocols showed two major problems: restrictions in throughput which arise from the use of windows as a flow control mechanism, and the difficulty in handling timers. The problem with windows is that they are both a data flow control and an error recovery mechanism. The problem with timers is estimating an appropriate timer value. These issues are considered in turn.

By definition, the goal of flow control in a transport protocol is to match the data transmission *rate* with the receiver's data consumption *rate*. Windows control the flow of data by bounding the number of data units which the transmitter may send to the receiver. In terms of the state information stored at each end, the window size is the SOS region boundary. As we showed earlier, a large window must be opened to achieve high throughput over long delay channels; however, this does not imply a full window of data should go all at once, but only that buffering for the data is ready. The transmission ought to be evenly distributed over an RTD time period to match the receiver's consumption speed. Unfortunately, windows only convey the former information - *how much* data can be buffered, rather than the latter - *how fast* the transmission should go. Using windows both as the flow control and the SOS bound often leads to a conflict -- the size is either too small to achieve high throughputs over long delay networks, or too large to have any control effect on the instant data rate.

To achieve reliable delivery of the window authorization, the authorization is coupled to the SOS synchronization message, the acknowledgment. Although the transmission state could include the status of every packet within the window region, a window scheme (in most definitions) takes a simplified approach to state synchronization in which the synchronization message is a single number, the number of the largest data item below which all units have arrived at the receiver. This restriction permits a simple, but perhaps inefficient form of synchronization. An acknowledgment with a sequence number N only tells the transmitter that all packets up to N have been successfully received, even in a case when the transmitter has sent N+W packets (where W is the window size) and the receiver has received all but the N+1th packet. This form of acknowledgment is often called a cumulative acknowledgment, as opposed to a selective acknowledgment (as used in NETBLT).

When a cumulative acknowledgment for N is returned, a window authorization is returned as an offset relative to N. That is, an authorization to send W packets means that the next W after N may be sent. But this means that, since a single lost packet prevents the cumulative acknowledgment from being advanced, a lost packet prevents the window from being opened until the error is recovered. An acknowledgment can be returned only after a correct reception of data. The window mechanism, by its nature, ties the flow control and error control together, and therefore becomes vulnerable in the face of data losses. The throughput is controlled by how quickly the recovery can be performed.

Unfortunately, existing mechanisms for error recovery do not operate quickly. When packets are lost, most reliable transport protocols use timers to trigger the transmission state resynchronization. If the RTD were constant, the retransmission timer could detect a loss promptly after an exact RTD time period. In practice, however, the RTD varies. This variation means that the timer must be set to longer than one RTD, otherwise it may cause excessive false alarms. Setting the timer is based on an unknown statistical distribution of the RTD and the exact causes of packet losses are usually unknown to the host (e.g. whether the network has a high-loss channel or whether the net is congested). Finding a good balance between a timer value that is too short and one that is too long can therefore be very difficult.

This problem is an intrinsic limitation of using timers, rather than a result of any specific timer algorithm being used [6]. The performance loss due to timers is particularly high when the round trip time is long (such as across a satellite link, where every loss costs a long wait), or when the channel is noisy and the error rate is high (the transmission will stop and wait too often)

These timer problems interact poorly with windows, since both false alarms and long waits cause window performance degradation. The effect of long timer delays is obvious; a lost packet prevents any acknowledgment, and thus stops data flow until the timer expires and the packet is retransmitted. A short timer has a different effect. The window controls the number of new packets which can be sent; it specifies nothing about how retransmissions are to be sent. Needless retransmission occurring at an unregulated rate can easily congest the network and the receiver. In this respect, windows do not really control the flow, but only control a parameter (the number of packets outstanding) which indirectly relates to flow.

---

[1]Strictly speaking, TFTP is an application protocol. Because it uses UDP, an unreliable protocol at the transport layer, TFTP faces the same network delay and unreliability problems to ensure the transmission reliability itself.

We draw the following conclusions from the previous experience:
- Window and timers perform poorly in synchronizing the end state. To achieve fast resynchronization of the end state, we need better mechanisms than the cumulative acknowledgment, and we must reduce reliance on timers.
- Flow control must be independent from error control. Mixing the two in one mechanism can only make the flow control vulnerable to transmission errors and delays.
- The goal of flow control is to match the speed at the two ends; the SOS region is a side effect of reliable data transmission. It is a mistake that window mechanism uses the SOS region as the flow control parameter. As a flow control mechanism, windows are too vulnerable to errors; as an SOS mechanism, it does not carry enough information for good performance; being both, it faces conflicts when a large SOS region is needed over a long delay network path while a small window size is desired to restrict the data flow rate.

4. NETBLT Design

4.1. Design Goals

We want a high throughput protocol that is robust in face of a network's long delay and high loss of the network. Seeing the problems with window flow control and timers, we decided that our goal was achievable only by employing a new flow control mechanism. A goal of NETBLT was to check the validity of the rate-based flow control mechanism, and to gain implementation and testing experience with rate control.

4.1.1. Flow Control by Rate

If NETBLT is to provide high throughput for its application, it must be able to transmit constantly, no matter what the status of previously-transmitted data. Provided that there is sufficient buffering in the protocol module, rate control provides this functionality.

Unlike window-based flow control, rate control works independently of the network round-trip delay (an exception to this is of course that changes to the rate take one round-trip delay to take effect). Thus no matter what the network state, the NETBLT sender of data simply transmits at the current rate. Of course if the network is congested, the rate must decrease, and the synchronization of this rate change between sending and receiving NETBLTs takes one RTD.

Rate control is also designed to work independently of error recovery. It places data to be retransmitted in the same queue with new data; all data leave the queue at the current transmission rate. Thus unlike window flow control mechanisms, there is no notion of error recovery working outside of the standard flow-control mechanism, and the load placed on the network does not change when data are retransmitted.

Rate control reduces reliance on timers and timer setting algorithms. Since retransmission is not RTD-based (as it is in TCP), an incorrect RTD estimate does not result in unneeded retransmissions. Retransmission timer estimation is instead based on the current transmission rate, which is fixed within any one RTD and known by both sender and receiver.

Currently most data loss in the network is due to congestion. Rate-based flow control can reduce this congestion in a number of ways. First, since packet retransmissions occur "in-band", they cause no extra load in the network. Second, since retransmission timers are based on the packet rate (or better yet on the packet inter-arrival time) rather than the network RTD, timers can be estimated more accurately, resulting in fewer unnecessary retransmissions. Finally, the rate can be adjusted to reflect the network's current ability to transport data.

4.1.2. Error Recovery/End State Synchronization

NETBLT's design goals include the ability to continuously transmit data in the face of long-delay networks. This means NETBLT connections must be able to maintain a large SOS region, and require efficient mechanisms to quickly synchronize the end state. NETBLT has several ways to speed up the synchronization.

NETBLT uses selective acknowledgment to convey as much information as possible to the sending NETBLT. By providing the status of each packet in the transmission, unneeded retransmissions are avoided. Obviously, the overhead incurred with a packet-for-packet ACKing scheme is too high; NETBLT therefore splits its out-of-synchronization region into "buffers", which become the synchronization point and recovery block. The sending and receiving NETBLTs synchronize state either upon successful transmission of a buffer or upon determination by the receiver that information is missing from a particular buffer. In the first case, a single message ACKs all packets contained in a particular buffer. In the second case, a single message tells the sender of data exactly which packets to retransmit.

Thus, by aggregating information into large units, NETBLT solves the ACK dilemma in window flow control mechanisms: do you incur high overhead by sending a separate ACK for each packet, or do you incur unneeded retransmissions by failing to provide complete information to the sender of data?

NETBLT also makes error recovery more efficient by placing the data retransmission timer at the receiving end. At any given moment, the receiver knows which packets have arrived and which have not. When a timeout occurs, the receiver can eliminate unnecessary retransmissions because it knows exactly which packets need retransmission. In addition, the timer value is easy for the receiver to estimate, since it is based on the transmission rate and the number of packets expected in a particular buffer. Error recovery and state synchronization both occur on the same (receiving) end; it therefore never matters when the receiver sends ACKs to the sender. Of course long waits between a timeout and a subsequent state resynchronization mean lowered performance, but there are never spurious retransmissions because a retransmit timer expires before an ACK is received.

Even with the above ACKing schemes, the minimum time of an error recovery by requesting retransmission remains an RTD period. In order to insure that error recovery and state synchronization be kept as close as possible to a single RTD, control messages containing ACK information must be transmitted with high reliability.

An affordable reliability in control transmissions is particularly necessary in NETBLT, because single control messages can ACK many data packets (depending on the number of packets per buffer). NETBLT uses such redundancy, at the same time reducing to almost nil the overhead incurred by processing duplicate control messages.

Even with efficient error recovery, continuous transmission is not possible over long-delay networks without a large SOS region. For this reason, NETBLT implementations must make the SOS region as large as resources permit. This is not possible with a window flow-control mechanism; in order to enjoy a large SOS region using window-based flow control, a protocol must in effect eliminate flow control by using extremely large window sizes. NETBLT uses rate control to meter the transmission rate; SOS region management operates independently of flow control.

4.1.3. Coping with Delay

Transmission delay is one of the most difficult problems that a transport protocol faces, because it causes the SOS problem. Resynchronization and error recovery are performed via timers, but in other transport protocols, the timer itself suffers from the delay variations since it is delay-based. This causes a positive feedback cycle of the delay-dependency, lowering performance.

NETBLT's solution to this problem has several parts. First, it uses a large SOS region, to make it unlikely that the transmission is forced to stop due to reaching the region boundary. Second, NETBLT speeds up the state synchronization using the mechanisms discussed above. This allows the SOS region to move forward quickly along the transmission stream, so that the transmission will not be forced to stop due to reaching the region boundary. Third, NETBLT reduces reliance on timers, limiting their use to a last resort in ensuring reliability. Because of the large SOS region, timer values can be set loosely and the protocol can transmit continuously while awaiting a retransmission timeout. Of course, if the SOS region cannot be large (due perhaps to system limitations), then more care must be taken in estimating retransmission timer values.

4.2. NETBLT Protocol Design

Having discussed some of the design philosophies behind NETBLT, we move on to a slightly more detailed discussion of the protocol. NETBLT works by opening a connection between two "clients" (the sender and the receiver), transferring data in a series of large numbered blocks (buffers), and then closing the connection. Because the amount of data to be transferred can be very large, the client is not required to provide at once all the data to the protocol module. Instead, the data is provided by the client in buffers. The NETBLT layer transfers each buffer as a sequence of packets; each buffer is composed of a large number of packets, so the per-buffer interaction between NETBLT and its client is far more efficient than a per-packet interaction would be.

In its simplest form, a NETBLT transfer works as follows: the sending client provides a buffer of data for the NETBLT layer to transfer. NETBLT breaks the buffer up into packets and sends the packets across the network in Internet datagrams. The receiving NETBLT layer loads these packets into a matching buffer provided by the receiving client. When the last packet in the buffer has arrived, the receiving NETBLT checks to see that all packets in that buffer have been correctly received. If some packets are missing, the receiving NETBLT requests that they be resent. When the buffer has been completely transmitted, the receiving client is notified by its NETBLT layer. The receiving client disposes of the buffer and provides a new buffer to receive more data. The receiving NETBLT notifies the sender that the new buffer is ready, and the sender prepares and sends the next buffer in the same manner. This continues until all the data has been sent; at that time the sender notifies the receiver that the transmission has been completed. The connection is then closed.

The above transfer model has an SOS region of one buffer; the model operates in lock-step fashion. Because of network delay, NETBLT typically maintains a large SOS region of a number of buffers (the exact number depends on the network error rate and RTD). This allows the sender to transmit new data while acknowledgments and error recovery for old data take place, and improves performance markedly.

Obviously, the above style of transmission also does not address issues of error recovery or flow control. The following sections detail NETBLTs implementation of the rate control and error recovery schemes described earlier.

4.2.1. Flow Control

NETBLT uses two strategies for flow control--one internal and one at the client level. The sending and receiving NETBLTs transmit data in buffers; client flow control is therefore at a buffer level. Before a buffer can be transmitted, NETBLT confirms that both clients have set up matching buffers, that one is ready to send data, and that the other is ready to receive data. Either client can therefore control the flow of data by not providing a new buffer. Clients cannot stop a buffer transfer once it is in progress.

Since buffers can be quite large, there has to be another method for flow control that is used during a buffer transfer. The NETBLT layer provides this form of flow control. As discussed above, the flow control method used is rate control. The transmission rate is negotiated by the sending and receiving NETBLTs during connection setup and after each buffer transmission. The sender uses timers, instead of messages from the receiver, to maintain the negotiated rate.

In its simplest form, rate control specifies a minimum time period per packet transmission. This can cause performance problems for several reasons. First, the transmission time for a single packet is very small, frequently smaller than the granularity of the timing mechanism. Also, the overhead required to maintain timing mechanisms on a per packet basis is relatively high and lowers performance.

The solution is to control the transmission rate of groups of packets, rather than single packets. The sender transmits a burst of packets over a negotiated time interval, then sends another burst. In this way, the overhead decreases by a factor of the burst size, and the per-burst transmission time is long enough that timing mechanisms will work properly. NETBLT's rate control therefore has two parts, a burst size and a burst rate, with (burst size)/(burst rate) equal to the average transmission time per packet. The burst interval is the number of milliseconds between the start of one burst transmission and the start of the next. The burst size is the number of data packets in a burst.

These two values reflect more accurately than a window the resources available to the receiver of data. They can reflect, for instance, a slow machine with little buffer space (long burst interval, small burst size), or a faster machine with a high process-scheduling overhead (short burst interval, large burst size). Note that the rate control parameters only deal with buffering at a very low level (the burst size can be based on the number of packet buffers available to the protocol module). Higher level buffering is decoupled from flow control, unlike TCP's window flow control strategy.

4.2.2. State Synchronization and Error Recovery

The receiving and sending NETBLTs synchronize their connection states via three different control messages: GO, RESEND, and OK. When the receiving NETBLT has a buffer N ready to receive data, it transmits a GO[N] message to the sender; this message tells the sender to begin transmission of buffer N. As soon as the first data packet in N arrives at the receiver, the receiver sets the "data timer"[2] belonging to N. The timer estimates how long it will take for the remainder of the buffer to arrive. The timer is fairly easy to estimate, because of NETBLT's "priority pipe" method of transmission: all buffers are transmitted in order by buffer number (buffers are given monotonically increasing numbers, from first buffer through last buffer). Once the sending NETBLT begins transmission of a buffer, it guarantees to transmit the entire buffer at the current rate before transmitting any later buffers. The remaining packets are therefore expected to arrive at the determined rate unless they are lost or delayed by the network. The timer value can be based either on the negotiated rate or the inter-packet arrival time.

The receiver now waits for one of two events. Either all packets for the buffer arrive, or the data timer expires. In the first case, the receiver clears the buffer's data timer and sends an OK[N] message, telling the sender that it can release buffer N. It may follow this with a GO[N+M] message, starting the transfer of another buffer. In the second case, the receiver looks at which packets in buffer N have arrived, and sends a RESEND[N] message containing a list of the missing packets. The sender retransmits these packets along with possible new data from subsequent buffers, all at the negotiated rate. Because all outgoing data are ordered by buffer number, retransmitted data are sent before new data. Assuming all the retransmitted packets arrive safely, the receiver sends an OK[N] message and deactivates N's data timer.

In order for the sending and receiving NETBLTs to synchronize their states as quickly as possible, control messages must be delivered reliably and in a timely fashion. NETBLT insures control message reliability in two ways. First, it uses a highly redundant message transmission algorithm. In NETBLT, multiple control messages can be packed into a single packet; the receiving NETBLT maintains a single long-lived control packet containing multiple messages, which is transmitted every time a group of new messages is generated by the receiver. ACKed control messages are pushed off the front of the packet, and new messages are added at the back of the packet, so a given message is transmitted as a member of the control packet until it is ACKed by the sender of data. Control message ACKs are by sequence number. Each control message has a unique sequence number which increases by one for each message sent. The sender of data receives these messages and notes the highest sequence number below which all messages have been received. It returns this "high ACK sequence number" in all packets flowing back to the receiver of data. When the receiver gets a high ACK sequence number, it pushes off the front of the control packet all messages with a sequence number less than or equal to the high ACK number.

The above message transmission algorithm gives high redundancy, which increases as the network delay increases. The sending NETBLT has been designed to throw away duplicate control messages with almost no overhead. Also, individual control messages are very short in length, so the bandwidth consumed by these messages is quite low. The cost of this redundancy is therefore fairly low and the benefits valuable.

Even with the redundant transmission algorithm described above, a control message will occasionally get lost. The receiving NETBLT therefore maintains a control message retransmit timer. The timer value is based on the network RTD, and is reset every time the control packet is transmitted. The timer is cleared whenever all messages in the control packet have been ACKed by the sender of data. Obviously, being based on the network RTD, this timer algorithm falls prey to the same problems that the TCP retransmit timer does. In NETBLT's case, however, the reliance on the control timer is so reduced (by the redundant transmission algorithm), that the retransmit timer almost never expires, and its value can be quite loose.

5. NETBLT Experience

In order to test NETBLT's effectiveness at providing high throughput over noisy or long-delay networks, extensive testing was conducted over a number of different networks. The current NETBLT test implementations run under UNIX (via the user-accessible raw IP socket, not the kernel) on a SUN-3 workstation, and under MS-DOS on an IBM PC/AT. A third implementation for the Symbolics Lisp Machine was also briefly tested[3].

Over high-bandwidth, short-delay LANs, NETBLT performed extremely well, achieving application memory-to-memory transfer rates of up to 1.75 megabits per second between two IBM PC/ATs on a 10 megabit-per-second Proteon Token Ring. Throughputs of up to 1.46 megabits per second were achieved over a heavily used 10 megabit-per-second Ethernet. When running memory-to-memory transfers over a Microvax-II-based C gateway connecting a Proteon Token Ring and an Ethernet, NETBLT achieved throughputs of up to 1.43 megabits per second. Since the above network environments are relatively hospitable, this came as no great surprise.

---

[2] The actual data timer mechanism is more complicated than this, but the added detail tends to obscure rather than clarify.

[3] A document describing in detail NETBLT implementation tests over a variety of networks is forthcoming.

A more accurate measure of NETBLT's abilities was in transmissions across the 3 megabit-per-second Wideband satellite network. This network provides high bandwidth with long (1.8 second) round-trip delay. In addition, the Wideband network possesses some interesting packet re-ordering and delay characteristics that resulted in substantial changes to the original NETBLT protocol design.

5.1. Coping with Delay

NETBLT's ability to handle large SOS regions proved invaluable in coping with the Wideband network's 1.8 second round-trip delay. Most tests used an SOS region ("window") of over 300,000 bytes with no performance loss due to state management overhead. Obviously not all systems will have that much available buffer space; the interesting point is that it proves large SOS regions do indeed provide high throughputs, and in NETBLT's case, the management of such a large region did not inhibit performance any. The large SOS region allowed NETBLT to transmit constantly, overlapping error recovery and ACK waits with the transmission of new data.

NETBLT was also eventually able to handle the Wideband network's tendency towards large delay variances. Under heavy load, the Wideband network can vary the delay of groups of packets by 600-700 milliseconds, due to its packet reservation scheme. The NETBLT receiver's data timers initially did not tolerate this delay well, and initially there were many spurious retransmission requests as data timers timed out due to delayed packets.

A solution to this problem was to base the data timer value on the inter-packet arrival time, rather than the negotiated rate. The receiver could then immediately increase its data timer values to reflect packet delay caused by congestion. The result was fewer false data timeouts and spurious retransmissions. Another solution is to set the data timer very loosely and correspondingly enlarge the SOS region. Obviously, machines which take the latter step will require large amounts of memory dedicated to NETBLT.

5.2. Packet Re-ordering

During initial testing, the Wideband network re-ordered groups of packets in a range of up to 100 (i.e. packet 100 would arrive before packet 1). Eventually, NETBLT was able to deal with this problem with a minimum of performance degradation. It forced us to rely more heavily on data timers, but this seems to have had little effect on performance over the Wideband network. Initially, NETBLT attempted to make retransmit "guesses" ahead of the data timer in order to improve efficiency. One such guess involved immediately generating a retransmit request if data packets were missing at the time the last packet in a buffer was received. Because of packet re-ordering, this "last packet" would frequently arrive before the first packet, causing a spurious retransmit for the entire buffer. This guess was eliminated, forcing retransmissions only upon expiration of the data timer.

NETBLT would also generate retransmit requests if packets for a buffer N+M arrived while packets for a buffer N were still missing (because the sending NETBLT transmits buffers in sequence, lowest number first, this was a reasonable guess on networks with little packet re-ordering). Again, packet re-ordering would cause spurious retransmission requests, so this guess was eliminated in favor of a slightly more complicated guess that involved resetting buffer N's data timer rather than generating a retransmit request.

5.3. Rate Control

Because of the Wideband network's long RTD, a window-based flow control mechanism would need to use a window so large that the flow control effect was essentially nonexistent. By decoupling the SOS region and the flow control, NETBLT was able to eliminate this problem. Rate control proved to work extremely well[4]. Instead of the transmission "hanging" while its window waited to open, NETBLT transmitted constantly at the negotiated rate with no slowdowns. In fact, rate control was ideally suited to the wideband network, which transmits packets internally in the form of timed bursts. By matching NETBLT's bursts to the network's, an high percentage of the network's bandwidth was utilized.

5.4. Results

NETBLT performed extremely well over the Wideband network. Out of a maximum available bandwidth of approximately 1 megabit per second[5], NETBLT managed a consistent steady-state throughput of 920,000 to 945,000 bits per second at the network's maximum transmission rate. At slower transmission rates, NETBLT worked at close to 100% efficiency.

Although rate control provides a neat solution to many problems, two important hurdles must be crossed before rate control can be used in production protocols. First, the protocol must be able to set an initial transmission rate based on the available network bandwidth and the speed at which the receiver can process data. The protocol must be also able to dynamically change the transmission rate in the face of changing network and receiver load. No matter how congested a network is, NETBLT will currently happily transmit packets at the negotiated rate until it reaches its SOS region boundary. The protocol has the ability to re-negotiate transmission rates at buffer boundaries; unfortunately if NETBLT uses internal state information to change the rate, it must make guesses based on incomplete information, and could start oscillations in the transmission rate. The guesses would permit dynamic changes to the transmission rate, but would still require a "blind" guess for an initial transmission rate. It is therefore important that support for rate selection exist at the network level. Of course this would require modifications to network gateways; even with the necessary modifications, the assumption must be made that the network load changes slowly enough that information gotten from the gateways is meaningful by the time it arrives.

There has been some work attempting to analyze the problem of adjusting the rate of a number of simultaneous flows [1]. But the problem is difficult, and both practical and analytical experience will be needed to identify a suitable approach.

A second problem is packet loss due to the lack of flow control in the link layer. NETBLT provides high enough performance that it uncovers previously hidden low-level network problems. For

---

[4]The next section discusses some enhancements that must be made for rate control to work correctly all the time.

[5]Obviously far less than the network's stated raw bandwidth. Unfortunately network overhead consumed fully 2/3 of the available bandwidth at the time we were testing.

example, the current NETBLT implementation operates on a machine with a fairly unsophisticated Ethernet network interface. It is possible, using NETBLT, to exceed the network interface's receiving speed when receiving bursts of packets. On a single-wire link, this problem can be eliminated by judicious choice of burst size and interval. If there are gateways along the transmission path, however, the transport layer no longer has control over the speed at which bursts of packets arrive. Also, congestion may occur anywhere along a transmission path -- within gateways or along a single Ethernet cable. If the NETBLT layer has enough low-level knowledge of its link level's capabilities, it can cope with the lack of flow control in the link layer. This is not, however, a good solution since it violates protocol layering. This problem can only be solved by developing link-layer flow control mechanisms.

Clearly, rate control can only offer optimal throughput if it is supported by all lower protocol layers. The network must be able to offer load information which NETBLT can use to determine an optimal initial transmission rate. It must also constantly update this information so that the transmission rate can be adjusted if the network load changes.

6. Summary

In this section we first summarize the above discussions to a few guidelines for reliable transport protocol design; we then look at a couple of existing protocols, followed by a brief conclusion of the paper.

We consider that the following can be used as guidelines in future reliable transport protocol designs:
1. Employ separate mechanisms for data flow control and error recovery.
2. Use a rate flow control to match the data transmission and consumption rates at the two communicating ends.
3. Set as large an SOS region as resources permit.
4. Explore feasible mechanisms, such as explicit information exchange between the transmitter and receiver about each other's behavior, using SACK instead of simple ACKs, and redundancy in data or control transmissions, to help speed up the end state resynchronization.
5. Coordinate with the underlying network traffic control.

Design efforts should be directed to synchronize the end state as quickly as possible. On the other hand, there is also a concern with the overhead involved in the synchronization, and we need a good judgment on balance.

Now we look at the approaches taken by a few existing protocols. As mentioned earlier, TFTP sets an SOS region of one packet, and hence loses throughput over long delay channels. At the other extreme, Blast [4] sets the SOS region to the total amount of data being transmitted. Based on the assumption of a low loss, low delay communication channel, the transmitter sends all data at once, under some rate flow control (the intention is to match incoming data with the disk operations), then recovers transmission errors according to SACKs from the receiver. Since there is no overlap between data transmission and error recovery phases, the latter can cause a long tail in the transmission process, if the channel is noisy or the delay is long, dragging the throughput value over the total transmission period to a very low average[6].

To manage the transmission state, there is a question of what basic data unit should be used in the transmission state management. The smaller the unit, the larger the state space needed to cover the same amount of data. For example, TCP uses the byte as the basic unit, while TP4 uses the packet, therefore improving TCP's performance by adding a SACK mechanism may be slightly more complex and costly than doing so to TP4.

Much work has been done on the performance issues of transport protocols. The flow control, transmission error recovery, and buffer space management issues seem to interact in a rather complicated way [5]. We showed in the above that once we understand the impact of network delays and errors on the transport protocol performance, and decouple flow control from error recovery mechanism, the problem is simplified and solutions are revealed.

NETBLT experience has helped us reach a better understanding on transport protocol performance issues. Remaining research topics are related to the flow control interactions with the network:
1. How good a performance can the end hosts achieve by tuning the control rate, under varying network conditions?
2. How does one design a network architecture to support rate-based traffic control?

References

[1] D. Bertsekas and R. Gallager.
Flow Control Schemes Based on Input Rate Adjustment.
Data Networks.
Prentice-Hall, Inc., 1987, Chapter 6.4.

[2] David Clark, Mark Lambert, and Lixia Zhang.
NETBLT: A Bulk Data Transfer Protocol.
Network Information Center RFC-998, SRI International.
March, 1987

[3] Karen Sollins.
The TFTP Protocol.
Network Information Center RFC-783, SRI International.
June, 1981

[4] Dan Theriault.
BLAST, an Experimental File Transfer Protocol.
MIT-LCS Compuer System Research Group RFC-217.
March, 1982

[5] R. Watson and S. Mamrak.
Gaining Efficiency in Transport Services by Appropriate Design and Implementation Choices.
ACM Transactions on Computer Systems 5(2):97-120, May, 1987.

[6] Lixia Zhang.
Why TCP Timers Don't Work Well.
In *Proceedings of Symposium on Communication Architectures and Protocols.* ACM SIGCOMM, 1986.

---

[6]A common misconception is that NETBLT and Blast look similar to each other. Actually the two are very different except that both protocols use separate flow control and error recovery mechanisms.

Measurement Management Service

Paul D. Amer
Lillan N. Cassel
Department of Computer and Information Sciences
University of Delaware, Newark DE 19716*

1 Introduction

This paper describes a facility for communicating between a controlling device and one or more measurement devices distributed in an internet. The facility includes placement of a command file at each device that is to participate in a monitoring event. The content of command files is deliberately unspecified to allow a user freedom to use the capabilities of each device to meet the current monitoring requirement.

The facility provided by the Measurement Management Protocol includes coordination of interactions between a controlling device and an arbitrary set of measurement devices. Section 2 provides an overview of the environment in which the Measurement Management Protocol operates, and of the services it provides. The remainder of the paper is a detailed specification of the service provided by an implementation of the Measurement Management Protocol.

2 Environment and Service

The Measurement Management Protocol provides a user with the facility to conduct a monitoring activity that involves any number of measurement devices distributed over an internetwork. Each measurement device involved in a monitoring activity is assumed to be capable of receiving packets from a network and examining the content of each packet. When a measurement device is collecting packets, it takes them directly from a network interface unit. The measurement application software keeps or discards any levels of heading on each packet. Packets are not decoded prior to reception by the measurement application software. The measurement devices are not gateways or other internetwork communication devices. The measurement devices are able to undertake measurement activities without having to give higher priority to other activities.

A controlling device is any computer that supports the ISO protocols and provides the services required by the Measurement Manageement Protocol.

The Measurement Management Protocol provides a user the ability to

- establish a Measurement Environment consisting of a controlling device and one or more measurement devices.

- place a command file at each measurement device in the environment.

*Supported, in part by the Office of Naval REsearch contract 83-K-0320

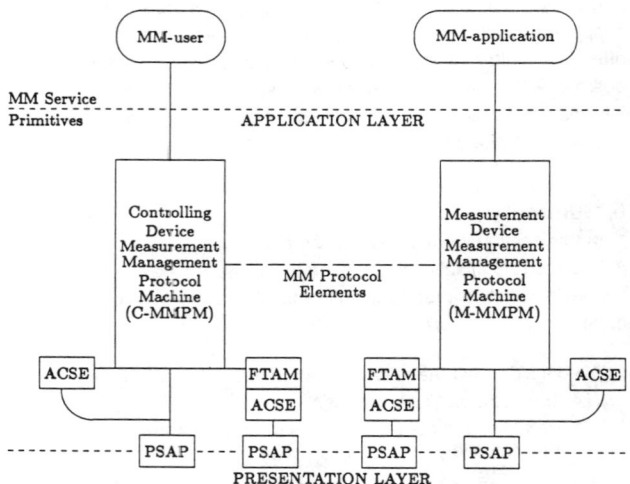

Figure 1: Relationship of this Protocol to OSI Standards

- initiate the monitoring event at all of the measurement devices included in the environment

- be notified when the resulting alarms or files of data are returned to the controlling device.

The measurement Management Service is provided in the Application Layer by the Measurement Management (MM) Protocol, making use of services available from the Association Control Service Entity (ACSE) in the Application Layer and the Presentation Service. Use is also made of the File Transfer Access and Management (FTAM) in the Application Layer. This specification also defines the Measurement Management characteristics which the MM-user may exploit. The relationship between the specifications for Measurement Management Service, Measurement Management Protocol, ACSE, FTAM, and the user of the Measurement Management Service is illustrated in Figure 1.

3 Scope and Field of Application

3.1 Scope

The rest of this paper defines the externally visable aspects of the Measurement Management Service within the OSI Application Layer in terms of

- a model defining the interaction between a user of the service and a controlled Measurement Device.

- the primitive actions and events of the service

- the parameter data associated with each primitive action and event
- the relationship between, and the valid sequences of, these actions and events.

This specification does not define the content of the command file that specifies the actions of the Measurement Device. It does specify the vehicle by which the command file is presented to a Measurement Device and the results of the Measurement Device activity are returned to the Controlling Device.

3.2 Field of Application

This service and its protocol apply to applications requiring command specifications to be delivered to and accepted by one or more remote devices, and the return of data or alarms from the remote devices to the controlling device initiating the application. The commands in the form of a command file, specify

- whether the remote device is to collect packets and store them for eventual transmission to the site that initiates the measuring activity, or is to issue an alarm to the initiator on the occasion of a specified event being detected in the network observed by the remote device.
- what event is to generate an alarm, in the event that alarms are required.
- what information in what packets is to be collected and stored, in the event that traffic collection is required.
- what computations, if any, are to be performed by the Measurement Device and reported to the service user.

4 Measurement Management Service Definitions

1. Controlling Device: Any host in a network or internet on which the MM service is available can be a Controlling Device.
2. Measurement Device: A special system processor attached to a network and able to monitor and/or capture information in response to instructions.
3. MM-user: A user of the Measurement Management service at a controlling device.
4. MM-application: An application process consisting of traffic monitoring activities at a Measurement Device (i.e., a user of the Measurement Management service at a Measurement Device).
5. Command File: A file containing specifications of the measurement activity to be undertaken by one or more Measurement Devices at the direction of a Controlling Device.
6. Information File: A file containing data collected at a Measurement Device for transmission to a Controlling Device.
7. MM-association: An application association between a Controlling Device and a Measurement Device.
8. Monitoring Event: All associations, communications and actions that result from one use of the Measurement Management service by an MM-user.
9. MM-environment (MME): Addresses specifying a set of Measurement Devices controlled by a Controlling Device during a Monitoring Event.
10. MM-parameter: An individual parameter of a Monitoring Event. Parameters include the identity of Measurement Devices to be included in a particular Monitoring Event, and specifications of the characteristics of the Monitoring Event.
11. Service: A distinct part of the total MM Service that is composed of a sequence of primitives taken from the set {request primitive, indication primitive, response primitive, confirm primitive}.
12. Collection mode: A characteristic of a Monitoring Event requiring storage of packet contents by a Measurement Device in an Information File and transmission of the file to the Controlling Device by the Measurement Device.
13. Alarm mode: A characteristic of a Monitoring Event requiring immediate notification of the Controlling Device by the Measurement Device when an indicated event is detected.
14. Measurement Management Protocol Machine: An instantiation of the Measurement Management Protocol executing in a Controlling Device or a Measurement Device.

5 Abbreviations

ISO International Organization for Standardization

OSI Open Systems Interconnection

ACSE Association Control Service Entity

FTAM File Transfer Access and Management

MMPM Measurement Management Protocol Machine

C-MMPM Controlling Device MMPM

M-MMPM Measurement Device MMPM

6 Overview of Measurement Management Service

6.1 General Features

6.1.1 Introduction

The Measurement Management Service supports specification of monitoring activities at distributed measurement devices by a single Controlling Device and the return of collected data or alarm indications to the Controlling Device.

Two modes of operation are defined, collection mode and alarm mode.

6.1.2 Features of the Service

The Measurement Management Service offers the following services to the MM-user:

- The means to establish an MM-association between a Controlling Device and one or more Measurement Devices for the purposes of collecting traffic or requesting alarms related to traffic detected on the networks to which the Measurement Devices are attached.
- The means to reserve the use of remote Measurement Device resources either between occurrences of specified events or during specified periods of time.
- The means to specify the data collection or alarm generating activities of remote Measurement Devices.
- The means to terminate an MM-association either at or before the completion of a Monitoring Event.
- The means to place a current version of a command file at each Measurement Device associated with a Monitoring Event.

6.1.3 MME Parameters

The specification and execution of a particular Monitoring Event takes place within an MM-environment and are defined by MM parameter values. The measurement activity of the Monitoring Event is specified in one or more command files specified by Monitoring Event parameters.

6.2 Communication Facilities

6.2.1 Establishment Facility

The establishment facility establishes an MM-association and an initial MME for that MM-association when an MM-user first invokes the Measurement Management Service.

6.2.2 Termination Facility

The termination facility provides services that enable an MM-user to terminate an MM-association. The termination facility provides for a destructive cancellation of an MME for one or more of the Measurement Devices participating in a Monitoring Event. The cancellation is initiated at the Controlling Device by the MM-user. The termination facility also provides for the release of a Measurement Device from an MME when the Measurement Device has indicated completion of its part in a Monitoring Event.

6.2.3 Commitment Facility

The commitment facility provides services that enable a Controlling Device to gain a commitment from a set of Measurement Devices to participate in a Monitoring Event.

6.2.4 Data Transfer Facility

The data transfer facility provides a service that enables an MM-user to assure that a current version of a command file is available at each Measurement Device participating in a Monitoring Event. The data transfer facility also provides for the collection at the Control Device of the data or alarms provided by each Measurement Device.

6.2.5 Status Check Facility

The status check facility provides service that enables an MM-user to determine the state of a specified Measurement Device within the context of a Monitoring Event. It includes provision for an MM-application to update the status of its MMPM as its execution progresses.

7 General Description of MM Service

7.1 Modes of Operation

The Measurement Management Service allows an MM-user to specify a Monitoring Event to be based on the collection and retention of parts of packets, or on the issuance of an alarm when an event is detected.

7.1.1 Collection-mode

Collection-mode (Packet-collection mode) has the following characteristics:

- Collection-mode operates when selected in the command file.
- Collection-mode requires that the command file include a pattern identifying those traffic packets to be selected when monitored, a specification of the information that is to be retained from each selected packet, and a description of any computations to be performed on the retained information. Data and results of the calculations are to be delivered to the Controlling Device.
- Collection-mode can be continuous during a specified interval of time, or between two specified events.
- Collection-mode implies an end-of-collection condition when allotted storage resources at the Measurement Device have been exceeded.

7.1.2 Alarm-mode

Alarm-mode has the following characteristics:

- Alarm-mode operates when selected in the command file.
- Alarm-mode requires that the command file include a pattern that identifies the event that is to generate an alarm.
- Alarm-mode can be continuous during a specified interval of time, between two specified events, or can be a single occurrence.
- Alarm-mode implies immediate notification to the Controlling Device when an alarm event occurs.

8 MM-Environment

8.1 The MME Model

A Monitoring Event occurs within the context of a Measurement Management environment. An MM-environment consists of a Controlling Device and one or more associated Measurement Devices. At each device an instance of the Measurement Management Protocol is active and operates as a Measurement Management Service Provider. At the Controlling Device the MM Service Provider receives commands from an MM-user. The user defines the Monitoring Event and specifies all needed parameters. At each Measurement Device an MM Service Provider receives commands in the form of protocol elements from a C-MMPM and in the form of service elements from a measurement application program. Figure 2 illustrates the MME model.

8.2 MM Event Parameters

The parameters required in the specification of a Measurement Event are described in Table 1.

- The monitor-id is used by a C-MMPM to identify for a user which M-MMPM is the source of a particular command indication, response, or confirm.
- The monitor list is used by a user to identify which monitors are to receive a command.
- The file designation is used by a user to identify a command file for transmission to one or more Measurement Devices.
- The start and stop conditions specify when packet collection or alarming is to begin at the Measurement Device participating in a Monitoring Event, and when it is to end. Start and/or stop may be based on clock time (at the Measurement Device), the arrival of a packet that matches a given pattern, or a specific event counter reaching or passing a specified value. The necessary patterns and counters must be defined in the command file sent to each participating Measurement Device.

9 Communication Facilities

9.1 Communication Model

This specification uses an abstract model for communication in which interactions take place between an MM-user, an MM-application, and an MM service provider. These interactions take the form of services that pass information in MM service parameters.

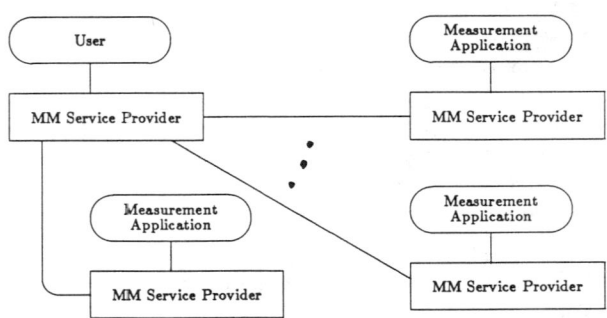

Figure 2: Service Model

Facility	Service	Structure
Establishment	MM-OPEN	Confirmed
Termination	MM-FINISH-WORK	Confirmed
	MM-ABORT	Non-confirmed
Data Transfer	MM-LOAD	Confirmed
	MM-ALARM	Confirmed
Commitment	MM-EXECUTE	Confirmed
Status Check	MM-STATUS	Confirmed
	MM-START	Non Confirmed
	MM-STOP	Non Confirmed

Table 2: Measurement Management Services

9.2 MM Services

Table 2 lists the services of the Measurement Management Service and the service facility to which each belongs.

The MM services are composed of MM service primitives. A service primitive is an atomic event and cannot be interrupted by any other event. The MM services defined in later sections use the following notation for the service parameters:

M: Presence of service parameter is mandatory

A: Service parameter specified by ISO (ACSE)

=: Service parameter value is unchanged by the service provider

blank: Service parameter is absent

9.2.1 MM Service Semantics: An Overview

This section describes informally the function served by each of the MM Services:

MM-OPEN requests an association be established between the Controlling Device and one or more Measurement Device.

MM-FINISH-WORK terminates the role in the Monitoring Event of the Measurement Devices specified. If the Measurement Device had been collecting packets, all information collected at the time of the MM-FINISH-WORK service request is sent to the Controlling Device.

MM-ABORT terminates the Monitoring Event at all specifed Measurement Devices. The effect is immediate and no information that may have been collected is returned to the Controlling Device.

MM-LOAD causes a current copy of a command file, which contains a description of the work to be done by a Measurement Device, to be in place at the designated Measurement Device.

MM-ALARM is used by a Measurement Device during an Alarm-mode Monitoring Event to notify its Controlling Device of the occurrence of a specified event.

MM-EXECUTE specifies the start and stop conditions for a Monitoring Event and notifies all associated Measurement Devices that the specification of a Monitoring Event is complete.

MM-STATUS requests that specified Measurement Devices report their status relevant to the current Monitoring Event.

MM-START is used by an MM-application to notify its M-MMPM that the start condition specified in the MM-EXECUTE is satisfied.

MM-STOP is used by an MM-application to notify its M-MMPM that the stop condition is satisfied and that the application has completed its activity. MM-stop may also be used by an MM-application to terminate a measurement activity due to other causes, such as exhausted resources.

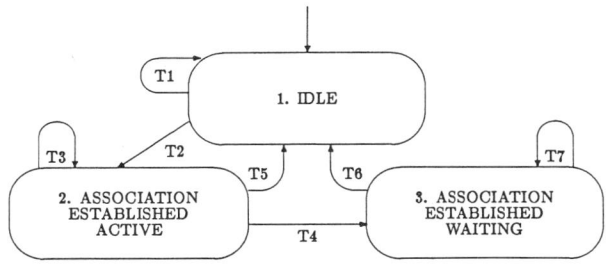

Figure 3: State transitions for Controlling Device MM Service

9.2.2 Controlling Device States and Transitions

The states and transitions of a C-MMPM differ from those of M-MMPMs. A C-MMPM is concerned with accepting commands from a user and coordinating communication between the user and multiple applications at remote sites. An M-MMPM is concerned with establishing an environment in which an application can carry out the measurement task specified by a remote user.

This section describes the states and transitions of a C-MMPM. Those of an M-MMPM are described in Section 9.2.3. Figure 3 indicates the normal sequence of transitions among states of the MM service provider at the Controlling Device. The states are

1. IDLE, when no MM association exists

2. ASSOCIATION ESTABLISHED - ACTIVE, when one or more Measurement Devices are associated with the Controlling Device and accepting work descriptions (that is, command files and start and stop conditions).

3. ASSOCIATION ESTABLISHED - WAITING, when a Monitoring Event has been specified and monitors have committed to its execution. The Controlling Device is awaiting data or alarms to be returned from the Measurement Devices.

The state transitions are:

T1 Use of the MM-OPEN service when the MM-OPEN-result parameter of each Measurement Device = "failure"

T2 Use of the MM-OPEN service when one or more MM-OPEN-result parameter = "success"

T3 Use of any MM service with a monitor list that is not the same as the complete monitor list for this Monitoring Event

T4 Use of the MM-EXECUTE service, which always involves all Measurement Devices in the monitor list for the current Monitoring Event, when at least one MM-EXECUTE-result parameter = "success"

T5 Use of the MM-FINISH-WORK service or the MM-ABORT service with monitor list that is the same as the complete monitor list for this event, when every MM-EXECUTE-result parameter = "failure"

T6 Use of the MM-FINISH-WORK, or MM-ABORT service such that the MME becomes empty

T7 Use of the MM-FINISH-WORK, or MM-ABORT service such that the MME does not become empty.

9.2.3 Measurement Device States and Transitions

The state transitions of a Measurement Device are shown in Figure 4. The states are:

1. IDLE, when no MM-association exists.

2. ASSOCIATION ESTABLISHED, when a Measurement Device is associated with a Controlling Device and is accepting work descriptions.

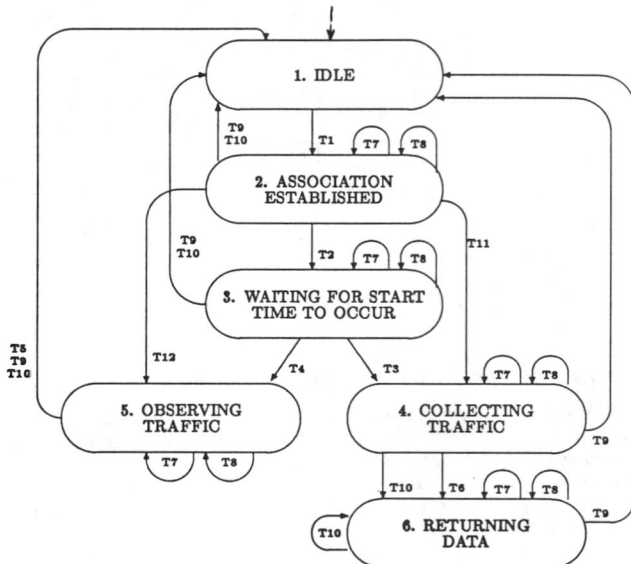

Figure 4: State transitions for Measurement Device MM Service

Service	IDLE	ASSOCIATION ESTABLISHED ACTIVE	ASSOCIATION ESTABLISHED WAITING
MM-OPEN	AVAILABLE	AVAILABLE	-
MM-LOAD	-	AVAILABLE	-
MM-ABORT	-	AVAILABLE	AVAILABLE
MM-FINISH-WORK	-	AVAILABLE	AVAILABLE
MM-EXECUTE	-	AVAILABLE	-
MM-STATUS	-	AVAILABLE	AVAILABLE

Table 3: Availability of MM-User Services according to Controlling Device state

Service	AWAITING START	OBSERVING TRAFFIC	RETURNING DATA
MM-COMPLETE	-	-	AVAILABLE
MM-SEND	-	-	AVAILABLE
MM-ALARM	-	AVAILABLE	-
MM-START	AVAILABLE	-	-
MM-STOP	-	AVAILABLE	AVAILABLE

Table 4: Availability of MM Application Services according to Measurement Device state

3. WAITING FOR START TIME TO OCCUR, when the Measurement Device is committed to a Monitoring Event and is waiting for the time when it is to begin monitoring traffic.

4. COLLECTING TRAFFIC, when the Measurement Device is collecting information and performing calculations to be stored for later return to the Controlling Device (used in Collection-mode).

5. OBSERVING TRAFFIC, when the Measurement Device is collecting packets and sending an alarm back to the Controlling Device when an alarm condition is detected (used in alarm mode).

6. RETURNING DATA, when the Measurement Device is in the process of transmitting a file to the Controlling Device.

The transitions are:

T1: Arrival of MM-OPEN to which Measurement Device responds with "success"

T2: Arrival of MM-EXECUTE when start value is a clock time

T3: Use of MM-START when Monitoring Event is Collection-mode

T4: Use of MM-START when Monitoring Event is Alarm-mode

T5: Use of MM-STOP when event is in Alarm-mode

T6: Use of MM-STOP when event is in Collection-mode

T7: Use of MM-OPEN or MM-EXECUTE to which Measurement Device responds with "failure"

T8: Arrival of MM-STATUS

T9: Arrival of MM-ABORT

T10: Arrival of MM-FINISH-WORK

T11: Arrival of MM-EXECUTE when start value is a condition (not a clock time) and the Monitoring Event is Collection-mode.

T12: MM-EXECUTE when start value is a condition (not a clock time) and Monitoring Event is Alarm-mode.

9.3 Availability and Usage Conditions of MM Services

MM Service availability is dependent on the state of the MM service provider. The service availability for the MM-user and the MM-application is shown in Tables 3 and 4. (States not listed in Table 4 have no service availability).

No service may be initiated by an MM-user if that user has initiated a confirmed service for which a confirm primitive has not been received.

9.4 Establishment Facility

9.4.1 MM-OPEN Service

Purpose: To establish an association with each Measurement Device listed in the monitor-list parameter.

Structure: Confirmed.

Service Parameters: Table 5 specifies the service parameters for the MM-OPEN service, together with an indication of when each parameter is required. A brief description of each parameter follows:

Monitor list is a list of internet addresses of Measurement Devices to be included in a Measurement Management environment as a result of this MM-OPEN service.

Monitor-id is the internet address of a particular Measurement Device whose response to an MM-OPEN service request is being confirmed to an MM-user.

Called Application Entity Title is the application entity title of the application entity with which an MM-association is to be established.

Calling Application Entity Title is the application entity title of the application entity initiating this MM-association.

Responding Application Entity Title is the application entity title of the application entity responding to an MM-association request.

MM-result indicates the result of the service; it takes values "success" or "failure" depending upon the outcome of the association effort. Neither failure reason is present if the MM-result is "success".

MM-application-failure-reason may contain the MM-application (at the Measurement Device)-specified rejection reason as an ASN.1 PrintableString [?] [?] if the MM-result is "failure" due to the MM-application rejecting the MM-OPEN.

MM-provider-failure-reason contains the rejection reason supplied by the MM-service provider if the MM-result is not "success" due to the service provider rejecting the MM-OPEN.

Usage and Effects: A user employs MM-OPEN to establish an association with one or more Measurement Devices. An MM-OPEN may be issued by an MM-user at any time prior to issuing an MM-EXECUTE. Each Measurement Device from which a response is received that con-

Parameter Name	Request	Indication	Response	Confirm
Monitor list	M			
Monitor-id				M
Called Application Entity Title	A			
Calling Application Entity Title		A		
Responding Application Entity Title			A	A=
MM-OPEN-result			M	M=
MM-OPEN-application-failure-reason			C	C=
MM-OPEN-provider-failure-reason				C

Table 5: MM-OPEN Service Parameters

Parameter Name	Request	Confirm
Monitor list	M	
Monitor-id		M
MM-FINISH-result		M

Table 6: FINISH-WORK Service Parameter List

tains MM-OPEN-result = "success" becomes associated with the Controlling Device.

All devices that have become associated with the Controlling Device in the context of this Monitoring Event become part of the environment (MME) of the event.

The MM-user must wait for a confirm from each of the monitors in the monitor list before proceeding with further specification.

9.5 Termination Facility

The termination facility provides the ability to end an association between the Controlling Device and an associated Measurement Device.

9.5.1 Services

Termination is achieved using one of three termination services. MM-FINISH-WORK and MM-ABORT are initiated by an MM-user. MM-STOP is initiated by an MM-application.

9.5.2 MM-FINISH-WORK

Purpose: To terminate the association of the Controlling Device with one or more monitors with a requirement that any data collected by the Measurement Device be returned to the Controlling Device, if the event is of collection mode.

Structure: Non-confirmed.
Service Parameters: See Table 6.

Monitor list is a list of internet addresses of Measurement Devices whose participation in the current Monitoring Event is to be terminated.

Monitor-id is the internet address of a Measurement Device whose response to an MM-FINISH-WORK service request is being confirmed to an MM-user.

MM-FINISH-result contains a description of the Measurement Device response to an MM-FINISH-WORK service request. The content of MM-FINISH-result is one of the following strings:

- Measurement activity terminated; no data transferred
- Measurement activity terminated; information file transfer initiated

Usage and Results: MM-FINISH-WORK may be issued by an MM-user at any time after an association is established. Each Measurement Device included in the Monitor list will cease all traffic monitoring activities. Any information file or portion of one that has been accumulated will be transferred to the Controlling Device.

Parameter Name	Request	Indication
Monitor list	M	
Monitor-id		M
MM-file designation	M	
MM-file result		M
MM-file failure reason		C

Table 7: LOAD Service Parameter List

9.5.3 MM-ABORT

Purpose: The MM-ABORT service allows the MM-user to terminate the association of one or more Measurement Devices in the Monitoring Event, with immediate effect.

Structure: Non-confirmed.
Service Parameters: Monitor list in the MM-ABORT service request.

Monitor list is a list of internet addresses of Measurement Devices whose participation in the Monitoring Event is to be terminated.

Usage and Effects: The MM-user may issue an MM-ABORT at any time. The association with the indicated monitors is broken and the monitors are removed from the MME. MM-ABORT takes precedence over any other service that might be active and causes immediate cancellation of any active process at the Measurement Device. No information file or partial file is returned from a Measurement Device that receives an MM-ABORT.

9.5.4 MM-STOP

Purpose: To notify an M-MMPM that the stop condition specified in the MM-EXECUTE request has occurred, and that the application has ended its measurement activity.

Structure: Non Confirmed
Parameters: none.

Usage and Effects: A measurement application issues the MM-STOP service request to indicate that the Monitoring Event has ended. An M-MMPM responds by sending a COMPLETE request if it is in Alarm mode. If an M-MMPM is in Collect mode, it responds by initiating the steps needed to transfer the collected data to the Controlling Device.

9.6 Data Transfer Facility

9.6.1 MM-LOAD

Purpose: To establish the existence of a current version of a command file at each Measurement Device participating in a Monitoring Event. A command file contains specifications of activities to be undertaken by a Measurement Device during a Monitoring Event.

Structure: Confirmed.
Service Parameter: See Table 7.

Monitor list is a list of internet addresses of Measurement Devices at which a current copy of the command file identified by a *file designation* is to be placed.

Monitor-id is the internet address of a Measurement Device whose reception of the command file is being indicated.

MM-file designation is identification of a file whose placement at each Measurement Device in the monirot list is requested.

MM-file result is the content of the result field of a confirm received from FTAM in response to a request to place the indicated file.

MM-file failure reason is the failure reason returned by FTAM if placement of the file at a particular Measurement Device has failed.

Usage and effect: The MM-user service LOAD causes the application sublayer FTAM to be invoked. Through use of FTAM commands, a designated Measurement Device is examined to see if it has a copy of the specified file that is older than one existing at the Controlling Device. If such is the case, the file copy at the Measurement Device is replaced by the file copy at the Controlling Device, by means of an FTAM file transfer. If there is no more recent copy of the designated file at the Controlling Device than at the Measurement Device, then no transfer occurs. This service is available any time after an association has been established and before the monitors are committed to the Monitoring Event.

Parameter Name	Request	Indication
Monitor-id		M
MM-ALARM reason	M	M

Table 8: ALARM Service Parameter List

9.6.2 MM-ALARM

Purpose: To notify an MM-user of the occurrence of an event for which an alarm has been requested.
Structure: Non-confirmed.
Parameter List: See Table 8.
Monitor-id is the internet address of a measurement Device from which an alarm is indicated to a user.
MM-ALARM-reason is a string supplied by an MM-application and identifying the condition that caused the alarm to be sent.
Usage and Effects: The MM-ALARM service is requested by an MM-application when an event for which an alarm was requested has been recognized. Alarm events are designated in the command file.

9.7 Commit Facility

The commit facility allows the MM-user to request a commitment from each monitor in the MM-environment to carry out the monitoring activity that has been specified.

9.7.1 MM-EXECUTE

Purpose: To allow the specification of the start and stop conditions associated with the Monitoring Event, and to obtain a commitment from each Measurement Device associated with the Monitoring Event to carry out the measurement instructions provided.
Structure: Confirmed.
Service Parameters: See Table 9.
Monitor-id is the internet address of the Measurement Device whose response to an MM-EXECUTE request is being confirmed to an MM-user.
MM-file designation is identification of the command file for this monitoring event.
MM-start condition indicates when the monitoring activity is to begin at each Measurement Device.
MM-stop condition indicates when the monitoring activity is to cease at each Measurement Device.
MM-result is either "success" or "failure" and indicates whether a particular Measurement Device is committed to the current Monitoring Event.
MM-denial reason is an explanation of the failure of a Measurement Device to commit to a Monitoring Event.
Usage and Effect: The start and stop conditions included as parameters of the MM-EXECUTE service are transmitted to all associated Measurement Devices. On receipt of the MM-EXECUTE, each Measurement Device attempts to begin an MM-application as defined by a command file and the start and stop parameters of EXECUTE. If the specification of the Monitoring Event provided by the command file and the parameters of EXECUTE is such that the Measurement Device cannot carry out the indicated activity, a failure notice is sent to the associated Controlling Device. The Measurement Device is deleted from the Measurement Management Environment.

9.8 Status Checking Facility

The status checking facility allows an MM-user to interrogate a designated subset of the Measurement Devices associated with a Monitoring Event. Each Measurement Device reports its state within the context of the Monitoring Event.

9.8.1 MM-STATUS

Purpose: To allow an MM-user to determine the progress of a Monitoring Event at one or more Measurement Devices in an MM-environment.
Structure: Confirmed.
Service Parameters: See Table 10.
Monitor list is a list of internet addresses of Measurement Devices the status of which are to be reported.

Parameter Name	Request	Indication	Response	Confirm
Monitor-id				M
MM-file designation	M	M=		
MM-start condition	M	M=		
MM-stop condition	M	M=		
MM-result			M	M=
MM-denial reason			C	C=

Table 9: EXECUTE Service Parameter List

Monitor-id is the internet address of the Measurement Device from which a response is being confirmed to an MM-user.
MM-STATUS-result is a string supplied by an M-MMPM in response to an MM-STATUS request and describing the state of the M-MMPM. Possible MM-STATUS-result contents are

- Not Associated
- Awaiting command file
- Awaiting execute response
- Awaiting occurrence of start condition
- Alarm mode - monitoring
- Collection mode - monitoring
- Returing information file

Usage and Effects: An MM-user may request an MM-STATUS at any time. The MM-STATUS service request may designate one or more of the Measurement Devices from the monitor list of the current Monitoring Event. A Measurement Device, on receiving an MM-STATUS service request, responds by reporting its current state. The MM-STATUS request has no effect on the Monitoring Event.

Parameter Name	Request	Indication	Response	Confirm
Monitor-list	M			M
Monitor-id				M
MM-STATUS-result			M	M=

Table 10: STATUS Service Parameter List

9.8.2 MM-START

Purpose: To notify M-MMPM that the start condition specified in the EXECUTE request has occurred, and that the application has begun the monitoring activity specified in the command file.
Structure: Non Confirmed
Parameters: none.
Usage and Effects: A measurement application issues an MM-START service request to indicate that a Monitoring Event has begun. An M-MMPM records the fact that the start condition has occurred and responds appropriately if a status request is received.

10 Summary

The facilities of the Measurement MANAGEMENT SERVICE allow a user to specify a measurement application to be carried out at one or more remote monitoring facilities in an interconnected network. Defined facilities include

- establishment of an association between a user at a Controlling Device and measurement applications at distributed Measurement Devices,
- data transfer for establishing command files at remote sites and for returning alarms and information files from remotes,
- commitment for confirming the participation of each measurement application in a Monitoring Event, and
- termination for ending a Monitoring Event before its defined stopping condition, at the discretion of the user.

The Measurement Management Service allows freedom to describe the monitoring activity to be undertaken by each Measurement Device by requiring the placement of a command file at each device. Content of a command file is unrestricted, except as follows:

- A command file must specify Alarm or Collection mode for activities of a measurement application.
- If a pattern or counter is referenced in a start or stop condition parameter, that pattern or counter must be defined in the command file.

References

[1] *Information processing systems − Open systems interconnection - Specification of Abstract Syntax Notation One (ASN.1).1*. International Organization for Standardization. Draft International Standard DIS 8824.

[2] *Information processing systems − Open systems interconnection - Specification of Basic encoding rules for Abstract Syntax Notation One (ASN.1).1*. International Organization for Standardization. Draft International Standard DIS 8825.

PART 12. NETWORK INTERCONNECTION AND SWITCHING

Y. Wang

Tongzi University, China

LAN-HUB
AN ETHERNET COMPATIBLE LOW COST/HIGH PERFORMANCE COMMUNICATION SOLUTION

Imrich Chlamtac and Alex Herman*

Department of Electrical & Computer Engineering
University of Massachusetts
Amherst, MA 01003

*Codex Corporation
Mansfield, MA 02067

ABSTRACT

The LAN-HUB is a new local area network designed to combine the properties of several existing LAN standards to provide highly reliable communication at a relatively lower cost per station, improve network capacity/delay performance and increase the LAN user's flexibility in configuring his network. The LAN-HUB network is configured around the CODEX 4320 LAN-HUB communication controllers which allow up to eight Ethernet/IEEE 802.3 stations to transparently share one network transceiver or RF Modem. Each LAN-HUB controller executes a fair, collision free, arbitration among its *local* stations attached to its LAN ports, using a patented collision avoidance algorithm. The HUB's rear panel further provides a Network port which can be attached to a standard 802.3 transceiver, to another HUB or terminated in a loop back mode. The HUBs, thus, allow stations to be organized in a standalone star network, in a "cascading" star configuration, or as an integrated bus/star network. When organized as star or cascaded star networks, the HUB controllers provide highly reliable and controlled, collision free, bandwidth allocation suitable for applications such as CPU room clusters. Alternately, in a bus configuration the HUBs support an Ethernet type bus network, with random access channel control. In the latter configuration the HUBs provide a lower cost/higher performance solution for bursty traffic users, since they reduce cabling requirements, decrease cost by sharing each transceiver among several LAN stations and improve network throughput/delay performance by eliminating local collisions. The LAN-HUB is thus effective in creating a local communication solution with a significant degree of flexibility in choosing the network layout and the type of service, random or deterministic, provided to the network users.

1. Introduction

In recent years the local area communication has witnessed the emergence of several (IEEE 802) LAN standards based on competing approaches [2,3,5]. Motivated by the need to support a wide range of dissimilar to span variable communication distances and to connect devices of highly varying cost, the existing standards differ significantly in their bandwidth allocation philosophies, resulting in selective efficiency in supporting different communication environments [4]. To obtain an efficient and overall cost effective service a customer may consequently, face the need to incorporate several LAN types on premises, each targeted towards a different application type. This in turn not only increases the total cost of communication, but also introduces new problems of network interconnection, integration and management [8,9].

The LAN-HUB described in this paper is a new local communication solution developed to bridge the gap between existing standards. Compared to existing LAN standards, the LAN-HUB was designed to provide a high reliability communication at lower cost per individual station and to improve network capacity/delay performance. And, not less importantly, it provides the LAN user with a flexibility in configuring his local area network in terms of topology and type of service provided, a feature not found in current LAN standards.

The HUB-LAN network is configured around the CODEX 4320 LAN-HUB [1]. The HUB is a communication device supporting Ethernet-format packet communication among its attached stations and between its stations and a network. In its basic configuration each 4320 LAN-HUB allows up to eight Ethernet/IEEE 802.3 devices to transparently share one transceiver or RF Modem, acting as a LAN port sharing device. The HUB rear panel provides a Network port which can be attached to an 802.3 transceiver, to another HUB or a loop back plug. The transceivers can be connected to baseband, broadband and fiber optic cables, giving the flexibility to choose different media. The 4320 LAN-HUB executes a fair, collision free arbitration among its locally attached stations using a patented Collision Avoidance (CA) algorithm [13]. Among the arriving packets the HUB chooses one packet which is given an immediate access to the Network port, while remaining transmitting stations are issued a (HUB generated) collision presence signal. In this way all potential collisions among the stations attached to the HUB's LAN ports are avoided so that, for example, in a standalone configuration a fair deterministic access is provided. At the same time, by providing its stations with collision information, the HUB fully emulates the CSMA/CD protocol. A station can thus be connected transparently, via a HUB over a 802.3 network, while experiencing a reduced probability of collision due to the HUB's filtering out of all collisions among its locally attached stations. The resulting network capacity is thus superior to conventional Ethernet or other IEEE 802.3 systems.

By appropriate setting of Network and LAN ports connections, the LAN-HUBs can be used to obtain various network configurations varying not only in topology and network size, but also in the channel access method. By attaching several stations to a HUB or several HUBs to the LAN ports of one HUB, star and cascaded star network configurations are easily generated. Networks created in this way have controlled, collision free bandwidth allocation suitable, e.g. for CPU room clusters. Alternately, by connecting the network port to a standard 802.3, the HUBs can be used to configure an Ethernet type bus network, with random access channel control transceiver. In the latter configuration the HUBs provide a lower cost/ higher performance solution for bursty traffic users by reducing the cabling requirements, lowering the cost by sharing each transceiver among several LAN stations, and by improving the network throughput/delay performance through the elimination of local collisions. The LAN-HUB controller can thus be used to configure low cost network architectures which are better tailored to users applications.

The LAN-HUB performance has been evaluated by measurement and simulation. In a standalone configuration a 4320 HUB based network has been shown to provide full utilization of the channel. When using HUB connections over a 802.3 network, the performance improvement was found to be relative to the reduction in the number of competing devices, reduced in this case to the total number of connected HUBs as opposed to the number of stations in a standard network. Given the improved performance and its relatively low station connection cost, the LAN-HUB is thus effective for attaching clusters of Ethernet/IEEE 802.3 compatible devices to a LAN with a significant flexibility in choosing the network layout and in the type of service (random or deterministic) provided to network users.

In subsequent sections we first describe the HUB 4320 operation and its hardware and software features. We then consider different network configurations and applications that can be build around the HUB controllers. For each configuration a detailed performance is evaluated and compared to that of existing LANs.

2. Hub Operation

The CODEX 4320 LAN-HUB allows up to eight Ethernet or IEEE 802.3 entryways (bridges, gateways or stations) to share one transceiver or RF modem. The HUB rear panel provides one network port and eight user ports. The network port can be attached to any Ethernet or IEEE 802.3 Media Access Unit. The purpose of the user ports is to provide an efficient Ethernet compatible channel access whose efficiency, cost and reliability are however superior to the Ethernet. In the Ethernet or IEEE 802.3 local area network system access to the transmission medium is distributed and regulated by the CSMA/CD random access protocol. The CSMA/CD protocol operation is well known and documented [2,7,8]. We shall therefore only highlight its principles as needed for describing the operation of the LAN-HUB. In the CSMA/CD protocol all stations connected to the network (known as Network Interface Units – NIU) "listen" to the trunk cable to determine if it is in use. An NIU will not interrupt another NIU who's transmission is detected on the trunk cable. Only when the trunk is sensed idle, an NIU that has a packet to send will transmit. In a IEEE 802.3 network the propagation delay time between any two NIU's can reach 52 microseconds. Therefore the trunk maybe sensed idle by one NIU while another NIU has already started a transmission. As a result packet collisions will occur. The Media Access Units attaching the NIU's to the trunk will detect the collision and in return will generate an IEEE 802.3 Collision signal to all NIUs. The transmitting NIUs will stop the transmission of the packet and jam the network for about 3.2 microseconds in order to enforce collision signal among all network NIUs. Following the jam the transmitting NIUs will "back off" and wait a randomly generated time before retransmission. Clearly, during periods of increased load, the collision probability increases significantly, reducing channel utilization and increasing the average packet delay [4,8].

The Codex 4320 LAN-HUB improves bandwidth utilization and increase capacity by preventing collisions among its attached NIUs. Collision are avoided by means of a patented Collision Avoidance Unit (CAU) [13]. When several stations attached to the HUB become ready for transmission they follow the CSMA/CD protocol. In the HUB configuration too, the nonnegligible distance of NIU's from the HUB can cause several NIU's to transmit during overlapping periods of time. However, unlike in Ethernet, in this case the HUB's station management is employed to resolve collisions. Specifically, the HUB will choose one packet among any colliding packets from the user ports and grant it immediate access to the network port. The other colliding packets are blocked and their generating NIUs receive a Private Collision signal. The CAU arbitration is fair so that if the NIUs collide again other NIU is given access to the trunk. Thus, one device can not "hog" the network. The end result is that the time usually taken up by the collision and the subsequent execution of the "back off" involving all colliding stations, is now available for packet transmission.

Lastly, the HUB function is transparent with respect to all devices attached to it, while completely supporting the standard Ethernet or IEEE 802.3 Access Unit Interface (AUI). To this end each HUB port provides 802.3 Transmit, Receive and Collision signals. The SQE (heartbeat) test signal of the 802.3 can be originated by the HUB itself.

3. Hardware Functional Requirements

The most fundamental functional requirement for the HUB is IEEE 802.3 compatibility. Figure 1 contains a representation of the interfaces that are defined under the 802.3 standard and a graphic representation of where the HUB fits with respect to these interfaces. The Attachment Unit Interface (AUI) as defined in 802.3 consists of a drop cable through which data and control are passed between the Medium Attachment Unit (MAU), which is a transceiver in the case of a baseband Ethernet, and the Network Interface Unit (represented in the diagram by the generic term DTE). It is at the level of this AUI interface that the HUB is interposed within the 802.3 hierarchy. The advantage to situating the HUB in such a manner lies in the flexibility in the applications that this arrangement allows. The HUB is consequently media independent, allowing broadband and baseband applications and is compatible with any 802.3 entryway or NIU that supports the AUI interface.

Another important requirement is for some providing means of handling collisions at the sub-network level. There are essentially two methods available to achieve this function: Local collision can be passed up to the main 802.3 (Ethernet) trunk, jamming the whole system, or collision within the sub-network can be arbitrated without notifying the trunk. The second of these approaches has been incorporated in the HUB in the form of a Collision Avoidance Unit (CAU). By avoiding collisions in the sub-network, a system wide enhancement in effective throughput can be achieved. In order to maintain full 802.3 compatibility, this collision avoidance mechanism must function transparently with respect to the entryways or NIU's attached to the HUB user ports. The collision avoidance mechanism incorporated in the HUB design provides this transparency through a private collision signal which is used to arbitrate collision in the sub-network without passing such collisions to the main trunk.

Configurable loopback capability is another required feature in order to provide the HUB with the flexibility to support the various applications for which it is intended. The loopback feature allows the HUB to be configured such that packets transmitted from the output port (the AUI port usually attached to the medium attachment unit) would be looped back to the receive channels of the other AUI ports. This function is necessary to allow the HUB to serve in stand-alone applications and would also be useful in system diagnostics. There are two approaches available to provide this function: Loopback can be manually selected via a switch or strapping arrangement, or loopback can occur automatically if the sharing unit senses that there is no medium attachment unit attached to to it. Because automatic loopback can cause timing problems in cascaded HUB applications (i.e. when HUBs are plugged into other HUBs) and in broadband applications, an external or internal manually-configurable loopback capability has been incorporated in the HUB design.

The HUB may be installed in wiring closet, alcoves, or other unattended non-airconditioned spaces, therefore high reliability is a must. A design that utilize repetitive use of highly reliable circuits was chosen.

4. Hardware Description

Figure 2 depicts the HUB's schematic block diagram. The hardware consists of three major components: Ten Squelched Receivers circuits, nine Half-Step Drivers circuits and a CAU (Collision Avoidance Unit).

The HUB consists of repeated instances of a very few functional blocks. Repeated functional blocks simplify reliability calculations; in the case of the HUB, the predicted MTBF (Mean Time Between Failures) is 140000 hours.

4.1 Squelched Receivers (SR)

The SR has two inputs: data from the AUI port and an internally generated Transmit Data lines emanating from the eight user ports SRs are "wired or" therefore creating an internal Transmit Data Bus. Each Transmit Enable signal gates the incoming packets from a user port to the Transmit Data Bus. Nine Carrier Detect lines (eight from the user port SR's and one from the network port collision signal SR) are fed into the Collision Avoidance Unit. These are all the inputs necessary for the CAU to arbitrate collisions. The tenth SR is connected to the network port receive line and gates the eight user port half step drivers.

4.2 Collision Avoidance Unit (CAU)

The CAU is a fast state machine which senses energy on the eight user port transmit lines via the Carrier Detect logic signals. Depending on the current state of the trunk (IDLE or BUSY), it decides whether to enable a user packet to propagate to the internal Transmit Data Bus and therefore to be transmitted to the 802.3 trunk. On the next data packet the state machine 'remembers' the user AUI port which last transmitted, and will grant transmission to a different AUI port, unless that last serviced port is the only currently active user port. The CAU samples its incoming Carrier Detect lines at the rate of 10 megasamples per second. In return the CAU gates the SR Transmit Data line within a bit time or less via the Transmit Enable lines that individually select/deselect the user AUI port for transmission on the 802.3 trunk. When the transmission of one or more user packets arrive 'simultaneously' (within the decision window of the CAU) only one user packet will be gated out to the internal Transmit Data Bus (and therefore to the 802.3 trunk). The AUI user port most recently granted trunk access will be the least preferred in the next contention, so a degree of fairness is maintained.

The private collision lines are the Collision signal to the user ports. The CAU state machine sends this signal to any user AUI port attempting to transmit while another user port in the HUB has been granted access to the 802.3 trunk. Private collision will remain active as long as the contending user AUI ports exhibits transmission energy.

The general collision signal is the 802.3 Collision signal from the transceiver/RF modem. It is gated to all user AUI ports not receiving a private collision signal. The SQE test burst (heartbeat) will thus be seen by the last transmitting entryway or NIU.

Trunk state (busy line) is an internal machine state signal which may take the values IDLE or BUSY. It is determined by the SR circuits as well as the previous machine state.

The CAU contains the SQE test generator. The internal SQE (heartbeat) test is manually enabled usually only in loopback situation. In looped-back cascaded HUB applications, only the header HUB may have internal heartbeat enabled.

4.3 Half Step Driver

All nine AUI port connections are fully compatible with ANSI/IEEE 802.3 standard and therefore feature half-step line drivers. The motive for the half-step feature comes from the low frequency behavior of 802.3 AUI pulse transformer. The latter provides up to 2000 volts isolation between the MAU and the entryway or NIU. All the nine AUI ports are isolated by the above pulse transformer. The HUB therefore is isolated from its MAU as well as from its entryways or NIUs.

In summary the HUB hardware is transparent to the user DTE as well as to the network trunk. The network AUI port looks to a transceiver/RF modem exactly like an entryway or NIU AUI port and each of the eight user ports looks to a an entryway or NIU exactly like a transceiver/RF modem AUI port. Neither of the above hardware components buffers data packets. The total delay of the hardware is less then a bit and an arriving packet may lose up to two preamble bits.

5. Network Configuration

The Network port of the HUB is connected to an AUI cable up to 50 meters (164 feet) long. One end of the AUI cable is plugged into the Network port. The other end is connected to the standard AUI connector on a transceiver. The HUB and the transceiver can be up to 50 meters apart.

Eight Ethernet or IEEE 802.3 devices may be connected to a single LAN HUB. From 1 to 50 meters of AUI cable connects the HUB to each of the attached NIU's. Thus, eight devices are attached to one trunk cable location. These eight Ethernet or IEEE 802.3 NIU are located within 100 meters of the trunk cable location (50 meters between the transceiver and HUB plus another 50 meters between the HUB and each device.)

By attaching HUBs to HUBs, they are "cascaded" as shown in figure 3. This is done by attaching the Network port of one HUB to the user port of another HUB. Thus, several HUBs can be attached to one trunk cable location. In a trunk cable based system, the cascade can be two LAN HUBs deep as shown in figure 3. A total of 64 Ethernet or IEEE 802.3 devices can be attached to one cable location. The Ethernet or IEEE 802.3 NIUs can be as far as 150 meters from the cable (three 50 meter cables).

The HUB can be used to make a standalone network without cable. A loop-back plug is attached to the Network port of one LAN-HUB. Again, it is "cascaded" by attaching the Network port of one LAN-HUBs to the user port of the other HUB. Without trunk cable, the cascade can be four levels deep. Up to 4096 Ethernet devices can be connected within a 820 foot radius of the central HUB. Depending on application, the cascade can be deeper and the distance greater. Configuring a standalone network cluster is similar to a cable based system. The user ports are connected in the same manner. The difference is that a loopback connector is attached to the Network port of the HUB rather than a transceiver cable (figure 3). The loopback capability is also selectable internal to the unit. In loopback, the HUB offers an alternative to coaxial cable media for Local Area Networks.

A small standalone LAN is easily connected to a larger coax-based system, by simple replace of the loopback connector at the Network port of the LAN-HUB with a transceiver cable. The transceiver cable is attached to a transceiver, RF modem, or any other standard LAN device.

The flexibility of configuration combined with the freedom to choose between a random access, or collision free channel access control, can be utilized to tailor the HUB-LAN based network to the requirements of specific applications.

Clustered Devices: LAN installations often include areas where many devices are located in a limited space. Examples of such areas include CPU rooms and wiring closets. When used together with nested asynchronous LAN entryways each LAN-HUB allows all 8 of these entryways to share one transceiver, significantly reducing system cost. Furthermore, while Ethernet specifications require a 2.5 meter spacing between transceiver cable locations, in the HUB LAN configuration cabling is reduced since 8 devices can share one cable location.

PC Networks: Figure 5 illustrates another common application for the LAN HUB. Here, the HUB's functions are used as an inexpensive means of connecting personal computers and/or workstations. The LAN-HUB can support any Ethernet or IEEE 802.3 compatible PC entryway card or engineering workstation. With one LAN-HUB, eight workstations can be connected. This is the size of a typical PC LAN.

Large HUB Networks: The cascaded configuration obtained by connecting the Network port of up to eight LAN-HUBs to the LAN ports of another HUB. Since the cascade can be four units deep, up to 4096 computers within a 1640 foot diameter can be connected without coaxial cable. The Codex 4320 LAN-HUB can replace LAN cable and transceivers to provide a "Star Wired" LAN solution. The patented collision avoidance capability here gives the simplicity of Ethernet with the added benefit of collision avoidance.

Integrated 802.3/HUB Network Interconnect: Lastly, the HUB LAN can be used to inexpensively connect any one of the above described LAN-HUB based networks to an existing Ethernet or 802.3 network as shown in figure 4. In this case the HUB LAN at each Ethernet trunk connection will fulfil a double role. As a local arbiter it is responsible for resolving collisions coming from its directly attached NIUs. In the "opposite" direction the HUB will pass to its NIUs all collision signals detected on the Ethernet cable, thus insuring complete compatibility of the NIUs with respect to the CSMA/CD protocol execution in the interconnect.

6. System Evaluation

The design of a new communication system requires comprehensive performance evaluation based on measurement and simulation. The objective of such evaluation is to understand the new network behavior, to verify its protocol operation, to establish rules for network configuration and use, to evaluate the support given to existing and potential LAN applications and to provide data for comparison with existing LAN solutions. For creating a versatile simulation tool a network model was generated using the software emulation approach introduced in [10,12]. With this approach the network simulation model can be generated automatically from network hardware and protocol specification. As a result the model correctness is guaranteed while simulation programming time is drastically reduced.

To evaluate the integrated system several dozens of models, with varying traffic loads have been run. The issues addressed included:

1. The basic throughput/delay system performance of single and multiple HUB network under varying traffic conditions in terms of load, packet size and population.
2. The performance of the network under different configurations in terms of station clustering, station distribution, network distances and topologies.
3. The comparison of the LAN-HUB network with other LANs in providing specific services and applications.

6.1 LAN-HUB Performance

For purposes of verification, the system behavior produced by the simulated system model, in which each HUB controller connects a single station, has been compared with Ethernet network operation. The verification of the LAN-HUB operation on an event by event basis with the 802.3 standard was used to validate the system. Following protocol analysis the LAN-HUB simulator was used to produce performance results shown in figure 5. The derived behavior is seen to be close but slightly better than that obtained in the past for Ethernet [4,8,11]. The discrepancy can be attributed to the fact that the HUB's circuitry is significantly faster than the transceiver/controller operation of the standard Ethernet.

For validation of the throughput/delay system performance the traffic load was characterized by exponential interarrival distribution and by 150 byte packets of user data. When transmitted, a 26 byte overhead is added as required by the 802.3 standard. The network configuration in this and the following models is documented in a table accompanying each figure. The table specifies the network topology, the network parameters setting and the traffic. Thus, for example, in case of figure 5 a 100 m cable is used for Ethernet while for the HUB models the cable length, referred to in the case of NIU to HUB connection as ray length, changes between 30 to 300 meters in each HUB cluster. The remaining network parameters are set to the values specified by the 802.3 standard. Figure 5a shows the average packet delay as a function of the network arrival rate, i.e., the load generated by 32 NIU's. The average packet delay represents the time a packet spends in the system from its generation and until the packet has been successfully received by its destination station. Notice that this measure can be only taken over all successfully transmitted packets. Therefore at very high loads, where the station's generated loads can not be supportable by the CSMA/CD protocol, the packet delay in itself is not a sufficient criterion to evaluate the system performance. Figure 5b thus gives the average packet delay as a function of the system throughput. The throughput is defined as the fraction of time the system is busy with successful transmissions.

6.1.1 Population Size

This model considers the effect of changing the number of station's connected over a system on the system performance. We consider the case of a single HUB-cluster configuration versus the 802.3 (Ethernet) mode, i.e., when each HUB connects a single station. For meaningful comparison of models with different number of stations the load is kept invariant, i.e., for the same system load value it is assumed that each station generates a larger load as the number of station's decreases.

Figure 6 shows that for both systems, the Ethernet as

well as the single HUB cluster, the performance slightly improves as the number of stations becomes smaller. While this behavior is well known for Ethernet networks it is observed here for the first time with respect to the HUB cluster. Unlike in Ethernet the phenomenon here is related to mutual collisions and to the need to observe interframe spacing when experiencing a busy HUB. The comparison of the two systems shows that a relative performance advantage of the HUB cluster is shown to be preserved over all population sizes. The clear reason for the improved performance in the HUB network is the total avoidance of collisions. Theoretically the HUB cluster can, therefore, provide a full utilization of the bandwidth. The reason that the measured system throughput does not reach the value of 1 is that each data packet requires an overhead of 26 bytes. The system capacity is thus limited to approximately 0.85 as confirmed by the simulation results presented in Figure 6.

6.1.2 The Effect of Network Span

In this case we consider the effect of communication distances on the performance of each system. We consider two network configurations. One in which stations are closely spaced – all 32 NIU's can be interconnected by using a 100 m Ethernet cable or 10–50 m rays respectively. In the other configuration a 1000 m cable is needed, corresponding to combined rays' lengths of 30 to 500 meters. The results produced by these models, shown in Figure 7, show a better performance of the HUB cluster for both short cable and long cable configurations.

It can further be observed that the HUB cluster performance is only slightly affected by the average ray length. (A significant effect is noticeable only when most of the mutual collisions in the HUB result in damaged packets. This is not the case in either of the two configurations considered in this model). On the other hand, in the case of an Ethernet network the average relative station distances define the effective CSMA/CD "collision window" given by maximum round trip propagation delay. Therefore, the performance of an Ethernet based system is heavily dependent on the cable length and deteriorates with increasing cable length as also seen from Figure 7. In conclusion the relative performance advantage of the HUB over Ethernet grows with the 'size of the system' which is to be spanned by the communication network.

Lastly, the performance of an integrated, multiple HUB over Ethernet, network is also affected by the cable length. The results show a noticeable performance degradation with the use of HUBs, although the overall degradation is milder than in a pure Ethernet network. Taking a single station per HUB a network with 16 HUBs will suffer delays of 7.86 msec for 500 m cable but delays of 15.6 msec for a 2500 m cable. Similarly, for 46 byte frames the throughput for a load of 0.4 will be 0.36 for 500 m but only 0.31 for 2500 m. With the use of 2 HUB clusters with 8 stations in each will deteriorate in delay from 7.53 msec to 13.86 msec and in throughput form 0.36 to 0.34 for the above change of cable length. This behavior is not intuitively straightforward since collision "on Ethernet" are also "transmitted" into each cluster by the HUB when acting as transceiver.

6.1.3. Packet Length Related Performance

The performance of an Ethernet LAN is negatively affected by shortening the data packet length. This is due to the worsening of the ratio between user information (data) and the constant control overhead (26 bytes in the case of Ethernet). In addition, the contention based protocol suffers further degradation with reduced packet length for a given load the number of packets present the system at any time will grow as their length decreases.

Due to the combination of the above reasons the maximum Ethernet throughput for the minimum (46 bytes) packet length cannot exceed 37% [11]. On the other hand, a HUB cluster operates as a queueing system and therefore does not suffer from the increased collision probability effect. Consequently for small packets (46 bytes), a HUB cluster has a maximum throughput advantage of over 30% while for larger packets (600 bytes) the difference between the two systems is approximately 10%. As shown in Figure 8, the performance of a HUB cluster is thus much less sensitive to packet size changes than Ethernet, and its relative performance advantage will increase as to average packet size decreases.

Since longer packets improve performance for both an Ethernet and a HUB cluster system, it is not surprising that in an integrated HUB/Ethernet network the same observation continues to hold. For example, for a 16 station, 2 HUB network with 8 stations per cluster and a load of 0.6 we obtain for 46 bytes frames the net throughput of the system is 0.36 with delays of 7.53 msec. On the other hand, for 600 byte packets the throughput is increased significantly to 0.585 with delays of 0.60 msec only.

6.1.4. Probability of Aborting Packets

In a single or multiple HUB system local collisions are used as the means for in–cluster HUB access management. To evaluate the effect of these collisions in the probability that packets will be aborted (discarded after 15 collisions) even when the network is not overloaded, we observe a network with 16 stations connected in four different configurations:

    a. in a single HUB

    b. 8 station's on each HUB (total of 2 HUB clusters)

    c. 2 station's per HUB cluster (total of 8 clusters)

    d. 1 station per HUB (16 HUB's on Ethernet)

The network behavior was observed for packet length of 46,150,600 and 1500 bytes and for variable traffic loads. It is very interesting to notice that for a given load the number of aborted packets is higher when Ethernet is involved in spite of the fact that with larger clusters (more stations per HUB) the number of private collisions in each cluster increases. This behavior can be ascribed to the fact that "during" a private collision the HUB will still correctly transfer the packet of the winning station on the Ethernet cable. Therefore, the HUB acts as an order introducing agent in the system – as collisions which would have otherwise occurred on a standard Ethernet are "solved (without performance penalty) at the HUB level before reaching the CSMA/CD protocol. Thus, for any given load, the probability of "global – Ethernet type" collisions is traded against the in–HUB private collision probability and higher total channel utilization. As a result, the overall probability of collision at each station becomes smaller and the probability of aborted packets for a given system load is reduced.

6.2 Configuring a HUB Based Network

Given the user's flexibility to assign stations to HUBs, it must be determined how different station to HUB assignments affect the delay/throughput behavior of the system. We investigate the effect of assigning a different number of stations to each HUB, the effect the uniformity of station assignment has on the delay and throughput and the tradeoffs between cabling requirements and system performance.

6.2.1. Station to HUB Assignment

In this model we consider a population of 32 station. The distance between every two stations connected in a HUB configuration does not exceed 300 meters. We consider station interconnection over a single cascaded HUB, over two cascaded HUBs with 16 stations in each cluster and over an Ethernet. In Figure 5a and 5b we give the average system performance for the different network models given above. Figure 5a shows the average packet delay as a function of the network arrival rate, i.e., the load generated by 32 stations. Figure 5b gives the average packet delay as a function of the system throughput. The results shown in Figures 5a and 5b provide the basis for the following observations:

a. For all load values the average packet delay is the smallest when all stations reside within a single HUB cluster.

b. The performance of an Ethernet model with two HUBs is very similar to that of the standard Ethernet. In fact, the improvement is commensurate with the reduction in the number of transceivers (in this case the number of HUBs) which compete for channel access. Therefore, any other station clustering using between 3 to 31 HUBs would produce performance curves bounded from below by the standard Ethernet curve and from above by the 2 cluster model. In other words, the exact number of HUB clusters for a given number of stations does not vary significantly with effect the system performance. The only significant effect is associated with the transition form a single HUB cluster system to a multiple HUB system.

A similar observation is supported by observing the system throughput/delay behavior shown in figure 5b. While the single HUB can operate at throughput values of at least 72% the Ethernet network throughput levels out at about 62%. This phenomenon can clearly be translated into other network characterizations. Thus, for example due to the higher throughput/lower delay of the HUB system at 50% system utilization the HUB cluster provides an average packet delay of 600 microseconds, while in a similarly loaded Ethernet the packets will suffer an average delay of 3000 microseconds.

6.2.2. Distributing the Stations among HUBS

One of the interesting questions arising from the EWC/Ethernet integrated system is the allocation of stations to clusters. Should the number of NIU's in each cluster be equal? Should, instead, the total load in each cluster be equalized by aggregating stations into clusters according to their arrival rates? To test the importance of determining the station to cluster allocation four different models were defined. All models represent the connection of 64 stations by 8 HUB clusters over a 500 m Ethernet cable with rays of 30 to 170 meters.

Model a: Eight stations in each HUB cluster. The arrival rates at all stations are equal.

Model b: 56 stations connected to a single HUB. Remaining HUBs support a single station each. All stations have the same arrival rate.

Model c: Similarly to model a, every eight stations are connected to one of the HUBs, however, the eight stations in HUB generate 56/64 of the total arrival rate.

Model d: A "realistic" unbalanced model.

For lack of space we shall not include the performance curves of all above models, but rather summarize the significant results as reported in [14]. We first consider the "optimally" balanced network of model a. where the system is balanced with respect to the number of stations in each cluster and with respect to the cluster arrival rates. We then compare the balanced with the unbalanced models b. and c.

The performance study provides the following observations; The performance of models b. and c., is significantly better than the performance of the balanced model. The reason for this counterintuitive behavior can be understood from observing the role of each HUB as a control introducing agent. Namely, the majority (about 90%) of frames in models b. and c. are generated within a single HUB. Since, however, every HUB (including the heavily loaded one) acts as an arbiter for the stations it supports, most collisions which would otherwise occur on "Ethernet network" will be solved within the single HUB as private collisions. Thus, the number of collisions on Ethernet in the unbalanced models is significantly smaller.

It is reasonable to assume that distribution of these stations on user premises will be random. Assuming that stations are randomly distributed at an average distance of 100 m from each HUB in model a., a model (d) was constructed in which rays of 380 m to 520 m are allocated for the connection of 56 stations to one cascaded HUB cluster as in model a. In this way, the average distance between any two stations in the system in models a. and d. is equal. The produced results show that while in comparison to model b, model d is relatively worse (due to increased ray length), when compared to model a., model d has still displays a significantly better performance. This observation supports the intuition gained earlier. It demonstrates that although the Ethernet cable remains the same (in al models) i.e., the connection of additional ray length (model d) the performance is still improved due to increased clustering of stations in model d.

6.3 Comparing HUB Performance with other Ethernet Extensions

The need to provide services and support applications not well addressed by the random access nature of the Ethernet protocol has lead to a number of "scaled up" Ethernet compatible products. In this section we address two popular LAN issues – priorities and CPU interconnection by a LAN.

6.3.1 Prioritized Service

As demonstrated in preceding models the standard Ethernet provides a service which is heavily dependent on network configurations and traffic characterization. A number of Ethernet extensions have thus been proposed where the quality of service can be assigned on a pre-application priority basis. Probably the most popular among solutions suggested for improving the Ethernet performance is Intel 82586 which provides a VLSI solution [6,11]. To provide a prioritized service, stations based on the 82586 component can be assigned between one to eight priorities. The so-called "exponential priority" provides a mechanism by which high priority users can draw a backoff value with a lower average wait time (following collision) than others. It is, therefore, interesting to compare this Ethernet extension with the HUB cluster provided service. Figure 9 shows the packet delay for a standard Ethernet, the prioritized Ethernet [11] and a single HUB cluster. The following observations hold for these systems:

a. The highest priority users in the prioritized Ethernet system obtain an improved response time relatively to the standard.

b. (However), the performance of the prioritized Ethernet averaged over all priority classes worse than that of the standard. This is due to the fact that in a prioritized system the improved performance for one class of customers comes at the expense of lower priority classes.

c. The HUB cluster performance is better than that obtained for the highest priority class in the 82586 based system.

6.3.2 A Serial Backplane Application

The connection of a small number of CPU modules within a cabinet or a room with cables of up to 100 m is a large application area. The Ethernet can, on one hand, replace dozens of users in a volume service area but cannot, on the other hand, guarantee low response times for typically short packets. In this case a single HUB cluster can easily meet the restrictions of limited number of stations per each HUB and the limited ray length. Depending on the packet length size distribution and the needed response times the single HUB cluster may potentially provide an inexpensive solution for this application area. Figure 10 shows the performance of a single HUB cluster with ray length of 10–50 meters and compares it with an Ethernet network using a 100 m cable for packet lengths of 46 and 150 bytes. For both packet sizes the LAN-HUB provides lower delay, higher throughput performance than both standard and prioritized Ethernet networks, due to providing collision free, reliable communication.

SUMMARY

This paper has presented the CODEX 4320 LAN-HUB. The HUB operation creates a low cost LAN solution by connecting several stations to one IEEE 802.3 transceivers and by significantly reducing the cabling requirements. The HUB's architecture was described and its use for configuring different types of LANs was given. The HUB's versatility was demonstrated by showing how it can be utilized to provide a controlled access star communication system, support IEEE 802.3 standard network operation with random access CSMA/CD protocol or can be used to generate any combination of the two. The HUB's performance was analyzed in detail. It was shown that in a single HUB cluster configuration the channel can be fully utilized. In an integrated HUB/Ethernet network the performance improvement was seen to be commensurate with the degree of station clustering.

References

1. The 4320 LAN-HUB Reference Guide, Codex Co., Division of Motorola, Canton, MA, First Printing, October 1986.
2. IEEE Comp. Soc., Local Network Standards, (Ethernet) 802.3, 1983.
3. Local Area Network (CMSA/CD Baseband), Coaxial Cable System, Standards ECMA-80-2, Euro. Comput. Manuf. Assoc., Switzerland, September 1982.
4. W. Bux, "Local Area Subnetworks; A Performance Comparison", *IEEE Trans. Comm.*, 29(10), 1981.
5. IEEE Local Network Standards, (Token ring and Token bus) IEEE 802.4 and 802.5, 1983.
6. The Complete VLSI LAN Solution INTEL Corp., Report #210783-001, October 1982.
7. The Ethernet: A Local Area Network: Data Link Layer and Physical Layer Specifications, DEC, INTEL, Xerox Comp., 1980.
8. W.R. Franta, I. Chlamtac, <u>Local Networks: Motivation, Technology and Performance</u>, Lexington Books, USA 1981.
9. A.S. Tanenbaum, <u>Computer Networks</u>, Prentice Hall, 1981.
10. I. Chlamtac and A. Rozenboim, "CONSIP – Concurrent Network Simulation Package", in <u>Computer Networks and Simulation</u>, editor, S. Schoemaker, North-Holland-Elsevier Science Pub., 1986.
11. I. Chlamtac, "A Programmable VLSI Controller for Standard and Prioritized Ethernet Local Networks", in <u>Local Area & Multiple Access Networks</u>, Computer Science Press, Inc., 1986.
12. I. Chlamtac, "A Concurrent Network Simulator for Automated Protocol Development and Performance Evaluation", *The Euromicro Journal*, Vol. 18, December 1986.
13. LAN-HUB U.S Patent number 4 602 364, Herman et.al., July 1986.
14. Comparative Performance Evaluation of the LAN-HUB, Internal Report, Codex Co., October 1985.

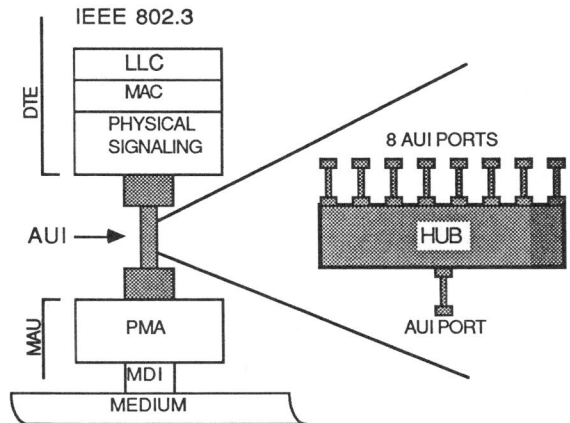

Fig. 1. IEEE 802.3 system representation

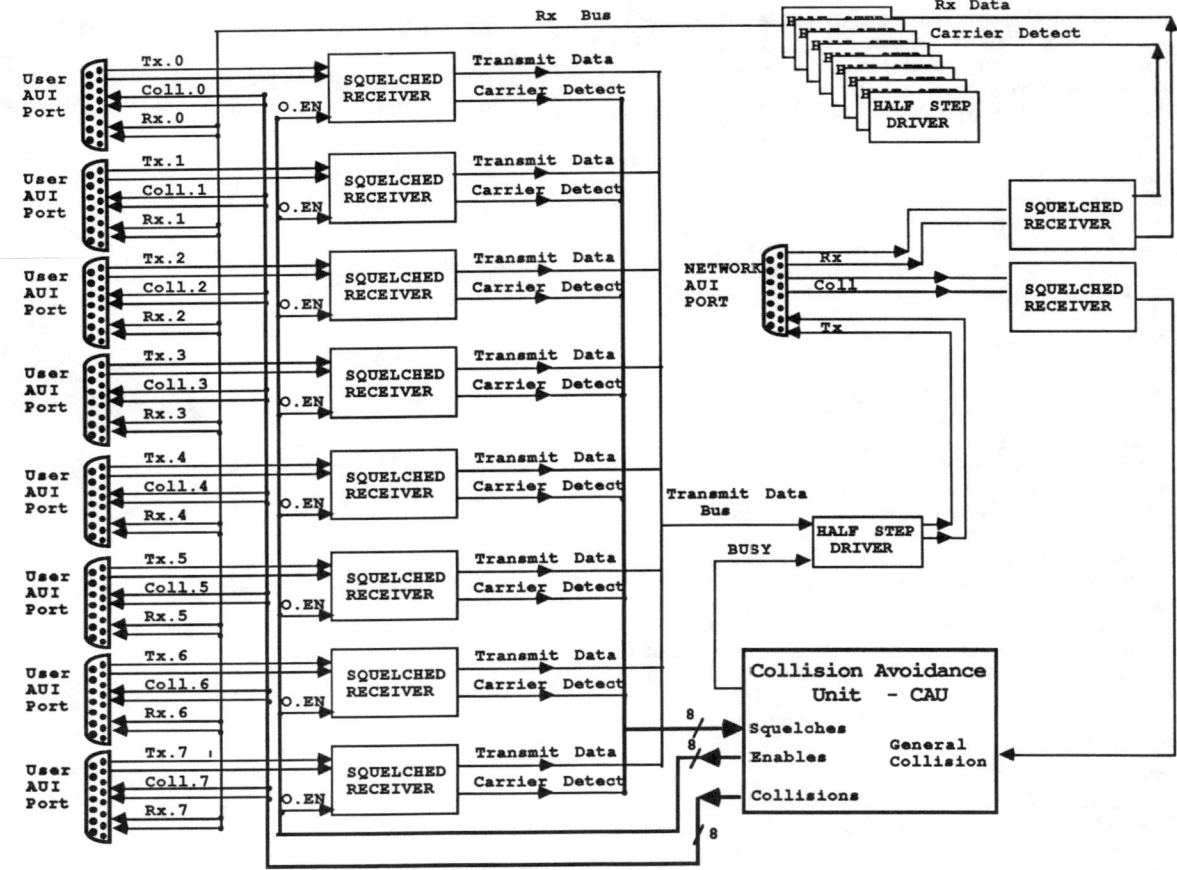

FIG. 2.   HUB BLOCK DIAGRAM SHOWING DATA FLOW

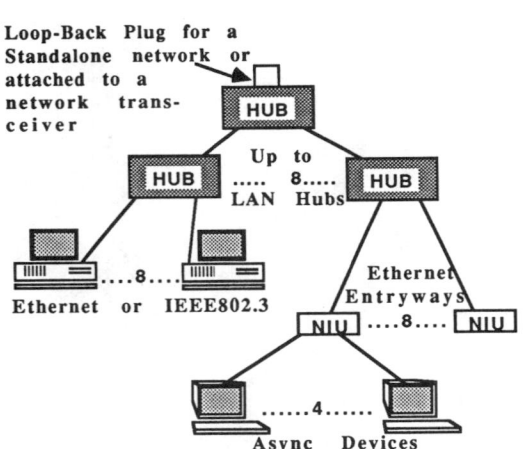

Fig. 3.   Cascaded operation

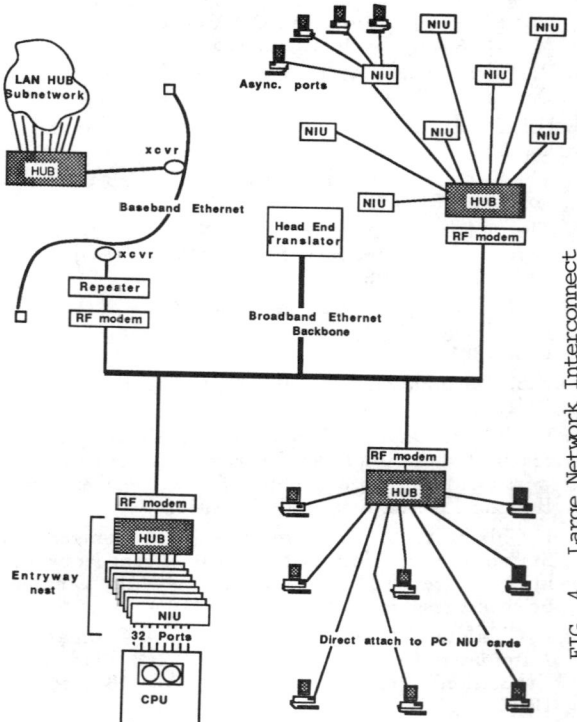

FIG. 4. Large Network Interconnect

CABLE LENGTH:	1000 m
NUMBER OF STATIONS (NIU)	32
SLOT TIME:	51.2 μsec
INTERFRAME SPACING:	9.6 μsec
NUMBER OF RETRIES:	15
NUMBER OF OVERHEAD	26 bytes
NUMBER OF HUBS	Specified below
CABLE LENGTH	Specified below
NUMBER OF NIU'S PER HUB	Specified below
INTERARRIVAL DISTRIBUTION:	Exponential
PACKET LENGTH DISTRIBUTION:	Constant: 150 bytes

PARAMETER	VALUE	PARAMETER	VALUE	SIGN
Standard IEEE 802.3	Current model	Cable length	100 m	-o-o-o-
Standard IEEE 802.3	Published results	Cable length	100 m	*******
Cascaded HUBs	1	Ray length	30 - 300 m	————
Cascaded HUBs	2	Ray length	30 - 170 m	- - - -

Fig. 5. Basic HUB and IEEE 802.3 performance

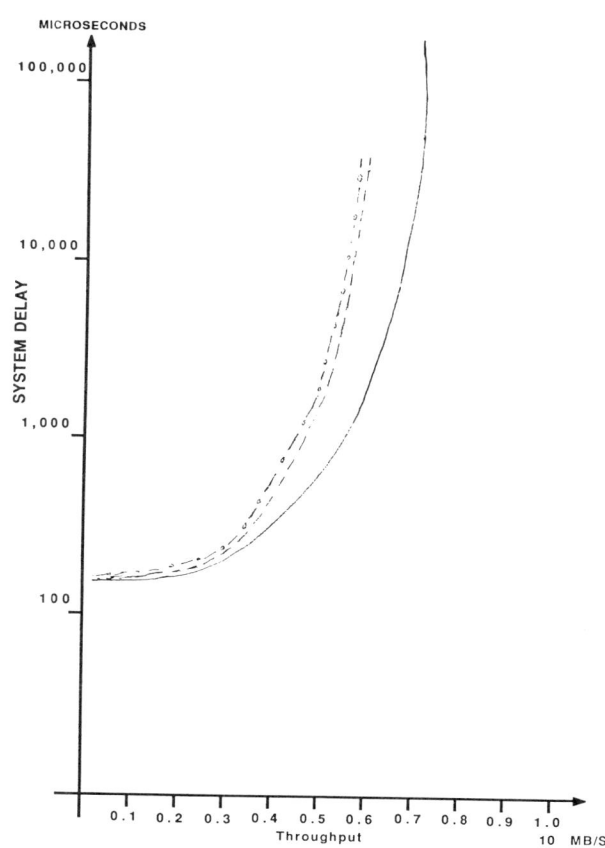

Fig. 5b Throughput / delay performance

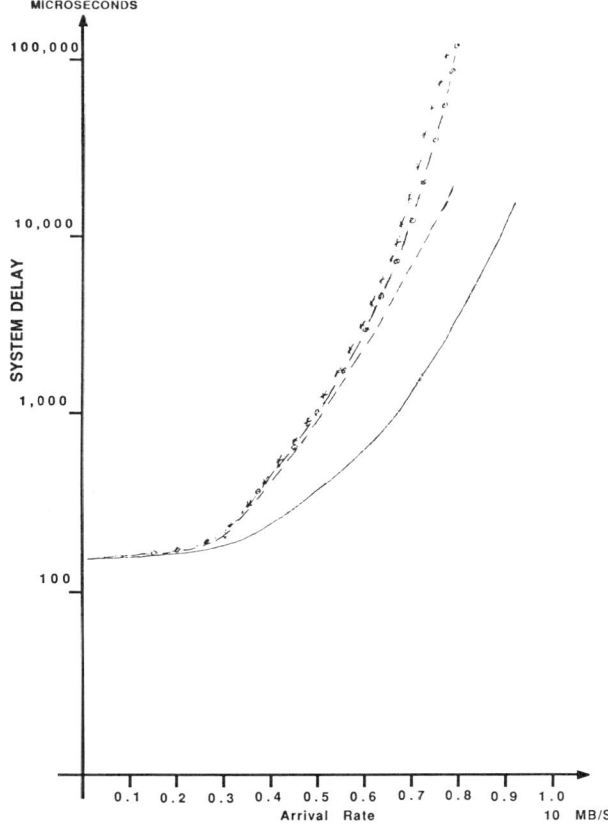

Fig. 5a Arrival rate / delay performance

CABLE LENGTH:	500 m
NUMBER OF STATIONS (NIU)	Specified below
SLOT TIME:	51.2 μsec
INTERFRAME SPACING:	9.6 μsec
NUMBER OF RETRIES:	15
NUMBER OF OVERHEAD	26 bytes
NUMBER OF HUBS	Specified below
RAY LENGTH	30 - 300 m
NUMBER OF NIU'S PER HUB	Specified below
INTERARRIVAL DISTRIBUTION:	Exponential
PACKET LENGTH DISTRIBUTION:	150 bytes

PARAMETER	VALUE	PARAMETER	VALUE	SIGN
IEEE 802.3	Standard	Number of NIUs	32	ooooooooo
IEEE 802.3	Standard	Number of NIUs	16	▯▯▯▯▯▯▯▯▯
IEEE 802.3	Standard	Number of NIUs	8	*******
HUB	1 cluster	Number of NIUs	32	△△△△△△
HUB	1 cluster	Number of NIUs	16	
HUB	1 cluster	Number of NIUs	8	++++++++++

Fig. 6. Population size effect on performance

CABLE LENGTH:	Specified below
NUMBER OF STATIONS (NIU)	32
SLOT TIME:	51.2 μsec
INTERFRAME SPACING:	9.6 μsec
NUMBER OF RETRIES:	15
NUMBER OF OVERHEAD	26 bytes
NUMBER OF HUBS	1
RAY LENGTH	Specified below
NUMBER OF NIU'S PER HUB	32
INTERARRIVAL DISTRIBUTION:	Exponential
PACKET LENGTH DISTRIBUTION:	150 bytes

PARAMETER	VALUE	PARAMETER	VALUE	SIGN
IEEE 802.3	Standard	Cable length	100 m	- - - - -
IEEE 802.3	Standard	Cable length	100 m	▯▯▯▯▯▯▯▯▯
HUB Cluster		Ray length	10-50 m	*******
HUB Cluster		Ray length	10-50 m	

Fig. 7. Network span effect

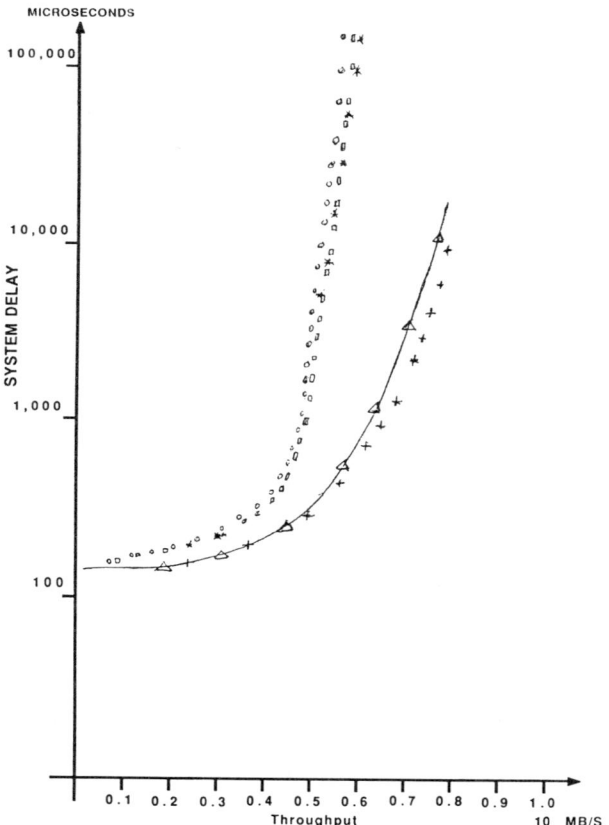

Fig. 6 Population size effect on performance

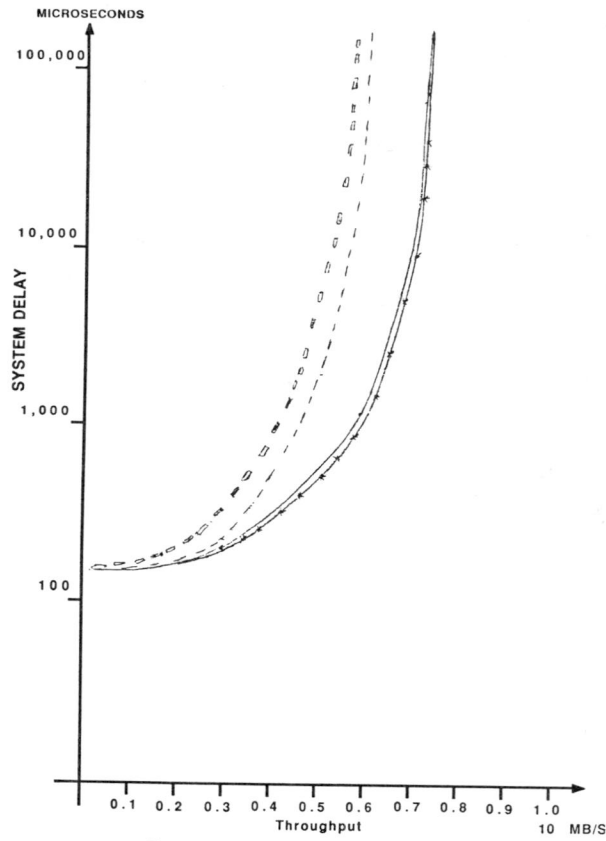

Fig. 7 Network span effect

CABLE LENGTH:	500 m
NUMBER OF STATIONS (NIU)	32
SLOT TIME:	51.2 μsec
INTERFRAME SPACING:	9.6 μsec
NUMBER OF RETRIES:	15
NUMBER OF OVERHEAD	26 bytes
NUMBER OF HUBS	Specified below
RAY LENGTH	Specified below
NUMBER OF NIU'S PER HUB	Specified below
INTERARRIVAL DISTRIBUTION:	Exponential
PACKET LENGTH DISTRIBUTION:	Specified below

PARAMETER	VALUE	PARAMETER	VALUE	SIGN
IEEE 802.3	Standard	Packet length	600 bytes	ooooo600
IEEE 802.3	Standard	Packet length	46 bytes	ooooo46
HUB	8 clusters w/4 NIUs ea	Packet length	600 bytes	- - -600
HUB	8 clusters w/4 NIUs ea	Packet length	46 bytes	- - -46
HUB	1 cascaded cluster	Packet length	600 bytes	———600
HUB	1 cascaded cluster	Packet length	46 bytes	———46

Fig. 8. Packet length effect

CABLE LENGTH:	500 m
NUMBER OF STATIONS (NIU)	32
SLOT TIME:	51.2 μsec
INTERFRAME SPACING:	9.6 μsec
NUMBER OF RETRIES:	15
NUMBER OF OVERHEAD	26 bytes
NUMBER OF HUBS	Specified below
RAY LENGTH	30 - 300 m
NUMBER OF NIU'S PER HUB	32
INTERARRIVAL DISTRIBUTION:	Exponential
PACKET LENGTH DISTRIBUTION:	150 bytes

PARAMETER	VALUE	PARAMETER	VALUE	SIGN
IEEE 802.3	Standard			- - - -
Ethernet	Intel 82585	Exponential priority	Average	ooooooooo
Ethernet	Intel 82585	Exponential priority	1 (Highest)	+++++++++
HUB cluster				———

Fig. 9. Comparison with Ethernet Extensions

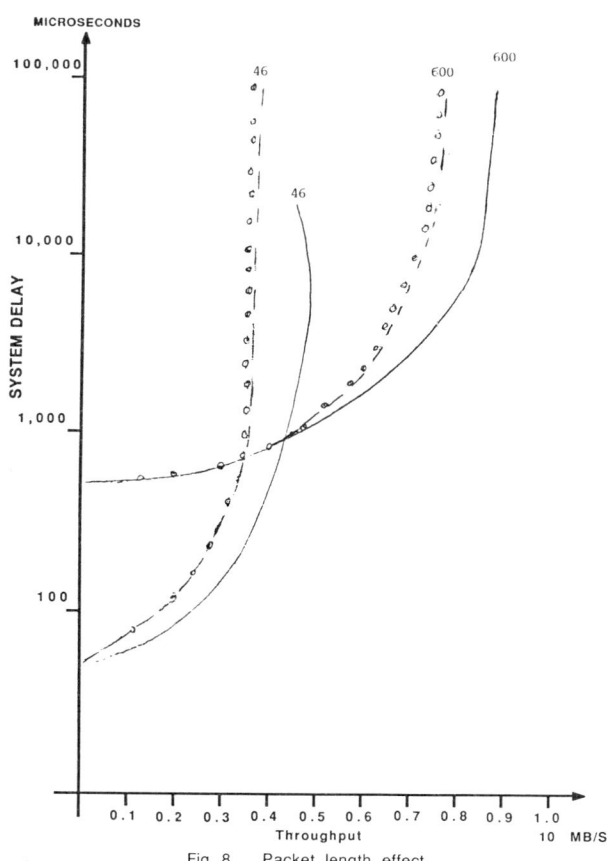

Fig. 8 Packet length effect

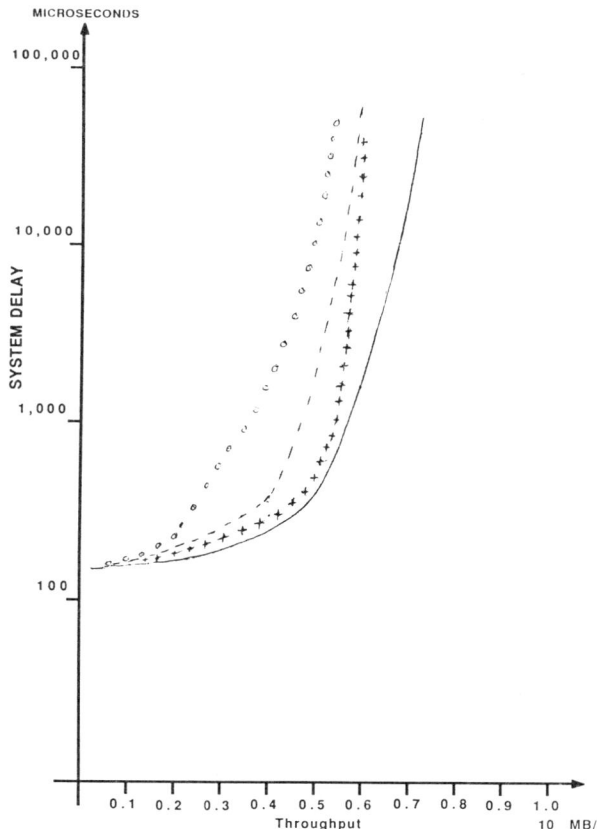

Fig. 9 Comparison with Ethernet extensions

CABLE LENGTH:	100 m		
NUMBER OF STATIONS (NIU)	32		
SLOT TIME:	51.2 μsec		
INTERFRAME SPACING:	9.6 μsec		
NUMBER OF RETRIES:	15		
NUMBER OF OVERHEAD	26 bytes		
NUMBER OF HUBS	1		
RAY LENGTH	10 – 50 m		
NUMBER OF NIU'S PER HUB	32		
INTERARRIVAL DISTRIBUTION:	Exponential		
PACKET LENGTH DISTRIBUTION:	Specified below		

PARAMETER	VALUE	PARAMETER	VALUE	SIGN
IEEE 802.3	Standard	Packet size	46	————
IEEE 802.3	Standard	Packet size	150	- - - - -
Cascaded HUB		Packet size	46	ooooooooooo
Cascaded HUB		Packet size	150	–*–*–*–*–*

Fig. 10. Serial backplan application

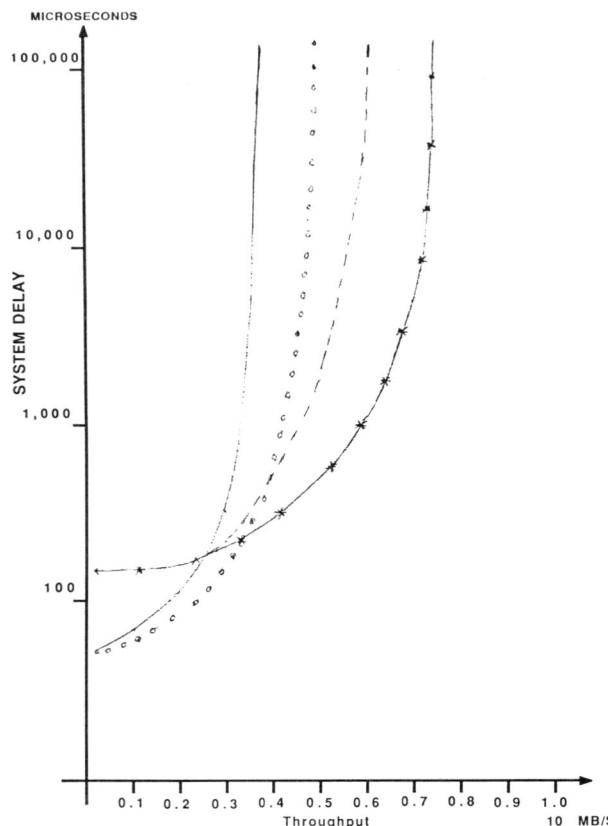

Fig. 10 Serial backplane application

Transparent Interconnection of Incompatible Local Area Networks Using Bridges

George Varghese and Radia Perlman

Distributed Systems Architecture and Advanced Development
Digital Equipment Corporation
Littleton, Massachusetts 01460

Abstract

No single LAN technology is sufficient to interconnect all the computers in a given plant, campus, or site. Thus it is desirable to combine different types of LANs, using a device called a **Bridge**, to produce an **Extended LAN**. Some LANs in the Extended LAN may have incompatible Data Link formats. Thus a bridge may need to encapsulate a frame originating on LAN A inside the Data Link header of another (incompatible) LAN B in order to allow the type A frame to travel over LAN B. In general, frames sent between any pair of LANs in the Extended LAN must be encapsulated across every incompatible LAN in the path betwen the LANs.

Bridges **learn** their routing information from information contained in frames they forward. Besides the problems of distinguishing various kinds of encapsulated and unencapsulated frames, the encapsulating protocol used by bridges must also solve the learning problem. This leads to a new set of considerations and solutions. We begin with a rough solution, and refine it using informal arguments and examples to lead to the final description. The stages in the description roughly mimic the design process.

1 TERMINOLOGY AND NOTATION

The major terminology is collected below. Some terms are explained in detail later, but are briefly defined here for convenience.

Data Link - the protocol on a single LAN used to:

- delimit the bits sent into messages (also called frames at this level)
- Do error detection (and possibly error correction).
- synchronize access to the LAN

- address frames to intended recipients on the LAN.

Bridge a node connected to two or more LANs so that it can transparently forward frames between these LANs. Bridges are transparent to stations on the LAN in that stations on different LANs can exchange frames as if they were on the same LAN.

Link a connection from a bridge to a single LAN.

Extended LAN the collection of LANs connected by bridges.

End Station a node in the Extended LAN that does not forward frames, but needs to communicate with other End Stations.

Translation the process by which the required information in the Data Link header of LAN A is converted into the Data Link header of LAN B, when A and B have different Data Link header formats.

Encapsulation the process by which a frame originating on a LAN of type B is placed inside a frame of type A, so that the the type B frame can travel over a LAN of type A.

Encapsulating Bridge a bridge that connects at least two LANs of different types, and cannot translate between the two Data Link formats.

We use the notation shown in Figures 1 and 2 to describe the relevant fields of unencapsulated and encapsulated frames. The meaning and use of these fields will be clarified in later sections.

2 INTRODUCTION

Consider a single LAN (e.g. an Ethernet) as shown in Fig. 3:

Assume that X1 and X2 are computers belonging to one manufacturer (say Xerox) and D1 and D2 stations that belong to another manufacturer (say DEC). Since DEC and XEROX both support Ethernet interfaces, X1 can send a message to X2 using the format shown in Fig. 1 with Destination Address (DA) = X2, and Source Address (SA) = X1.

The actual Ethernet header represents Layer 2, the Data Link layer, in the ISO model [1]. The Higher level protocols represent Levels 3 through 6 in the ISO model. Now while XEROX and DEC both use the same Data Link Protocol on the Ethernet, they **do not** use the same higher level protocols; for example, the

---

Permission to copy without fee all or part of this material is granted provided that the copies are not made or distributed for direct commercial advantage, the ACM copyright notice and the title of the publication and its date appear, and notice is given that copying is by permission of the Association for Computing Machinery. To copy otherwise, or to republish, requires a fee and/or specfic permission.

© 1988 ACM 0-89791-245-4/88/0001/0381 $1.50

DEC computer may use DECNET while the XEROX computer may use XNS.

Thus until the ISO committee standardises the higher level protocols needed for applications in computers to communicate, and manufacturers adopt these standards, the situation is as follows:

An alternative interconnect device is the bridge described in [7,8,9]. Bridges interconnect local networks transparently - no end station to router/ gateway protocol is needed - to form an **Extended LAN** (ELAN). In ISO terminology, a bridge is a Data Link layer relay. A bridge participates as a station on each of the LANS it interconnects, and receives a copy of all frames sent on these LANS (using the so-called "promiscuous" mode).

The physical topology of the Extended LAN is allowed to be an arbitrary mesh. However, bridges dynamically prune the physical topology ([8]) to create a logical topology that is a tree. Because the logical topology is a tree, there is only one path between 2 stations on the ELAN.

Consequently, to forward a frame, a bridge need only know which of its links a destination is reachable through. This information is stored by a bridge in a **Forwarding Database**. The **Forwarding Database** is an association between **source addresses** in received frames and the links the frames are received on.

When a frame arrives on link L, the bridge makes an entry (corresponding to the source address in the received frame) in the Forwarding Database. The entry states that the source address is reachable through link L. The bridge then looks up the frame destination address in the **Forwarding Database**. If there is such an entry, and the link associated with this address is the same as the link the frame was received on, the frame is discarded; if the link is different, the frame is handed to the controller of link L for transmission.

Finally, if the destination address is not in the Database, the frame is flooded - i.e. it is transmitted on all the local networks the bridge is attached to, except the one it was received on. Frames sent to a group address are also flooded to ensure that the frame reaches all possible members of the group.

In essence, the bridges described in [7] forward frames based on destination Data Link addresses, and learn forwarding information from source Data Link addresses. By doing so, bridges interconnect LANs transparently: end stations do not need to communicate with the bridges, and are, in fact, unaware of them.

Consider Fig. 5 with a bridge replacing the router in Fig. 4.

When X1 sends a frame to X2 using the format of Fig. 1, it sets DA = X2 and SA = X1.

The bridge operates in promiscuous mode and receives this frame. Assuming it has no entry for X2, the bridge floods the frame, thus sending it to X2 on link 2. The bridge also makes an entry for X1 as belonging on link 1. When X2 replies to X1, if the bridge does not have an entry for X1, it will flood the reply which reaches X1. It also make an entry for X2 as belonging on Link 2. From this point, any messages to X2 and X1 are only forwarded if necessary. Thus if X3 sends a frame to X1, the bridge will not forward the frame.

In sum, multiple vendors can use the Extended LAN as a common data highway; the result is an effective LAN with a larger bandwidth, distance, and number of nodes.

2.1 Encapsulation and Translation

Customers can use bridges to overcome the limitations of a single LAN. More interestingly, they can combine various types of LANS (e.g. [3, 4, 5]) in an Extended LAN, using each LAN where it is best suited. For example, an 802.3 CSMA/CD [3] network allows a large number of attachments but a physical extent of only 1.8 km; a token bus [4] can span greater distances but allows a smaller number of stations to be attached. Performance results also indicate that CSMA/CD networks work well for bursty traffic while token passing schemes do better when the traffic is more steady. The two can be combined synergistically if CSMA/CD networks are used as local access networks and bridged together by a token bus backbone.

The different types of LANs lead to 3 categories of bridge operation:

- **Pass-through:** A bridge between two local networks whose Data Link functions and addressing are identical can pass frames through unchanged.

- **Translation:** A bridge between two local networks whose Data Link functions and addressing are suficiently similar (but not identical) may translate Data Link protocols so that stations can communicate between these dissimilar networks.

- **Encapsulation:** A bridge between 2 local networks whose Data Link functions and addressing are sufficiently dissimilar to make translation impossible or infeasible may encapsulate a frame received on Link A in the Data Link format of Link B so that the frame can travel on link B. By encapsulation, we mean that the whole of the Link B frame is put into the Data field of a Link B frame.

The first two categories of bridge operation fall naturally within the bridge algorithm described above. This paper will focus on encapsulating bridges, and the additional protocol needed to accomodate them.

3 Problem Description

Figure 6 shows the simplest type of encapsulating bridge.

Assume that we need to interconnect two BLUE networks (LANs 1 and 2) using a RED network, and that it is infeasible to translate between RED and BLUE Data Link formats.

If there are no end stations on the Backbone Network, the solution is simple: B1 encapsulates any frames destined for LAN 2 in the RED Data Link format, and decapsulates any frames received on the RED Network to uncover the BLUE frames sent by LAN 2. B2's algorithm is identical. This algorithm easily extends to any number of similar bridges that are interconnected by a "pure backbone network": a pure backbone network is one that does not have any stations other than bridges. Satellite bridges [2] use this solution.

If the Backbone Network has end stations, then we immediately have a problem. How does B1 distinguish between frames that originated on the RED network, and those that originated on LAN 2 but were encapsulated by B2?

Going a step further, it may be that frames originating on the RED network need to be encapsulated across the BLUE networks in order to travel to other RED networks. Thus, the BLUE networks could be used as backbones by the RED networks, and the RED networks could be used as backbones by the BLUE networks. In [10], a similar problem is described in the context of Wide Area Networks (using gateways, not bridges), and is called **Mutual Encapsulation**.

Despite this similarity of concept, the protocols used by bridges to **implement** mutual encapsulation are necessarily different from those described in [10] for Wide Area Networks. First, as we show in the next section, the bridge encapsulation protocol needs an encapsulation header which is not needed in [10].

Second, and most important, Wide Area Networks have no concept of learning as described for bridges. Typically, a separate routing process obtains forwarding information in a Wide Area Network. It is the additional requirement that bridges be able to learn forwarding information from encapsulated frames that distinguishes the problem in this paper from that in [10].

4 INITIAL SOLUTION

Before we describe an initial solution, we make 2 general observations:

1. Data Link frames are not self-describing. By looking at the Data Link header of a message, we cannot tell what tell what type of Data Link the frame originated on; bits in the header of one Data Link can be mistaken for that of another Data Link. We need an encapsulating bridge protocol header to hold this information.

2. Frames must never be encapsulated more than once. Otherwise, the protocol would only work for a symmetrical arrangement of bridges and networks. In Figure 7 assume the frame sent by S1 to S2 is encapsulated by the first Bridge 1 in the GREEN Data Link format, and this frame is again encapsulated by Bridge 2 in the BLUE Data Link format. When the frame arrives at Bridge 3, Bridge 3 can only remove the BLUE Data Link header. Bridge 3 cannot remove the GREEN header because it does not understand the GREEN Data Link format. The only alternative for Bridge 2 is to remove the GREEN header (decapsulate) and put on the BLUE header (encapsulate).

In general, in order to allow mutual encapsulation across Extended LANs, bridges must distinguish 3 kinds of frames. We illustrate this using the example topology in Figure 8.

Let us focus on bridge B3. For each type of frame described below that arrives to B3 on its GREEN network, the action taken by B3 before transmitting the frame on the RED network is different:

1. Decapsulation plus Encapsulation – BLUE Frames sent by S1 to S2 which arrive at B3: B3 must decapsulate the GREEN frame it receives, and then re-encapsulate the underlying BLUE frame in the RED format.

2. Decapsulation Only – RED Frames sent by S3 to S4 which arrive at B3: B3 must decapsulate the GREEN frame it receives.

3. Encapsulation Only – GREEN Frames sent by S5 to S6 which arrive at B3: B3 must encapsulate the GREEN frame in the RED format.

First we must distinguish unencapsulated frames (i.e S5-S6 at B3) from encapsulated frames. Assume all Data Link headers have a source and destination address field. Further assume that the source address field contains the address of the originating station. Then the only degree of freedom is the destination address. Bridges can identify encapsulated frames if the destination address field:

a) Contains a special, well-known group (multicast) address for "All Encapsulating Bridges".

OR

b) Contains the address of the bridge that needs to decapsulate the frame; in the example above, it would be B3.

Next, for encapsulated frames, bridges like B3 need to know the original frame format before encapsulation since B3 must re-encapsulate frames that were originally BLUE, but not those that were originally RED. To distinguish between these frames, we attach an Encapsulation Header to encapsulated frames that contains the original Frame type. The frame format for an encapsulated frame now must change as shown in Fig. 9:

With this frame format, bridges have sufficient information to send frames originating on a network of Type X to any other network of type X. In the example above (Figure 8) if S1 sends a frame to S2:

1. B1 receives it and encapsulates it with C = BLUE, DA = AEB, SA = B1

2. B2 receives the encapsulated frame sent to AEB; it looks into the Encapsulation Header. Because C = Blue and its other Local Network is GREEN, it strips off the RED header and adds a GREEN header with DA = AEB and SA = B2

3. B3 receives it and strips off the GREEN header, and adds a RED header with DA = AEB and SA = B3

4. B4 receives it and strips off the RED header. Since C = BLUE and its other Local Network is BLUE, B4 strips off the Encapsulation Header and transmits the original BLUE frame ("naked as the day it was born").

5. S2 receives the frame

We call this Scheme 1

5 IMPROVING THE SOLUTION

For correctness, bridges can simply repeat all received frames to all local networks to which they are attached. However, to work **efficiently**, the ELAN must satisfy the following **Learning paradigm**:

Consider a pair of stations A and B in the Extended LAN that are exchanging frames in a conversation. After the first pair of frames exchanged by them, all frames sent between them should be sent only on the Local Networks on the path between A and B.

It is precisely this additional requirement that distinguishes the problem in [10] from the one described here.

Thus the flooding mechanism used initially must disappear after A sends a frame to B, and B sends one to A. However, Scheme 1 described above has an important flaw: it does not satisfy the **Learning paradigm** in all cases.

Consider the frame sent by S1 to S2 in the example topology of Fig. 8 using Scheme 1. B1 learns that S1 is to the left; but when the frame arrives at B2, B2 cannot learn about S1 because it does not understand the BLUE Data Link format. Consequently, all frames sent by S1 to S2 must be flooded by B2.

The problem arises because B2, which is connected to a GREEN and RED network, cannot be expected to understand the BLUE Data Link format. If this information were available in a canonical format (that all bridges understood), then B2 could learn about S1.

This leads to a simple improvement of Scheme 1. Since the Encapsulation Header is a canonical form, we expand it to include information about the original source and destination. If we assume that all station addresses in the Extended LAN can be mapped into a uniform address space (e.g. using the 48 bit 802 MAC Address Space or by concatenating the network type with the address), then we can repeat the original destination and source in the Encapsulation Header. The new header becomes as shown in Fig. 10:

Scheme 1 is modified as follows - when an encapsulating bridge receives an encapsulated frame it:

1. Learns the direction of SA from the outermost header.
2. Learns the direction of ES from the Encapsulation header
3. Forwards the encapsulated frame based on the direction of ED

Ordinary bridges (those that do not encapsulate) only learn and forward based on the outermost header. All encapsulated frames are addressed to "All Encapsulating Bridges" in the outermost header.

We call this Scheme 2: it should be clear that Scheme 2 satisfies the **Learning Paradigm**.

6 A Refinement

A property of Scheme 2 is that encapsulating bridges potentially need to store the addresses of all End Stations in the ENET. This includes End Stations on LANs whose Data Link format the Encapsulating Bridge does not recognize. It is, however, desirable that a bridge between a RED and a BLUE LAN keep track of only BLUE and RED station addresses, and not MAUVE, VIOLET, and INDIGO station addresses. This would reduce considerably the storage and lookup time in bridges; the total number of entities eligible for the learning table of a Bridge B would then become the number of stations of the same type as the Data Links attached to B, plus all bridges.

To this end, we define a Source Encapsulating Bridge as the bridge that adds the encapsulating header on a frame. A BLUE frame can go through a RED network, and arrive on a BLUE network with its encapsulation header removed. If the frame is then re-encapsulated for travel over a GREEN network, the second bridge that adds the encapsulating header is also a Source Encapsulating Bridge. Similarly, a Destination Encapsulating Bridge is defined as a bridge that takes off the Encapsulation Header.

More concretely, we change the frame format for encapsulated frames as shown in Fig. 11:

We illustrate this version, Scheme 3, with an example. Once again refer to Figure 8.

Consider first a frame sent by S1 to S2; none of the bridges have entries for S1 and S2 yet.

1. B1 receives the frame. Since it has no entry for S2 it floods the frame. It encapsulates the frame on its RED link with DA = "AEB", SA = B1, C = BLUE, ED = "AEB", and ES = B1. It also learns S1 is to the left.

2. B2 receives the frame. Because the frame is addressed to "AEB", it strips off the outer RED header. It learns B1 is to the left from the ES field in Encapsulation Header Because BD = "AEB" it floods the frame. It reencapsulates the frame on the GREEN link with DA = "AEB", SA = B2, C = Blue, ED = "AEB", and ES = B1. Note that ES is unchanged.

3. B3 receives the frame. Because the frame is addressed to "AEB", it strips off the outer GREEN header. It learns B2 is to the left from the SA field in the Outer GREEN Header It learns B1 is to the left from the ES field in Encapsulation Header Because BD = "AEB" it floods the frame. It reencapsulates the frame on the RED link with DA = "AEB", SA = B3, C = BLUE, ED = "AEB" and ES = B1

4. B4 receives the frame. Because frame is addressed to "AEB", it strips off the outer RED header. It learns B3 is to the left from the SA field in the outer Header It also learns that S1 (from original frame) can be reached through B1 by looking at the encapsulation header and OS in the original frame. Because ED = "AEB", it floods the frame. Because C = BLUE, it removes the encapsulation header and sends out the original frame on its BLUE network; this gets to S2.

5. B5 receives the frame. Because it has no entry for S2, it floods the frame onto the GREEN network with DA = "AEB", SA = B5, C = BLUE, ED = "AEB", ES = B5 Note change in ES. B5 learns S1 is to the left from the BLUE header.

Note that A4 calls for a special type of Database entry. Previously, bridges had Database entries of the form:

```
(Address, Link in bridge)
```

Now, some entries will be a triple:

```
(Address, Link, Next DEB)
```

Next DEB is the next Destination Encapsulating Bridge on the path to the destination.

To see how the Learning Paradigm operates using this new form of Database Entry, we now consider a frame going from S2 to S1 immediately after the frame from S1 to S2 we considered above.

1. B5 promiscuously receives the frame. Since B5's entry for S1 says S1 is to the left, it discards the frame. B5 learns S2 is to the left.

2. B4 promiscuously receives the frame addressed to S1. B4's Database (see above) says that S1 is on the left. Since the left Data Link is RED, B4 encapsulates with DA = "AEB", SA = B4, C = BLUE, ES = B4. For ED it uses the third component in the entry for S1 i.e. the Destination Encapsulating Bridge. Thus ED = B1. B4 learns that S2 is to the right.

3. B3 receives the frame addressed to "AEB". B3 strips the RED header. Its entry for ED = B1 says that B1 is to the left. Since C = BLUE, B3 puts on a GREEN header with DA = "AEB" and SA = B3 B3 learns that B4 is to the right.

4. B2 receives the frame addressed to "AEB". B2 strips the GREEN header. Its entry for ED = B1 says that B1 is to the left. Since C = BLUE, B3 puts on a RED header with DA = "AEB" and SA = B2. B2 learns that B4 and B3 are on the right.

5. B1 receives the frame addressed to "AEB". B1 strips the RED header Since BD = B1 = itself, it is the Destination Encapsulating Bridge: so it strips off the encapsulating header. Since its entry for B1 says it is on the left, it sends the frame to S1. From the encapsulation and BLUE headers, B1 learns that S2 is reachable through B4.

Thus after the first pair of messages, all the bridges in the path between S1 and S2 have entries for S1 and S2, or their corresponding Destination Encapsulating Bridges.

We call this Scheme 3.

7 Final Touches

One flaw shared by Schemes 1, 2, and 3 is that all encapsulated frames are multicast to "AEB" in the outermost header. Thus Encapsulating Bridges must receive all frames sent on their LANs (normal frames received promiscuously and Encapsulated Frames sent to "AEB"). This is undesirable if the Backbone Networks are of much higher speed than the Local Access networks.

Further, if Non-Encapsulating Bridges (bridges that simply forward between similar networks) are to coexist with Encapsulating Bridges, then they must flood encapsulated frames sent to "AEB". This would lead to poor performance.

We observe, however, that this effect disappears if frames could be addressed, after the initial learning exchange, to the next bridge on the path. Recall that a bridge will look into a frame if the frame is addressed to it.

This can be achieved by modifying Scheme 3. In Scheme 3, Encapsulating bridges between a Source Encapsulating Bridge ES and the next Destination Encapsulating Bridge ED only remember the direction of S. This can be extended to remember the direction of S as well as the bridge S is reachable through: the information is available from SA in the outermost header. Then, instead of sending encapsulated frames to "AEB", if an entry exists for ED, the frame is sent to the next bridge in the path.

Thus after an initial learning period, encapsulated frames are not multicast. We call this Scheme 4. Note that the new type of entry required to support Scheme 4 is identical to the triple required for Scheme 3.

8 CONCLUSIONS

In this paper we have presented a simple protocol that can be used by bridges to encapsulate frames over foreign Data Links. Rather than present the final version, we have attempted to reconstruct informally the reasoning behind the design of this protocol. We hope this gives the reader some flavor of the process by which this protocol was designed.

The final solution (Scheme 4) has the following properties:

- Generality and Correctness: It allows encapsulation in its fullest generality for arbitrary topologies of interconnected LANs. Frames can be exchanged between any pair of LANs, and are encapsulated across any intermediate incompatible LANs.

- Efficiency: It preserves the Learning Paradigm required by bridges for efficient operation: after the first pair of frames exchanged by 2 stations A and B in the Extended Network, all subsequent frames in the conversation are sent only on the Local Networks on the path between A and B. After the initial learning exchange, Encapsulating Bridges need to examine the Encapsulating Header of only those Encapsulated Frames they must forward.

- Compatibility : It allows efficient coexistence with Non-Encapsulating Bridges that do not participate in the Encapsulation Protocol.

- Minimal Storage: Bridges need to have storage for only Stations of the same type as the Data Links to which it is attached, plus all other bridges.

- Extensibility: Adding New Bridges that connect to Data Links with new colors does not involve reprogramming the old bridges.

While the concept of **Mutual Encapsulation** has been studied in [10], the final protocol described in this paper is very different from that in [10]. For example, of the five properties listed above, only the first and the last are applicable to the solution in [10]. This is simply because the requirements of Extended LAN and Internet environments are different.

9 ACKNOWLEDGEMENTS

John Hart of Vitalink Corp originally suggested that the Source Bridge Address be placed in the Encapsulating header. This protocol has been reviewed and discussed by him and by Alan Kirby, Mike Soha, and Bob Stewart of the NAC A/D group at DEC, all of whom contributed to the ideas in this paper in many ways.

10 REFERENCES

1. H. Zimmerman, "OSI Reference Model - The ISO Model of Architecture for Open Systems Interconnection," IEEE Trans. Commun., vol. COM-28, April 1980

2. J. Hart, "Bridges smooth troubled waters for wide-area networking", Data Communications, vol. 14, no. 3, March 1985

3. ANSI/IEEE Standard 802.3, "CSMA/CD Specification"

4. ANSI/IEEE Standard 802.4, "Token Bus Specification"

5. ANSI/IEEE Standard 802.5, "Token Ring Speciication"

6. "DNA Routing Layer Functional Specification", Version 2.0, Order No. AA-X435A-TK

7. W. Hawe, A. Kirby, and B. Stewart, "Transparent Interconnection of Local Area Networks with Bridges," Journal of Telecommunication Networks, September 1984

8. R. Perlman, "An Algorithm for Distributed Computation of a Spanning Tree", Proceedings of the Ninth Data Comunications Symposium, Montreal, 1984

9. B. Hawe and G. Varghese, "Extended Local Area Network Management Principles", Digital Equipment Coroporation, technical paper submitted to IEEE 802 Standards committee, October, 1984

10. J. Shoch, D. Cohen, and E. Taft, "Mutual Encapsulation of Internetwork Protocols," Proceedings of Trends and Applications: Computer Network Protocols, Gaithersburg, MD, 1980

```
---------------   . . . . . .
| DA |  SA  |   Rest of frame   |
---------------   . . . . . . .|
```

DA = Destination Address on LAN frame is being sent on
SA = Source Address on LAN frame is being sent on

Fig. 1 - Unencapsulated Frame Format

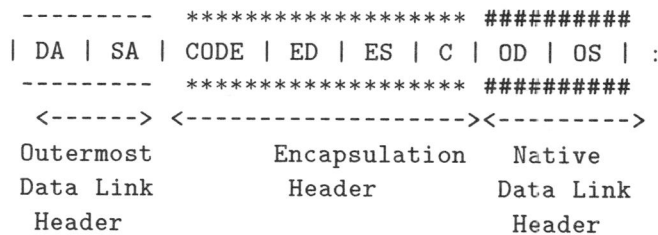

```
--------  ******************* #########
| DA | SA | CODE | ED | ES | C | OD | OS | :
--------  ******************* #########
 <------> <------------------><---------->
 Outermost    Encapsulation      Native
 Data Link       Header         Data Link
  Header                         Header
```

OD = Original Data Link Destination Address
OS = Original Data Link Source Address Header
ED = Destination Address in Encapsulation Header
ES = Source Address in Encapsulation Header
CODE = Value that identifies frame as being encapsulated
C = Value that identifies type of LAN frame originated on

Fig. 2 - Encapsulated Frame Format

Fig.3 - A single LAN with 4 stations

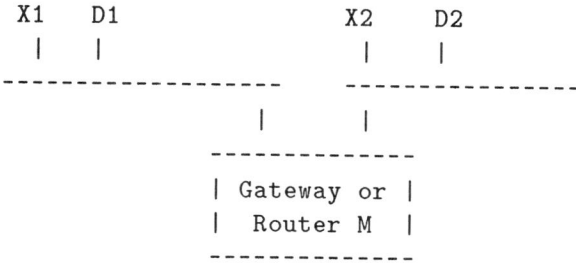

Fig. 4 - Interconnecting LANs with a gateway/router

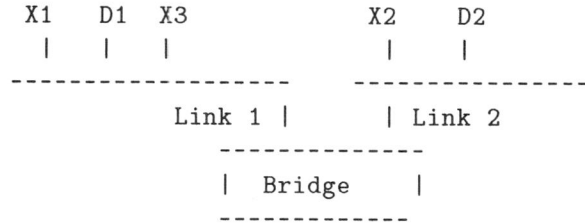

Fig. 5 - 2 LANs interconnected with a bridge

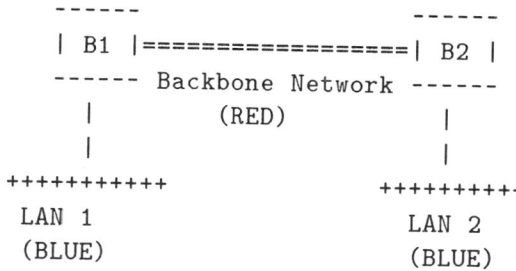

Figure 6: Encapsulating over a Backbone Network

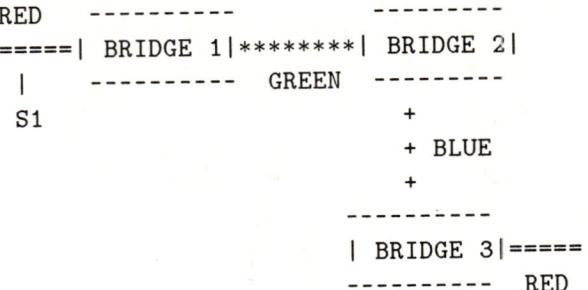

```
RED        ----------           ---------
=====| BRIDGE 1|********| BRIDGE 2|
 |         ----------   GREEN    ---------
 S1                              +
                                 + BLUE
                                 +
                                 ----------
                                 | BRIDGE 3|=====
                                 ----------   RED
```

Figure 7: An example to illustrate the
infeasibility of multiple levels of encapsulation

```
         S1        S5      S2              S7
    BLUE  |  GREEN  |       |  BLUE         |
    ++++++   *******    ++++++++++++    ========
      |    |    |          |         |    | RED
    ----  ---  ----      ----      ----  ----
    |B1| |B2| |B3|      | B4 |    | B5 | | B6 |
    ----  ---  ----      ----      ---    ---
      |    |    |          |         |      |
      |    |    |          |         |      |
    ==========  ===========    **************
      |  RED      |  RED       |  GREEN
        S3           S4           S6
```

Figure 8: Example Topology

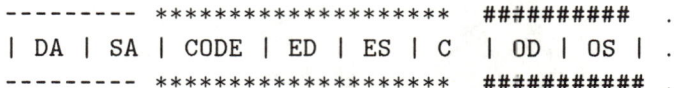

```
--------- ******************* ##########  .
| DA | SA | CODE | ED | ES | C | OD | OS | .
--------- ******************* ##########  .
```

ED = Mapped (into canonical address space)
     Original Destination Address

ES = Mapped (into canonical address space)
     Original Source Address

Fig. 10: Encapsulated Frame format for
Scheme 2

```
 --------  ********  #############
| DA | SA | CODE| C  | OD | OS | . .
 --------  ********  #############
```

```
<-------><---------><------------>
Current   Encapsulation  Original
Data Link Header         Data Link
Header                   Header
```

DA   =   "All Encapsulating Bridges(AEB)"
         or a specific bridge address

CODE =   Code to distinguish this frame from
         other frames addressed to bridges -
         e.g. management frames

C   =   Encodes the type of network the frame
         originated on (e.g. GREEN, RED, BLUE)

Fig. 9: Encapsulated Frame format for Scheme 1

```
 --------  *******************   ##########   .
| DA | SA | CODE | ED | ES | C  | OD | OS | .
 --------  *******************   ##########   .
```

ED = If known, the next Destination
     Encapsulating Bridge in the frame path;
     else ``AEB''.

ES = Address of previous Source Encapsulating
     Bridge in frame path

Fig. 11: Encapsulated Frame format for
         Scheme 3

Fragmentation Considered Harmful

Christopher A. Kent
Jeffrey C. Mogul

Digital Equipment Corporation
Western Research Lab

Abstract

Internetworks can be built from many different kinds of networks, with varying limits on maximum packet size. Throughput is usually maximized when the largest possible packet is sent; unfortunately, some routes can carry only very small packets. The IP protocol allows a gateway to *fragment* a packet if it is too large to be transmitted. Fragmentation is at best a necessary evil; it can lead to poor performance or complete communication failure. There are a variety of ways to reduce the likelihood of fragmentation; some can be incorporated into existing IP implementations without changes in protocol specifications. Others require new protocols, or modifications to existing protocols.

1. Introduction

Internetworks built of heterogeneous networks are valuable because they insulate higher-level protocols from changes in network technology, because they allow universal communication without the expense of constructing a homogeneous universal infrastructure, and because they allow the use of different network technologies as appropriate to both local-area and long-haul links. Most datagram networks set a maximum limit on the size of packets they carry, to simplify packet buffering in the nodes and to limit how long one packet can tie up the link. In a heterogeneous internet, such as the DARPA IP Internet, these packet-size limits, known as MTUs (for *maximum transmission unit*) vary widely: from 254 bytes for Packet Radio networks to 2000 bytes for the Wideband Satellite Network [22]; since nobody knows exactly what is connected to the Internet, the range in MTUs may be even broader.

In general, it is better to use a few large packets instead of many small packets to carry a given amount of data, because much of the cost of packetized communication is per-packet rather than per-byte. On a high-speed LAN, throughput can increase almost linearly with packet size over a wide range of sizes. Therefore, we prefer to make our packets as large as possible.

This desire for large packets conflicts with the variation in MTUs across an internet. We want to send large packets but some network along the packets' path may not be able to carry them. One approach to this dilemma is *fragmentation*: when a node must transmit a packet that is larger than the MTU of the network, it breaks the packet into several smaller *fragments* and sends them instead. If the fragments are all sent along the same data link and are immediately reassembled at the next node, this is called *transparent* or *intra-network* fragmentation. If the fragments are allowed to follow independent routes, and are reassembled only upon reaching their ultimate destination, this is called *inter-network* fragmentation. A good discussion of both methods, in more detail, may be found in Shoch [23].

In this paper, drawing on experience with a large heterogeneous internetwork, we examine fragmentation in the context of the IP protocol [18]. IP supports the use of inter-network fragmentation. (Transparent fragmentation may be also be used as long as it is invisible to the IP layer.) Fragmentation appears at first to be an elegant solution to the problem, but subtle complications arise in real networks that can result in poor performance or even total communication failure.

Experience with inter-network fragmentation in the IP Internet has convinced us that it is something to avoid. In section 2 we compare the advantages and disadvantages of fragmentation, in order to justify this assertion. We then discuss, in section 3, a variety of schemes for avoiding or recovering from fragmentation.

Permission to copy without fee all or part of this material is granted provided that the copies are not made or distributed for direct commercial advantage, the ACM copyright notice and the title of the publication and its date appear, and notice is given that copying is by permission of the Association for Computing Machinery. To copy otherwise, or to republish, requires a fee and/or specfic permission.

© 1988 ACM 0-89791-245-4/88/0001/0390 $1.50

2. What is wrong with fragmentation?

The arguments in favor of fragmentation are straightforward. Fragmentation allows higher level protocols to be unconcerned with the characteristics of the transmission channel, and to send data in conveniently sized pieces. Sending larger quantities of data in each IP datagram minimizes the bookkeeping overhead associated with managing the data. (See section 3.5 for a specific example.)

Fragmentation allows the source host to deal with routes having different MTUs without having to know what path packets are taking. The safest strategy is for the source to send very small datagrams, at a great loss of efficiency. Fragmentation allows the source to choose a size that is "reasonable" and, when that size proves to be too large, provides a mechanism that allows data to continue to get through.

Finally, fragmentation allows protocols to optimize performance for high bandwidth connections. Emerging network technologies have larger and larger MTUs. Most local networks have MTUs large enough to send 1024 bytes of user data plus associated overhead in a single packet; new technologies will allow ten times that. Fragmentation provides a mechanism for deciding the actual packet size as late as possible. It especially allows protocols to avoid choosing to send small datagrams until absolutely necessary. Protocols can choose large segment sizes to take advantage of the large MTU in a local network, and rely on fragmentation at gateways to send the segments through networks with small MTUs when needed. If datagrams must traverse a route consisting of several high-MTU links followed by a low-MTU link, by delaying the use of small packets until the low-MTU link is reached, fragmentation allows the use of large packets on the initial high-MTU links, and thus uses those links more efficiently.

The arguments against fragmentation fall into three categories:

- **Fragmentation causes inefficient use of resources:** Poor choice of fragment sizes can greatly increase the cost of delivering a datagram. Additional bandwidth is used for the additional header information, intermediate gateways must expend computational resources to make additional routing decisions, and the receiving host must reassemble the fragments.

- **Loss of fragments leads to degraded performance:** Reassembly of IP fragments is not very robust. Loss of a single fragment requires the higher level protocol to retransmit all of the data in the original datagram, even if most of the fragments were received correctly.

- **Efficient reassembly is hard:** Given the likelihood of lost fragments and the information present in the IP header, there are many situations in which the reassembly process, though straightforward, yields lower than desired performance.

2.1. An overview of fragmentation in IP

IP is a protocol providing unreliable delivery of *datagrams*. IP datagrams are encapsulated in network-specific *packets*. Gateways may fragment an incoming packet if it will not fit in a single outgoing packet; in this case, each *fragment* is sent as a separate packet. The IP header contains several fields that are used to manage fragmentation [18]:

- **Identification:** A 16-bit field assigned by the sender to aid in assembling the fragments of a datagram. The tuple (*source*, *destination*, *protocol*, *identification*) for a given datagram must be unique over all existing datagrams. When a packet is fragmented, the value of the Identification field of the original packet is copied into each fragment.

- **Time to live** (TTL): An 8-bit field that specifies the maximum time, measured in seconds, that the packet may remain in the Internet system. If TTL contains the value zero, the packet must be discarded. The TTL must be decreased by at least one every time the packet passes through a gateway, even if the time required to process the packet is less than a second. Thus, the TTL field is an upper bound on packet lifetime.

- **Fragment offset:** A 13-bit field that identifies the fragment location, relative to the beginning of the original, unfragmented datagram. Fragment offsets are in units of 8 bytes.

- **More fragments:** A 1-bit field that indicates whether or not this is the last fragment of the datagram.

The reassembly process consists of matching the protocol and identification fields of incoming fragments with those of fragments already held, and coalescing the data into complete datagrams. Fragments must be discarded if their TTL expires while they are held for reassembly. (For more details of the reassembly algorithm, see [5].)

Higher level protocols such as TCP (Transmission Control Protocol) [19] use IP as a basis to implement a reliable connection between two client processes. Portions of the data stream known as *segments* are sent in individual IP datagrams, along with control information used by the cooperating TCP processes to ensure reliable communication. In particular, TCP uses a sequence number that covers individual bytes in the data stream, and an acknowledgement mechanism that allows the receiving process to tell the sender "I have correctly received all data up to and including sequence number *n*."

2.2. Fragmentation causes inefficient resource usage

Consider the costs associated with sending a packet. Each time it passes through a gateway, there is some constant computational overhead to make routing decisions, modify the packet header, compute the new checksum, and move the packet between the appropriate incoming and outgoing queues. In addition, a portion of the available bandwidth on the incoming and outgoing interfaces is consumed. In many cases, the constant computational overhead dominates the cost. Input and output may be overlapped using DMA devices; in a typical uniprocessor gateway, there is no way to parallelize the computational overhead.

Fragmenting at an IP gateway, rather than having the host choose the appropriate segment size to avoid fragmentation, may lead to suboptimal use of gateway resources and network bandwidth. Consider a TCP process that tries to send 1024 data bytes across a route that includes the ARPAnet, which has an MTU of 1006 bytes. The IP and TCP headers are at least 40 bytes long, leading to a total unfragmented IP datagram 1064 bytes in length. To cross the ARPAnet, this will be broken into a 1006 byte fragment, followed by a 78 byte fragment. These short fragments amortize the fixed overhead per ARPAnet packet over very few bytes of data, and the total packet count is much higher than needed. If the sending TCP instead chooses segments that fit in a 1006 byte ARPAnet packet, the total packet count is minimized, and the total overhead is as low as possible.

For example, consider sending 10 Kbytes of data. Sending 1024-byte TCP segments generates 10 IP datagrams, each 1064 bytes long. Each datagram is fragmented into two ARPAnet packets, one 1006 bytes long and the other 78 bytes, for a total of 20 packets. If the originating TCP instead sends 966 byte segments (the largest that will fit in a single ARPAnet packet), only 11 packets are sent.

Another limit to utilizing available bandwidth lies in the interaction of the TTL and Identification fields. Assume that a reasonable initial value for the TTL field is 32 (the maximum hop count from edge to edge of the DARPA Internet is currently estimated to be between 15 and 20). If we allow fragmentation, we must ensure that all datagrams in flight have unique values for the Identification field. Thus, the maximum datagram rate is $2^{16}/32$, or 2048 datagrams per second. Current gateways can forward nearly 1000 packets per second; high performance workstations and interfaces can generate packets much more rapidly, and can probably forward 4000 packets per second. We are certainly within five years of having commonly available processor and network technology that pushes against the limit imposed by the 16-bit Identification field.

This limit implies that, to increase bandwidth in the presence of fragmentation, hosts should send larger datagrams, so as to carry more data per value of the Identification field. This is a bad idea, because large datagrams lead to more fragments, and we shall show that this increases the likelihood of a severe decrease in performance. If we simply avoid fragmented datagrams, values of the Identification field need not be unique, and there is no bandwidth limit imposed by its size.

2.3. Poor performance when fragments are lost

When segments are sent that are large enough to require fragmentation, the loss of any fragment requires the entire segment to be retransmitted. This can lead to poorer performance than would have been achieved by originally sending segments that didn't require fragmentation.

Gateways in the Internet must drop packets when congested. If the gateways are congested, dropping fragments only makes the situation worse. Dropped fragments mean increased retransmissions, which leads to more fragments. As the loss rate goes up due to heavy congestion, the total throughput drops dramatically, since the loss of any one fragment means that the resources expended in sending the other fragments of that datagram are entirely wasted.

Even when congestion is not the problem, retransmission does not necessarily increase the likelihood that all the fragments that make up the segment will arrive unscathed. In particular, network idiosyncrasies may conspire to cause the same fragment or fragments to be lost on successive retransmission. We call this *deterministic fragment loss*.

An example of deterministic fragment loss occurs in the 4.2BSD Unix implementation of TCP when datagrams pass between a local network (typically an Ethernet or a Proteon ring, with MTUs of 1500 or 2046 bytes, respectively) and the ARPAnet. The TCP prefers to send 1024 byte data segments, which are transmitted in 1064 byte IP datagrams. As seen earlier, this results in two fragments, 1006 and 78 bytes long.

The receiving gateway receives both fragments and sends them out over the local Proteon ring. The Proteon ring interface does not have sufficient buffering to receive back-to-back packets, so it consistently drops the second fragment. The sending TCP times out, and retransmits the 1024 byte segment, which will again be fragmented. The second fragment is again lost, the segment times out, and eventually the connection is broken.

In addition, many of the gateways in the Internet today are derived from 4.2BSD Unix. This implementation of IP does not properly fragment a previously fragmented packet, preventing some fragments from ever reaching their destination, which might better be called *guaranteed* fragment loss.

2.4. Efficient reassembly is difficult

Reassembling fragments into datagrams at the IP layer is considerably less robust than constructing a reliable stream at the TCP layer. The window mechanism in TCP allows the reassembly process to accurately gauge how much buffer space to allocate for the current stream of unacknowledged data bytes. Also, because in TCP the data stream is covered by a sequence number for each data byte, once a contiguous sequence of bytes at the beginning of the outstanding data stream has been reassembled, it can be acknowledged and handed up to the next layer. Thus, progress can always be made, even if in small amounts.

At the IP layer, there is no indication in the header of a fragmented packet of how many other fragments follow, or of the length of the entire datagram. The More Fragments bit tells only if this the last fragment of the datagram, and the Fragment Offset field tells only the position of this fragment in the complete datagram. If the total size of the incoming datagram is too large to fit available buffer space, no progress can be made. The IP specification requires hosts to be able to reassemble datagrams at least 576 bytes in length; larger segment sizes must be explicitly negotiated by higher level protocols.

Even if there is sufficient buffer space to reassemble a very large datagram, conflicts can occur. In the Internet, it is possible for fragments of the same datagram to take different routes to their ultimate destination. Depending on queue management strategies at gateways along the way, a fragment of a small datagram may arrive intermixed with the fragments of a large datagram. More concretely, assume two datagrams, L (large) and S (small), are fragmented as $L_1 L_2 L_3 L_4 L_5 L_6 L_7 L_8$ and $S_1 S_2$. If there are only eight buffers available, and the reception order is $L_1 L_2 L_3 L_4 L_5 L_6 L_7 S_1 L_8 S_2$, reassembly of L cannot succeed, despite adequate buffer space. Upon reception of S_1, the reassembly process could discard L_1 through L_7, which would leave six free buffers and allow S to be reassembled when S_2 arrives. Or, it could discard L_8 (and subsequently S_2), blocking reassembly of both L and S; the buffers would be kept full until the fragments expire. In either case, the work done to transport all the fragments of L is entirely wasted. It is not possible to coalesce a complete initial string of fragments and partially acknowledge receipt of the datagram in order to free some of the buffer space. (Dave Mills first pointed out this behavior in [13].)

It is difficult to decide how long to hold on to received fragments. The only firm limit is the TTL field; the reassembly process must discard fragments as their TTLs expire. Since each gateway decrements the TTL field, it must be set high enough to traverse the longest possible route, and thus may still be quite high when the packet arrives at its destination. Naive use of the received TTL as a reassembly timeout will cause some fragments to occupy buffer space for a much longer time than necessary. Use of too short a reassembly timeout will cause fragments to be dropped too quickly, leading to unnecessary retransmissions.

Because IP is a datagram protocol, there is no guarantee that a given fragment will ever arrive. A higher level protocol may retransmit a lost IP datagram. If a retransmitted datagram does not have the same value for the IP Identification field, its data will not be recognized as being the same as that in previously received fragments. The old fragments will occupy buffer space until timed out or forced out by incoming packets, and cannot fill holes left by fragments dropped from the second datagram. This suggests that higher level protocols should attempt to use the same value for the IP Identification on both the original and retransmitted data. (This idea was proposed by John Shriver [24].)

3. Avoiding fragmentation

We believe that, in most circumstances, the potential disadvantages of fragmentation far outweigh the expected advantages. Thus, hosts should avoid sending datagrams that are so large that they will be fragmented. The length limit can be determined by a variety of general approaches:

- **Always send small datagrams:** There is some datagram size that is small enough to fit without fragmentation on any network; we could simply send no datagrams larger than this limit.
- **Guess minimum MTU of path:** Use a heuristic to guess the minimum MTU along the path the datagram will follow.
- **Discover actual minimum MTU of path:** Use a protocol to determine the actual minimum MTU along the path the datagram will follow.
- **Guess or discover MTU and backtrack if wrong:** Since an estimate might be wrong, and a discovered MTU may change if a route changes, sometimes we may have to adjust the length limit. This requires both a mechanism for detecting errors, and a mechanism for correcting them.

Later in this section we will discuss more specific fragmentation avoidance schemes.

All these strategies assume that the route the datagrams will follow is independently determined. If multiple routes are available between source and destination, one might instead try to avoid fragmentation by using source-routing to avoid data links with small MTUs. Suitable alternate routes seldom exist, however, and even when they do we see no efficient way for an IP host to obtain enough information to choose a good source-route.

IP is a layered protocol architecture, and fragmentation avoidance must be done at the right layer. It makes little sense to build redundant mechanisms into several layers if it is possible to do it once. This implies that the right place for fragmentation avoidance is the layer common to all IP communication, the IP datagram layer itself (and its partner, the ICMP protocol). It would be a poor idea to put the entire fragmentation avoidance mechanism in, say, the TCP layer, because both the mechanism and any additional protocol would have to be duplicated in parallel layers, such as UDP [17], NETBLT [6], and VMTP [3], and because it would be awkward for a TCP-based mechanism to share knowledge with other layers and across connections.

This is not to say that layers above IP should be uninvolved in fragmentation avoidance. Architectural layering does not mean that higher layers must be kept ignorant of fragmentation issues. Optimal performance depends upon cooperation between layers: for example, the TCP layer should not send huge segments if the IP layer knows that they will be fragmented.

Most of the fragmentation-avoidance schemes we will propose depend on keeping some knowledge about the minimum MTU (MINMTU) on the path a datagram will follow. A MINMTU value could be associated with a specific destination network, a specific destination host, a specific route (there may be several routes to one destination, with differing MINMTUs), or a specific connection (since for different applications, we may want to choose between optimizing for maximum bandwidth versus minimum delay, and thus might want to accept different risks of fragmentation for different connections to the same host). The MINMTU values could be kept in the IP routing database, or in a separate database, especially if per-connection MINMTUs are wanted. To support per-connection MINMTUs, the IP layer must obtain a connection identifier from connection-oriented higher layers.

It is our belief that a per-connection scheme (degenerating to a per-route-to-specific-host scheme for connectionless protocols) is the most flexible one. While it is true that by keeping per-destination-network information one might be able to pool information about several hosts, this is not necessarily safe. Because many networks are subnetted [15], because MTUs may vary among the subnets of a given network, and because one cannot tell whether a remote network is subnetted or not, it is not true that knowing the MINMTU for one host reliably gives you the MINMTU for all other hosts on the same network.

Routes in a datagram network are not necessarily symmetric; the route a packet takes may not be the reverse of the route taken by a packet traveling in the opposite direction. Because of this, it is not safe for a host to assume that it can send a datagram as large as the one it has received from its peer. An independent MINMTU determination must be made for each direction, although the peer hosts may assist each other in doing so.

When the IP layer has determined the MINMTU for a connection or destination, it can make this information available to higher layers, such as TCP, that are generating segments to be sent as IP datagrams. Segment-generating layers should ask the IP layer for a MINMTU before sending a segment; connection-based layers should either check periodically that the MINMTU has not changed, or should be able to handle asynchronous notification of a change.

3.1. Fragmentation avoidance without protocol changes

In this section we describe several fragmentation avoidance schemes that can be implemented without changing existing protocol specifications or creating new protocols. There are obvious advantages to such approaches, since they can be taken immediately by individual sites or vendors; further, we have sufficient experience with one of them to believe that it works fairly well. On the other hand, none of these schemes can make use of exact knowledge of MINMTUs, and so may not provide optimal performance.

3.1.1. Always send tiny datagrams

If a host always sent datagrams no larger than the minimum MTU over the entire internet, these datagrams would never be fragmented. In the IP Internet the limit is no higher than 254 bytes, and might be lower. Since almost all of the Internet supports larger MTUs, and since performance depends so strongly on packet size, this approach can't provide reasonable performance. It is worth invoking only as a temporary diagnostic measure: if performance actually increases when the datagram size is decreased, this is a clear indication that inappropriate fragmentation is taking place for larger datagrams.

Alternatively, one might assume that using a 576-byte limit is small enough to avoid fragmentation in virtually all cases (we hope that in the future, all new IP network links would be capable of handling packets of this size). 576 bytes is set forth in the IP specification [18] as the maximum size a host can send without explicit permission from the receiving host, so it is reasonable as an arbitrary value.

3.1.2. Send 576-byte datagrams if the route goes via a gateway

The IP layer can determine if the route for a connection or destination goes via a gateway. If it does, then the size limit is set to 576 (our favorite arbitrary value); otherwise, any size up to the MTU of the data-link layer may be used.

This approach provides maximum performance for local connections, and reasonable assurance that on most non-local connections, datagrams will not be fragmented. It is not perfect, since

1. It does not avoid fragmentation on every path.

2. It may unnecessarily limit packet size, especially on subnetted collections of high-speed LANs that all support large packets.

3. If proxy ARP is used [14] then the IP layer may be fooled into believing that a non-local path is local, and thus use large datagrams when they are not necessarily safe.

However, it is quite easy to implement and in general provides good performance. A variant of this scheme, implemented in the TCP layer, has been used for several years at many sites and is now incorporated in 4.3BSD Unix [12]. This is the method we recommend in the absence of protocol changes.

3.1.3. Send 576-byte datagrams if the route goes off-net

Instead of checking whether a destination is behind a gateway, the IP layer can examine the destination's network number to decide if it is local or non-local. In a subnetted environment, this trades a higher risk of guessing too high a MINMTU for higher performance within the local collection of subnets.

3.2. Fragmentation avoidance with protocol changes

In this section we describe several fragmentation avoidance schemes that require changes to existing protocol specifications or the creation of new protocols. Mostly, these involve changes to gateways and some minor changes to IP-layer software; all are designed so as to coexist with unmodified gateways and hosts.

3.2.1. Probe mechanisms

Ideally, for a host to be able to send the largest possible datagrams that will not be fragmented, it must have perfect information as to the MINMTU along the path the datagrams will follow. Since most IP hosts do not even know what that route is, much less what the MTUs are along the route, we need a mechanism for discovering MINMTU.

The most straightforward kind of mechanism is to send a packet along the route, collecting MTU information as it goes; we call these *probe mechanisms*. Probe mechanisms require support from gateways: each gateway along the route must update the probe according to the MTU of the hop it is about to take. Probe mechanisms also require support from peer hosts; since paths are asymmetric, once a probe reaches the end of its route, the information it has collected must be returned to the source host.

A probe may either gather a list of all the MTUs along the path (somewhat analogous to the IP ''Record Route'' option), with which the host can determine the MINMTU, or the probe may simply carry only the lowest MTU value seen along the route. The former method provides a little more information; the latter method is easier to implement and results in shorter packets.

A probe may be made only once, at the beginning of a connection or the use of a route, or it may be made periodically. Periodic probes are preferable if the MINMTU is kept per-destination or per-connection, since the route may change. If MINMTU information is kept per-route, then it will not change and consequently probes need not be repeated.

Probe mechanisms are useful for discovering other path characteristics besides MINMTU. As long as one is processing a probe, it makes sense to collect a variety of information, since it comes at little additional cost. This information could include:

Minimum bandwidth
Useful for determining appropriate transmission rates; if a host knows that a 9600-baud link is part of the path, it should behave differently than if the path is entirely via 100 Mbit fiber networks.

Maximum delay
Useful for determining realistic round-trip times; if a satellite channel is in use, with a delay of several hundred milliseconds, a host should not retransmit as quickly as if the end-to-end delay were several milliseconds.

Maximum queue length
A high value implies congestion; if measured using the ''fair-queueing'' algorithm [16] it indicates to a host whether it is sending too much. Alternatively, a ''congestion-encountered'' flag could be set if any gateway along the path is experiencing congestion.

Maximum error rate
When a link along the path is experiencing a high error rate, a host might choose to send shorter packets (so as to reduce the likelihood that an entire datagram is dropped because of a single error) or use error-correcting codes.

Hop Count
The total number of links traversed along the route may be of interest, for example, in choosing a value for the ''Time To Live'' field. (Collection of hop counts was proposed by Mike Karels [10].)

It is not necessary for every gateway along the path to support probing, providing they all forward the probe. Gaps in the probe information are not fatal; at worst, host behavior is the same as if no probing is done. A gateway that does support probing can cover up for an occasional uncooperative gateway by looking at the incoming link as well as the outgoing link when determining the MINMTU.

Since route choices may depend on the IP ''Type of Service'' and perhaps the IP ''Security'' option, probes should carry the same Type of Service and Security as the data packets will [4]; gateways should observe Type of Service and Security when updating values in probes.

3.2.2. Probing with ICMP messages

A probe can be done using a separate packet; in the IP architecture, we would do this using a new ICMP "Probe Path" message. This is described in detail in appendix I.

Briefly, a host wishing to probe a path sets initial values for the fields of the Probe Path message, then sends it to the destination host. Each gateway along the route updates various fields of the message. When the destination host receives the message, it copies the recorded information into a different area of the message, reinitializes the recording fields, and returns the message to the original host. If the second host requests, the message may make one more trip, after which both hosts will have the path information, including MINMTU.

3.2.3. Probes piggybacked on IP headers

It is not necessary to send a separate packet to probe the path. Instead, the probe information can be piggybacked on the actual data packets, as part of the IP header. In appendix II we describe new IP header options for recording and returning MINMTU information. (Additional options could be defined for recording other path characteristics.)

In this case, a host wishing to probe a path sets initial values for the "Probe MTU" option in the IP header of a datagram it is sending. Each gateway along the route may update the value carried in this option. When the destination host receives the datagram, it copies the recorded information into a "MTU Reply" option and attaches it to the next datagram going back to the source host. When this reply is received, the first host knows the MINMTU; the second host may pass its own Probe MTU option along with the MTU Reply, so after one more datagram both hosts can know the MINMTU.

Because the piggyback method does not involve additional packets, it may be cheaper than the ICMP method; it should be cheap enough that one can send it frequently, to react to changes in the route. The drawback is that it adds overhead to the processing of data packets, and may be harder to implement, since when a host wants to return a MINMTU value it must find an outgoing datagram to which it can attach the MTU Reply option.

3.3. Recovery from fragmentation

Instead of avoiding fragmentation by trying to predict when it will occur, a host could instead detect when it occurs and recover by shrinking the datagram size. Detection can be accomplished with or without the use of new protocols.

All methods start by assuming a large datagram size, and adjusting the datagram size based on indications of fragmentation. After a few iterations of this process using a binary search on the datagram size, and after receiving acknowledgements from the remote host to verify that the datagrams are actually arriving, the source host can have arbitrarily precise knowledge of the MINMTU for the path.

Detection methods have the advantage that they cause no additional overhead unless fragmentation occurs. They have the disadvantage that they can create lots of useless traffic if not carefully implemented.

3.3.1. Use of "Don't Fragment" flag

One such approach is to set the "Don't Fragment" flag on every datagram, and use the MTU of the first hop as the initial datagram size. If a datagram reaches a gateway that would have to fragment it, the gateway (obeying the "Don't Fragment" flag) must drop the datagram and return an ICMP "Destination Unreachable/Fragmentation Needed and DF Set" message [20]. The source host, upon receiving this ICMP, should try a smaller datagram size and retransmit any unacknowledged data. (A variant of this scheme was first proposed by Geof Cooper [7].)

This method requires no protocol changes, but the drawback is that until the proper MINMTU is discovered, many datagrams will be dropped, and thus it may take a long time to set up a connection. Since many connections transfer only a few data packets (mail, for example), this is a significant overhead; it would only be useful for long connections.

3.3.2. Passive detection of fragmentation

A complementary approach is to allow fragmentation of any datagram, but to detect when this happens and adjust the datagram size accordingly. While this might take longer to arrive at the proper MINMTU, it does not force gateways to drop any datagrams in the meantime; thus it improves performance on long connections without harming brief ones. One way to do this without changing protocols is to observe the retransmission rate; from a high retransmission rate one might deduce that deterministic fragment loss is occurring. The datagram size can be lowered until the retransmission rate drops noticeably.

The problem is that a high retransmission rate may also be caused by other problems, especially congestion. Cutting the datagram size is exactly the wrong approach when fragmentation is not occurring and the path is congested, since it increases the number of packets required to send the same data and thus increases the congestion. This approach should therefore be used only when an independent mechanism is used to detect or suppress congestion, such as the use of ICMP source quenches, Nagle's *fair-queueing* algorithm [16], or statistical properties of the round-trip delays [9].

3.3.3. Proper use of "Time Exceeded" ICMP messages

The receiving host can tell if it is losing fragments because partial datagrams waiting on its reassembly queue will time out. The ICMP protocol currently includes a "Time Exceeded" message, including a code that can be set to indicate "fragment reassembly time exceeded." While this message does not convey complete information on the MINMTU of the path, it is a clear indication that the source host has guessed too high and should reduce the size of the datagrams it is sending. Apparently, many IP implementations do not send this message, nor do many know what to do with it.

3.3.4. "Fragmentation Warning" ICMP messages

In this scheme, when a gateway fragments a datagram, it forwards the fragments as usual but also sends a message back to the source host. This "Fragmentation Warning" ICMP message would carry the maximum allowable datagram size, so that the source host could reduce the datagram size to fit through the link in question. The process may have to be repeated if a subsequent link has a slightly smaller MTU. (A variant of this scheme was first proposed by Art Berggreen [1].)

This scheme has a serious danger: if the source host does not receive or act upon the warning message, not only will fragmentation continue to occur, but a lot of useless traffic will be created by subsequent warning messages. A gateway could avoid sending multiple warnings to the same host, at the cost of maintaining a cache of recently warned host addresses. Alternatively, we could introduce a new "Warn if Fragmented" flag in the IP header, analogous to the "Don't Fragment" flag. Only if this flag is set would a warning be issued, and a source host setting this flag should take care to heed warnings.

3.3.5. "Fragments Received" ICMP messages

A similar approach generates warnings at the destination, rather than the gateways. If a host receives a fragmented datagram, it can send a "Fragments Received" ICMP message back to the source host. This warning would carry the size of the largest fragment of the datagram; this is a lower bound on MINMTU, although it is possible that larger datagrams could be sent without fragmentation. Again, some mechanism is needed to limit unheeded warnings, so as to prevent congestion. (A variant of this scheme was first proposed by Charles Lynn [11].)

3.4. Use of Transparent Fragmentation

The need for inter-network fragmentation, and consequently its dangers, can be reduced or eliminated by the use of transparent fragmentation (sometimes called intra-network fragmentation). If all the fragments of a datagram are sent to a unique next-hop gateway for reassembly, and if the fragmenting and reassembling gateways use a low-level protocol that increases the chances of complete delivery, two benefits are obtained:

1. Deterministic fragment loss is unlikely, if the protocol between the two gateways supports acknowledgements of individual fragments. It need not be completely reliable, since the end hosts are willing to accept occasional lost or mis-sequenced datagrams.
2. If the (reassembled) datagram subsequently traverses a network with a larger MTU, it makes more efficient use of that network than a collection of smaller fragments.

On the other hand, transparent fragmentation has many drawbacks: (1) a datagram may be repeatedly reassembled and refragmented; (2) gateway implementations become more complex and require much more buffer memory; (3) the performance gains are limited because a datagram cannot be larger than the MTU of the first-hop network and because a maximum size must be enforced to provide a limit on gateway reassembly buffer space. Most important, in the IP world a destination host may still have to perform reassembly, since the MTU of the last-hop link may be smaller than the datagram size; this means that most of the problems associated with inter-network fragmentation would still be present, although to a lesser degree. (Transparent fragmentation was successful in the Pup architecture because almost all non-gateway Pup hosts were attached to networks with MTUs larger than the maximum allowed Pup datagram size [2].)

Since transparent fragmentation is invisible except to the gateways involved, it can be used in an IP internet wherever the benefits outweigh the drawbacks; this is specifically allowed by the IP specification [18]. We encourage designers of gateways and networks to consider the use of transparent fragmentation, especially if the natural MTU of the network is unusually small. For example, the actual IMP-to-IMP messages on the ARPAnet are only 1008 bits long; the 1007-byte MTU of the ARPAnet is an illusion created by transparent fragmentation and reassembly within the IMPs [8].

3.5. Careful use of intentional fragmentation

In certain restricted cases, and with a little luck, one can obtain significant performance improvements by sending such large datagrams that they must be fragmented immediately by the source host, before being transmitted on their first hop. This is done in Sun Microsystems' implementation of their NFS protocol [21]. Throughput is improved because fewer datagrams are handled in the layers above IP, and because end-to-end acknowledgements are done only in the RPC layer, rather than in the transport layer as well. This performance improvement is extremely unstable;

because it is vulnerable to deterministic fragment loss, performance may drop radically if gateways or interfaces with insufficient buffering are in use. In some cases, the protocol fails entirely.

We do not believe that intentional fragmentation is a good idea, since careful protocol design and implementation should be able to provide similar peak performance without anywhere near the risk. It is especially irresponsible to use over an internet prone to congestion, since congestion may cause deterministic fragment loss and the resulting retransmission of long packet trains can only worsen the congestion.

Intentional fragmentation, in spite of its risk, is appealing because as long as it works it requires no implementation modifications beyond some parameter tuning. If it is used, we think the risk can be reduced by approaches analogous to those we have suggested for determining MINMTU.

For example, intentional fragmentation could be restricted to those destinations that are on the local network, or those without an intervening gateway. Alternatively, the source host could observe the retransmission rate and cease intentional fragmentation if the rate is high; since intentional fragmentation is worse for congestion than the use of undersized datagrams, this is a good idea even when one cannot distinguish retransmissions caused by congestion from those caused by deterministic fragment loss.

If accurate information, say from a probe mechanism, shows that somewhere along the path the fragments will be re-fragmented, one would clearly not want to use intentional fragmentation. Aside from the problem that many existing gateways derived from 4.2BSD code cannot properly fragment a fragment, this results in a great expansion in the total number of fragments and consequently the risks of congestion and deterministic fragment loss.

4. Summary and Recommendations

We believe that future heterogeneous internetworks will include networks with a wide range of bandwidths, because economics force long-haul networks to have lower bandwidths than local-area networks. The MTU that maximizes performance varies with bandwidth: on low-bandwidth links, a small MTU is used to limit the time the link can be occupied by one packet; on high-bandwidth links, a large MTU allows per-packet overheads to be amortized over many bytes. Therefore, link-level MTUs will always vary within heterogeneous internetworks.

In this paper, we have explored the use of inter-network fragmentation as a solution to the problem of differing MTUs. Fragmentation frees higher level protocols from having to alter their behavior based on the route over which packets flow. To the designers of IP, inter-network fragmentation appeared to be the right choice. Unfortunately, as we have shown, blind reliance on fragmentation in IP can be costly in both performance and reliability.

4.1. Recommendations

In section 3 we described a broad variety of schemes for avoiding or ameliorating fragmentation. Not all of these schemes are worthwhile, and not all of the good ones should be adopted together. Here we suggest what we believe are the most appropriate steps to take.

We are proposing engineering modifications to a large, heterogeneous internetwork where there is a tremendous delay in disseminating change to all sites; some sites may never catch up. Stability is important; this means that whenever possible, a change should not disrupt those hosts that are not yet updated.

Since a robust host implementation should simply ignore packets and options that it does not understand, one might think it safe to make changes that involve sending additional packets on the off chance that the receiver knows what to do with them. In the larger context of an internetwork prone to congestion, however, we should worry about injecting useless packets. We thus favor approaches that do not repeatedly send packets that might be ignored.

4.1.1. Recommendations not involving protocol changes

Some solutions can be implemented immediately, without changes to protocol specifications. Most effective is the one described in section 3.1.2, limiting the datagram size to 576 bytes whenever the packet is routed via a gateway. This should be implemented in the IP layer, rather than in the TCP layer as in 4.3BSD.

Somewhat more difficult, but still possible without protocol changes at the IP layer or above, is the use of transparent fragmentation (that is, immediate reassembly) over networks with small MTUs. Effectively, this means increasing the MTU of such networks as viewed by hosts on other networks.

Finally, we strongly encourage implementors who use intentional fragmentation to do so only when packets are sent directly, with no gateway along the route. Also, intentional fragmentation should cease when the retransmission rate increases beyond a certain level.

We do not recommend the use of the ICMP "fragment reassembly time exceeded" message since it appears that most hosts simply ignore it; this is a shame but it may be too late to correct.

4.1.2. Recommendations for protocol changes

If protocol changes were to be considered, we would recommend the adoption of both the ICMP "Probe Path" message described in appendix I, and the IP "Probe MTU" option described in appendix II. Both of these changes require support from gateways and from host IP layers, but they can be incrementally adopted without confusing existing implementations. On the other hand, the ICMP "Probe Path" message can still cause the "useless packets" problem.

We suggest implementing both probe mechanisms because the cost of doing so is not much higher than that of implementing one, and we cannot predict which is more effective. Each may be optimal for certain applications.

4.1.3. Recommendations for new architectures

The IP Internet was intended as an experiment, and from this experiment we can extract some lessons to use in designing new architectures. Any large heterogeneous datagram internetwork is likely to require fragmentation at times; careful design can make fragmentation normally unnecessary, and can avert its most serious drawbacks. We do not believe that fragmentation should be completely hidden from hosts; to do so would be to fall into the trap of providing reliable stream protocols at too low a level. Rather, fragmentation should simply be as robust as possible, so that it does not lead to performance disasters.

We urge consideration of transparent fragmentation whenever possible. There is little value in the ability to send fragments of one datagram along different routes, and reassembly by gateways should not be prohibitively expensive. Main memory sizes and costs are improving so rapidly that buffer space should no longer be considered the limiting resource; reassembly might actually improve the switching rates of gateways by reducing the number of individually switched fragments. We suggest that a source host be able to turn off transparent fragmentation by setting a flag in the datagram header, analogous to the IP "Don't Fragment" flag.

We also believe that the ability to record path information — not only about MTU but also about congestion, bandwidth, etc.— is so valuable that it should be done on every packet. The header overhead could be reduced by encoding the numerical information, either by reducing resolution or by using a logarithmic scale. By doing recording in standard rather than optional header fields, its cost could be made negligible.

Finally, since transparent fragmentation cannot entirely obviate the use of inter-network fragmentation, there must be a way to recover from inappropriate fragmentation. The receiving host can detect the problem, through repeated reassembly timeouts, and should notify the sending host via something akin to the ICMP "fragmentation reassembly time exceeded" message. If support for this message had been mandatory in IP, it would have eliminated the problem of complete communication failure due to deterministic fragment loss.

Acknowledgements

This paper was inspired by a flurry of messages on the TCP-IP electronic mailing list, which provoked us to write down some thoughts we had been harboring for several years. Many of the ideas in this paper come from TCP-IP participants; we have tried to cite specific references. Other participants whose important contributions are not otherwise cited include Bob Braden, Hans-Werner Braun, Vint Cerf, Doug Kingston, John Wobus, and Lixia Zhang. We would also like to thank Dave Boggs for continually reminding us that Pup got it right.

Appendix I. ICMP "Probe Path" message

The format of the proposed ICMP "Probe Path" message is shown in figure I-1.

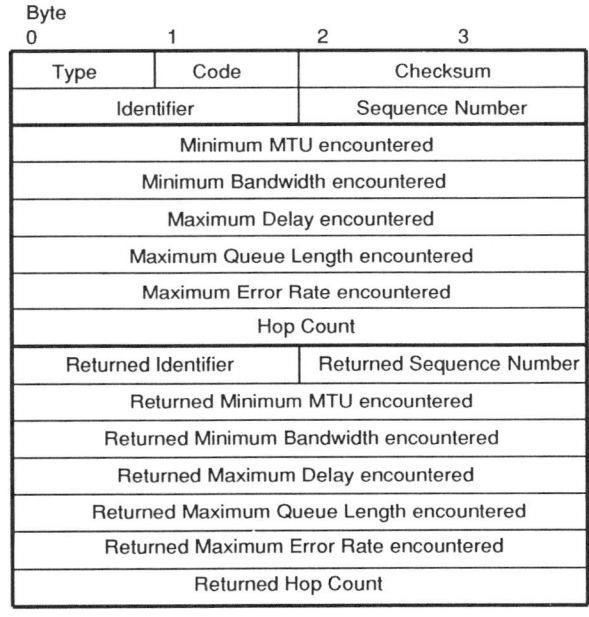

Figure I-1: Format of ICMP "Probe Path" message

The fields of a Probe Path message are:

Type
To be assigned.

Code
Indicates how far through a "three-way" handshake this message is:
1 = Initial message: don't believe "Returned" values; please reply.

2 = Second message: believe "Returned" values; please reply.

3 = Third message: believe "Returned" values; no reply expected.

For codes 1 and 2, gateways must update values in other fields as specified. For code 3, gateways need not update values in other fields.

Checksum
   The usual ICMP checksum. It must be updated when a gateway modifies any of the other fields.

Identifier
   An identifier to aid in matching probes with replies, may be zero.

Sequence Number
   A sequence number to aid in matching probes with replies, may be zero.

If the Code is 1 or 2, the following six fields are updated by gateways as the message follows its route; they are all 32-bit two's complement (signed) integers. Their initial values are set by the source host, as indicated. Gateways should observe the Type of Service field and Security option in the IP header of the Probe Path message when updating these fields.

Minimum MTU encountered
   Initially set to the MTU of the first hop data link, or to MAXINT ($2^{31}-1$). Each gateway compares this value to the MTU of the incoming and outgoing links for the message, and reduces the recorded value, if necessary. MTU is measured in octets.

Minimum Bandwidth encountered
   Initially set to the bandwidth of the first hop data link, or to MAXINT. Each gateway compares this value to the bandwidth of the incoming and outgoing links for the message, and reduces the recorded value, if necessary. Bandwidth is measured in bits per second.

Maximum Delay encountered
   Initially set to the delay of the first hop data link, or to zero. Each gateway compares this value to the time it will take the packet to traverse the incoming and outgoing links, and increases the recorded value, if necessary. Delay is measured in microseconds. For networks, such as CSMA/CD, where the delay is not a simple function of the packet length, use the expected value of the delay for an average packet.

Maximum Queue Length encountered
   Initially set to the length of the output queue of the source host when the packet is placed on that queue, or to zero. Each gateway compares this value to the length of the queue in which the packet is placed, and increases the recorded value, if necessary.

Maximum Error Rate encountered
   Initially set to the error rate of the first hop data link, or to zero. Each gateway compares this value to the error rate of the incoming and outgoing links, and increases the recorded value, if necessary. Error rate is measured as the reciprocal of the bit-error rate; i.e., it is the expected value of the number of bits between errors.

Hop Count
   Initially set to 1. Each gateway increments this value by one.

If the Code of an incoming message is 1 or 2, the following eight ("returned") fields are used to return the previous eight ("incoming") fields to the probing host:

Returned Identifier
Returned Sequence Number
Returned Minimum MTU encountered
Returned Minimum Bandwidth encountered
Returned Maximum Delay encountered
Returned Maximum Queue Length encountered
Returned Maximum Error Rate encountered
Returned Hop Count

The destination host copies the appropriate fields (e.g., "Minimum MTU encountered" is copied to "Returned Minimum MTU encountered"), re-initializes the incoming fields, sets the code field to 2 or 3 depending on whether it needs path information, recomputes the checksum, reverses the source and destination addresses, and returns the message. When a host receives a Code 2 or Code 3 message, it can use the values in the returned fields to update its path information database. The 32-bit wide fields are interpreted as two's complement integers; a negative value means that the field value is not valid.

Appendix II. IP "Probe MTU" options

The format of the proposed IP "Probe MTU" option is shown in figure II-1. The option type code is *to be assigned*; it is not copied on fragmentation, it is of option class 2 (debugging and measurement). This option is always 8 octets long.

010xxxx0	Length	Minimum MTU encountered	Identifier
Type=yyy	Length=8		

Figure II-1: Format of IP "Probe MTU" option

The value of the Probe MTU option is the minimum MTU encountered along the route followed by the packet, measured in octets. It is initialized by the source host to the MTU of the first hop data-link, or it may be initialized to $2^{31}-1$. Each gateway compares this value to the MTU of the incoming and outgoing links for the packet, and reduces the recorded value, if necessary. Gateways should observe the Type of Service field and Security option in the IP header when updating this value. The source host should set the Identifier field to allow it to match the reply to this option with the appropriate connection or route.

When a destination host receives a packet with the Probe MTU option, it creates an "MTU Reply" option, whose format is shown in figure II-2. The option type code is *to be assigned*; it is not copied on fragmentation, it is of option class 2 (debugging and measurement). This option is always 8 octets long. The "Returned Minimum MTU" and "Identifier" fields are copies of the corresponding fields in the received Probe MTU option.

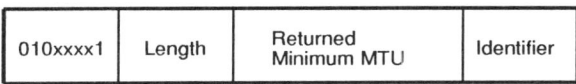

Type=zzz   Length=8

Figure II-2: Format of IP "MTU Reply" option

The destination host returns this option attached to the next packet sent to the originating host. Because several Probe MTU options may arrive before one is sent, the MTU Reply option may appear more than once in a packet. A packet carrying an MTU Reply option may also carry a Probe MTU option.

When a host receives an MTU Reply option, it uses the Identifier field to associate the Minimum MTU value with a particular connection or destination.

References

1. Art Berggreen. IP Datagram Sizes. Electronic distribution of the TCP-IP Discussion Group, no Message-ID.

2. David R. Boggs, John F. Shoch, Edward A. Taft, and Robert M. Metcalfe. "Pup: An internetwork architecture." *IEEE Transactions on Communications COM-28*, 4 (April 1980), 612-624.

3. David R. Cheriton. VMTP: A transport protocol for next generation communication systems. SIGCOMM '86, ACM SIGCOMM, August, 1986.

4. J. Noel Chiappa. IP Datagram Sizes. Electronic distribution of the TCP-IP Discussion Group, Message-ID <12304502322.33.JNC@XX.LCS.MIT.EDU>.

5. David D. Clark. IP Datagram Reassembly Algorithms. RFC 815, Network Information Center, SRI International, July, 1982.

6. David D. Clark, Mark L. Lambert, and Lixia Zhang. NETBLT: A Bulk Data Transfer Protocol. RFC 998, Network Information Center, SRI International, March, 1987.

7. Geof Cooper. IP Datagram Sizes. Electronic distribution of the TCP-IP Discussion Group, Message-ID <8705230517.AA01407@apolling.imagen.uucp>.

8. F. E. Heart, R. E. Kahn. S. M. Ornstein, W. R. Crowther, and D. C. Walden. The interface message processor for the ARPA computer network. Proc. AFIPS Spring Joint Computer Conference, May, 1970, pp. 551-567.

9. Van Jacobson. Retransmit Timers: Theory and Practice. In preparation.

10. Mike Karels. IP Datagram Sizes. Electronic distribution of the TCP-IP Discussion Group, Message-ID <8705262316.AA08021@okeefe.Berkeley.EDU>.

11. Charles Lynn. IP Datagram Sizes. Electronic distribution of the TCP-IP Discussion Group, Message-ID <[G.BBN.COM]22-May-87 20:11:55.CLYNN>.

12. M. Kirk McKusick, Mike Karels, and Sam Leffler. Performance Improvements and Functional Enhancements in 4.3BSD. Proc. Summer USENIX Conference, June, 1985, pp. 519-531.

13. Dave Mills. IP Datagram Sizes. Electronic distribution of the TCP-IP Discussion Group, Message-ID <8705261315.a029301@Huey.UDEL.EDU>.

14. Jeffrey Mogul. Internet Subnets. RFC 917, Network Information Center, SRI International, October, 1984.

15. Jeffrey Mogul and Jon Postel. Internet Standard Subnetting Procedure. RFC 950, Network Information Center, SRI International, August, 1985.

16. John B. Nagle. "On Packet Switches with Infinite Storage." *IEEE Transactions on Communications COM-35*, 4 (April 1987), 435-438.

17. Jon Postel. User Datagram Protocol. RFC 768, Network Information Center, SRI International, August, 1980.

18. Jon Postel. Internet Protocol. RFC 791, Network Information Center, SRI International, September, 1981.

19. Jon Postel. Transmission Control Protocol. RFC 793, Network Information Center, SRI International, September, 1981.

20. Jon Postel. Internet Control Message Protocol. RFC 792, Network Information Center, SRI International, September, 1981.

21. Russel Sandberg, David Goldberg, Steve Kleiman, Dan Walsh, and Bob Lyon. Design and Implementation of the Sun Network Filesystem. Proc. Summer USENIX Conference, June, 1985, pp. 119-130.

22. Alan Sheltzer, Robert Hinden, and Mike Brescia. "Connecting different types of networks with gateways." *Data Communications* (August 1982), 119-126.

23. John Shoch. "Packet Fragmentation in Inter-Network Protocols." *Computer Networks 3*, 1 (February 1979), 3-8.

24. John A. Shriver. IP Datagram Sizes. Electronic distribution of the TCP-IP Discussion Group, Message-ID <8705261623.AA12946@monk.proteon.com>.

A CASE FOR PACKET SWITCHING IN HIGH-PERFORMANCE WIDE-AREA NETWORKS

Zygmunt Haas
Electrical Engineering Department
Stanford University, CA 94305

David R. Cheriton
Computer Science Department
Stanford University, CA 94305

Abstract

The large capacity of optical fibers suggests that circuit-switching may become a more attractive switching method in future communication networks. We show, however, that under some reasonable assumptions the delays associated with circuit-switching make the technique inferior to packet-switching in a high-performance, distributed environment. A network design that demonstrates the feasibility of packet-switching in high-performance environment is also presented.

This work was sponsored in part by the Defense Advanced Research Projects Agency under contract N00039-86-K-0431, by the Digital Equipment Corporation, by ATT Information Systems and by Bell Northern Research.

1 Introduction

The potential of computer communication is, at present, severely handicapped by the poor performance of wide-area networks. The geographically dispersed clusters of machines operated by military, commercial, government, and research organizations are information and resource "islands" that limit the efficiency, capability, and responsiveness of these organizations. Moreover, distributed environments and more performance-demanding applications will characterize future wide-area communication. Consequently, wide-area networks that are matched in delay and bandwidth to the performance of local area and metropolitan area networks are required to solve today's and tomorrow's communication needs.

Optical fiber provides a long distance channel technology that makes this goal feasible. As a consequence, communication networks are evolving towards a new physical layer. Fibers are being installed rapidly [3], replacing twisted pairs and coaxial cables, and bringing with them the benefit of very high bandwidth, two or three orders of magnitude higher than that of the existing networks. However, these benefits can easily be wasted if an inappropriate switching technique is used for these high-bandwidth networks.

At the first glance it seems that circuit-switching would be the preferred switching technique in high-bandwidth networking. We claim, however, that circuit-switching is a poor choice for high-speed, distributed-environment computer traffic, and we make the case for packet-switching. The challenge is, consequently, to provide switching nodes that handle high data rates with minimal delay and at a reasonable cost. In particular, a switching node must minimize the packet routing decision delay. Also, it must be able to make switching decisions at the packet rate determined by the traffic on the incoming channels.

To support the claim that packet-switching can be performed in high-speed networks, we describe *Blazenet*, a packet-switched network based on optical fiber and high-performance switching nodes. *Blazenet* provides an appropriate solution to the problem of networking in high-performance environments. The network is presented here as a wide-area network. We see it as a backbone network, whose nodes are gateways to other networks. Nevertheless, the concept of *Blazenet* is easily applied to smaller networks and, with some constraints on maximum packet size, even to local area networks.

Section 2 justifies through examples the need for high-performance networks for the future communication. Section 3 discusses switching techniques for high-performance networks. Section 4 describes the *Blazenet* network architecture, addressing the issues of packet-switching, packet

Permission to copy without fee all or part of this material is granted provided that the copies are not made or distributed for direct commercial advantage, the ACM copyright notice and the title of the publication and its date appear, and notice is given that copying is by permission of the Association for Computing Machinery. To copy otherwise, or to republish, requires a fee and/or specfic permission.

© 1988 ACM 0-89791-245-4/88/0001/0402 $1.50

blockage, and switching node design. Final section summarizes our perception of future networking and its implications.

2 High-performance communication

High-performance communication will become essential in future computing environments, which will be characterized by distributed processing. By high-performance communication we mean low-delay, multi-point, *on-demand* delivery of large amounts of data. By on-demand we mean access (request) of data in an unpredictable manner. This section presents some examples of applications that illustrate the need for high-performance communication.

Large-scale distributed data base systems in general, and file systems in particular, are applications that require high-performance communication. Cashing the data in a file system is usually an unpredictable process. Thus, access to the data in a file system is done on an on-demand basis. Moreover, large cache sizes, which tend to have improved performance, need to communicate large amounts of data. Thus high-throughput is required. Furthermore, in order to keep the data base consistent, fast communication is needed. Also, because the data base is distributed and replicated, multi-point communication is important.

Another example of the need for high-performance communication is multi-media conferencing. Such systems obviously require multi-point communication. Various mixtures of transmission are involved: image, high-resolution graphics, voice, etc. Some data types require communication of large amounts of data. Most of the communication is done on an on-demand basis by the current speaker, who upon receiving the "floor", may send a large chunk of data that includes mixture of multiple types of data.

High-capacity systems are not sufficient to provide high-performance communication, because high-capacity systems are not necessarily low-delay systems. For example, high-capacity satellite communication still suffers from long delays. Moreover, the on-demand characteristic of high-performance communication is crucial. The following example illustrates this point.

Site A needs to process medical image data with a powerful processor located at site B. The processing is done on pictures composed of 1000×1000 pixels each. Assuming 8 bit/pixel representation, each picture requires 1 Mbyte. The processing requires that the data of a whole picture be present before the processing on this picture starts. Suppose that the time to process a single picture is 100 msec. A satisfactory solution is to provide a low-speed, low-throughput, channel (1 Mbps, for example) that constantly sends the data from A to B. B buffers the data and passes it to the processor at processor pace. However, if the next picture to be processed depends on the results of the computation done on the previous one, the effective rate at which the whole process is performed is the sum of the two serially done processes: transmission over the network and processing at the processor. Because the link is a low-speed one, each 100 msec of the processor operation will be interleaved with 8 sec of waiting for the next picture to arrive. Note that we have assumed that the network introduces no delay. In reality, if the channel is low-speed, there is additional delay encountered. Another solution is to provide a high-speed, high-throughput channel (suppose 1 Gbps), used only when B issues a request for the next picture of data. Now the rate at which the whole process is done is approximately the processing rate only, since the transmission is done at very high speed. Thus the processor receives the next picture only 8 msec after the request is initiated (neglecting the delay introduced by the high-speed channel) and the 100 msec processing periods are interleaved with only 8 msec transmission overhead. Moreover, retransmissions, required because of errors, have a minor effect on the whole process rate in this case.

We have presented a few examples of applications where the need for high-performance communication exists. These are only representative ones; we expect many other applications to arise when high-performance wide-area communication is truly available.

3 Packet- vs circuit- switching

Packet-switching and circuit-switching are two possible techniques to be used in high-performance communication. Circuit-switching is characterized by static allocation of communication resources. Packet-switching, on the other hand, exercise dynamic allocation of the communication channel.

The following simple analysis compares the delay encountered by a chunk of information of d bits, transmitted over a path of l links, once when the network uses packet-switching technique, and once when the network links are divided into N sub-channels working in the circuit-switching mode. We assume links of capacity C [bps] each, low network load, and "cut-through" ([10,11]) mode of operation for the packet-switched version. The low-load assumption is justified by the large capacity C. (Also note that in the circuit-switching arrangement C is divided into N sub-channels carring *bursty* traffic and, thus, being underutilized.)

The delay encountered on the packet-switched link constitutes of:

- Path propagation delay, T_{prop}.

- Transmission time, d/C.

- The delay encountered in each one of the l switching nodes on the transmission path due to packets contention, T_q.

- The delay encountered in each one of the switching nodes on the transmission path to perform the switching decision.

Assign ϵ to the number of bits that a packet is delayed by at each switching node in order to perform the switching decision. The total delay of the packet-switched version is:

$$D^{PS} = T_{prop} + \frac{d}{C} + (T_q + \frac{\epsilon}{C}) \cdot l \qquad (1)$$

The same data transmitted over the circuit-switched channel encounters the following delay components:

- Propagation delay over the path, T_{prop}.
- Waiting time to obtain an idle sub-channel, T_{wait}, if there is no circuit set up to the destination. Assign p_w to the probability there is no idle sub-channel.
- Circuit set up time, T_{setup}. Assign p_s to the probability that no circuit to the destination already exists.
- Transmission over a channel of capacity C/N.

Thus the total delay for the circuit-switched arrangement is:

$$D^{CS} = T_{prop} + p_s \cdot (p_w T_{wait} + T_{setup}) + \frac{d \cdot N}{C} \qquad (2)$$

When a network operates under light load, $T_q \approx 0$ for packet-switching and $p_w \approx 0$ for circuit-switching (there is always an idle sub-channel available). This results in the following low-load approximations:

$$D^{PS}_{low\ load} = T_{prop} + \frac{d}{C} + \frac{\epsilon}{C} l \qquad (3)$$

$$D^{CS}_{low\ load} = T_{prop} + p_s \cdot T_{setup} + \frac{d \cdot N}{C} \qquad (4)$$

Under these approximations and the assumption that fast packet-switching is performed (i.e, $(\epsilon \cdot l)/C \approx 0$), the comparision of $D^{PS}_{low\ load}$ to $D^{CS}_{low\ load}$ leads to the important conclusion that $D^{PS}_{low\ load} \leq D^{CS}_{low\ load}$ for finite C. Note also that in the improved circuit-switching scheme where the header of the transmission performs the set-up procedure, the conclusion that $D^{PS}_{low\ load} \leq D^{CS}_{low\ load}$ remains still valid. In this later case, although T_{setup} term is eliminated, nevertheless, because of the increased transmission time due to smaller capacity of the sub-channels, circuit-switching scheme encounters longer delays.

Next, we demonstrate through an example that $D^{CS}_{low\ load}$ might be considerably greater then $D^{PS}_{low\ load}$ for reasonable parameters values and that an attempt to bring both closely together results in unreasonable capacity requirements.

Consider the following case: a coast-to-coast network (4000 km span) with clusters of M hosts on each coast, and 40 switching nodes on the coast-to-coast path. As a particular example, assume that:

- $C = 1$ Gbps.
- Low-load network operation.

- $M = 10$.
- 1 Mbit (=125 kbyte) is to be transmitted.
- 100 bit switching delay at each node in the packet-switching mode.
- The propagation speed of light on fiber is 200 000 km/sec.
- T_{setup} is on the order of round trip delay, i.e negligible processing time comparing to T_{prop}.

Consequently,

$$T_{prop} = 20\ msec \qquad (5)$$

$$d/C = 1\ msec \ll T_{prop} \qquad (6)$$

$$\frac{\epsilon}{C} l = 4\ \mu sec \ll T_{prop} \qquad (7)$$

$$T_{setup} \approx 2 \cdot T_{prop} = 40\ msec \qquad (8)$$

Thus,

$$D^{PS}_{low\ load} = 21\ msec\ \approx T_{prop} \qquad (9)$$

Let us turn now to circuit-switching. Let us assume that a circuit remains set until some traffic needs the line for a new circuit. In this case the circuit is closed with negligible delay. Note that all these assumptions are conservative, in the sense that they decrease the circuit-switching delay.

The maximum number of sub-channels required between the two clusters of hosts is $M \times M = M^2$. Assign η to the fraction of the maximum M^2 sub-channels that are actually built, that is $\eta = N/M^2$. Further assume that the traffic between any two hosts is random and independent of all the other host-host pairs. Thus the probability that there is an established channel upon traffic arrival is approximately equal to η. Substituting all the assumptions into the formula for $D^{CS}_{low\ load}$ yields:

$$D^{CS}_{low\ load} = T_{prop} + T_{setup} + \eta \cdot (\frac{d \cdot M^2}{C} - T_{setup}) \qquad (10)$$

And for our particular example,

$$D^{CS}_{low\ load} \approx 60 + 60 \cdot \eta\ [msec] \qquad (11)$$

Choosing $\eta = 1/M^2$ in order to minimize the $D^{CS}_{lowload}$ yields $D^{CS}_{lowload} \approx 60\ msec$, that is three times the packet-switching delay.

As C increases, $D^{CS}_{low\ load}$ becomes closer to $D^{PS}_{low\ load}$. By increasing the value of N, p_w and p_s decrease. $p_w = 0$ and $p_s = 0$ as N reaches the maximum number of concurrently required connections on this link. In this case, the value of C, required to bring $D^{CS}_{low\ load}$ within 90% of $D^{PS}_{low\ load}$, is given approximately by:

$$C \approx 10 \cdot (\frac{N \cdot d}{T_{prop}}) \qquad (12)$$

Now, suppose that $N = 100$, $d = 1$ Mbyte, and that the two closest nodes in our network are 100 km apart. This yields C equal to 16 Tbps (!). Thus extremely large capacity is required to bring $D^{CS}_{low\ load}$ closely to $D^{PS}_{low\ load}$.

The argument of circuit-switching advocates is that when $C \to \infty$, formulas (3) and (4) both approach the same limit (since $C \to \infty$ implies $p_s \to 0$):

$$\lim_{C \to \infty} D^{PS}_{low\ load} = T_{prop} \qquad (13)$$

$$\lim_{C \to \infty} D^{CS}_{low\ load} = T_{prop} \qquad (14)$$

Consequently, the circuit-switching advocates claim that in these circumstances the preferred switching techniques has to be determined based on other then the delay consideration. We will show, however, that when $C \to \infty$ an attempt to minimize the delay of a circuit-switched network for a reasonable range of parameters values (and under the assumption of low load) results in a single-channel solution of the total capacity C (i.e, $N_{opt} = 1$). Thus, we show that in these circumstances the packet-switching is the optimal solution.

Consider a channel of capacity C divided into N sub-channels. Assign N_{max} to the maximum number of sub-channels that can ever be simultaneously required. Using the formula (4) with $p_s = 1 - N/N_{max}$ and $T_{setup} = 2 \cdot T_{prop}$ gives:

$$D^{CS}_{low\ load} = 3 \cdot T_{prop} + N \cdot (\frac{d}{C} - \frac{2 \cdot T_{prop}}{N_{max}}) \qquad (15)$$

The optimal value of N, N_{opt}, depends on the sign of the term $\frac{d}{C} - \frac{2T_{prop}}{N_{max}}$ in the following manner:

- if $2T_{prop} > \frac{dN_{max}}{C}$, then $N_{opt} = N_{max}$
- else, then $N_{opt} = 1$ \qquad (16)

(for equality both solutions are possible)
Concentrating on the expression:

$$\frac{d \cdot N_{max}}{C} - 2 \cdot T_{prop} \qquad (17)$$

we notice that increasing C tends to prefer the maximum number of sub-channels as an optimal solution, while the increase in both amount of data to transmit, d, as well as the maximal number of sub-channels, N_{max}, prefers the single-channel solution. Note that in general N_{max} equals to the second power of the number of possible network destinations. We claim that due to the very nature of the distributed systems, the number of hosts on the network will rapidly increase in the future networks. Moreover, future high-performance communication will have high-throughput traffic, increasing the d parameter. Therefore, the value of the expression (17) will increase overall. Consequently, an attempt to optimize the circuit-switching arrangement for future environment yields a single channel, which is simply the packet-switching solution with unnecessary set-up overhead. In the next example we use some quite conservative parameters values (in the sense that they tend towards the $N_{opt} = N_{max}$ solution) and show that even in this case the optimal solution is a single channel of total capacity C.

- $C = 100$ Gbps.
- $d = 10.01$ Mbit (≈ 1.25 Mbyte).
- Path of 1000 km.
- $N_{max} = 100$.
- The propagation speed of light on fiber is 200 000 km/sec.

Substituting these values into (17) yields positive value of the expression. (Actually, $d=10$ Mbit is the breaking point between the two solutions.) Thus, even for such high-speed channel, so long path, so small number of hosts on the network, and relatively small amount of data to communicate, the single-channel solution is still preferred.

In case of the improved circuit-switching (mentioned before) the optimal solution is $N_{opt} = 1$. However, in this case the $N_{opt} = 1$ solution is precisely the packet-switching solution, since no set-up procedure is performed. Thus, also for the improved circuit-switching technique an attempt to minimize the delay for a reasonable range of parameters values results in the packet-switching scheme.

As C increases the transmission time decreases and the propagation delay dominates in the value of the total delay of a packet-switched network. It is reasonable to ask what is the point beyond which any further increase in total channel capacity yields only a marginal improvement in the delay. The breaking point (defined as the value of C which results in transmission time to be equal to 10% of the propagation time) can be found from (3), which, assuming fast packet switching, results in:

$$C_{break} = \frac{10 \cdot d}{T_{prop}} \qquad (18)$$

Suppose 10 Mbit needs to be communicated over a path of length 1000 km. Assuming 200 000 km/sec as a speed of light on optical fiber, results in $C_{break} = 20$ Gbps. Therefore, to reach the breaking point, even for such a long path, requires large capacity. However, if very large capacities will become available with the progress of the technology in the future, the argumentation presented in this section supports the usage of a number of packet-switched networks operating in concurrency, rather then a single circuit-switched network. Such a solution possesses the additional advantages of increased reliability and lower dependency on future growth of the network.

Circuit-switching has some other disadvantages as compared to packet-switching which are emphasized when used in environments requiring high-performance communication.

Suppose it is necessary to multicast (sending the same packet to many destinations) to k destinations. If the link multiplexes N circuits in the circuit-switching method and $k > N$, some of the circuits will have to be closed and reopened to new destinations, in order to perform the multicast operation. Thus, the delay significantly increases in such a case. In contrast, packet-switching allows a multicast packet to travel as a single packet up to the point where it has to be replicated. Thus, delay, as well as throughput, are improved in the packet-switched multicast as opposed to the circuit-switched one.

Accommodation of bursts of high priority traffic when a network is congested (all sub-channels are busy) is difficult to cope with when circuit-switching technique is used. Since priority is assigned on a per packet basis in packet-switching techniques, traffic priority is easily changed in the middle of a transmission. Moreover, because of the dynamic sharing of the channel, packet-switching can accommodate higher priority traffic by reducing the service level for lower priority traffic when the network is congested.

Some of the other disadvantages of circuit-switching technique in a high-performance environment include: lower utilization of the channel, lower sharing capability, and more complex implementation.

The reasoning of some authors, favoring circuit-switching that supports traffic of long duration with high bit rate for the future high-speed networks, is that the switching speed will be limited by "... the time required to electronically calculate or look-up in a table the next path configuration to be realized by the switching array"[15]. However, traffic that looks like *stream* traffic may turns out to be more of the bursty type when used on a very high speed channel. (Stream traffic is traffic with average to peak data rate ratio close to unity. In bursty traffic the ratio is considerably smaller then 1. The characteristic is done on a channel.) For example, traffic like packetized voice, which on a 64 kbps channel is apparently of the stream type, changes to bursty traffic on 100 Mbps link. Consequently, high-speed links in future networks will see traffic that is more of the bursty type. In the next section we present the design of *Blazenet*, a packet-switching network that can perform packet switching on the fly, and is, therefore, not limited by the calculation or look-up procedure of a packet routing operation. Thus, we show that fast packet-switching is, in fact, possible.

From the comparison of packet-switching with circuit-switching technique we conclude that for future data networks, packet-switching is the better switching method to use. However, since very large memories operating at the speed of future optical fiber links might be impossible or highly expensive (see [13,14]), conventional packet-switching cannot be used. Some adjustments to the packet-switching technique should be made in order to accommodate the lack of conventional memory within the switching nodes. Also, because of the high speed requirement, the processing done on a packet should be reduced to minimum. For example, error detection and flow control could

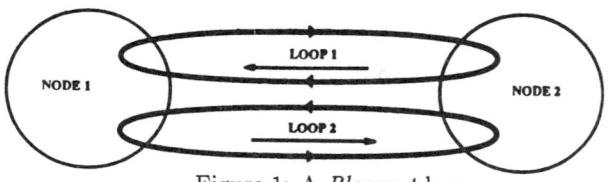

Figure 1: A *Blazenet* loop

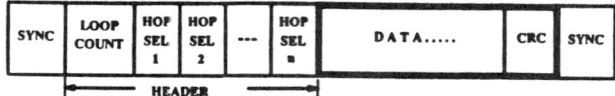

Figure 2: The *Blazenet* packet format

be deleted from the physical layer, routing algorithms simplified and network management facilities reduced. In the limit, the whole Data Link Layer and a portion of Network Layer could be removed. *Blazenet*, presented in the next section, incorporates some of these guidelines, leading to a packet-switched photonic implementable data network.

4 Blazenet

Blazenet is a wide-area packet-switching network based on optical fiber links. It is, essentially, the direct implementation of the principles described in the previous section. The idea behind *Blazenet* is the use of the storage inherently present in the fiber links; the special structure of the links (formed by creating loops, as shown in figure 1) provides the temporary storage for blocked packets in transit. A packet that cannot be forwarded in the switching node it arrived at, is returned to its previously visited node. After being sent once more, the packet will arrive at the blocking node again one round trip time later for a new attempt to be forwarded. The procedure will repeat itself until the packet successfully makes its way to the next node on its path.

The *Blazenet* packet format, shown in figure 2, is composed of two delimiting synchronization fields (*sync*s), a header, and a data portion. Within the header, the *loopcount* limits the packet lifetime within the network (as described later) and the *hop-select*s dictate the hop-by-hop route for the packet to reach its destination. The data portion contains higher level protocol data and can, optionally, be protected by a checksum.

Blazenet, as a network, is composed of switching nodes that are connected by point-to-point logical links formed by the fiber loops. The hosts and gateways on the periphery of the network act as sources and sinks for the network traffic. Thus *Blazenet* is a forwarding type network. Packets are generated by hosts and passed to the switching nodes, to which they are connected. The packets are then forwarded from node to node till they arrive at the switching node connected to the destination host. The packets are then removed from the network by the switching node and passed to the destination host. An example of a four node *Blazenet* is shown in figure 3.

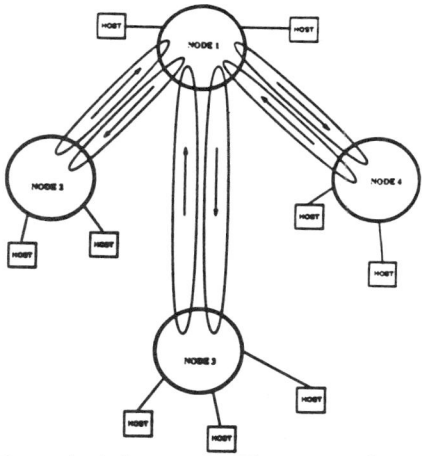

Figure 3: A four node *Blazenet* configuration

4.1 Fast Packet Switching in *Blazenet*

Blazenet uses source routing. Each packet contains a series of *hop-select*s, specified by the source host. The *hop-select*s represent the switching operations that will be taken in the subsequent nodes along the packet path from its source to its destination through the network. Each *hop-select* field indicates the output link on which the packet is to be forwarded for that hop. When a packet arrives at a switching node, the first *hop-select* field in the packet is examined to determine the next output link for the packet. If that output link is available for transmission of a new packet, the first *hop-select* field is zeroed and the packet is immediately routed to the available output link. The zeroing of the first *hop-select* field during the forwarding process means that the first non-zero *hop-select* field in the packet always represents the current hop selection.

This design has several advantages. First, because of the simple logic required to make the hop selection, it is feasible to perform the switching function at gigabit per second data rates. Second, the delay for switching in a node is limited to the time required to interpret the packet header, check the availability of the output link, and perform the actual switching operation (if the output link is available). Since the extra delay introduced by a switching node is estimated to be about 20 bits, this delay is only a small fraction of the propagation delay of a few kilometer long link. Finally, the simplicity of the node logic suggests that a photonics implementation is feasible. Photonic implementation, as opposed to a conventional electronic implementation, offers increased switching speeds [6,5]. (Note that the lack of need of conventional memory within a switching node increases the photonic implementation feasibility, since optical memory is still in the laboratory stage [4].) An optical realization would have high immunity to interference and security benefits.

4.2 Packet Blockage

A packet is blocked when it is to be forwarded on an unavailable output link. When a packet is blocked by a switching node, it is routed back to the previous switching node on the return portion of the input loop. Upon its arrival at the previous switching node, the returned packet is sent again to arrive at the blocking switching node one round-trip time after its first arrival at this node. Thus, the loop effectively provides short-term storage of the packet, causing the packet to reappear at the blocking switching node a short time later. The *loopcount* field is decremented and examined each time the packet is returned. When *loopcount* reaches zero, the packet is removed from the network. This mechanism prevents a packet from indefinitely looping within the network under some failure or load conditions.

This approach to handling blockage has several advantages. First, as opposed to a design in which the packet is simply dropped when blocked at the outgoing link (such a network is referred to here as a *lossy* network), *Blazenet* dramatically reduces the average packet delay through a loaded network and increases the network efficiency. When a packet is dropped in a *lossy* network, it has to be retransmitted by the source after some timeout, at least one round-trip time long. Since the probability of a packet being blocked increases with path length, as does the network investment in the blocked packet, dropping the packet seriously degrades the network performance under load for networks with a large hop span. Second, the design does not require memory in the switching node of the size and speed required to store all blocked packets, such as would be needed for a conventional store-and-forward design. Several megabytes of memory operating at 1 Gbps would significantly increase the cost of the switching nodes and make their realization in optics infeasible, at least in the near future. The combination of the high data rates, the wide-area span of the links, and the low-cost of the fiber makes this form of storage attractive. For example, a 100 km link (= 200 km loop) operating at 1 Gbps can store nearly 1 Mbits or 125 packets of 1 kbyte each. Finally, the loopback technique exerts back pressure on the link over which the packet was received, because the loop is then less available for new packets to be forwarded on it. In the extreme, this back pressure extends back from the point of contention to one or more packet sources. Besides alerting the packet source of congestion, the back pressure provides fast feedback to the source routing mechanism, allowing it to react quickly to network load and topological changes.

A potential disadvantage arises when the link between switching nodes is very long, since the round-trip delay on the loop may be excessive. We avoid this problem by including loopback support in the optical repeaters that are already placed every few tens of kilometers on a fiber optic link. Thus, a packet that is blocked at a switching node is looped back either to the previous switching node or to the previous repeater, whichever is closer. If, for example, the distance between adjacent switching nodes is 100 km, the round-trip delay is approximately 1 msec. Because a *Blazenet* switching node includes the regeneration function between the input and output ports, it can be used as

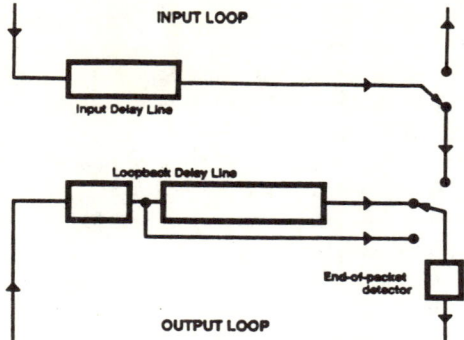

Figure 4: The switching node design

a repeater, thereby automatically supporting the loopback function. (In this use, only two input and two output loops are used.) The network is then built from one type of interconnection component, rather than two. By using such a design, packets can loop at intermediate loops on a long link, reducing its delay through the network (assuming the congestion clears before the packet is dropped). Consequently, the packet is delayed in time units corresponding to the round trip time on the intermediate loop rather than that for the entire link.

4.3 *Blazenet* node design

Figure 4 shows the block design of a *Blazenet* switching node. Each *Input Loop* has a Delay Line (*Input Delay Line*), built, possibly, of a piece of fiber. The *Input Delay Line* is long enough to contain the leading *sync*, the *loop-count*, the *hop-selects*, and the length corresponding to the time the control logic needs to do the actual switching.

Each *Output Loop* also has its own Delay Line, the *Loopback Delay Line*. The *Loopback Delay Line* must be of the length of the maximum packet size. The *Loopback Delay Line* is considered to be free if it does not contain a packet or any part of a packet.

When a packet is to be forwarded to the *Output Loop* the availability of the *Output Loop* and its *Loopback Delay Line* is checked. If both are free, the packet from the *Input Loop* is clocked onto the *Output Loop*. If, on the other hand, the *Output Loop* and/or the *Loopback Delay Line* are busy, the packet is blocked and returned by being clocked out on the return portion of the *Input Loop* it arrived on. In case more than one packet tries to enter a specific *Output Loop*, only one packet wins (the one with the higher priority, or one chosen randomly in case of equal priorities), and the other(s) are clocked out on the return portion of their *Input Loop*s. Upon its arrival to the other end of the *Input Loop* (which changes its name to *Output Loop*), blocked packet is clocked into the corresponding *Loopback Delay Line*, blocking access to this *Output Loop* by any new arrival.

More detailed description of *Blazenet* can be found in [1,2].

5 Conclusions

In this paper we have argued that packet switching remains the more attractive switching technique for high-performance networking. We have also presented some of the specific problems that arise in such networks and suggested possible solutions. *Blazenet*, a packet-switching design that supports our conclusion, has also been presented.

Closer look on *Blazenet* reveals some of the network's salient characteristics: high-speed switching, the lack of conventional memories, good behavior under traffic load, self control of congestion, priority traffic, multicast delivery, and the possibility of photonic implementation. Specifically, *Blazenet* provides switching of multi-gigabit per second data rates, low delay, and good behavior under load. The use of source routing allows each switching node to make switching decisions on the fly, minimizing the switching delay. The use of a loopback channel, which effectively stores packets that are blocked at the switch, minimizes the packet loss under load without requiring additional memory within the switch. Finally, the simplicity of the switching node, as a result of the use of source routing and the absence of switching buffer memory, makes it feasible to realize the switching node through the use of photonics. Photonics makes the switching node more immune than electronics to electromagnetic monitoring or interference. It will also provides greater performance and reliability, especially as photonic technology matures.

However, the importance of *Blazenet* extends beyond the mere fact of the existence of another communication network design. The *Blazenet* concept demonstrates the feasibility of packet-switching in high speed networks. In the other words, the *Blazenet* design shows that it is not necessary to resort to circuit-switching to handle the data rates made possible by optical fiber. In fact, when computer traffic has to be carried, packet-switching has some crucial advantages over circuit-switching, advantages that are emphasized in high-speed networks. Consequently, *Blazenet* provides the basis for packet-switched, high-speed networks designs.

We see *Blazenet* as a representative of a future class of networks that behave as passive "light pipes" for data, offering very high throughput, low delay, and high reliability. With the introduction of this class of wide-area networks, we expect that the computer interfaces, rather than the networks, will appear to be the performance and functionality bottlenecks of the communication process. However, further research and development are required to make this perception of the future a reality. In particular, an actual photonic realization of the *Blazenet* concept is of great importance. Today's state of the art in photonic switching permits such a realization only to a limited degree. Nevertheless, this limited realization can serve as a first step towards a future all-photonic communication network.

References

[1] Z. Haas and D. R. Cheriton, "*Blazenet*: A High-Performance Wide-Area Packet-Switched Network Using Optical Fibers," in Proceedings of the IEEE Pacific RIM Conference on Communication, Computers and Signal Processing, Victoria, B.C., June 4-5, 1987

[2] Z. Haas and D. R. Cheriton, "*Blazenet*: A High-Performance Wide-Area Packet-Switched Network Using Optical Fibers," technical report, in preparation.

[3] A. Bellman, "Switching Architectures Towards the Nineties," in Proceedings of the International Seminar on *Digital Communications, New Directions in Switching and Networks,* Zürich, Switzerland, March 11-13, 1986.

[4] L. Thylén, "High Speed, Wide Bandwidth Digital Switching and Communications Utilizing Guided Wave Optics," in Proceedings of the International Seminar on *Digital Communications, New Directions in Switching and Networks,* Zürich, Switzerland, March 11-13, 1986.

[5] F. Guterl and G. Zorpette, "Fiber optics: poised to displace satellites," *IEEE Spectrum,* August 1985.

[6] P. R. Prucnal, D. J. Blumenthal and P. A. Perrier, "Photonic Switch with Optically Self-Routed Bit Switching," *IEEE Communication Magazine,* vol.25, No.5, May 1987.

[7] R. D. Rosener and B. Springer, "Circuit and packet switching," *Computer Networks 1,* 1976, 7-26.

[8] K. Kümmerle and H. Rudin, "Packet and Circuit Switching: Cost/Performance Boundaries," *Computer Networks 2,* 1978, 3-17.

[9] H. Miyahara, Y. Teshigawara, and T. Hasegawa, "Delay and Throughput Evaluation of Switching Methods in Computer Communication Networks," *IEEE TRANSACTIONS ON COMMUNICATIONS,* vol.COM-26, No.3, March 1978.

[10] P. Kermani and L. Kleinrock, "Virtual Cut-Through: A New Computer Communication Switching Technique," *Computer Networks 3,* 1979, 267-286.

[11] M. Ilyas and H. T. Mouftah, "Quasi cut-through: New hybrid switching technique for computer communication networks," *IEE PROCEEDINGS,* vol.131, No.1, Jan 1984.

[12] M. Ilyas and H. T. Mouftah, "Delay analysis of a modified cut-through switching for multipacket messages," *IEE PROCEEDINGS,* vol.132, No.1, Jan 1985.

[13] M. Sakaguchi and K. Kaede, "Optical Switching Devices Technologies," in Proceedings of the International Seminar on *Digital Communications, New Directions in Switching and Networks,* Zürich, Switzerland, March 11-13, 1986.

[14] R. I. MacDonald, "Optoelectronic Switching," in Proceedings of the International Seminar on *Digital Communications, New Directions in Switching and Networks,* Zürich, Switzerland, March 11-13, 1986

[15] H. S. Hinton, "Photonic Switching Using Directional Couplers," *IEEE Communication Magazine,* vol.25, No.5, May 1987.

NOTES

NOTES

NOTES